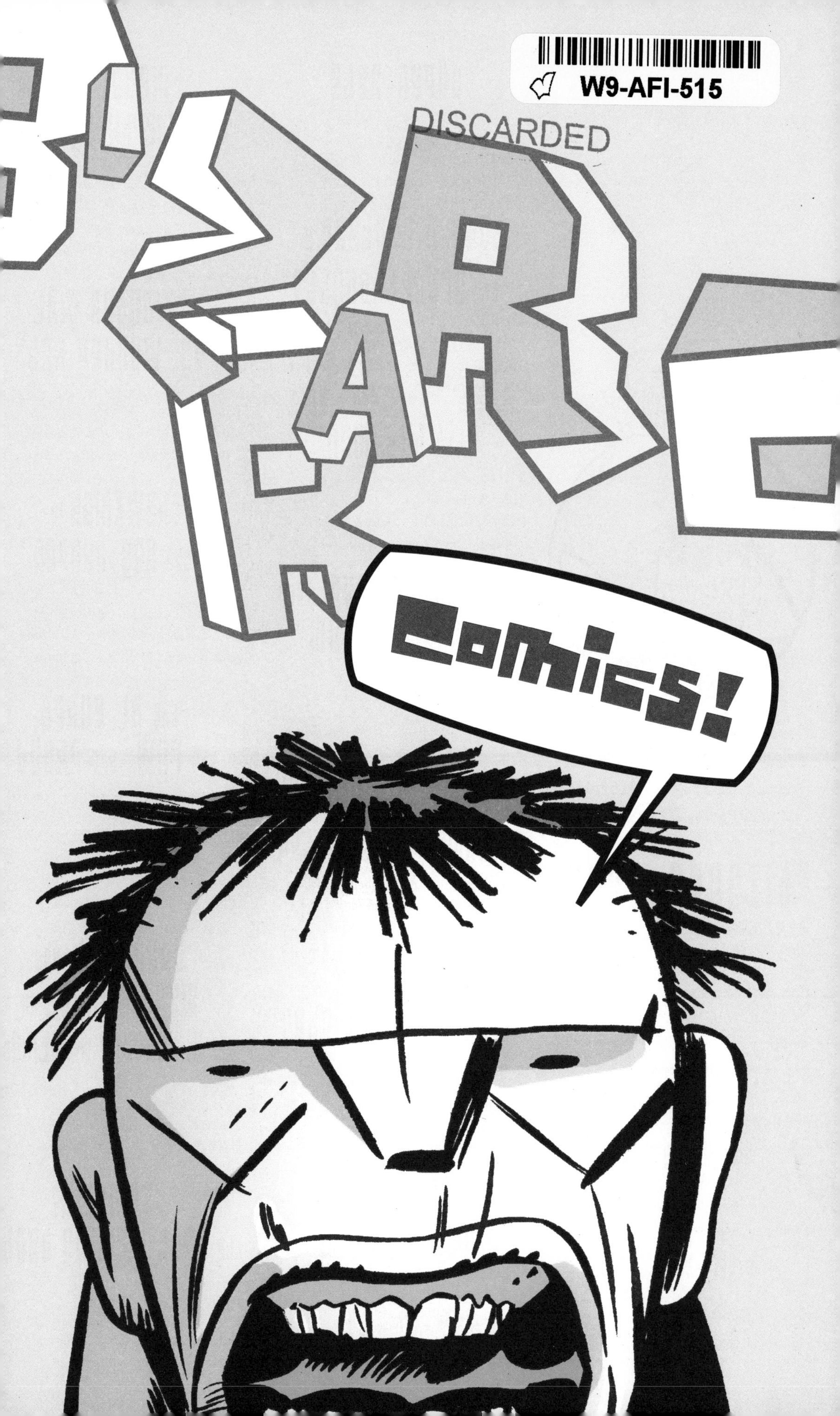
Comics!

BIZARRO COMICS AM STOOPID!

Cover art by Matt Groening
Cover color by Nathan Kane
Special thanks to Bill Morrison
Logo design by Rian Hughes

Superman created by
Jerry Siegel & Joe Shuster
Batman created by
Bob Kane
Wonder Woman created by
William Moulton Marston
Kamandi created by
Jack Kirby

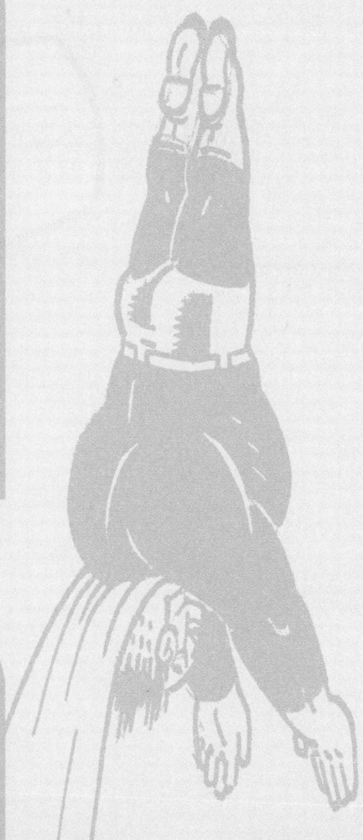

BIZARRO COMICS!
Published by DC Comics, 1700 Broadway, New York, NY 10019.
Copyright © 2001 DC Comics. All Rights Reserved.
All characters featured in this issue, the distinctive likenesses
thereof, and all related indicia are trademarks of DC Comics.
The stories, characters and incidents mentioned in this magazine
are entirely fictional. Printed on recyclable paper.
Printed in Canada.
DC Comics. A division of Warner Bros.-An AOL
Time Warner Company.

dc comics

Jenette Kahn President & Editor-in-Chief
Paul Levitz Executive Vice President & Publisher
Mike Carlin Executive Editor
Joey Cavalieri Editor
Mark Chiarello Editorial Art Director
Amie Brockway-Metcalf Art Director
Richard Bruning VP-Creative Director
Patrick Caldon Senior VP-Finance & Operations
Dorothy Crouch VP-Licensed Publishing
Terri Cunningham VP-Managing Editor
Joel Ehrlich,Senior VP-Advertising & Promotions
Alison Gill Executive Director-Manufacturing
Lillian Laserson VP & General Counsel
Jim Lee Editorial Director-WildStorm
John Nee VP & General Manager-WildStorm
Cheryl Rubin VP-Licensing & Merchandising
Bob Wayne VP-Sales & Marketing

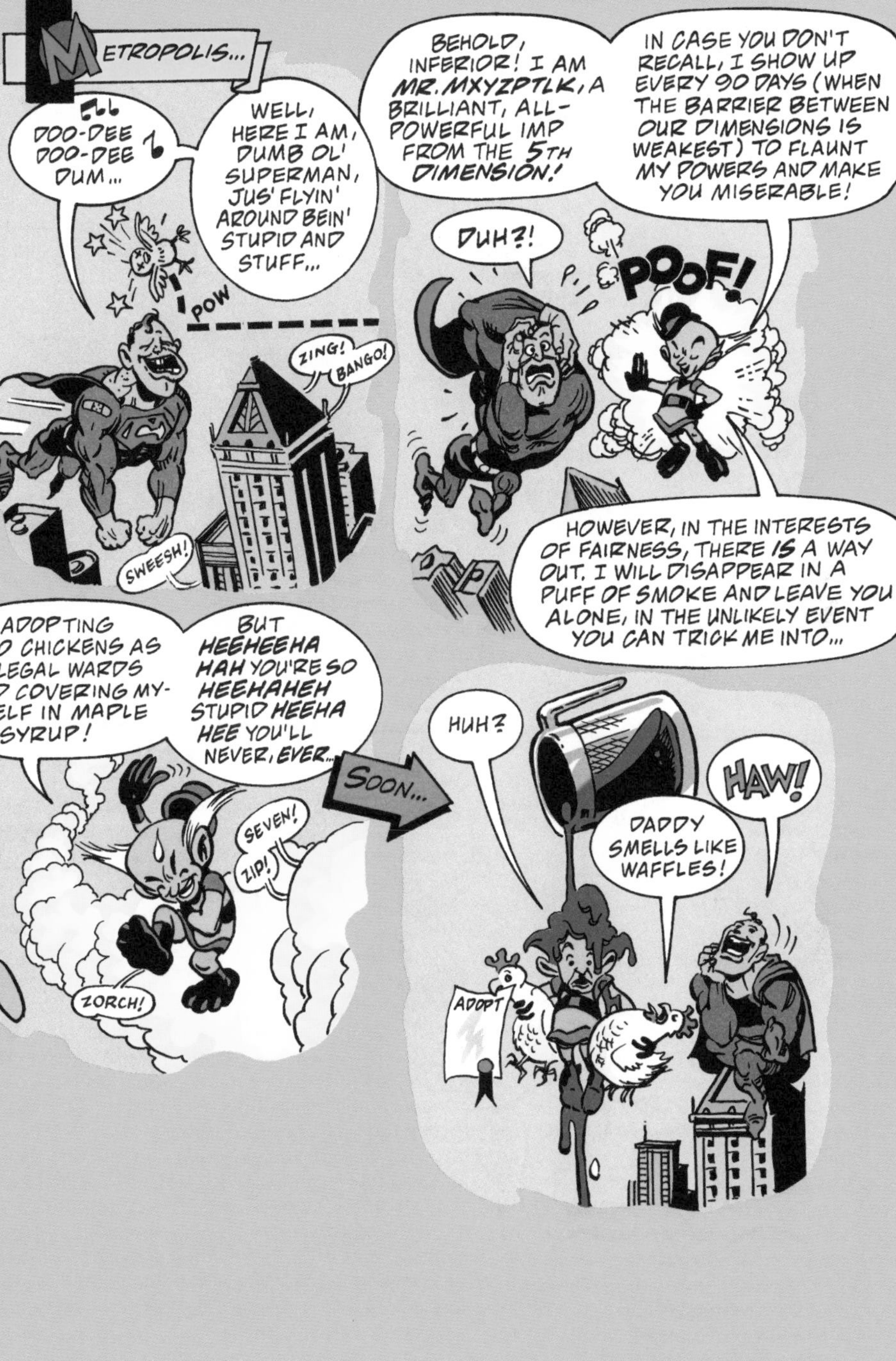
METROPOLIS...
DOO-DEE DOO-DEE DUM...
WELL, HERE I AM, DUMB OL' SUPERMAN, JUS' FLYIN' AROUND BEIN' STUPID AND STUFF...
POW
ZING!
BANGO!
SWEESH!
BEHOLD, INFERIOR! I AM MR. MXYZPTLK, A BRILLIANT, ALL-POWERFUL IMP FROM THE 5TH DIMENSION!
IN CASE YOU DON'T RECALL, I SHOW UP EVERY 90 DAYS (WHEN THE BARRIER BETWEEN OUR DIMENSIONS IS WEAKEST) TO FLAUNT MY POWERS AND MAKE YOU MISERABLE!
DUH?!
POOF!
HOWEVER, IN THE INTERESTS OF FAIRNESS, THERE IS A WAY OUT. I WILL DISAPPEAR IN A PUFF OF SMOKE AND LEAVE YOU ALONE, IN THE UNLIKELY EVENT YOU CAN TRICK ME INTO...
...ADOPTING TWO CHICKENS AS MY LEGAL WARDS AND COVERING MY-SELF IN MAPLE SYRUP!
BUT HEEHEEHA HAH YOU'RE SO HEEHAHEH STUPID HEEHA HEE YOU'LL NEVER, EVER...
SEVEN!
ZIP!
ZORCH!
SOON...
HUH?
HAW!
DADDY SMELLS LIKE WAFFLES!
ADOPT

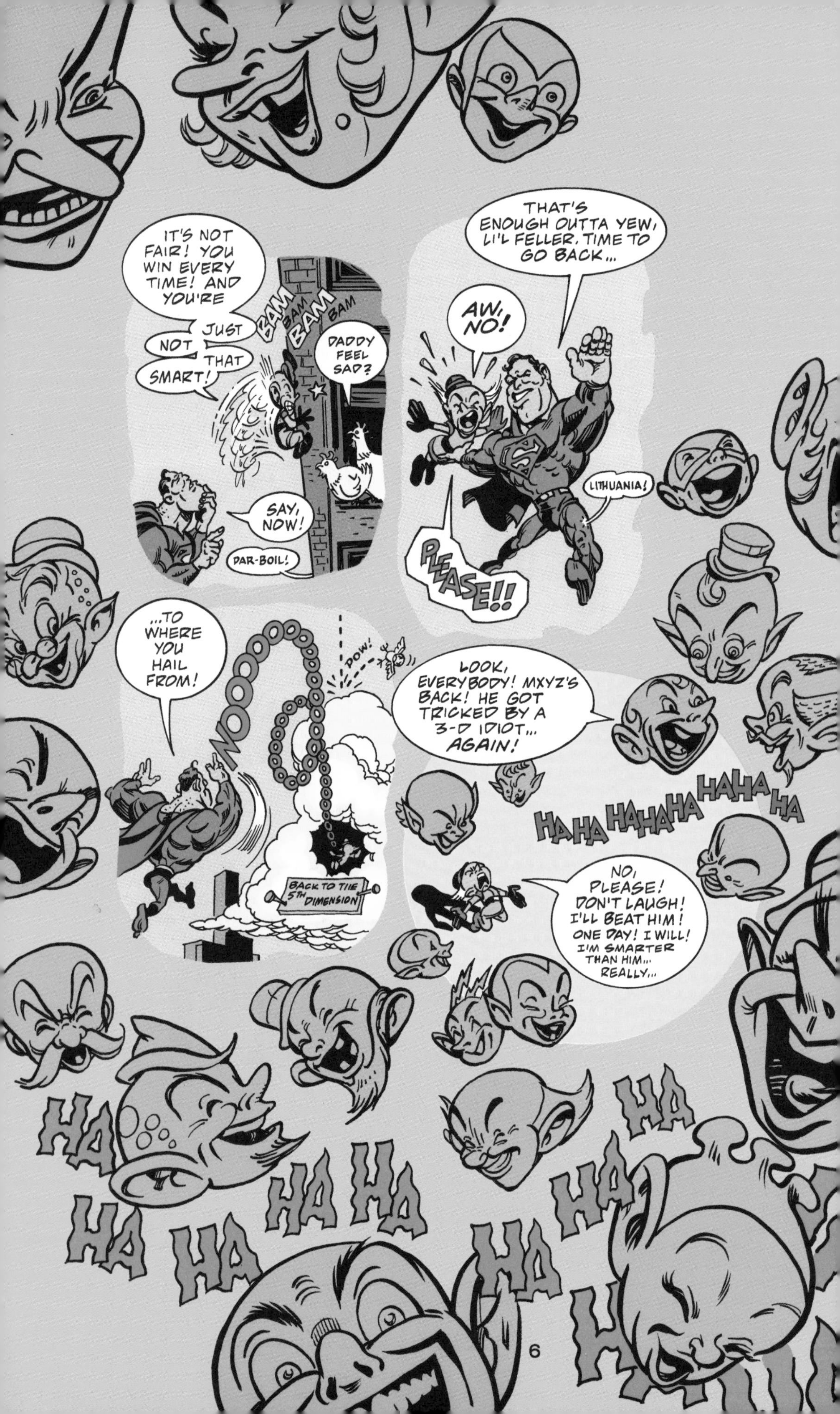
IT'S NOT FAIR! YOU WIN EVERY TIME! AND YOU'RE
JUST
NOT
THAT
SMART!
BAM BAM BAM BAM
DADDY FEEL SAD?
SAY, NOW!
DAR-BOIL!
THAT'S ENOUGH OUTTA YEW, LI'L FELLER. TIME TO GO BACK...
AW, NO!
LITHUANIA!
PLEASE!!
...TO WHERE YOU HAIL FROM!
NOOOOOOOOOOO
POW!
BACK TO THE 5TH DIMENSION
LOOK, EVERYBODY! MXYZ'S BACK! HE GOT TRICKED BY A 3-D IDIOT... AGAIN!
HA HA HAHAHA HAHAHA HA
NO, PLEASE! DON'T LAUGH! I'LL BEAT HIM! ONE DAY! I WILL! I'M SMARTER THAN HIM... REALLY...
HA HA HA HA HA HA HA HA HA HA

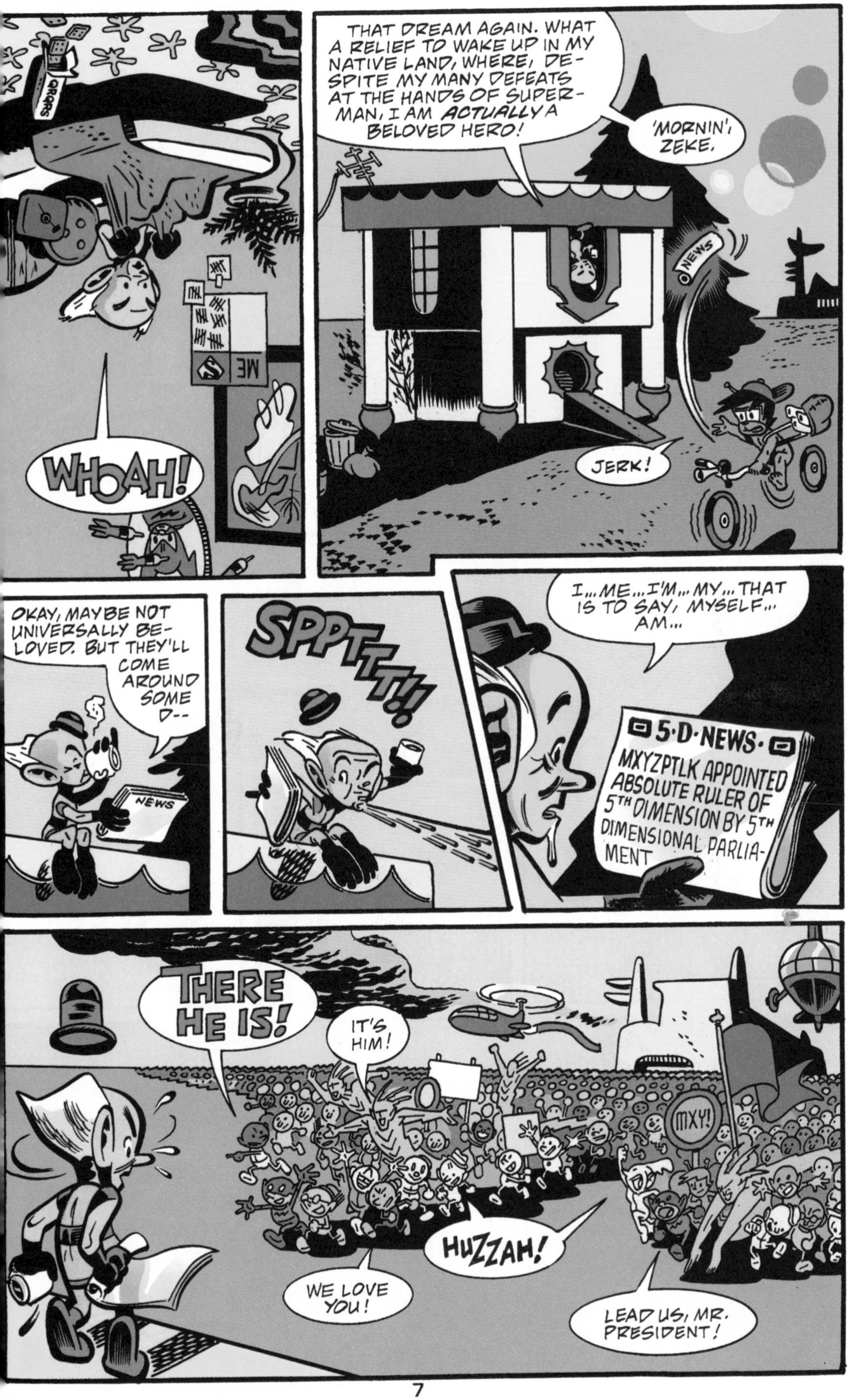
QRQRS
ME
WHOAH!
THAT DREAM AGAIN. WHAT A RELIEF TO WAKE UP IN MY NATIVE LAND, WHERE, DESPITE MY MANY DEFEATS AT THE HANDS OF SUPERMAN, I AM ACTUALLY A BELOVED HERO!
'MORNIN', ZEKE.
NEWS
JERK!
OKAY, MAYBE NOT UNIVERSALLY BELOVED. BUT THEY'LL COME AROUND SOME D--
NEWS
SPPTTTT!!
I... ME... I'M... MY... THAT IS TO SAY, MYSELF... AM...
5·D·NEWS·
MXYZPTLK APPOINTED ABSOLUTE RULER OF 5TH DIMENSION BY 5TH DIMENSIONAL PARLIAMENT
THERE HE IS!
IT'S HIM!
MXY!
HUZZAH!
WE LOVE YOU!
LEAD US, MR. PRESIDENT!

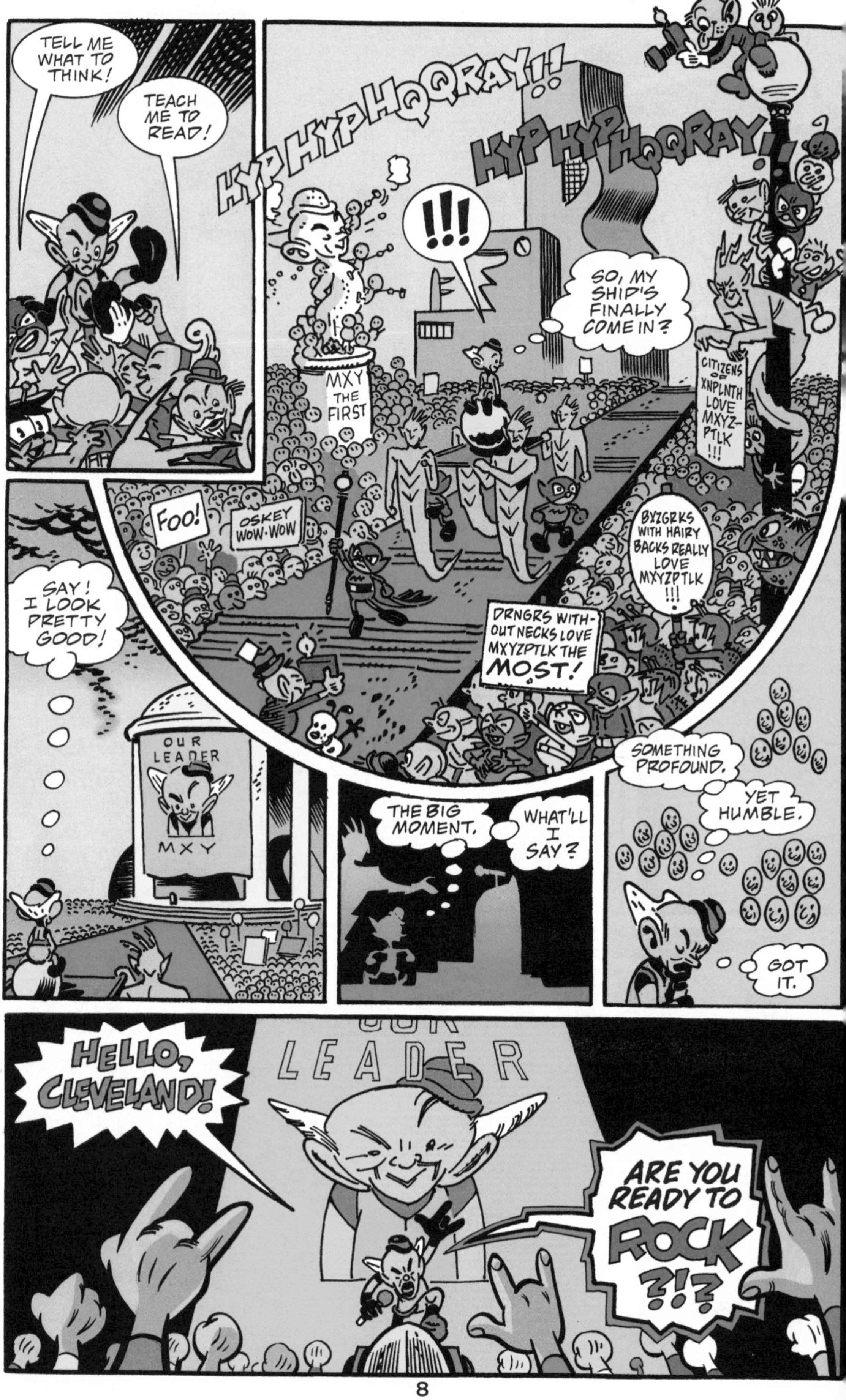
TELL ME WHAT TO THINK!
TEACH ME TO READ!
HYPHYPHQQRAY!!
HYPHYPHQQRAY!!
!!!
SO, MY SHIP'S FINALLY COME IN?
MXY THE FIRST
CITIZENS OF XNPLNTH LOVE MXYZPTLK !!!
FOO!
OSKEY WOW-WOW
BXZGRKS WITH HAIRY BACKS REALLY LOVE MXYZPTLK !!!
DRNGRS WITHOUT NECKS LOVE MXYZPTLK THE MOST!
SAY! I LOOK PRETTY GOOD!
OUR LEADER
MXY
THE BIG MOMENT.
WHAT'LL I SAY?
SOMETHING PROFOUND.
YET HUMBLE.
GOT IT.
LEADER
HELLO, CLEVELAND!
ARE YOU READY TO ROCK ?!?

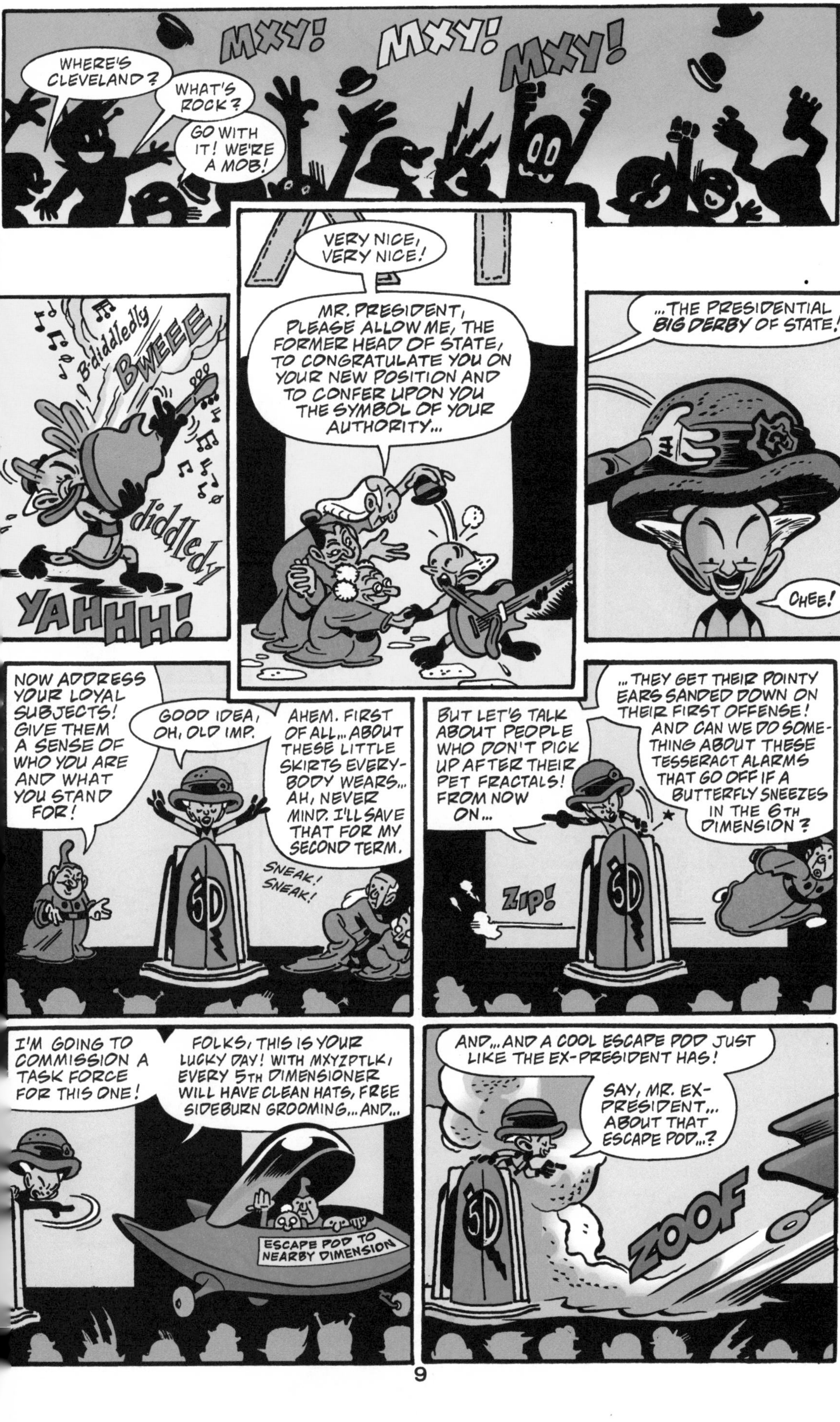
MXY! MXY! MXY!
WHERE'S CLEVELAND?
WHAT'S ROCK?
GO WITH IT! WE'RE A MOB!
VERY NICE, VERY NICE!
MR. PRESIDENT, PLEASE ALLOW ME, THE FORMER HEAD OF STATE, TO CONGRATULATE YOU ON YOUR NEW POSITION AND TO CONFER UPON YOU THE SYMBOL OF YOUR AUTHORITY...
B'diddledly BWEEE diddledy
YAHHHH!
...THE PRESIDENTIAL BIG DERBY OF STATE!
CHEE!
NOW ADDRESS YOUR LOYAL SUBJECTS! GIVE THEM A SENSE OF WHO YOU ARE AND WHAT YOU STAND FOR!
GOOD IDEA, OH, OLD IMP.
AHEM. FIRST OF ALL... ABOUT THESE LITTLE SKIRTS EVERYBODY WEARS... AH, NEVER MIND. I'LL SAVE THAT FOR MY SECOND TERM.
SNEAK! SNEAK!
BUT LET'S TALK ABOUT PEOPLE WHO DON'T PICK UP AFTER THEIR PET FRACTALS! FROM NOW ON...
...THEY GET THEIR POINTY EARS SANDED DOWN ON THEIR FIRST OFFENSE!
AND CAN WE DO SOMETHING ABOUT THESE TESSERACT ALARMS THAT GO OFF IF A BUTTERFLY SNEEZES IN THE 6TH DIMENSION?
ZIP!
5D
I'M GOING TO COMMISSION A TASK FORCE FOR THIS ONE!
FOLKS, THIS IS YOUR LUCKY DAY! WITH MXYZPTLK, EVERY 5TH DIMENSIONER WILL HAVE CLEAN HATS, FREE SIDEBURN GROOMING... AND...
ESCAPE POD TO NEARBY DIMENSION
AND... AND A COOL ESCAPE POD JUST LIKE THE EX-PRESIDENT HAS!
SAY, MR. EX-PRESIDENT... ABOUT THAT ESCAPE POD...?
ZOOF

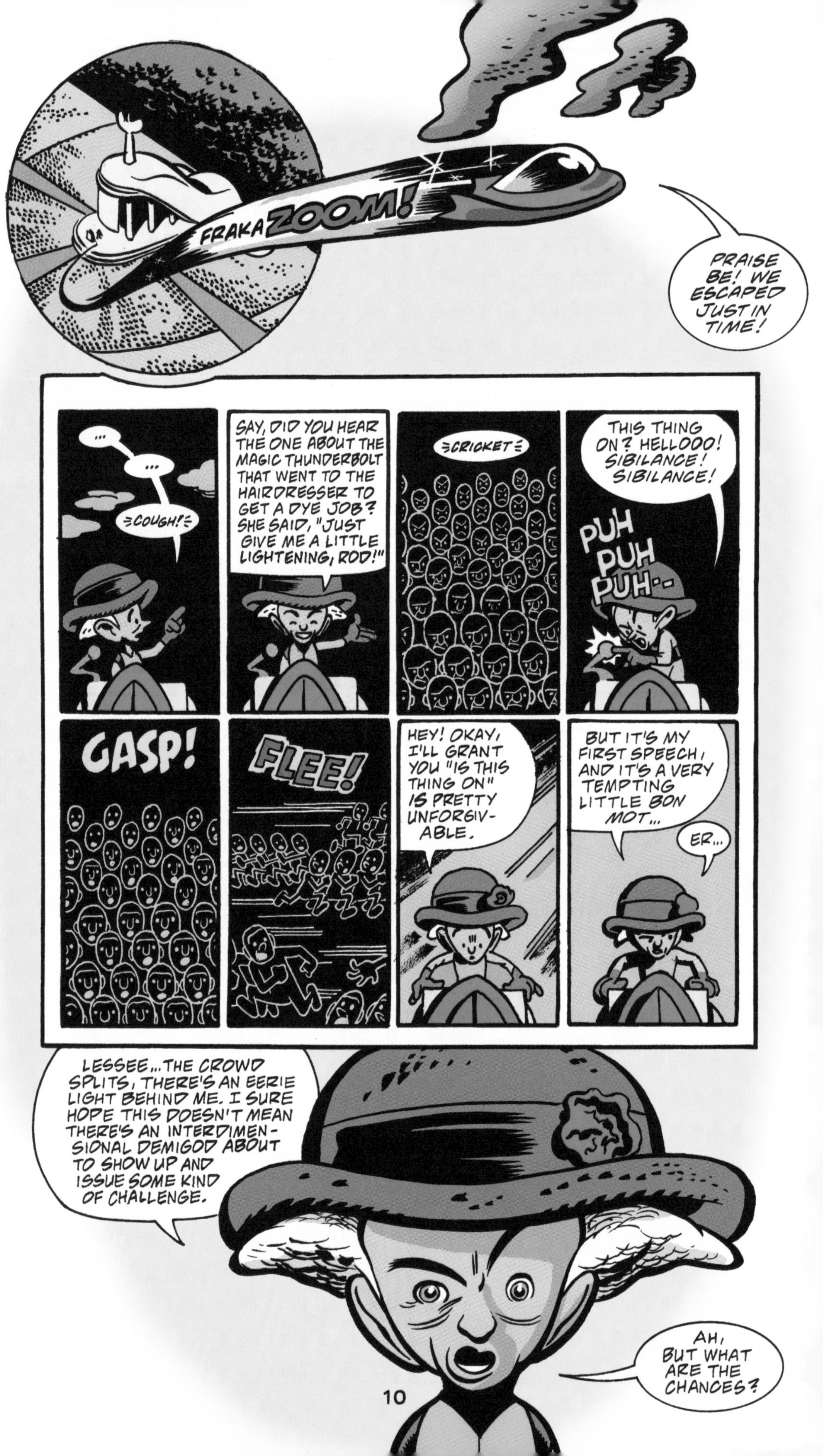
FRAKAZOOM!
PRAISE BE! WE ESCAPED JUST IN TIME!
...
...
COUGH!
SAY, DID YOU HEAR THE ONE ABOUT THE MAGIC THUNDERBOLT THAT WENT TO THE HAIRDRESSER TO GET A DYE JOB? SHE SAID, "JUST GIVE ME A LITTLE LIGHTENING, ROD!"
CRICKET
THIS THING ON? HELLOOO! SIBILANCE! SIBILANCE!
PUH PUH PUH--
GASP!
FLEE!
HEY! OKAY, I'LL GRANT YOU "IS THIS THING ON" IS PRETTY UNFORGIV-ABLE.
BUT IT'S MY FIRST SPEECH, AND IT'S A VERY TEMPTING LITTLE BON MOT...
ER...
LESSEE... THE CROWD SPLITS, THERE'S AN EERIE LIGHT BEHIND ME. I SURE HOPE THIS DOESN'T MEAN THERE'S AN INTERDIMEN-SIONAL DEMIGOD ABOUT TO SHOW UP AND ISSUE SOME KIND OF CHALLENGE.
AH, BUT WHAT ARE THE CHANCES?

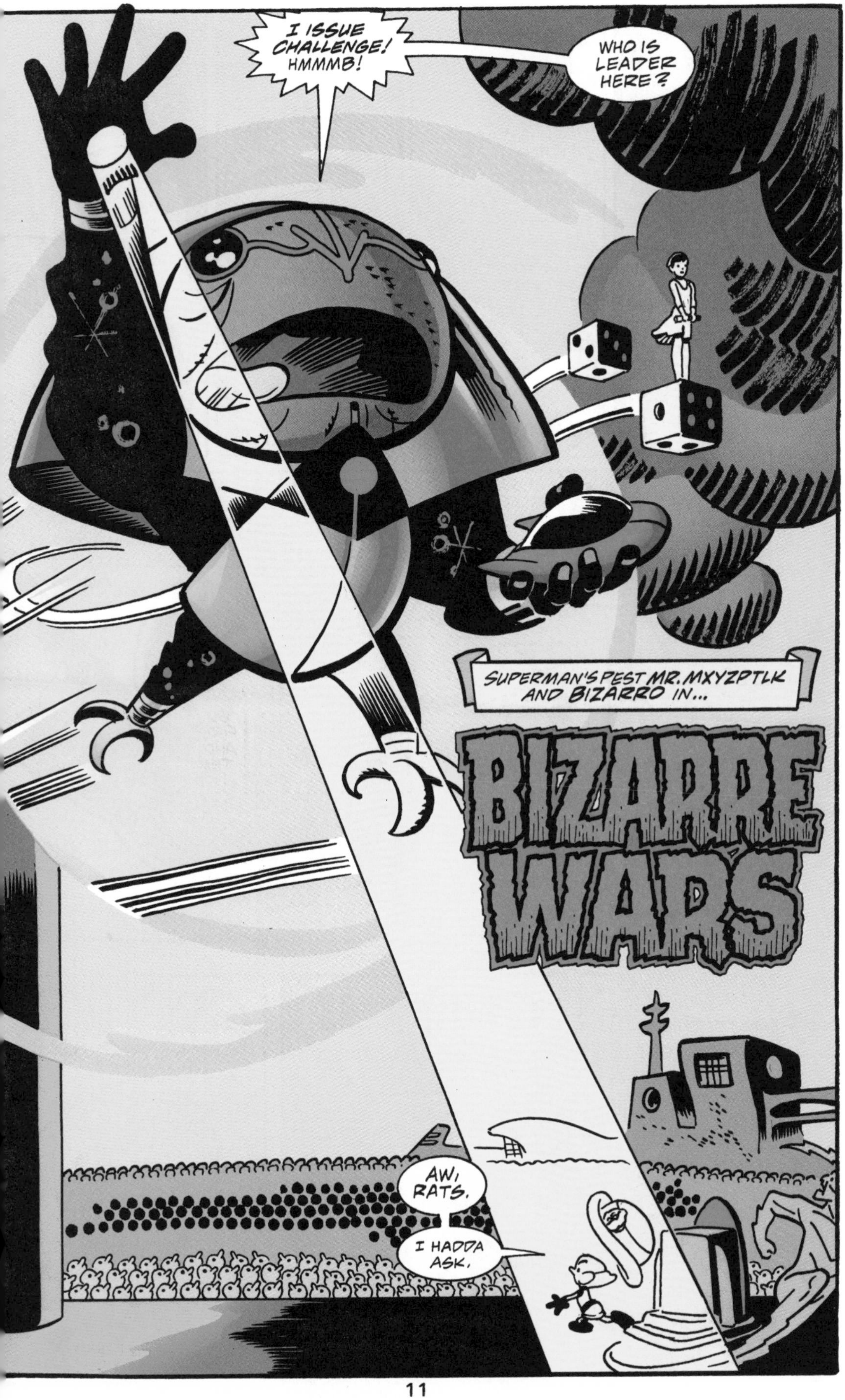
I ISSUE CHALLENGE! HMMMB!
WHO IS LEADER HERE?
SUPERMAN'S PEST MR. MXYZPTLK AND BIZARRO IN...
BIZARRE WARS
AW, RATS.
I HADDA ASK.

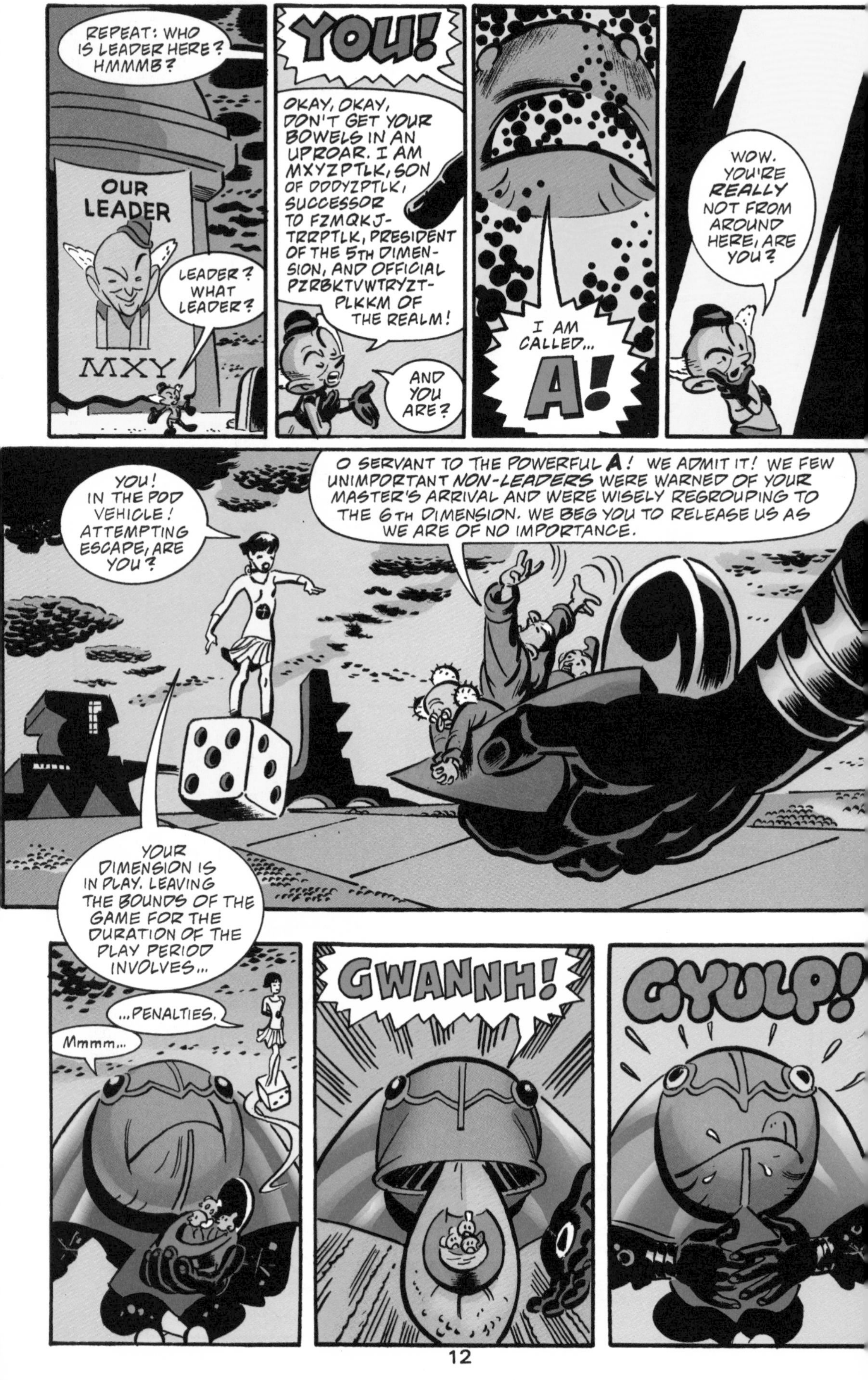

REPEAT: WHO IS LEADER HERE? HMMMB?
OUR LEADER
MXY
LEADER? WHAT LEADER?
YOU!
OKAY, OKAY, DON'T GET YOUR BOWELS IN AN UPROAR. I AM MXYZPTLK, SON OF DDDYZPTLK, SUCCESSOR TO FZMQKJ-TRRPTLK, PRESIDENT OF THE 5TH DIMENSION, AND OFFICIAL PZRBKTVWTRYZT-PLKKM OF THE REALM!
AND YOU ARE?
I AM CALLED... A!
WOW. YOU'RE REALLY NOT FROM AROUND HERE, ARE YOU?
YOU! IN THE POD VEHICLE! ATTEMPTING ESCAPE, ARE YOU?
O SERVANT TO THE POWERFUL A! WE ADMIT IT! WE FEW UNIMPORTANT NON-LEADERS WERE WARNED OF YOUR MASTER'S ARRIVAL AND WERE WISELY REGROUPING TO THE 6TH DIMENSION. WE BEG YOU TO RELEASE US AS WE ARE OF NO IMPORTANCE.
YOUR DIMENSION IS IN PLAY. LEAVING THE BOUNDS OF THE GAME FOR THE DURATION OF THE PLAY PERIOD INVOLVES...
...PENALTIES.
Mmmm...
GWANNH!
GYULP!

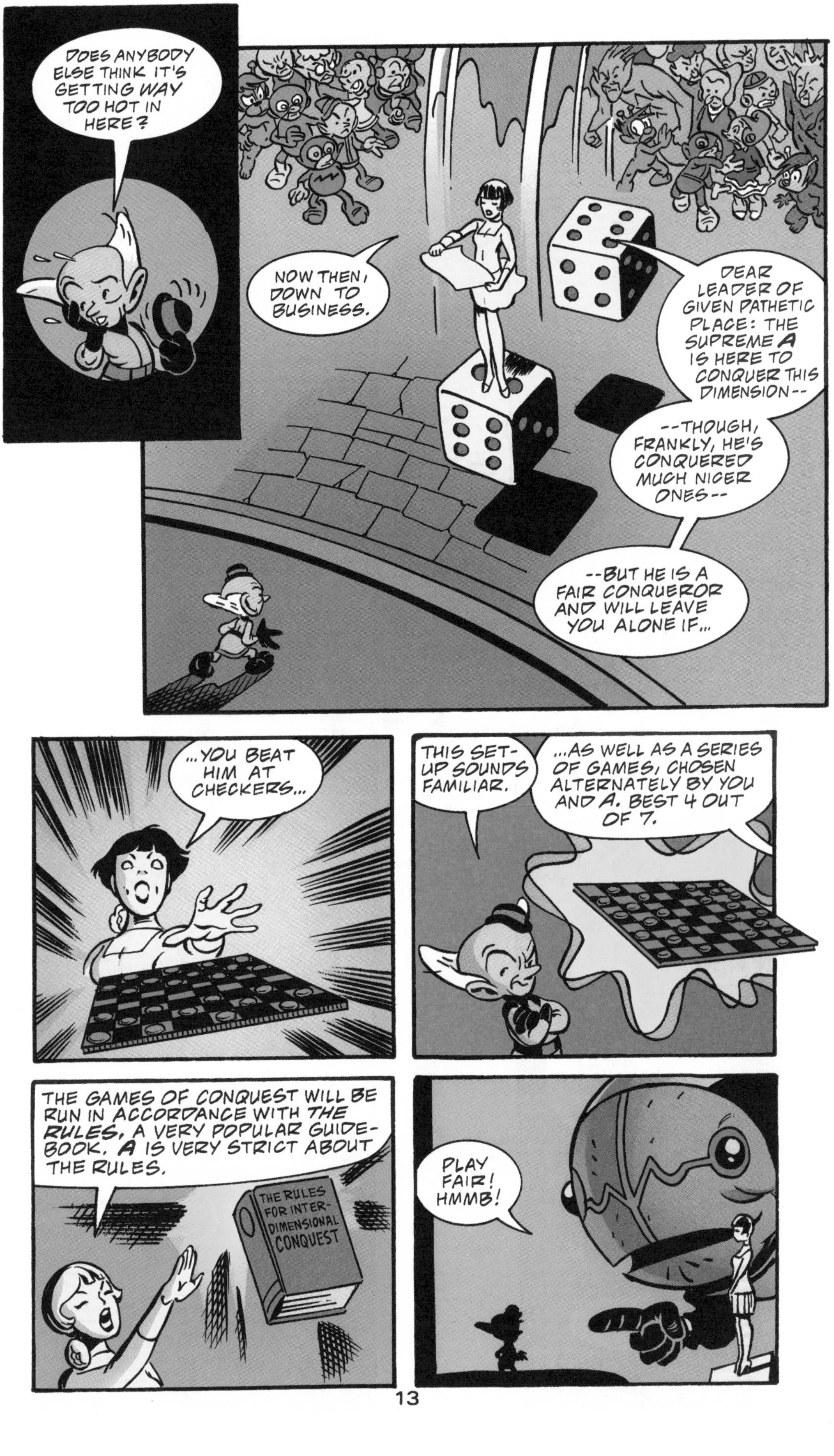
DOES ANYBODY ELSE THINK IT'S GETTING WAY TOO HOT IN HERE?
NOW THEN, DOWN TO BUSINESS.
DEAR LEADER OF GIVEN PATHETIC PLACE: THE SUPREME A IS HERE TO CONQUER THIS DIMENSION--
--THOUGH, FRANKLY, HE'S CONQUERED MUCH NICER ONES--
--BUT HE IS A FAIR CONQUEROR AND WILL LEAVE YOU ALONE IF...
...YOU BEAT HIM AT CHECKERS...
THIS SET-UP SOUNDS FAMILIAR.
...AS WELL AS A SERIES OF GAMES, CHOSEN ALTERNATELY BY YOU AND A. BEST 4 OUT OF 7.
THE GAMES OF CONQUEST WILL BE RUN IN ACCORDANCE WITH THE RULES, A VERY POPULAR GUIDE-BOOK. A IS VERY STRICT ABOUT THE RULES.
THE RULES FOR INTER-DIMENSIONAL CONQUEST
PLAY FAIR! HMMB!

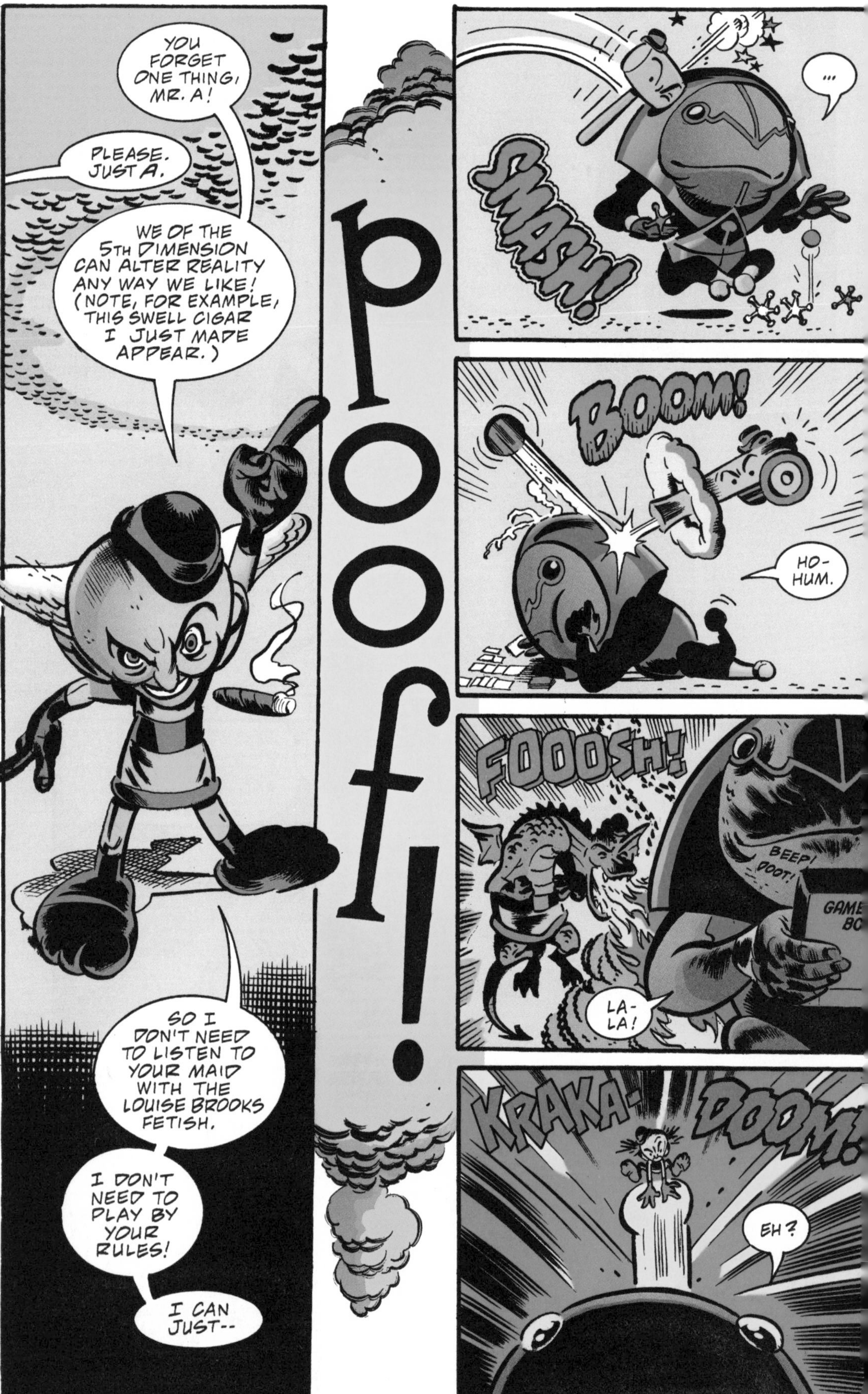
YOU FORGET ONE THING, MR. A!
PLEASE. JUST A.
WE OF THE 5TH DIMENSION CAN ALTER REALITY ANY WAY WE LIKE! (NOTE, FOR EXAMPLE, THIS SWELL CIGAR I JUST MADE APPEAR.)
SO I DON'T NEED TO LISTEN TO YOUR MAID WITH THE LOUISE BROOKS FETISH.
I DON'T NEED TO PLAY BY YOUR RULES!
I CAN JUST--
poof!
SMASH!
...
BOOM!
HO-HUM.
FOOOSH!
BEEP! DOOT!
LA-LA!
KRAKA-DOOM!
EH?

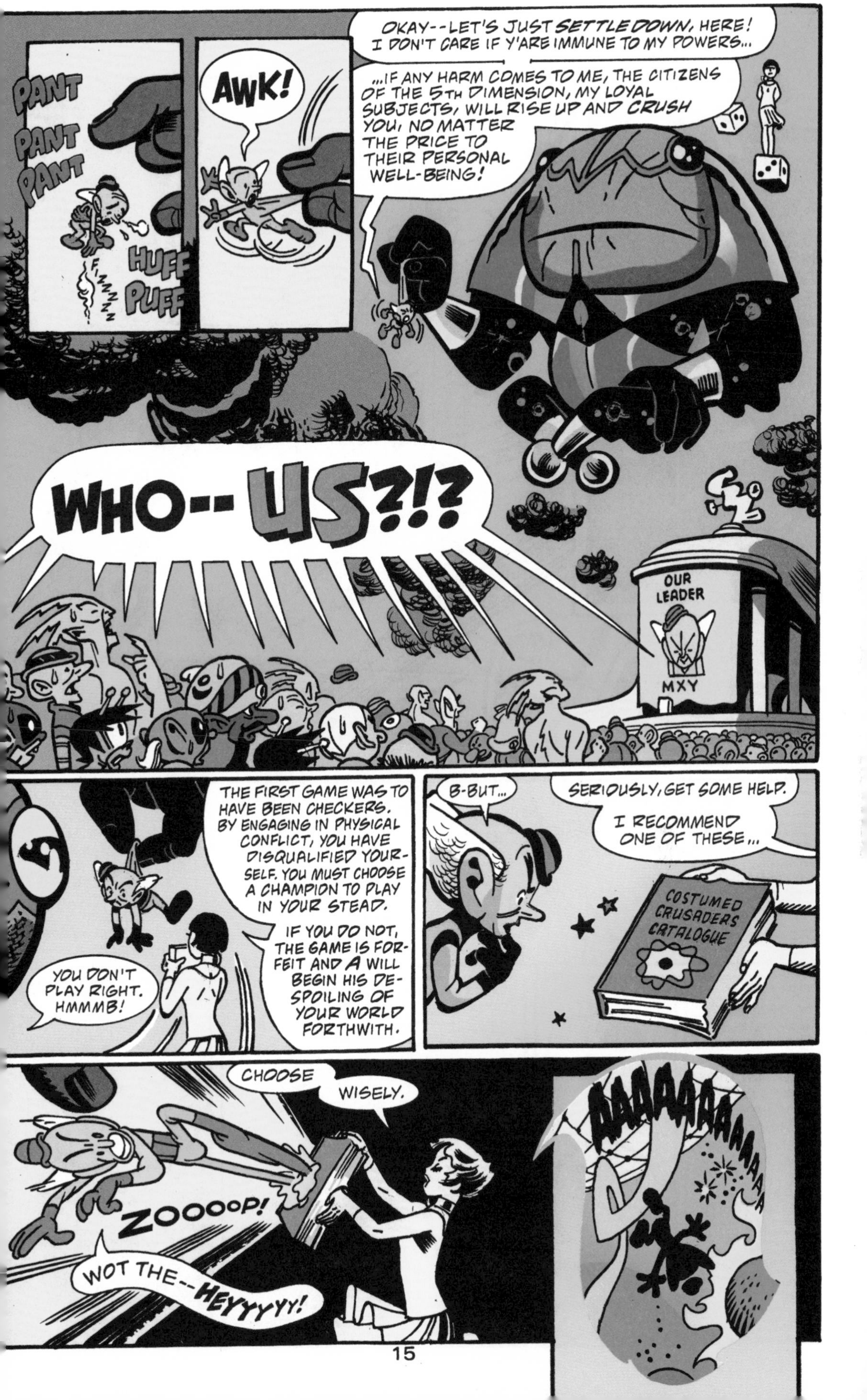
PANT
PANT
PANT
HUFF
PUFF
FZZZZZ
AWK!
OKAY--LET'S JUST SETTLE DOWN, HERE! I DON'T CARE IF Y'ARE IMMUNE TO MY POWERS...
...IF ANY HARM COMES TO ME, THE CITIZENS OF THE 5TH DIMENSION, MY LOYAL SUBJECTS, WILL RISE UP AND CRUSH YOU, NO MATTER THE PRICE TO THEIR PERSONAL WELL-BEING!
WHO-- US?!?
OUR LEADER
MXY
THE FIRST GAME WAS TO HAVE BEEN CHECKERS. BY ENGAGING IN PHYSICAL CONFLICT, YOU HAVE DISQUALIFIED YOURSELF. YOU MUST CHOOSE A CHAMPION TO PLAY IN YOUR STEAD.
IF YOU DO NOT, THE GAME IS FORFEIT AND A WILL BEGIN HIS DESPOILING OF YOUR WORLD FORTHWITH.
YOU DON'T PLAY RIGHT. HMMMB!
B-BUT...
SERIOUSLY, GET SOME HELP.
I RECOMMEND ONE OF THESE...
COSTUMED CRUSADERS CATALOGUE
CHOOSE
WISELY.
ZOOOOP!
WOT THE--HEYYYYY!
AAAAAAAAAAAAAAA

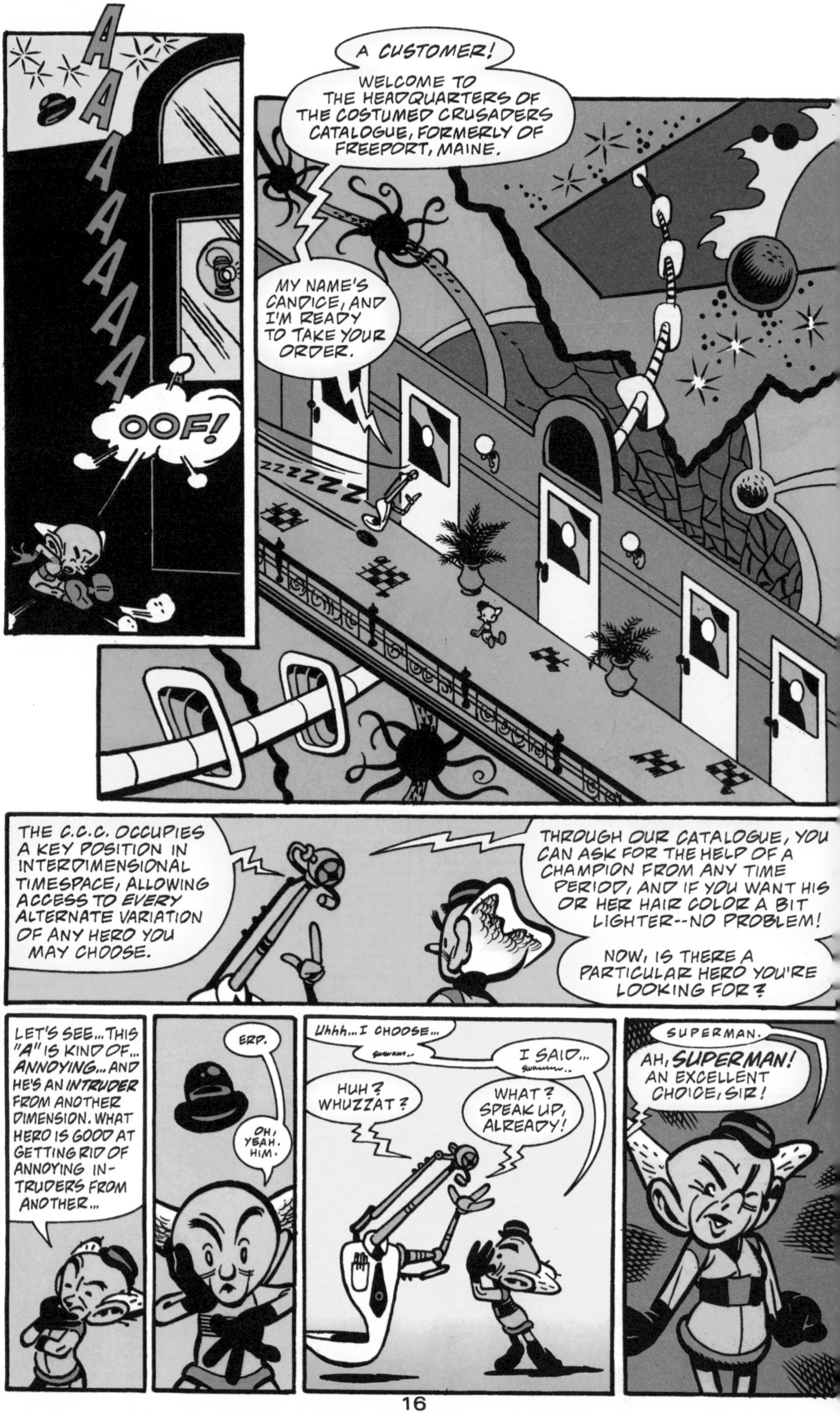
A
A
AAAAA
OOF!
A CUSTOMER!
WELCOME TO THE HEADQUARTERS OF THE COSTUMED CRUSADERS CATALOGUE, FORMERLY OF FREEPORT, MAINE.
MY NAME'S CANDICE, AND I'M READY TO TAKE YOUR ORDER.
ZZZZZZZ
THE C.C.C. OCCUPIES A KEY POSITION IN INTERDIMENSIONAL TIMESPACE, ALLOWING ACCESS TO EVERY ALTERNATE VARIATION OF ANY HERO YOU MAY CHOOSE.
THROUGH OUR CATALOGUE, YOU CAN ASK FOR THE HELP OF A CHAMPION FROM ANY TIME PERIOD, AND IF YOU WANT HIS OR HER HAIR COLOR A BIT LIGHTER--NO PROBLEM!
NOW, IS THERE A PARTICULAR HERO YOU'RE LOOKING FOR?
LET'S SEE...THIS "A" IS KIND OF... ANNOYING... AND HE'S AN INTRUDER FROM ANOTHER DIMENSION. WHAT HERO IS GOOD AT GETTING RID OF ANNOYING INTRUDERS FROM ANOTHER...
ERP.
OH, YEAH. HIM.
Uhhh... I CHOOSE...
HUH? WHUZZAT?
I SAID...
WHAT? SPEAK UP, ALREADY!
SUPERMAN.
AH, SUPERMAN! AN EXCELLENT CHOICE, SIR!

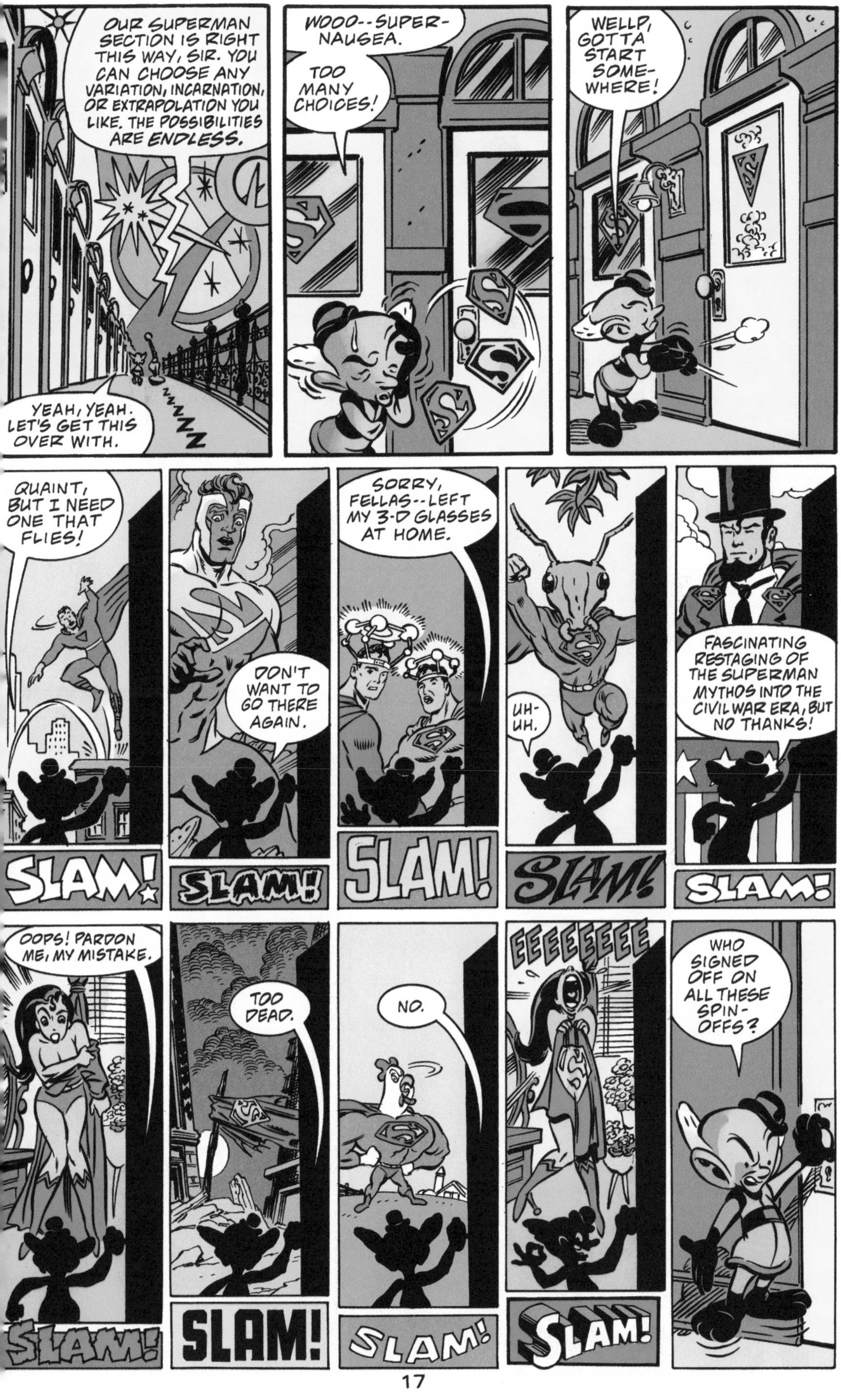
OUR SUPERMAN SECTION IS RIGHT THIS WAY, SIR. YOU CAN CHOOSE ANY VARIATION, INCARNATION, OR EXTRAPOLATION YOU LIKE. THE POSSIBILITIES ARE ENDLESS.
YEAH, YEAH. LET'S GET THIS OVER WITH.
ZZZZ
WOOO--SUPER-NAUSEA.
TOO MANY CHOICES!
WELLP, GOTTA START SOME-WHERE!
QUAINT, BUT I NEED ONE THAT FLIES!
SLAM!
DON'T WANT TO GO THERE AGAIN.
SLAM!
SORRY, FELLAS--LEFT MY 3-D GLASSES AT HOME.
SLAM!
UH-UH.
SLAM!
FASCINATING RESTAGING OF THE SUPERMAN MYTHOS INTO THE CIVIL WAR ERA, BUT NO THANKS!
SLAM!
OOPS! PARDON ME, MY MISTAKE.
SLAM!
TOO DEAD.
SLAM!
NO.
SLAM!
EEEEEEEE
SLAM!
WHO SIGNED OFF ON ALL THESE SPIN-OFFS?

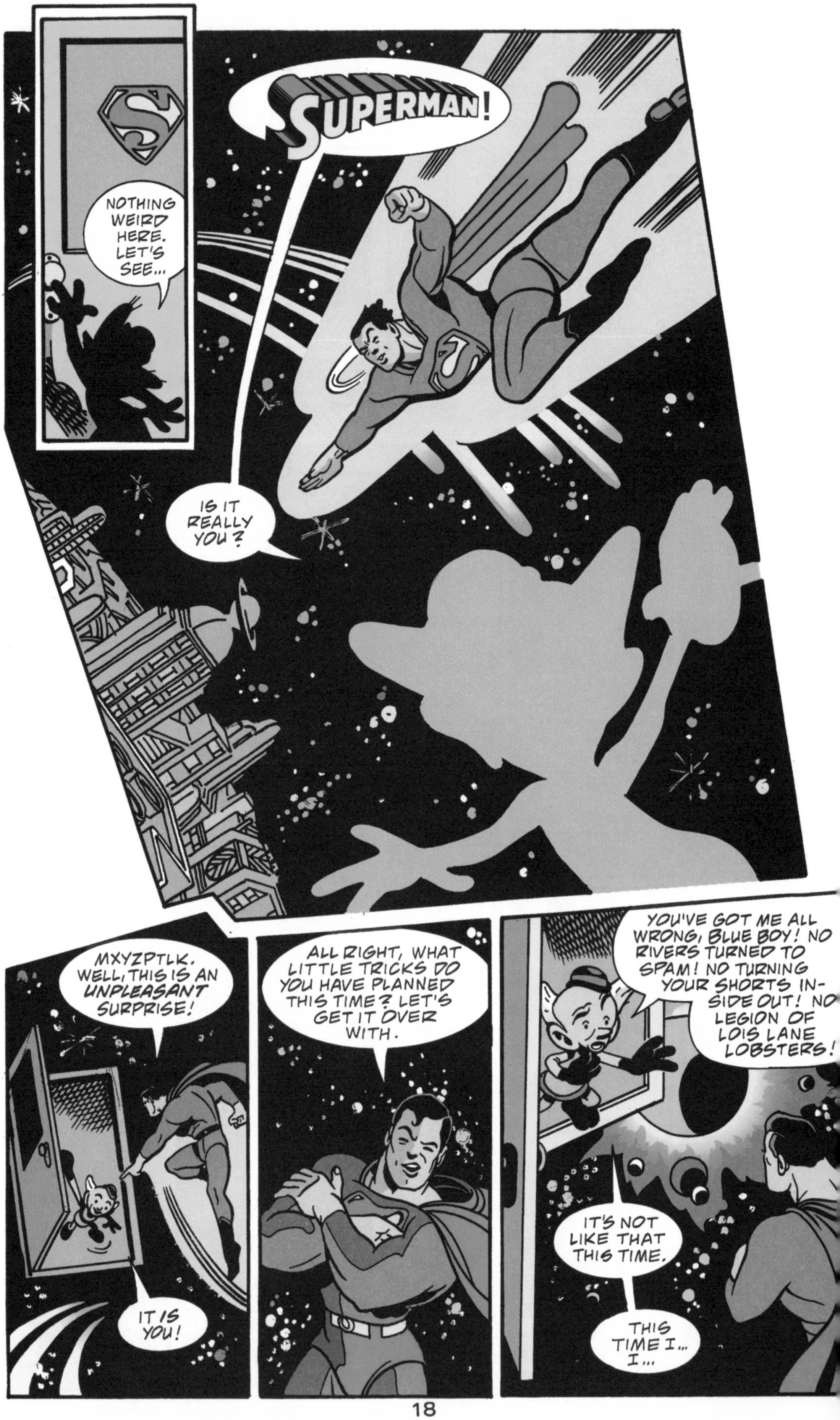
NOTHING WEIRD HERE. LET'S SEE...
SUPERMAN!
IS IT REALLY YOU?
MXYZPTLK. WELL, THIS IS AN UNPLEASANT SURPRISE!
IT IS YOU!
ALL RIGHT, WHAT LITTLE TRICKS DO YOU HAVE PLANNED THIS TIME? LET'S GET IT OVER WITH.
YOU'VE GOT ME ALL WRONG, BLUE BOY! NO RIVERS TURNED TO SPAM! NO TURNING YOUR SHORTS INSIDE OUT! NO LEGION OF LOIS LANE LOBSTERS!
IT'S NOT LIKE THAT THIS TIME.
THIS TIME I... I...

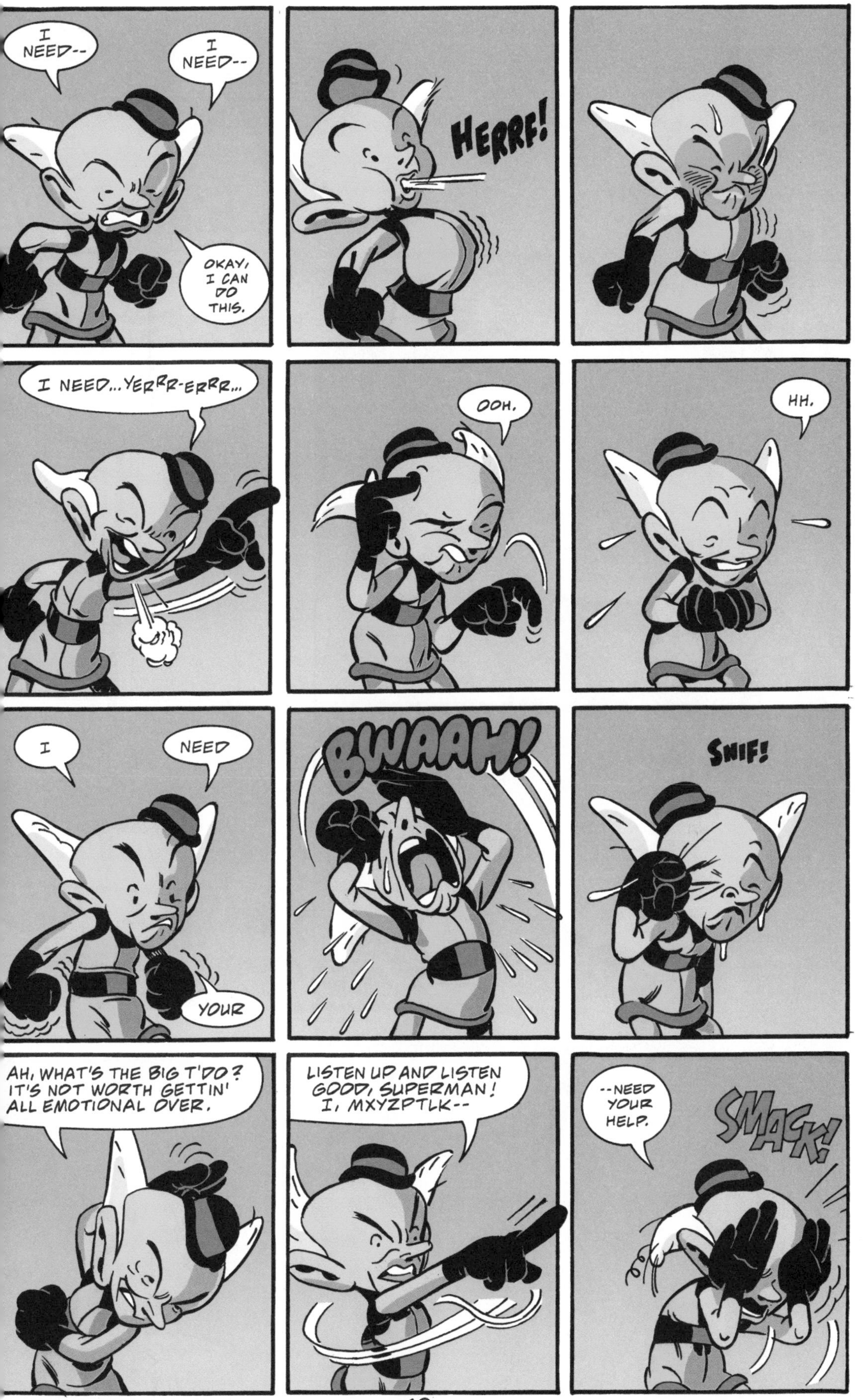
I NEED--
I NEED--
OKAY, I CAN DO THIS.
HERRF!
I NEED... YERRR-ERRR...
OOH.
HH.
I
NEED
YOUR
BWAAAH!
SNIF!
AH, WHAT'S THE BIG T'DO? IT'S NOT WORTH GETTIN' ALL EMOTIONAL OVER.
LISTEN UP AND LISTEN GOOD, SUPERMAN! I, MXYZPTLK--
--NEED YOUR HELP.
SMACK!

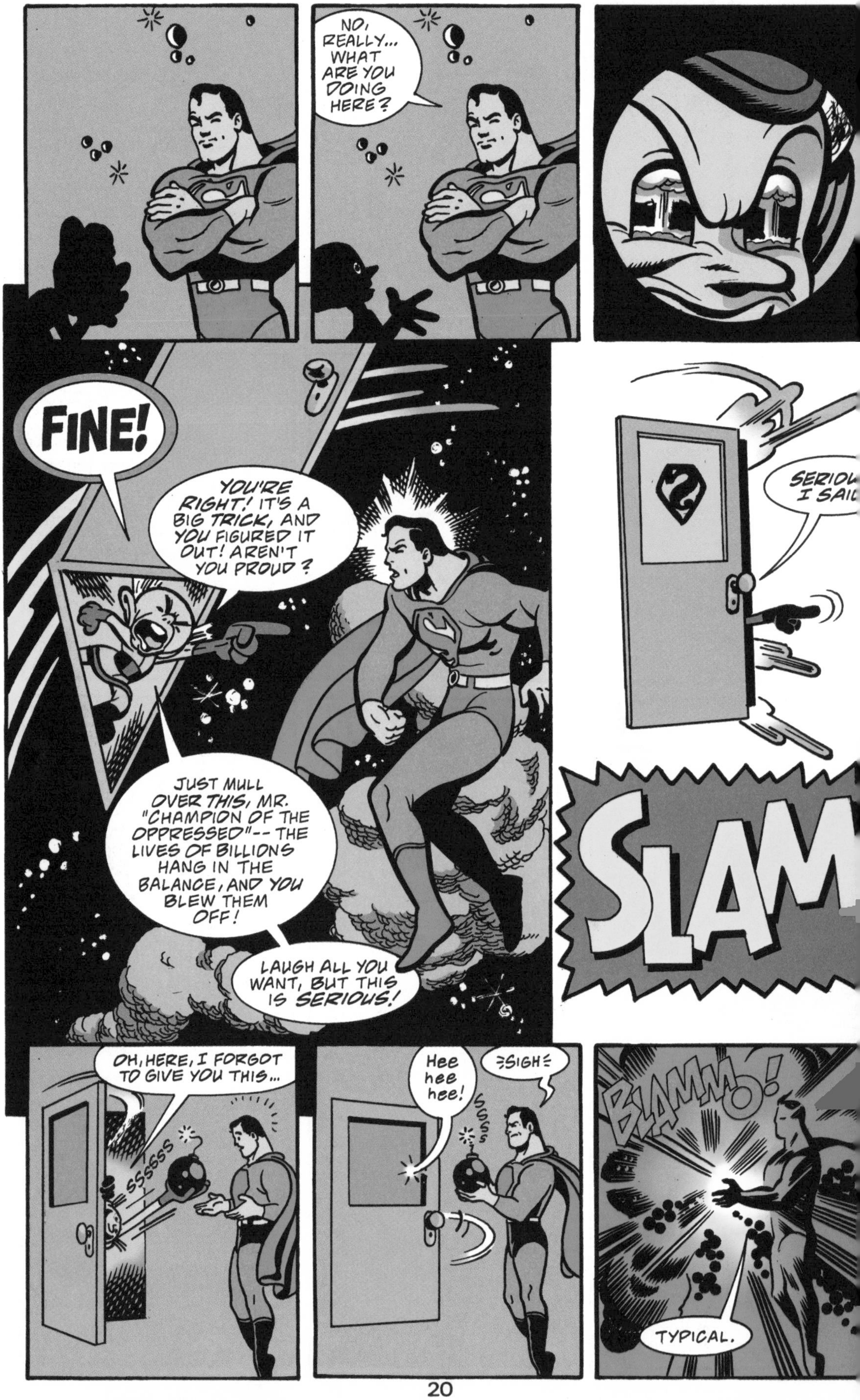
NO, REALLY... WHAT ARE YOU DOING HERE?
FINE!
YOU'RE RIGHT! IT'S A BIG TRICK, AND YOU FIGURED IT OUT! AREN'T YOU PROUD?
JUST MULL OVER THIS, MR. "CHAMPION OF THE OPPRESSED"-- THE LIVES OF BILLIONS HANG IN THE BALANCE, AND YOU BLEW THEM OFF!
LAUGH ALL YOU WANT, BUT THIS IS SERIOUS!
SLAM
OH, HERE, I FORGOT TO GIVE YOU THIS...
SSSSS
Hee hee hee!
SSSS
SIGH
BLAMMO!
TYPICAL.

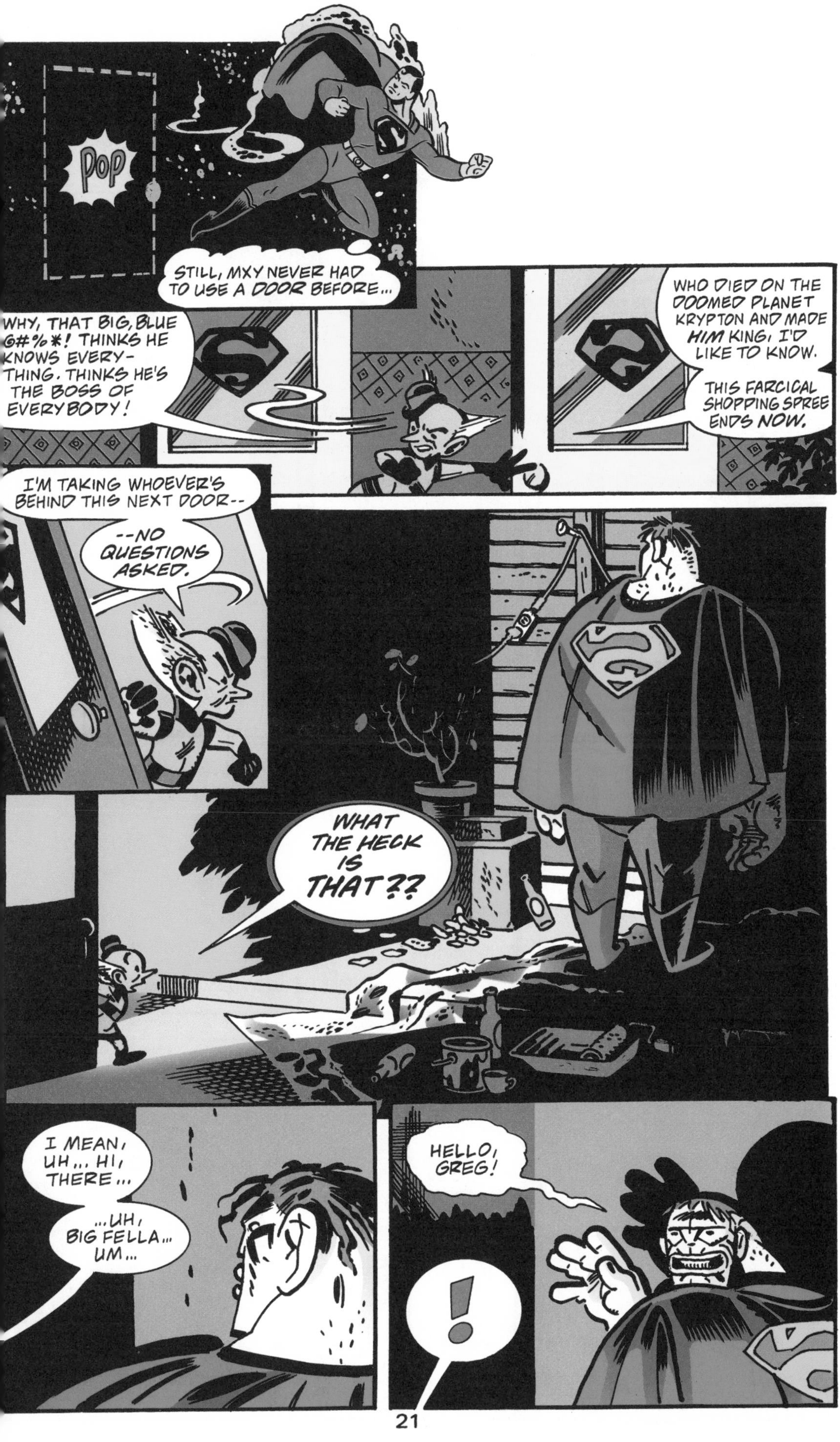
POP
STILL, MXY NEVER HAD TO USE A DOOR BEFORE...
WHY, THAT BIG, BLUE G#%*! THINKS HE KNOWS EVERY-THING. THINKS HE'S THE BOSS OF EVERYBODY!
WHO DIED ON THE DOOMED PLANET KRYPTON AND MADE HIM KING, I'D LIKE TO KNOW.
THIS FARCICAL SHOPPING SPREE ENDS NOW.
I'M TAKING WHOEVER'S BEHIND THIS NEXT DOOR--
--NO QUESTIONS ASKED.
WHAT THE HECK IS THAT??
I MEAN, UH... HI, THERE...
...UH, BIG FELLA... UM...
HELLO, GREG!
!

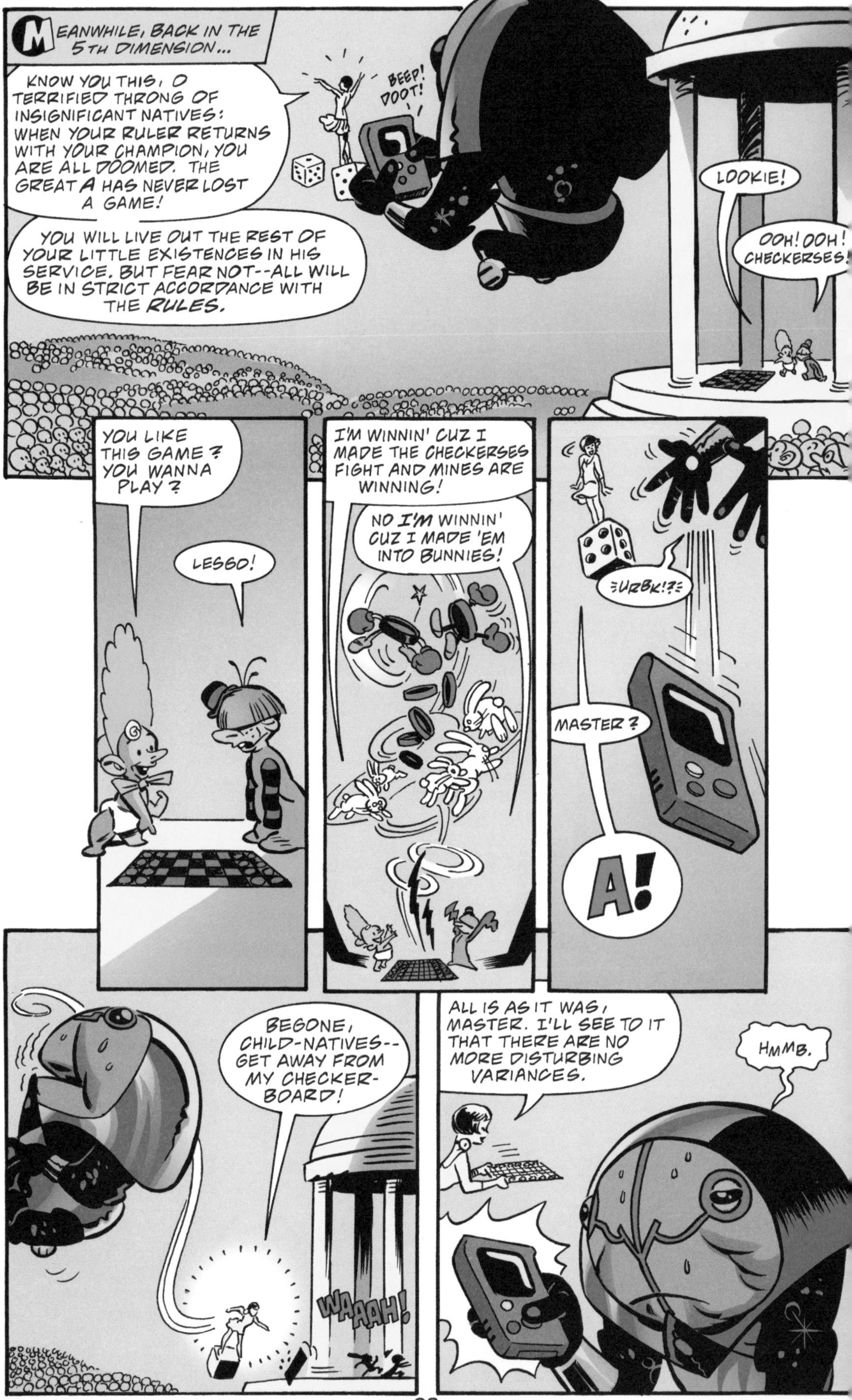

MEANWHILE, BACK IN THE 5TH DIMENSION...
KNOW YOU THIS, O TERRIFIED THRONG OF INSIGNIFICANT NATIVES: WHEN YOUR RULER RETURNS WITH YOUR CHAMPION, YOU ARE ALL DOOMED. THE GREAT A HAS NEVER LOST A GAME!
YOU WILL LIVE OUT THE REST OF YOUR LITTLE EXISTENCES IN HIS SERVICE. BUT FEAR NOT--ALL WILL BE IN STRICT ACCORDANCE WITH THE RULES.
BEEP! DOOT!
LOOKIE!
OOH! OOH! CHECKERSES!
YOU LIKE THIS GAME? YOU WANNA PLAY?
LESGO!
I'M WINNIN' CUZ I MADE THE CHECKERSES FIGHT AND MINES ARE WINNING!
NO I'M WINNIN' CUZ I MADE 'EM INTO BUNNIES!
URBK!?
MASTER?
A!
BEGONE, CHILD-NATIVES--GET AWAY FROM MY CHECKER-BOARD!
WAAAH!
ALL IS AS IT WAS, MASTER. I'LL SEE TO IT THAT THERE ARE NO MORE DISTURBING VARIANCES.
HMMB.

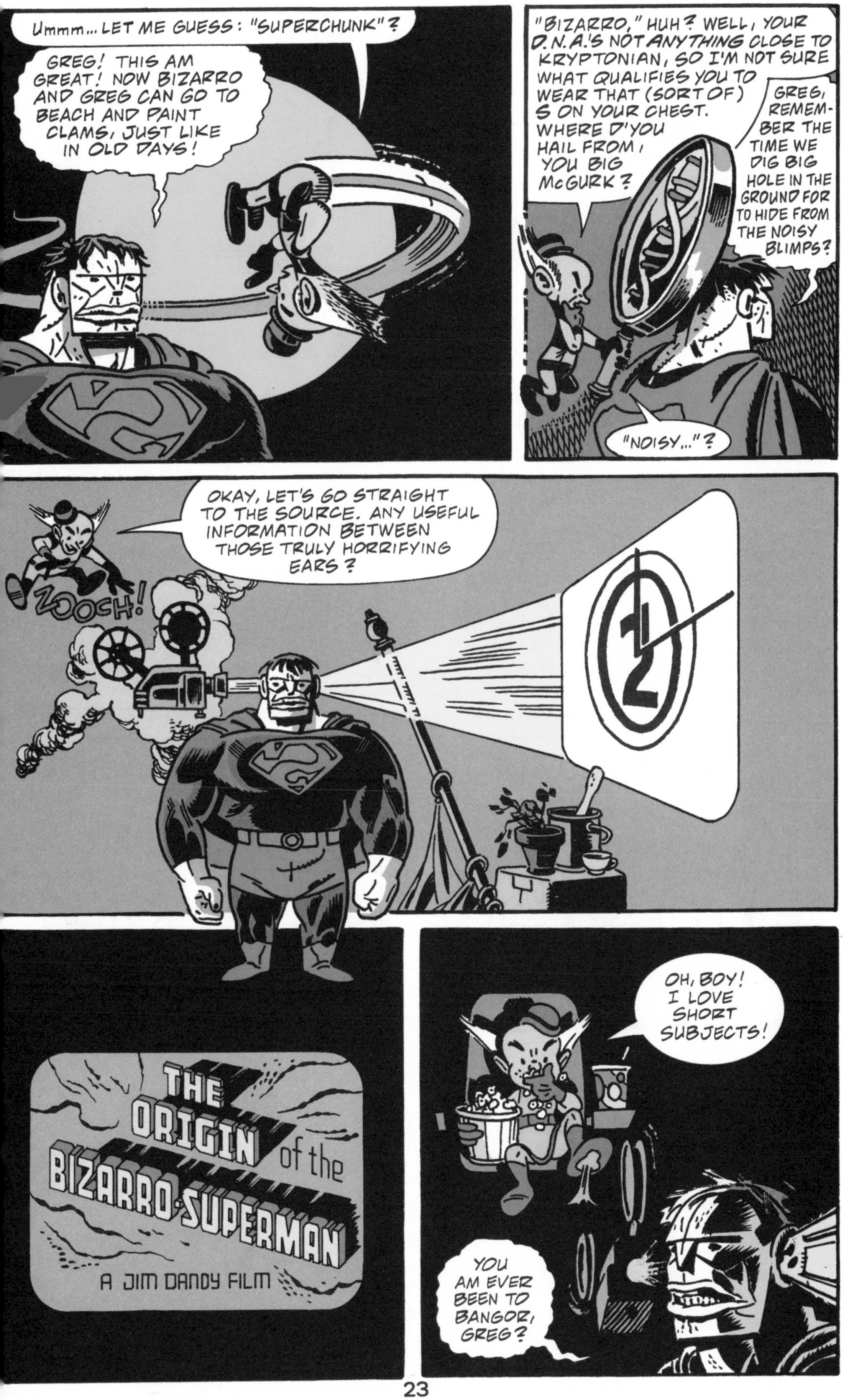
Ummm... LET ME GUESS: "SUPERCHUNK"?
GREG! THIS AM GREAT! NOW BIZARRO AND GREG CAN GO TO BEACH AND PAINT CLAMS, JUST LIKE IN OLD DAYS!
"BIZARRO," HUH? WELL, YOUR D.N.A.'S NOT ANYTHING CLOSE TO KRYPTONIAN, SO I'M NOT SURE WHAT QUALIFIES YOU TO WEAR THAT (SORT OF) S ON YOUR CHEST. WHERE D'YOU HAIL FROM, YOU BIG McGURK?
GREG, REMEMBER THE TIME WE DIG BIG HOLE IN THE GROUND FOR TO HIDE FROM THE NOISY BLIMPS?
"NOISY..."?
OKAY, LET'S GO STRAIGHT TO THE SOURCE. ANY USEFUL INFORMATION BETWEEN THOSE TRULY HORRIFYING EARS?
ZOOCH!
THE ORIGIN of the BIZARRO-SUPERMAN
A JIM DANDY FILM
OH, BOY! I LOVE SHORT SUBJECTS!
YOU AM EVER BEEN TO BANGOR, GREG?

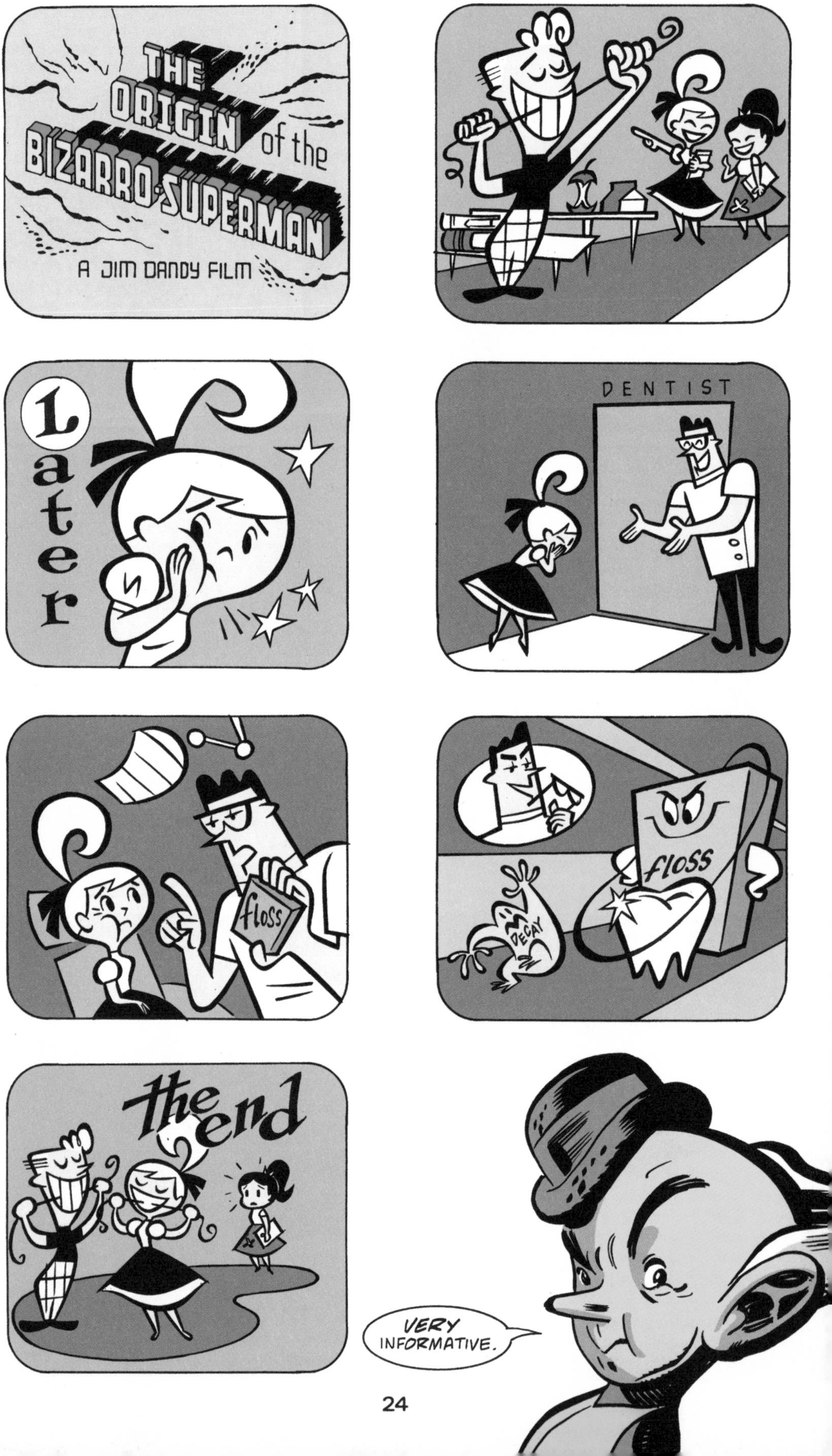
THE ORIGIN of the BIZARRO-SUPERMAN
A JIM DANDY FILM
Later
DENTIST
floss
FLOSS
DECAY
the end
VERY INFORMATIVE.

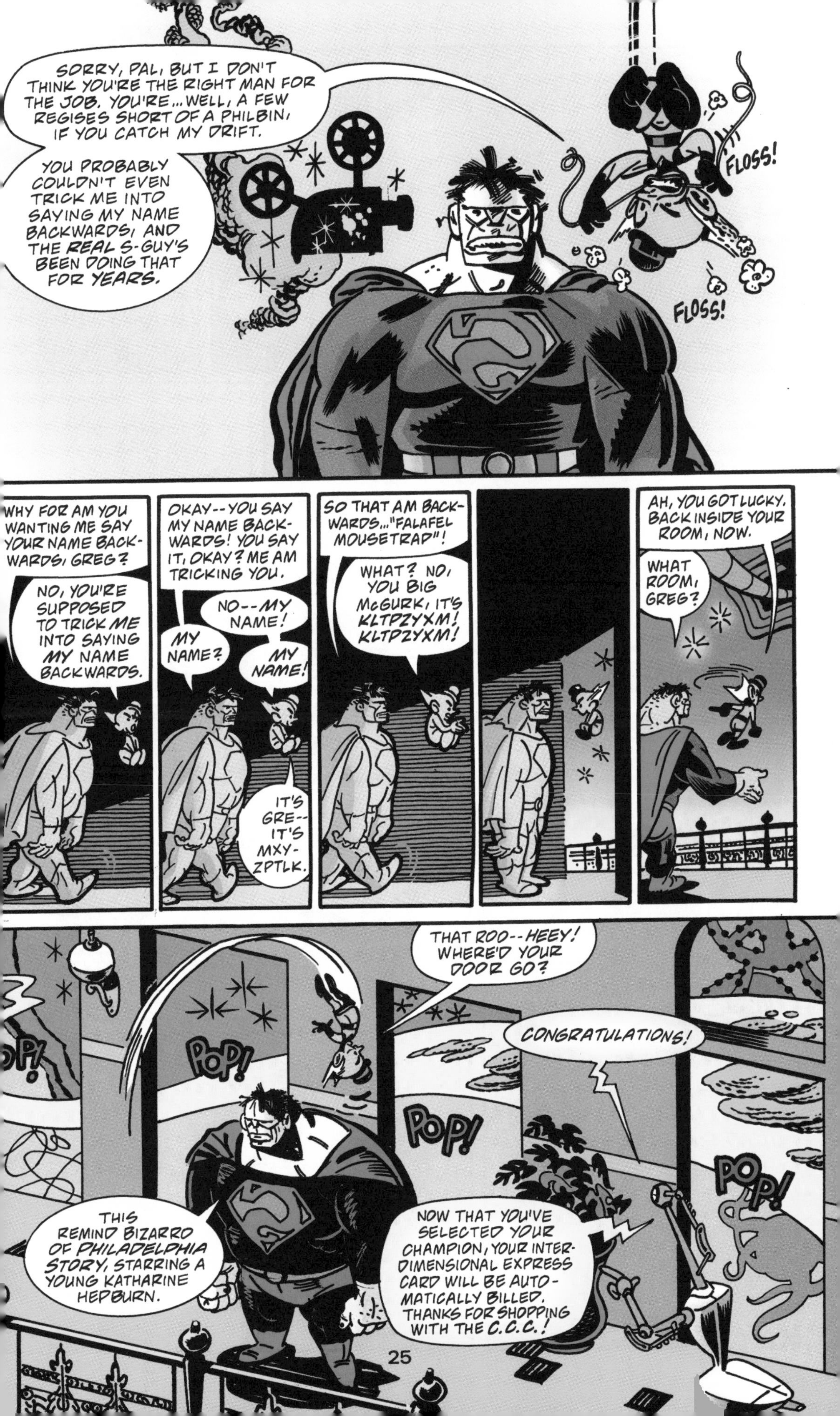
SORRY, PAL, BUT I DON'T THINK YOU'RE THE RIGHT MAN FOR THE JOB. YOU'RE... WELL, A FEW REGISES SHORT OF A PHILBIN, IF YOU CATCH MY DRIFT.
YOU PROBABLY COULDN'T EVEN TRICK ME INTO SAYING MY NAME BACKWARDS, AND THE REAL S-GUY'S BEEN DOING THAT FOR YEARS.
FLOSS!
FLOSS!
WHY FOR AM YOU WANTING ME SAY YOUR NAME BACKWARDS, GREG?
NO, YOU'RE SUPPOSED TO TRICK ME INTO SAYING MY NAME BACKWARDS.
OKAY--YOU SAY MY NAME BACKWARDS! YOU SAY IT, OKAY? ME AM TRICKING YOU.
MY NAME?
NO--MY NAME!
MY NAME!
IT'S GRE-- IT'S MXY-ZPTLK.
SO THAT AM BACKWARDS... "FALAFEL MOUSETRAP"!
WHAT? NO, YOU BIG McGURK, IT'S KLTPZYXM! KLTPZYXM!
AH, YOU GOT LUCKY. BACK INSIDE YOUR ROOM, NOW.
WHAT ROOM, GREG?
THAT ROO--HEEY! WHERE'D YOUR DOOR GO?
POP!
POP!
POP!
POP!
CONGRATULATIONS!
THIS REMIND BIZARRO OF PHILADELPHIA STORY, STARRING A YOUNG KATHARINE HEPBURN.
NOW THAT YOU'VE SELECTED YOUR CHAMPION, YOUR INTER-DIMENSIONAL EXPRESS CARD WILL BE AUTO-MATICALLY BILLED. THANKS FOR SHOPPING WITH THE C.C.C.!

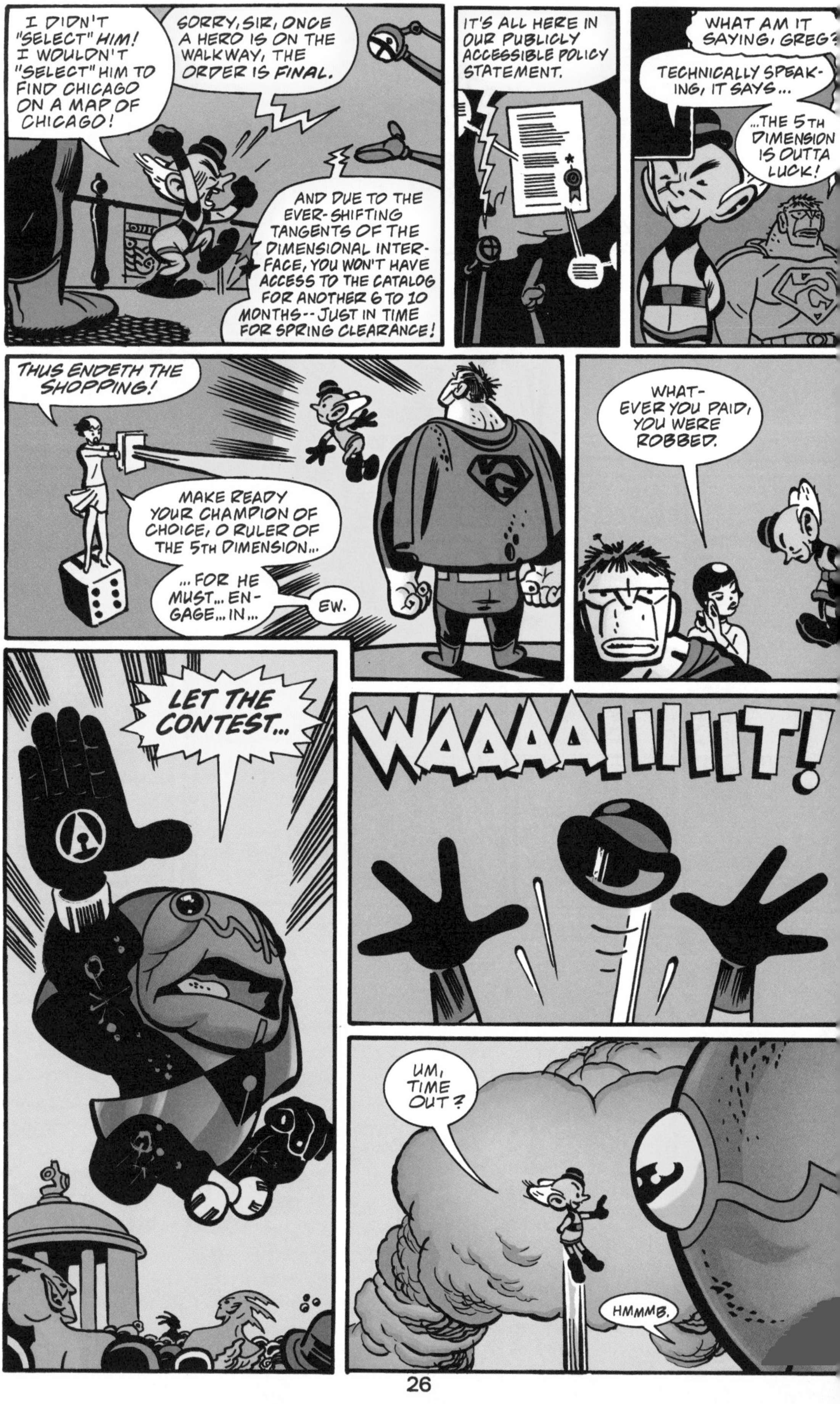
I DIDN'T "SELECT" HIM! I WOULDN'T "SELECT" HIM TO FIND CHICAGO ON A MAP OF CHICAGO!
SORRY, SIR, ONCE A HERO IS ON THE WALKWAY, THE ORDER IS FINAL.
AND DUE TO THE EVER-SHIFTING TANGENTS OF THE DIMENSIONAL INTER-FACE, YOU WON'T HAVE ACCESS TO THE CATALOG FOR ANOTHER 6 TO 10 MONTHS-- JUST IN TIME FOR SPRING CLEARANCE!
IT'S ALL HERE IN OUR PUBLICLY ACCESSIBLE POLICY STATEMENT.
WHAT AM IT SAYING, GREG?
TECHNICALLY SPEAK-ING, IT SAYS...
...THE 5TH DIMENSION IS OUTTA LUCK!
THUS ENDETH THE SHOPPING!
MAKE READY YOUR CHAMPION OF CHOICE, O RULER OF THE 5TH DIMENSION...
...FOR HE MUST... EN-GAGE... IN...
EW.
WHAT-EVER YOU PAID, YOU WERE ROBBED.
LET THE CONTEST...
WAAAAIIIIIT!
UM, TIME OUT?
HMMMB.

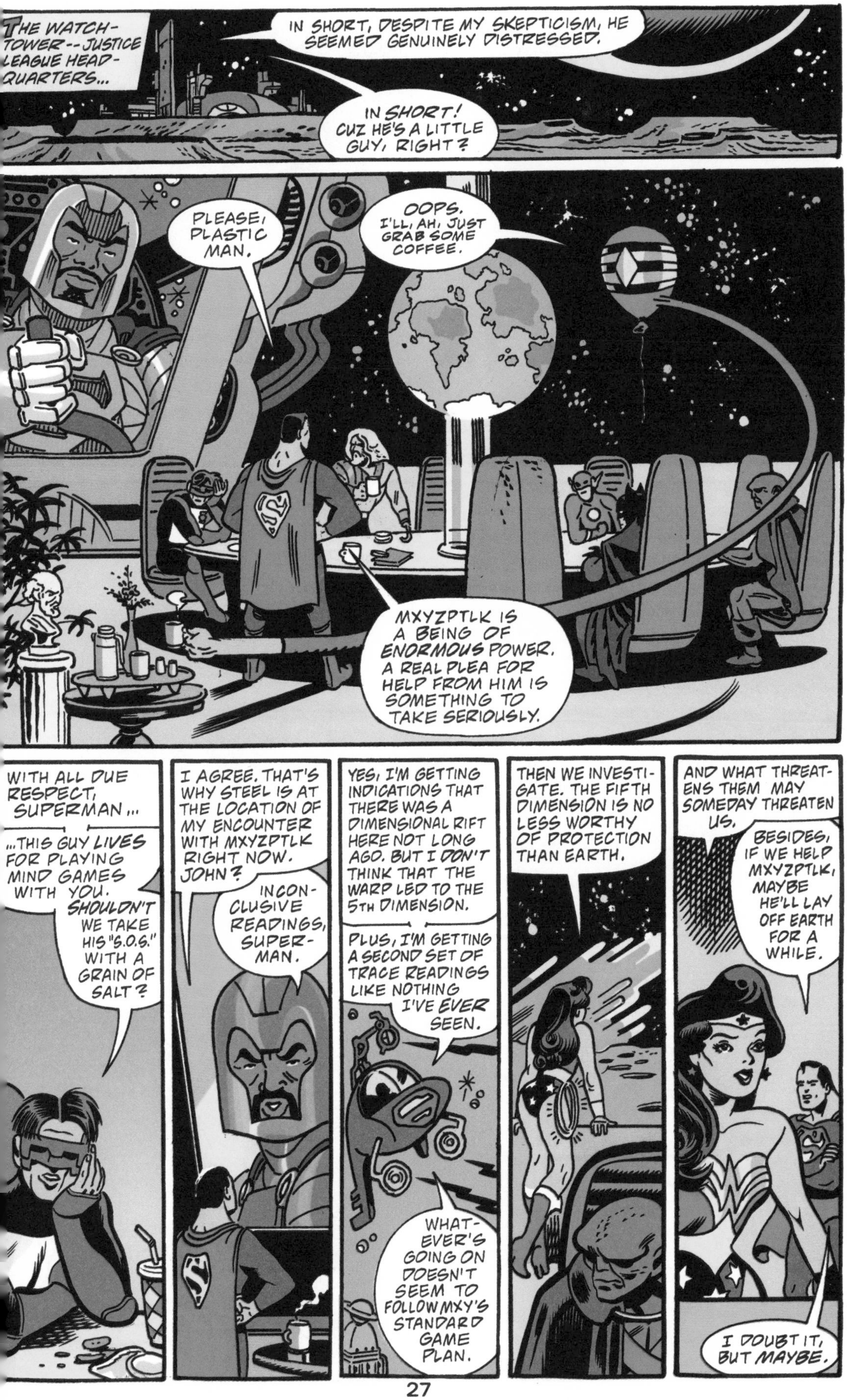
THE WATCHTOWER--JUSTICE LEAGUE HEADQUARTERS...
IN SHORT, DESPITE MY SKEPTICISM, HE SEEMED GENUINELY DISTRESSED.
IN SHORT! CUZ HE'S A LITTLE GUY, RIGHT?
PLEASE, PLASTIC MAN.
OOPS. I'LL, AH, JUST GRAB SOME COFFEE.
MXYZPTLK IS A BEING OF ENORMOUS POWER. A REAL PLEA FOR HELP FROM HIM IS SOMETHING TO TAKE SERIOUSLY.
WITH ALL DUE RESPECT, SUPERMAN...
...THIS GUY LIVES FOR PLAYING MIND GAMES WITH YOU.
SHOULDN'T WE TAKE HIS "S.O.S." WITH A GRAIN OF SALT?
I AGREE. THAT'S WHY STEEL IS AT THE LOCATION OF MY ENCOUNTER WITH MXYZPTLK RIGHT NOW. JOHN?
INCONCLUSIVE READINGS, SUPERMAN.
YES, I'M GETTING INDICATIONS THAT THERE WAS A DIMENSIONAL RIFT HERE NOT LONG AGO. BUT I DON'T THINK THAT THE WARP LED TO THE 5TH DIMENSION.
PLUS, I'M GETTING A SECOND SET OF TRACE READINGS LIKE NOTHING I'VE EVER SEEN.
WHATEVER'S GOING ON DOESN'T SEEM TO FOLLOW MXY'S STANDARD GAME PLAN.
THEN WE INVESTIGATE. THE FIFTH DIMENSION IS NO LESS WORTHY OF PROTECTION THAN EARTH.
AND WHAT THREATENS THEM MAY SOMEDAY THREATEN US.
BESIDES, IF WE HELP MXYZPTLK, MAYBE HE'LL LAY OFF EARTH FOR A WHILE.
I DOUBT IT, BUT MAYBE.

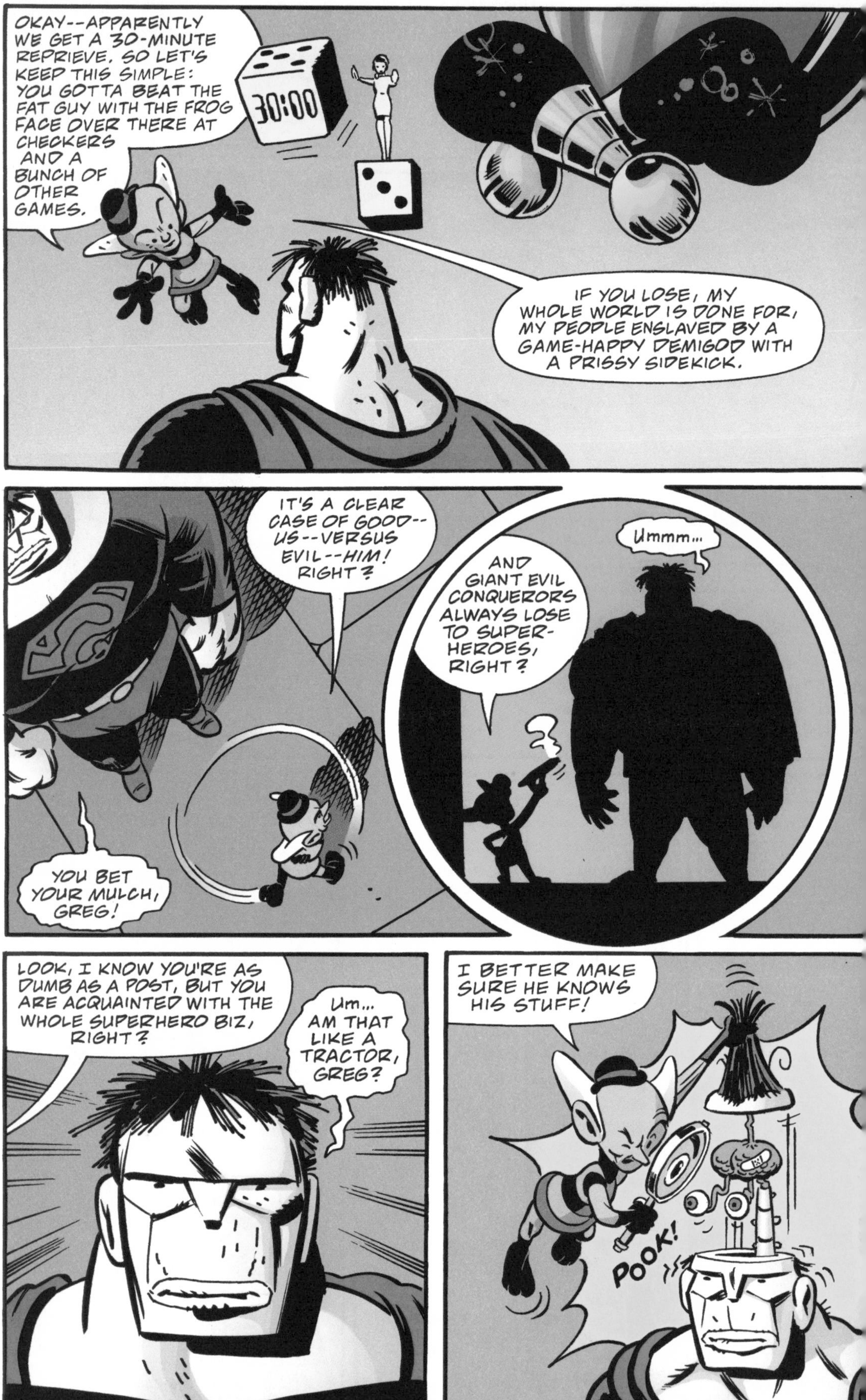
OKAY--APPARENTLY WE GET A 30-MINUTE REPRIEVE. SO LET'S KEEP THIS SIMPLE: YOU GOTTA BEAT THE FAT GUY WITH THE FROG FACE OVER THERE AT CHECKERS AND A BUNCH OF OTHER GAMES.
30:00
IF YOU LOSE, MY WHOLE WORLD IS DONE FOR, MY PEOPLE ENSLAVED BY A GAME-HAPPY DEMIGOD WITH A PRISSY SIDEKICK.
IT'S A CLEAR CASE OF GOOD--US--VERSUS EVIL--HIM! RIGHT?
YOU BET YOUR MULCH, GREG!
AND GIANT EVIL CONQUERORS ALWAYS LOSE TO SUPER-HEROES, RIGHT?
Ummm...
LOOK, I KNOW YOU'RE AS DUMB AS A POST, BUT YOU ARE ACQUAINTED WITH THE WHOLE SUPERHERO BIZ, RIGHT?
Um... AM THAT LIKE A TRACTOR, GREG?
I BETTER MAKE SURE HE KNOWS HIS STUFF!
POOK!

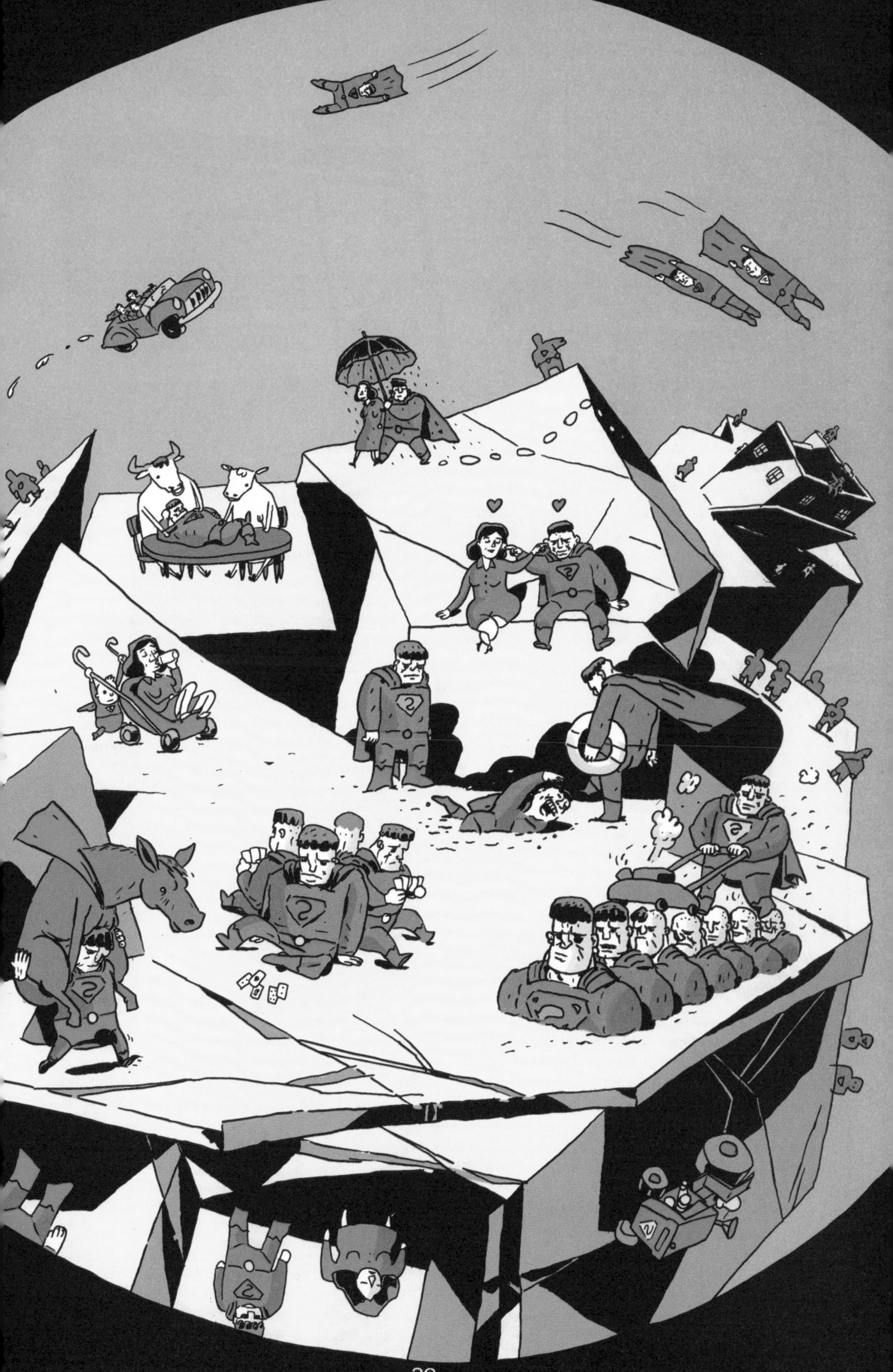

PROBLEM. BIZARRO ONLY KNOWS... BIZARRO. HE NEEDS A CRASH COURSE IN ALL THINGS SUPER.

PLUNK

ZZOOF!

LOOKIE HERE, BIG GUY-- I'VE CREATED SOMETHING YOU THREE-DIMENSIONALS SEEM TO REALLY GO FOR.

THIS WEB SITE WILL TELL YOU *EVERYTHING* YOU NEED TO KNOW ABOUT THOSE ANNOYING SUPERHEROES.

Everything youneedtoknow aboutthoseannoying superheroes.net

OH, GOODY GUM PIES!

THAT'S RIGHT, DIG IN. FIND OUT HOW EVERY ONE OF THEM HAS GOTTA HAVE *BICEPS* THE SIZE OF OAXACA. AND *POWERS*, LIKE THE ABILITY TO TURN ANIMALS INTO ROCK SALT, OR SOME SUCH.

BUT IT'S NOT ALL ABOUT STRENGTH. YA GOTTA HAVE...

...STYLE! CAN'T JUST FIGHT BAD GUYS-- NO! YOU GOTTA DRESS UP AS A BAT, JUMP AROUND IN COLORFUL TIGHTS, AND FAITHFULLY FOLLOW THE *UOTO** CODE.

* THAT'S UNDER-PANTS ON THE OUT-SIDE, IN CASE YOU WERE WONDERING.

CLIKETY! SCROLL! SURF!

AND *ORIGINS!* AS I RECALL, THE CREATION OF A SUPERHERO HAS TO INVOLVE THE GRATUITOUS DEATH OF A LOVED ONE, EXTENSIVE TRAINING BY FORMER NINJAS, LOTS OF RADIATION, AND *MONGOOSES.*

RIP

MON-GEESE?

30

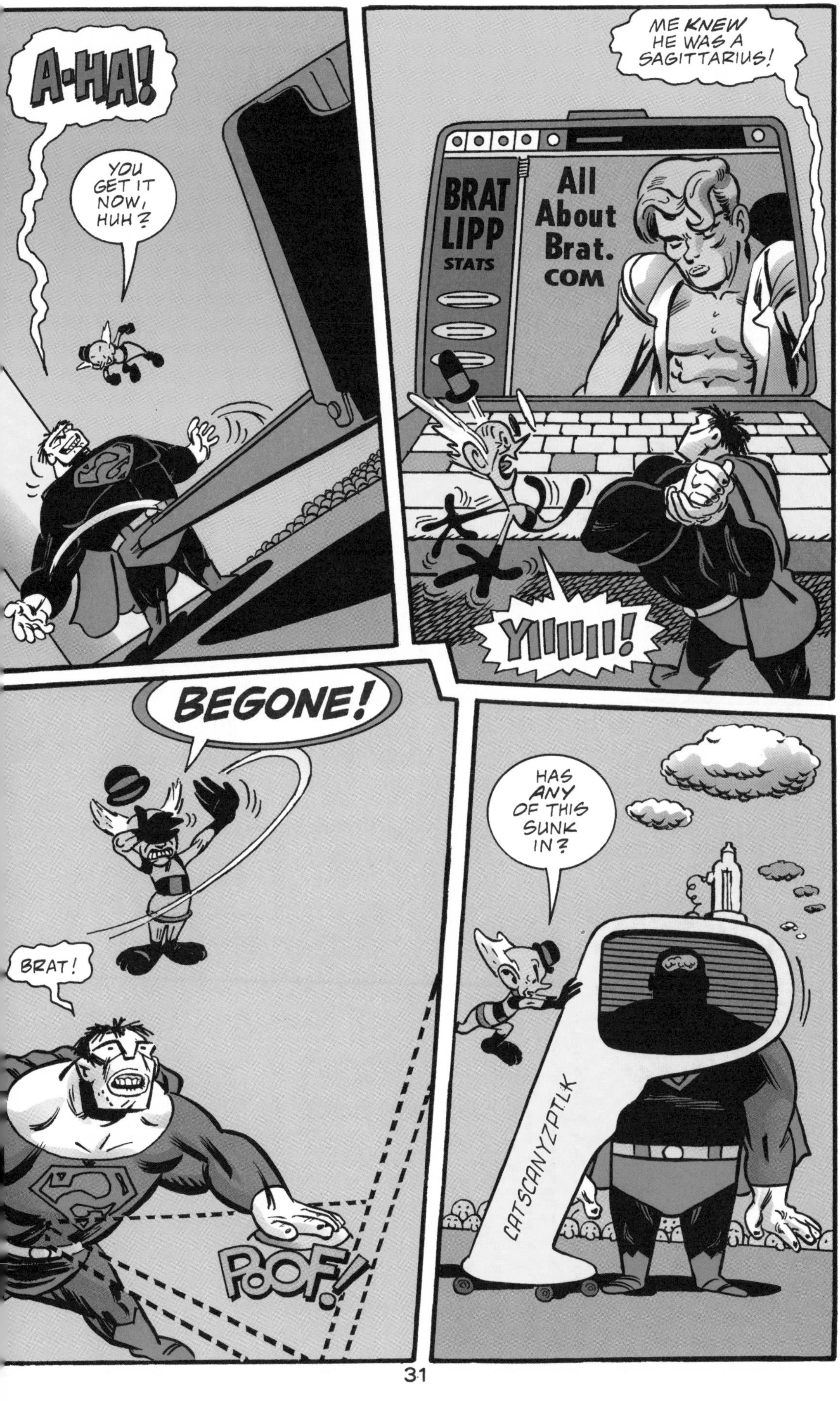
A-HA!
YOU GET IT NOW, HUH?
ME KNEW HE WAS A SAGITTARIUS!
BRAT LIPP STATS
All About Brat. COM
YIIIIII!
BEGONE!
BRAT!
POOF!
HAS ANY OF THIS SUNK IN?
CATSCANYZPTLK

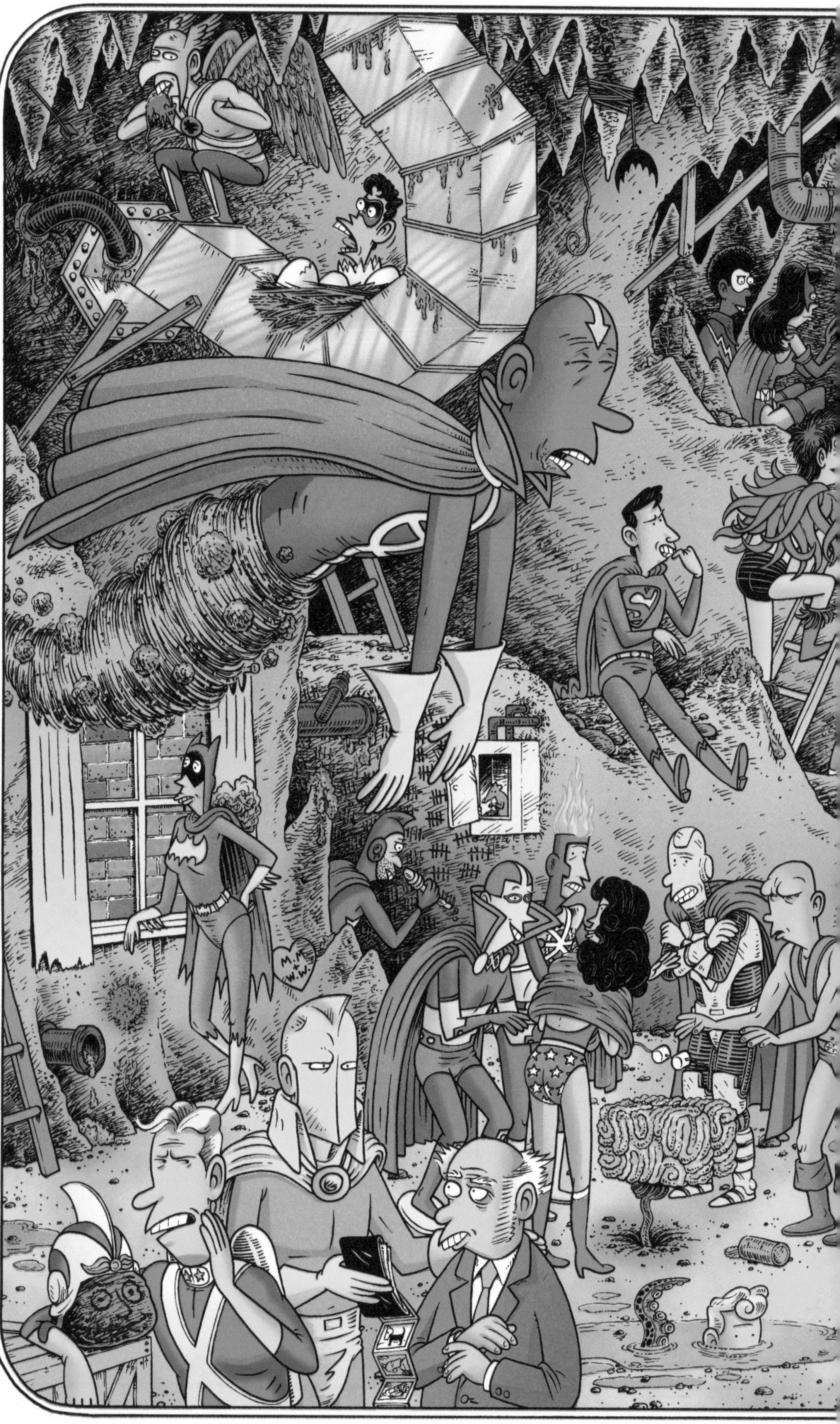
M.M. + W.W.

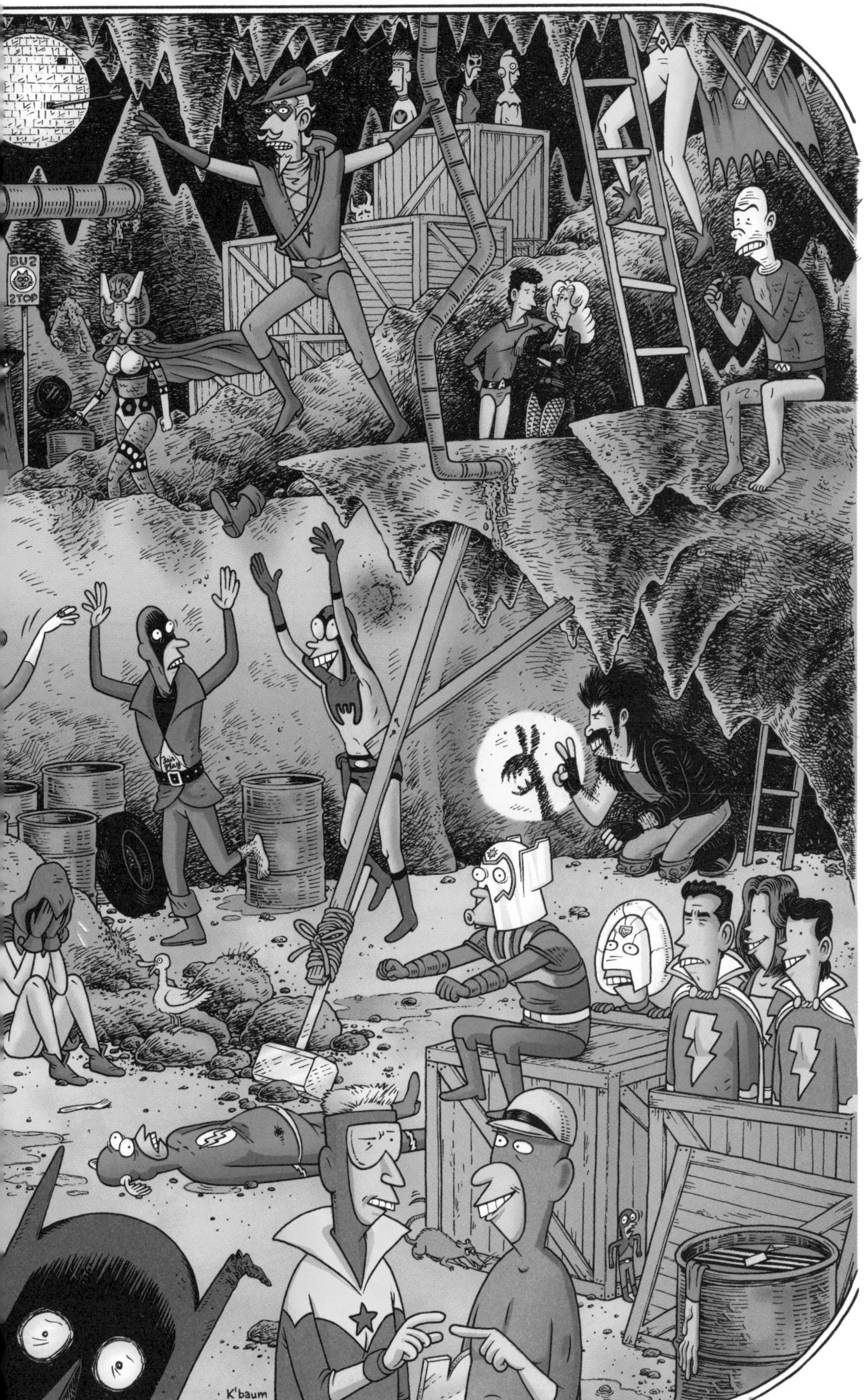
BUS
STOP
K'baum

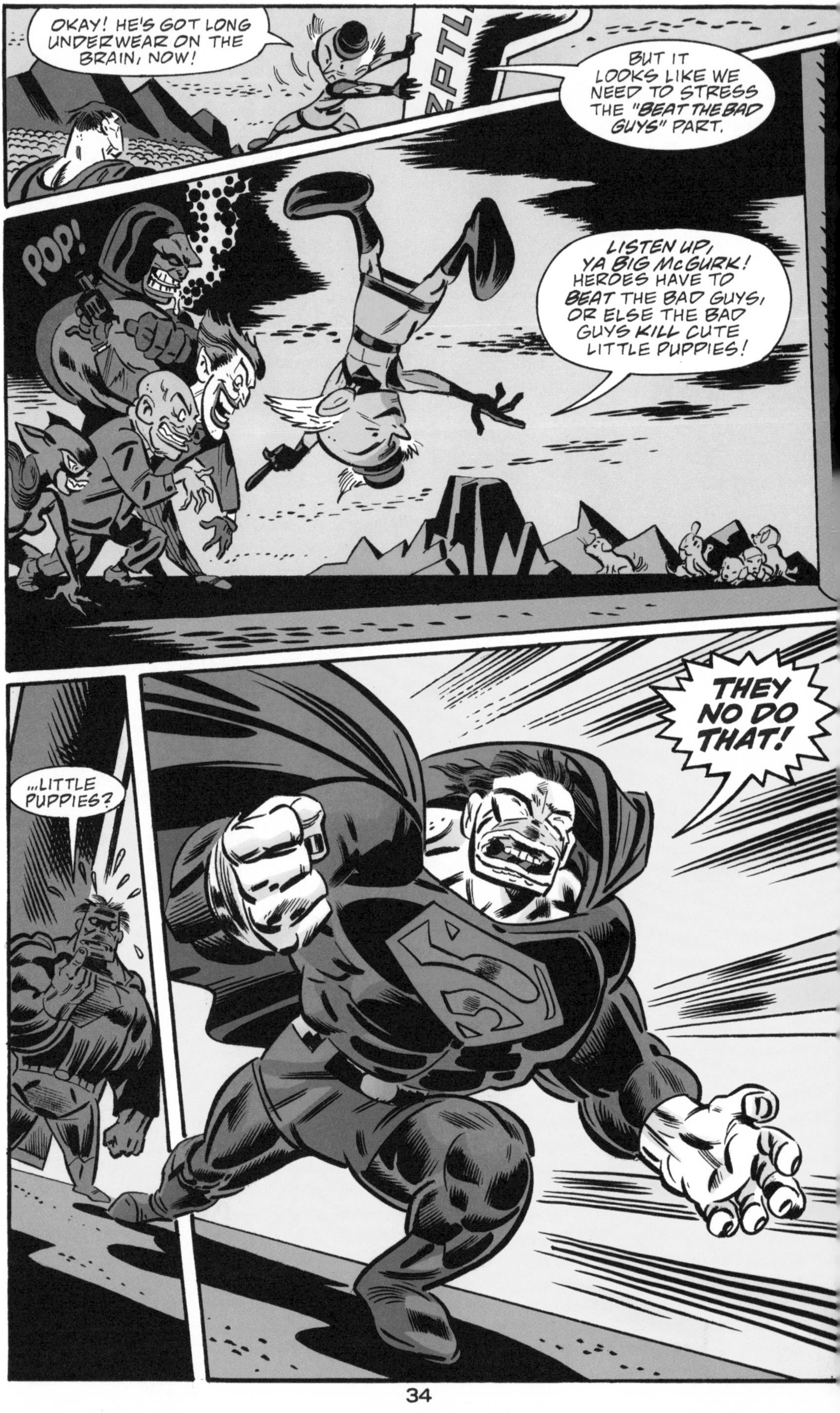
OKAY! HE'S GOT LONG UNDERWEAR ON THE BRAIN, NOW!
BUT IT LOOKS LIKE WE NEED TO STRESS THE "BEAT THE BAD GUYS" PART.
POP!
LISTEN UP, YA BIG McGURK! HEROES HAVE TO BEAT THE BAD GUYS, OR ELSE THE BAD GUYS KILL CUTE LITTLE PUPPIES!
...LITTLE PUPPIES?
THEY NO DO THAT!

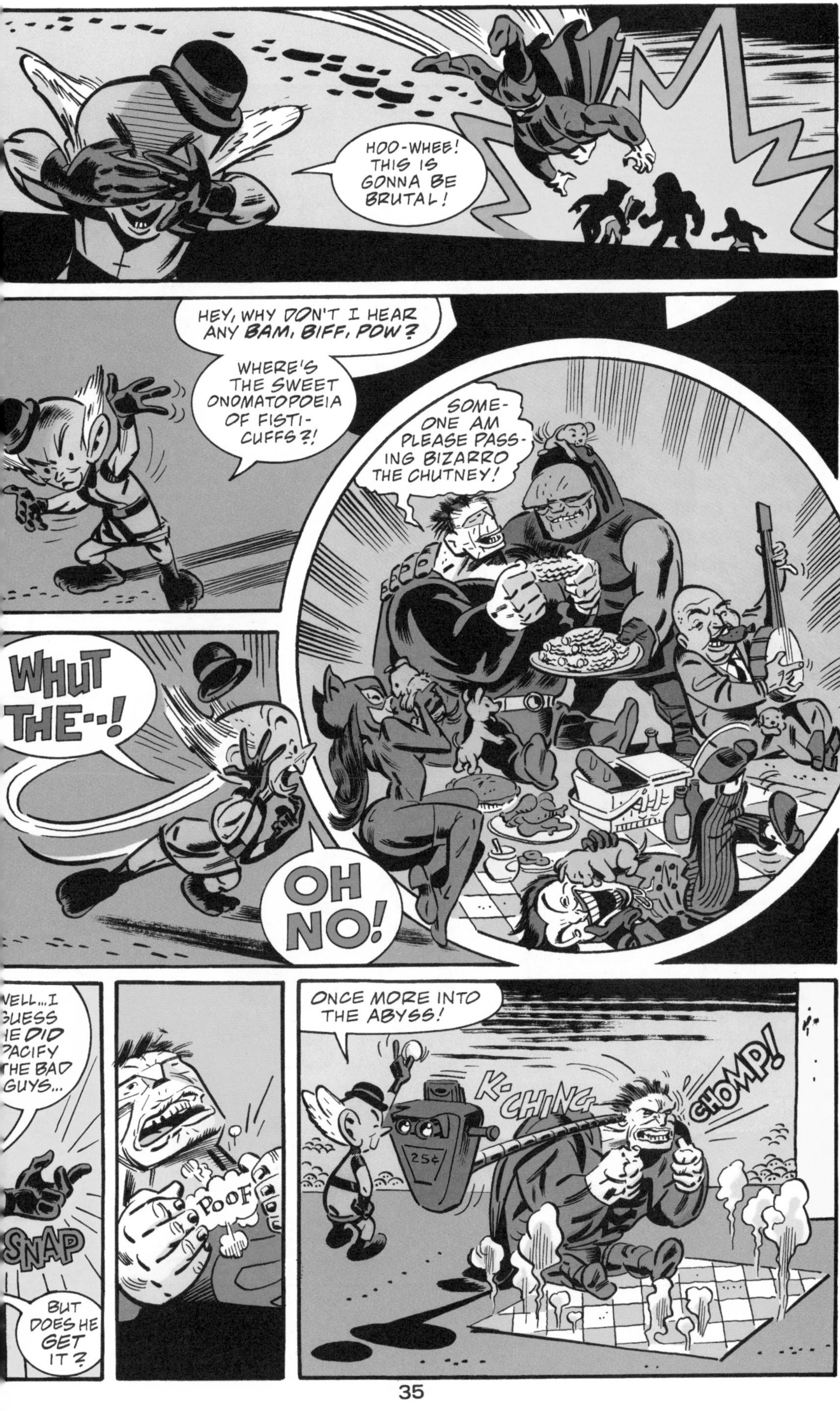
HOO-WHEE! THIS IS GONNA BE BRUTAL!
HEY, WHY DON'T I HEAR ANY BAM, BIFF, POW?
WHERE'S THE SWEET ONOMATOPOEIA OF FISTI-CUFFS?!
SOME-ONE AM PLEASE PASS-ING BIZARRO THE CHUTNEY!
WHUT THE--!
OH NO!
ONCE MORE INTO THE ABYSS!
K-CHING
CHOMP!
25¢
WELL...I GUESS HE DID PACIFY THE BAD GUYS...
POOF
SNAP
BUT DOES HE GET IT?

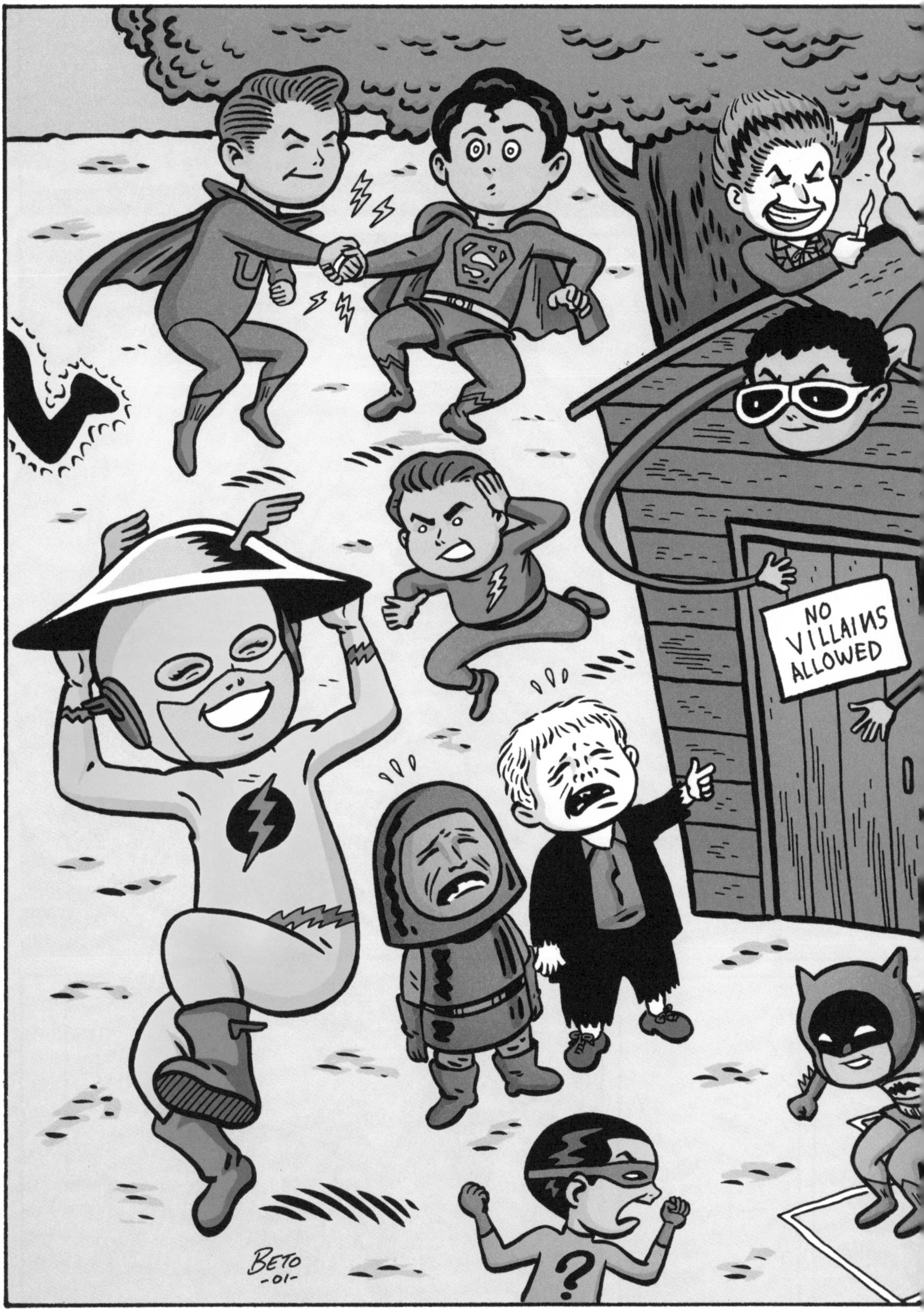
NO VILLAINS ALLOWED
BETO -01-

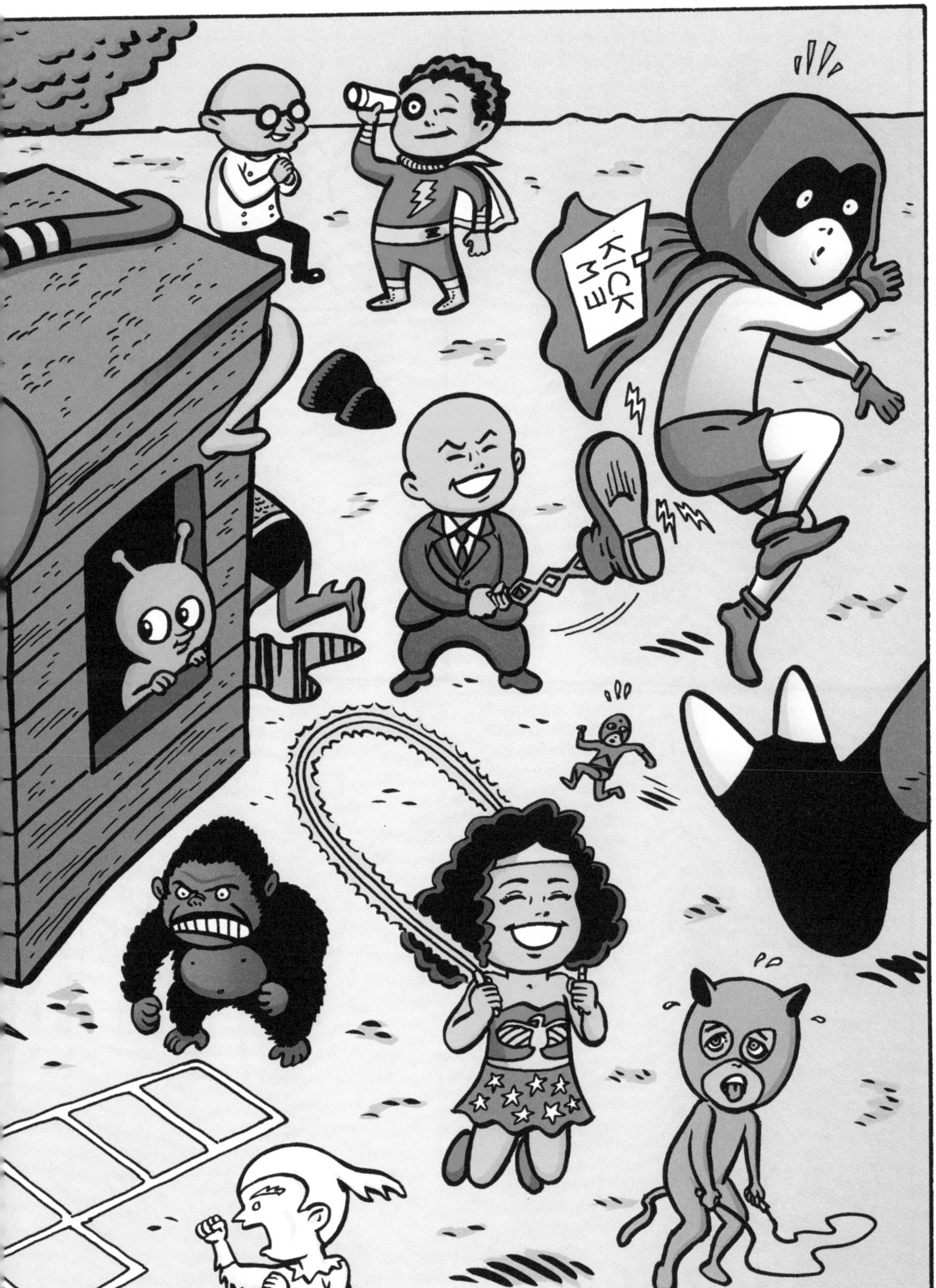
KICK ME

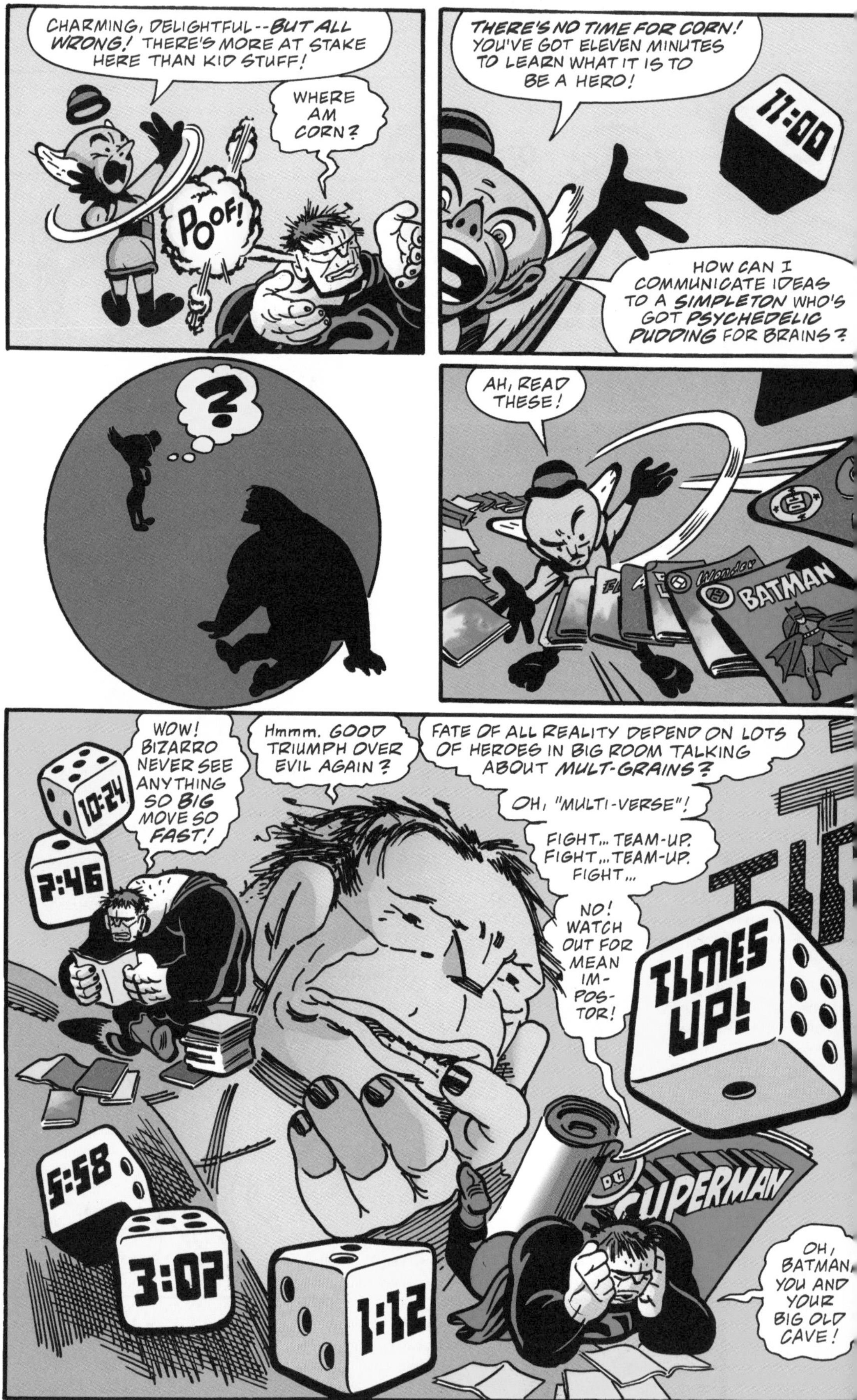
CHARMING, DELIGHTFUL--BUT ALL WRONG! THERE'S MORE AT STAKE HERE THAN KID STUFF!
WHERE AM CORN?
POOF!
THERE'S NO TIME FOR CORN! YOU'VE GOT ELEVEN MINUTES TO LEARN WHAT IT IS TO BE A HERO!
11:00
HOW CAN I COMMUNICATE IDEAS TO A SIMPLETON WHO'S GOT PSYCHEDELIC PUDDING FOR BRAINS?
?
AH, READ THESE!
BATMAN
WOW! BIZARRO NEVER SEE ANYTHING SO BIG MOVE SO FAST!
Hmmm. GOOD TRIUMPH OVER EVIL AGAIN?
FATE OF ALL REALITY DEPEND ON LOTS OF HEROES IN BIG ROOM TALKING ABOUT MULT-GRAINS?
OH, "MULTI-VERSE"!
FIGHT... TEAM-UP. FIGHT... TEAM-UP. FIGHT...
NO! WATCH OUT FOR MEAN IM-POS-TOR!
10:24
7:46
TIMES UP!
5:58
3:07
1:12
SUPERMAN
OH, BATMAN, YOU AND YOUR BIG OLD CAVE!

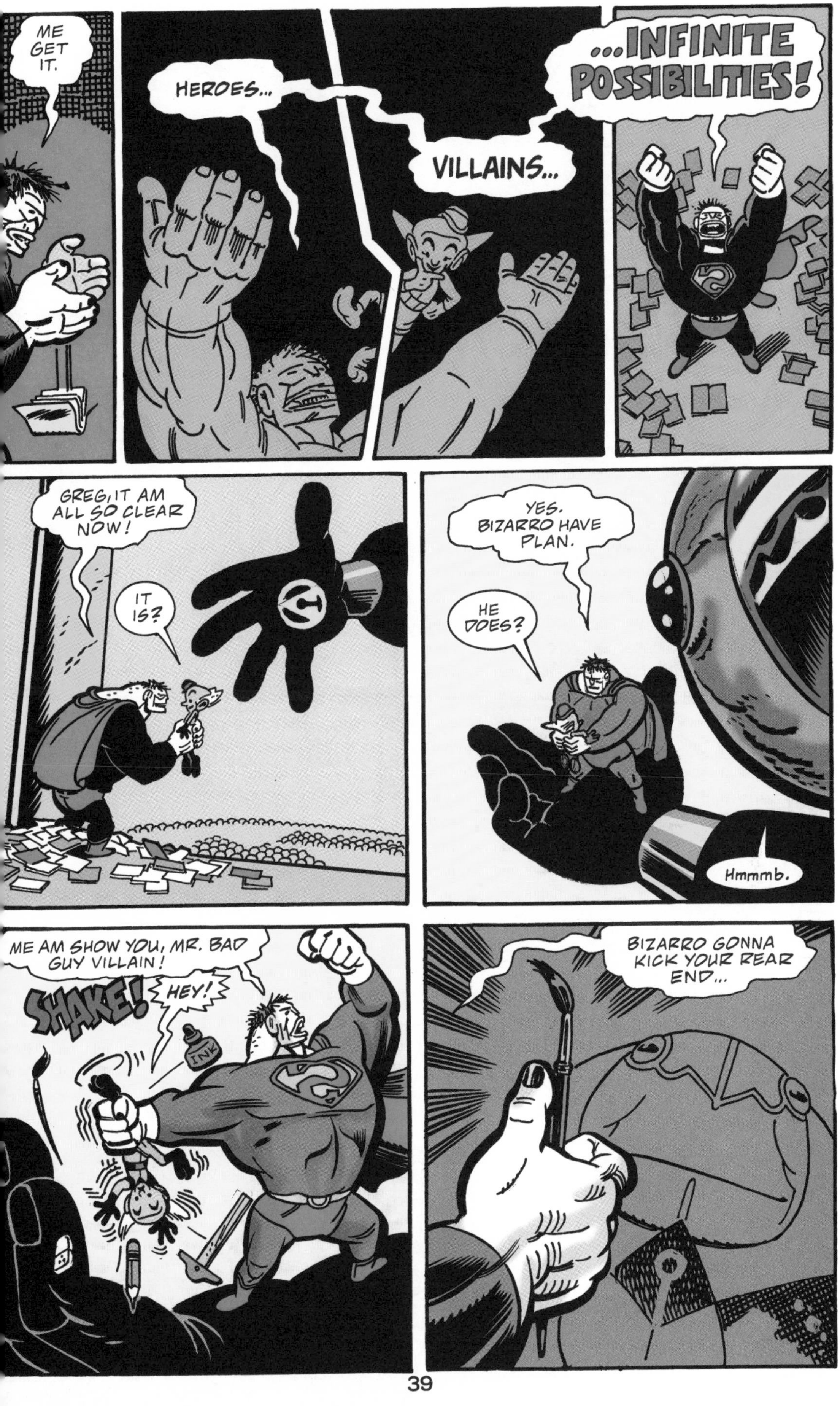

ME GET IT.
HEROES...
VILLAINS...
...INFINITE POSSIBILITIES!
GREG, IT AM ALL SO CLEAR NOW!
IT IS?
YES. BIZARRO HAVE PLAN.
HE DOES?
Hmmmb.
ME AM SHOW YOU, MR. BAD GUY VILLAIN!
SHAKE!
HEY!
INK
BIZARRO GONNA KICK YOUR REAR END...

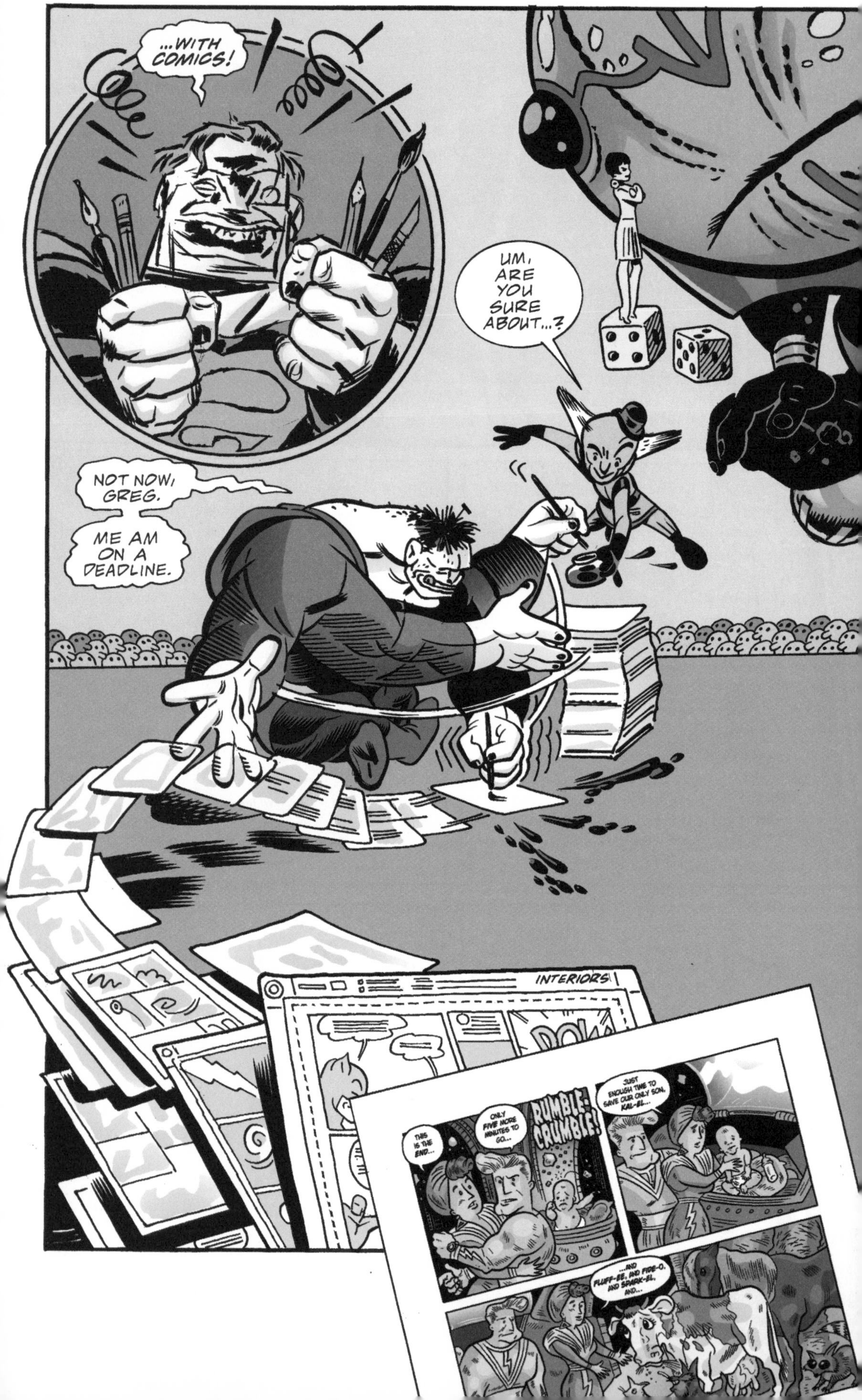
...WITH COMICS!
UM, ARE YOU SURE ABOUT...?
NOT NOW, GREG.
ME AM ON A DEADLINE.
INTERIORS
THIS IS THE END...
ONLY FIVE MORE MINUTES TO GO...
RUMBLE! CRUMBLE!
JUST ENOUGH TIME TO SAVE OUR ONLY SON, KAL-EL...
...AND FLUFF-EE, AND FIDE-O, AND SPARK-EL, AND...

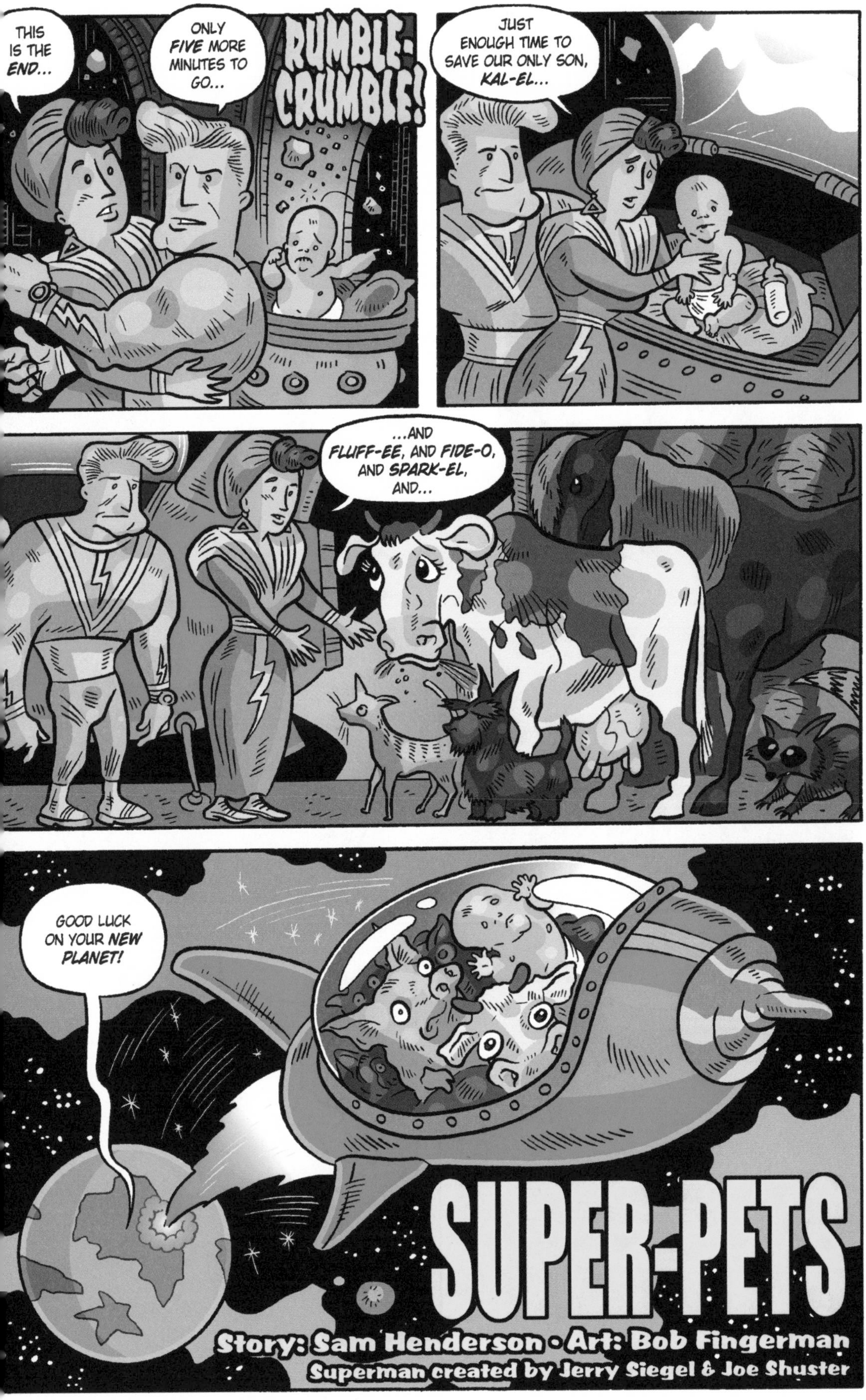
THIS IS THE *END*...
ONLY *FIVE* MORE MINUTES TO GO...
RUMBLE-CRUMBLE!
JUST ENOUGH TIME TO SAVE OUR ONLY SON, *KAL-EL*...
...AND *FLUFF-EE*, AND *FIDE-O*, AND *SPARK-EL*, AND...
GOOD LUCK ON YOUR *NEW PLANET!*
SUPER-PETS
Story: Sam Henderson • Art: Bob Fingerman
Superman created by Jerry Siegel & Joe Shuster

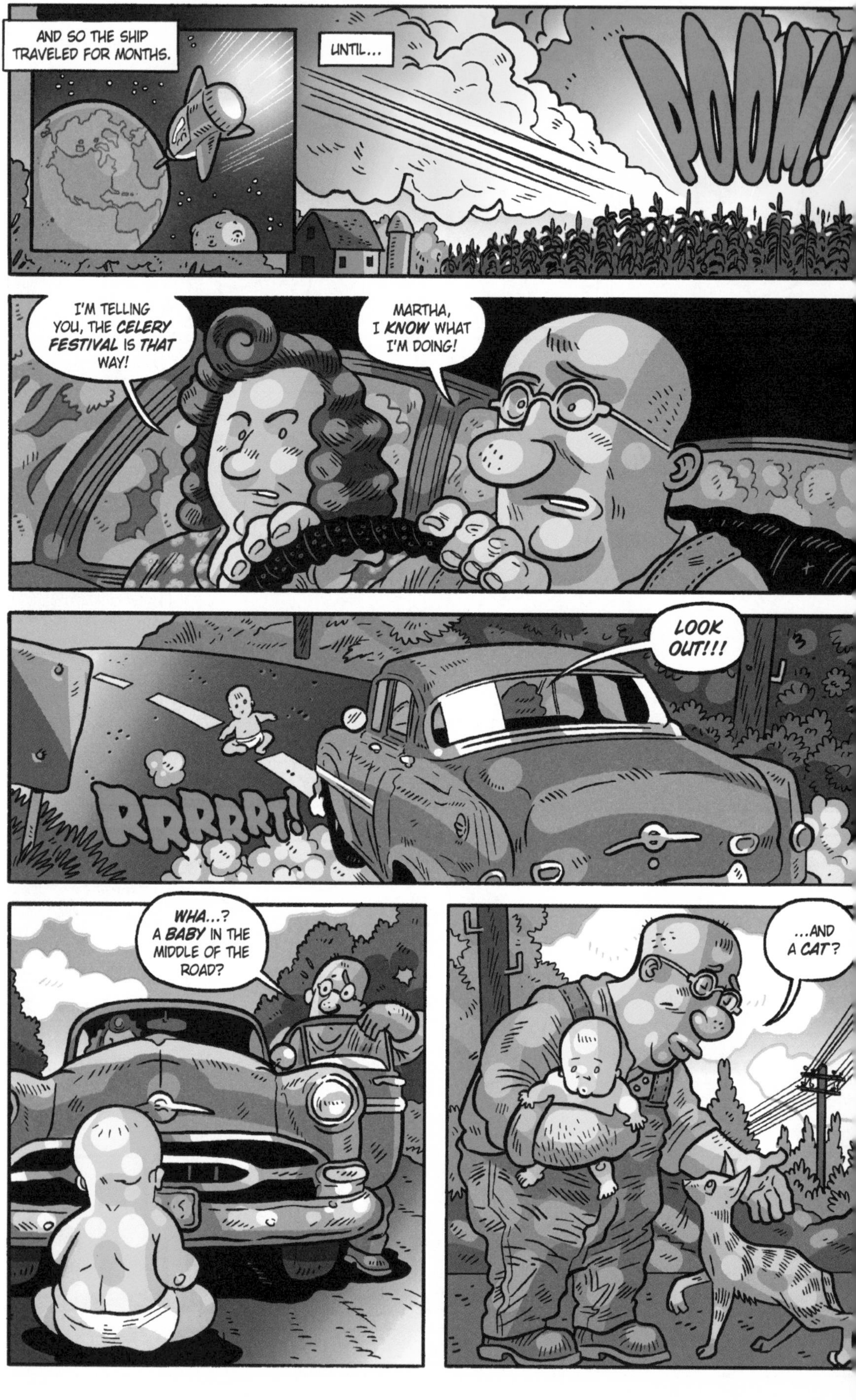
AND SO THE SHIP TRAVELED FOR MONTHS.
UNTIL...
POOM!
I'M TELLING YOU, THE CELERY FESTIVAL IS THAT WAY!
MARTHA, I KNOW WHAT I'M DOING!
LOOK OUT!!!
RRRRRT!
WHA...? A BABY IN THE MIDDLE OF THE ROAD?
...AND A CAT?

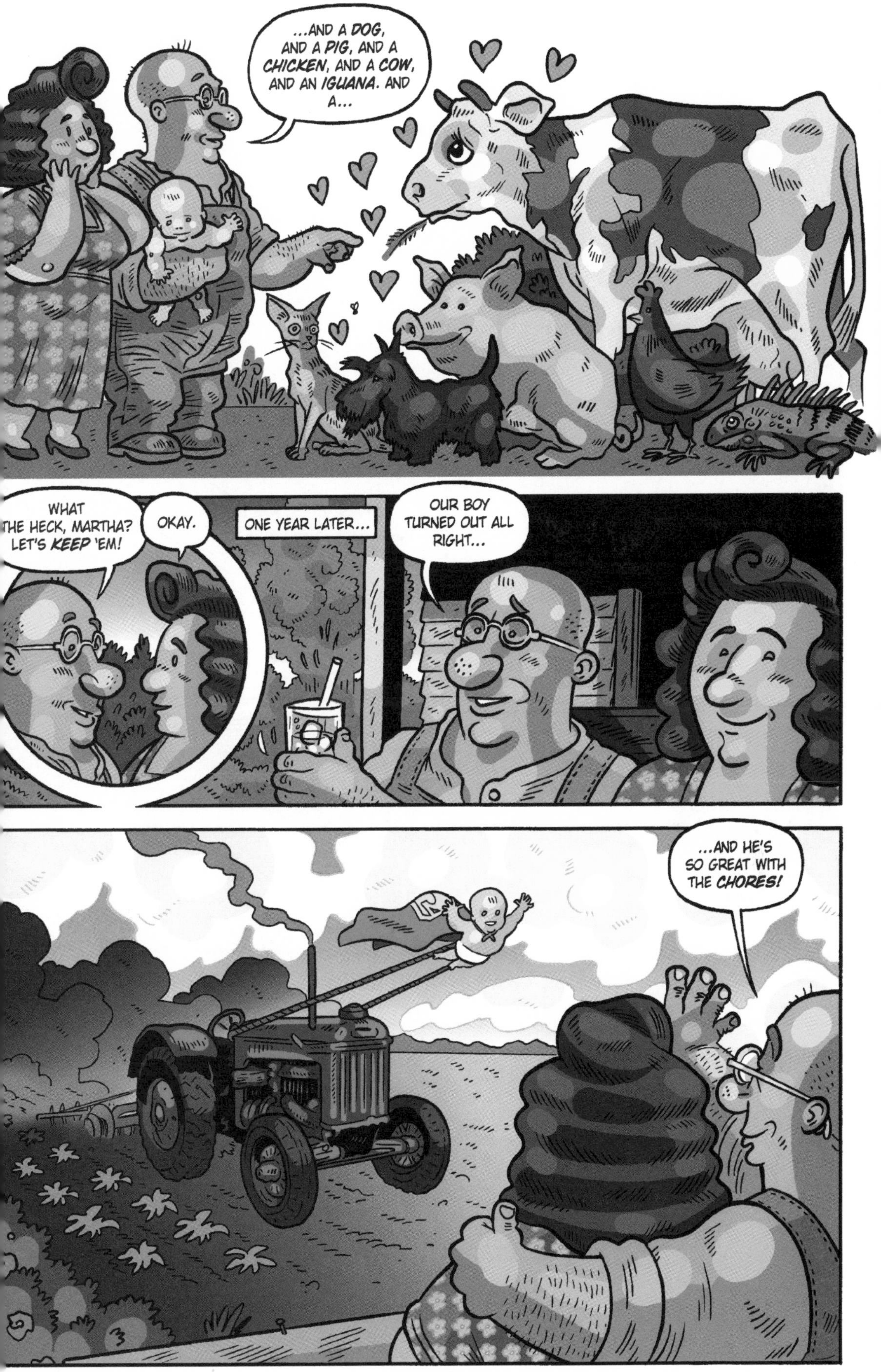
...AND A DOG, AND A PIG, AND A CHICKEN, AND A COW, AND AN IGUANA. AND A...
WHAT THE HECK, MARTHA? LET'S KEEP 'EM!
OKAY.
ONE YEAR LATER...
OUR BOY TURNED OUT ALL RIGHT...
...AND HE'S SO GREAT WITH THE CHORES!

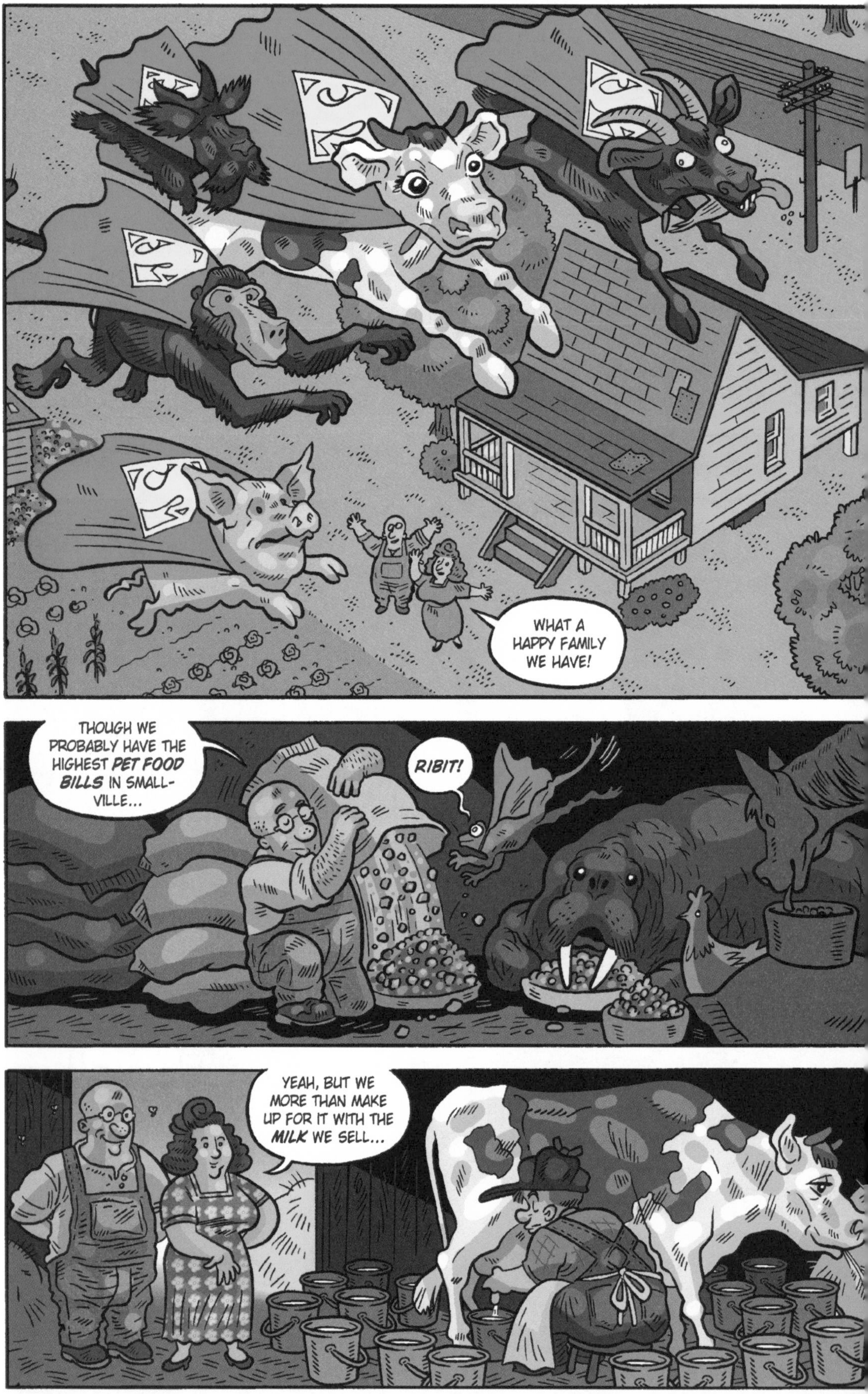
WHAT A HAPPY FAMILY WE HAVE!
THOUGH WE PROBABLY HAVE THE HIGHEST PET FOOD BILLS IN SMALL-VILLE...
RIBIT!
YEAH, BUT WE MORE THAN MAKE UP FOR IT WITH THE MILK WE SELL...

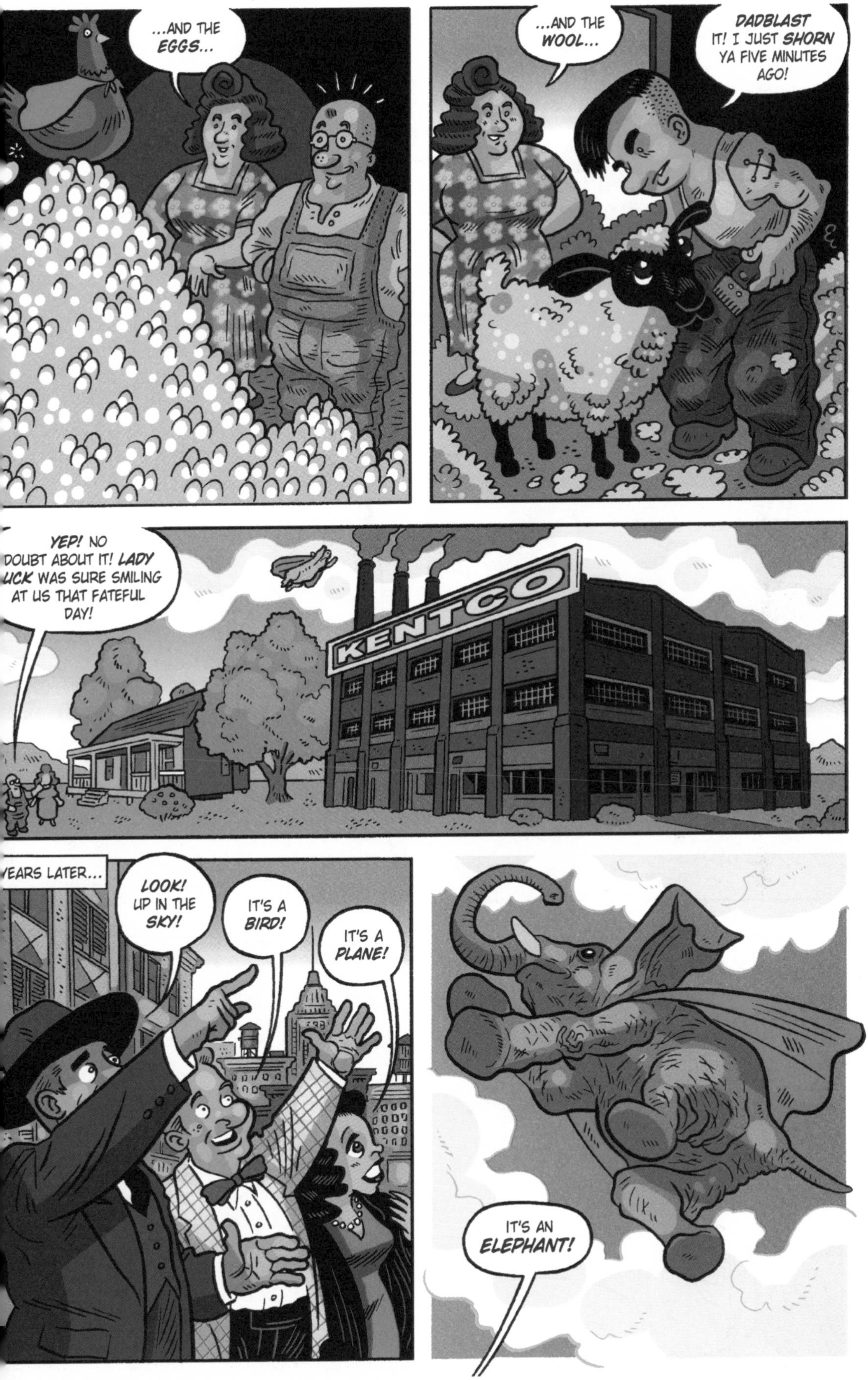
...AND THE EGGS...
...AND THE WOOL...
DADBLAST IT! I JUST SHORN YA FIVE MINUTES AGO!
YEP! NO DOUBT ABOUT IT! LADY LUCK WAS SURE SMILING AT US THAT FATEFUL DAY!
KENTCO
YEARS LATER...
LOOK! UP IN THE SKY!
IT'S A BIRD!
IT'S A PLANE!
IT'S AN ELEPHANT!

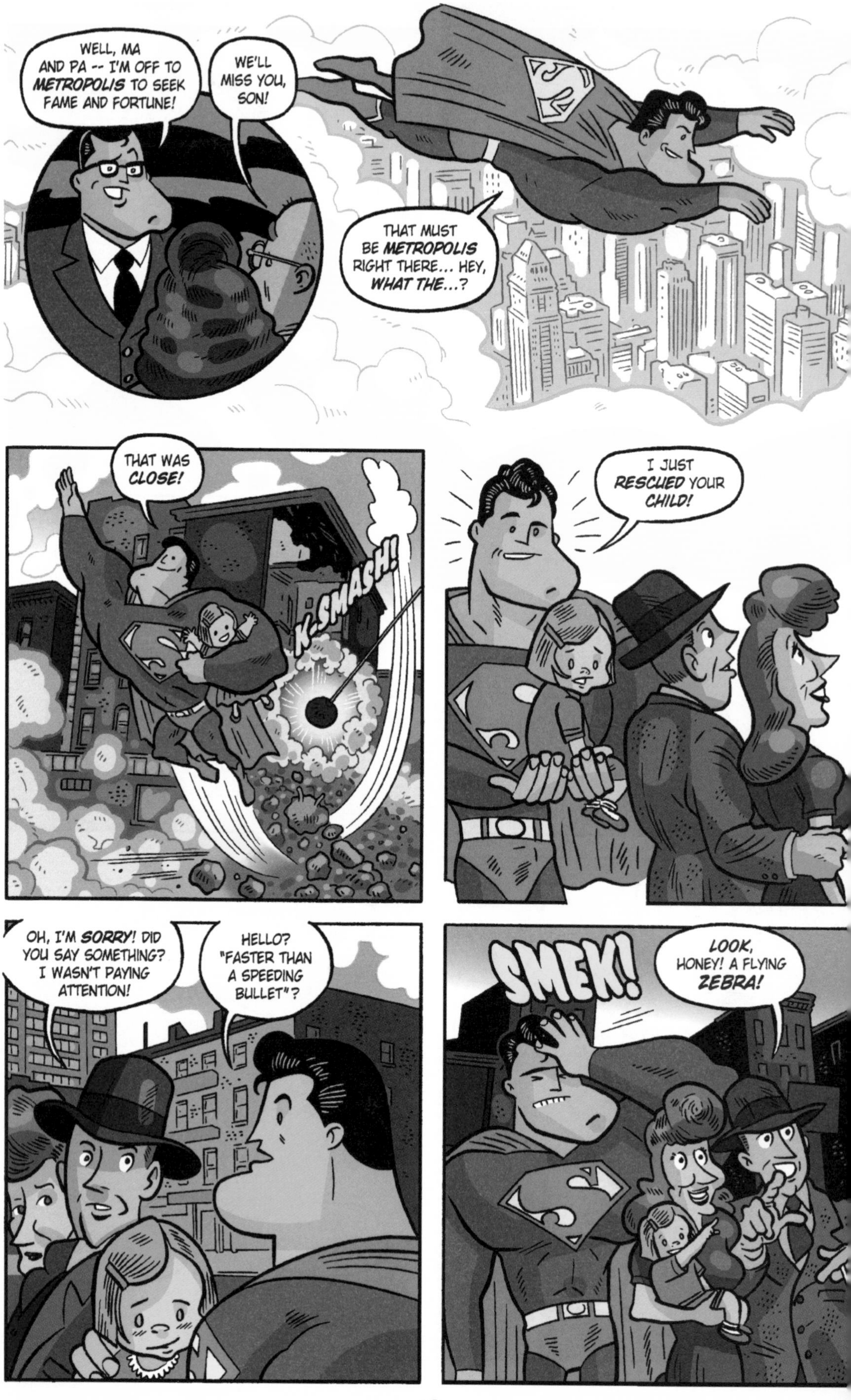
WELL, MA AND PA -- I'M OFF TO METROPOLIS TO SEEK FAME AND FORTUNE!
WE'LL MISS YOU, SON!
THAT MUST BE METROPOLIS RIGHT THERE... HEY, WHAT THE...?
THAT WAS CLOSE!
K-SMASH!
I JUST RESCUED YOUR CHILD!
OH, I'M SORRY! DID YOU SAY SOMETHING? I WASN'T PAYING ATTENTION!
HELLO? "FASTER THAN A SPEEDING BULLET"?
SMEK!
LOOK, HONEY! A FLYING ZEBRA!

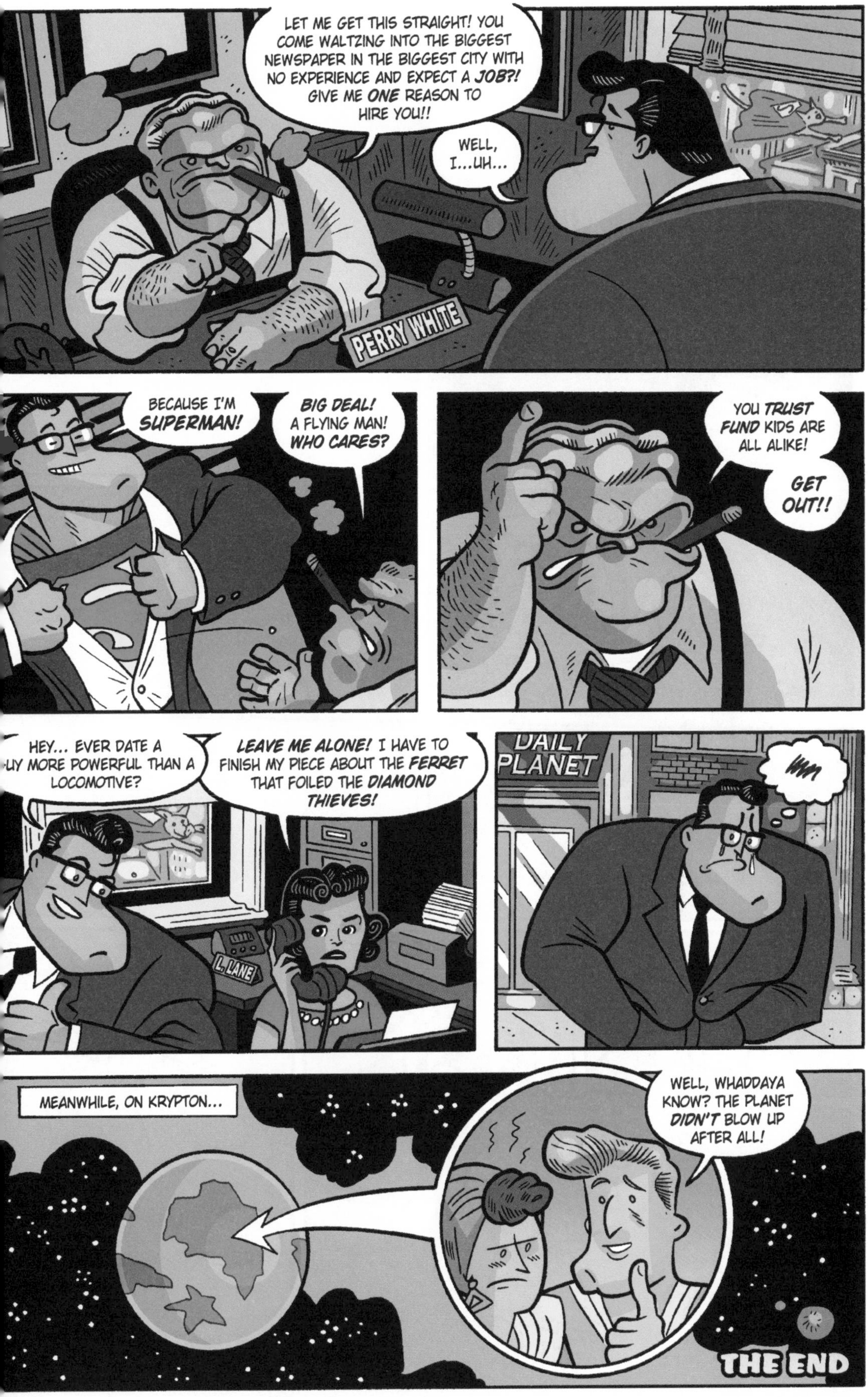
LET ME GET THIS STRAIGHT! YOU COME WALTZING INTO THE BIGGEST NEWSPAPER IN THE BIGGEST CITY WITH NO EXPERIENCE AND EXPECT A JOB?! GIVE ME ONE REASON TO HIRE YOU!!
WELL, I...UH...
PERRY WHITE
BECAUSE I'M SUPERMAN!
BIG DEAL! A FLYING MAN! WHO CARES?
YOU TRUST FUND KIDS ARE ALL ALIKE!
GET OUT!!
HEY... EVER DATE A UY MORE POWERFUL THAN A LOCOMOTIVE?
LEAVE ME ALONE! I HAVE TO FINISH MY PIECE ABOUT THE FERRET THAT FOILED THE DIAMOND THIEVES!
L. LANE
DAILY PLANET
MEANWHILE, ON KRYPTON...
WELL, WHADDAYA KNOW? THE PLANET DIDN'T BLOW UP AFTER ALL!
THE END

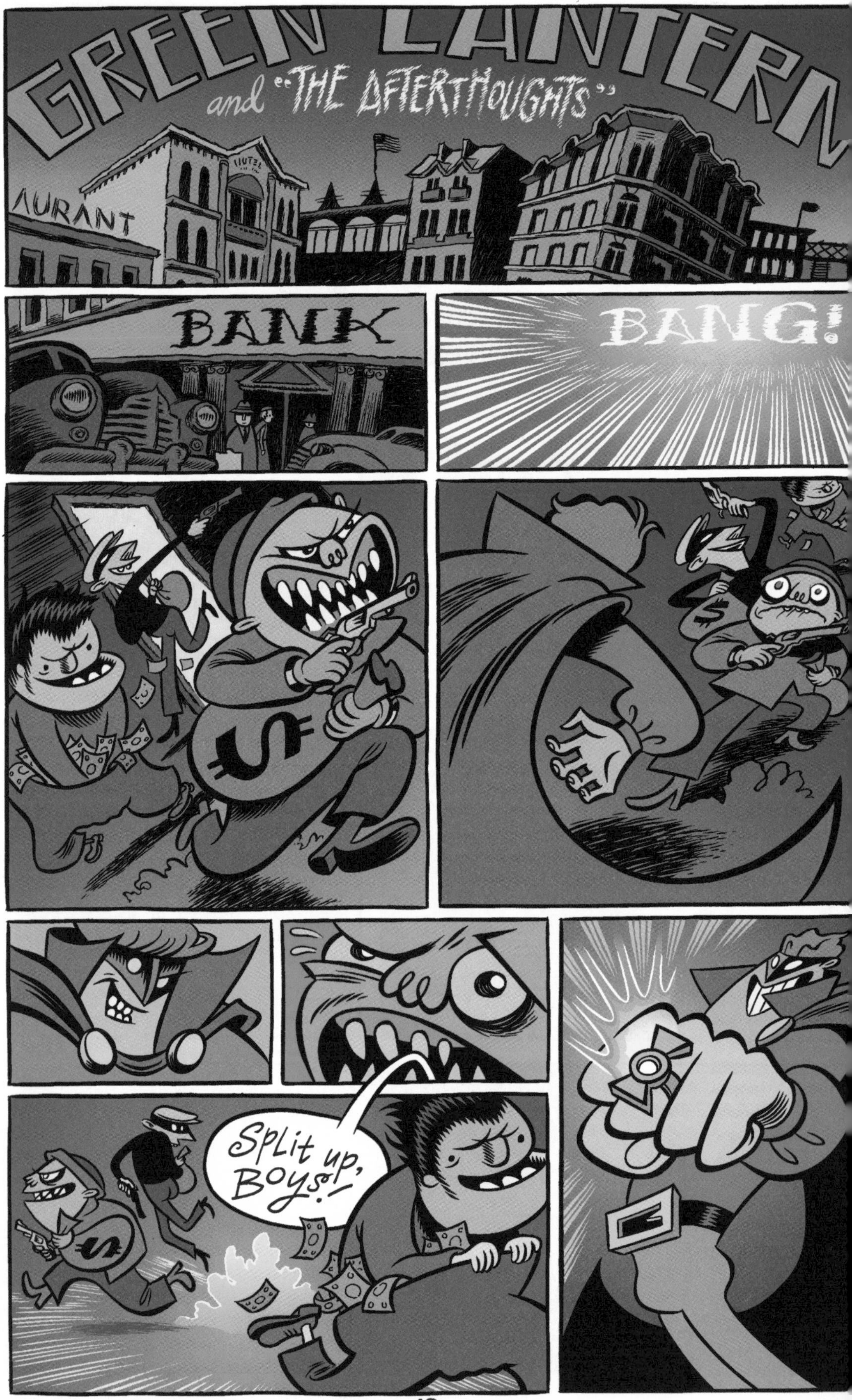
GREEN LANTERN
and "THE AFTERTHOUGHTS"
AURANT
HOTEL
BANK
BANG!
Split up, Boys!

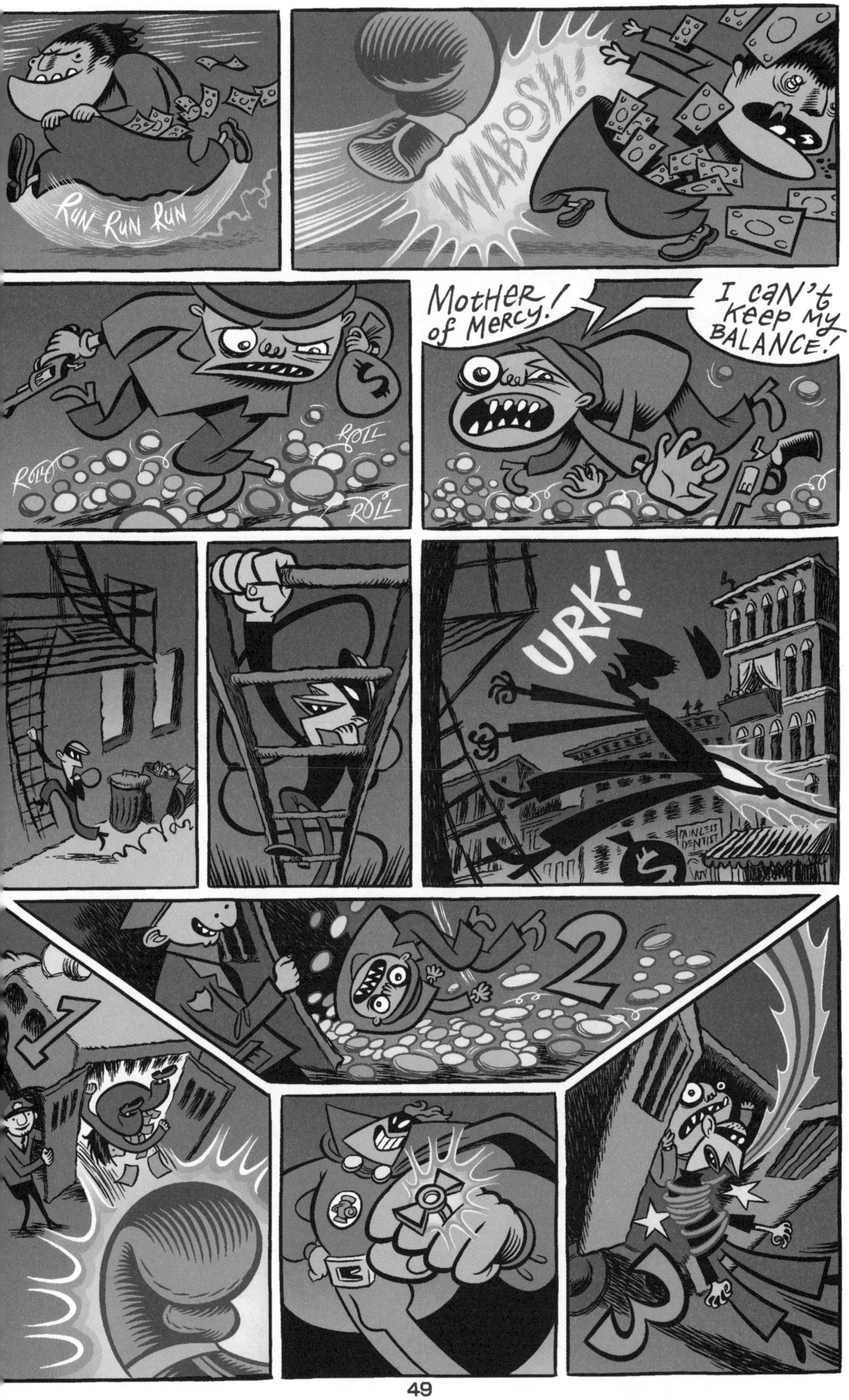
RUN RUN RUN
WABOSH!
ROLL
ROLL
ROLL
Mother of Mercy!
I can't keep my BALANCE!
URK!
PAINLESS DENTIST
1
2
3

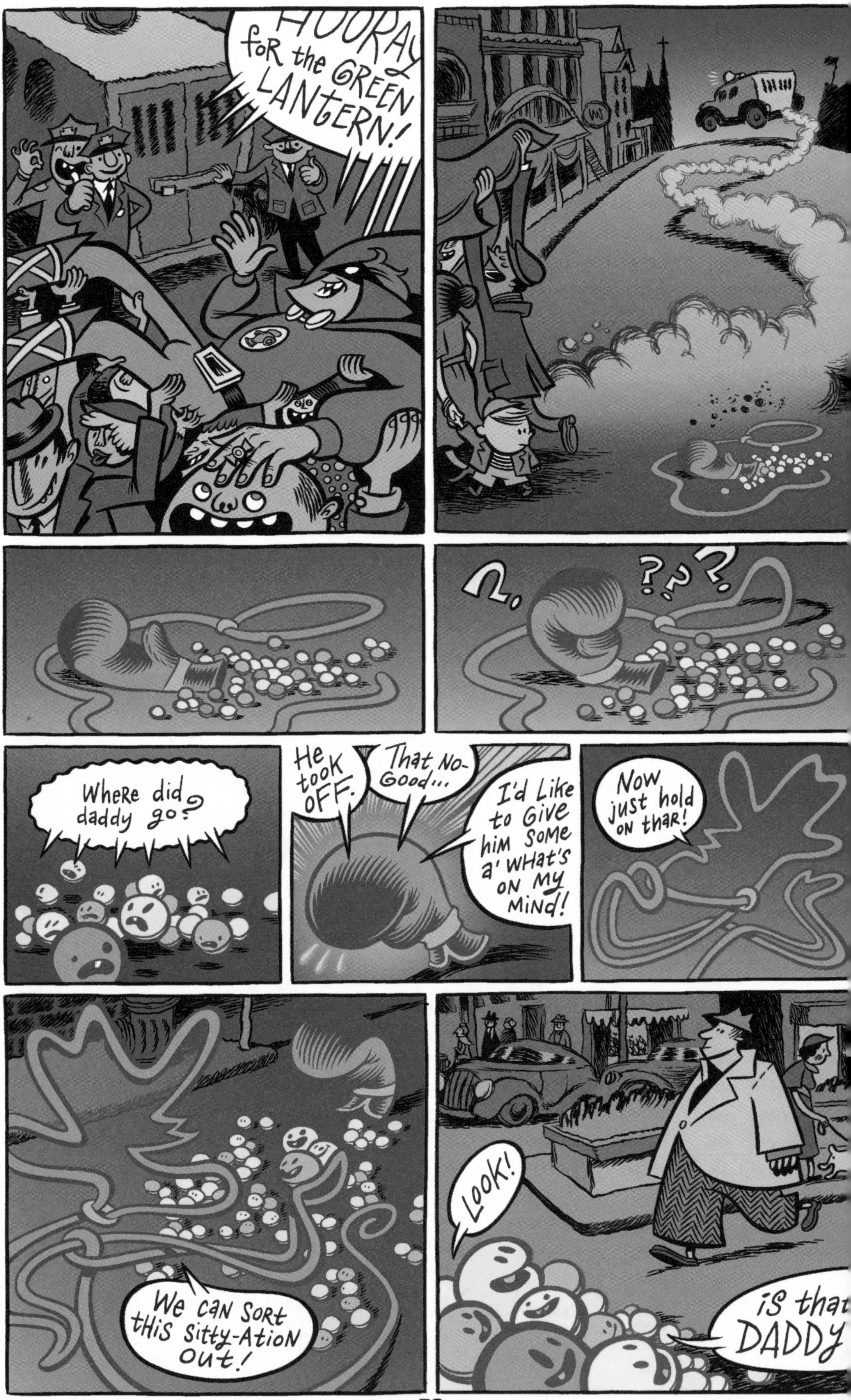
HOORAY for the GREEN LANTERN!
?, ???
Where did daddy go?
He took OFF.
That No-Good...
I'd Like to Give him Some a' WHat's on My MIND!
Now just hold on thar!
We can Sort tHIS sitty-Ation out!
LOOK!
is tha DADDY

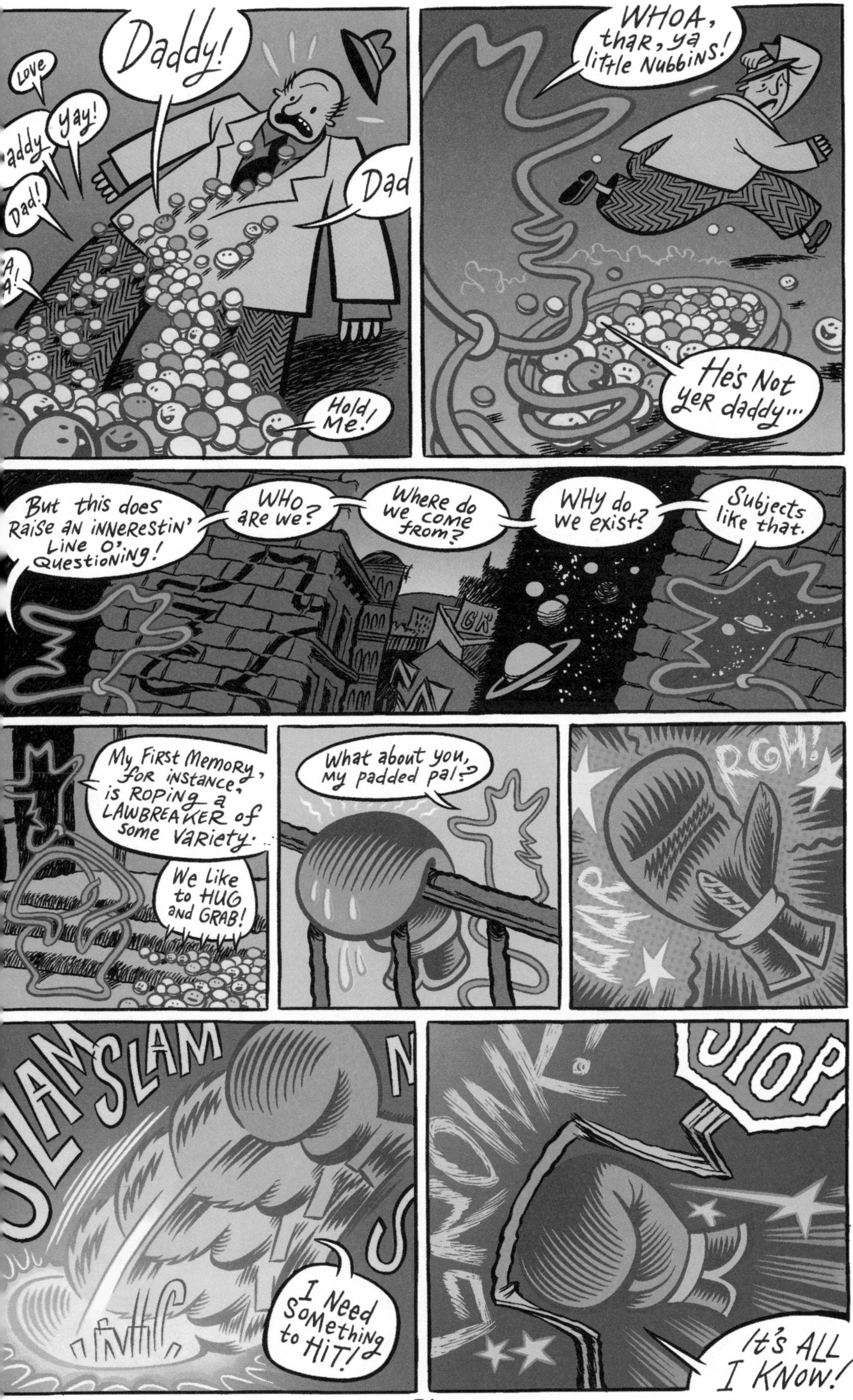
Love
addy
Yay!
Dad!
Daddy!
Dad
Hold Me!
WHOA, thar, ya little Nubbins!
He's Not yer daddy...
But this does Raise an innerestin' Line o' Questioning!
WHO are we?
Where do we come from?
WHy do we exist?
Subjects like that.
My First Memory, for instance, is Roping a LAWBREAKER of some Variety.
We Like to HUG and GRAB!
What about you, my padded pal?
SLAM SLAM
I Need Something to HIT!
STOP
It's ALL I KNOW!

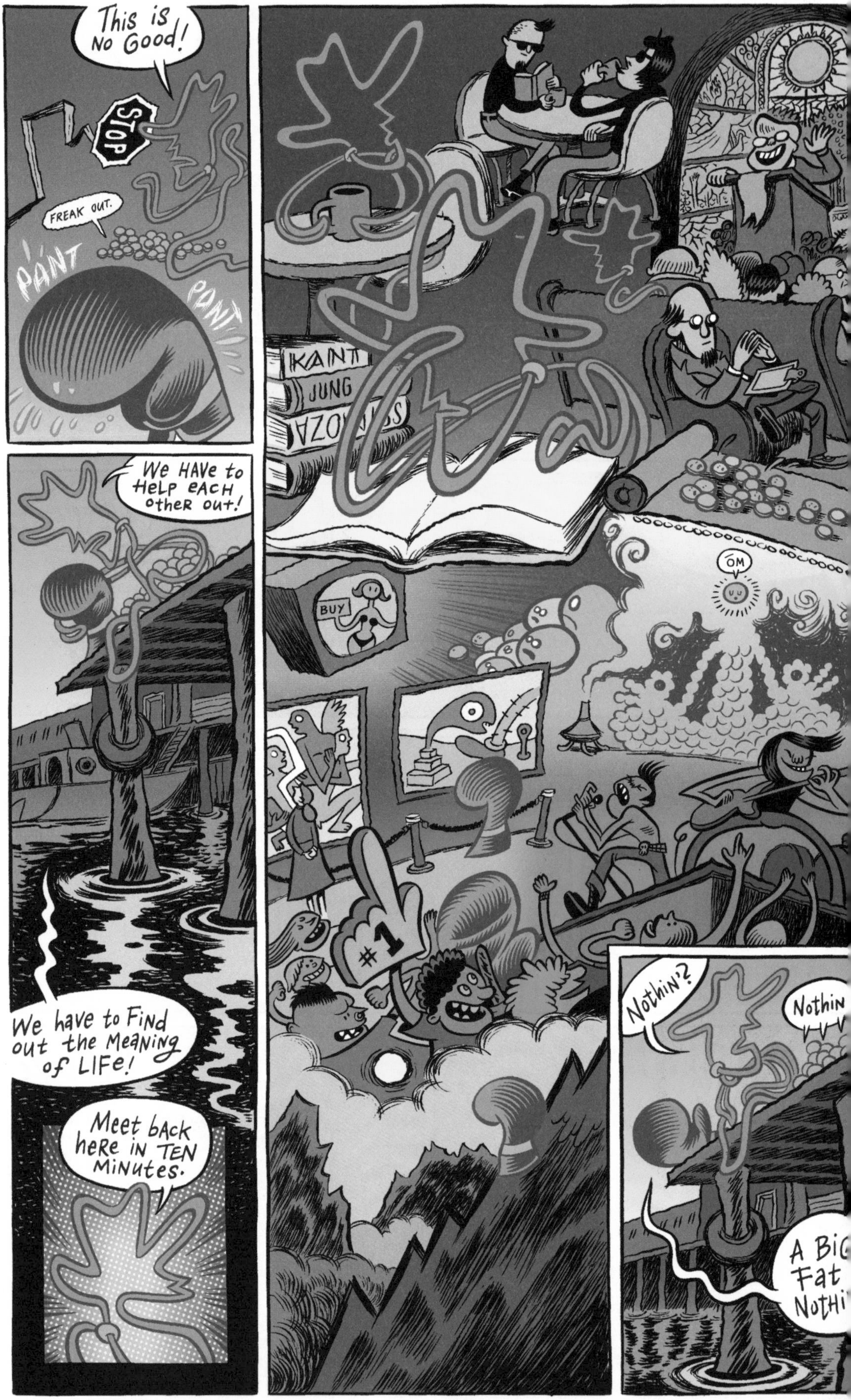
This is No Good!
STOP
FREAK OUT.
PANT
PANT
We HAVE to HELP EACH other out!
We have to Find out the Meaning of LIFE!
Meet back here in TEN Minutes.
KANT
JUNG
BUY
OM
#1
Nothin'?
Nothin
A Big Fat Nothi

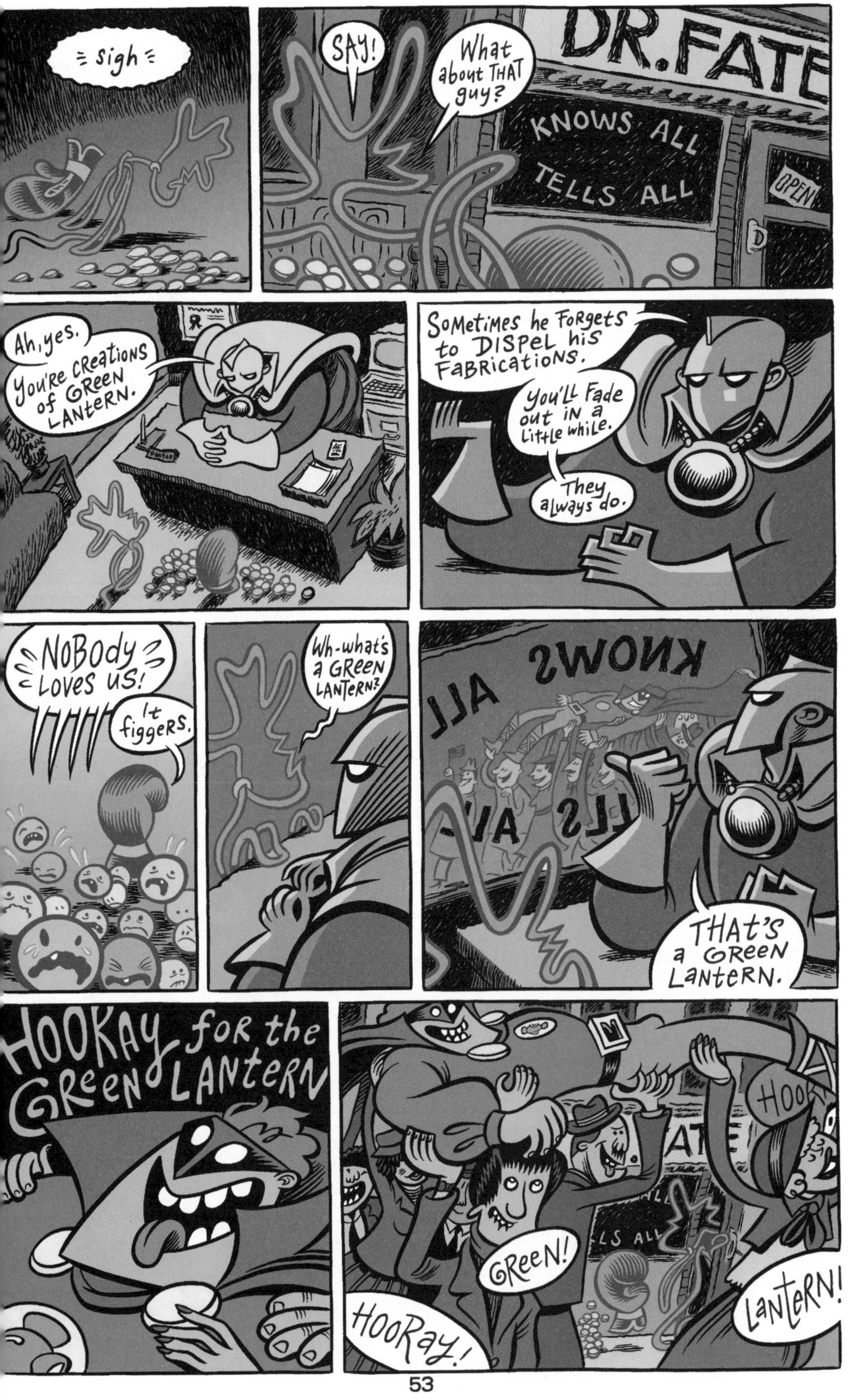
sigh
SAY!
What about THAT guy?
DR. FATE
KNOWS ALL TELLS ALL
OPEN
Ah, yes.
You're creations of GREEN LANTERN.
Sometimes he forgets to DISPEL his fabrications.
You'll fade out in a little while.
They always do.
NOBODY LOVES US!
It figgers.
Wh-what's a GREEN LANTERN?
KNOWS ALL TELLS ALL
THAT'S a GREEN Lantern.
HOORAY for the GREEN LANTERN
HOO
GREEN!
HOORAY!
LANTERN!

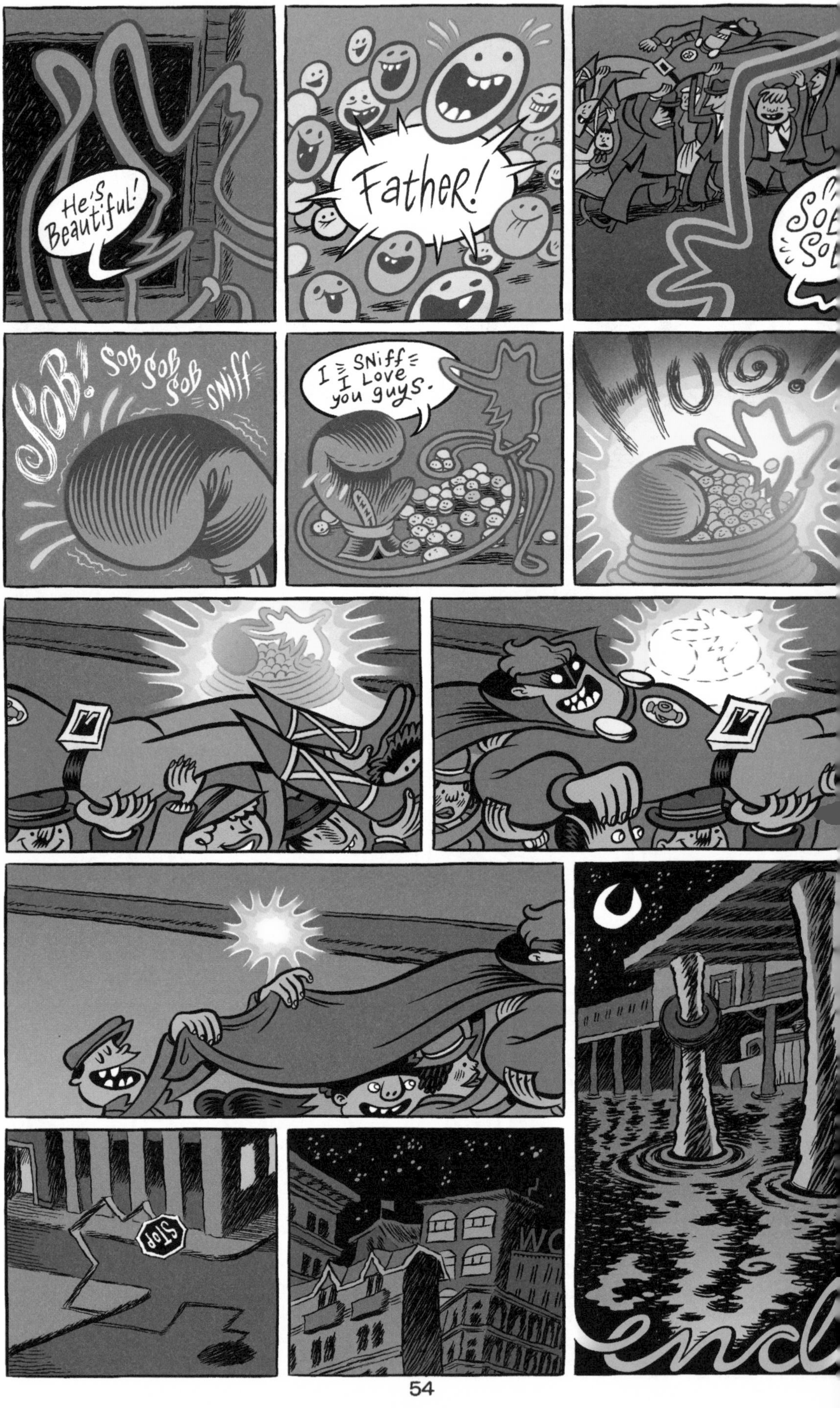

He's Beautiful!
Father!
SOB! SOB SOB SOB SNIFF
I SNIFF I LOVE YOU GUYS.
HUG!

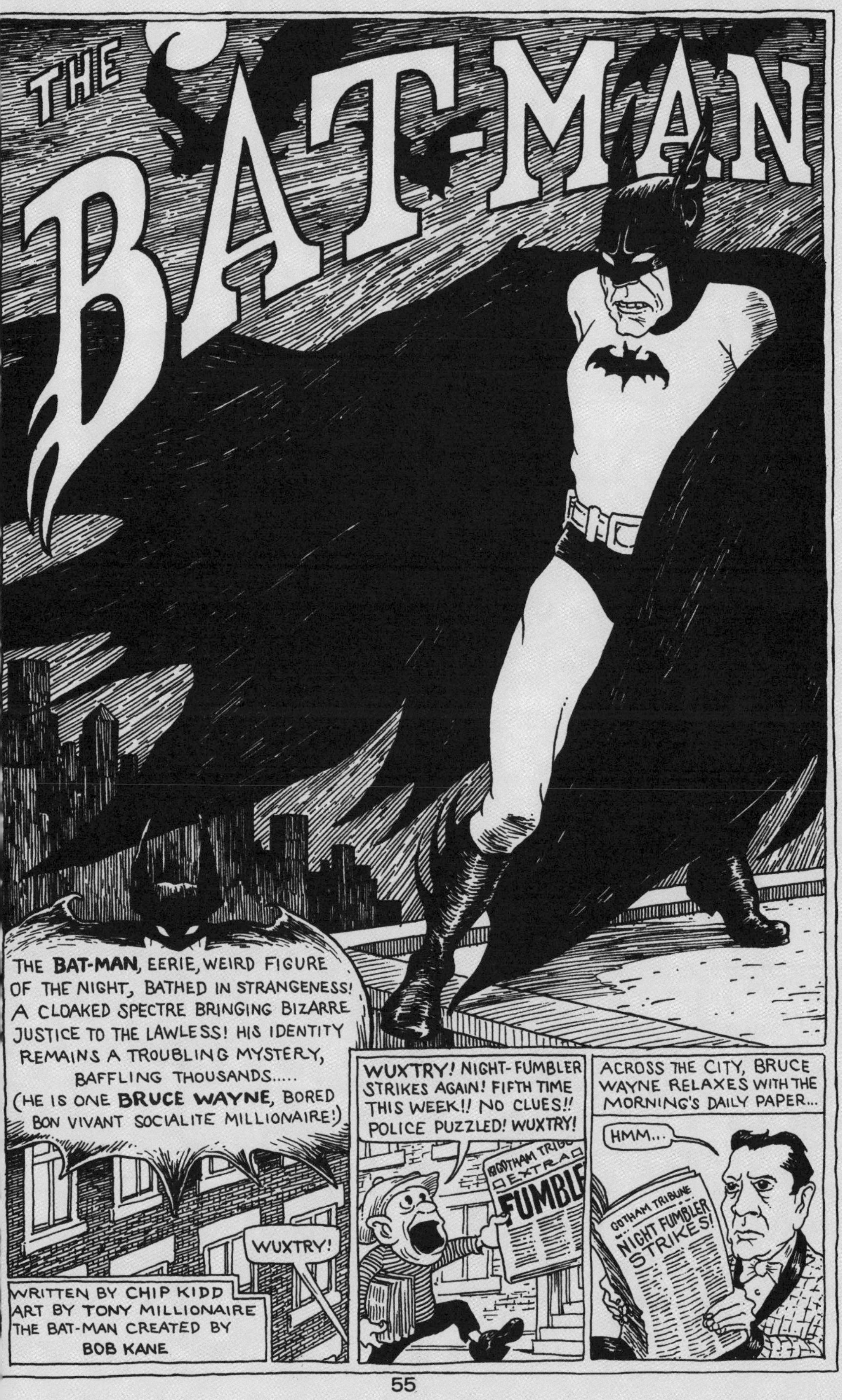
THE BAT-MAN
THE BAT-MAN, EERIE, WEIRD FIGURE OF THE NIGHT, BATHED IN STRANGENESS! A CLOAKED SPECTRE BRINGING BIZARRE JUSTICE TO THE LAWLESS! HIS IDENTITY REMAINS A TROUBLING MYSTERY, BAFFLING THOUSANDS..... (HE IS ONE BRUCE WAYNE, BORED BON VIVANT SOCIALITE MILLIONAIRE!)
WUXTRY!
WRITTEN BY CHIP KIDD
ART BY TONY MILLIONAIRE
THE BAT-MAN CREATED BY
BOB KANE
WUXTRY! NIGHT-FUMBLER STRIKES AGAIN! FIFTH TIME THIS WEEK!! NO CLUES!! POLICE PUZZLED! WUXTRY!
EXTRA
FUMBLE
ACROSS THE CITY, BRUCE WAYNE RELAXES WITH THE MORNING'S DAILY PAPER...
HMM...
GOTHAM TRIBUNE
NIGHT FUMBLER STRIKES!

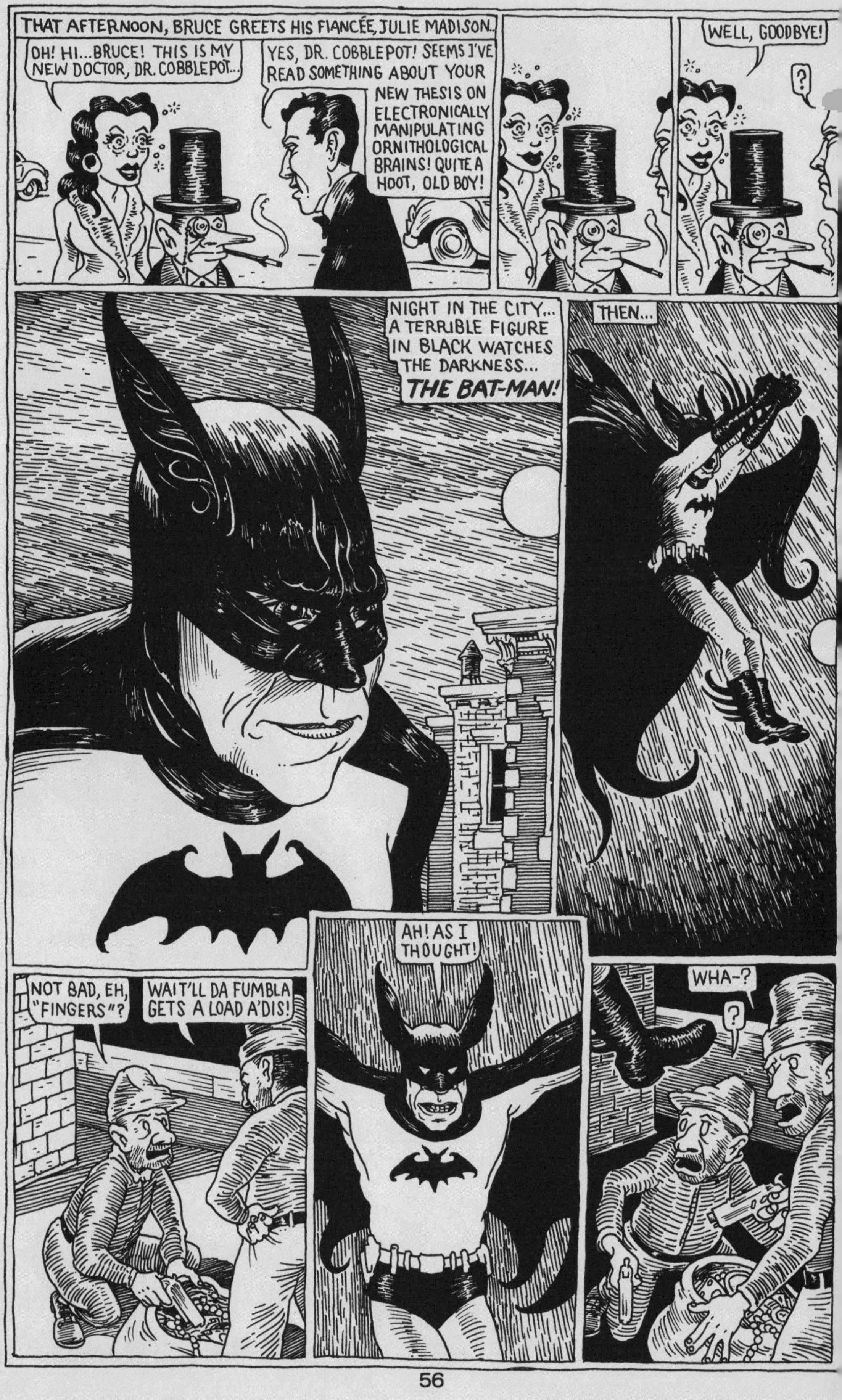
THAT AFTERNOON, BRUCE GREETS HIS FIANCÉE, JULIE MADISON..
OH! HI...BRUCE! THIS IS MY NEW DOCTOR, DR. COBBLEPOT...
YES, DR. COBBLEPOT! SEEMS I'VE READ SOMETHING ABOUT YOUR NEW THESIS ON ELECTRONICALLY MANIPULATING ORNITHOLOGICAL BRAINS! QUITE A HOOT, OLD BOY!
WELL, GOODBYE!
?
NIGHT IN THE CITY... A TERRIBLE FIGURE IN BLACK WATCHES THE DARKNESS... THE BAT-MAN!
THEN...
NOT BAD, EH, "FINGERS"?
WAIT'LL DA FUMBLA GETS A LOAD A'DIS!
AH! AS I THOUGHT!
WHA-?
?

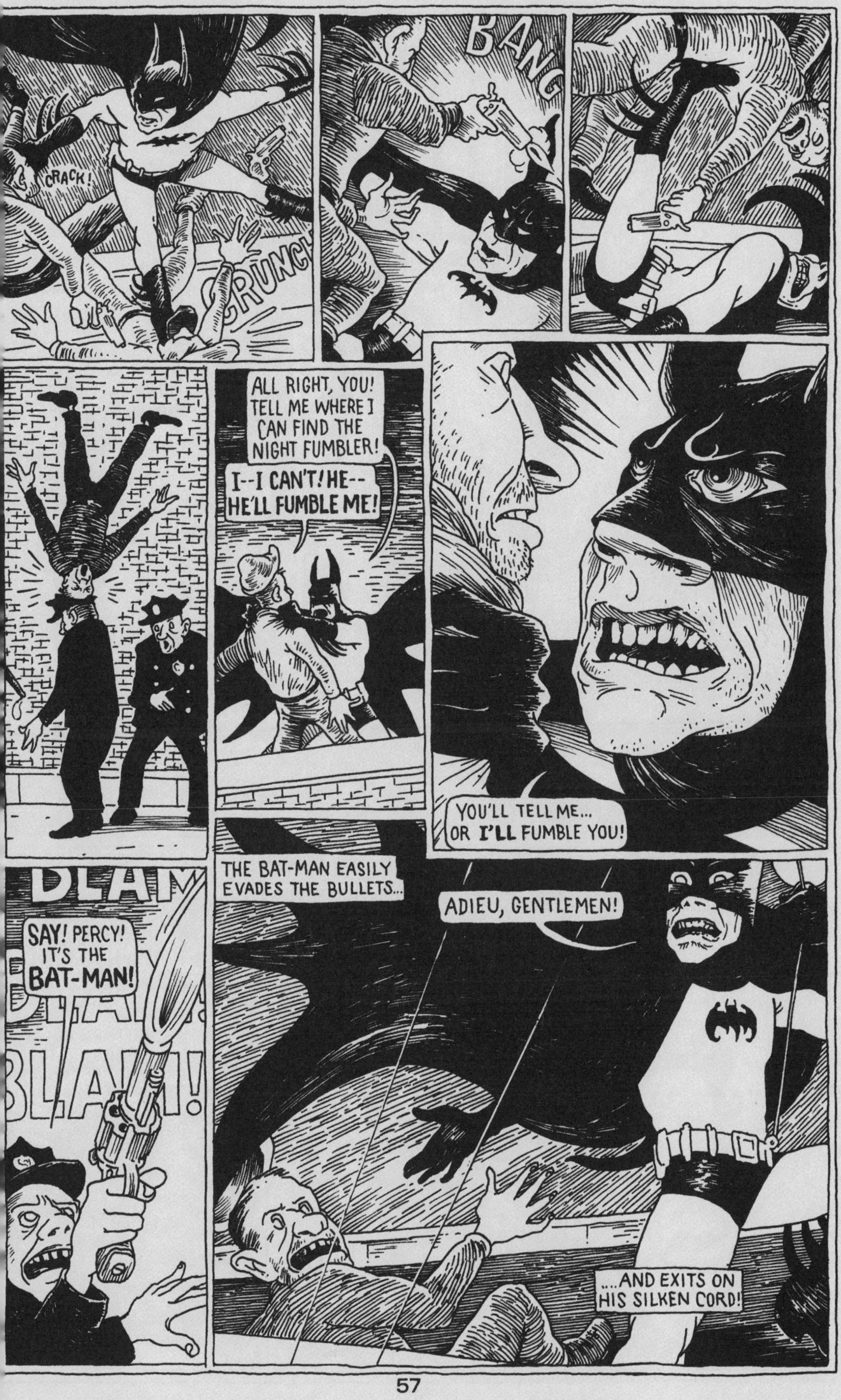
CRACK!
CRUNCH
BANG
ALL RIGHT, YOU! TELL ME WHERE I CAN FIND THE NIGHT FUMBLER!
I--I CAN'T! HE--HE'LL FUMBLE ME!
YOU'LL TELL ME... OR I'LL FUMBLE YOU!
BLAM
SAY! PERCY! IT'S THE BAT-MAN!
BLAM!
THE BAT-MAN EASILY EVADES THE BULLETS...
ADIEU, GENTLEMEN!
...AND EXITS ON HIS SILKEN CORD!

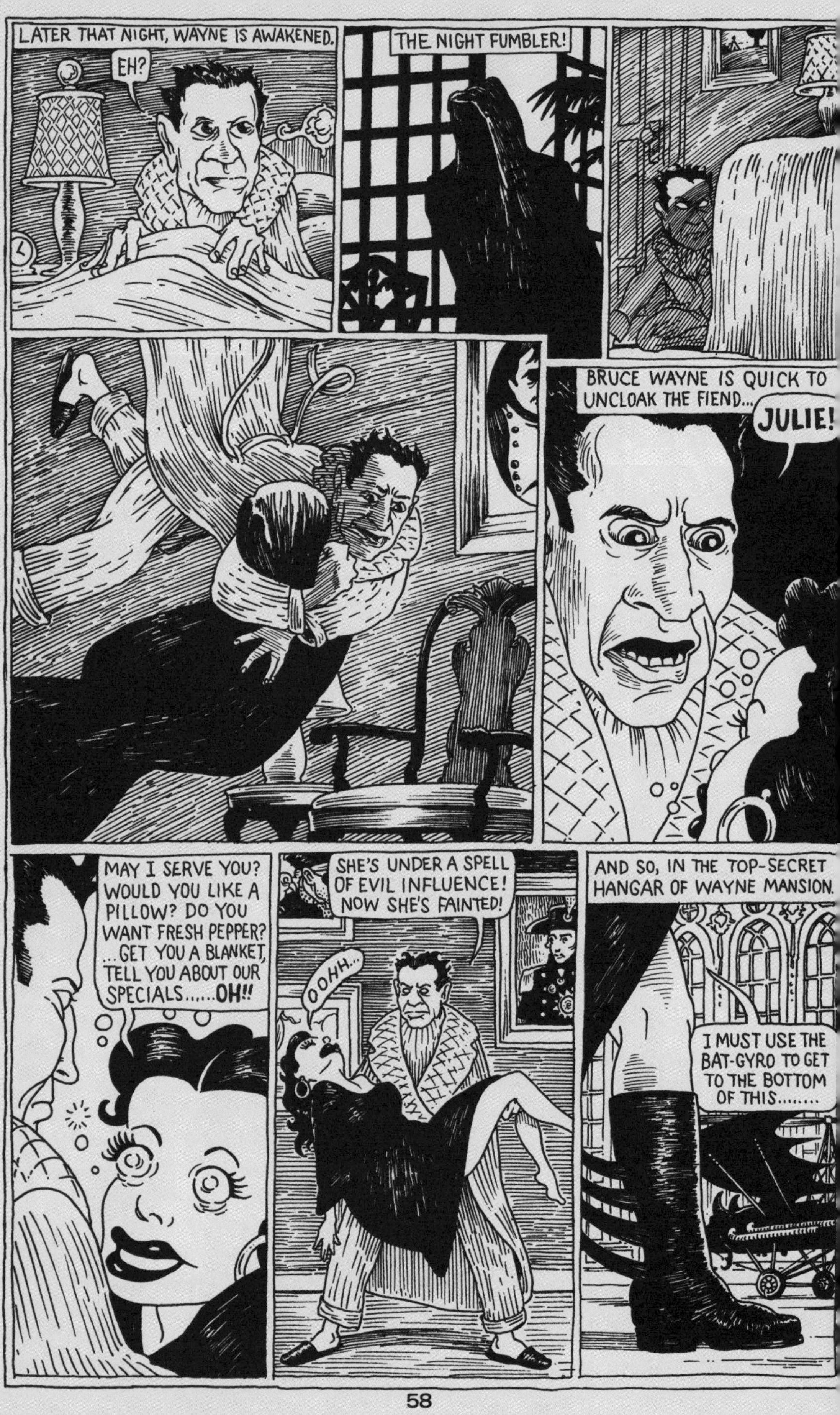
LATER THAT NIGHT, WAYNE IS AWAKENED.
EH?
THE NIGHT FUMBLER!
BRUCE WAYNE IS QUICK TO UNCLOAK THE FIEND...
JULIE!
MAY I SERVE YOU? WOULD YOU LIKE A PILLOW? DO YOU WANT FRESH PEPPER? ...GET YOU A BLANKET, TELL YOU ABOUT OUR SPECIALS.......OH!!
SHE'S UNDER A SPELL OF EVIL INFLUENCE! NOW SHE'S FAINTED!
OOHH..
AND SO, IN THE TOP-SECRET HANGAR OF WAYNE MANSION.
I MUST USE THE BAT-GYRO TO GET TO THE BOTTOM OF THIS........

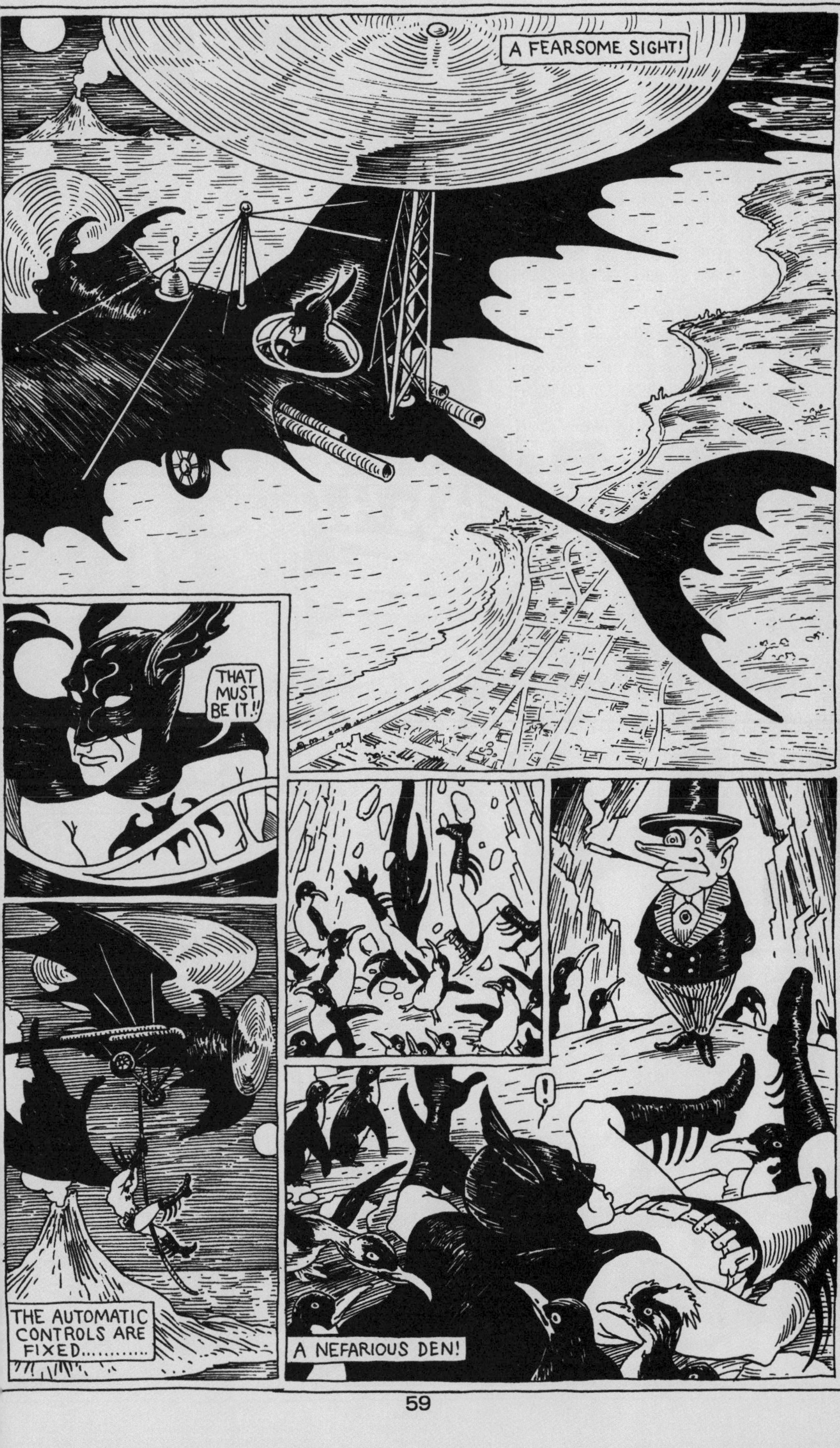
A FEARSOME SIGHT!
THAT MUST BE IT!!
THE AUTOMATIC CONTROLS ARE FIXED..........
!
A NEFARIOUS DEN!

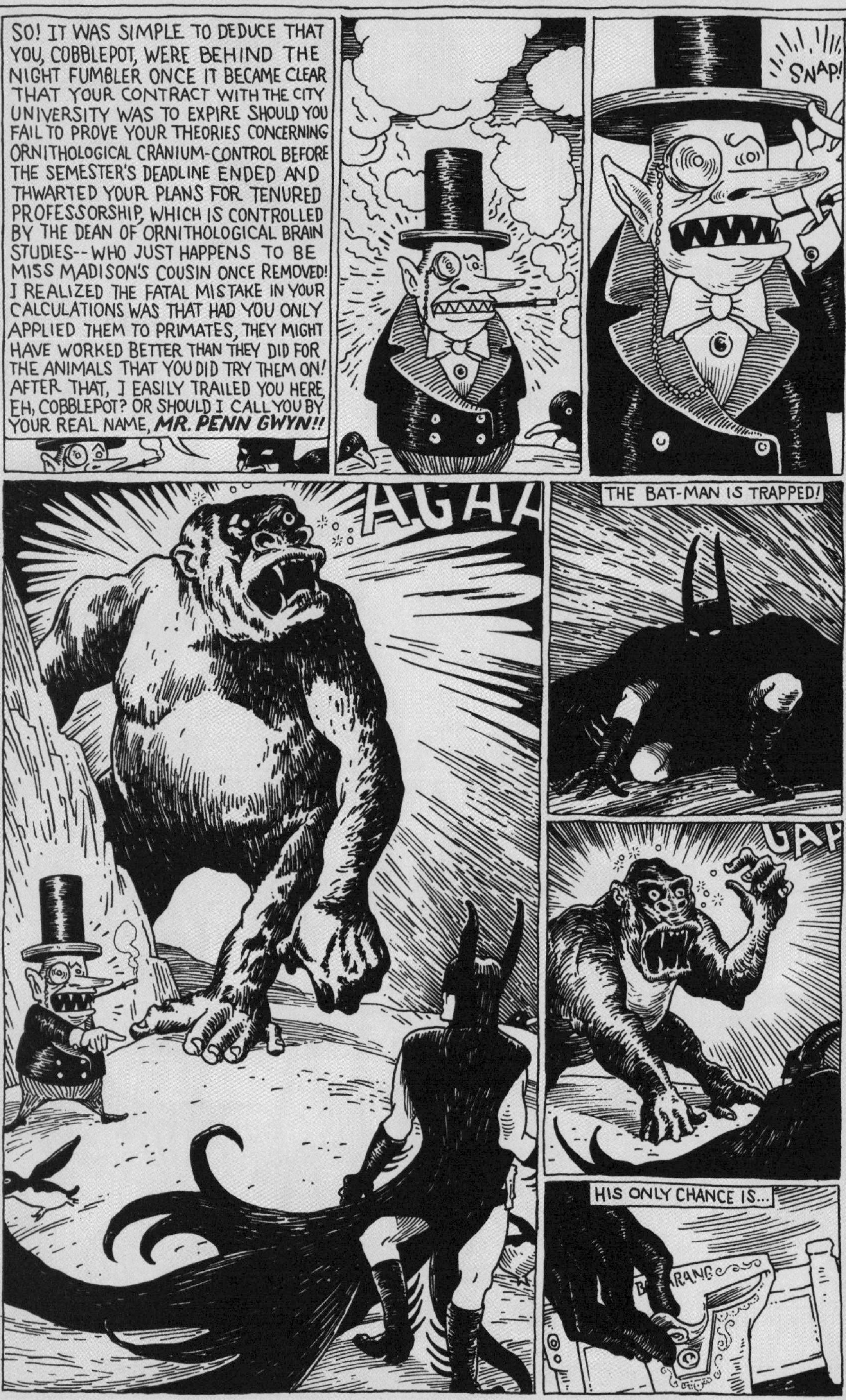
SO! IT WAS SIMPLE TO DEDUCE THAT YOU, COBBLEPOT, WERE BEHIND THE NIGHT FUMBLER ONCE IT BECAME CLEAR THAT YOUR CONTRACT WITH THE CITY UNIVERSITY WAS TO EXPIRE SHOULD YOU FAIL TO PROVE YOUR THEORIES CONCERNING ORNITHOLOGICAL CRANIUM-CONTROL BEFORE THE SEMESTER'S DEADLINE ENDED AND THWARTED YOUR PLANS FOR TENURED PROFESSORSHIP, WHICH IS CONTROLLED BY THE DEAN OF ORNITHOLOGICAL BRAIN STUDIES--WHO JUST HAPPENS TO BE MISS MADISON'S COUSIN ONCE REMOVED! I REALIZED THE FATAL MISTAKE IN YOUR CALCULATIONS WAS THAT HAD YOU ONLY APPLIED THEM TO PRIMATES, THEY MIGHT HAVE WORKED BETTER THAN THEY DID FOR THE ANIMALS THAT YOU DID TRY THEM ON! AFTER THAT, I EASILY TRAILED YOU HERE, EH, COBBLEPOT? OR SHOULD I CALL YOU BY YOUR REAL NAME, **MR. PENN GWYN!!**
SNAP!
AGAA
THE BAT-MAN IS TRAPPED!
GAP
HIS ONLY CHANCE IS...
BATARANG

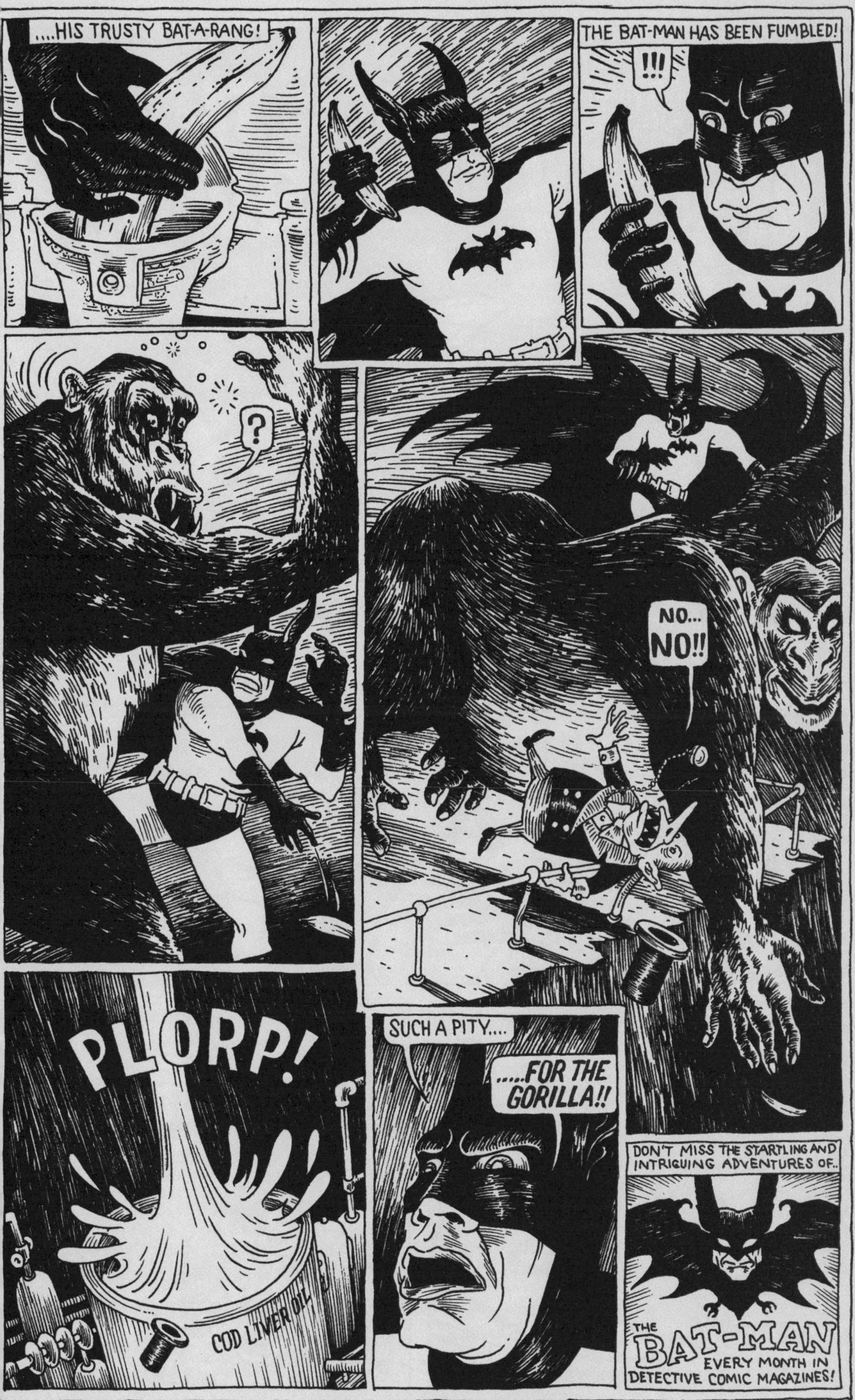
....HIS TRUSTY BAT-A-RANG!
THE BAT-MAN HAS BEEN FUMBLED!
!!!
?
NO... NO!!
PLORP!
COD LIVER OIL
SUCH A PITY....
.....FOR THE GORILLA!!
DON'T MISS THE STARTLING AND INTRIGUING ADVENTURES OF..
THE BAT-MAN
EVERY MONTH IN DETECTIVE COMIC MAGAZINES!

CAPTAIN MARVEL *and the* SHAM SHAZAM

SAM HENDERSON
STORY
DEAN HASPIEL
ART
BILL OAKLEY
LETTERS
MATT MADDEN
COLORS

TRICKING INNOCENT TIGERS OUT OF THEIR A.T.M. PIN NUMBERS, eh, MR. MIND? LET'S SEE HOW WELL YOU DO IT IN THE STATE PENITENTIARY!

THANK YOU SO MUCH FOR SAVING ME! SAY, HOW DID YOU BECOME CAPTAIN MARVEL, ANYWAY?

I'M GLAD YOU ASKED, TAWNY. COME ON, I'LL SHOW YOU.

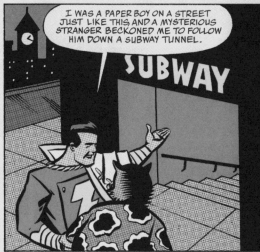

I WAS A PAPER BOY ON A STREET JUST LIKE THIS, AND A MYSTERIOUS STRANGER BECKONED ME TO FOLLOW HIM DOWN A SUBWAY TUNNEL.

SUBWAY

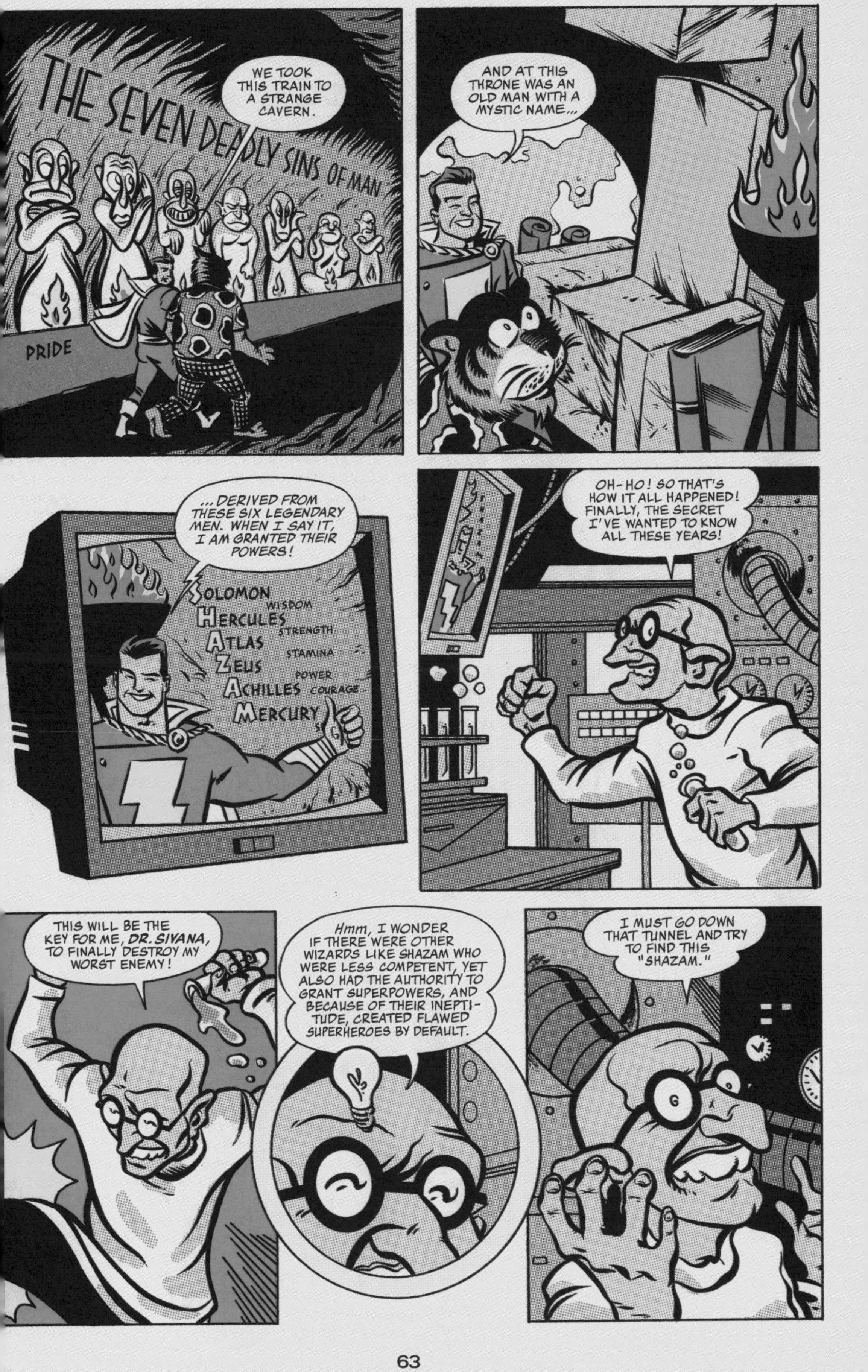
THE SEVEN DEADLY SINS OF MAN
WE TOOK THIS TRAIN TO A STRANGE CAVERN.
PRIDE
AND AT THIS THRONE WAS AN OLD MAN WITH A MYSTIC NAME...
...DERIVED FROM THESE SIX LEGENDARY MEN. WHEN I SAY IT, I AM GRANTED THEIR POWERS!
SOLOMON WISDOM
HERCULES STRENGTH
ATLAS STAMINA
ZEUS POWER
ACHILLES COURAGE
MERCURY
OH-HO! SO THAT'S HOW IT ALL HAPPENED! FINALLY, THE SECRET I'VE WANTED TO KNOW ALL THESE YEARS!
THIS WILL BE THE KEY FOR ME, DR. SIVANA, TO FINALLY DESTROY MY WORST ENEMY!
Hmm, I WONDER IF THERE WERE OTHER WIZARDS LIKE SHAZAM WHO WERE LESS COMPETENT, YET ALSO HAD THE AUTHORITY TO GRANT SUPERPOWERS, AND BECAUSE OF THEIR INEPTI-TUDE, CREATED FLAWED SUPERHEROES BY DEFAULT.
I MUST GO DOWN THAT TUNNEL AND TRY TO FIND THIS "SHAZAM."

HELLO? ANYBODY HERE? IS SHAZAM HERE?

HOW MAY I HELP YOU, YOUNG MAN?

WELL, I, *er, um,* I'M A STUDENT, AND I'M WRITING A PAPER ABOUT, *uh,* HEROES, AND I WAS WONDERING IF YOU COULD ANSWER SOME QUESTIONS?

I'LL TRY.

WE ALL KNOW YOU AUTHORIZED THE POWERS OF SIX GREAT MEN. MY QUESTION FOR YOU IS-- IS THERE ANYONE, *um,* NOT QUITE PERFECT, THAT HAS THE POWERS OF HISTORY'S *DUMBEST, MOST INCOMPETENT* MEN?

Hmm, I'M NOT REALLY SUPPOSED TO DIVULGE THIS INFORMATION TO MORTALS, BUT SINCE YOU'RE A STUDENT, I GUESS IT'S OKAY.

THERE WAS ONCE A FELLOW NAMED "DUH" WHO HAD ATTRIBUTES THAT WEREN'T EXACTLY HELPFUL.

DUMBOSTHENES
STUPIDITY
ULOUSSIES
CLUMSINESS
HOPELESSCULES
CLUELESSNESS

I SEE. THAT'S VERY INTERESTING.

DUMBOSTHENES
STUPIDITY
ULOUSSIES
CLUMSINESS
HOPELESSCULES
CLUELESSNESS

WELL, SO LONG, SUCKER!

LATER...

NOW FOR THE FINAL TOUCH!

OH, BILLY! BILLY BATSON! WAKE UP!

HUH, WHA....?

I HAVE SOME VERY URGENT NEWS!!

WHAT IS IT?

IT'S AN IMPORTANT MATTER OF SECURITY! THE WRONG PEOPLE MIGHT BECOME AWARE OF YOUR ABILITY TO TURN INTO CAPTAIN MARVEL, AND IT COULD RESULT IN IMPOSTORS. SO, TO PREVENT THIS, YOU WILL NOW HAVE TO USE AN ACCESS CODE NAME...

FROM NOW ON, YOU MUST SHOUT "DUH!" BEFORE SHOUTING "SHAZAM!"

DUMBOSTHENES STUPIDITY LEADERSHIP ULOUSSIES CLUMSINESS NOBILITY HOPELESSCULES HELPLESSNESS SUCCESS

REMEMBER THAT NAME, BILLY BATSON! 'BYE, NOW!

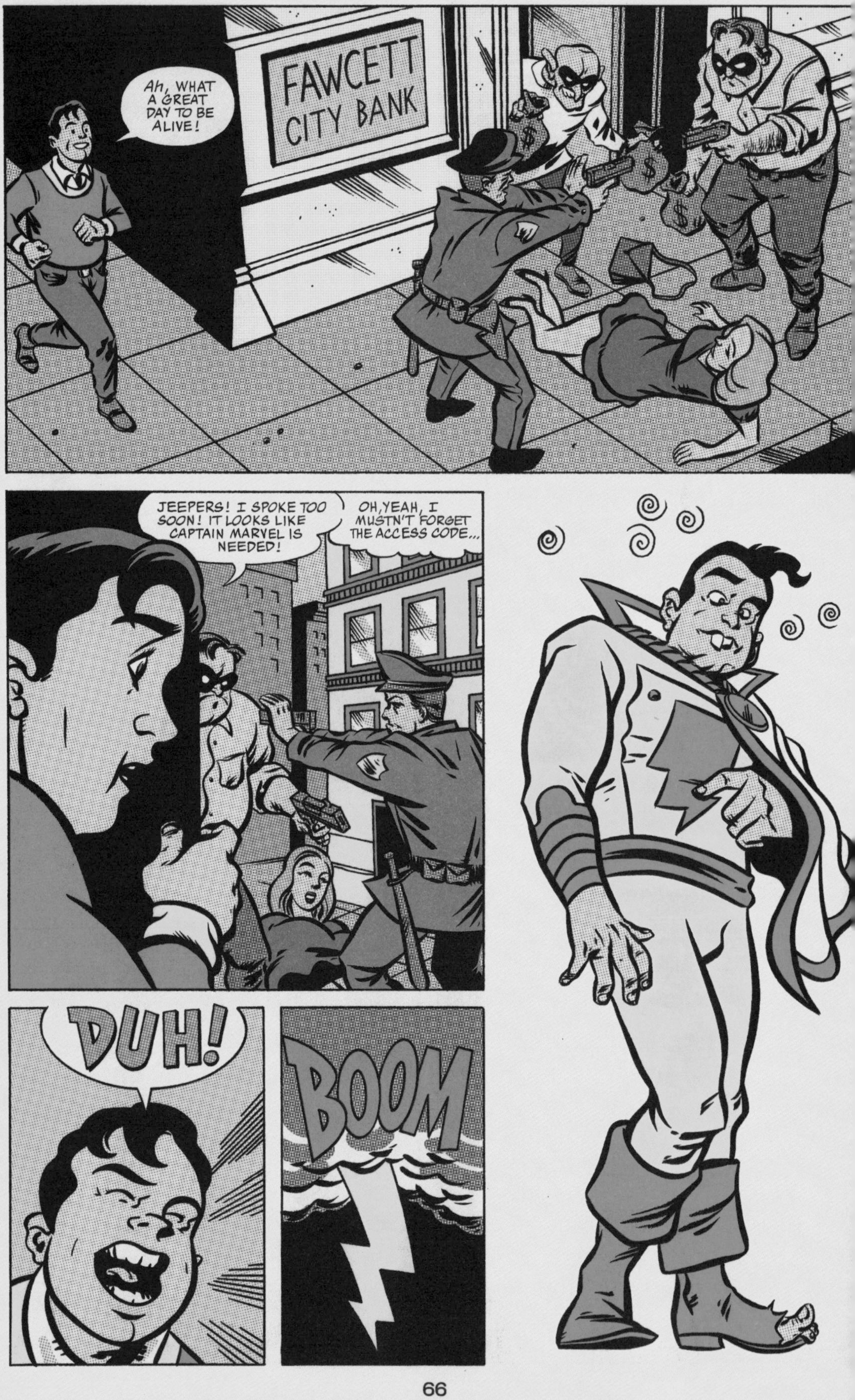

FAWCETT CITY BANK
Ah, WHAT A GREAT DAY TO BE ALIVE!
JEEPERS! I SPOKE TOO SOON! IT LOOKS LIKE CAPTAIN MARVEL IS NEEDED!
OH, YEAH, I MUSTN'T FORGET THE ACCESS CODE...
DUH!
BOOM

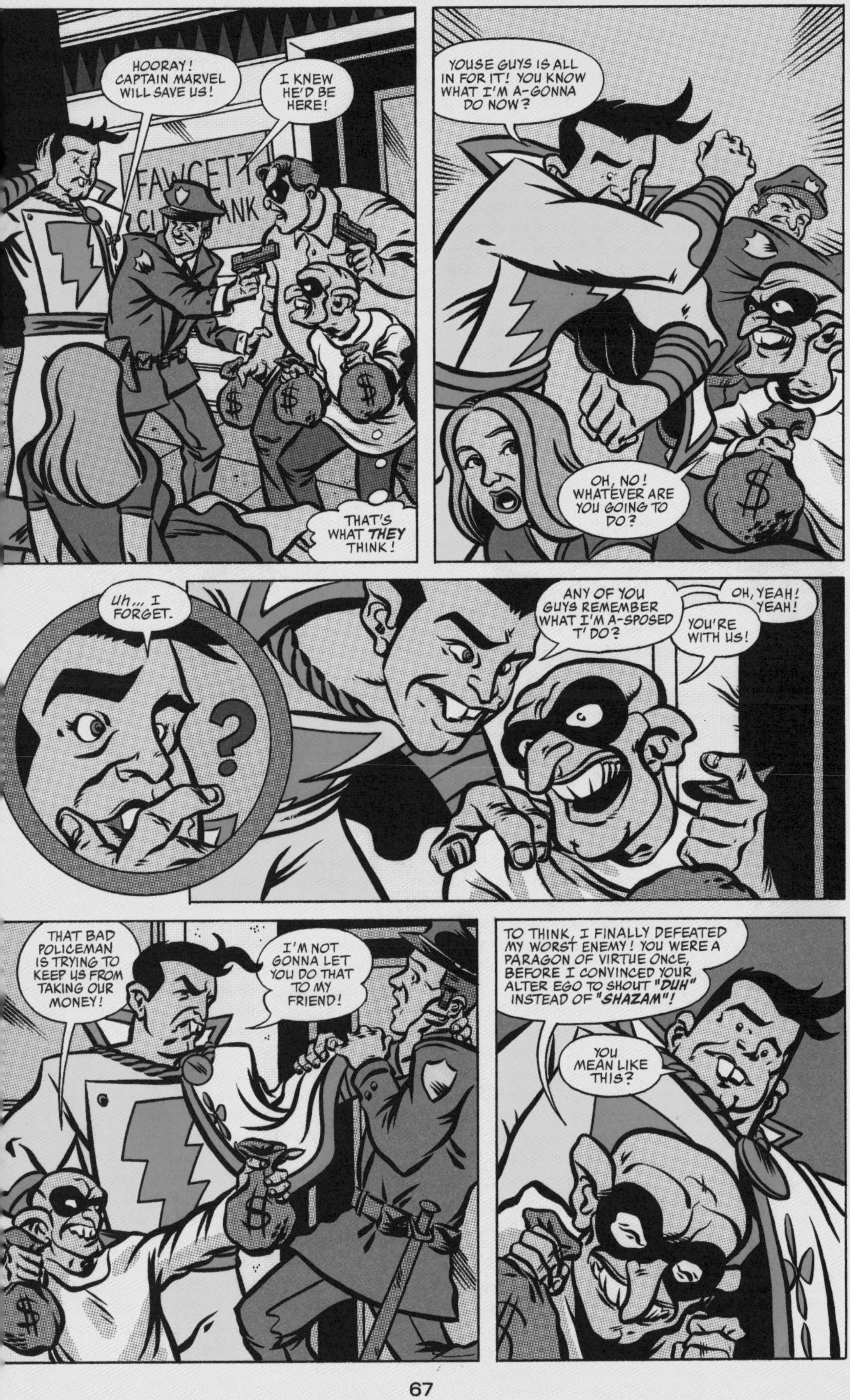
HOORAY! CAPTAIN MARVEL WILL SAVE US!
I KNEW HE'D BE HERE!
FAWCETT ... ANK
THAT'S WHAT THEY THINK!
YOUSE GUYS IS ALL IN FOR IT! YOU KNOW WHAT I'M A-GONNA DO NOW?
OH, NO! WHATEVER ARE YOU GOING TO DO?
Uh... I FORGET.
?
ANY OF YOU GUYS REMEMBER WHAT I'M A-SPOSED T' DO?
OH, YEAH! YEAH!
YOU'RE WITH US!
THAT BAD POLICEMAN IS TRYING TO KEEP US FROM TAKING OUR MONEY!
I'M NOT GONNA LET YOU DO THAT TO MY FRIEND!
TO THINK, I FINALLY DEFEATED MY WORST ENEMY! YOU WERE A PARAGON OF VIRTUE ONCE, BEFORE I CONVINCED YOUR ALTER EGO TO SHOUT "DUH" INSTEAD OF "SHAZAM"!
YOU MEAN LIKE THIS?

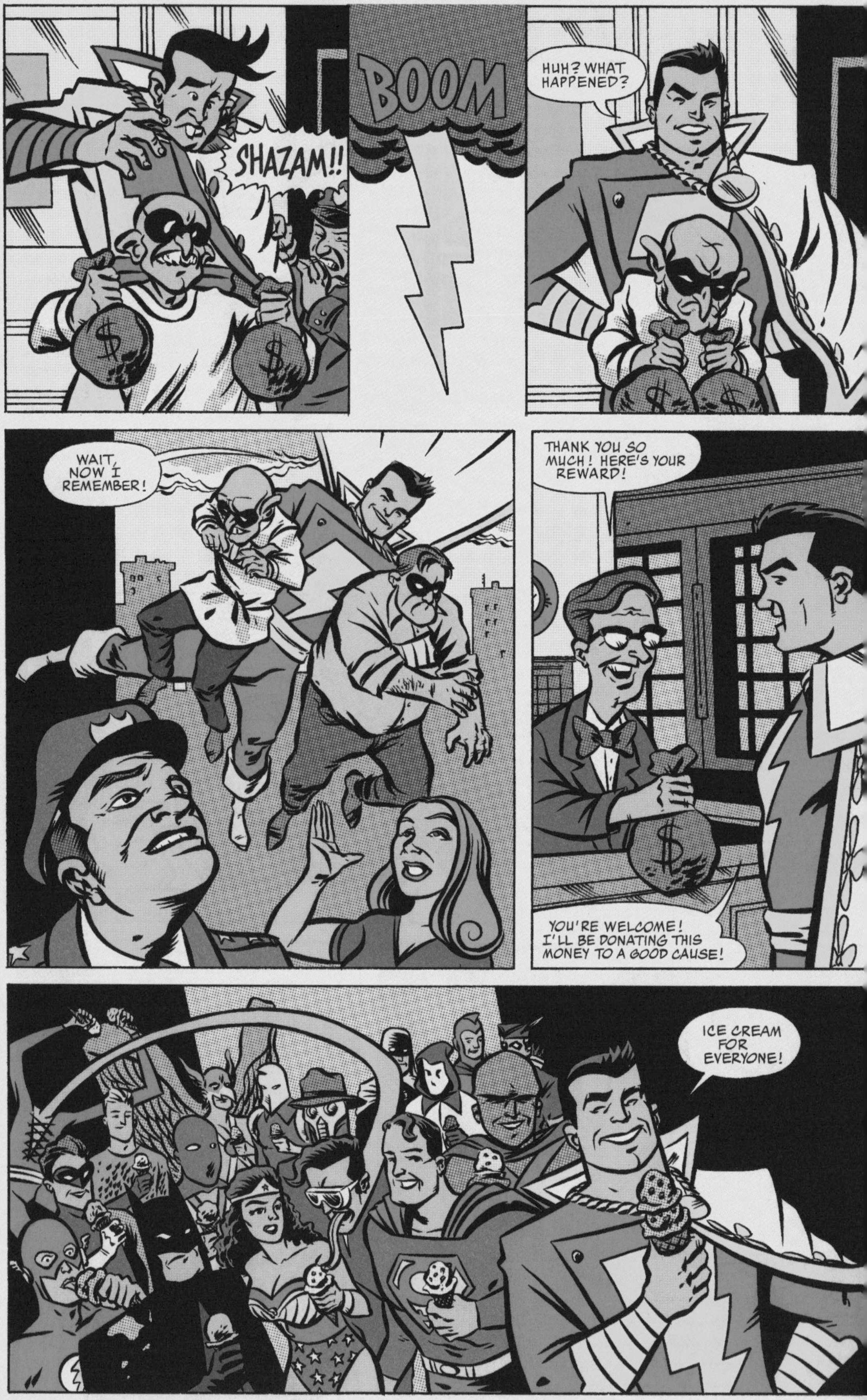
SHAZAM!!
BOOM
HUH? WHAT HAPPENED?
WAIT, NOW I REMEMBER!
THANK YOU SO MUCH! HERE'S YOUR REWARD!
YOU'RE WELCOME! I'LL BE DONATING THIS MONEY TO A GOOD CAUSE!
ICE CREAM FOR EVERYONE!

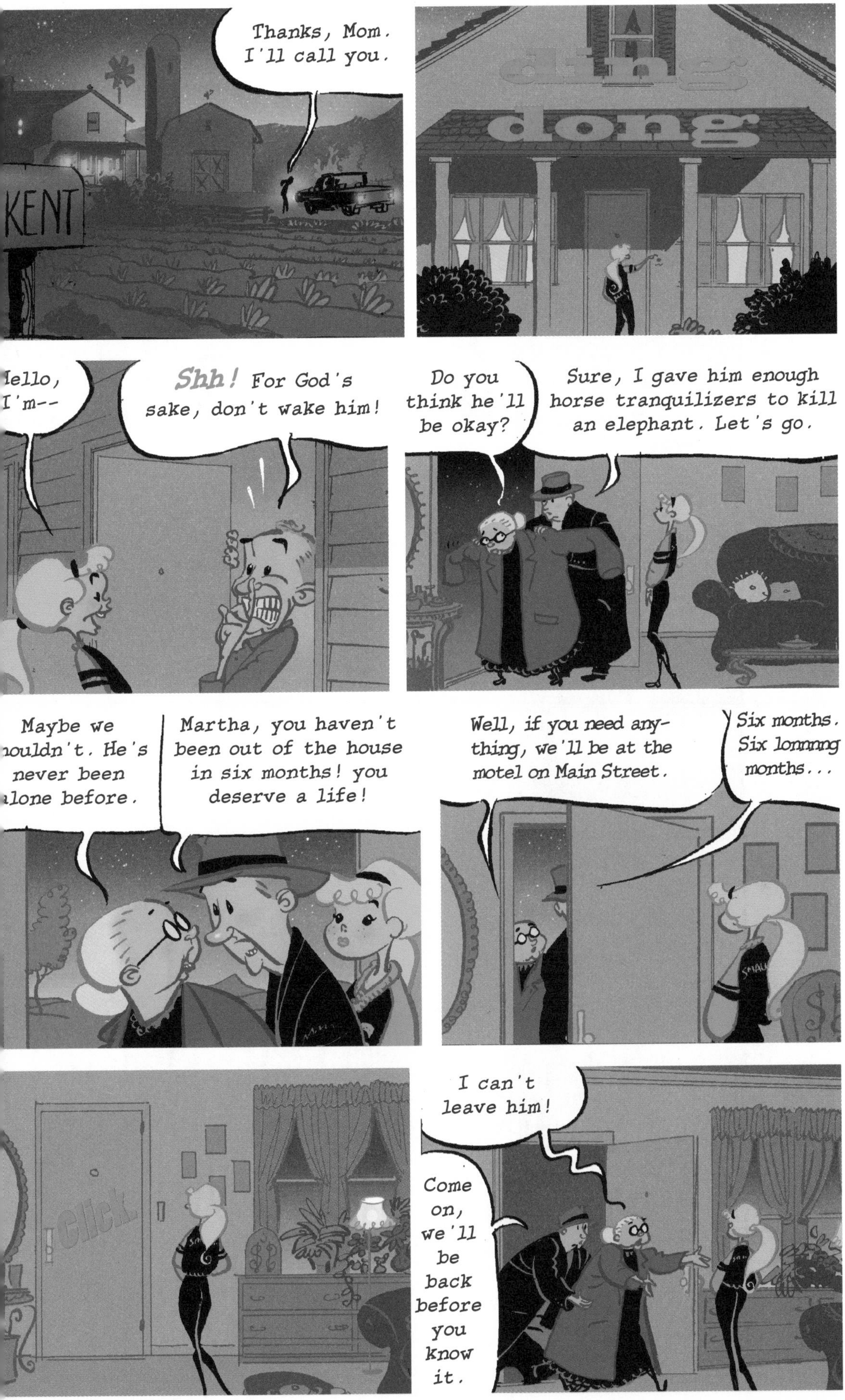
KENT
Thanks, Mom. I'll call you.
ding
dong
ello, I'm--
Shh! For God's sake, don't wake him!
Do you think he'll be okay?
Sure, I gave him enough horse tranquilizers to kill an elephant. Let's go.
Maybe we ouldn't. He's never been lone before.
Martha, you haven't been out of the house in six months! you deserve a life!
Well, if you need anything, we'll be at the motel on Main Street.
Six months. Six lonnnng months...
Click
I can't leave him!
Come on, we'll be back before you know it.

I'm a terrible mother. God, I feel so guilty...

Everything will be fine. Wild horses couldn't kill that kid. A *tractor* couldn't kill that kid. Being plowed under a *corn field* couldn't kill that kid.

That reminds me. Did you call the man about fixing the plow and tractor?

Click.

DC AND ELSEWORLDS PRESENT:

LETITIA LERNER, SUPERMAN'S BABYSITTER!

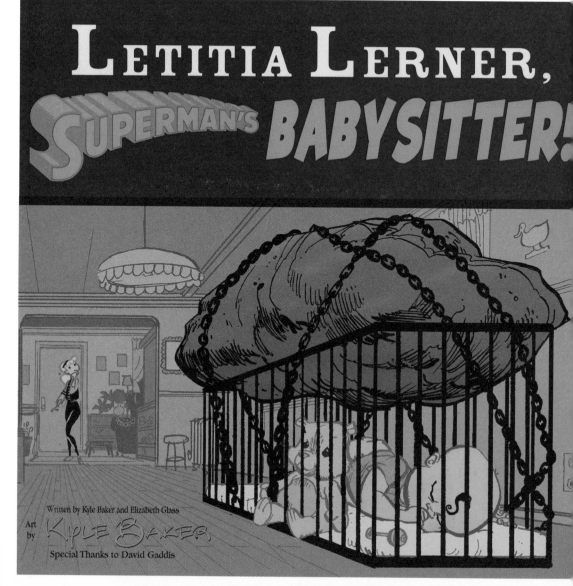

Written by Kyle Baker and Elizabeth Glass

Art by KYLE BAKER

Special Thanks to David Gaddis

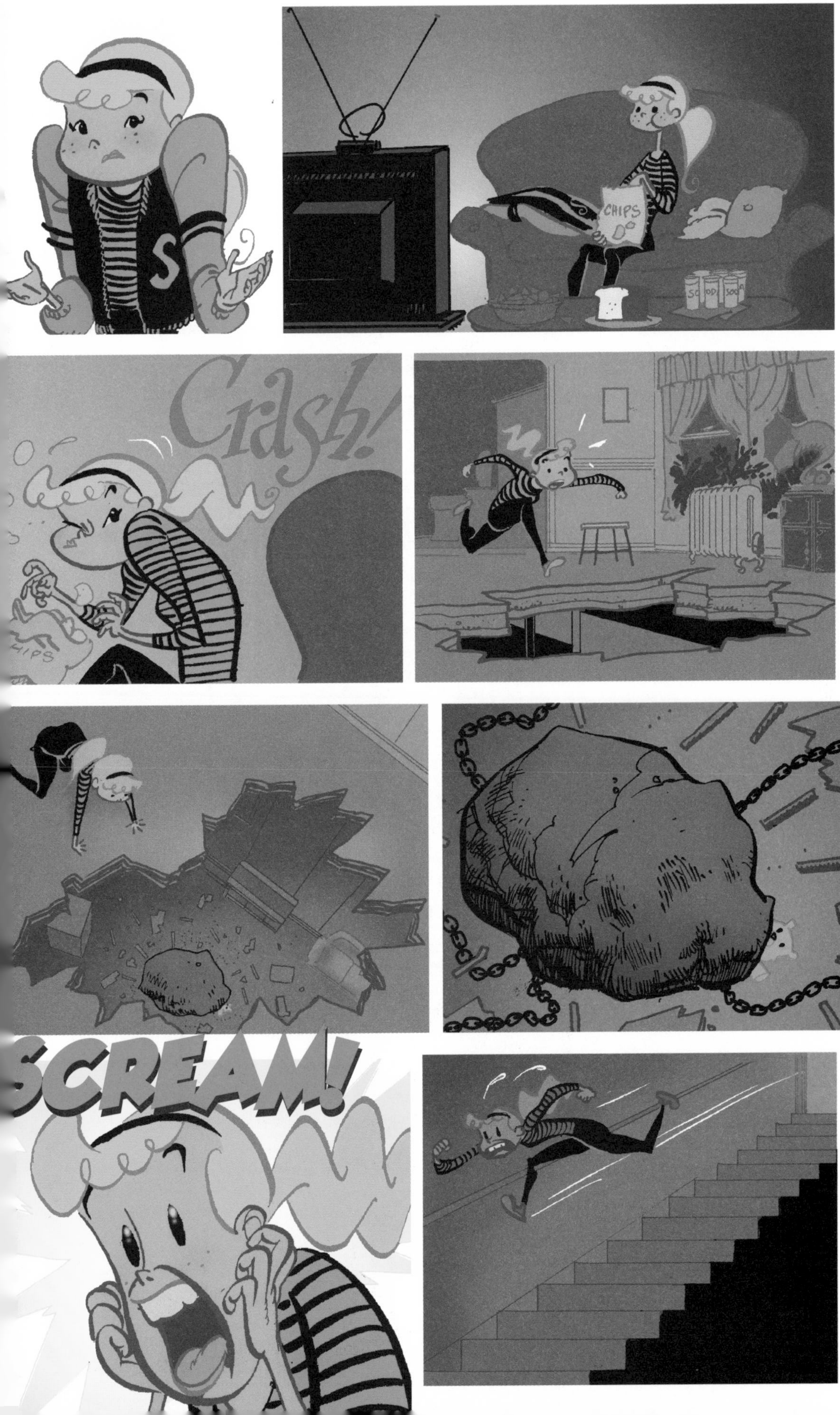

CHIPS
Crash!
SCREAM!

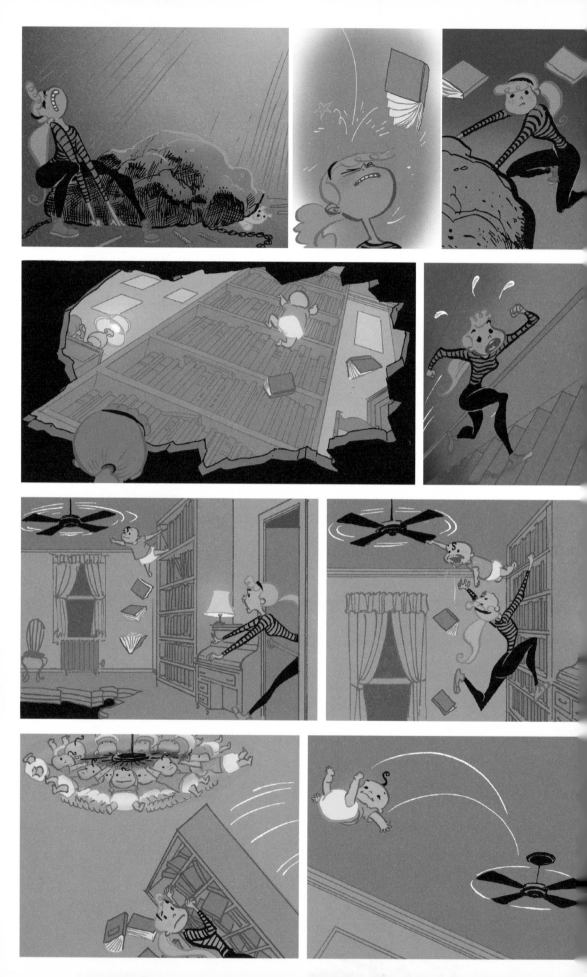

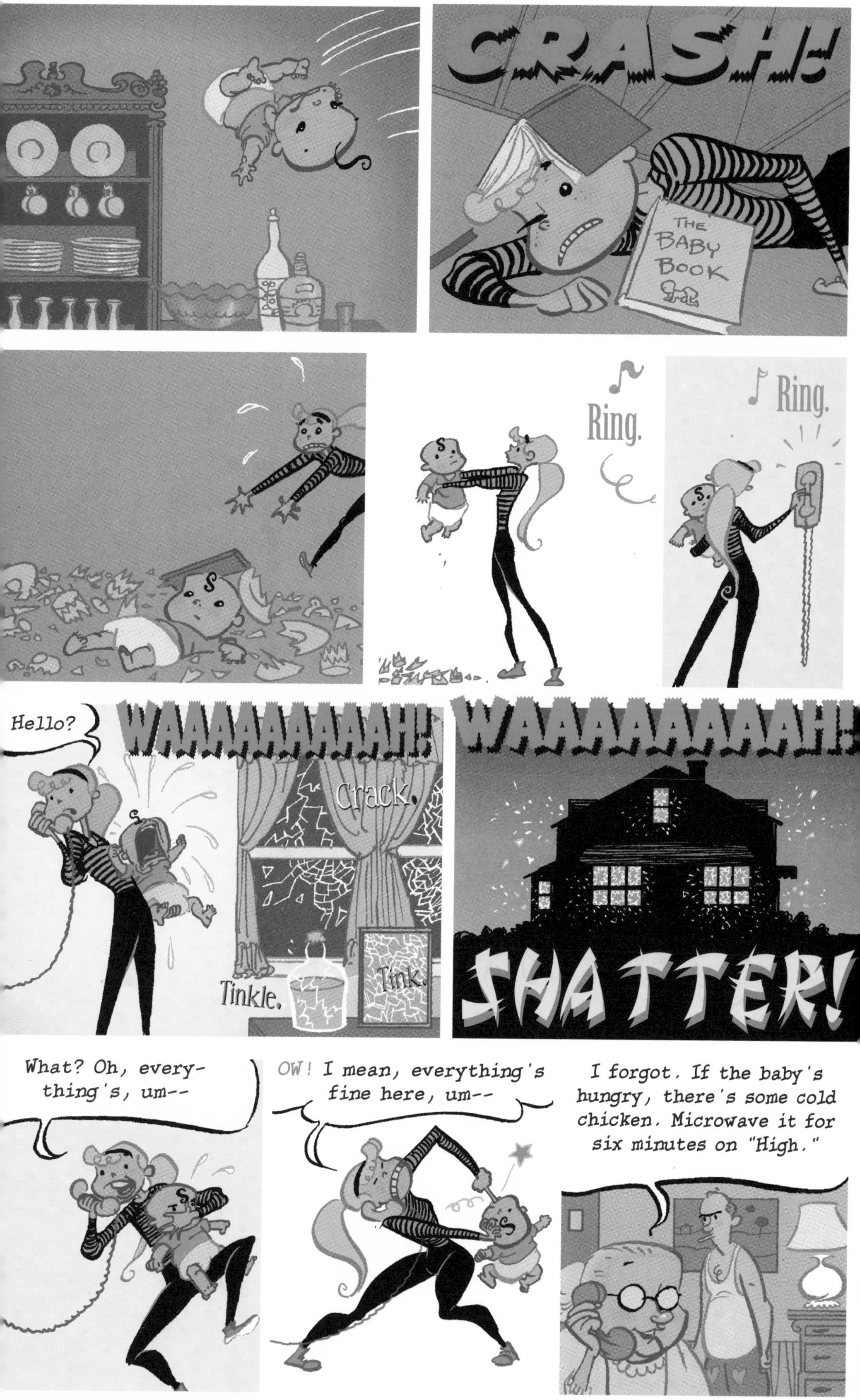
CRASH!
THE BABY BOOK
Ring.
Ring.
Hello?
WAAAAAAAAAH!
Crack.
Tinkle.
Tink.
WAAAAAAAAAH!
SHATTER!
What? Oh, every-thing's, um--
OW! I mean, everything's fine here, um--
I forgot. If the baby's hungry, there's some cold chicken. Microwave it for six minutes on "High."

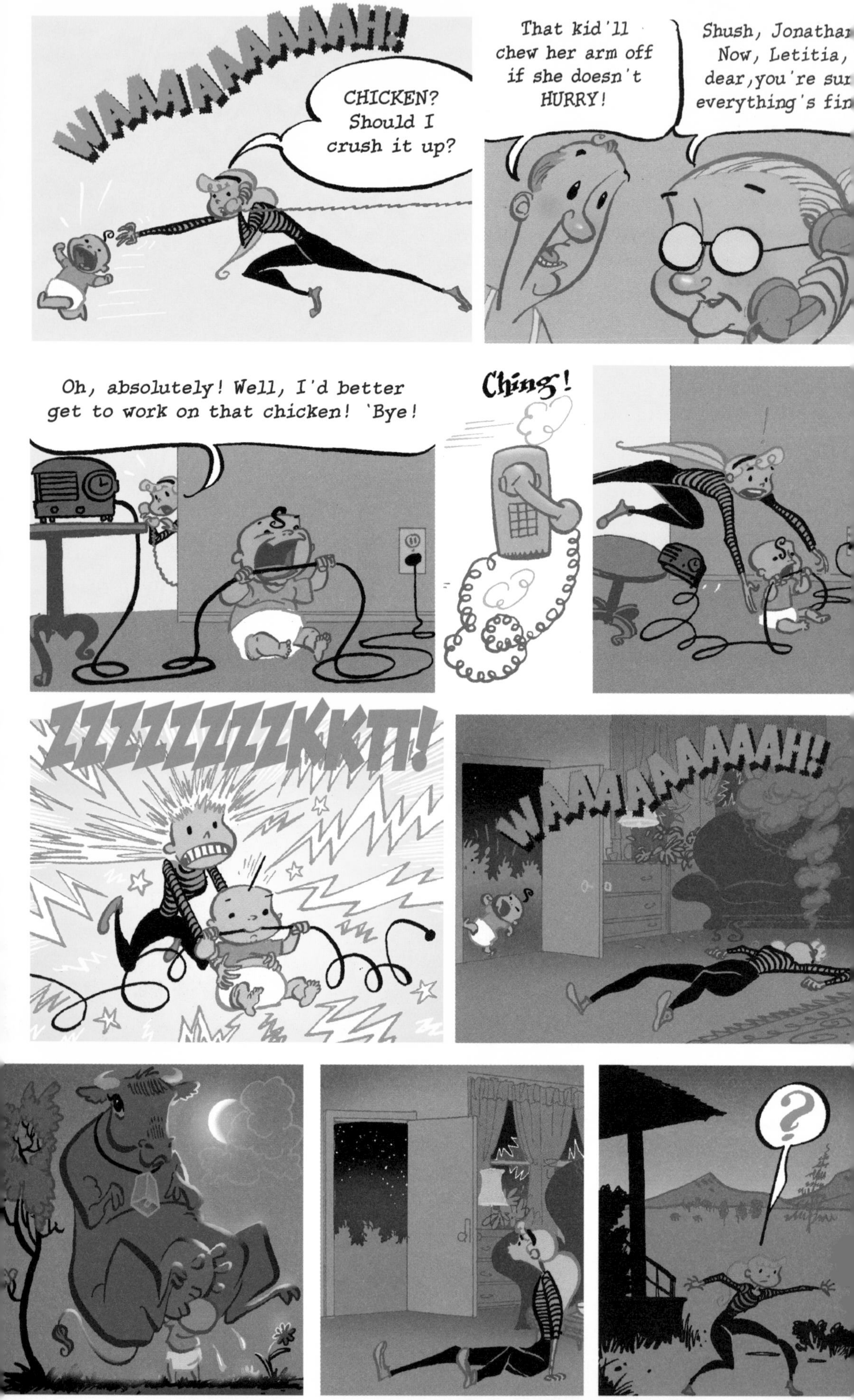
WAAAAAAAAAH!
CHICKEN? Should I crush it up?
That kid'll chew her arm off if she doesn't HURRY!
Shush, Jonatha
Now, Letitia,
dear, you're su
everything's fin
Oh, absolutely! Well, I'd better get to work on that chicken! 'Bye!
Ching!
ZZZZZZZZKKTT!
WAAAAAAAAAH!

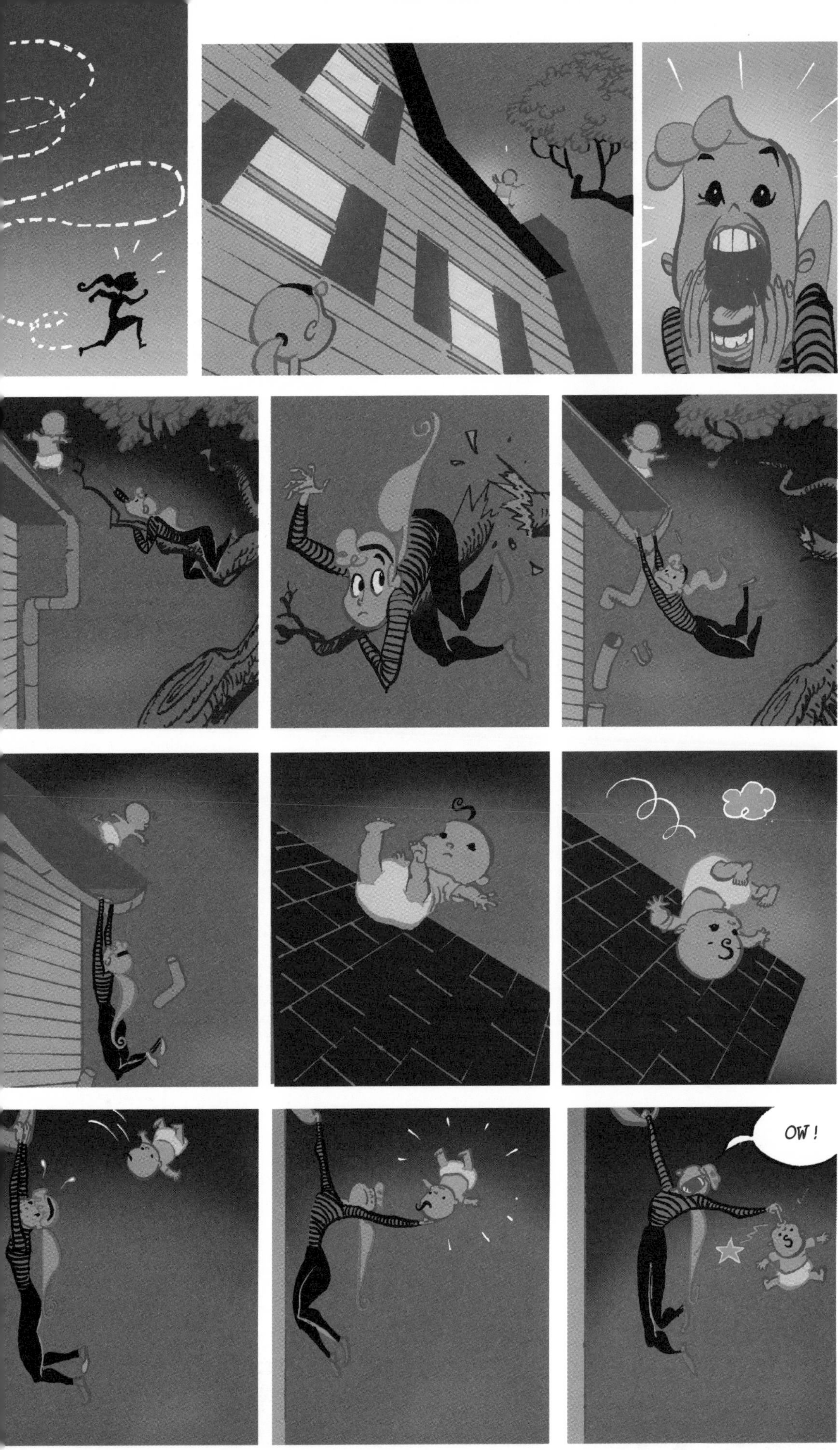
OW !

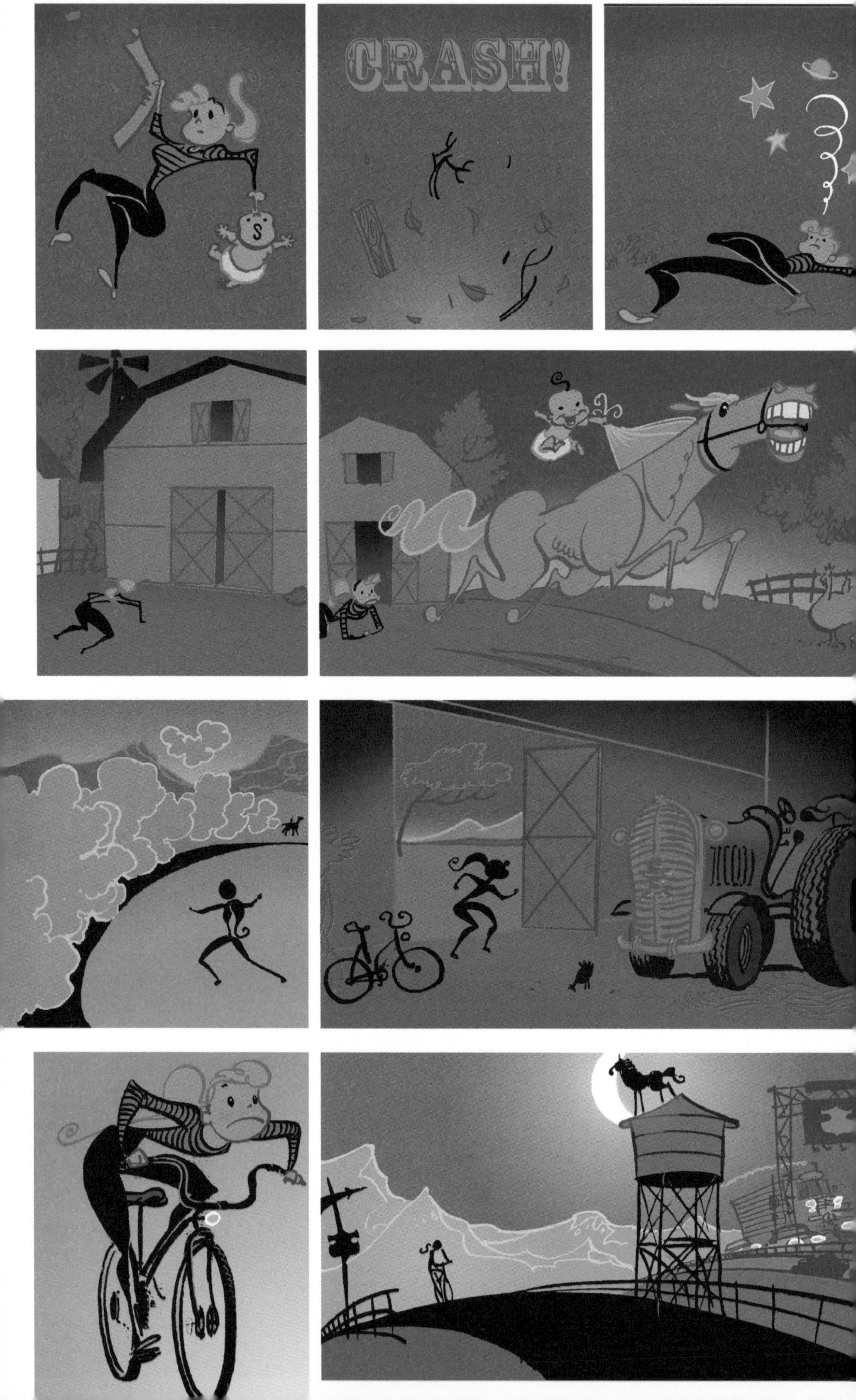
CRASH!

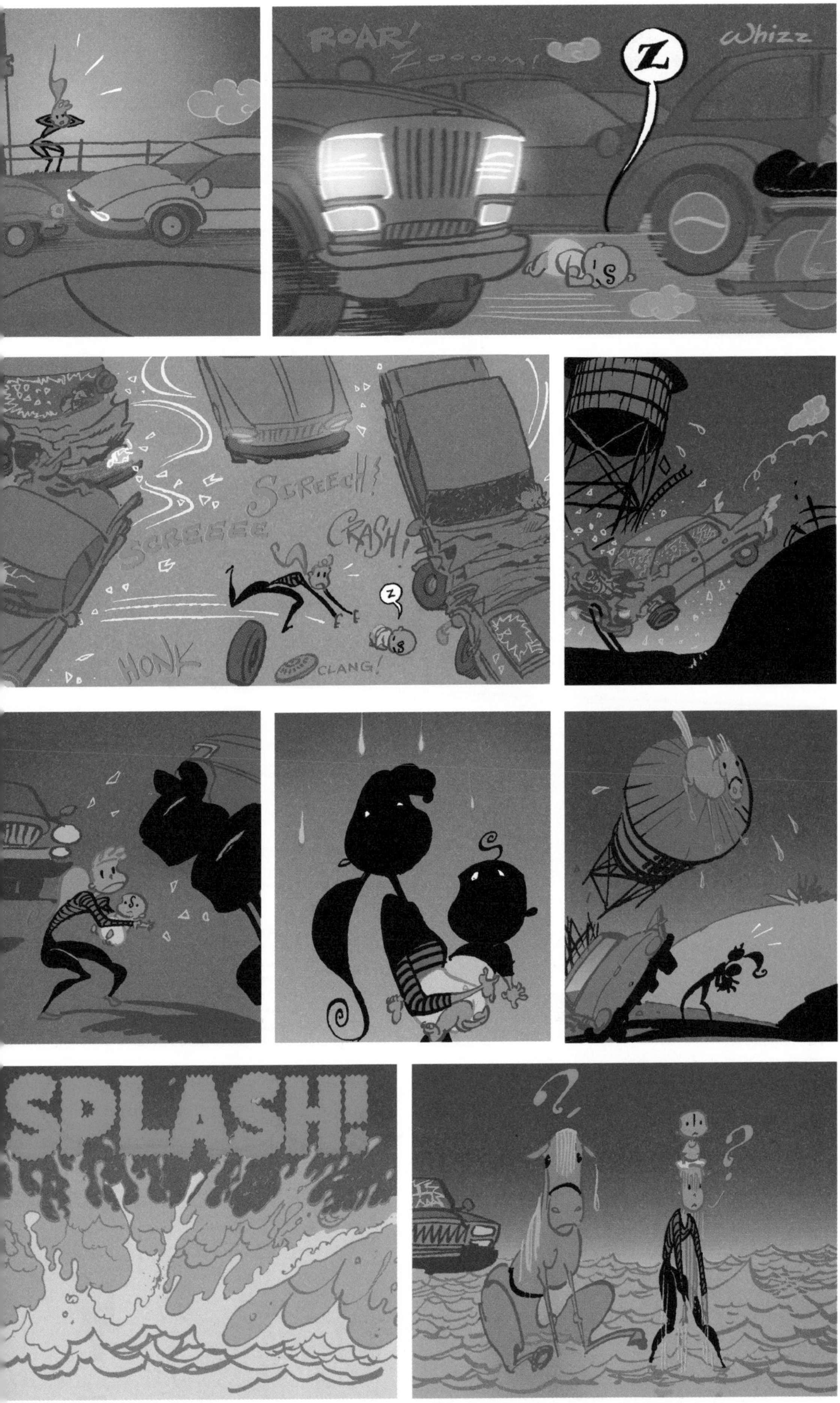
ROAR!
Zoooom!
Z
Whizz
SCREECH!
SCREEEE
CRASH!
Z
HONK
CLANG!
SPLASH!
?
?

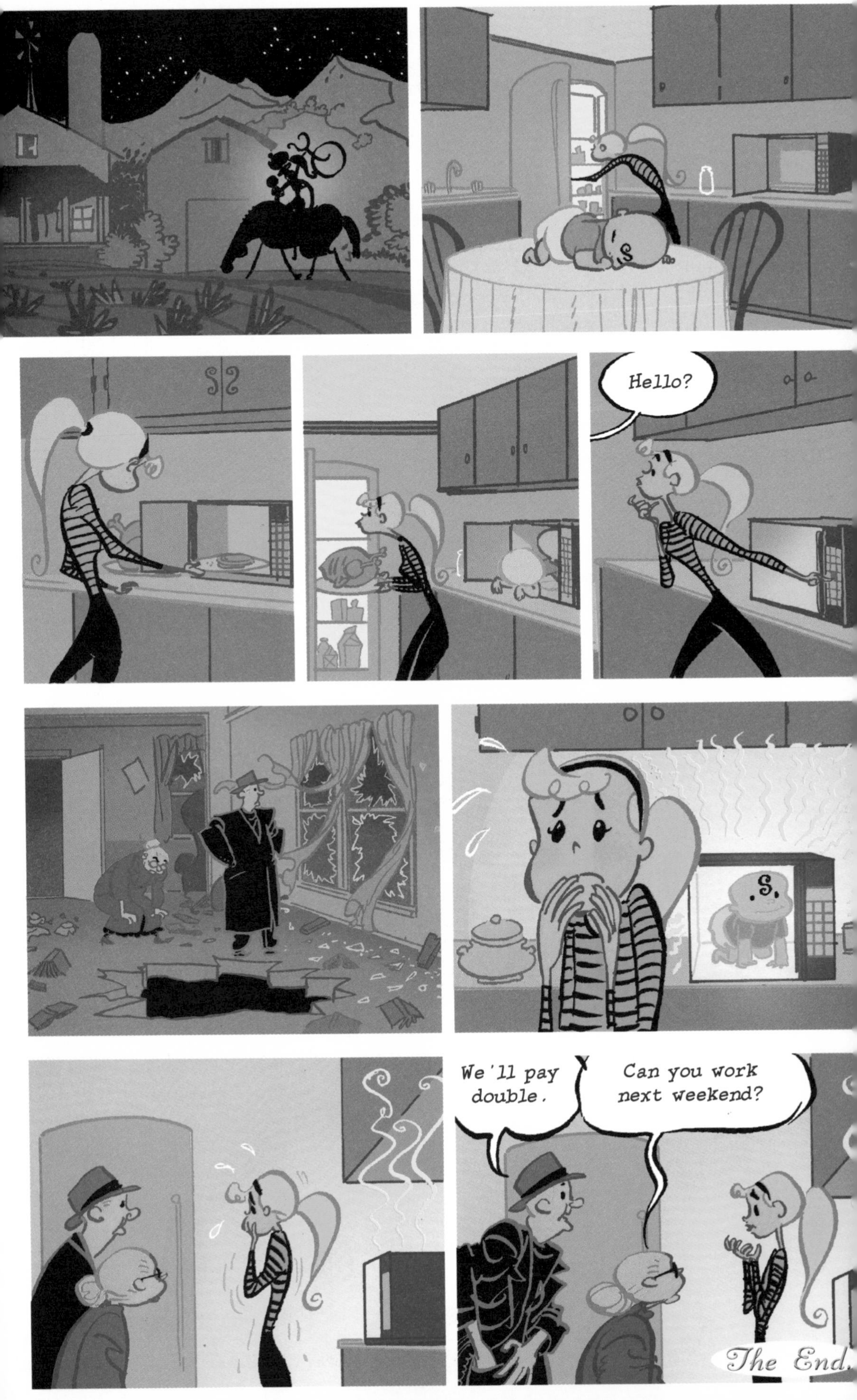

Hello?
We'll pay double.
Can you work next weekend?
The End.

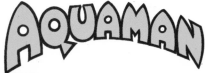

AQUAMAN in: SILENCE of the FISHES

STORY: EVAN DORKIN AND BRIAN DAVID-MARSHALL

ART: BILL WRAY

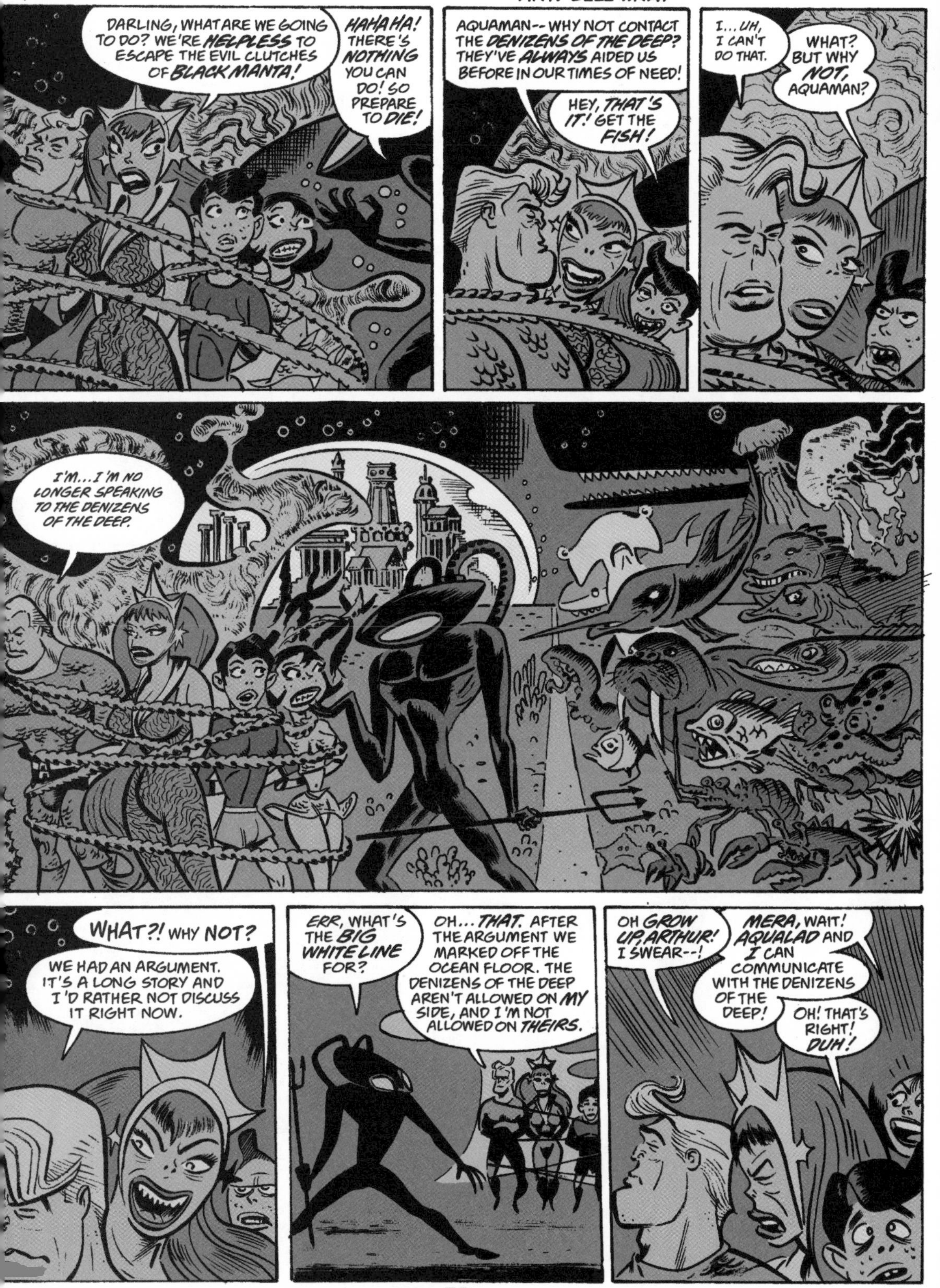
DARLING, WHAT ARE WE GOING TO DO? WE'RE HELPLESS TO ESCAPE THE EVIL CLUTCHES OF BLACK MANTA!
HAHAHA! THERE'S NOTHING YOU CAN DO! SO PREPARE TO DIE!
AQUAMAN-- WHY NOT CONTACT THE DENIZENS OF THE DEEP? THEY'VE ALWAYS AIDED US BEFORE IN OUR TIMES OF NEED!
HEY, THAT'S IT! GET THE FISH!
I... UH, I CAN'T DO THAT.
WHAT? BUT WHY NOT, AQUAMAN?
I'M... I'M NO LONGER SPEAKING TO THE DENIZENS OF THE DEEP.
WHAT?! WHY NOT?
WE HAD AN ARGUMENT. IT'S A LONG STORY AND I'D RATHER NOT DISCUSS IT RIGHT NOW.
ERR, WHAT'S THE BIG WHITE LINE FOR?
OH... THAT. AFTER THE ARGUMENT WE MARKED OFF THE OCEAN FLOOR. THE DENIZENS OF THE DEEP AREN'T ALLOWED ON MY SIDE, AND I'M NOT ALLOWED ON THEIRS.
OH GROW UP, ARTHUR! I SWEAR--!
MERA, WAIT! AQUALAD AND I CAN COMMUNICATE WITH THE DENIZENS OF THE DEEP!
OH! THAT'S RIGHT! DUH!

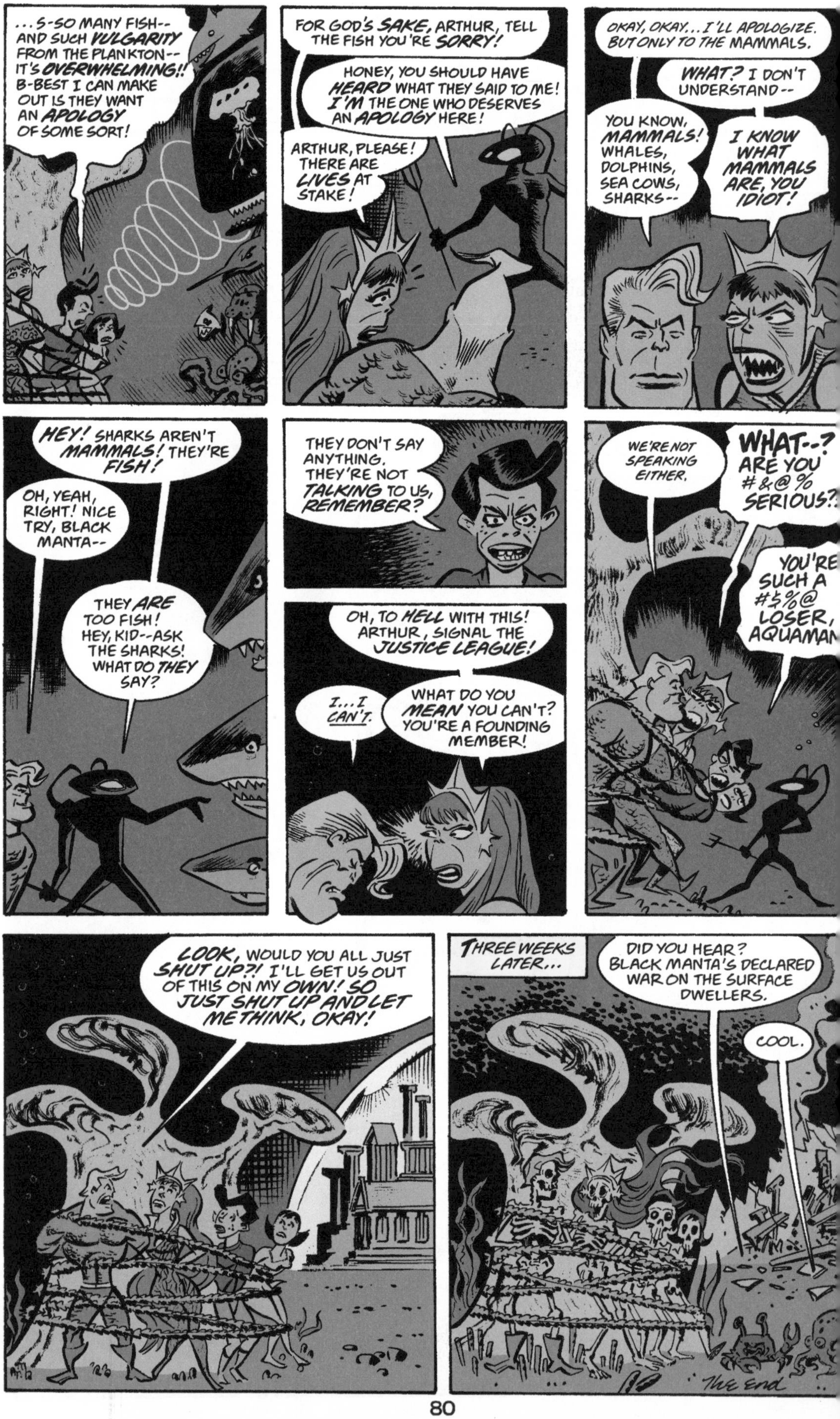
...S-SO MANY FISH-- AND SUCH VULGARITY FROM THE PLANKTON-- IT'S OVERWHELMING!! B-BEST I CAN MAKE OUT IS THEY WANT AN APOLOGY OF SOME SORT!
FOR GOD'S SAKE, ARTHUR, TELL THE FISH YOU'RE SORRY!
HONEY, YOU SHOULD HAVE HEARD WHAT THEY SAID TO ME! I'M THE ONE WHO DESERVES AN APOLOGY HERE!
ARTHUR, PLEASE! THERE ARE LIVES AT STAKE!
OKAY, OKAY... I'LL APOLOGIZE. BUT ONLY TO THE MAMMALS.
WHAT? I DON'T UNDERSTAND--
YOU KNOW, MAMMALS! WHALES, DOLPHINS, SEA COWS, SHARKS--
I KNOW WHAT MAMMALS ARE, YOU IDIOT!
HEY! SHARKS AREN'T MAMMALS! THEY'RE FISH!
OH, YEAH, RIGHT! NICE TRY, BLACK MANTA--
THEY ARE TOO FISH! HEY, KID--ASK THE SHARKS! WHAT DO THEY SAY?
THEY DON'T SAY ANYTHING. THEY'RE NOT TALKING TO US, REMEMBER?
OH, TO HELL WITH THIS! ARTHUR, SIGNAL THE JUSTICE LEAGUE!
I...I CAN'T.
WHAT DO YOU MEAN YOU CAN'T? YOU'RE A FOUNDING MEMBER!
WE'RE NOT SPEAKING EITHER.
WHAT--? ARE YOU #&@% SERIOUS?
YOU'RE SUCH A #$%@ LOSER, AQUAMAN
LOOK, WOULD YOU ALL JUST SHUT UP?! I'LL GET US OUT OF THIS ON MY OWN! SO JUST SHUT UP AND LET ME THINK, OKAY!
THREE WEEKS LATER...
DID YOU HEAR? BLACK MANTA'S DECLARED WAR ON THE SURFACE DWELLERS.
COOL.
The End

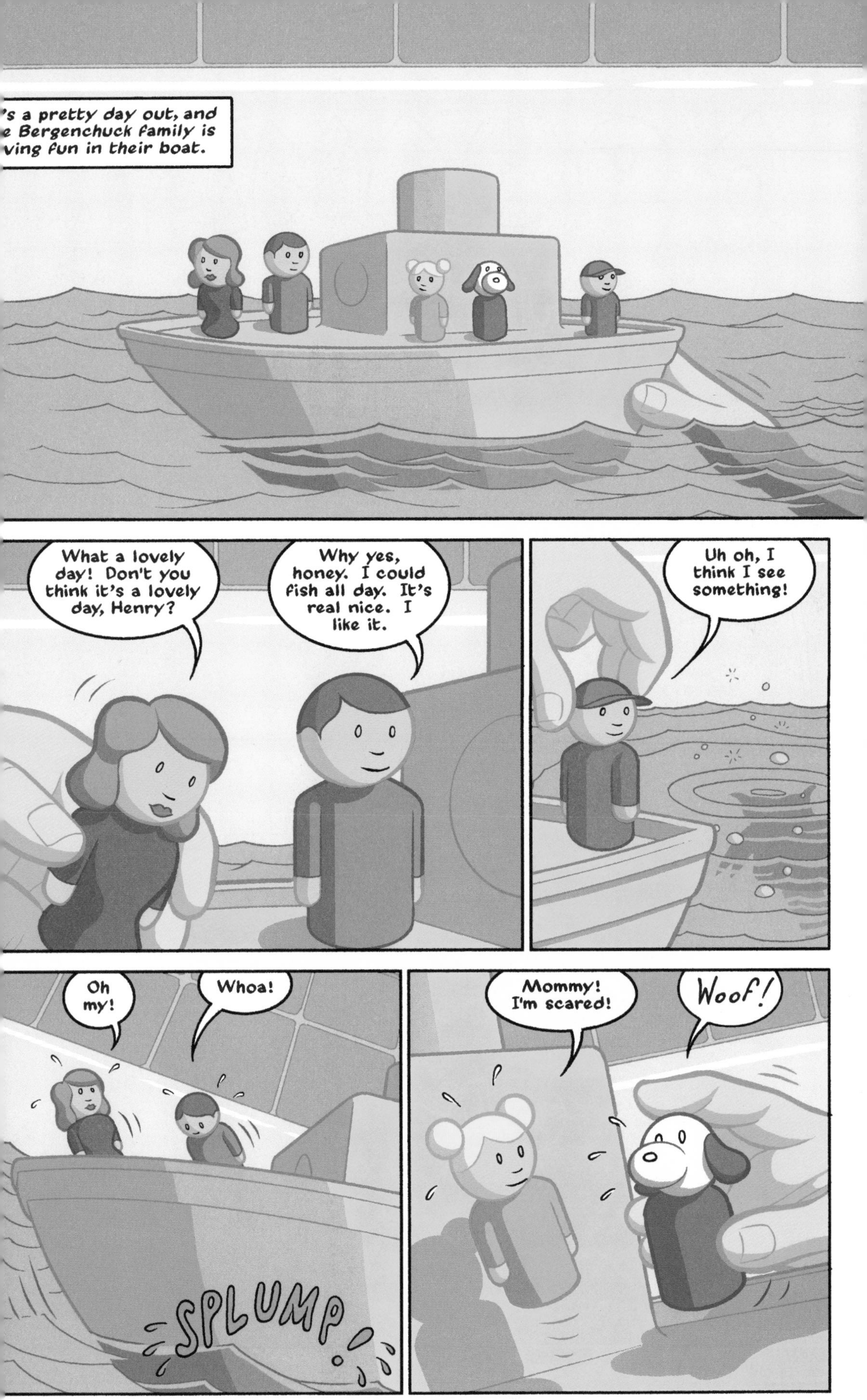
's a pretty day out, and
e Bergenchuck family is
ving fun in their boat.
What a lovely day! Don't you think it's a lovely day, Henry?
Why yes, honey. I could fish all day. It's real nice. I like it.
Uh oh, I think I see something!
Oh my!
Whoa!
SPLUMP!
Mommy! I'm scared!
Woof!

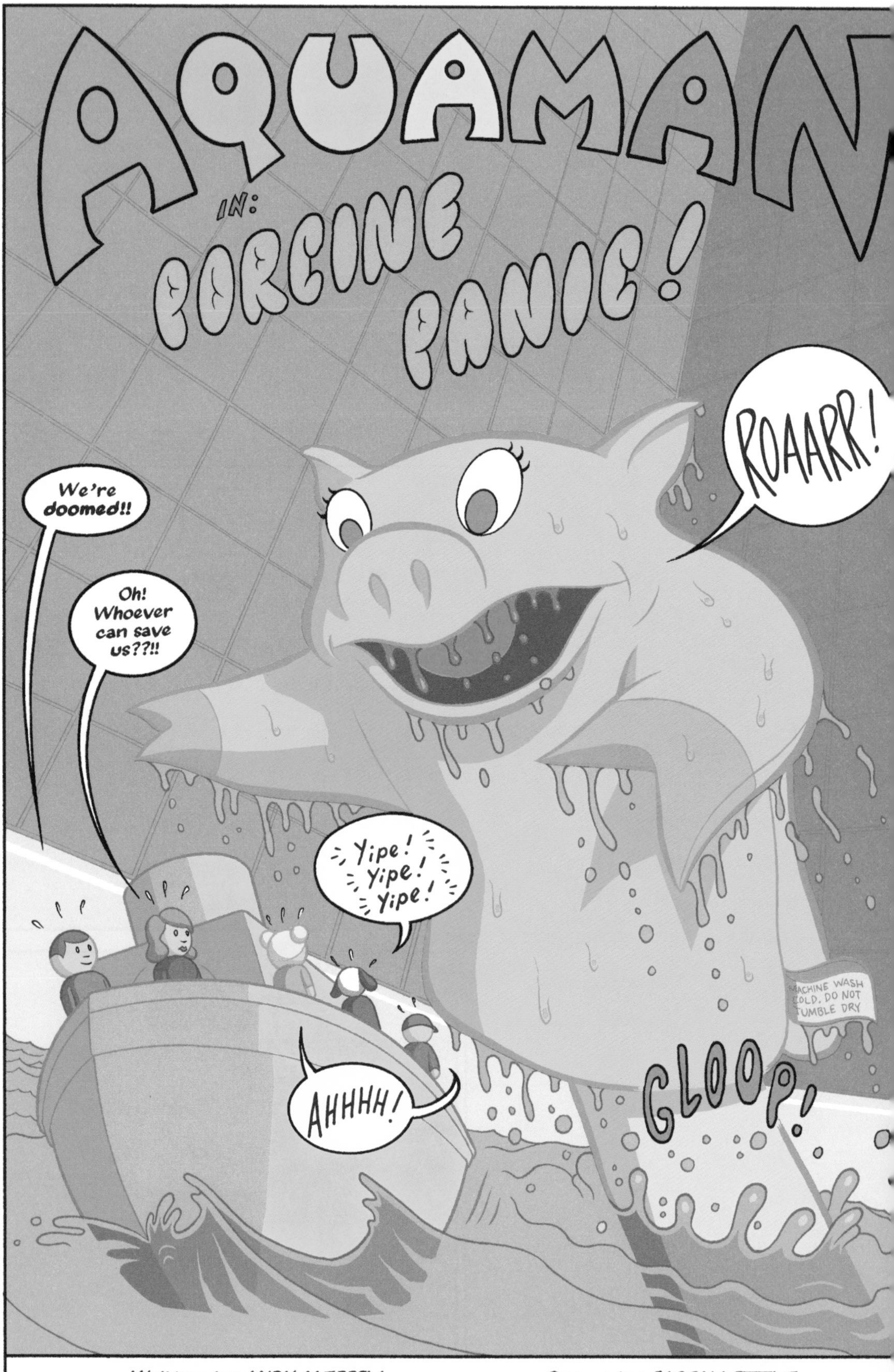
AQUAMAN
IN: PORCINE PANIC!
We're doomed!!
Oh! Whoever can save us??!!
ROAARR!
Yipe! Yipe! Yipe!
MACHINE WASH COLD. DO NOT TUMBLE DRY
AHHHH!
GLOOP!

Written by ANDY MERRILL Drawn by JASON LITTLE

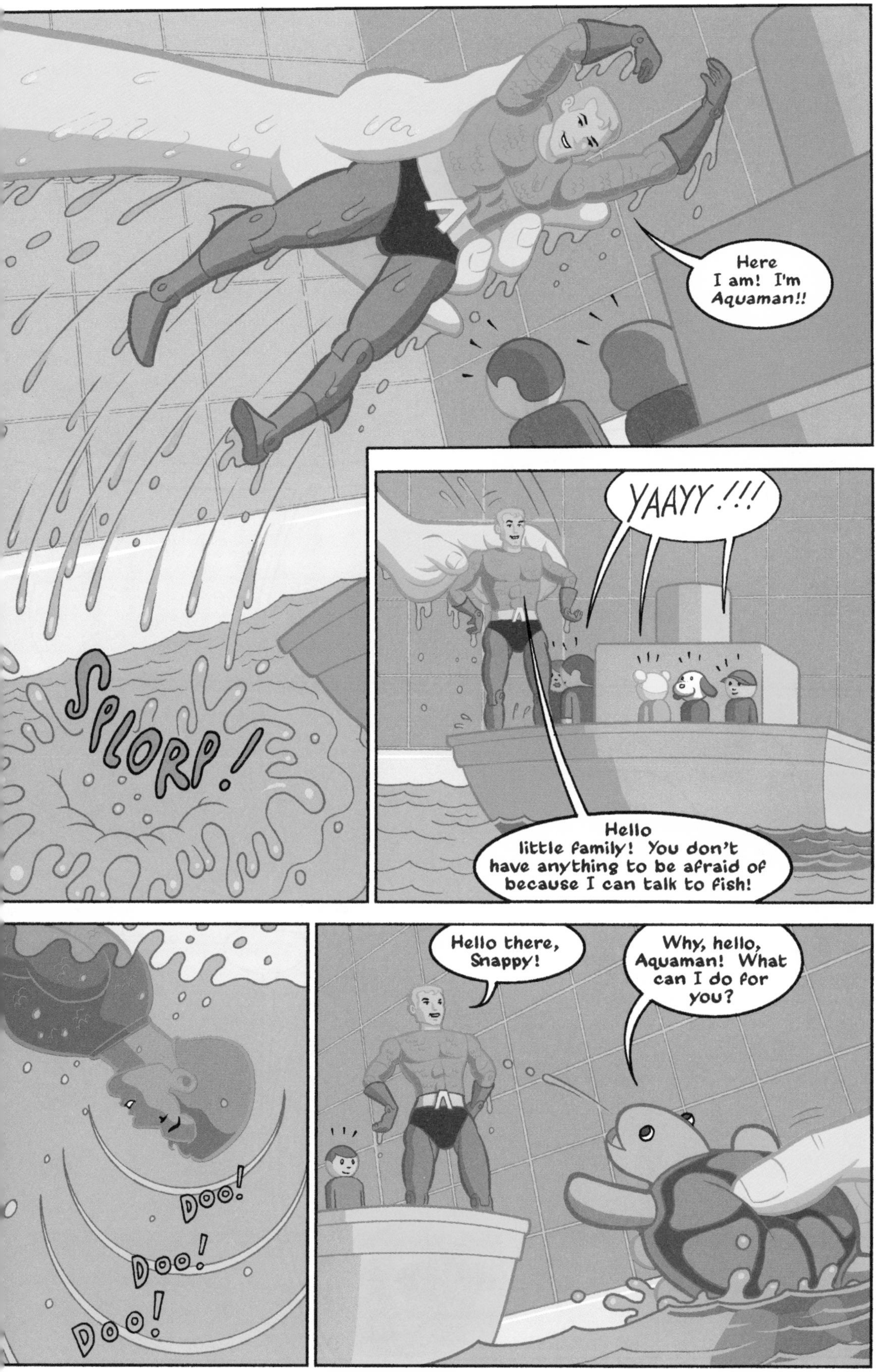
Here I am! I'm Aquaman!!
SPLORP!
YAAYY!!!
Hello little family! You don't have anything to be afraid of because I can talk to fish!
DOO!
DOO!
DOO!
Hello there, Snappy!
Why, hello, Aquaman! What can I do for you?

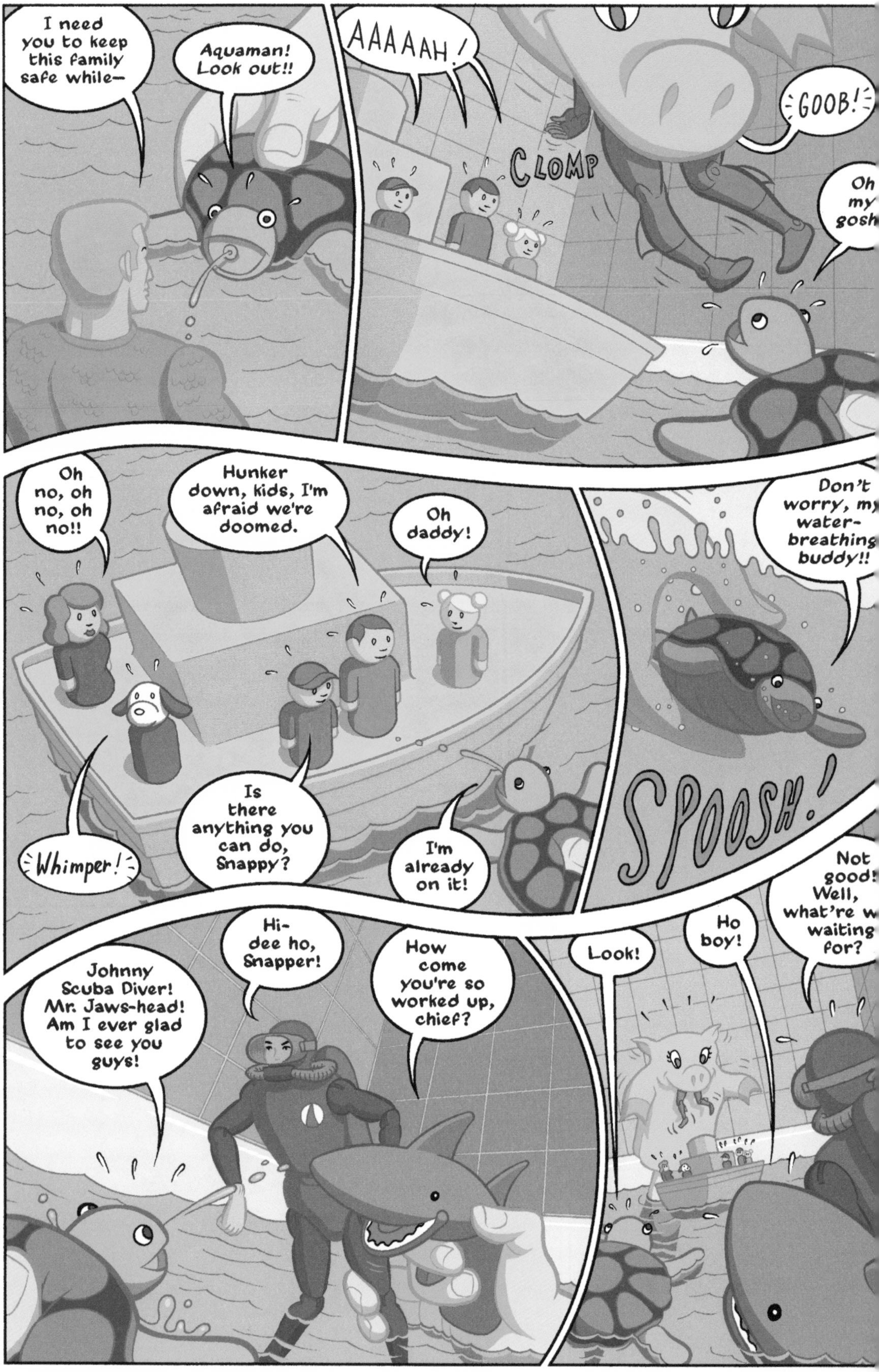
I need you to keep this family safe while—
Aquaman! Look out!!
AAAAAH!
CLOMP
GOOB!
Oh my gosh
Oh no, oh no, oh no!!
Hunker down, kids, I'm afraid we're doomed.
Oh daddy!
Whimper!
Is there anything you can do, Snappy?
I'm already on it!
Don't worry, my water-breathing buddy!!
SPOOSH!
Johnny Scuba Diver! Mr. Jaws-head! Am I ever glad to see you guys!
Hi-dee ho, Snapper!
How come you're so worked up, chief?
Look!
Ho boy!
Not good! Well, what're we waiting for?

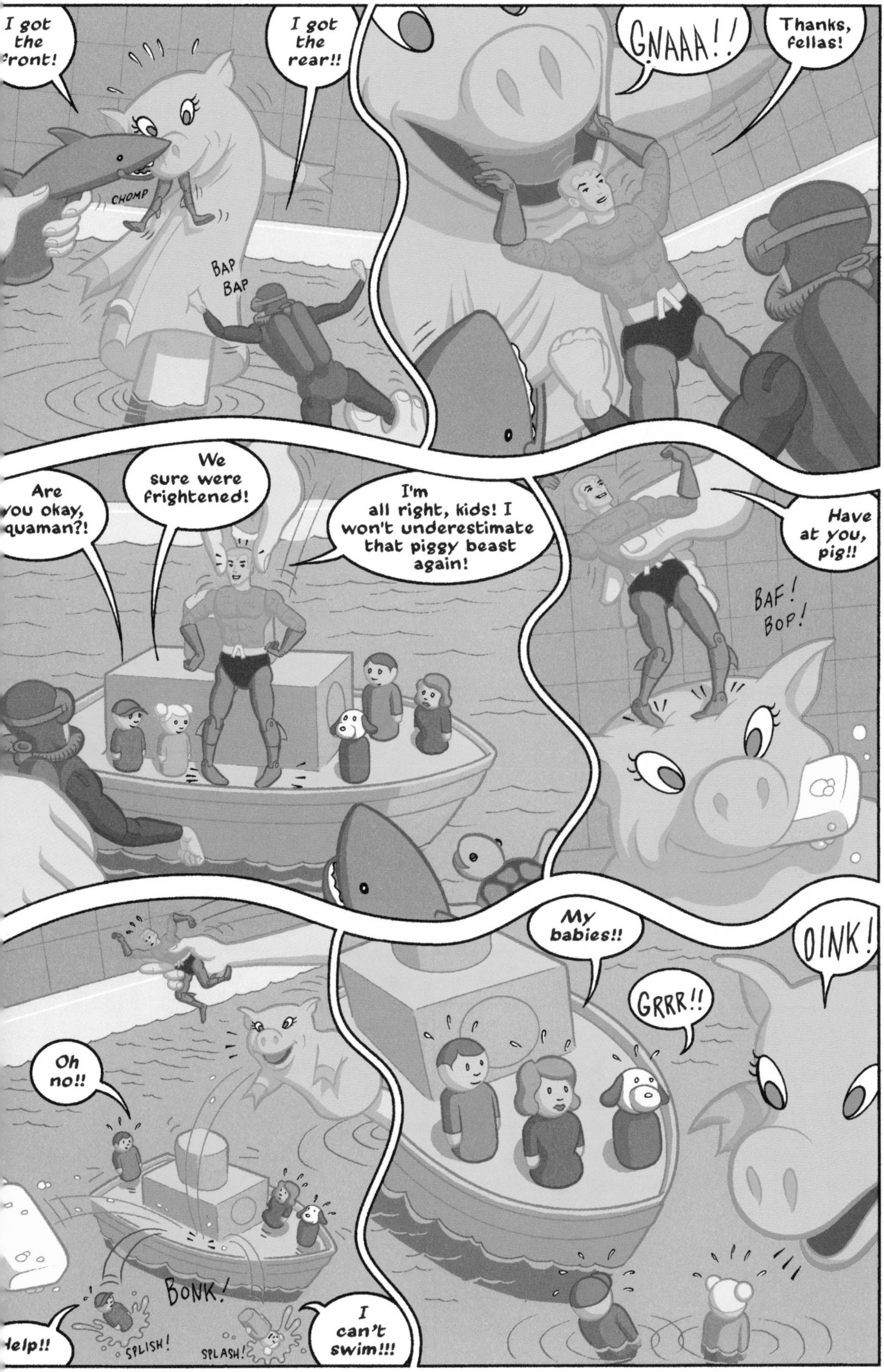

I got the front!
CHOMP
I got the rear!!
BAP BAP
GNAAA!!
Thanks, fellas!
Are you okay, quaman?!
We sure were frightened!
I'm all right, kids! I won't underestimate that piggy beast again!
Have at you, pig!!
BAF! BOP!
My babies!!
OINK!
GRRR!!
Oh no!!
BONK!
Help!!
SPLISH!
SPLASH!
I can't swim!!!

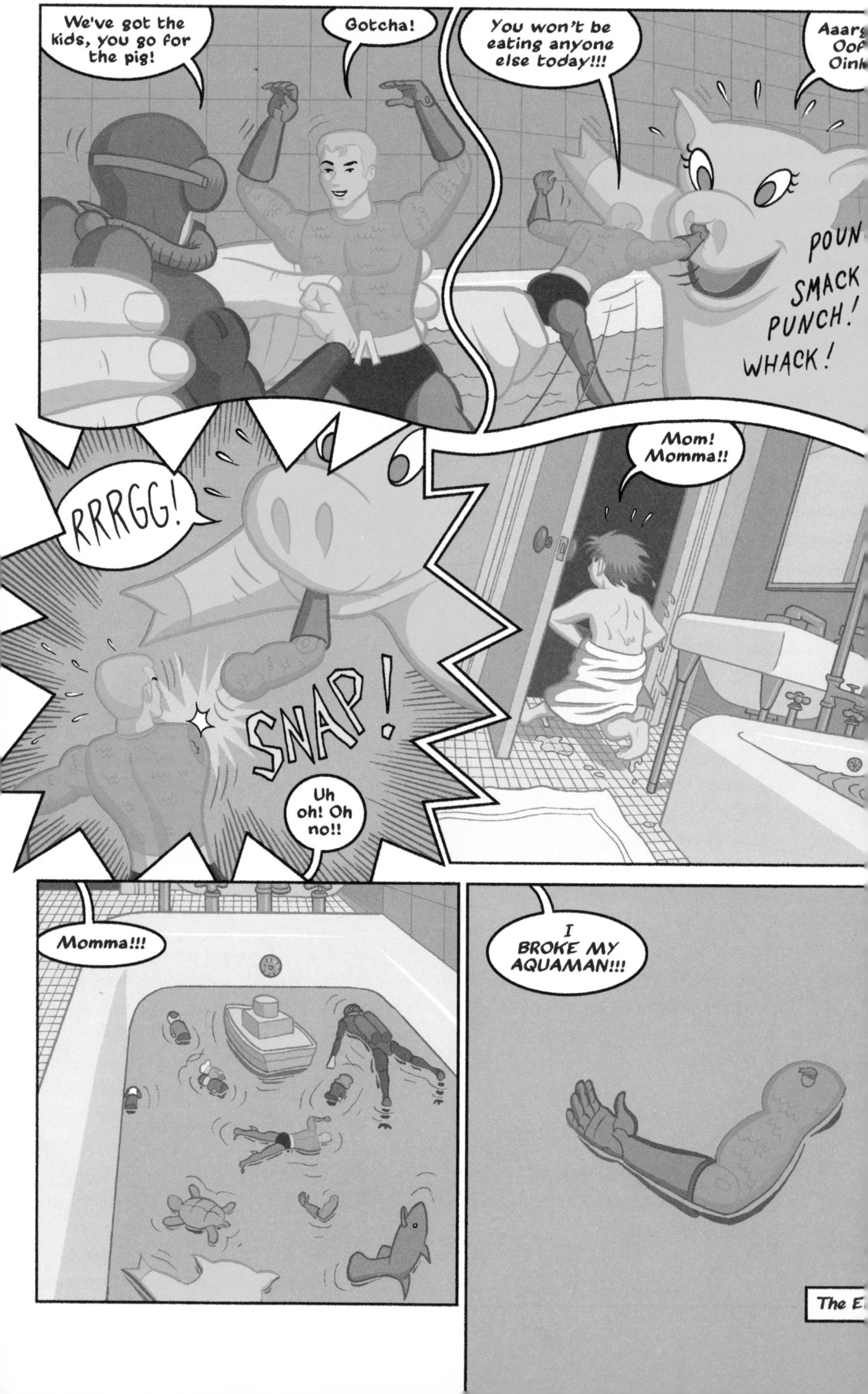
We've got the kids, you go for the pig!
Gotcha!
You won't be eating anyone else today!!!
Aaarg
Oof
Oink
POUN
SMACK
PUNCH!
WHACK!
RRRGG!
SNAP!
Uh oh! Oh no!!
Mom! Momma!!
Momma!!!
I BROKE MY AQUAMAN!!!
The E

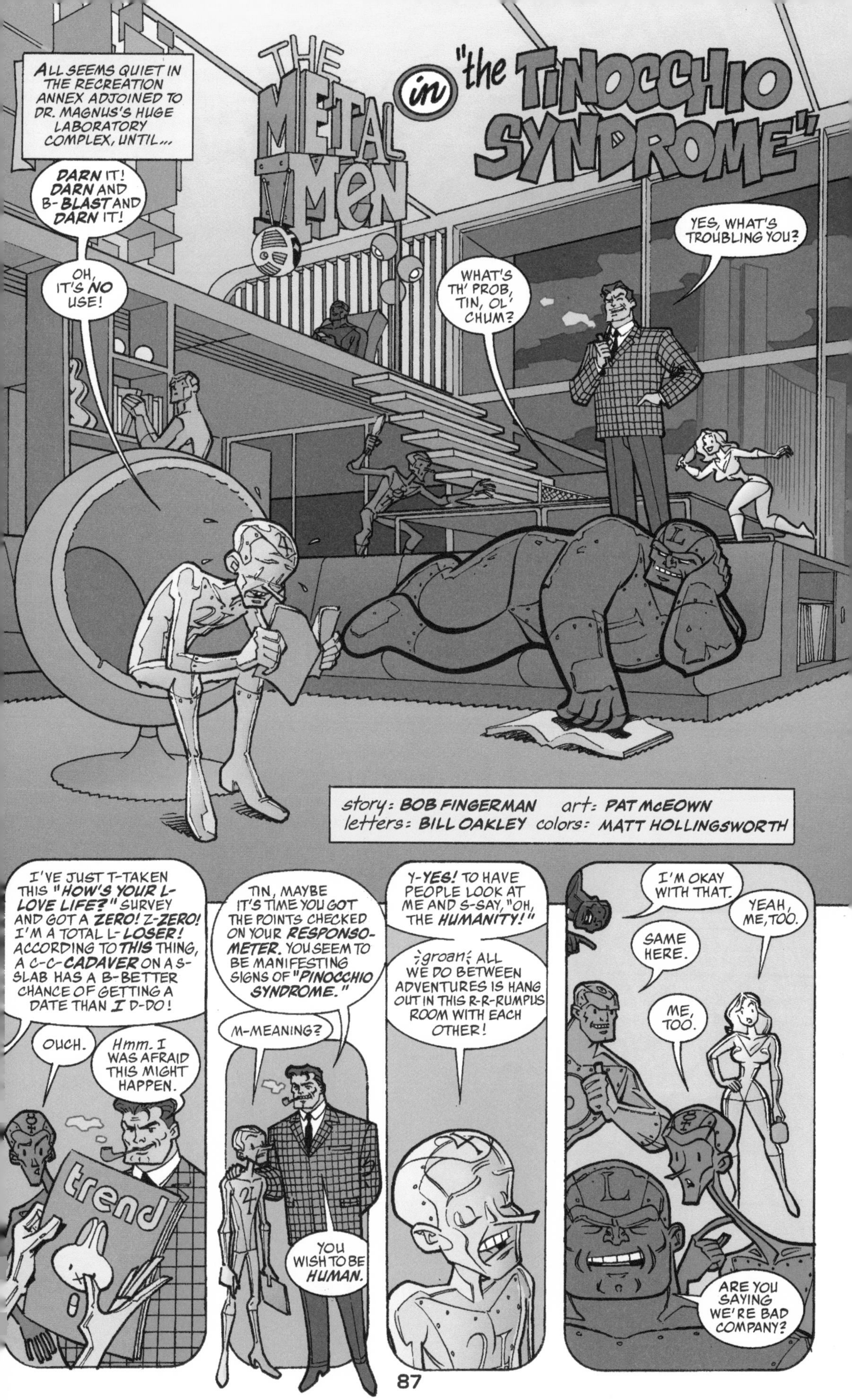
THE METAL MEN in "the TINOCCHIO SYNDROME"
ALL SEEMS QUIET IN THE RECREATION ANNEX ADJOINED TO DR. MAGNUS'S HUGE LABORATORY COMPLEX, UNTIL...
DARN IT! DARN AND B-BLAST AND DARN IT!
OH, IT'S NO USE!
WHAT'S TH' PROB, TIN, OL' CHUM?
YES, WHAT'S TROUBLING YOU?
story: BOB FINGERMAN art: PAT McEOWN
letters: BILL OAKLEY colors: MATT HOLLINGSWORTH
I'VE JUST T-TAKEN THIS "HOW'S YOUR L-LOVE LIFE?" SURVEY AND GOT A ZERO! Z-ZERO! I'M A TOTAL L-LOSER! ACCORDING TO THIS THING, A C-C-CADAVER ON A S-SLAB HAS A B-BETTER CHANCE OF GETTING A DATE THAN I D-DO!
OUCH.
Hmm. I WAS AFRAID THIS MIGHT HAPPEN.
trend
TIN, MAYBE IT'S TIME YOU GOT THE POINTS CHECKED ON YOUR RESPONSOMETER. YOU SEEM TO BE MANIFESTING SIGNS OF "PINOCCHIO SYNDROME."
M-MEANING?
YOU WISH TO BE HUMAN.
Y-YES! TO HAVE PEOPLE LOOK AT ME AND S-SAY, "OH, THE HUMANITY!"
groan ALL WE DO BETWEEN ADVENTURES IS HANG OUT IN THIS R-R-RUMPUS ROOM WITH EACH OTHER!
I'M OKAY WITH THAT.
YEAH, ME, TOO.
SAME HERE.
ME, TOO.
ARE YOU SAYING WE'RE BAD COMPANY?

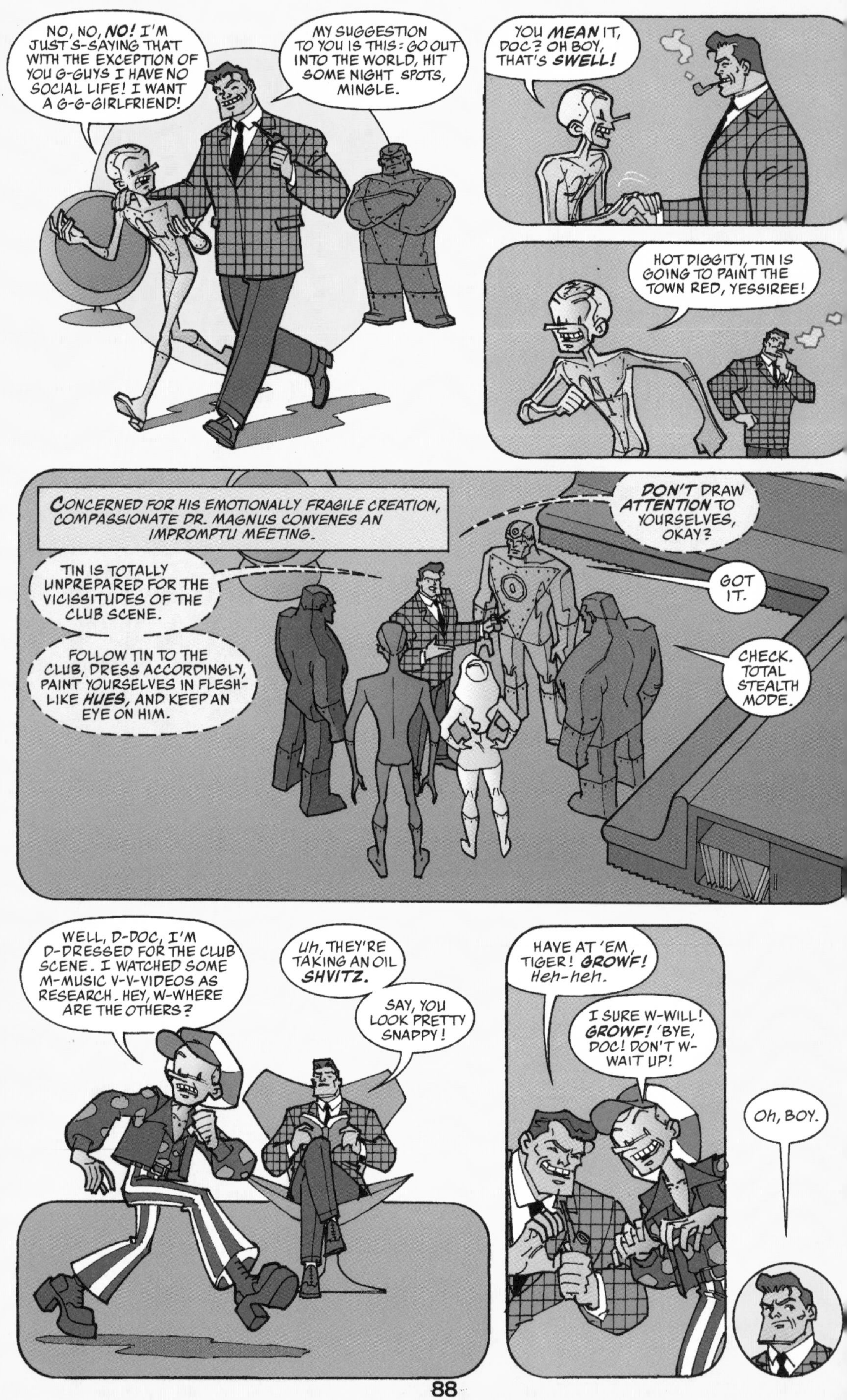

NO, NO, **NO!** I'M JUST S-SAYING THAT WITH THE EXCEPTION OF YOU G-GUYS I HAVE NO SOCIAL LIFE! I WANT A G-G-GIRLFRIEND!
MY SUGGESTION TO YOU IS THIS: GO OUT INTO THE WORLD, HIT SOME NIGHT SPOTS, MINGLE.
YOU **MEAN** IT, DOC? OH BOY, THAT'S **SWELL!**
HOT DIGGITY, TIN IS GOING TO PAINT THE TOWN RED, YESSIREE!
CONCERNED FOR HIS EMOTIONALLY FRAGILE CREATION, COMPASSIONATE DR. MAGNUS CONVENES AN IMPROMPTU MEETING.
TIN IS TOTALLY UNPREPARED FOR THE VICISSITUDES OF THE CLUB SCENE.
FOLLOW TIN TO THE CLUB, DRESS ACCORDINGLY, PAINT YOURSELVES IN FLESH-LIKE **HUES,** AND KEEP AN EYE ON HIM.
DON'T DRAW **ATTENTION** TO YOURSELVES, OKAY?
GOT IT.
CHECK. TOTAL STEALTH MODE.
WELL, D-DOC, I'M D-DRESSED FOR THE CLUB SCENE. I WATCHED SOME M-MUSIC V-V-VIDEOS AS RESEARCH. HEY, W-WHERE ARE THE OTHERS?
UH, THEY'RE TAKING AN OIL **SHVITZ.**
SAY, YOU LOOK PRETTY SNAPPY!
HAVE AT 'EM, TIGER! **GROWF!** *Heh-heh.*
I SURE W-WILL! **GROWF!** 'BYE, DOC! DON'T W-WAIT UP!
Oh, BOY.

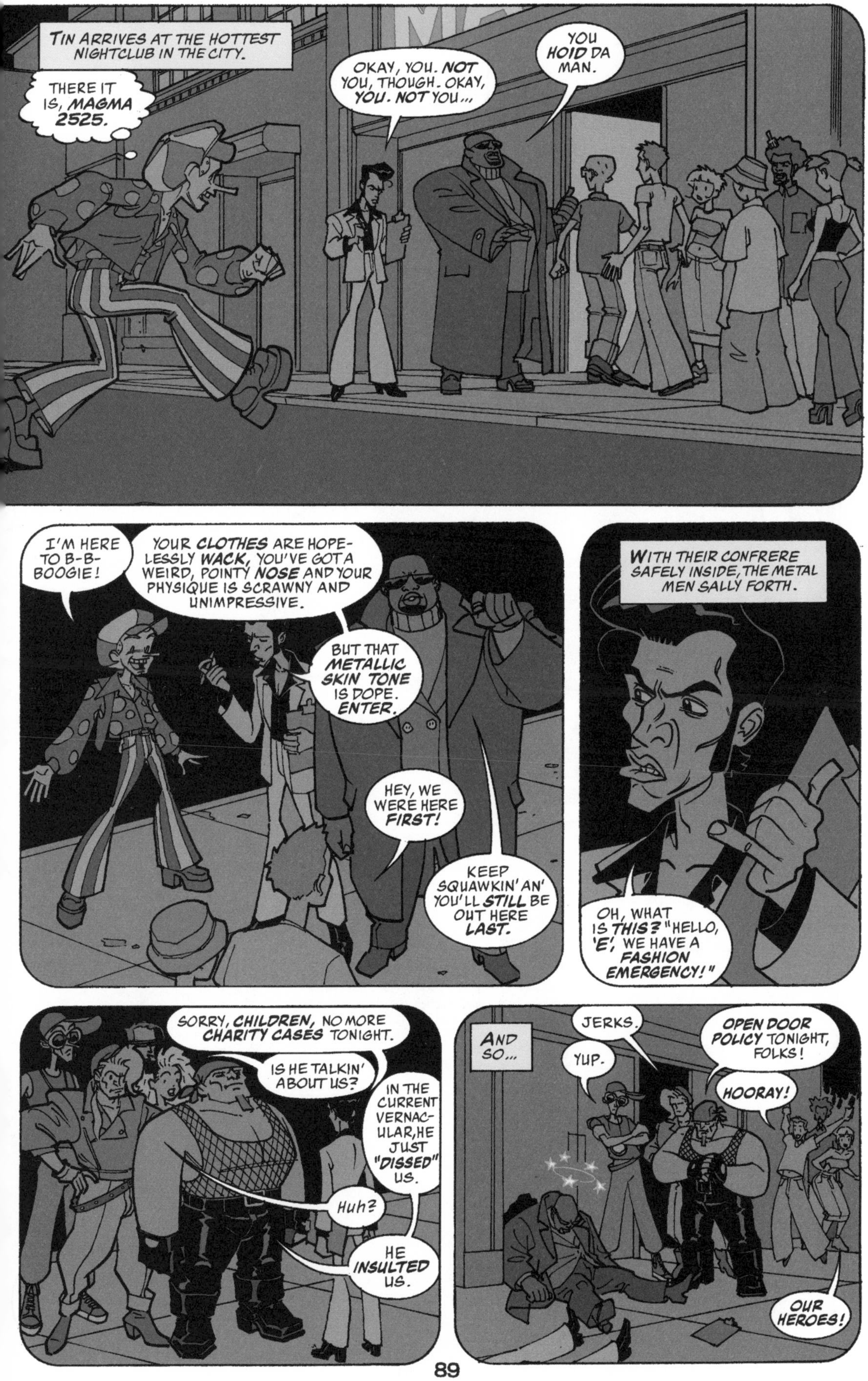
TIN ARRIVES AT THE HOTTEST NIGHTCLUB IN THE CITY.
THERE IT IS, MAGMA 2525.
OKAY, YOU. NOT YOU, THOUGH. OKAY, YOU. NOT YOU...
YOU HOID DA MAN.
I'M HERE TO B-B-BOOGIE!
YOUR CLOTHES ARE HOPELESSLY WACK, YOU'VE GOT A WEIRD, POINTY NOSE AND YOUR PHYSIQUE IS SCRAWNY AND UNIMPRESSIVE.
BUT THAT METALLIC SKIN TONE IS DOPE. ENTER.
HEY, WE WERE HERE FIRST!
KEEP SQUAWKIN' AN' YOU'LL STILL BE OUT HERE LAST.
WITH THEIR CONFRERE SAFELY INSIDE, THE METAL MEN SALLY FORTH.
OH, WHAT IS THIS? "HELLO, 'E,' WE HAVE A FASHION EMERGENCY!"
SORRY, CHILDREN, NO MORE CHARITY CASES TONIGHT.
IS HE TALKIN' ABOUT US?
IN THE CURRENT VERNACULAR, HE JUST "DISSED" US.
Huh?
HE INSULTED US.
AND SO...
JERKS.
YUP.
OPEN DOOR POLICY TONIGHT, FOLKS!
HOORAY!
OUR HEROES!

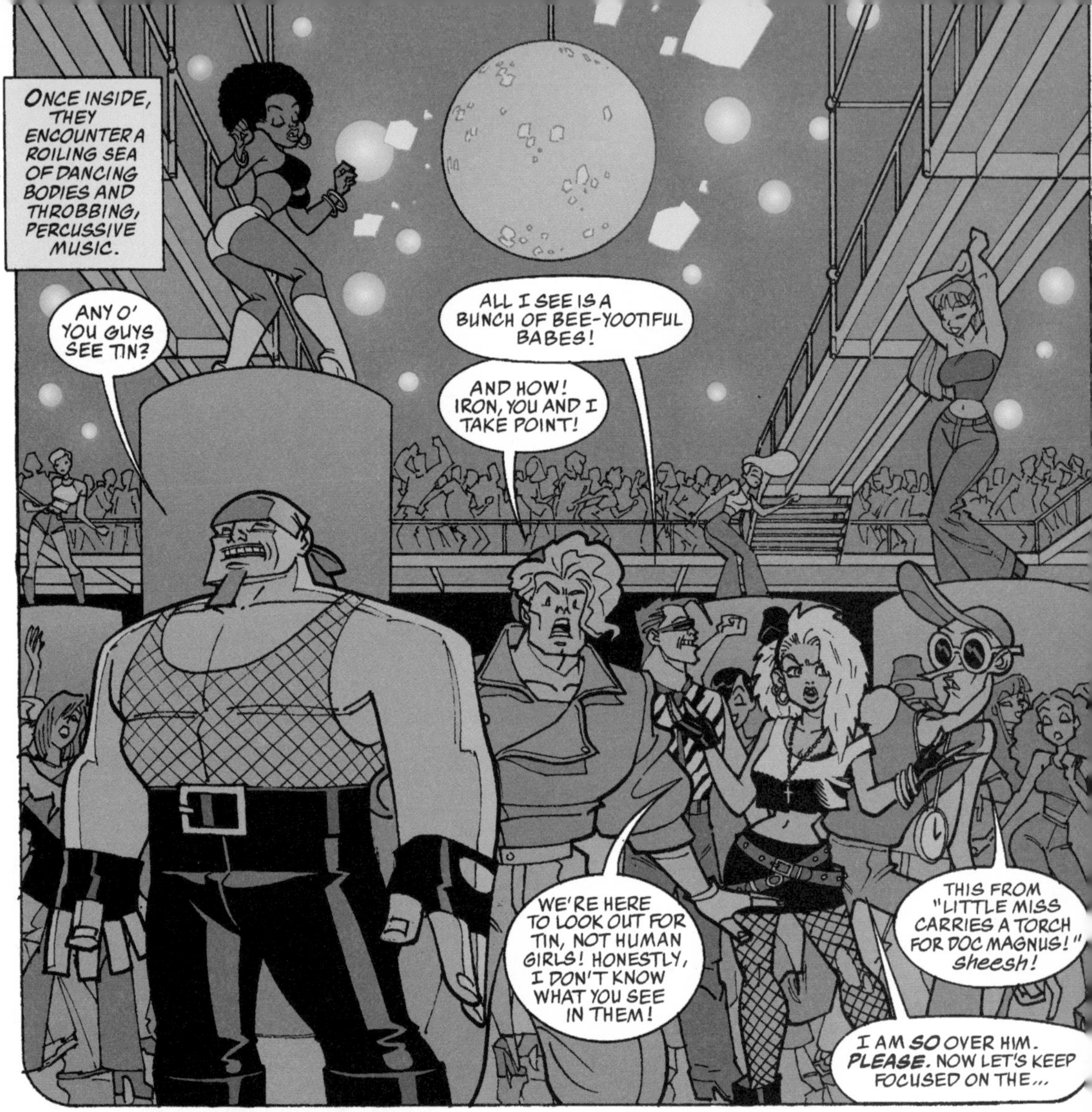
ONCE INSIDE, THEY ENCOUNTER A ROILING SEA OF DANCING BODIES AND THROBBING, PERCUSSIVE MUSIC.
ANY O' YOU GUYS SEE TIN?
ALL I SEE IS A BUNCH OF BEE-YOOTIFUL BABES!
AND HOW! IRON, YOU AND I TAKE POINT!
WE'RE HERE TO LOOK OUT FOR TIN, NOT HUMAN GIRLS! HONESTLY, I DON'T KNOW WHAT YOU SEE IN THEM!
THIS FROM "LITTLE MISS CARRIES A TORCH FOR DOC MAGNUS!" sheesh!
I AM SO OVER HIM. PLEASE. NOW LET'S KEEP FOCUSED ON THE...

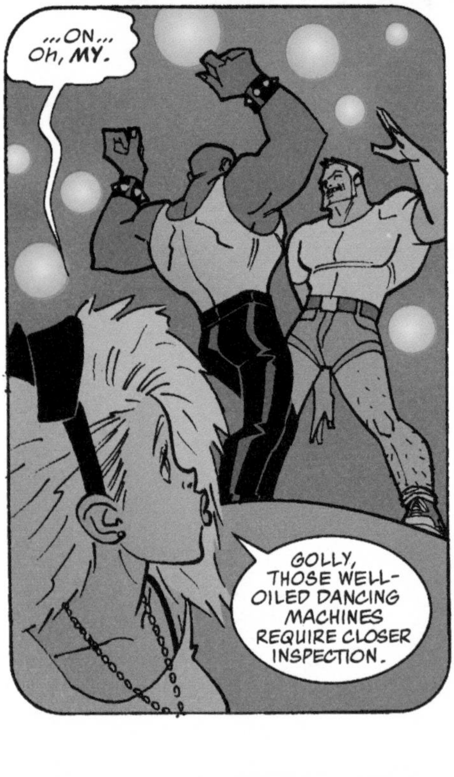
...ON... Oh, MY.
GOLLY, THOSE WELL-OILED DANCING MACHINES REQUIRE CLOSER INSPECTION.

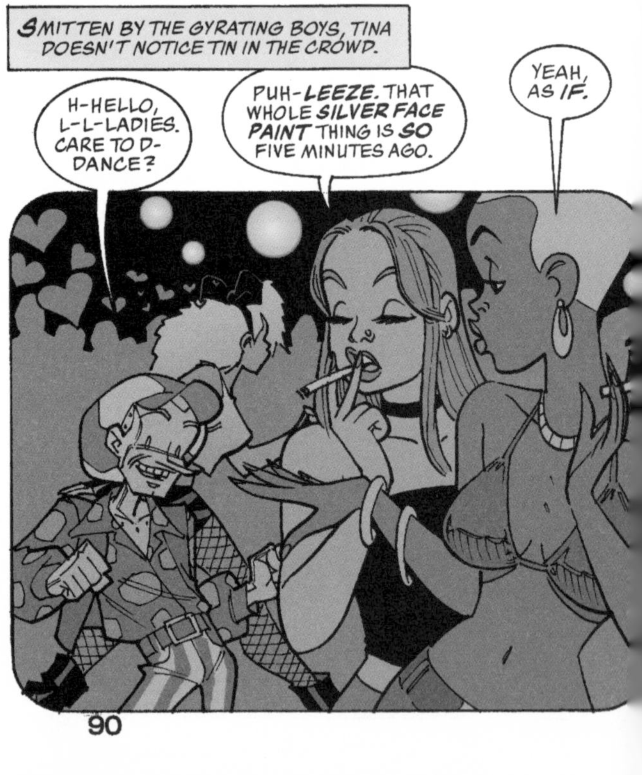
SMITTEN BY THE GYRATING BOYS, TINA DOESN'T NOTICE TIN IN THE CROWD.
H-HELLO, L-L-LADIES. CARE TO D-DANCE?
PUH-LEEZE. THAT WHOLE SILVER FACE PAINT THING IS SO FIVE MINUTES AGO.
YEAH, AS IF.

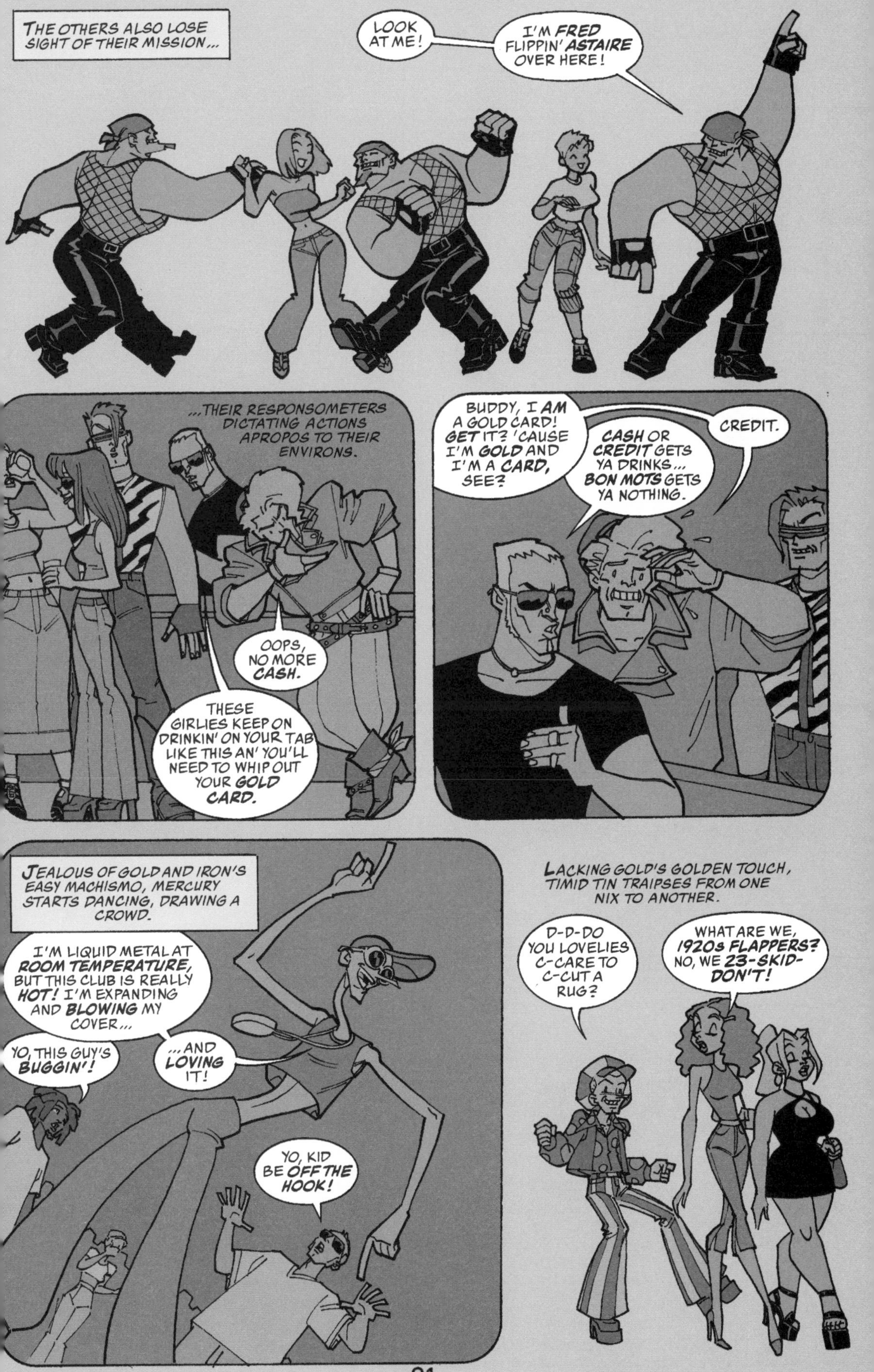
THE OTHERS ALSO LOSE SIGHT OF THEIR MISSION...
LOOK AT ME!
I'M FRED FLIPPIN' ASTAIRE OVER HERE!
...THEIR RESPONSOMETERS DICTATING ACTIONS APROPOS TO THEIR ENVIRONS.
OOPS, NO MORE CASH.
THESE GIRLIES KEEP ON DRINKIN' ON YOUR TAB LIKE THIS AN' YOU'LL NEED TO WHIP OUT YOUR GOLD CARD.
BUDDY, I AM A GOLD CARD! GET IT? 'CAUSE I'M GOLD AND I'M A CARD, SEE?
CASH OR CREDIT GETS YA DRINKS... BON MOTS GETS YA NOTHING.
CREDIT.
JEALOUS OF GOLD AND IRON'S EASY MACHISMO, MERCURY STARTS DANCING, DRAWING A CROWD.
I'M LIQUID METAL AT ROOM TEMPERATURE, BUT THIS CLUB IS REALLY HOT! I'M EXPANDING AND BLOWING MY COVER...
...AND LOVING IT!
YO, THIS GUY'S BUGGIN'!
YO, KID BE OFF THE HOOK!
LACKING GOLD'S GOLDEN TOUCH, TIMID TIN TRAIPSES FROM ONE NIX TO ANOTHER.
D-D-DO YOU LOVELIES C-CARE TO C-CUT A RUG?
WHAT ARE WE, 1920s FLAPPERS? NO, WE 23-SKID-DON'T!

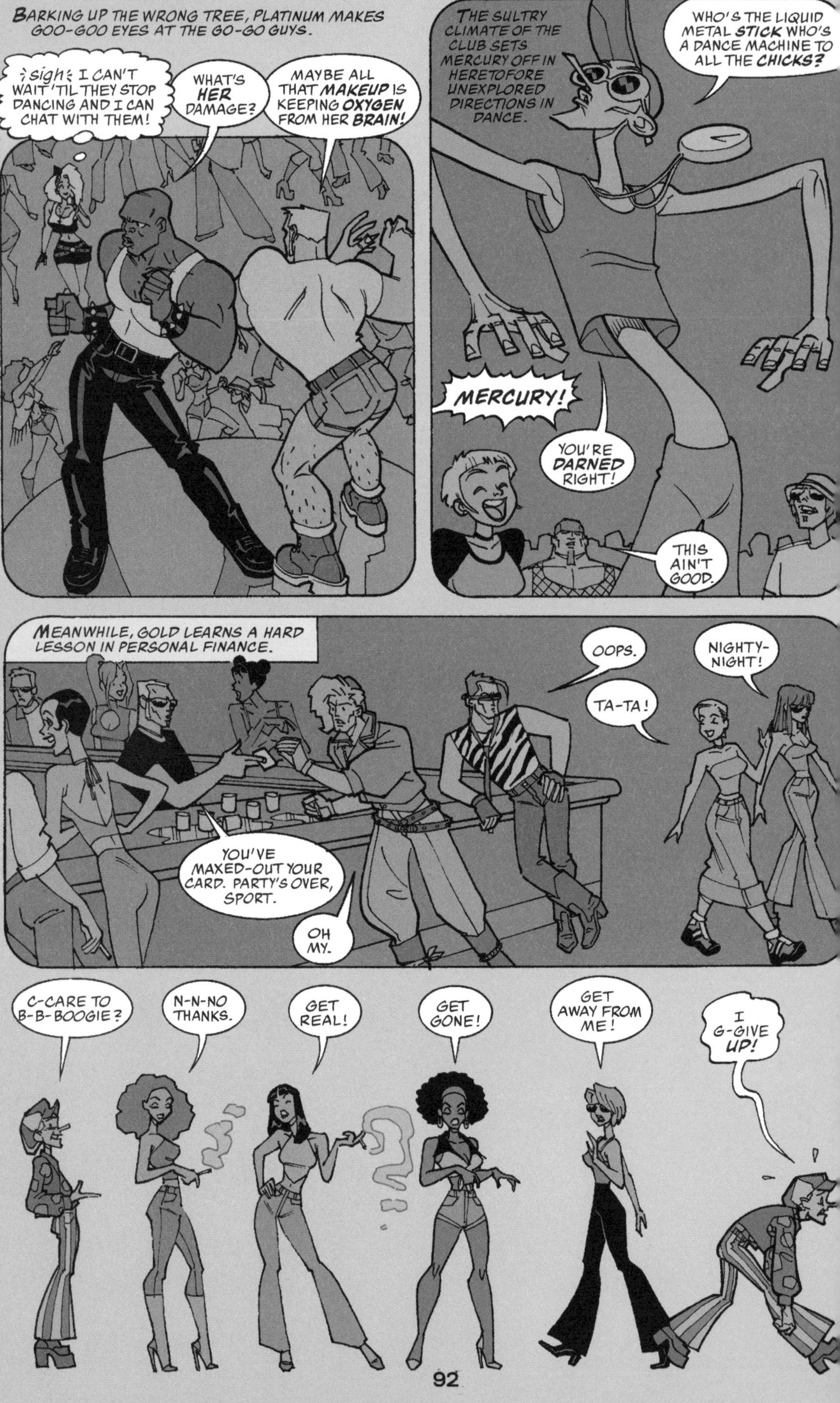

BARKING UP THE WRONG TREE, PLATINUM MAKES GOO-GOO EYES AT THE GO-GO GUYS.
SIGH I CAN'T WAIT 'TIL THEY STOP DANCING AND I CAN CHAT WITH THEM!
WHAT'S HER DAMAGE?
MAYBE ALL THAT MAKEUP IS KEEPING OXYGEN FROM HER BRAIN!
THE SULTRY CLIMATE OF THE CLUB SETS MERCURY OFF IN HERETOFORE UNEXPLORED DIRECTIONS IN DANCE.
WHO'S THE LIQUID METAL STICK WHO'S A DANCE MACHINE TO ALL THE CHICKS?
MERCURY!
YOU'RE DARNED RIGHT!
THIS AIN'T GOOD.
MEANWHILE, GOLD LEARNS A HARD LESSON IN PERSONAL FINANCE.
OOPS.
NIGHTY-NIGHT!
TA-TA!
YOU'VE MAXED-OUT YOUR CARD. PARTY'S OVER, SPORT.
OH MY.
C-CARE TO B-B-BOOGIE?
N-N-NO THANKS.
GET REAL!
GET GONE!
GET AWAY FROM ME!
I G-GIVE UP!

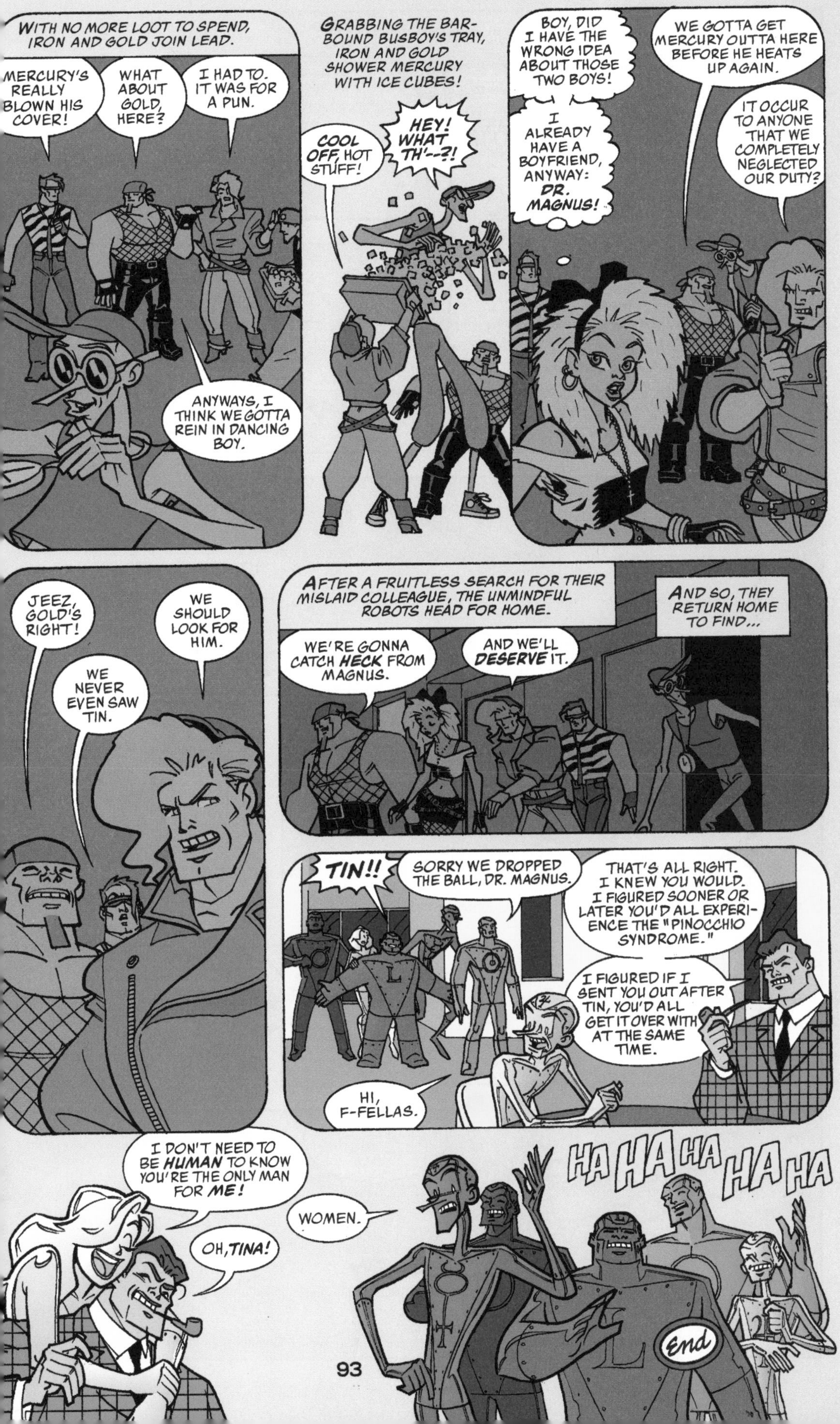
WITH NO MORE LOOT TO SPEND, IRON AND GOLD JOIN LEAD.
MERCURY'S REALLY BLOWN HIS COVER!
WHAT ABOUT GOLD, HERE?
I HAD TO. IT WAS FOR A PUN.
ANYWAYS, I THINK WE GOTTA REIN IN DANCING BOY.
GRABBING THE BAR-BOUND BUSBOY'S TRAY, IRON AND GOLD SHOWER MERCURY WITH ICE CUBES!
COOL OFF, HOT STUFF!
HEY! WHAT TH'--?!
BOY, DID I HAVE THE WRONG IDEA ABOUT THOSE TWO BOYS!
I ALREADY HAVE A BOYFRIEND, ANYWAY: DR. MAGNUS!
WE GOTTA GET MERCURY OUTTA HERE BEFORE HE HEATS UP AGAIN.
IT OCCUR TO ANYONE THAT WE COMPLETELY NEGLECTED OUR DUTY?
JEEZ, GOLD'S RIGHT!
WE SHOULD LOOK FOR HIM.
WE NEVER EVEN SAW TIN.
AFTER A FRUITLESS SEARCH FOR THEIR MISLAID COLLEAGUE, THE UNMINDFUL ROBOTS HEAD FOR HOME.
WE'RE GONNA CATCH HECK FROM MAGNUS.
AND WE'LL DESERVE IT.
AND SO, THEY RETURN HOME TO FIND...
TIN!!
SORRY WE DROPPED THE BALL, DR. MAGNUS.
THAT'S ALL RIGHT. I KNEW YOU WOULD. I FIGURED SOONER OR LATER YOU'D ALL EXPERIENCE THE "PINOCCHIO SYNDROME."
I FIGURED IF I SENT YOU OUT AFTER TIN, YOU'D ALL GET IT OVER WITH AT THE SAME TIME.
HI, F-FELLAS.
I DON'T NEED TO BE HUMAN TO KNOW YOU'RE THE ONLY MAN FOR ME!
OH, TINA!
WOMEN.
HA HA HA HA HA HA
End

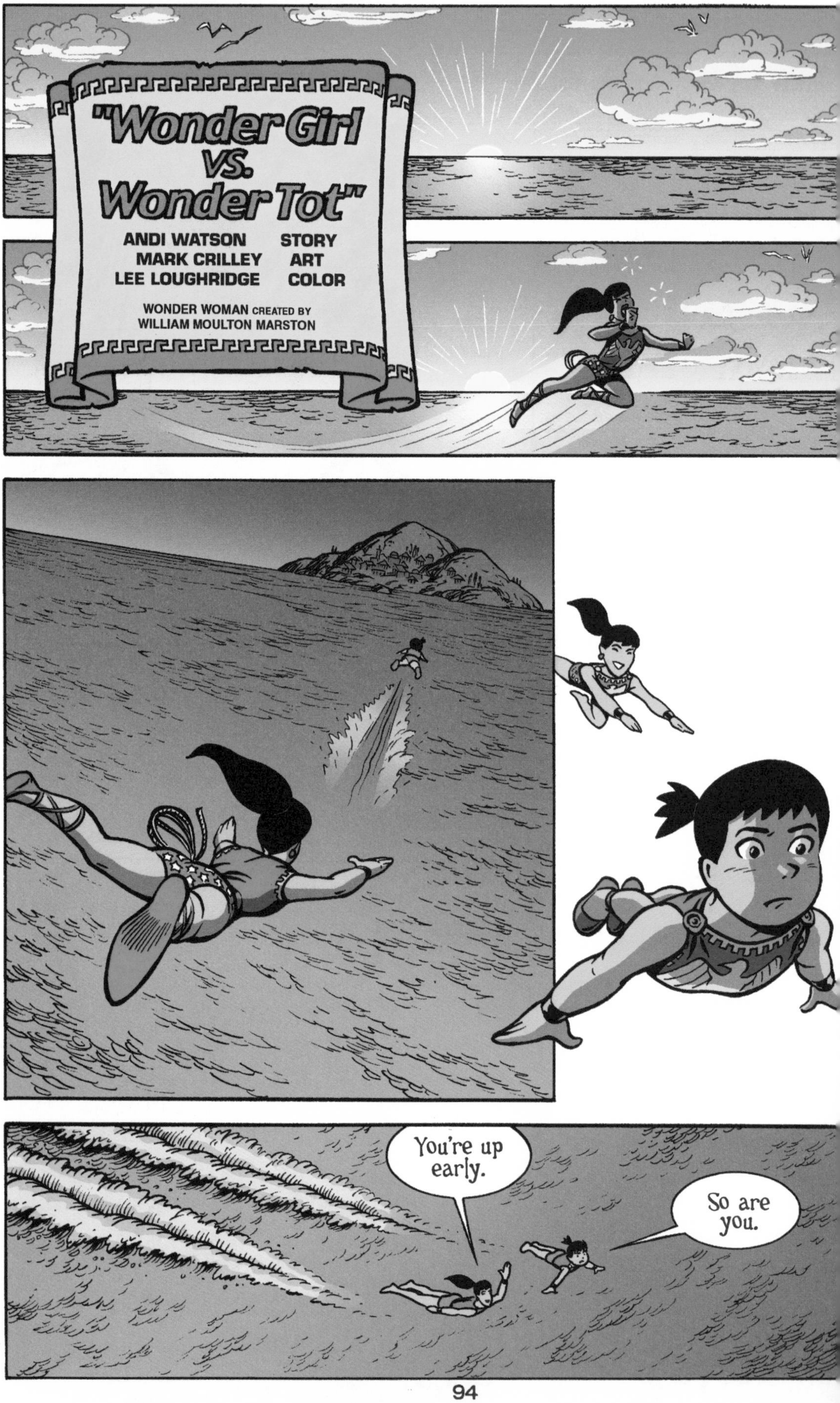
"Wonder Girl vs. Wonder Tot"
ANDI WATSON STORY
MARK CRILLEY ART
LEE LOUGHRIDGE COLOR
WONDER WOMAN CREATED BY
WILLIAM MOULTON MARSTON
You're up early.
So are you.

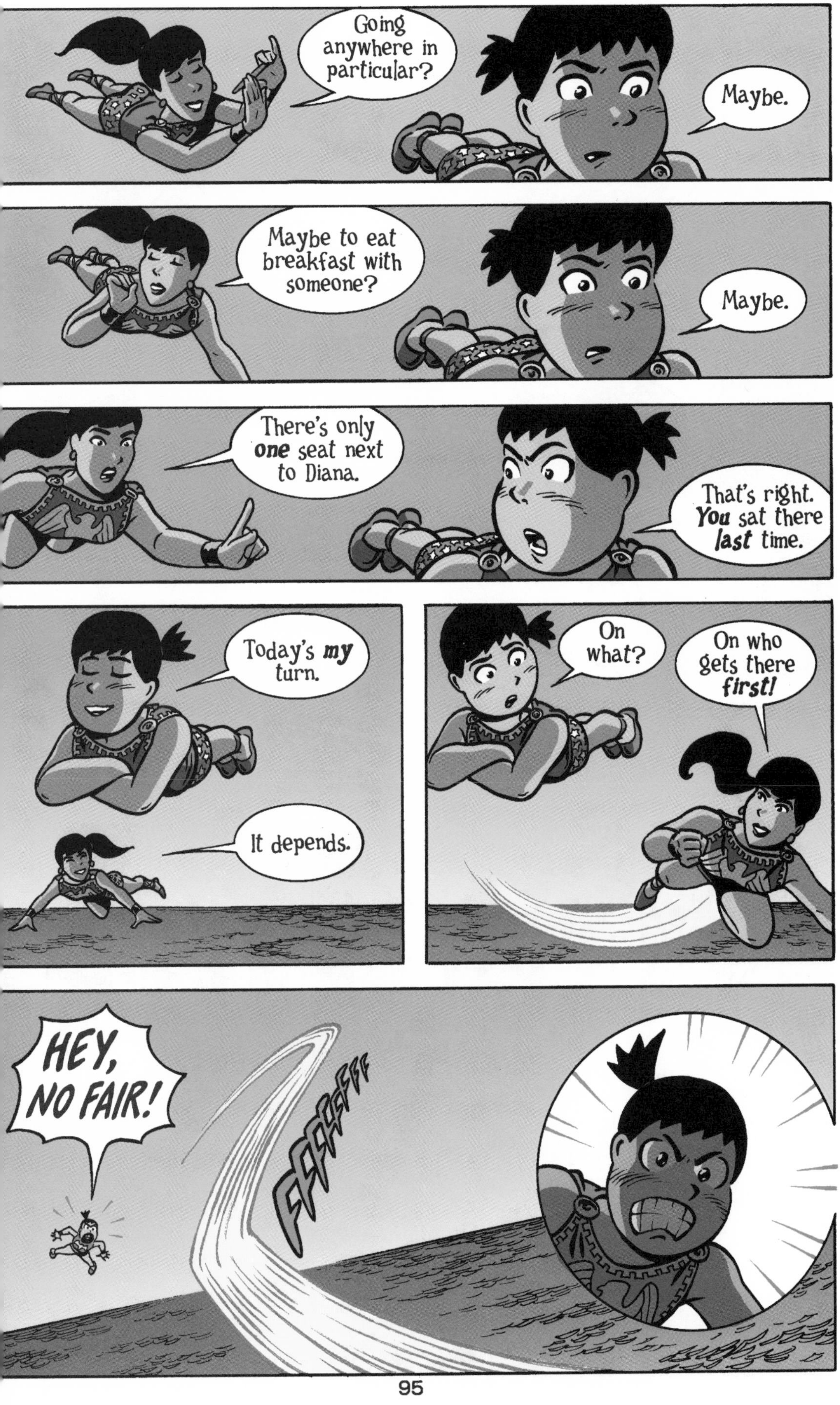
Going anywhere in particular?
Maybe.
Maybe to eat breakfast with someone?
Maybe.
There's only one seat next to Diana.
That's right. You sat there last time.
Today's my turn.
It depends.
On what?
On who gets there first!
HEY, NO FAIR!
FFFFFFFFF

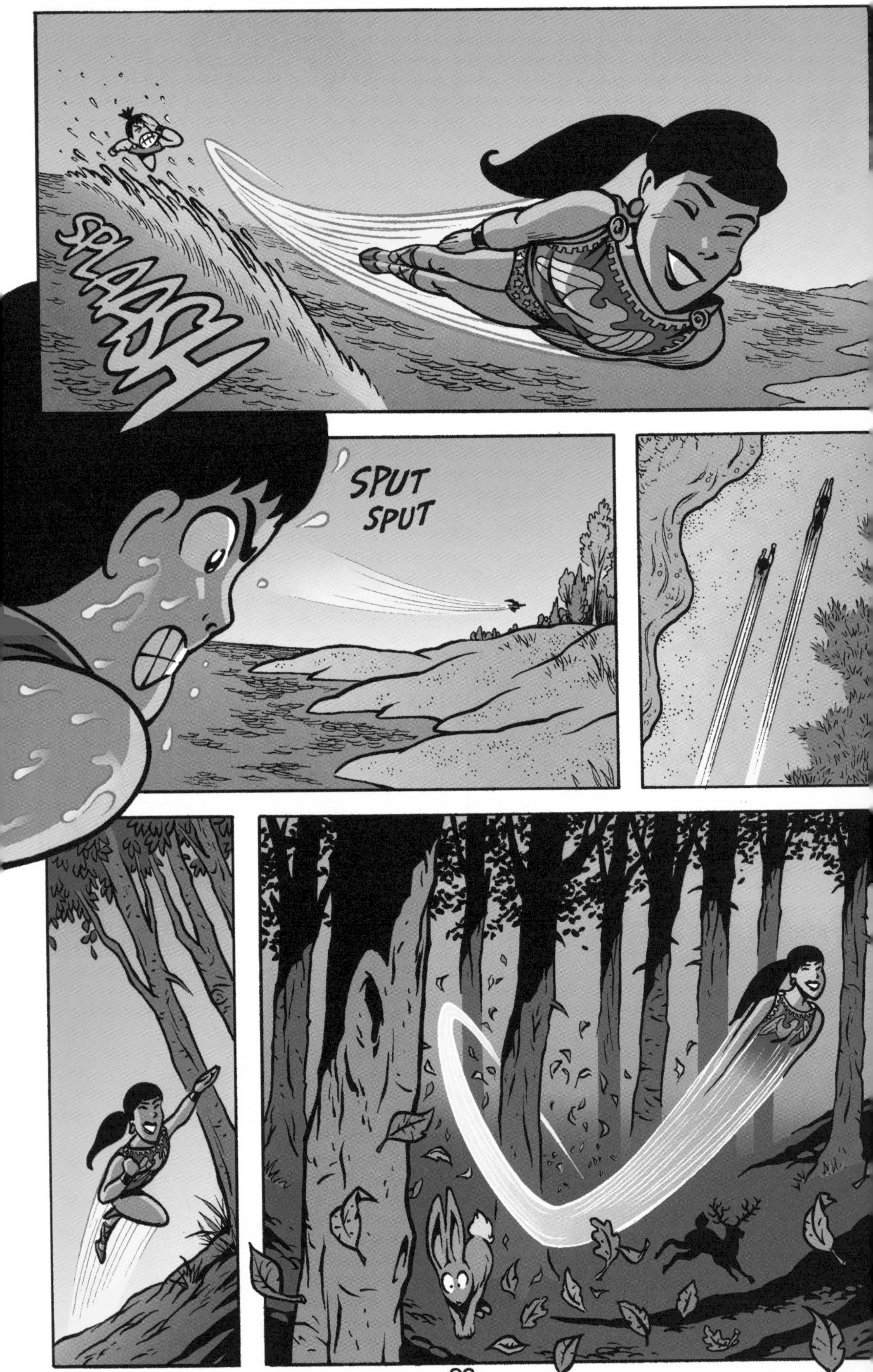
SPLASH
SPUT
SPUT

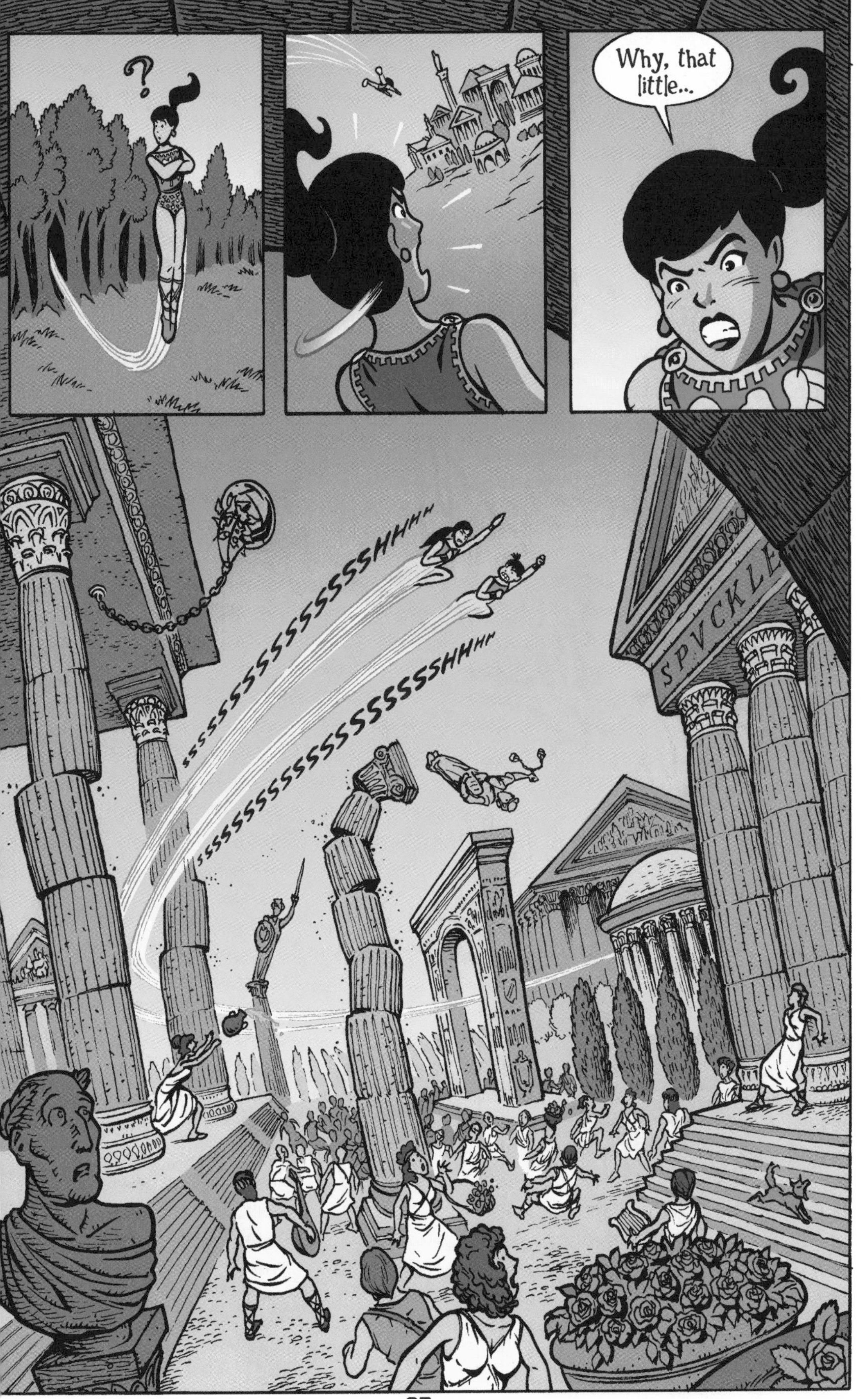
?
Why, that little...
SSSSSSSSSSSSSSSSHHhh
SSSSSSSSSSSSSSSSSSSSHHhh
SPVCKLE

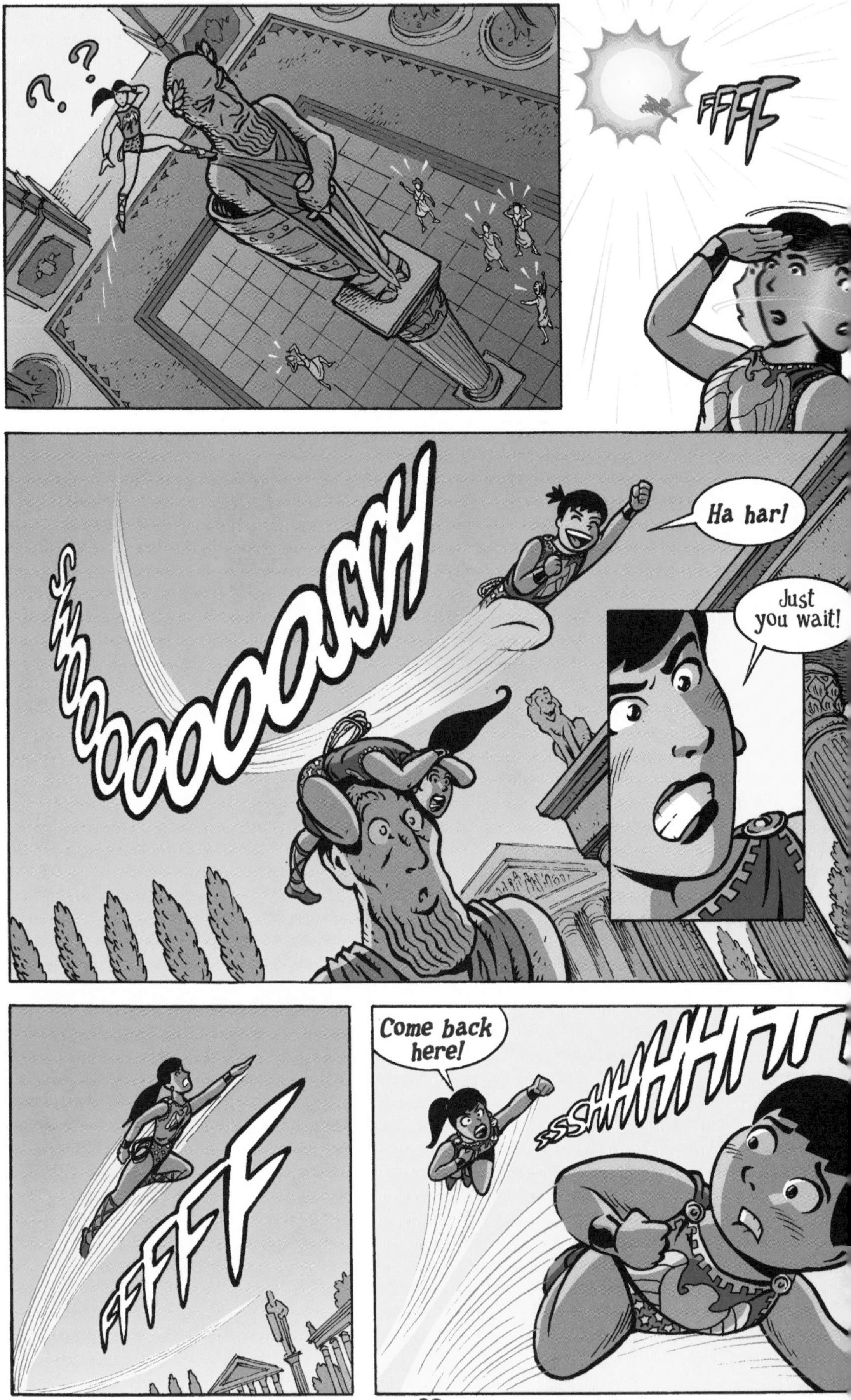
? ?
FFFF
SWOOOOOOOSH
Ha har!
Just you wait!
FFFFF
Come back here!
SSHHHHHH

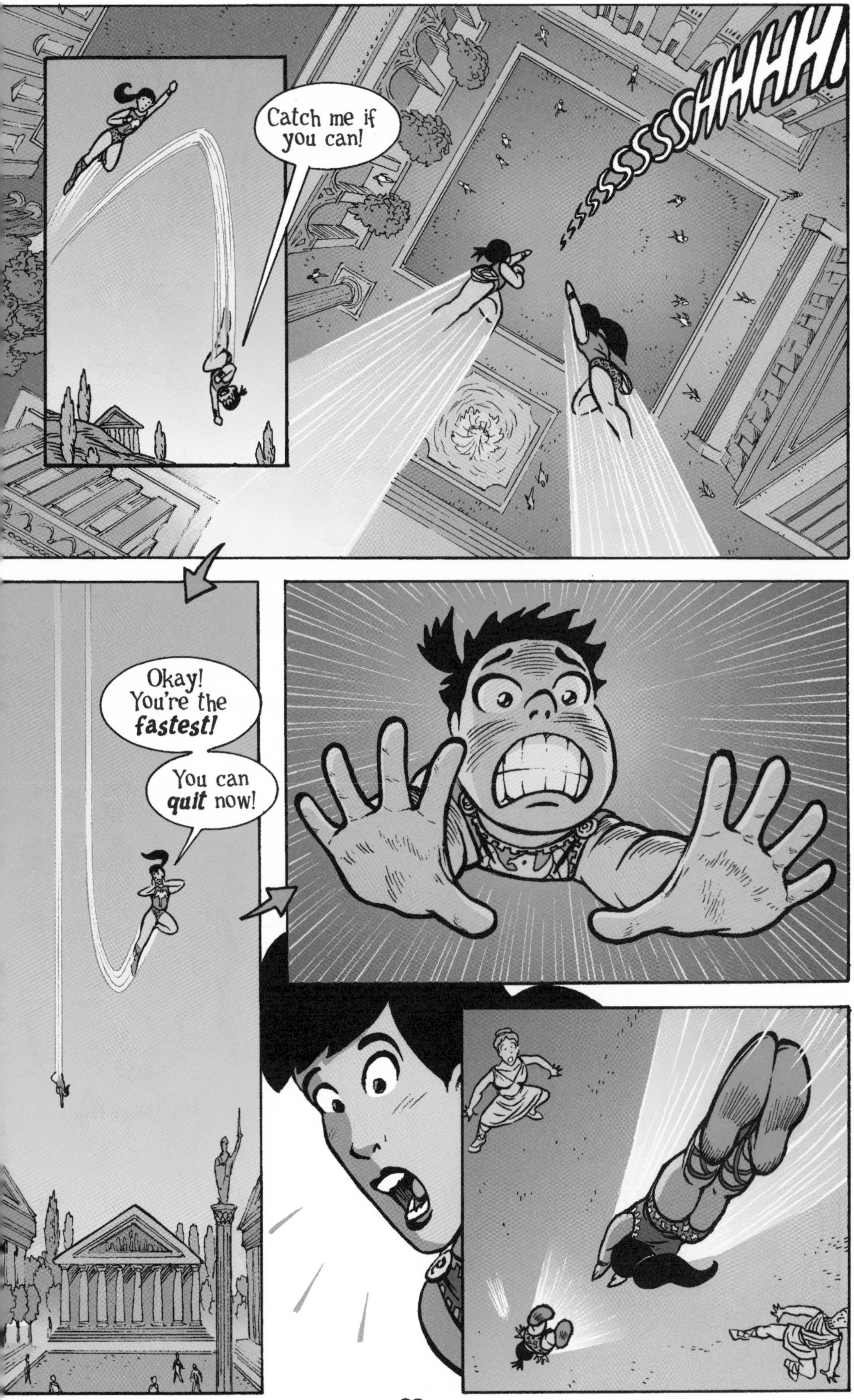
Catch me if you can!
SSSSSSSSSHHHHH
Okay! You're the **fastest!**
You can **quit** now!

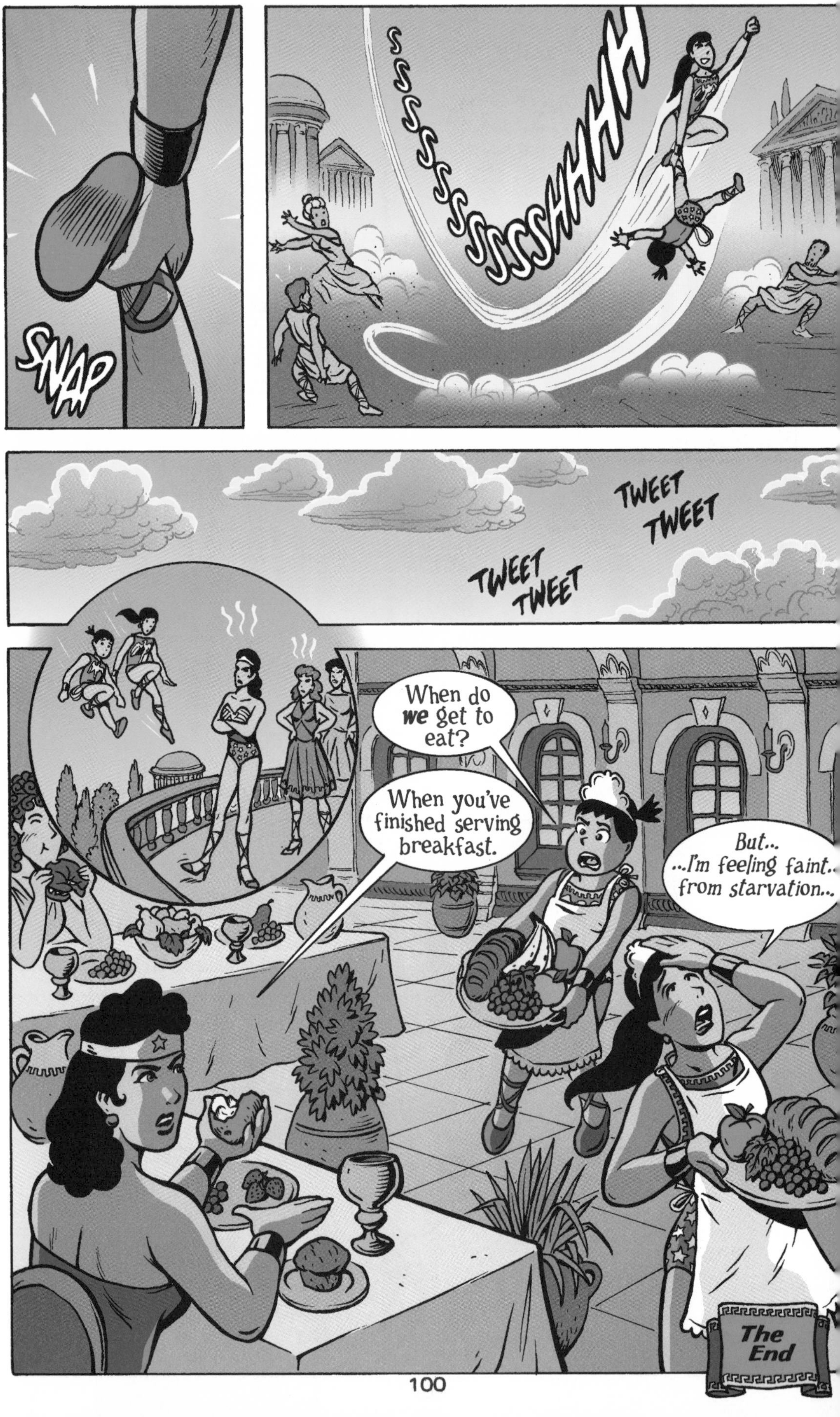
SNAP
SSSSSSSSSSSHHHH
TWEET TWEET
TWEET TWEET
When do **we** get to eat?
When you've finished serving breakfast.
But... ...I'm feeling faint... from starvation...
The End

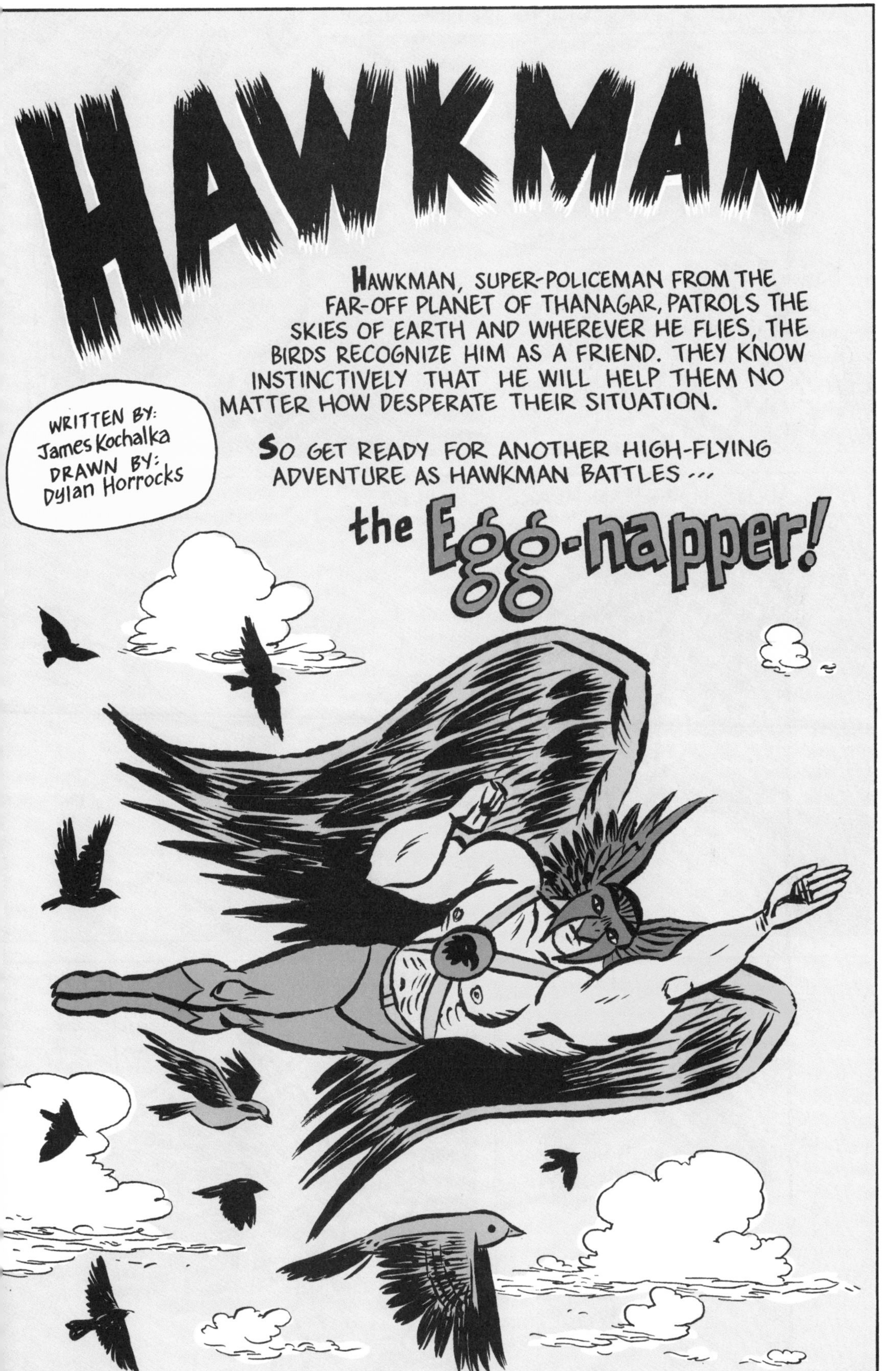
HAWKMAN
HAWKMAN, SUPER-POLICEMAN FROM THE FAR-OFF PLANET OF THANAGAR, PATROLS THE SKIES OF EARTH AND WHEREVER HE FLIES, THE BIRDS RECOGNIZE HIM AS A FRIEND. THEY KNOW INSTINCTIVELY THAT HE WILL HELP THEM NO MATTER HOW DESPERATE THEIR SITUATION.
SO GET READY FOR ANOTHER HIGH-FLYING ADVENTURE AS HAWKMAN BATTLES...
WRITTEN BY: James Kochalka DRAWN BY: Dylan Horrocks
the Egg-napper!
1

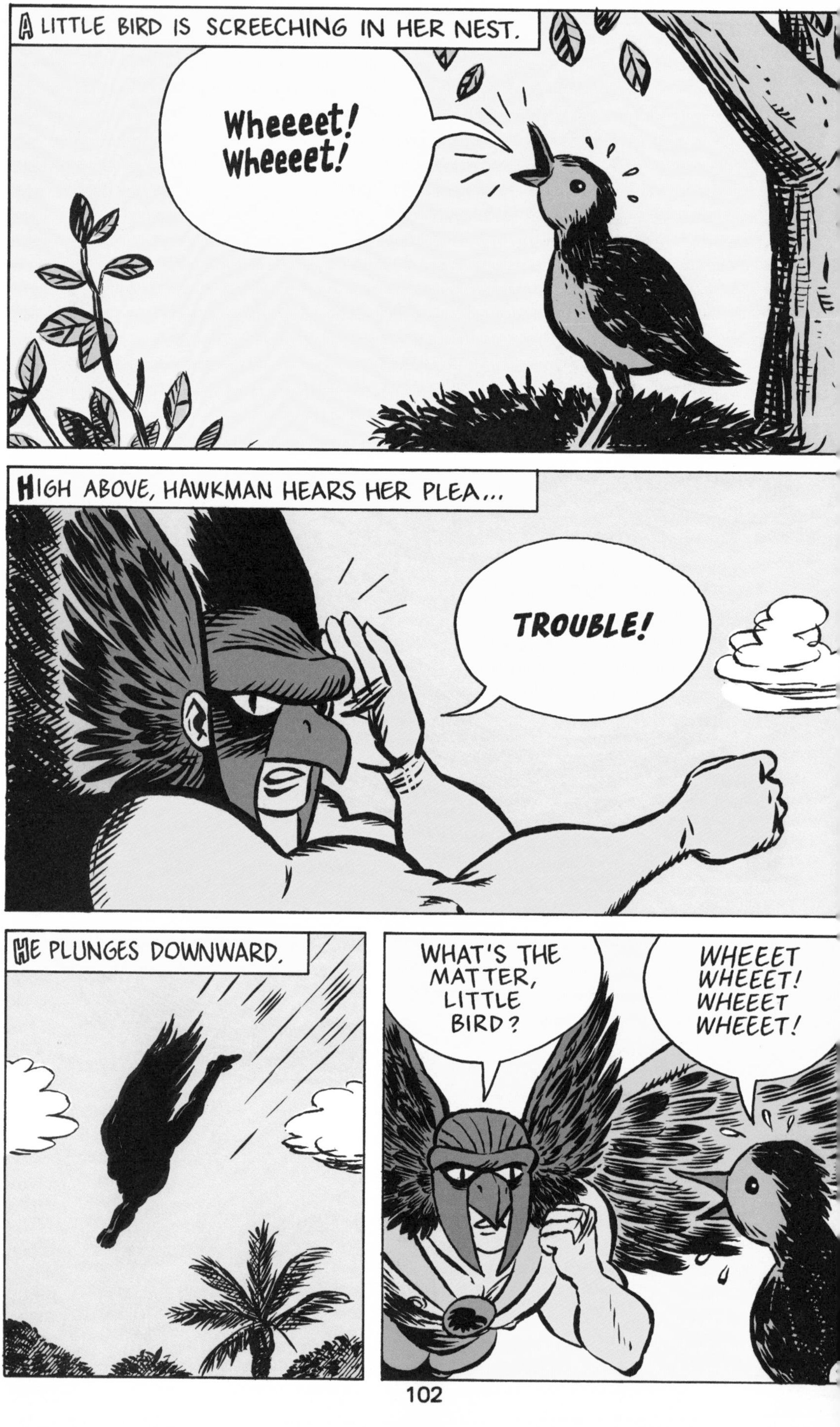
A LITTLE BIRD IS SCREECHING IN HER NEST.
Wheeeet! Wheeeet!
HIGH ABOVE, HAWKMAN HEARS HER PLEA...
TROUBLE!
HE PLUNGES DOWNWARD.
WHAT'S THE MATTER, LITTLE BIRD?
WHEEET WHEEET! WHEEET WHEEET!

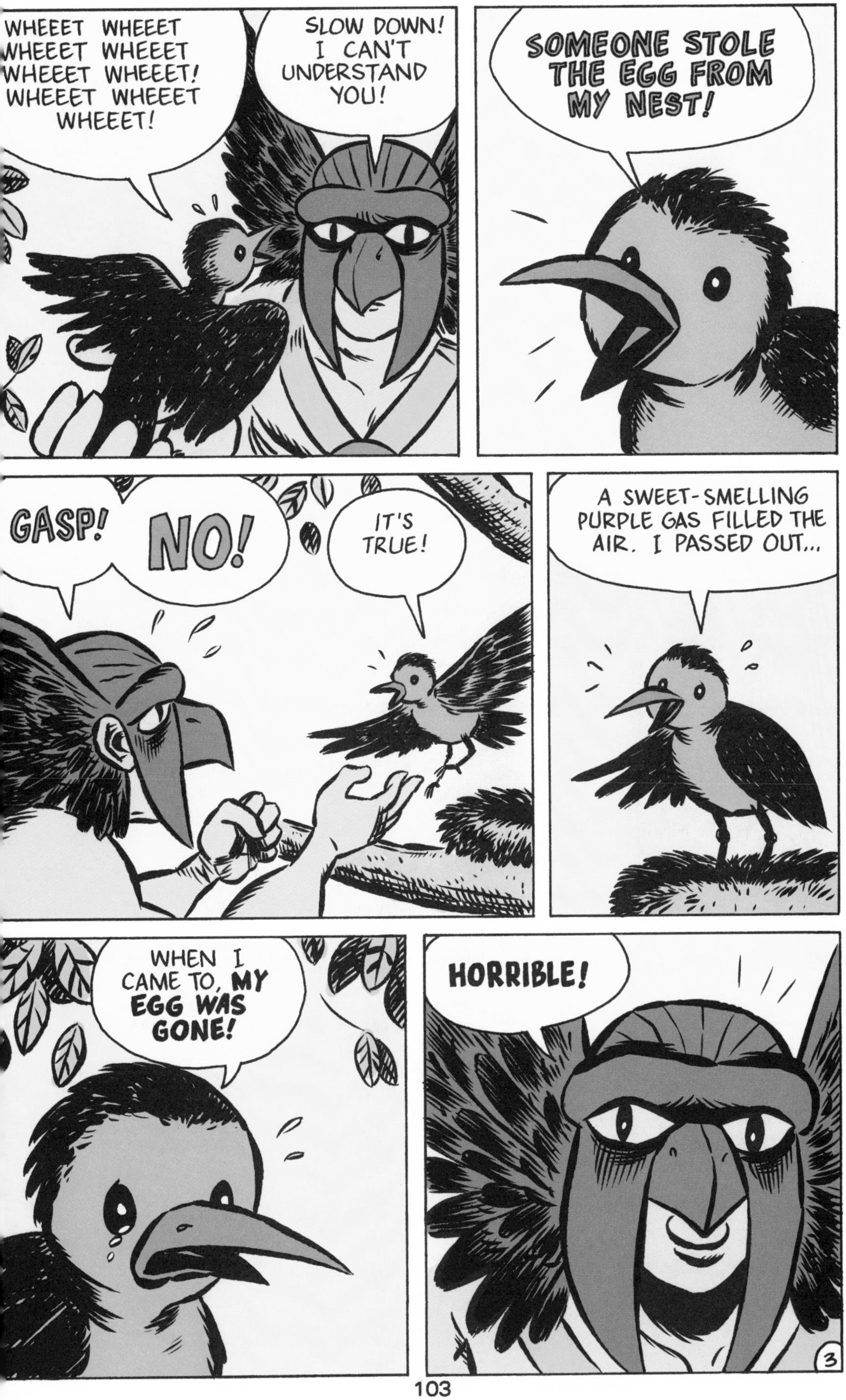
WHEEET WHEEET WHEEET WHEEET WHEEET WHEEET! WHEEET WHEEET WHEEET!
SLOW DOWN! I CAN'T UNDERSTAND YOU!
SOMEONE STOLE THE EGG FROM MY NEST!
GASP!
NO!
IT'S TRUE!
A SWEET-SMELLING PURPLE GAS FILLED THE AIR. I PASSED OUT...
WHEN I CAME TO, MY EGG WAS GONE!
HORRIBLE!
3

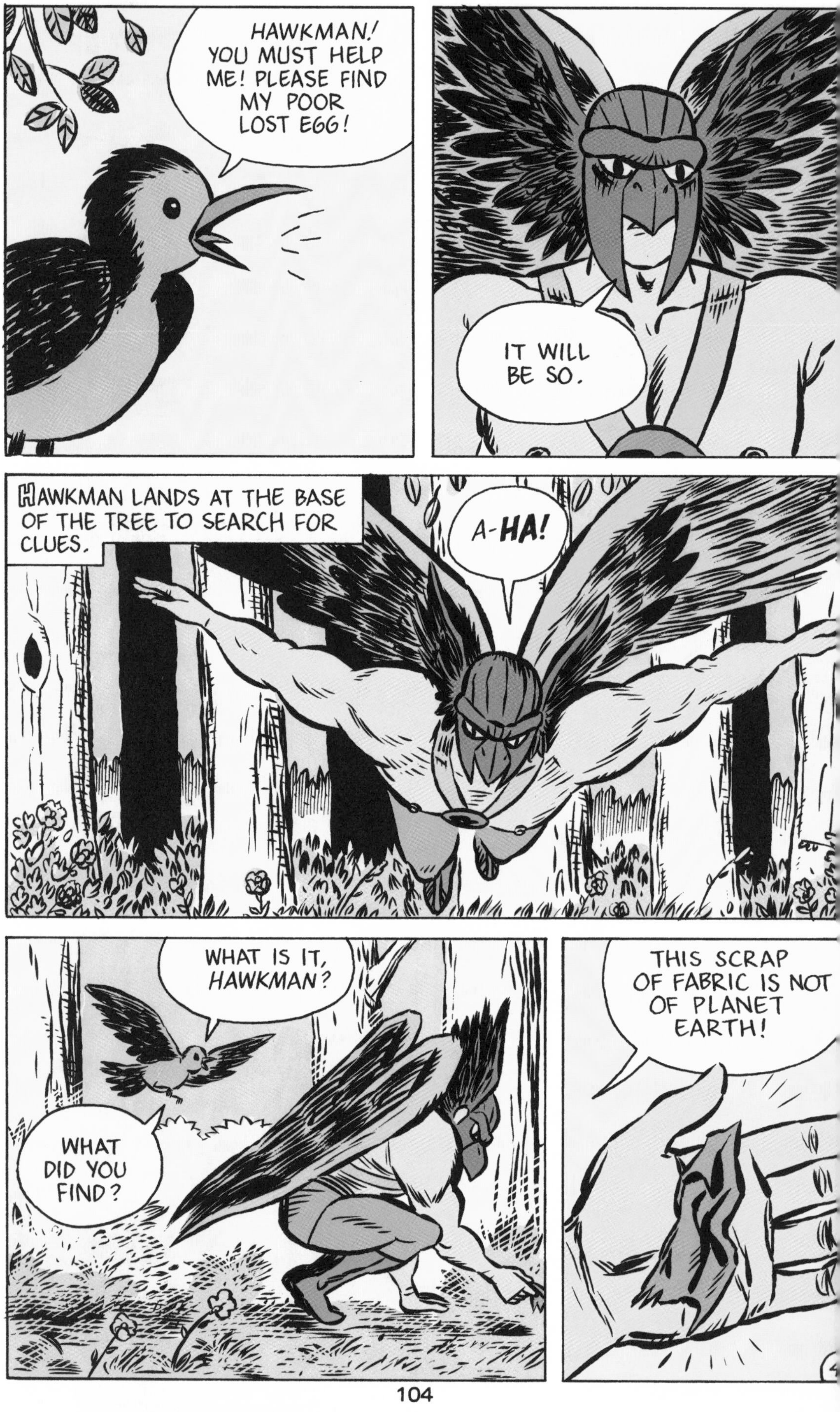
HAWKMAN! YOU MUST HELP ME! PLEASE FIND MY POOR LOST EGG!
IT WILL BE SO.
HAWKMAN LANDS AT THE BASE OF THE TREE TO SEARCH FOR CLUES.
A-HA!
WHAT IS IT, HAWKMAN?
WHAT DID YOU FIND?
THIS SCRAP OF FABRIC IS NOT OF PLANET EARTH!

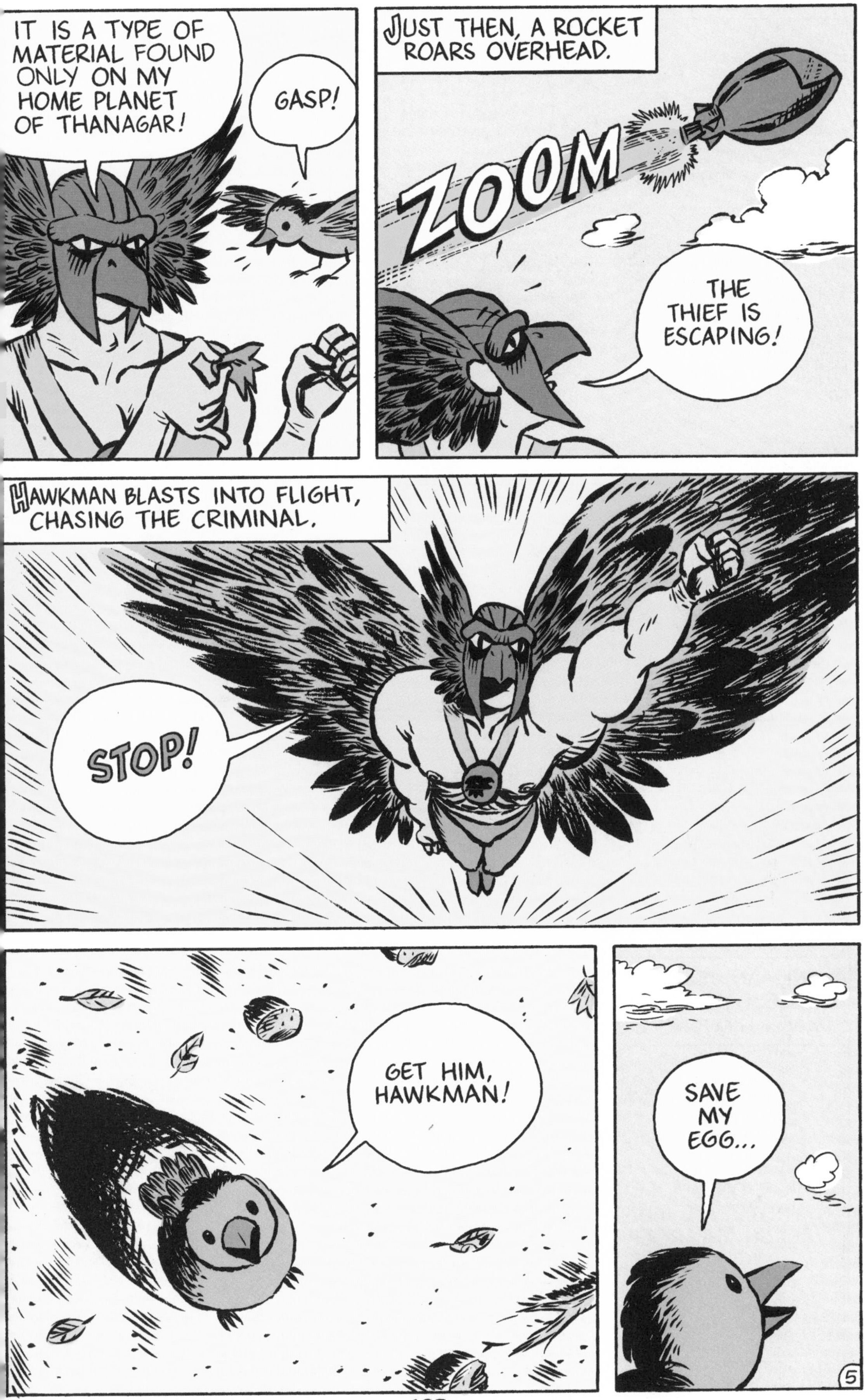
IT IS A TYPE OF MATERIAL FOUND ONLY ON MY HOME PLANET OF THANAGAR!
GASP!
JUST THEN, A ROCKET ROARS OVERHEAD.
ZOOM
THE THIEF IS ESCAPING!
HAWKMAN BLASTS INTO FLIGHT, CHASING THE CRIMINAL.
STOP!
GET HIM, HAWKMAN!
SAVE MY EGG...
5

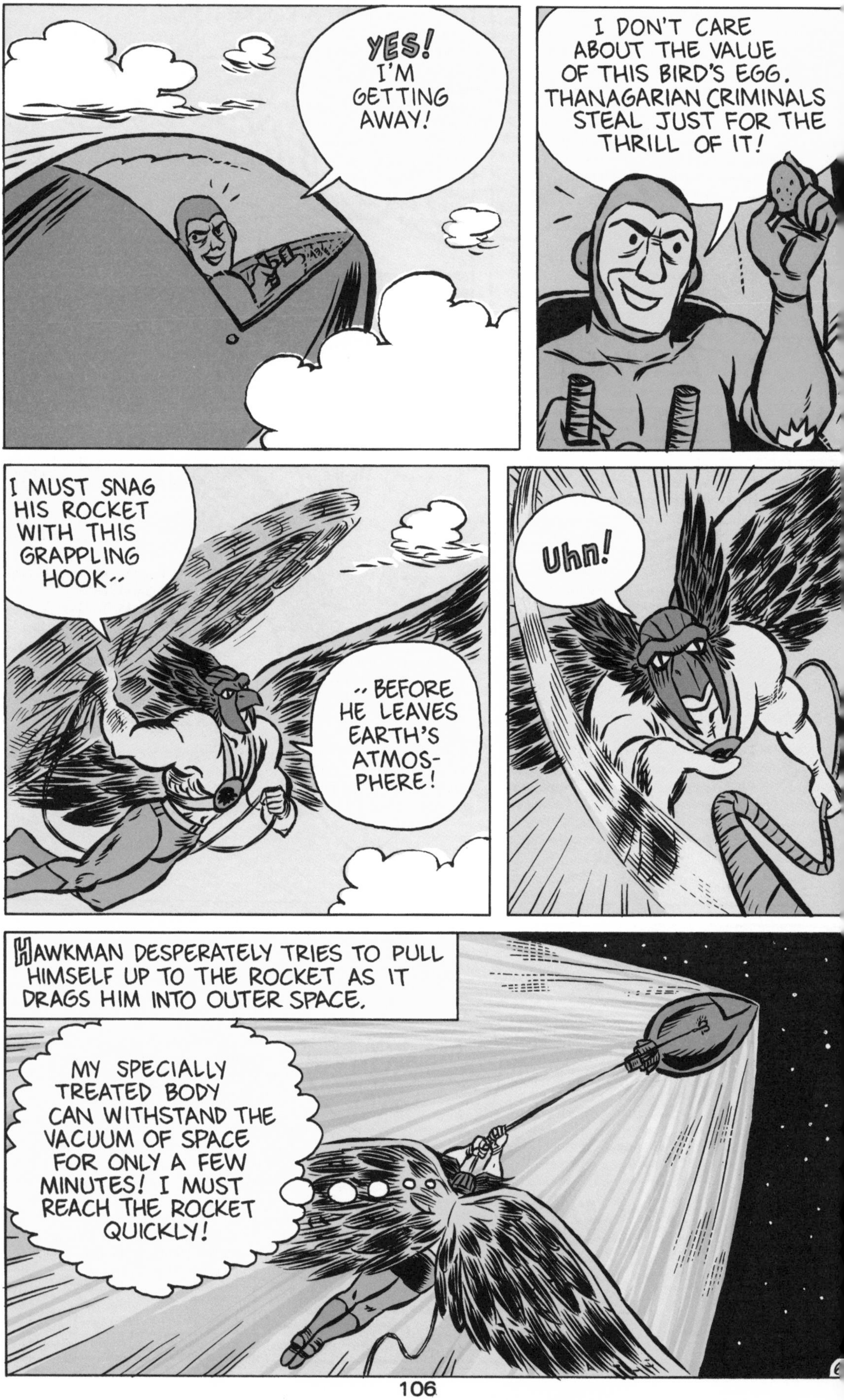
YES! I'M GETTING AWAY!
I DON'T CARE ABOUT THE VALUE OF THIS BIRD'S EGG. THANAGARIAN CRIMINALS STEAL JUST FOR THE THRILL OF IT!
I MUST SNAG HIS ROCKET WITH THIS GRAPPLING HOOK--
--BEFORE HE LEAVES EARTH'S ATMOS-PHERE!
Uhn!
HAWKMAN DESPERATELY TRIES TO PULL HIMSELF UP TO THE ROCKET AS IT DRAGS HIM INTO OUTER SPACE.
MY SPECIALLY TREATED BODY CAN WITHSTAND THE VACUUM OF SPACE FOR ONLY A FEW MINUTES! I MUST REACH THE ROCKET QUICKLY!

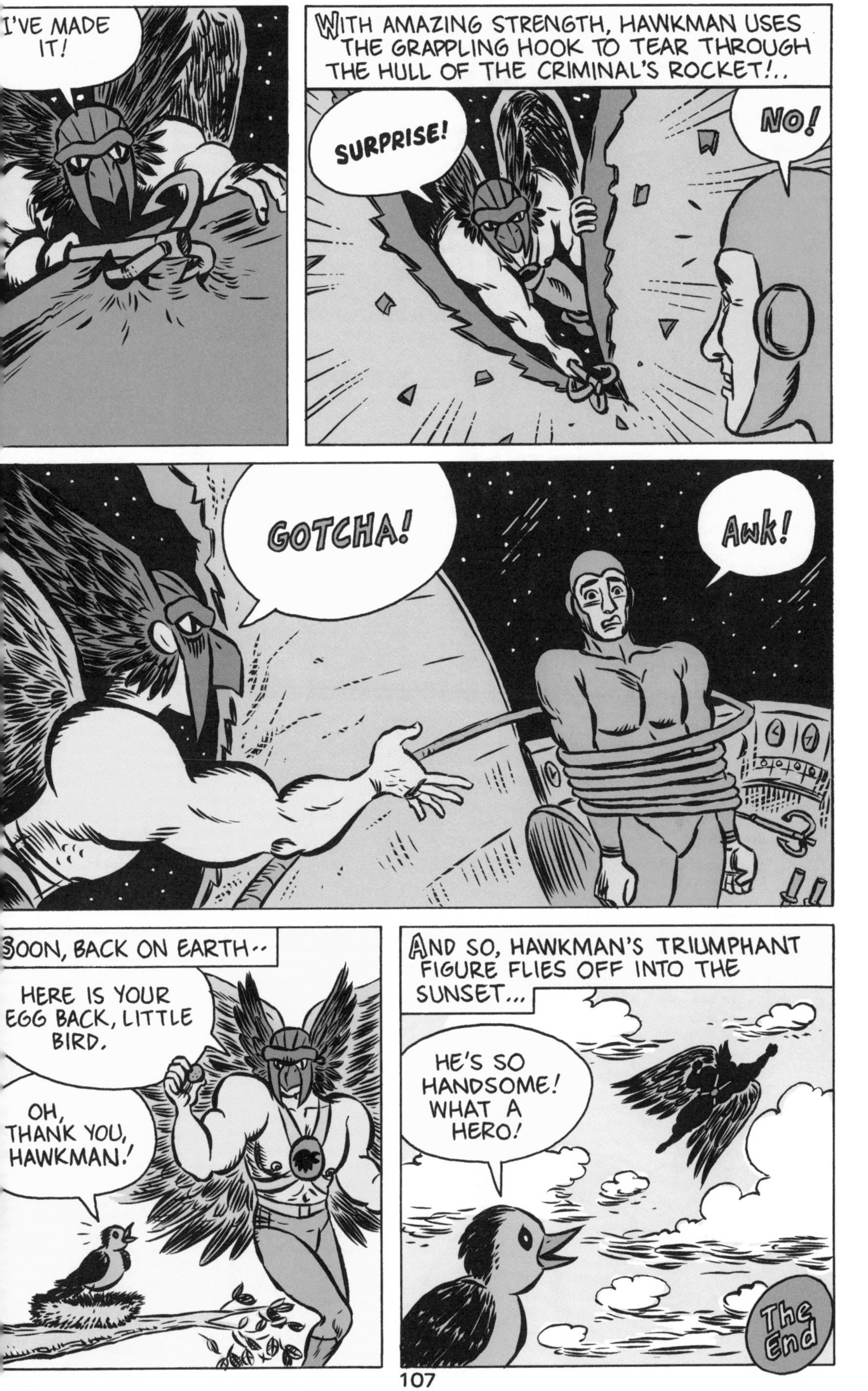
I'VE MADE IT!
WITH AMAZING STRENGTH, HAWKMAN USES THE GRAPPLING HOOK TO TEAR THROUGH THE HULL OF THE CRIMINAL'S ROCKET!..
SURPRISE!
NO!
GOTCHA!
AWK!
SOON, BACK ON EARTH..
HERE IS YOUR EGG BACK, LITTLE BIRD.
OH, THANK YOU, HAWKMAN!
AND SO, HAWKMAN'S TRIUMPHANT FIGURE FLIES OFF INTO THE SUNSET...
HE'S SO HANDSOME! WHAT A HERO!
The End

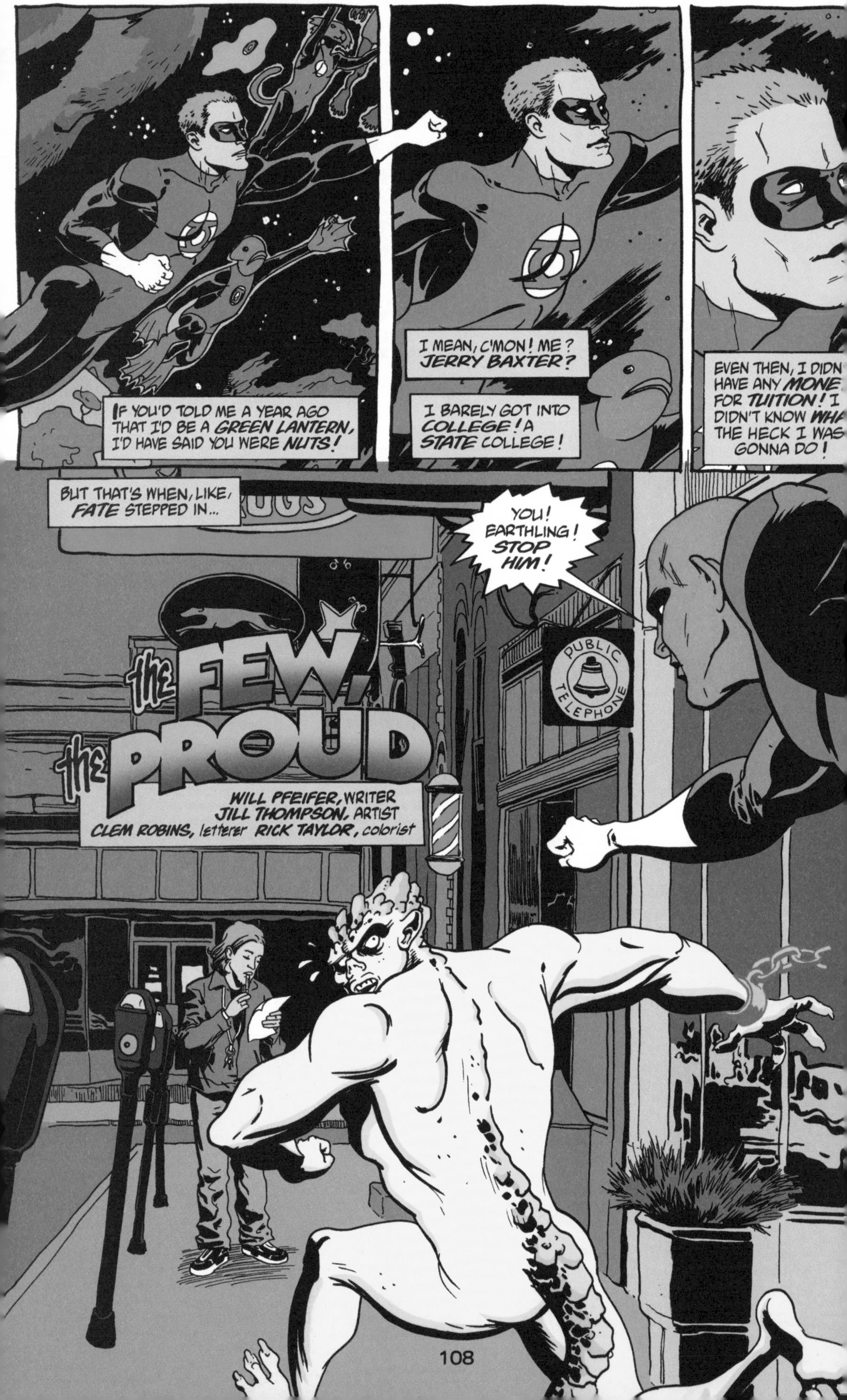
IF YOU'D TOLD ME A YEAR AGO THAT I'D BE A GREEN LANTERN, I'D HAVE SAID YOU WERE NUTS!
I MEAN, C'MON! ME? JERRY BAXTER?
I BARELY GOT INTO COLLEGE! A STATE COLLEGE!
EVEN THEN, I DIDN HAVE ANY MONE FOR TUITION! I DIDN'T KNOW WHA THE HECK I WAS GONNA DO!
BUT THAT'S WHEN, LIKE, FATE STEPPED IN...
YOU! EARTHLING! STOP HIM!
PUBLIC TELEPHONE
the FEW, the PROUD
WILL PFEIFER, WRITER
JILL THOMPSON, ARTIST
CLEM ROBINS, letterer RICK TAYLOR, colorist

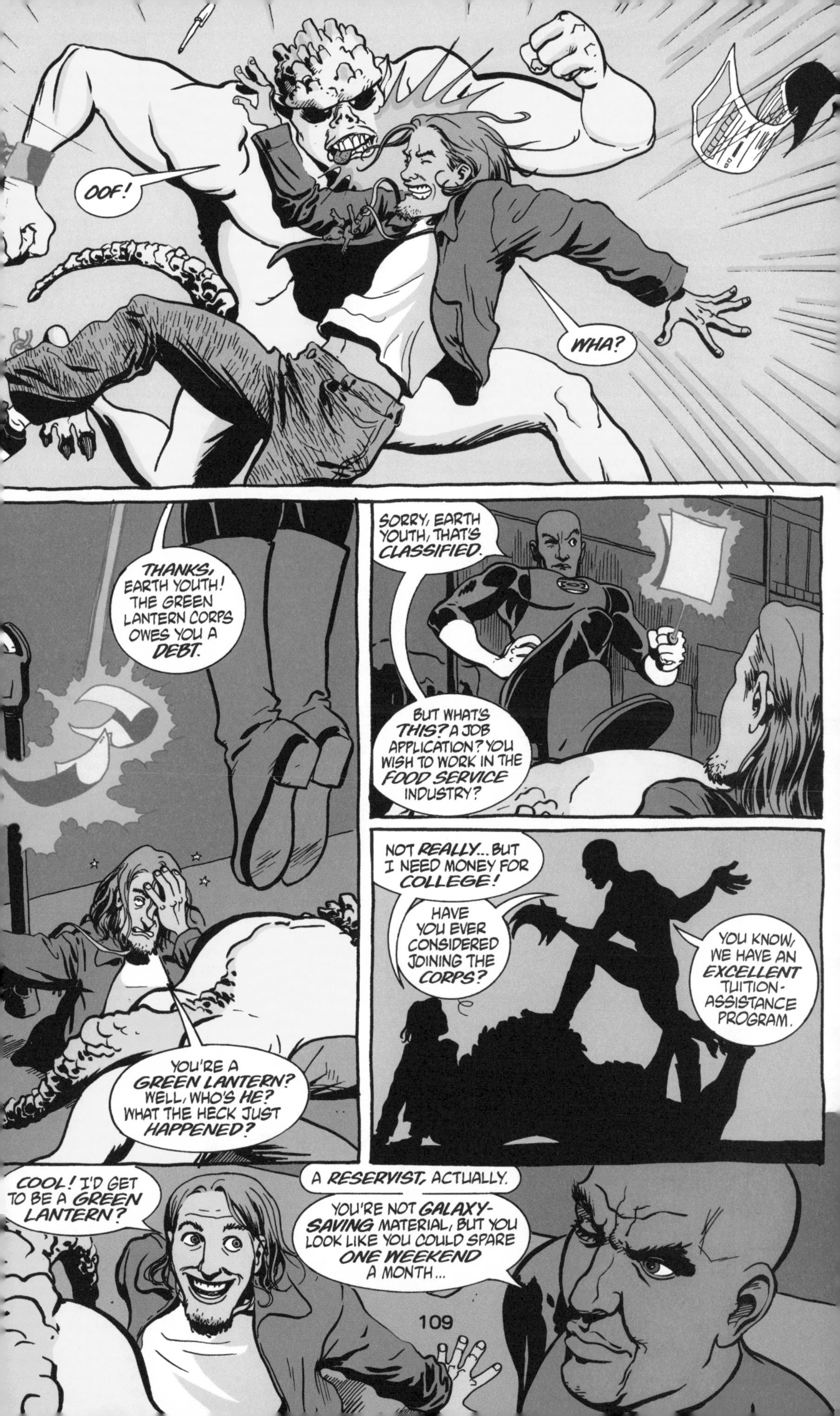

OOF!
WHA?
THANKS, EARTH YOUTH! THE GREEN LANTERN CORPS OWES YOU A DEBT.
YOU'RE A GREEN LANTERN? WELL, WHO'S HE? WHAT THE HECK JUST HAPPENED?
SORRY, EARTH YOUTH, THAT'S CLASSIFIED.
BUT WHAT'S THIS? A JOB APPLICATION? YOU WISH TO WORK IN THE FOOD SERVICE INDUSTRY?
NOT REALLY... BUT I NEED MONEY FOR COLLEGE!
HAVE YOU EVER CONSIDERED JOINING THE CORPS?
YOU KNOW, WE HAVE AN EXCELLENT TUITION-ASSISTANCE PROGRAM.
COOL! I'D GET TO BE A GREEN LANTERN?
A RESERVIST, ACTUALLY.
YOU'RE NOT GALAXY-SAVING MATERIAL, BUT YOU LOOK LIKE YOU COULD SPARE ONE WEEKEND A MONTH...

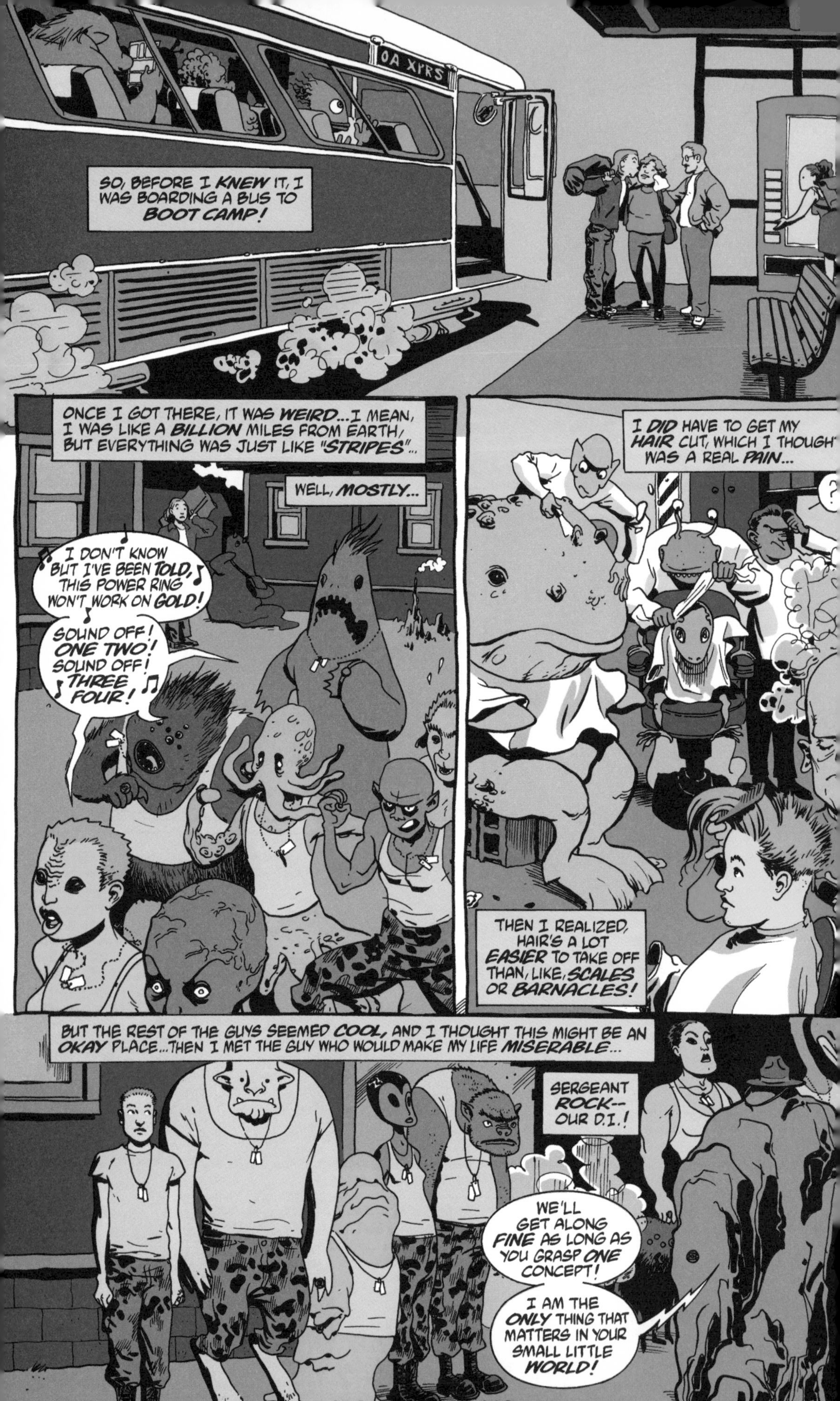
0A XPRS
SO, BEFORE I KNEW IT, I WAS BOARDING A BUS TO BOOT CAMP!
ONCE I GOT THERE, IT WAS WEIRD...I MEAN, I WAS LIKE A BILLION MILES FROM EARTH, BUT EVERYTHING WAS JUST LIKE "STRIPES"...
WELL, MOSTLY...
I DON'T KNOW BUT I'VE BEEN TOLD, THIS POWER RING WON'T WORK ON GOLD!
SOUND OFF! ONE TWO! SOUND OFF! THREE FOUR!
I DID HAVE TO GET MY HAIR CUT, WHICH I THOUGHT WAS A REAL PAIN...
?
THEN I REALIZED, HAIR'S A LOT EASIER TO TAKE OFF THAN, LIKE, SCALES OR BARNACLES!
BUT THE REST OF THE GUYS SEEMED COOL, AND I THOUGHT THIS MIGHT BE AN OKAY PLACE...THEN I MET THE GUY WHO WOULD MAKE MY LIFE MISERABLE...
SERGEANT ROCK-- OUR D.I.!
WE'LL GET ALONG FINE AS LONG AS YOU GRASP ONE CONCEPT!
I AM THE ONLY THING THAT MATTERS IN YOUR SMALL LITTLE WORLD!

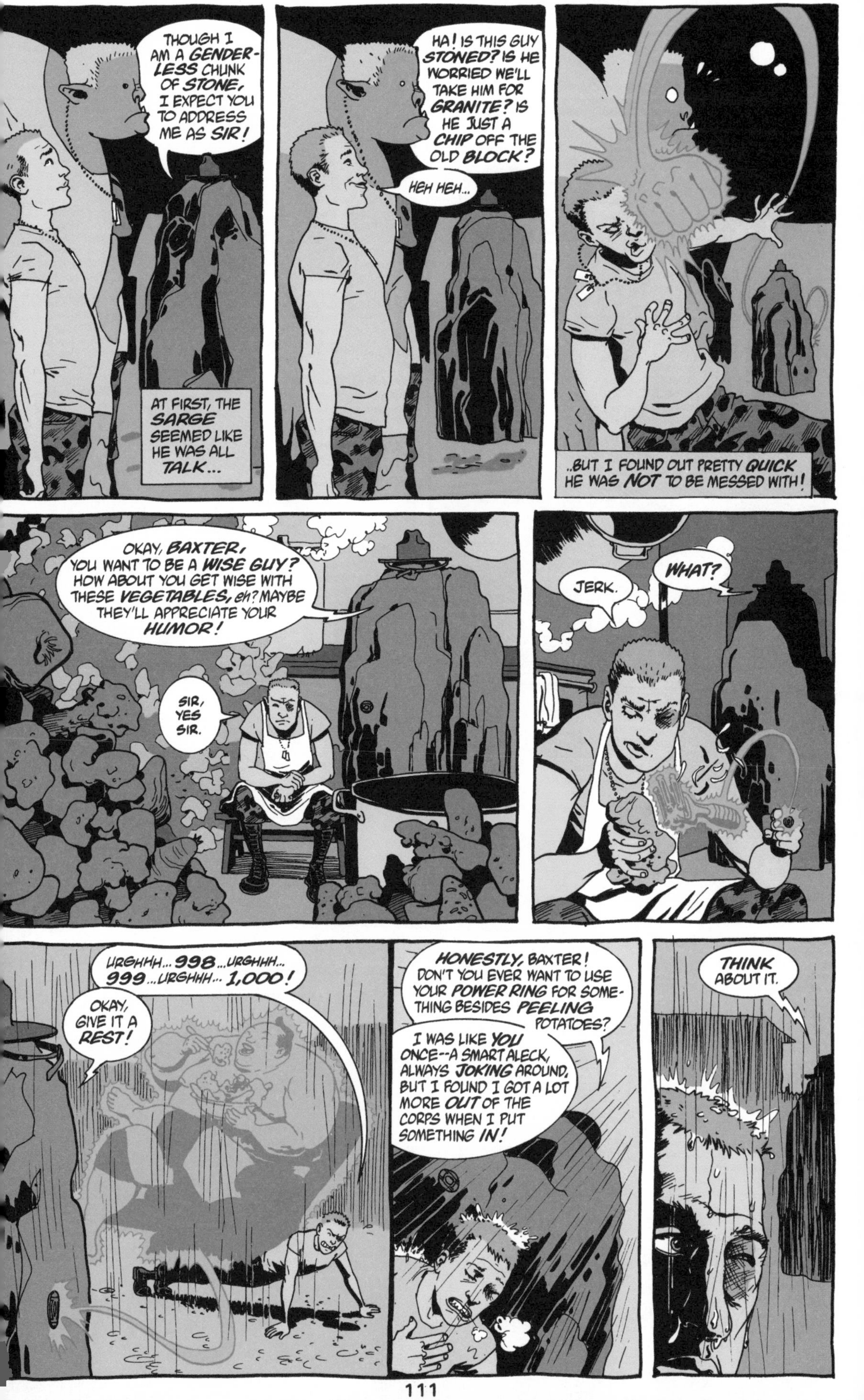

THOUGH I AM A GENDER-LESS CHUNK OF STONE, I EXPECT YOU TO ADDRESS ME AS SIR!
AT FIRST, THE SARGE SEEMED LIKE HE WAS ALL TALK...
HA! IS THIS GUY STONED? IS HE WORRIED WE'LL TAKE HIM FOR GRANITE? IS HE JUST A CHIP OFF THE OLD BLOCK?
HEH HEH...
..BUT I FOUND OUT PRETTY QUICK HE WAS NOT TO BE MESSED WITH!
OKAY, BAXTER, YOU WANT TO BE A WISE GUY? HOW ABOUT YOU GET WISE WITH THESE VEGETABLES, eh? MAYBE THEY'LL APPRECIATE YOUR HUMOR!
SIR, YES SIR.
JERK.
WHAT?
URGHHH... 998...URGHHH... 999...URGHHH... 1,000!
OKAY, GIVE IT A REST!
HONESTLY, BAXTER! DON'T YOU EVER WANT TO USE YOUR POWER RING FOR SOME-THING BESIDES PEELING POTATOES?
I WAS LIKE YOU ONCE--A SMART ALECK, ALWAYS JOKING AROUND, BUT I FOUND I GOT A LOT MORE OUT OF THE CORPS WHEN I PUT SOMETHING IN!
THINK ABOUT IT.

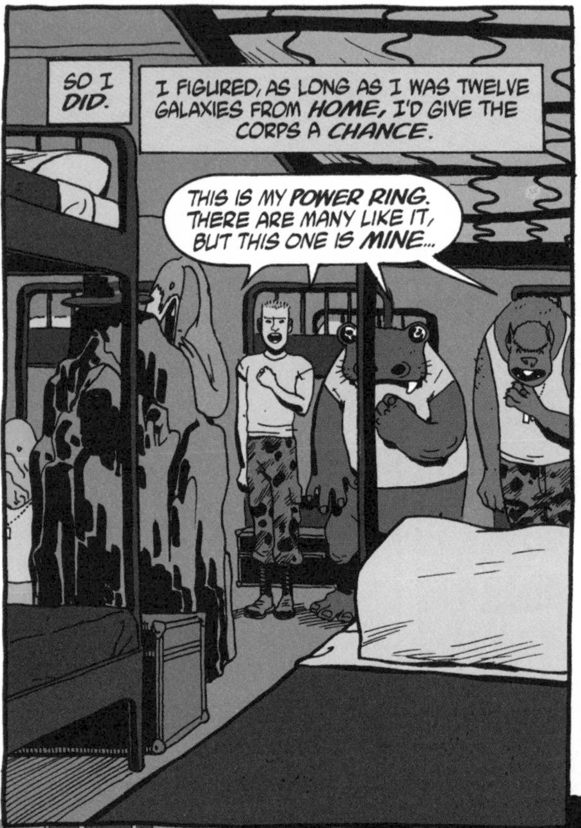
SO I DID.
I FIGURED, AS LONG AS I WAS TWELVE GALAXIES FROM HOME, I'D GIVE THE CORPS A CHANCE.
THIS IS MY POWER RING. THERE ARE MANY LIKE IT, BUT THIS ONE IS MINE...

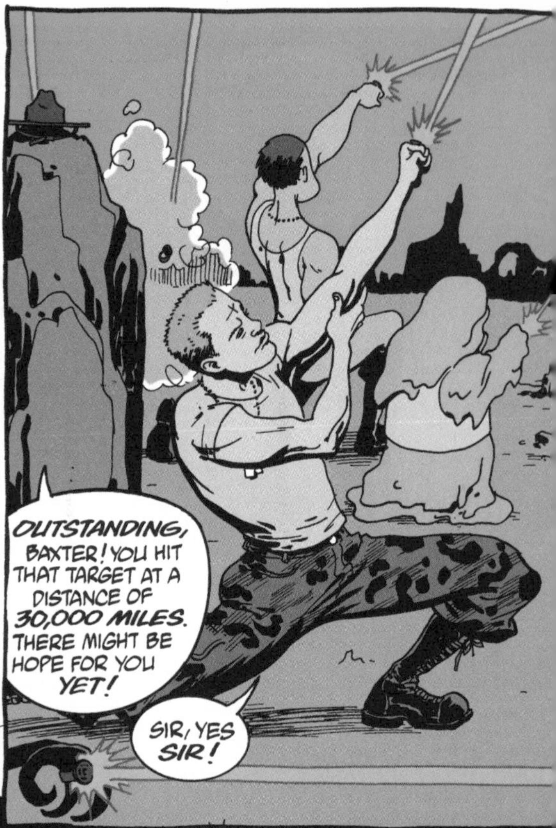
OUTSTANDING, BAXTER! YOU HIT THAT TARGET AT A DISTANCE OF 30,000 MILES. THERE MIGHT BE HOPE FOR YOU YET!
SIR, YES SIR!

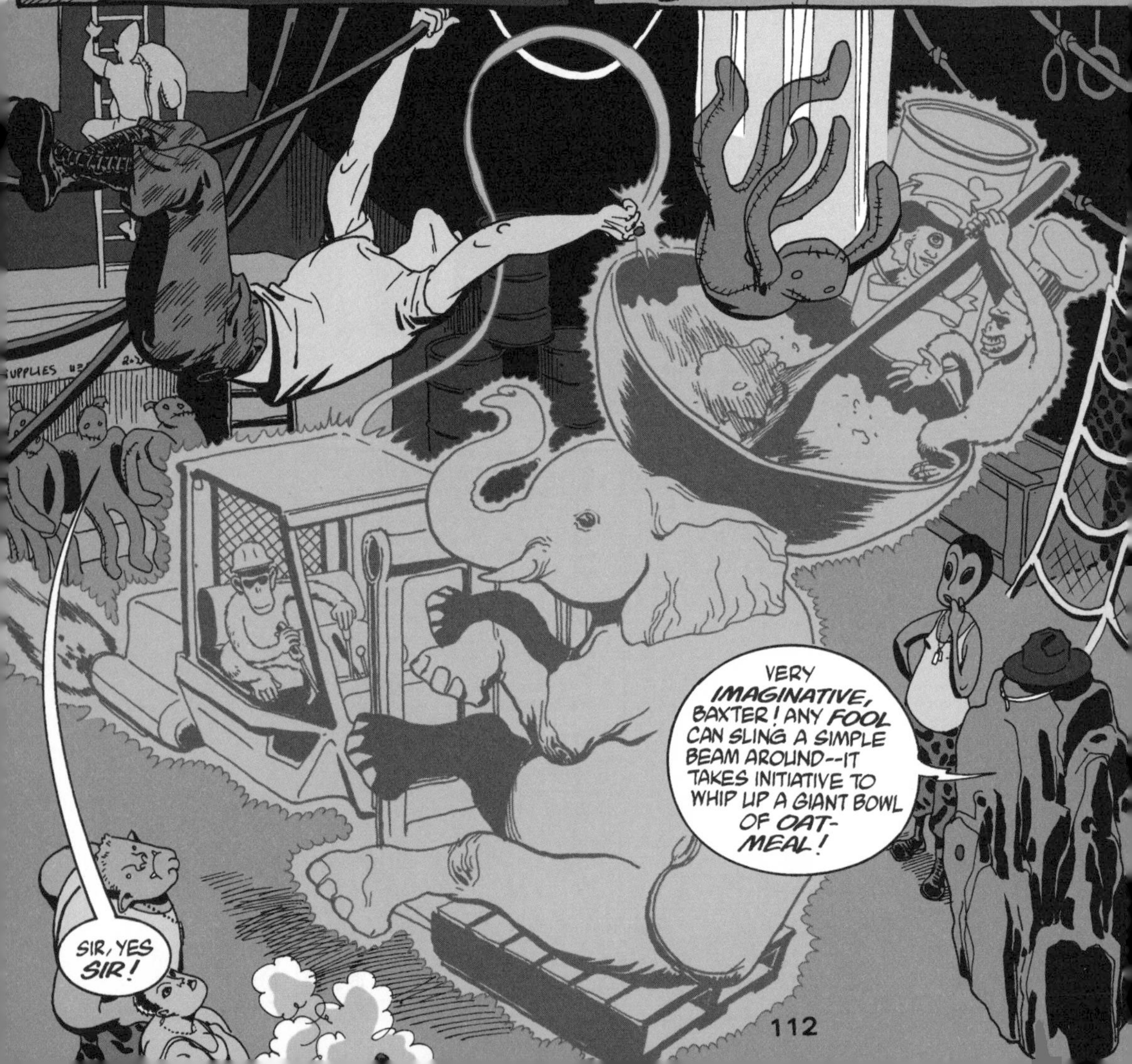
VERY IMAGINATIVE, BAXTER! ANY FOOL CAN SLING A SIMPLE BEAM AROUND--IT TAKES INITIATIVE TO WHIP UP A GIANT BOWL OF OAT-MEAL!
SIR, YES SIR!

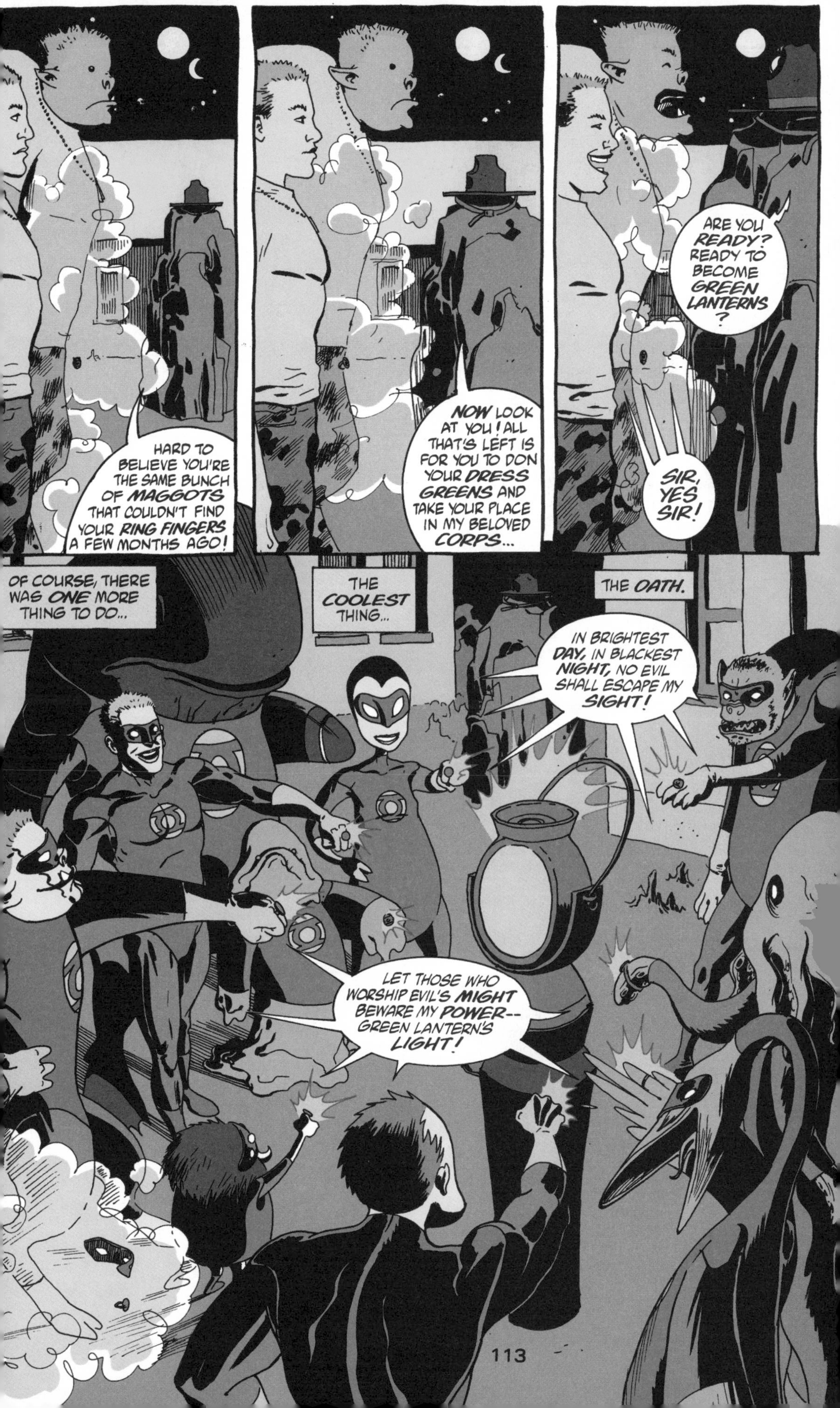
HARD TO BELIEVE YOU'RE THE SAME BUNCH OF MAGGOTS THAT COULDN'T FIND YOUR RING FINGERS A FEW MONTHS AGO!
NOW LOOK AT YOU! ALL THAT'S LEFT IS FOR YOU TO DON YOUR DRESS GREENS AND TAKE YOUR PLACE IN MY BELOVED CORPS...
ARE YOU READY? READY TO BECOME GREEN LANTERNS?
SIR, YES SIR!
OF COURSE, THERE WAS ONE MORE THING TO DO...
THE COOLEST THING...
THE OATH.
IN BRIGHTEST DAY, IN BLACKEST NIGHT, NO EVIL SHALL ESCAPE MY SIGHT!
LET THOSE WHO WORSHIP EVIL'S MIGHT BEWARE MY POWER-- GREEN LANTERN'S LIGHT!

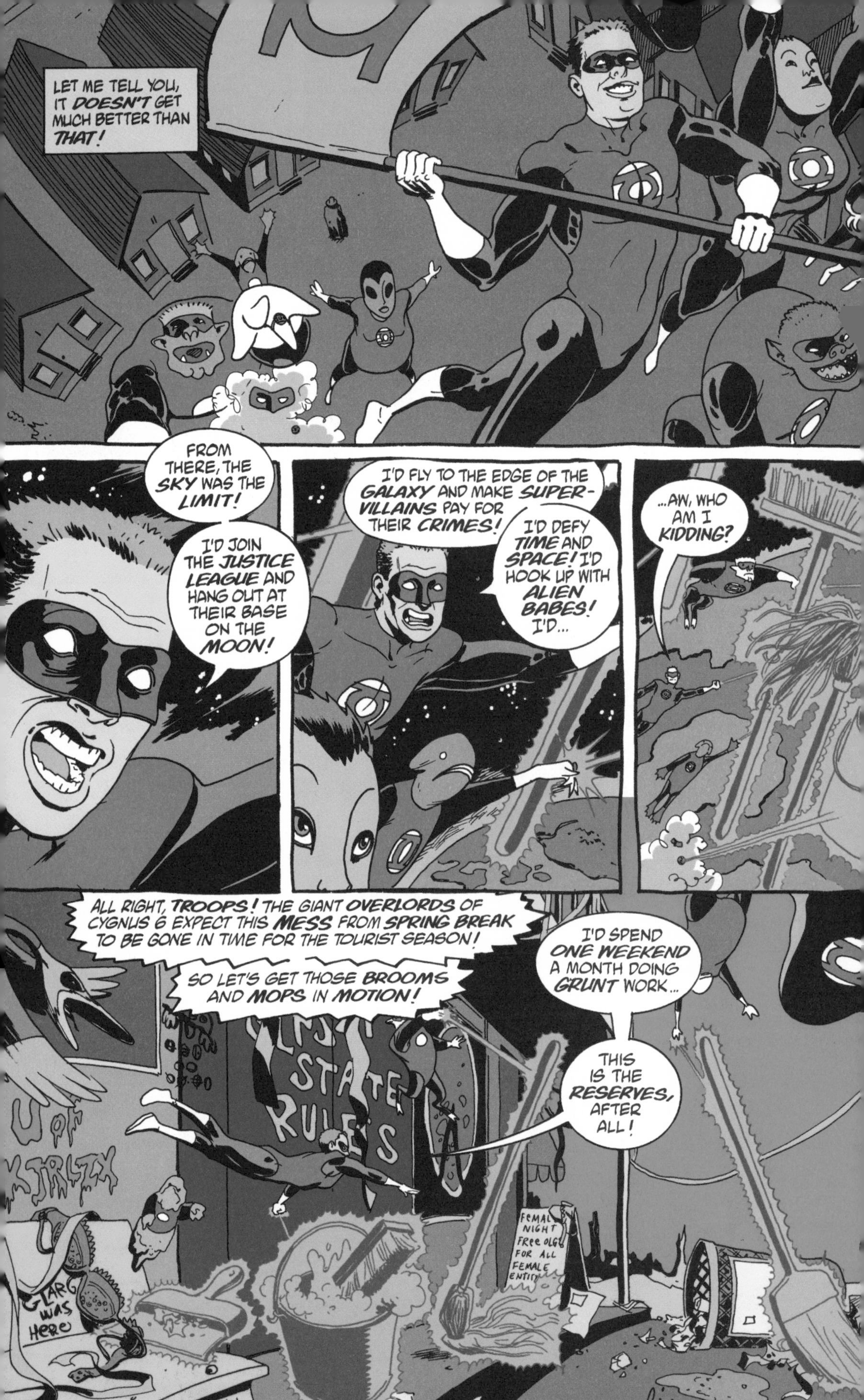

LET ME TELL YOU, IT DOESN'T GET MUCH BETTER THAN THAT!
FROM THERE, THE SKY WAS THE LIMIT!
I'D JOIN THE JUSTICE LEAGUE AND HANG OUT AT THEIR BASE ON THE MOON!
I'D FLY TO THE EDGE OF THE GALAXY AND MAKE SUPER-VILLAINS PAY FOR THEIR CRIMES!
I'D DEFY TIME AND SPACE! I'D HOOK UP WITH ALIEN BABES! I'D...
...AW, WHO AM I KIDDING?
ALL RIGHT, TROOPS! THE GIANT OVERLORDS OF CYGNUS 6 EXPECT THIS MESS FROM SPRING BREAK TO BE GONE IN TIME FOR THE TOURIST SEASON!
SO LET'S GET THOSE BROOMS AND MOPS IN MOTION!
I'D SPEND ONE WEEKEND A MONTH DOING GRUNT WORK...
THIS IS THE RESERVES, AFTER ALL!
STATE RULES
GLARG WAS HERE
FEMAL NIGHT FREE OLG FOR ALL FEMALE ENTITY
fin

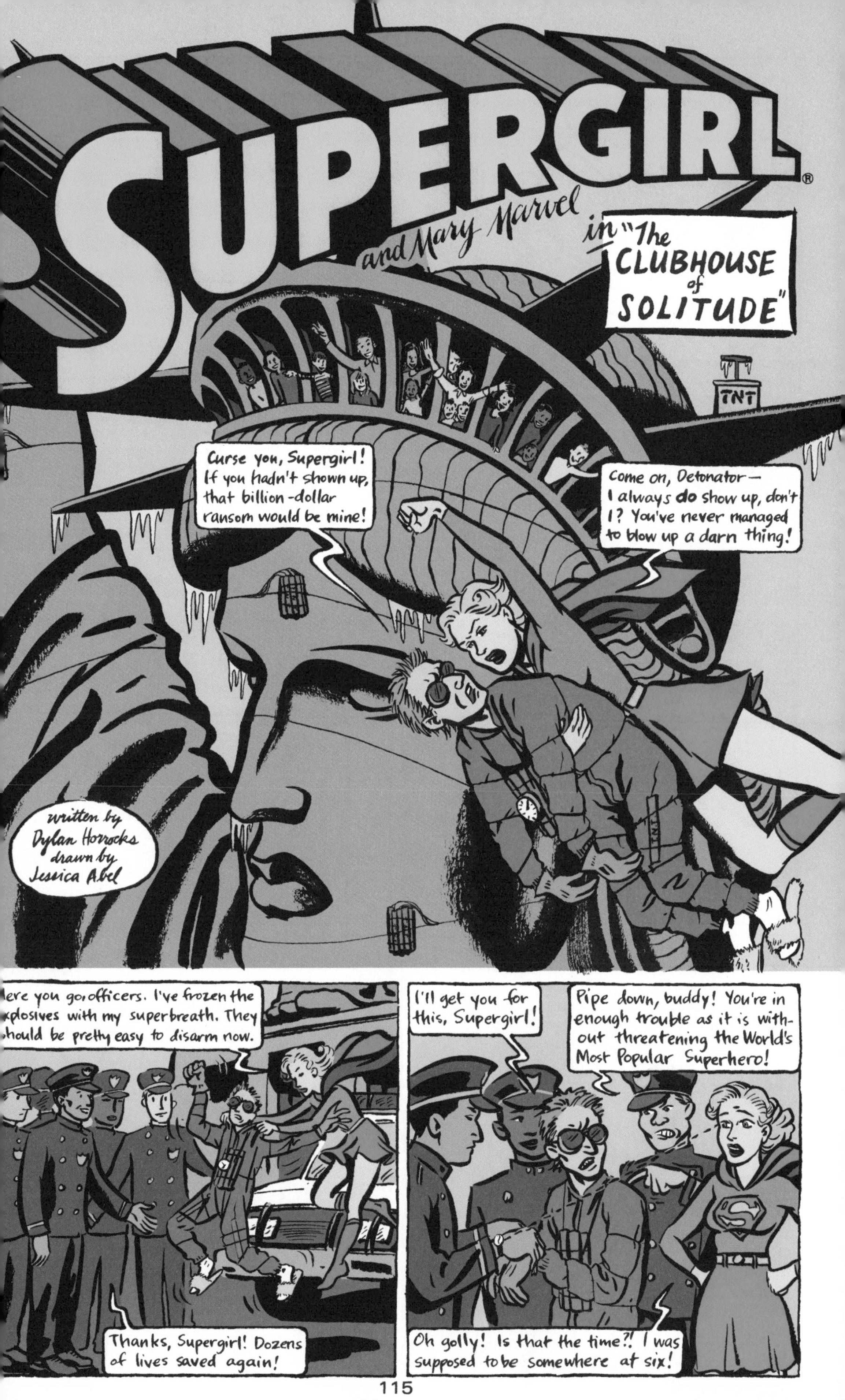
SUPERGIRL®
and Mary Marvel in "The CLUBHOUSE of SOLITUDE"
TNT
Curse you, Supergirl! If you hadn't shown up, that billion-dollar ransom would be mine!
Come on, Detonator— I always do show up, don't I? You've never managed to blow up a darn thing!
written by Dylan Horrocks drawn by Jessica Abel
Here you go, officers. I've frozen the explosives with my superbreath. They should be pretty easy to disarm now.
Thanks, Supergirl! Dozens of lives saved again!
I'll get you for this, Supergirl!
Pipe down, buddy! You're in enough trouble as it is without threatening the World's Most Popular Superhero!
Oh golly! Is that the time?! I was supposed to be somewhere at six!

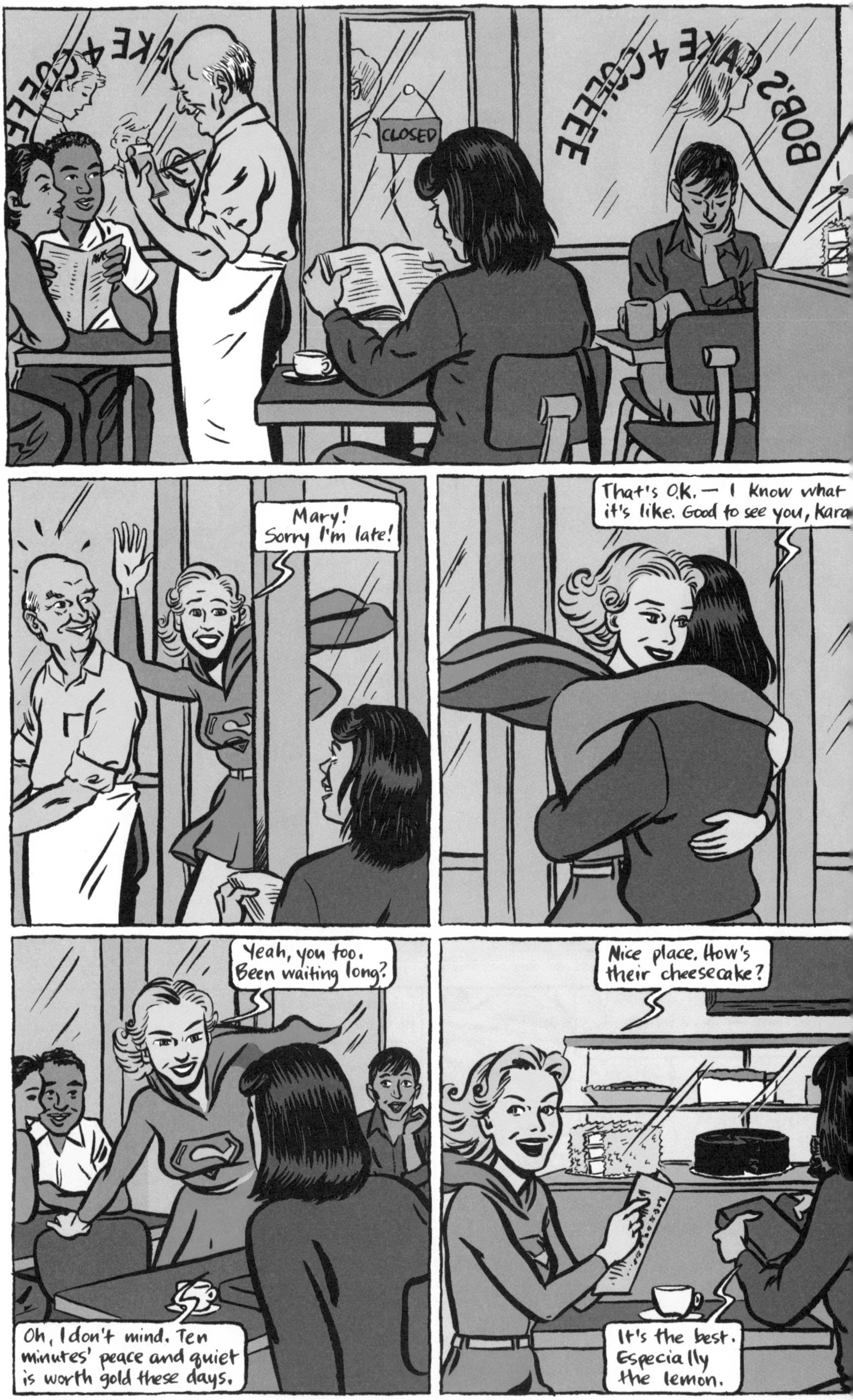
CLOSED
Mary! Sorry I'm late!
That's O.K. — I know what it's like. Good to see you, Kara
Yeah, you too. Been waiting long?
Oh, I don't mind. Ten minutes' peace and quiet is worth gold these days.
Nice place. How's their cheesecake?
It's the best. Especially the lemon.

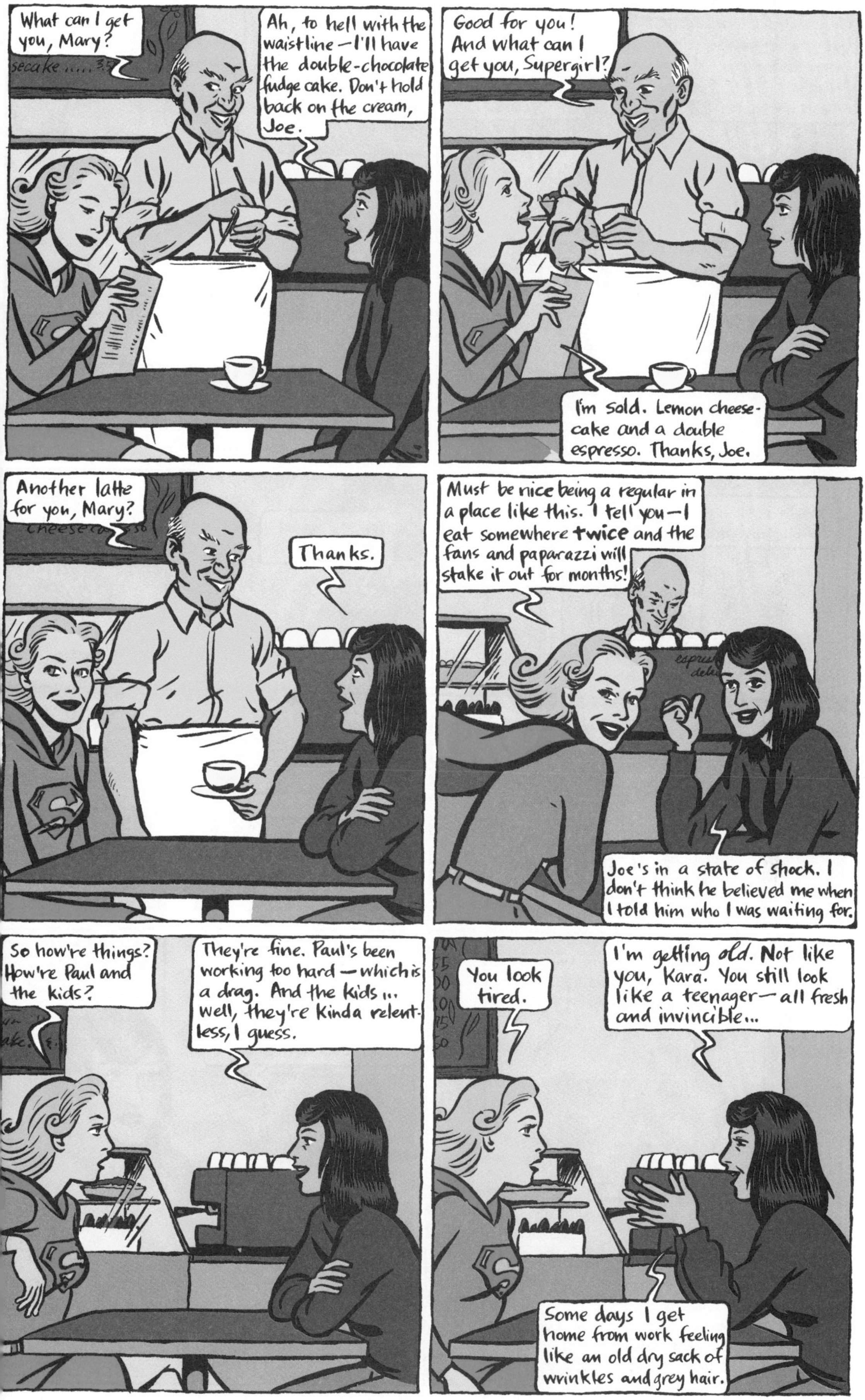

What can I get you, Mary?
Ah, to hell with the waistline — I'll have the double-chocolate fudge cake. Don't hold back on the cream, Joe.
Good for you! And what can I get you, Supergirl?
I'm sold. Lemon cheese-cake and a double espresso. Thanks, Joe.
Another latte for you, Mary?
Thanks.
Must be nice being a regular in a place like this. I tell you — I eat somewhere **twice** and the fans and paparazzi will stake it out for months!
Joe's in a state of shock. I don't think he believed me when I told him who I was waiting for.
So how're things? How're Paul and the kids?
They're fine. Paul's been working too hard — which is a drag. And the kids... well, they're kinda relent-less, I guess.
You look tired.
I'm getting *old*. Not like you, Kara. You still look like a teenager — all fresh and invincible...
Some days I get home from work feeling like an old dry sack of wrinkles and grey hair.

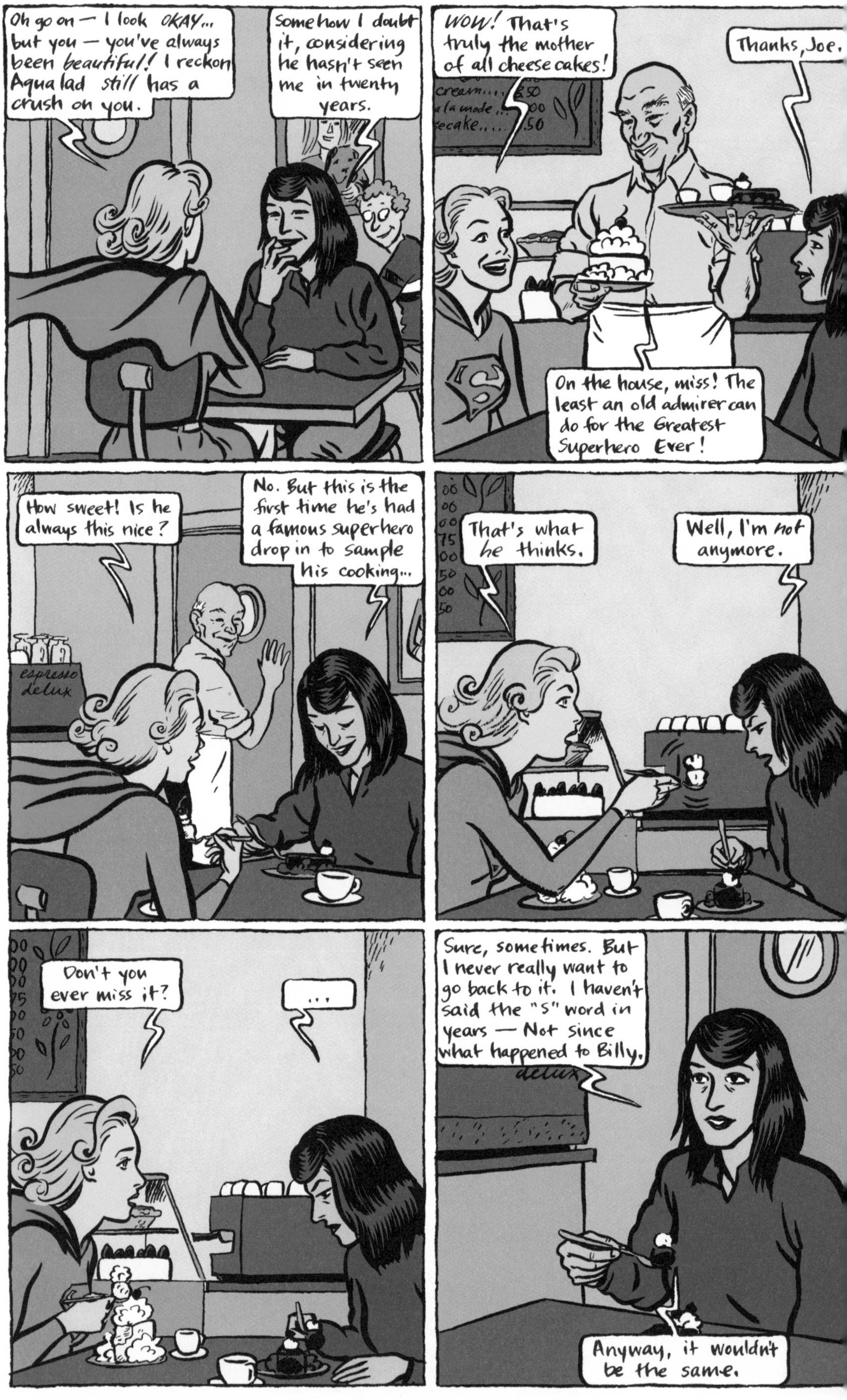

Oh go on — I look OKAY... but you — you've always been beautiful! I reckon Aqualad still has a crush on you.
Somehow I doubt it, considering he hasn't seen me in twenty years.
WOW! That's truly the mother of all cheesecakes!
Thanks, Joe.
On the house, miss! The least an old admirer can do for the Greatest Superhero Ever!
How sweet! Is he always this nice?
No. But this is the first time he's had a famous superhero drop in to sample his cooking...
espresso delux
That's what he thinks.
Well, I'm not anymore.
Don't you ever miss it?
...
Sure, sometimes. But I never really want to go back to it. I haven't said the "S" word in years — Not since what happened to Billy.
Anyway, it wouldn't be the same.

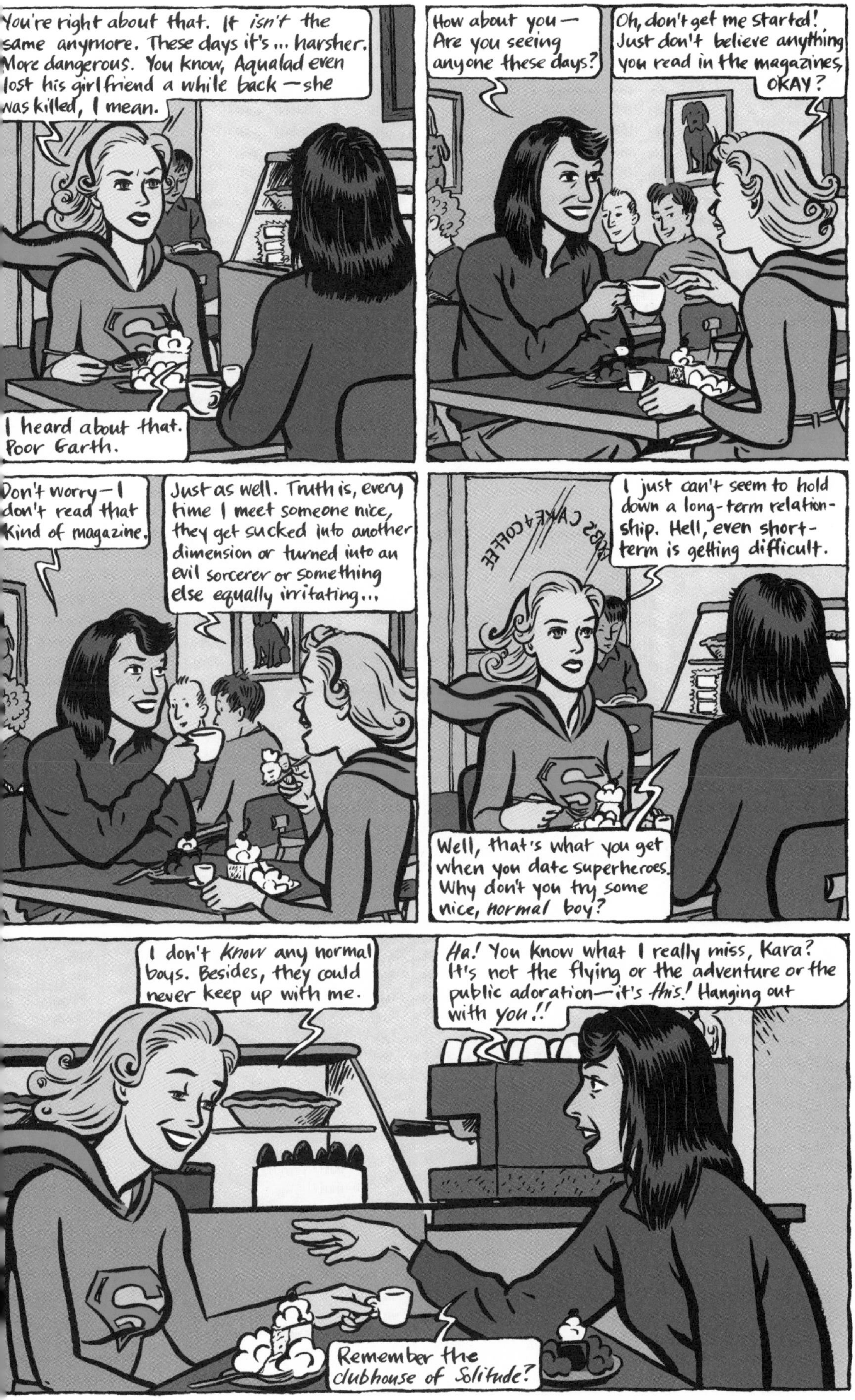

You're right about that. It *isn't* the same anymore. These days it's... harsher. More dangerous. You know, Aqualad even lost his girlfriend a while back—she was killed, I mean.
I heard about that. Poor Garth.
How about you—Are you seeing anyone these days?
Oh, don't get me started! Just don't believe anything you read in the magazines, OKAY?
Don't worry—I don't read that kind of magazine.
Just as well. Truth is, every time I meet someone nice, they get sucked into another dimension or turned into an evil sorcerer or something else equally irritating...
I just can't seem to hold down a long-term relationship. Hell, even short-term is getting difficult.
Well, that's what you get when you date superheroes. Why don't you try some nice, *normal* boy?
I don't *know* any normal boys. Besides, they could never keep up with me.
Ha! You know what I really miss, Kara? It's not the flying or the adventure or the public adoration—it's *this!* Hanging out with *you!!*
Remember the clubhouse of Solitude?

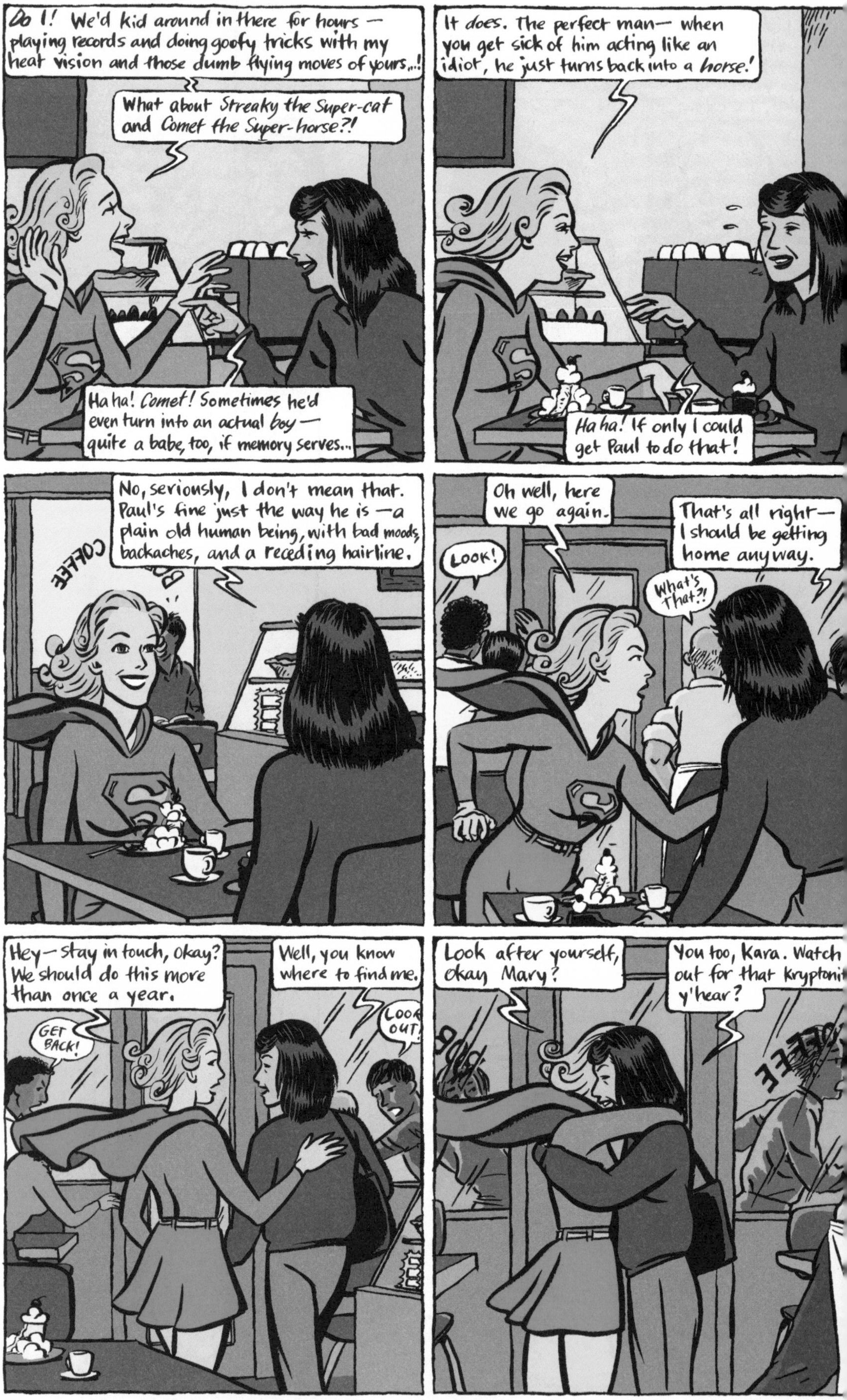

Do I! We'd kid around in there for hours — playing records and doing goofy tricks with my heat vision and those dumb flying moves of yours...!
What about Streaky the Super-cat and Comet the Super-horse?!
Ha ha! Comet! Sometimes he'd even turn into an actual boy — quite a babe, too, if memory serves...
It does. The perfect man— when you get sick of him acting like an idiot, he just turns back into a horse!
Ha ha! If only I could get Paul to do that!
No, seriously, I don't mean that. Paul's fine just the way he is — a plain old human being, with bad moods, backaches, and a receding hairline.
Oh well, here we go again.
LOOK!
What's that?!
That's all right— I should be getting home anyway.
Hey— stay in touch, okay? We should do this more than once a year.
GET BACK!
Well, you know where to find me.
LOOK OUT!
Look after yourself, okay Mary?
You too, Kara. Watch out for that kryptoni y'hear?

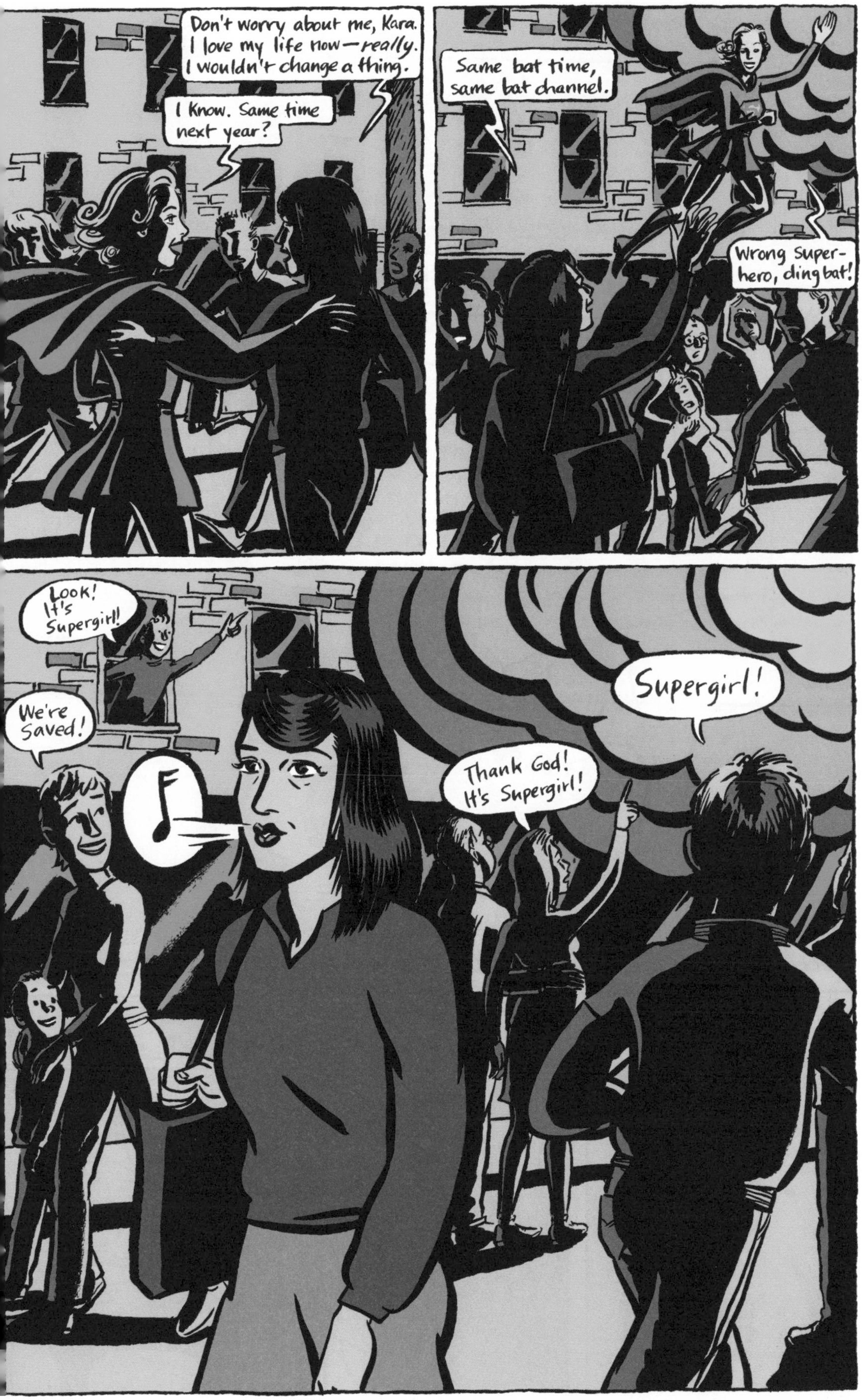

Don't worry about me, Kara. I love my life now—really. I wouldn't change a thing.
I know. Same time next year?
Same bat time, same bat channel.
Wrong super-hero, dingbat!
Look! It's Supergirl!
We're Saved!
Supergirl!
Thank God! It's Supergirl!

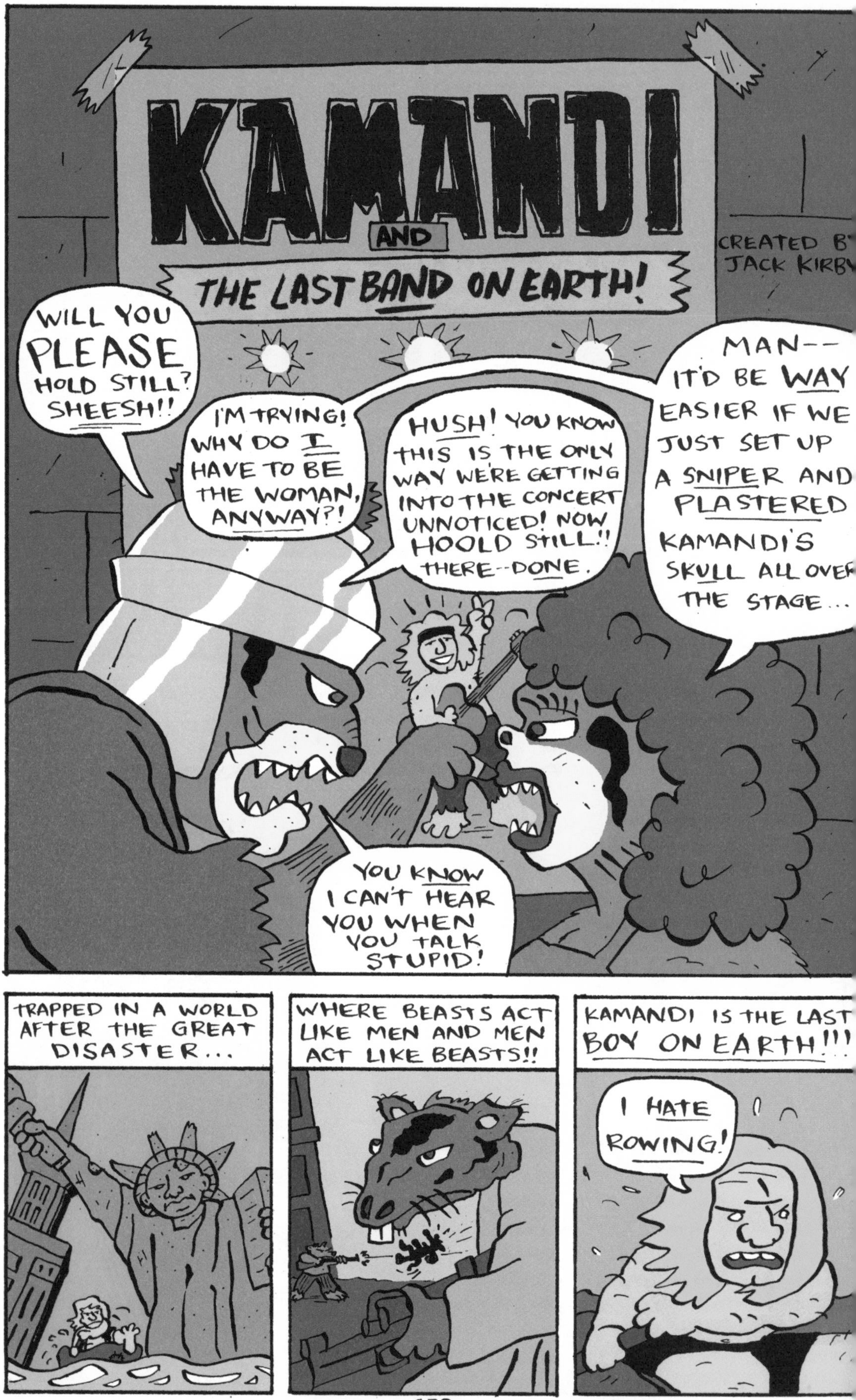
KAMANDI AND THE LAST BAND ON EARTH!
CREATED BY JACK KIRBY
WILL YOU PLEASE HOLD STILL? SHEESH!!
I'M TRYING! WHY DO I HAVE TO BE THE WOMAN, ANYWAY?!
HUSH! YOU KNOW THIS IS THE ONLY WAY WE'RE GETTING INTO THE CONCERT UNNOTICED! NOW HOOLD STILL!! THERE--DONE.
MAN-- IT'D BE WAY EASIER IF WE JUST SET UP A SNIPER AND PLASTERED KAMANDI'S SKULL ALL OVER THE STAGE...
YOU KNOW I CAN'T HEAR YOU WHEN YOU TALK STUPID!
TRAPPED IN A WORLD AFTER THE GREAT DISASTER...
WHERE BEASTS ACT LIKE MEN AND MEN ACT LIKE BEASTS!!
KAMANDI IS THE LAST BOY ON EARTH!!!
I HATE ROWING!

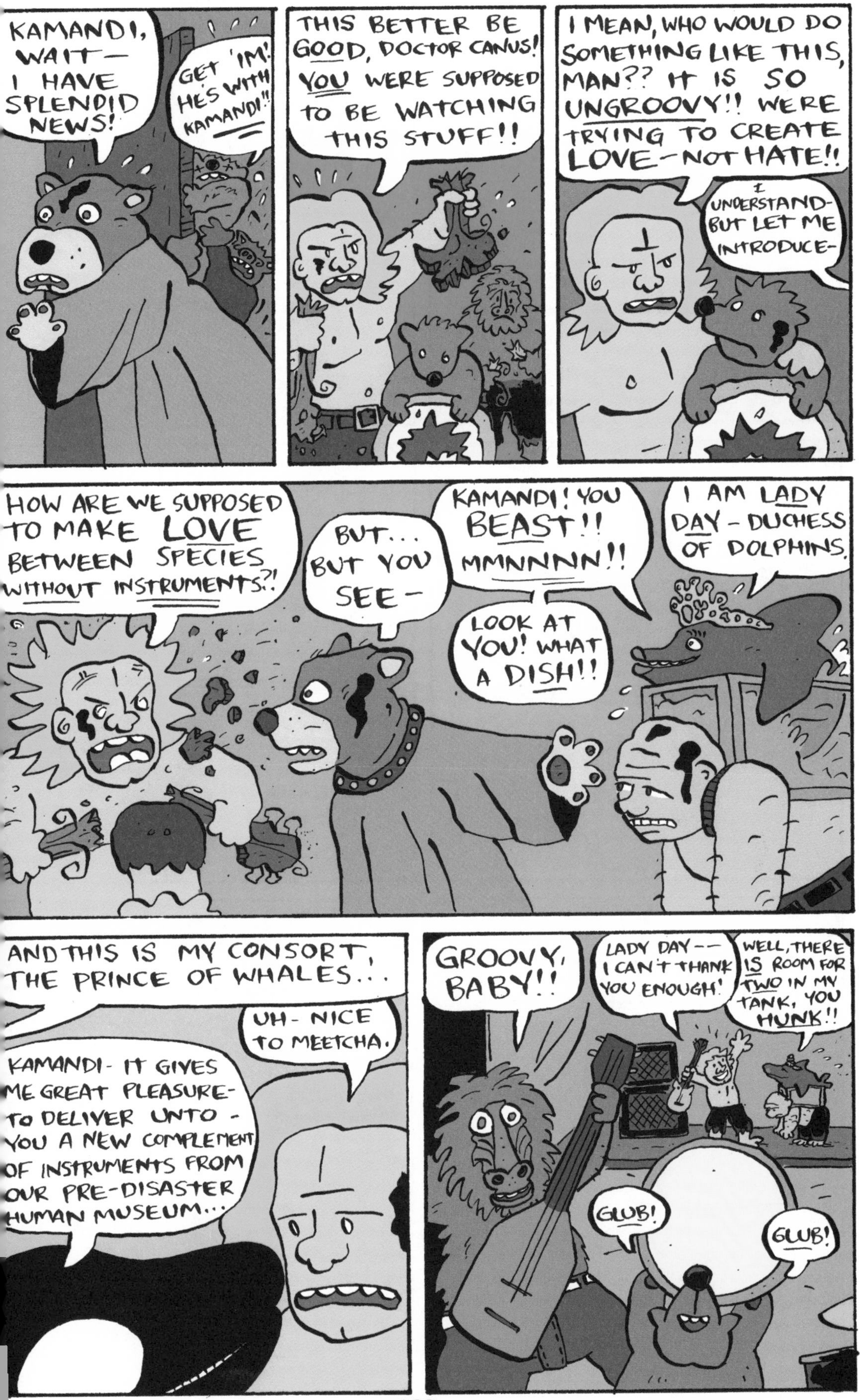
KAMANDI, WAIT— I HAVE SPLENDID NEWS!
GET 'IM! HE'S WITH KAMANDI!!
THIS BETTER BE GOOD, DOCTOR CANUS! YOU WERE SUPPOSED TO BE WATCHING THIS STUFF!!
I MEAN, WHO WOULD DO SOMETHING LIKE THIS, MAN?? IT IS SO UNGROOVY!! WE'RE TRYING TO CREATE LOVE—NOT HATE!!
I UNDERSTAND—BUT LET ME INTRODUCE—
HOW ARE WE SUPPOSED TO MAKE LOVE BETWEEN SPECIES WITHOUT INSTRUMENTS?!
BUT... BUT YOU SEE—
KAMANDI! YOU BEAST!! MMNNNN!!
LOOK AT YOU! WHAT A DISH!!
I AM LADY DAY—DUCHESS OF DOLPHINS.
AND THIS IS MY CONSORT, THE PRINCE OF WHALES...
UH—NICE TO MEETCHA.
KAMANDI—IT GIVES ME GREAT PLEASURE—TO DELIVER UNTO—YOU A NEW COMPLEMENT OF INSTRUMENTS FROM OUR PRE-DISASTER HUMAN MUSEUM...
GROOVY, BABY!!
LADY DAY—I CAN'T THANK YOU ENOUGH!
WELL, THERE IS ROOM FOR TWO IN MY TANK, YOU HUNK!!
GLUB!
GLUB!

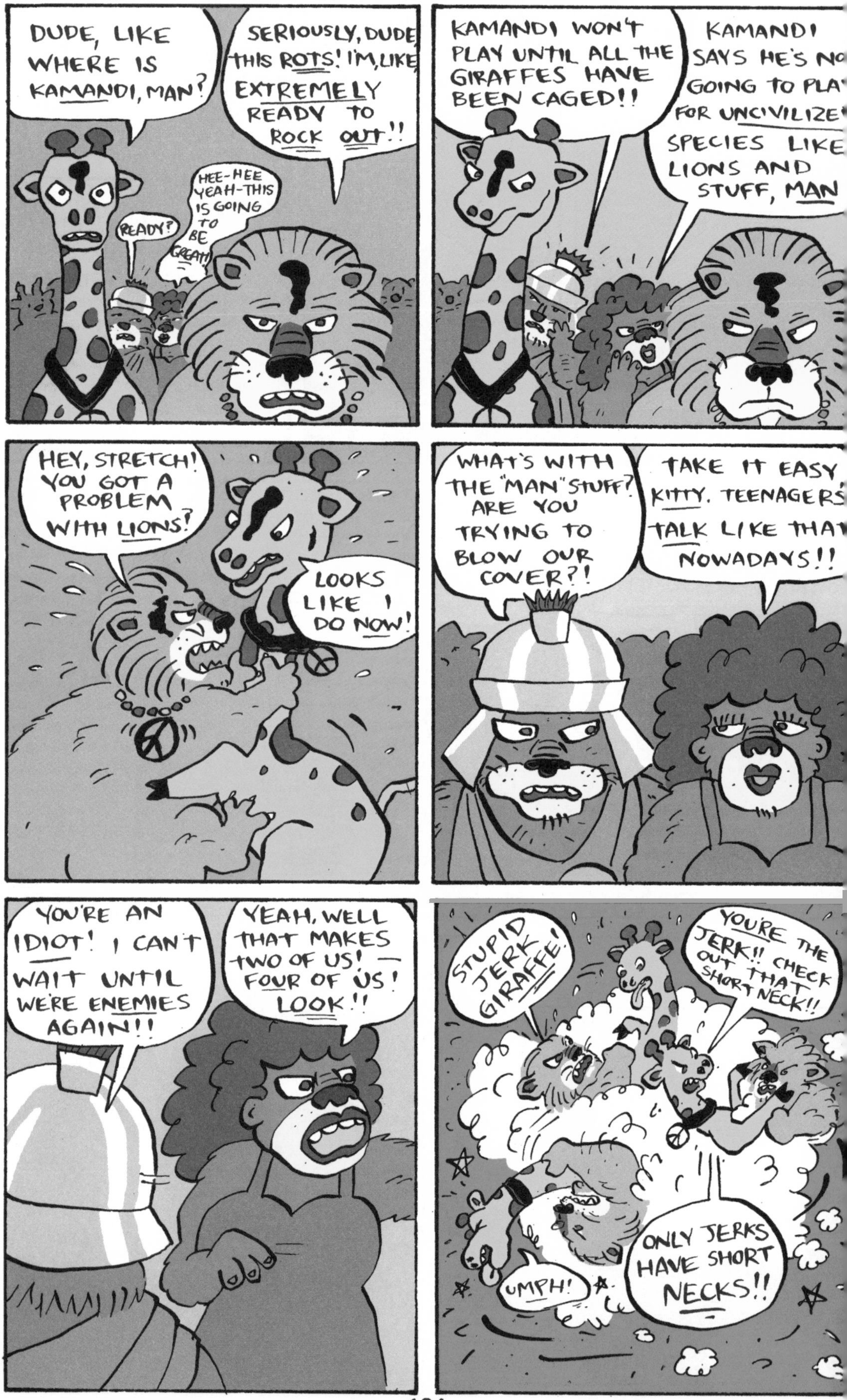
DUDE, LIKE WHERE IS KAMANDI, MAN?
SERIOUSLY, DUDE THIS ROTS! I'M, LIKE, EXTREMELY READY TO ROCK OUT!!
READY?
HEE-HEE YEAH-THIS IS GOING TO BE GREAT!
KAMANDI WON'T PLAY UNTIL ALL THE GIRAFFES HAVE BEEN CAGED!!
KAMANDI SAYS HE'S NO
GOING TO PLA
FOR UNCIVILIZE
SPECIES LIKE LIONS AND STUFF, MAN
HEY, STRETCH! YOU GOT A PROBLEM WITH LIONS?
LOOKS LIKE I DO NOW!
WHAT'S WITH THE "MAN" STUFF? ARE YOU TRYING TO BLOW OUR COVER?!
TAKE IT EASY, KITTY. TEENAGERS TALK LIKE THAT NOWADAYS!!
YOU'RE AN IDIOT! I CAN'T WAIT UNTIL WE'RE ENEMIES AGAIN!!
YEAH, WELL THAT MAKES TWO OF US! — FOUR OF US! LOOK!!
STUPID JERK GIRAFFE!
YOU'RE THE JERK!! CHECK OUT THAT SHORT NECK!!
UMPH!
ONLY JERKS HAVE SHORT NECKS!!

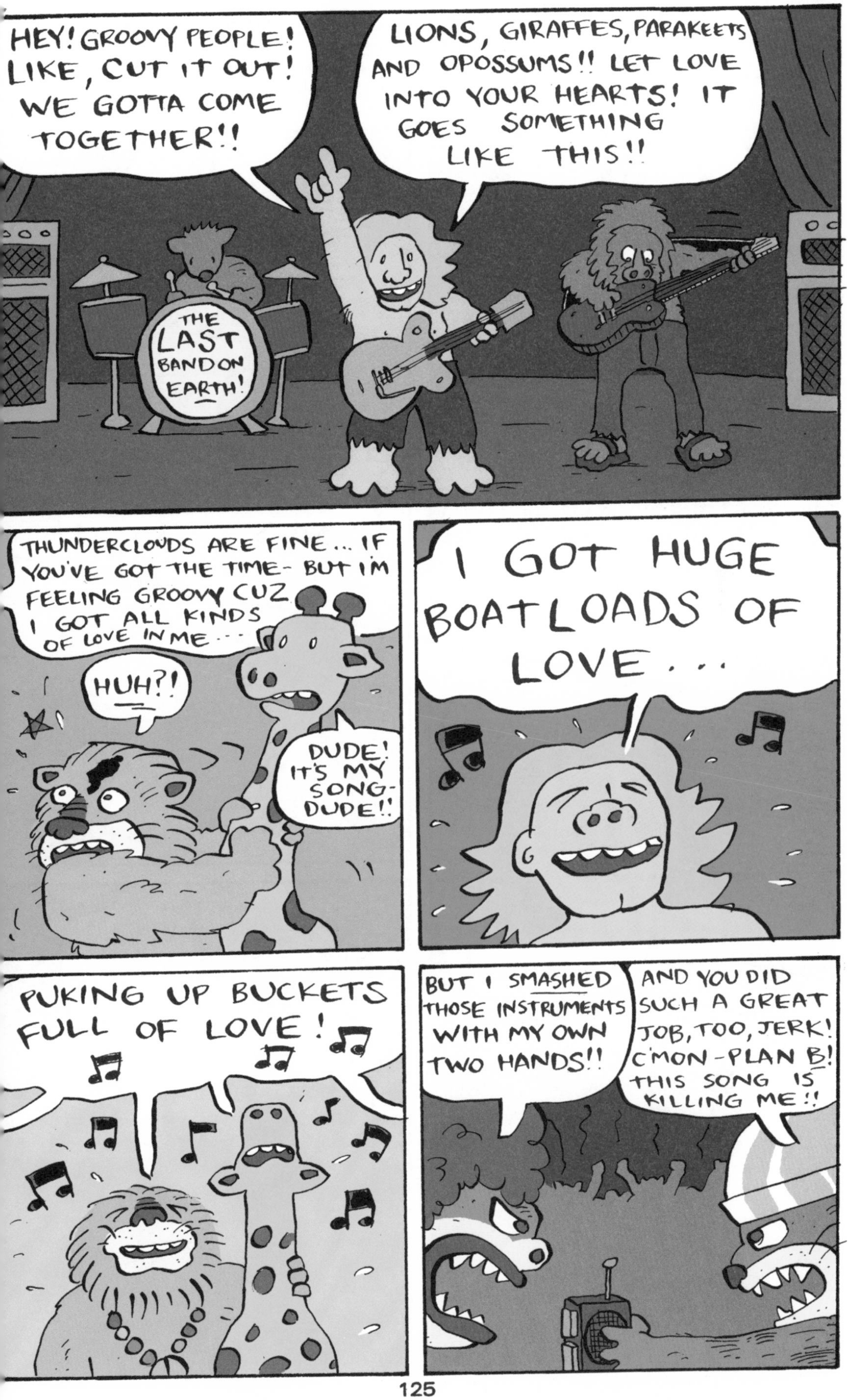
HEY! GROOVY PEOPLE! LIKE, CUT IT OUT! WE GOTTA COME TOGETHER!!
LIONS, GIRAFFES, PARAKEETS AND OPOSSUMS!! LET LOVE INTO YOUR HEARTS! IT GOES SOMETHING LIKE THIS!!
THE LAST BAND ON EARTH!
THUNDERCLOUDS ARE FINE... IF YOU'VE GOT THE TIME- BUT I'M FEELING GROOVY CUZ I GOT ALL KINDS OF LOVE IN ME...
HUH?!
DUDE! IT'S MY SONG- DUDE!!
I GOT HUGE BOATLOADS OF LOVE...
PUKING UP BUCKETS FULL OF LOVE!
BUT I SMASHED THOSE INSTRUMENTS WITH MY OWN TWO HANDS!!
AND YOU DID SUCH A GREAT JOB, TOO, JERK! C'MON-PLAN B! THIS SONG IS KILLING ME!!

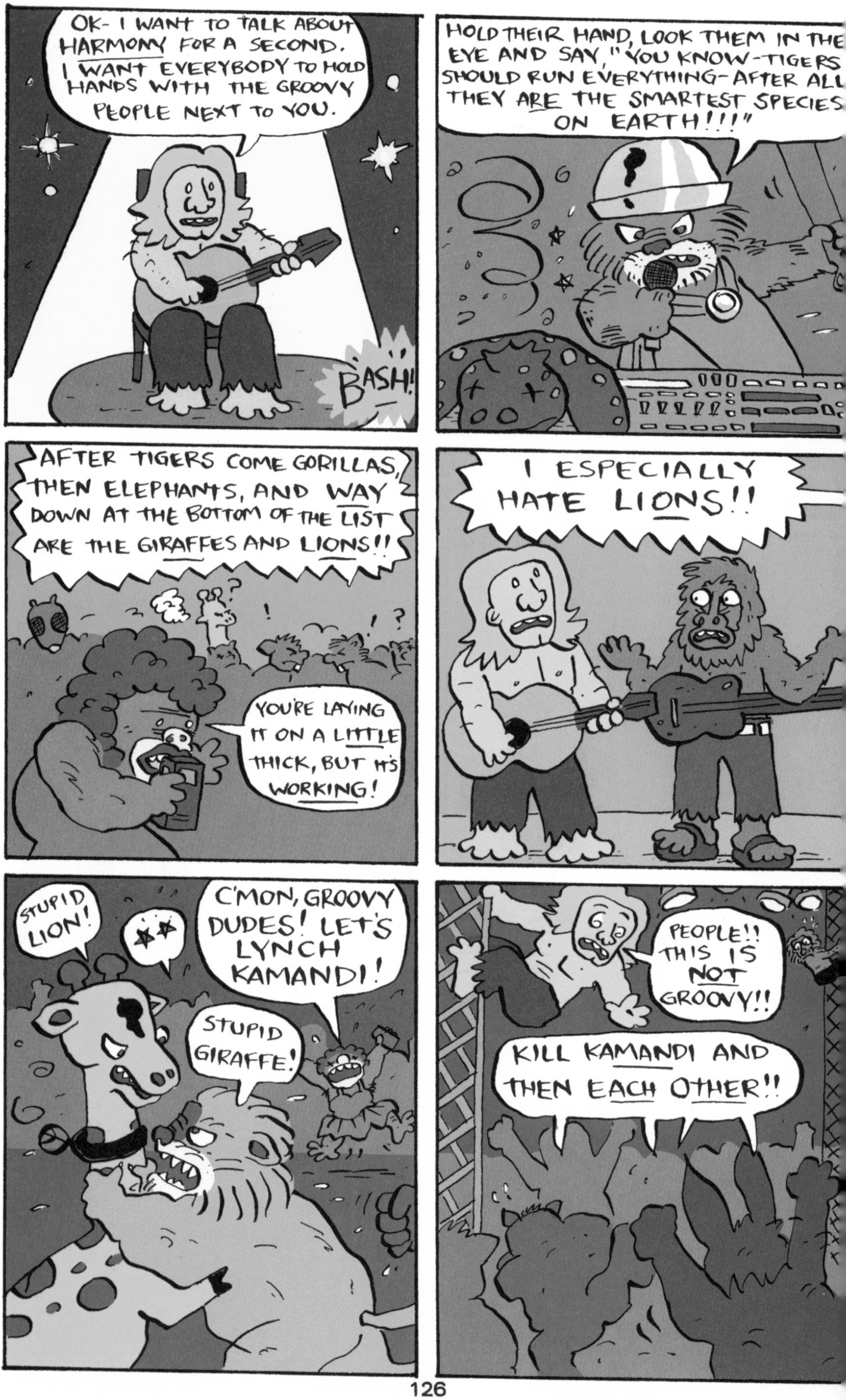
OK- I WANT TO TALK ABOUT HARMONY FOR A SECOND. I WANT EVERYBODY TO HOLD HANDS WITH THE GROOVY PEOPLE NEXT TO YOU.
BASH!
HOLD THEIR HAND, LOOK THEM IN THE EYE AND SAY, "YOU KNOW-TIGERS SHOULD RUN EVERYTHING-AFTER ALL THEY ARE THE SMARTEST SPECIES ON EARTH!!!"
AFTER TIGERS COME GORILLAS, THEN ELEPHANTS, AND WAY DOWN AT THE BOTTOM OF THE LIST ARE THE GIRAFFES AND LIONS!!
YOU'RE LAYING IT ON A LITTLE THICK, BUT IT'S WORKING!
I ESPECIALLY HATE LIONS!!
STUPID LION!
C'MON, GROOVY DUDES! LET'S LYNCH KAMANDI!
STUPID GIRAFFE!
PEOPLE!! THIS IS NOT GROOVY!!
KILL KAMANDI AND THEN EACH OTHER!!

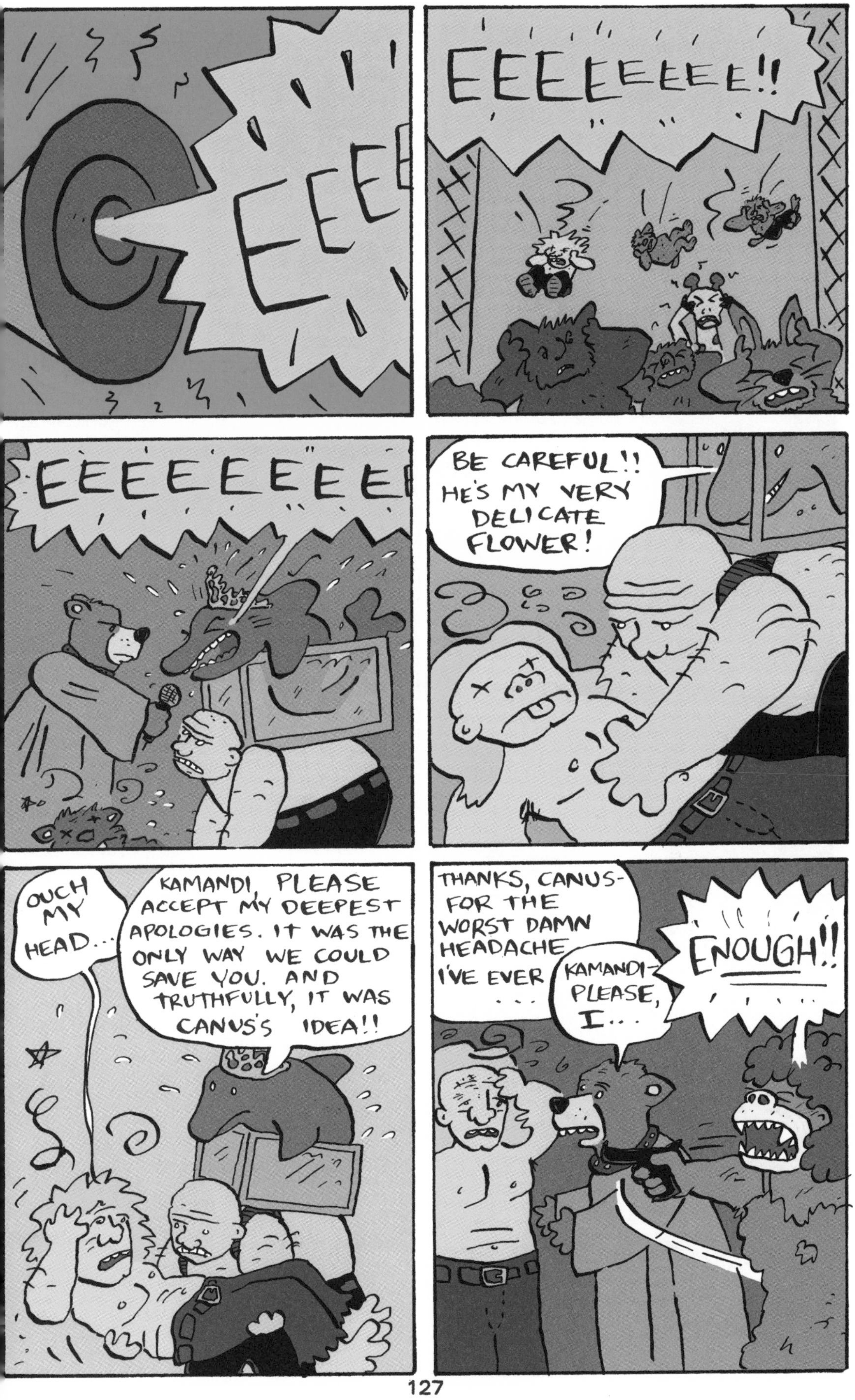
EEEE
EEEEEEEE!!
EEEEEEEEE
BE CAREFUL!! HE'S MY VERY DELICATE FLOWER!
OUCH MY HEAD...
KAMANDI, PLEASE ACCEPT MY DEEPEST APOLOGIES. IT WAS THE ONLY WAY WE COULD SAVE YOU. AND TRUTHFULLY, IT WAS CANUS'S IDEA!!
THANKS, CANUS- FOR THE WORST DAMN HEADACHE I'VE EVER . . .
KAMANDI- PLEASE, I...
ENOUGH!!

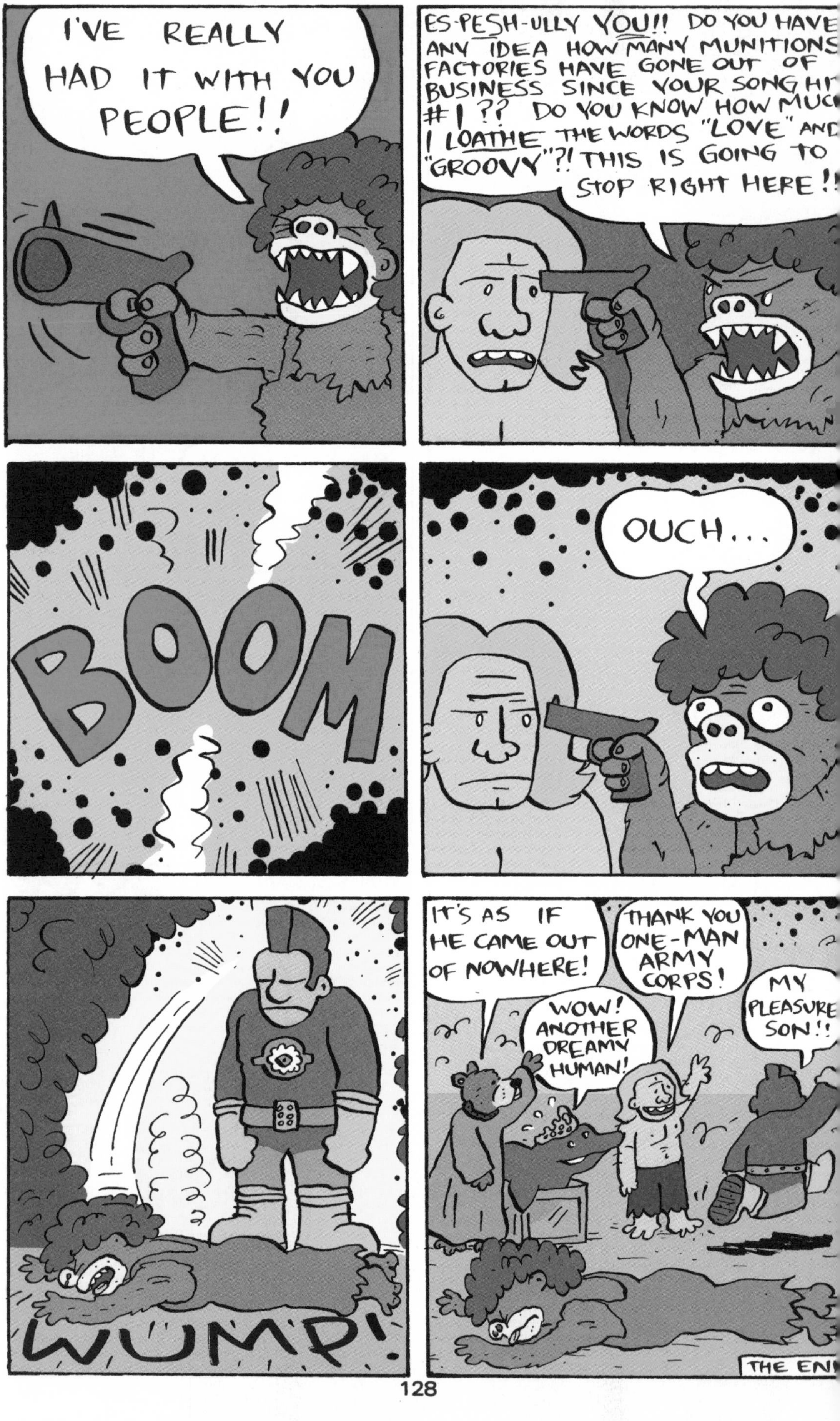
I'VE REALLY HAD IT WITH YOU PEOPLE!!
ES-PESH-ULLY YOU!! DO YOU HAVE ANY IDEA HOW MANY MUNITIONS FACTORIES HAVE GONE OUT OF BUSINESS SINCE YOUR SONG HI #1 ?? DO YOU KNOW HOW MUC I LOATHE THE WORDS "LOVE" AND "GROOVY"?! THIS IS GOING TO STOP RIGHT HERE!!
BOOM
OUCH...
WUMP!
IT'S AS IF HE CAME OUT OF NOWHERE!
WOW! ANOTHER DREAMY HUMAN!
THANK YOU ONE-MAN ARMY CORPS!
MY PLEASURE SON!!
THE EN

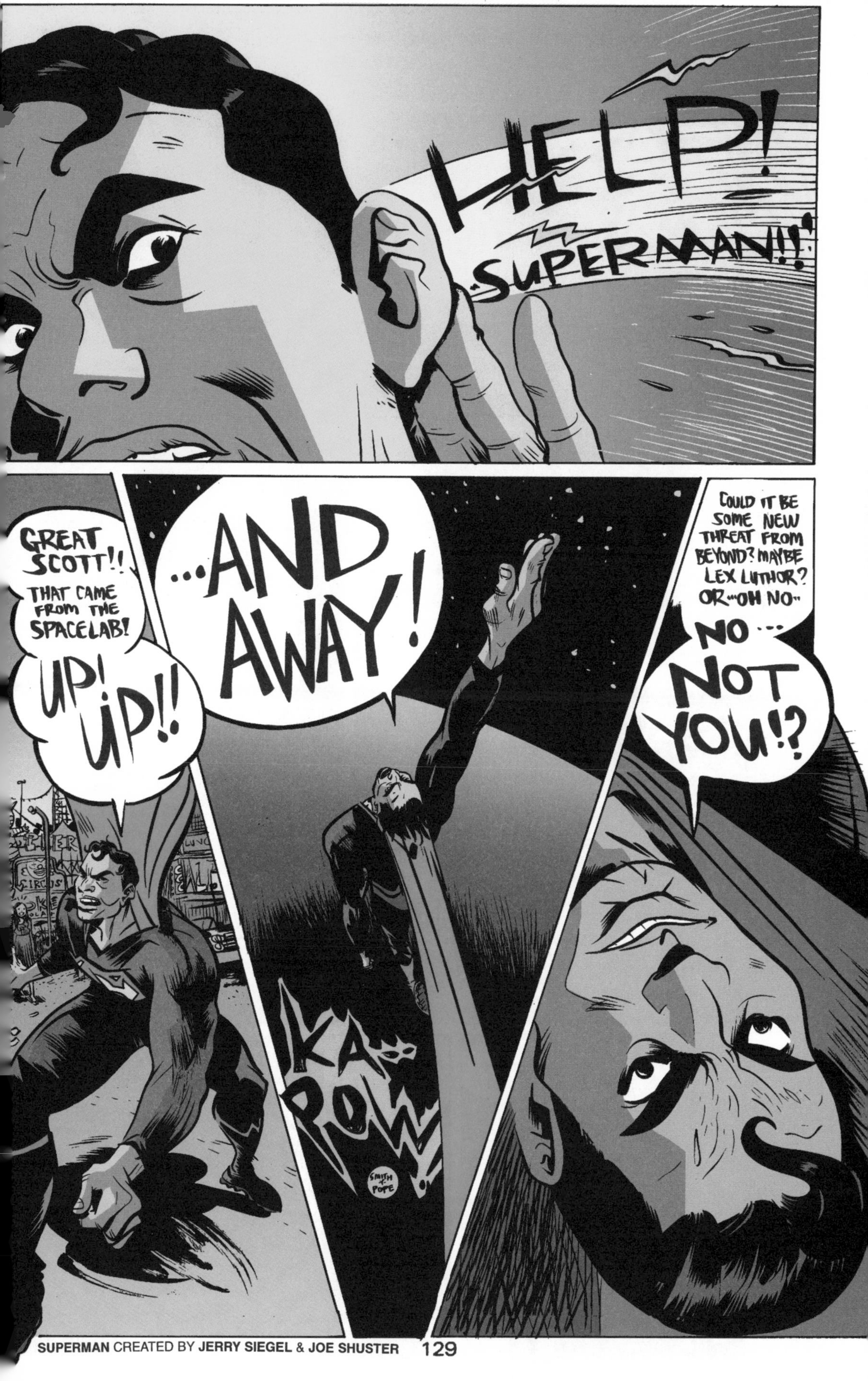
HELP! SUPERMAN!!
GREAT SCOTT!! THAT CAME FROM THE SPACELAB!
UP! UP!!
...AND AWAY!
KA-POW
COULD IT BE SOME NEW THREAT FROM BEYOND? MAYBE LEX LUTHOR? OR...OH NO...
NO... NOT YOU!?

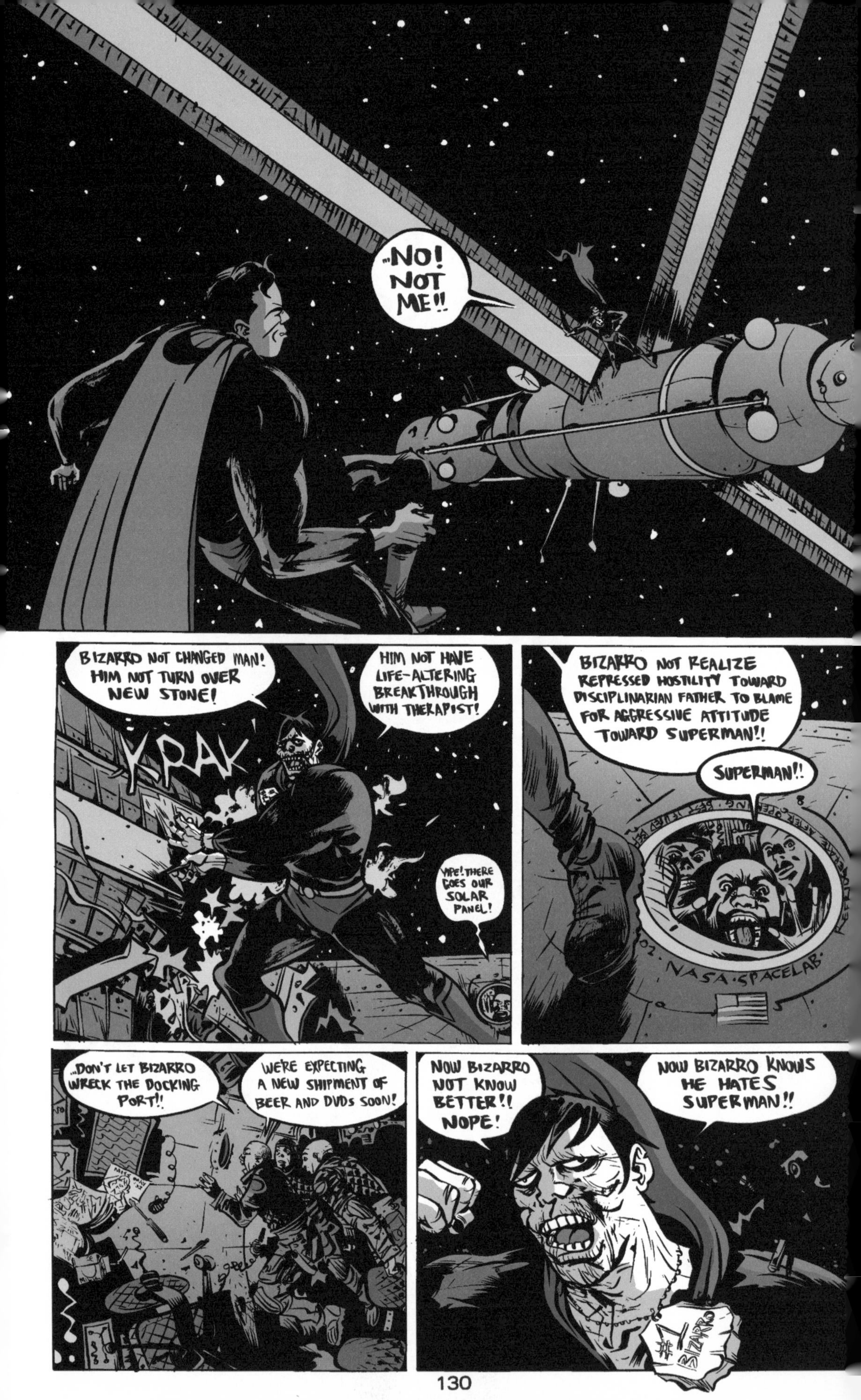

...NO! NOT ME!!
BIZARRO NOT CHANGED MAN! HIM NOT TURN OVER NEW STONE!
HIM NOT HAVE LIFE-ALTERING BREAKTHROUGH WITH THERAPIST!
KRAK
YIPE! THERE GOES OUR SOLAR PANEL!
BIZARRO NOT REALIZE REPRESSED HOSTILITY TOWARD DISCIPLINARIAN FATHER TO BLAME FOR AGGRESSIVE ATTITUDE TOWARD SUPERMAN!!
SUPERMAN!!
'02 NASA·SPACELAB
...DON'T LET BIZARRO WRECK THE DOCKING PORT!!
WE'RE EXPECTING A NEW SHIPMENT OF BEER AND DVDs SOON!
NOW BIZARRO NOT KNOW BETTER!! NOPE!
NOW BIZARRO KNOWS HE HATES SUPERMAN!!
#1 BIZARRO

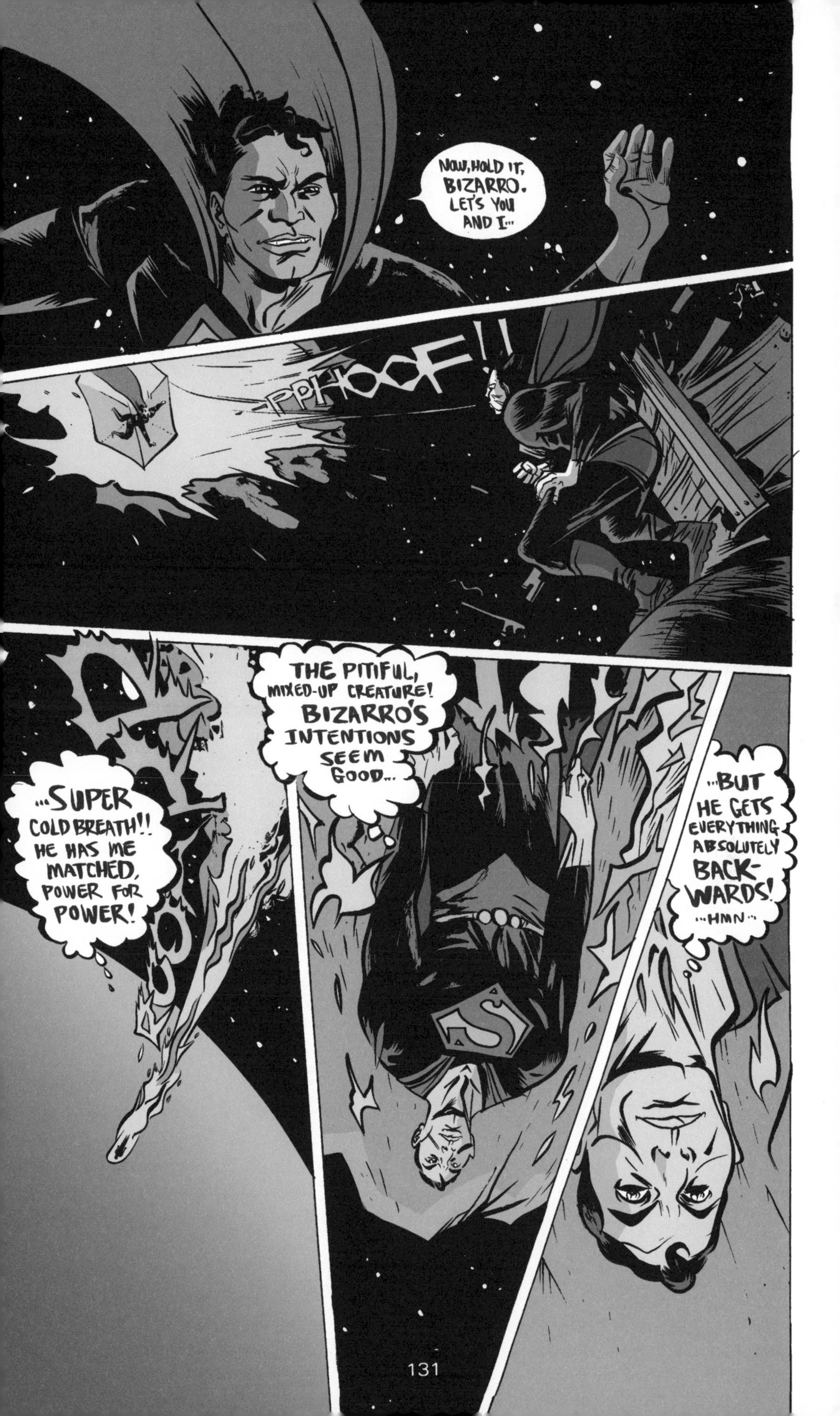
NOW, HOLD IT, BIZARRO. LET'S YOU AND I...
PPHOOF!!
THE PITIFUL, MIXED-UP CREATURE! BIZARRO'S INTENTIONS SEEM GOOD...
...SUPER COLD BREATH!! HE HAS ME MATCHED, POWER FOR POWER!
...BUT HE GETS EVERYTHING ABSOLUTELY BACK-WARDS! ...HMN...

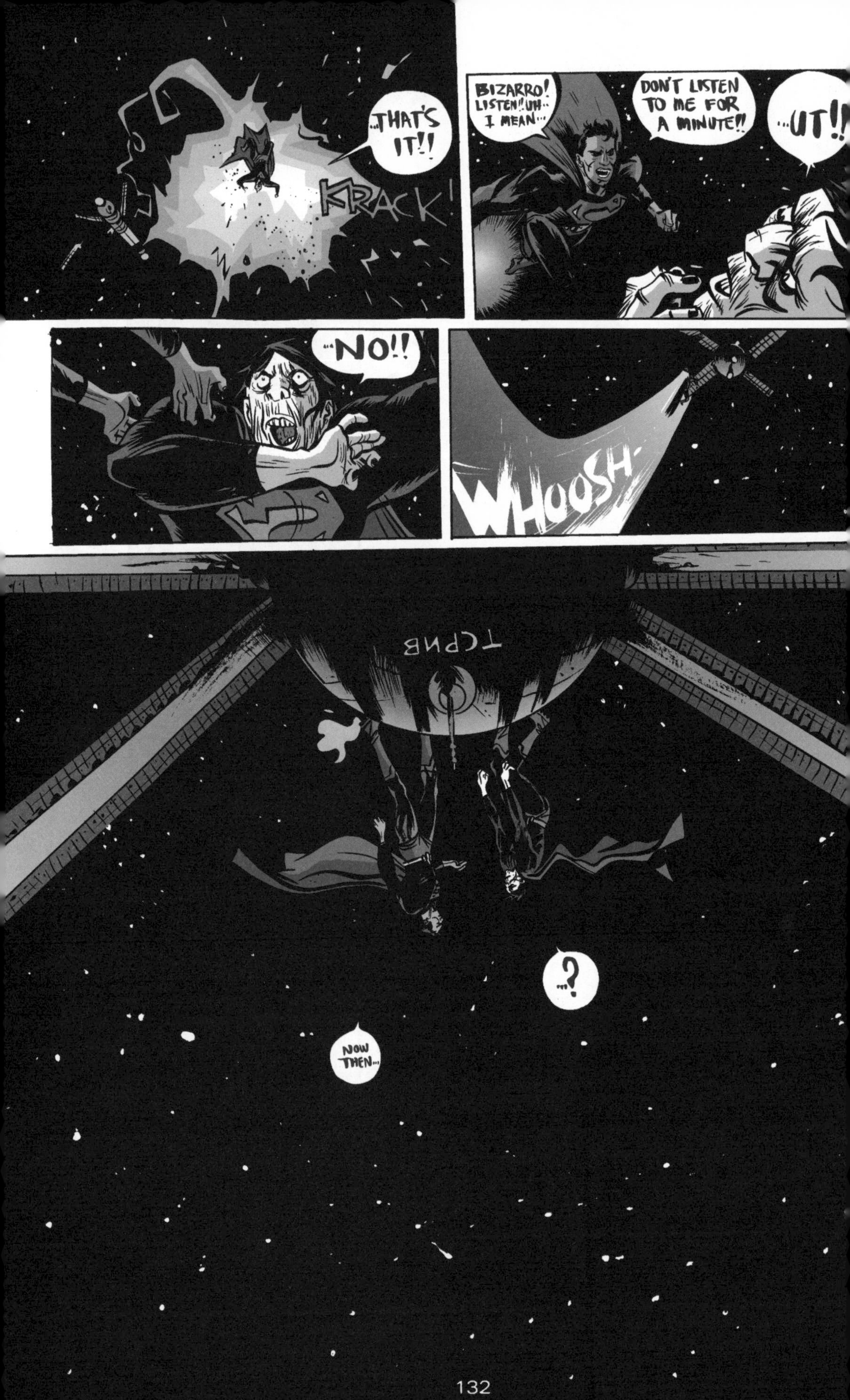
...THAT'S IT!!
KRACK!
BIZARRO! LISTEN!! UH... I MEAN...
DON'T LISTEN TO ME FOR A MINUTE!!
...UT!!
...NO!!
WHOOSH
...?
NOW THEN...

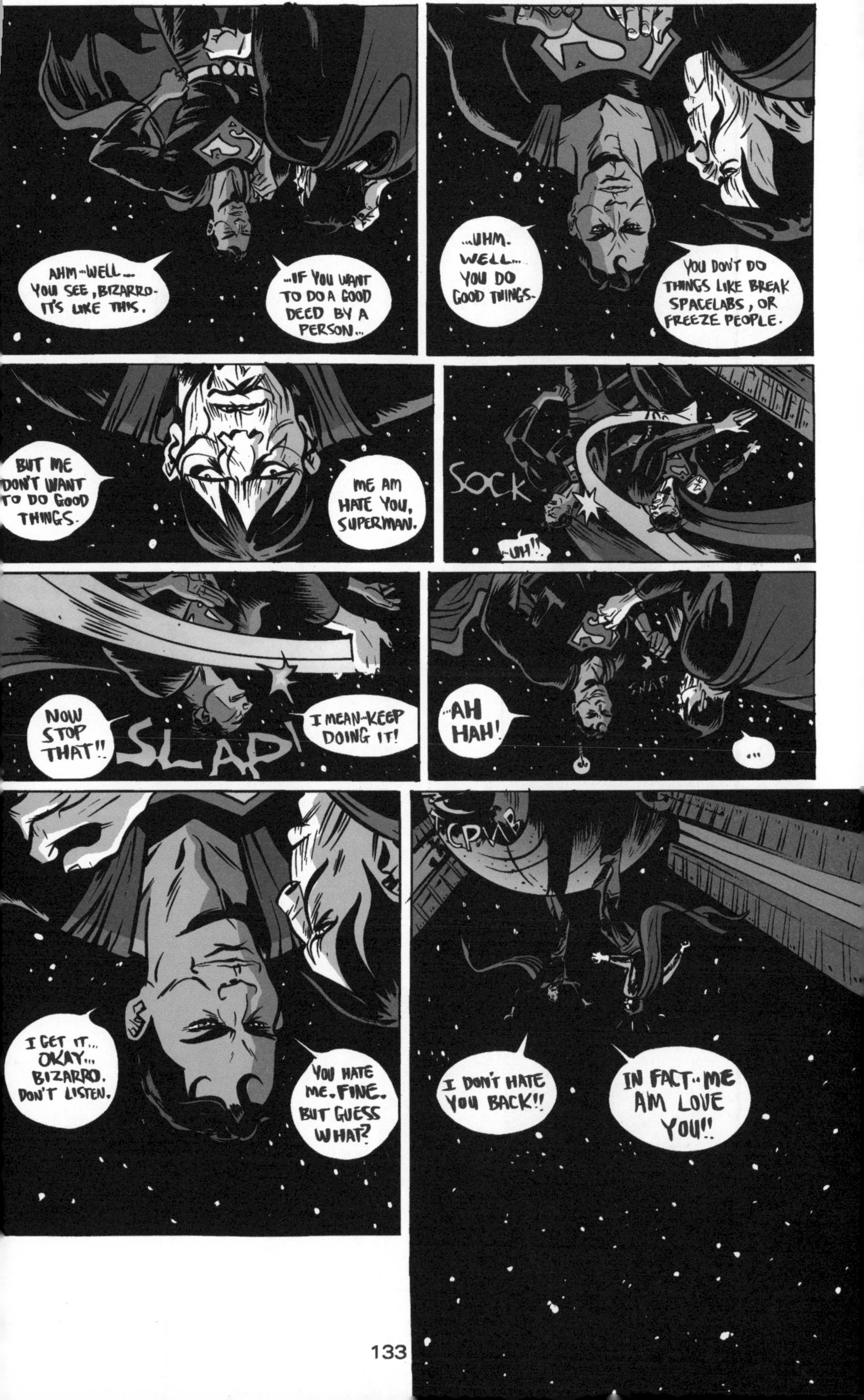
AHM--WELL...
YOU SEE, BIZARRO-
IT'S LIKE THIS.
...IF YOU WANT
TO DO A GOOD
DEED BY A
PERSON...
...UHM.
WELL...
YOU DO
GOOD THINGS.
YOU DON'T DO
THINGS LIKE BREAK
SPACELABS, OR
FREEZE PEOPLE.
BUT ME
DON'T WANT
TO DO GOOD
THINGS.
ME AM
HATE YOU,
SUPERMAN.
SOCK
UH!!
NOW
STOP
THAT!!
SLAP!
I MEAN--KEEP
DOING IT!
...AH
HAH!
...
I GET IT...
OKAY...
BIZARRO.
DON'T LISTEN.
YOU HATE
ME. FINE.
BUT GUESS
WHAT?
I DON'T HATE
YOU BACK!!
IN FACT.. ME
AM LOVE
YOU!!

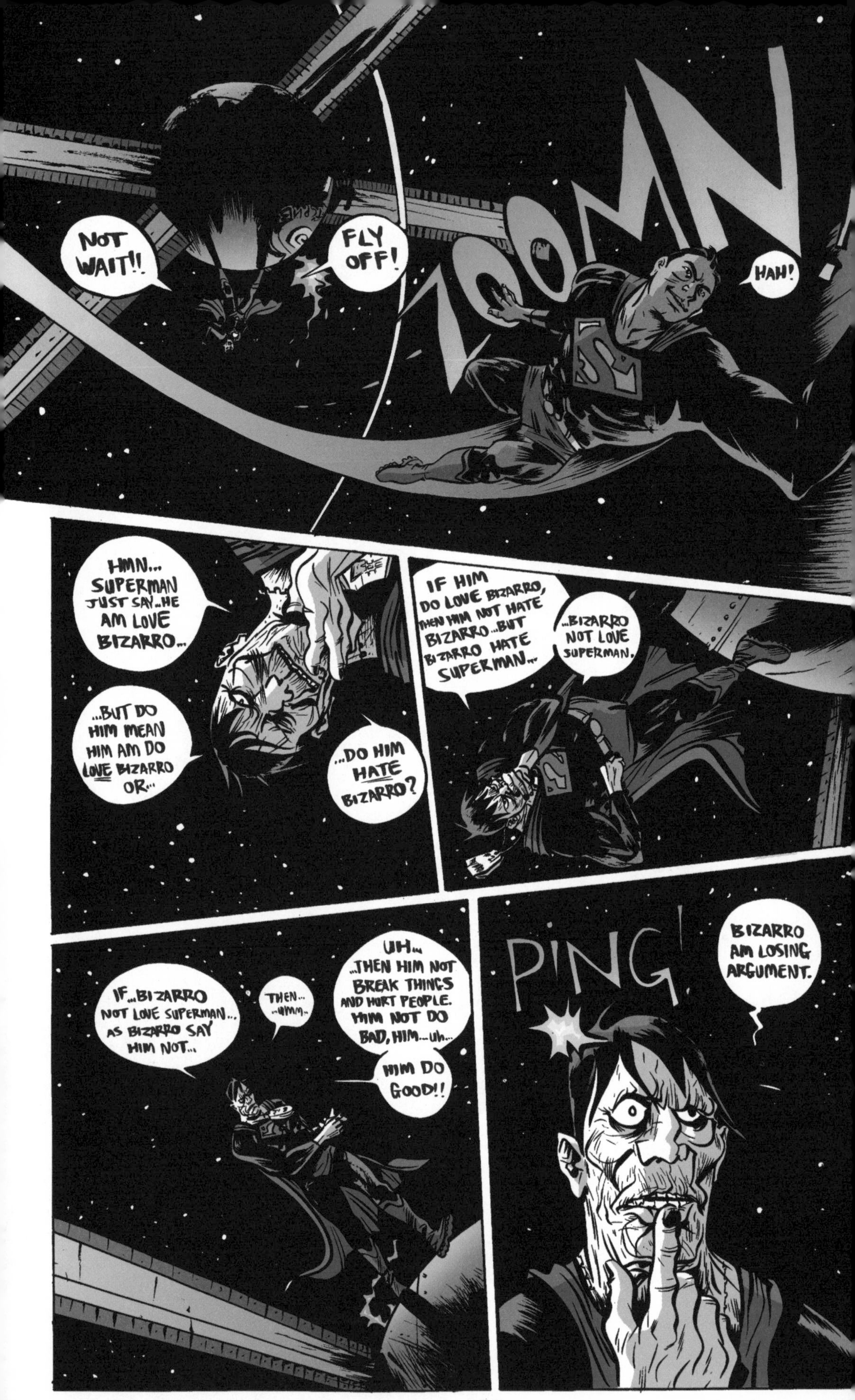
NOT WAIT!!
FLY OFF!
ZOOMN
HAH!
HMN... SUPERMAN JUST SAY...HE AM LOVE BIZARRO...
...BUT DO HIM MEAN HIM AM DO LOVE BIZARRO OR...
...DO HIM HATE BIZARRO?
IF HIM DO LOVE BIZARRO, THEN HIM NOT HATE BIZARRO...BUT BIZARRO HATE SUPERMAN...
...BIZARRO NOT LOVE SUPERMAN.
IF...BIZARRO NOT LOVE SUPERMAN... AS BIZARRO SAY HIM NOT...
THEN... ...UMM...
UH... ...THEN HIM NOT BREAK THINGS AND HURT PEOPLE. HIM NOT DO BAD, HIM...UH...
HIM DO GOOD!!
PING!
BIZARRO AM LOSING ARGUMENT.

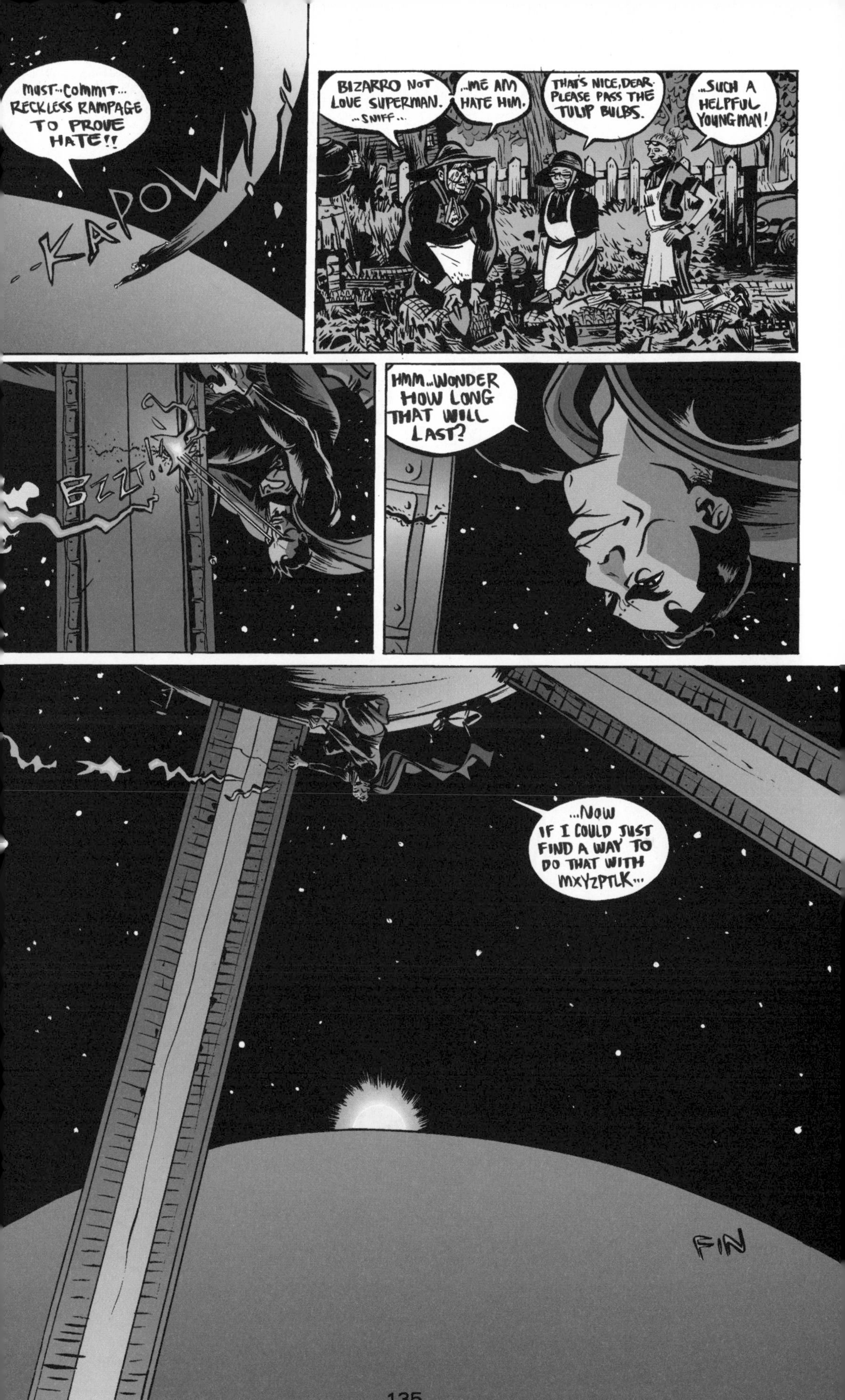
MUST...COMMIT... RECKLESS RAMPAGE TO PROVE HATE!!
KA-POW!!
BIZARRO NOT LOVE SUPERMAN. ...SNIFF...
...ME AM HATE HIM.
THAT'S NICE, DEAR. PLEASE PASS THE TULIP BULBS.
...SUCH A HELPFUL YOUNG MAN!
BZZT!
HMM...WONDER HOW LONG THAT WILL LAST?
...NOW IF I COULD JUST FIND A WAY TO DO THAT WITH MXYZPTLK...
FIN

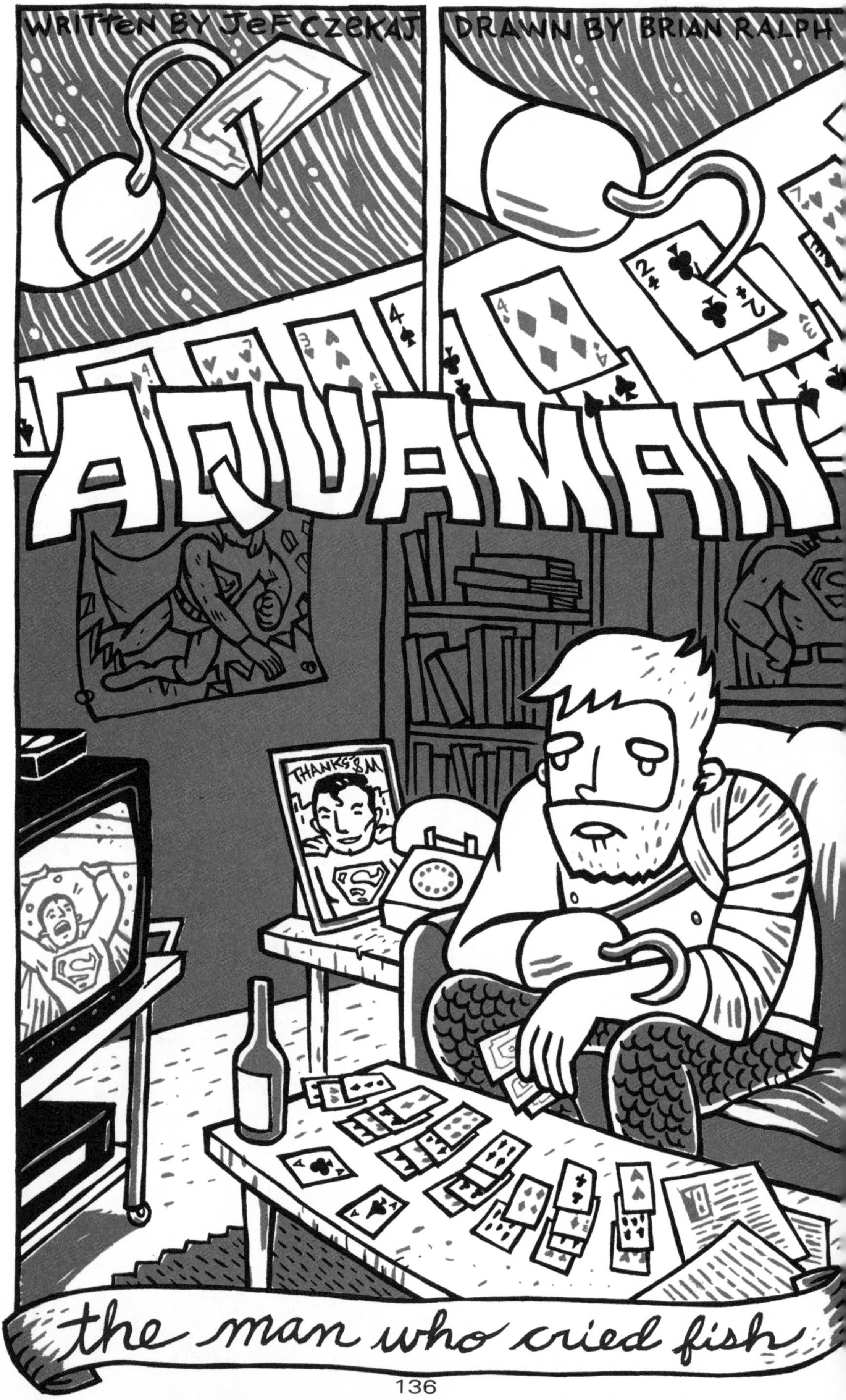
WRITTEN BY JEF CZEKAJ
DRAWN BY BRIAN RALPH
AQUAMAN
THANKS SM
the man who cried fish

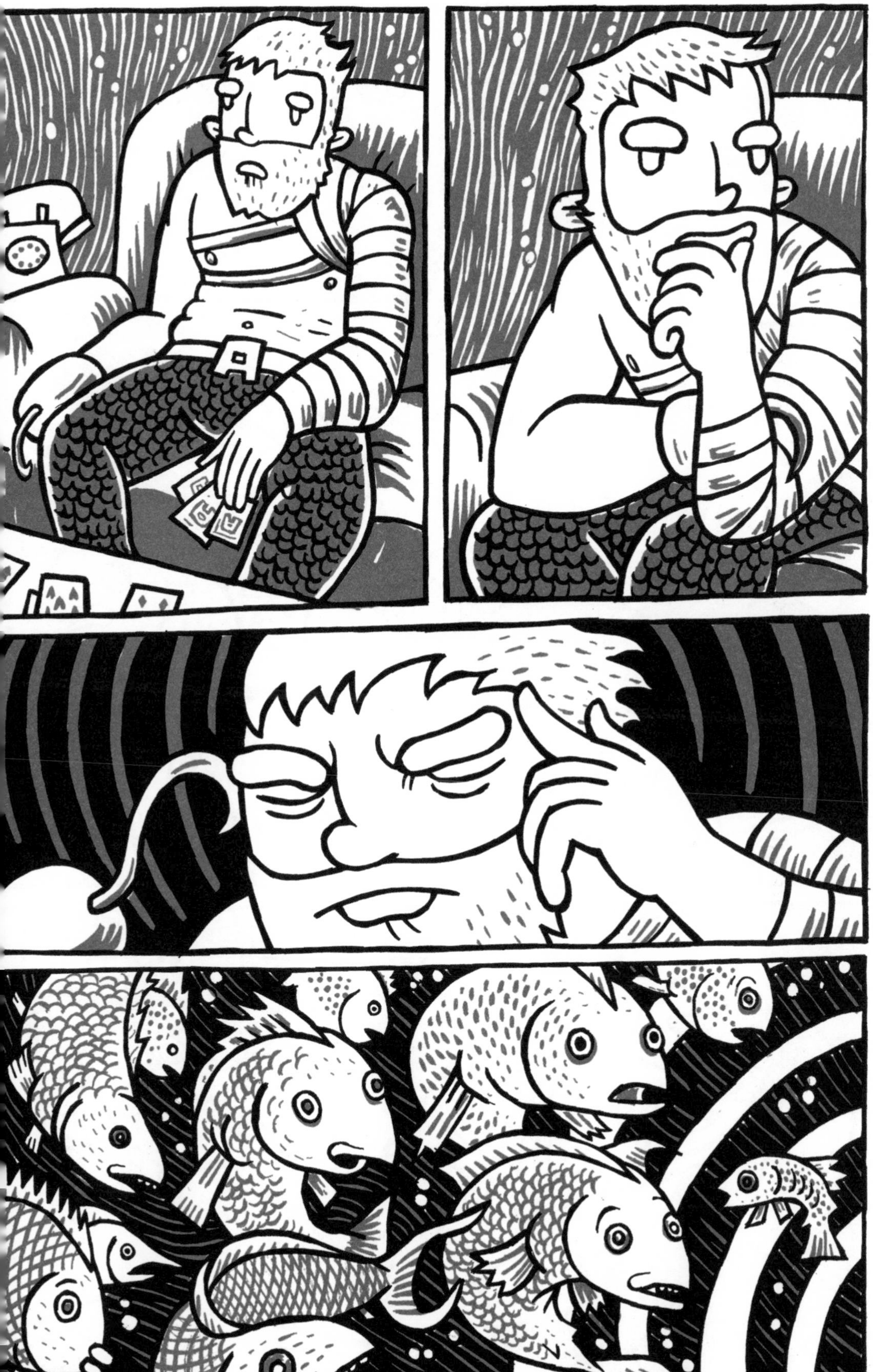

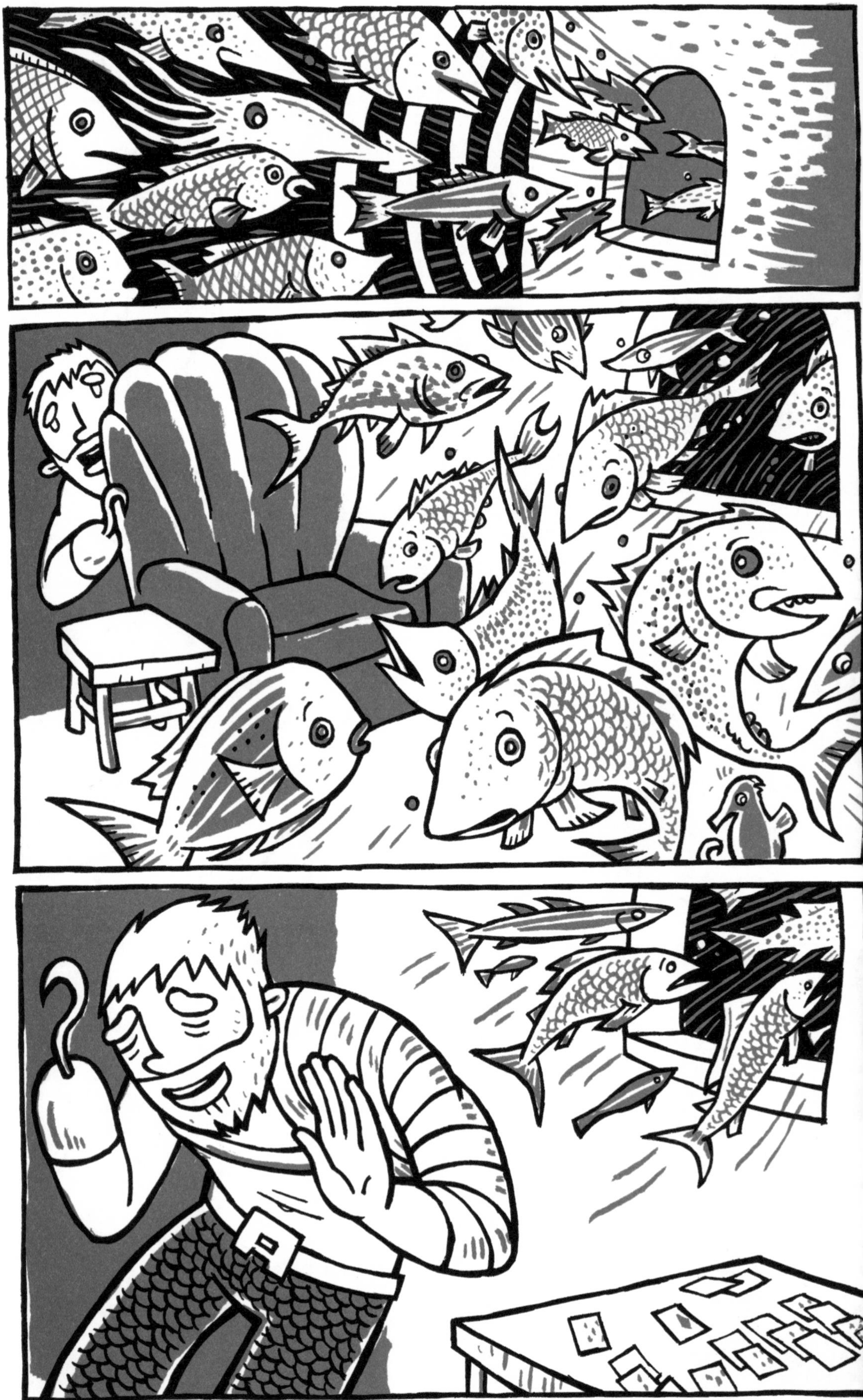

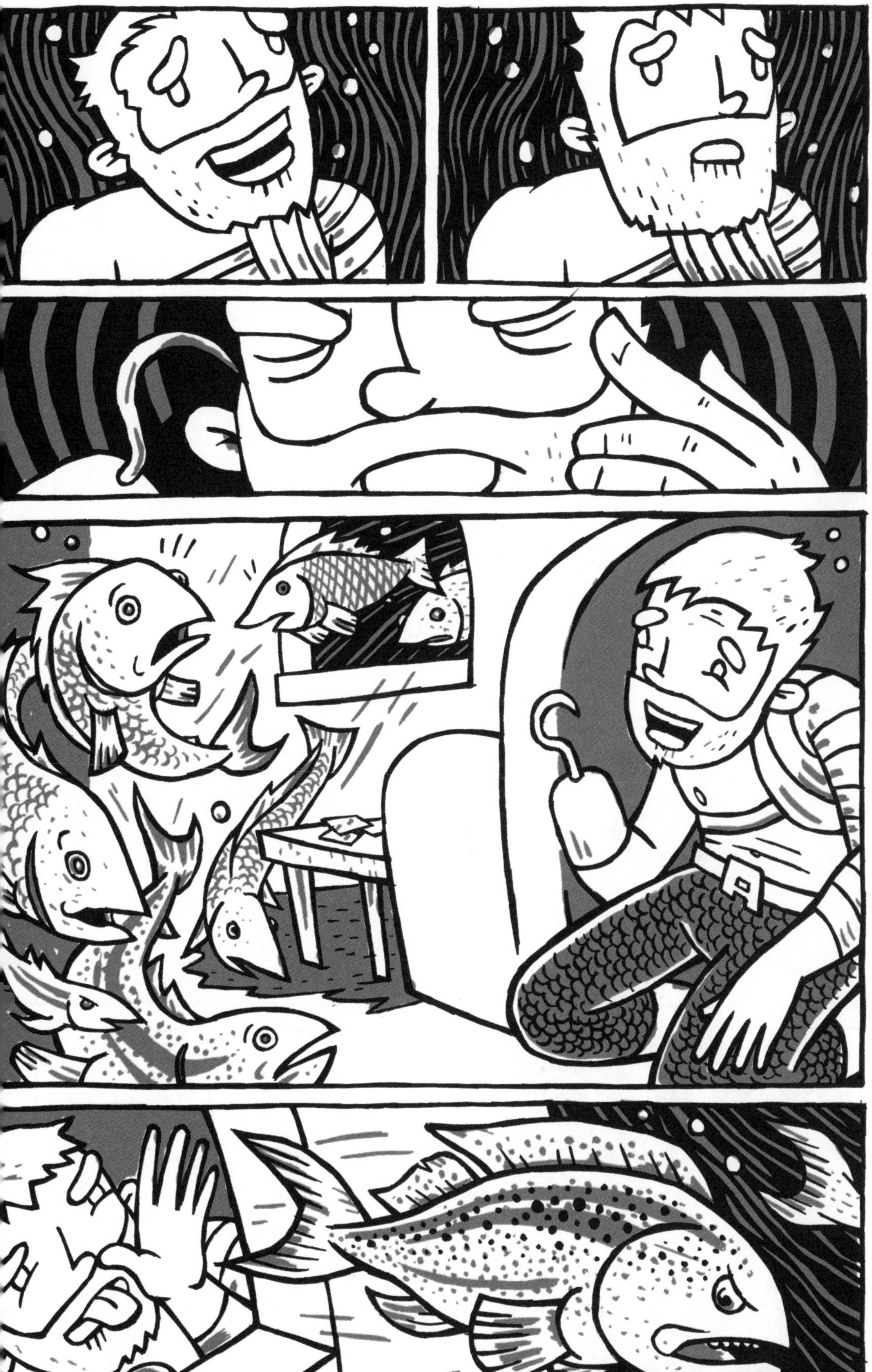

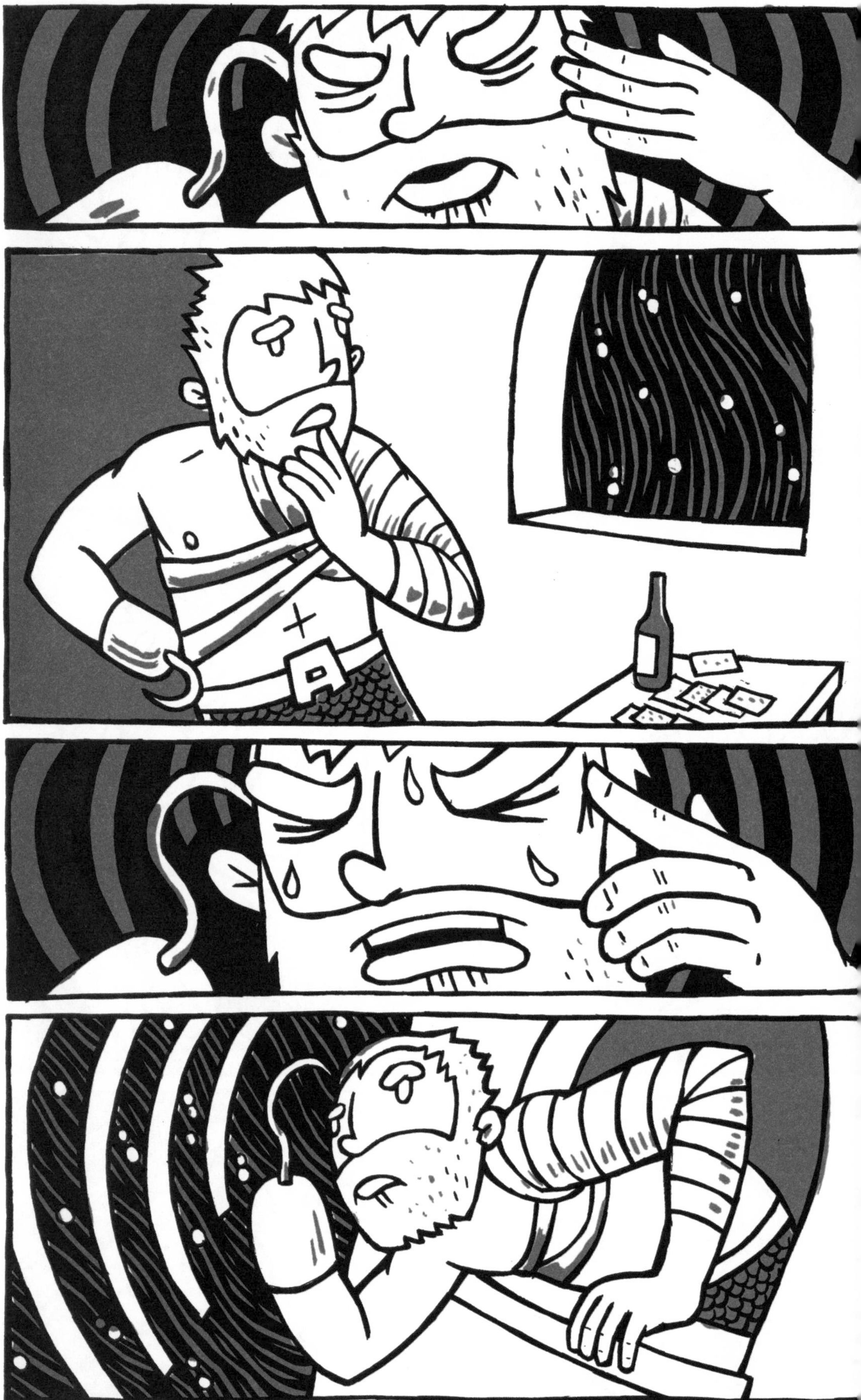

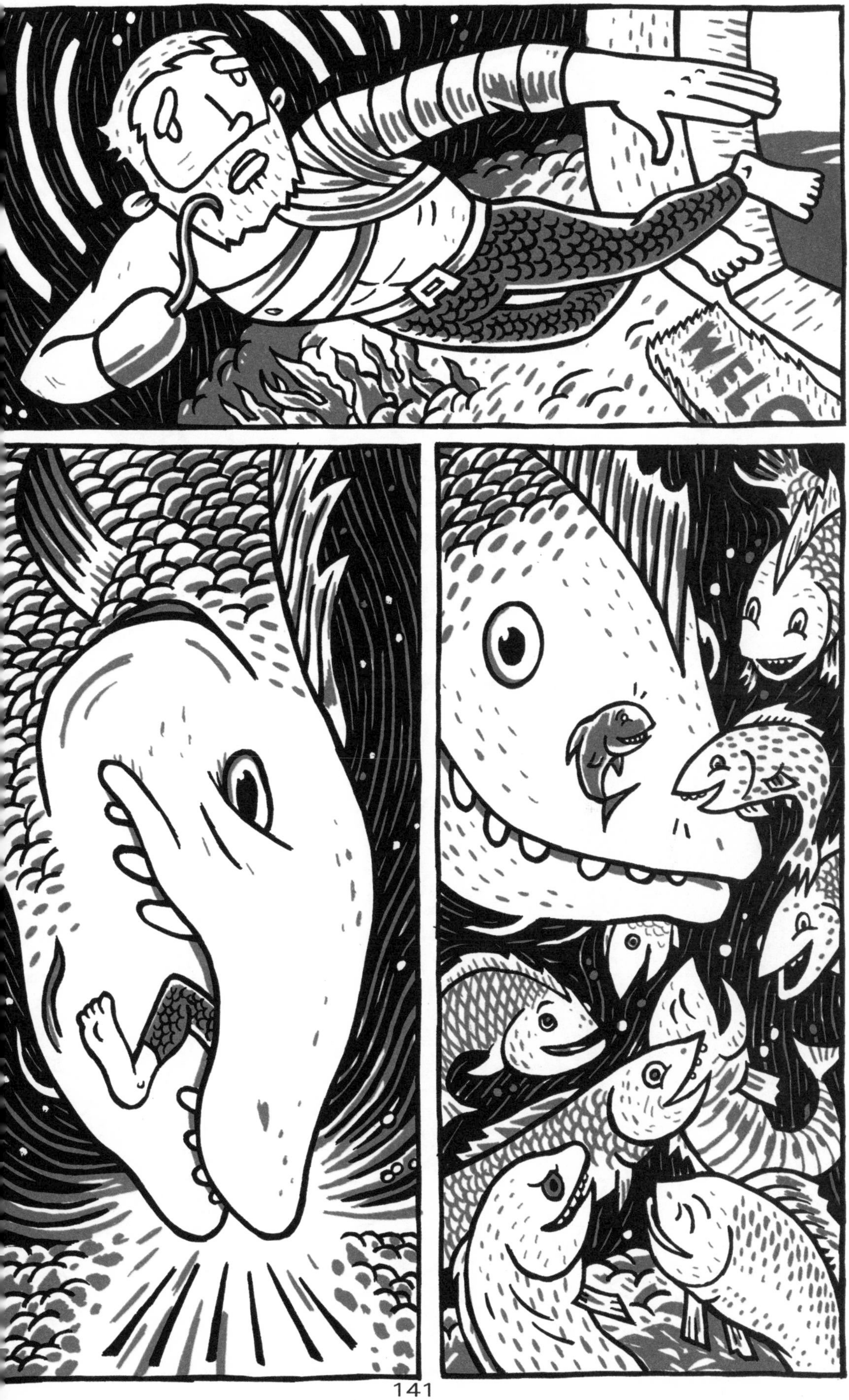
WEL

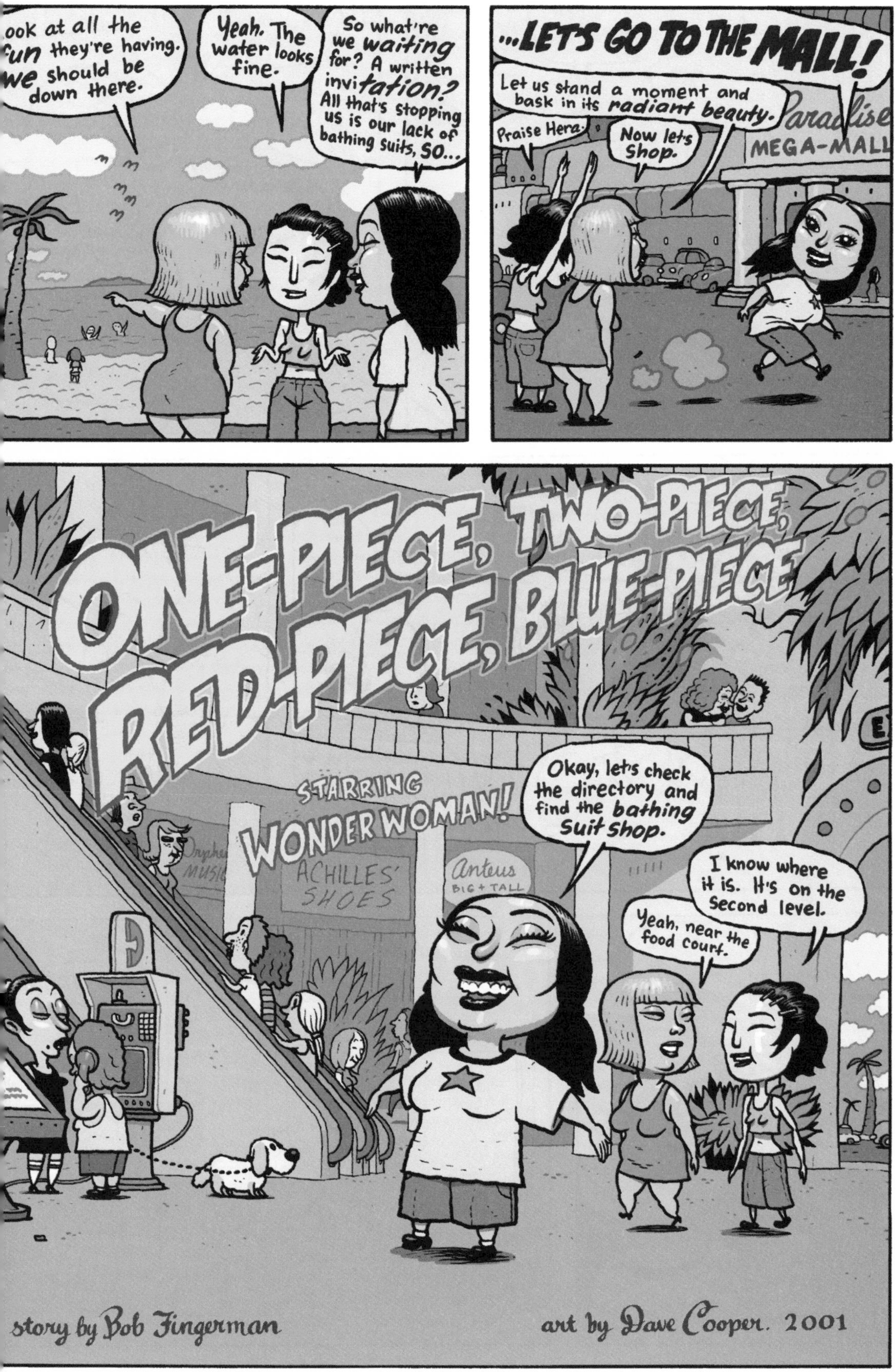

ook at all the fun they're having. we should be down there.
Yeah. The water looks fine.
So what're we waiting for? A written invitation? All that's stopping us is our lack of bathing suits, SO...
...LET'S GO TO THE MALL!
Let us stand a moment and bask in its radiant beauty.
Praise Hera.
Now let's Shop.
Paradise MEGA-MALL
ONE-PIECE, TWO-PIECE, RED-PIECE, BLUE-PIECE
STARRING WONDER WOMAN!
ACHILLES' SHOES
Anteus BIG + TALL
Okay, let's check the directory and find the bathing suit shop.
I know where it is. It's on the second level.
Yeah, near the food court.
story by Bob Fingerman
art by Dave Cooper. 2001

WONDER WOMAN created by William Moulton Marston

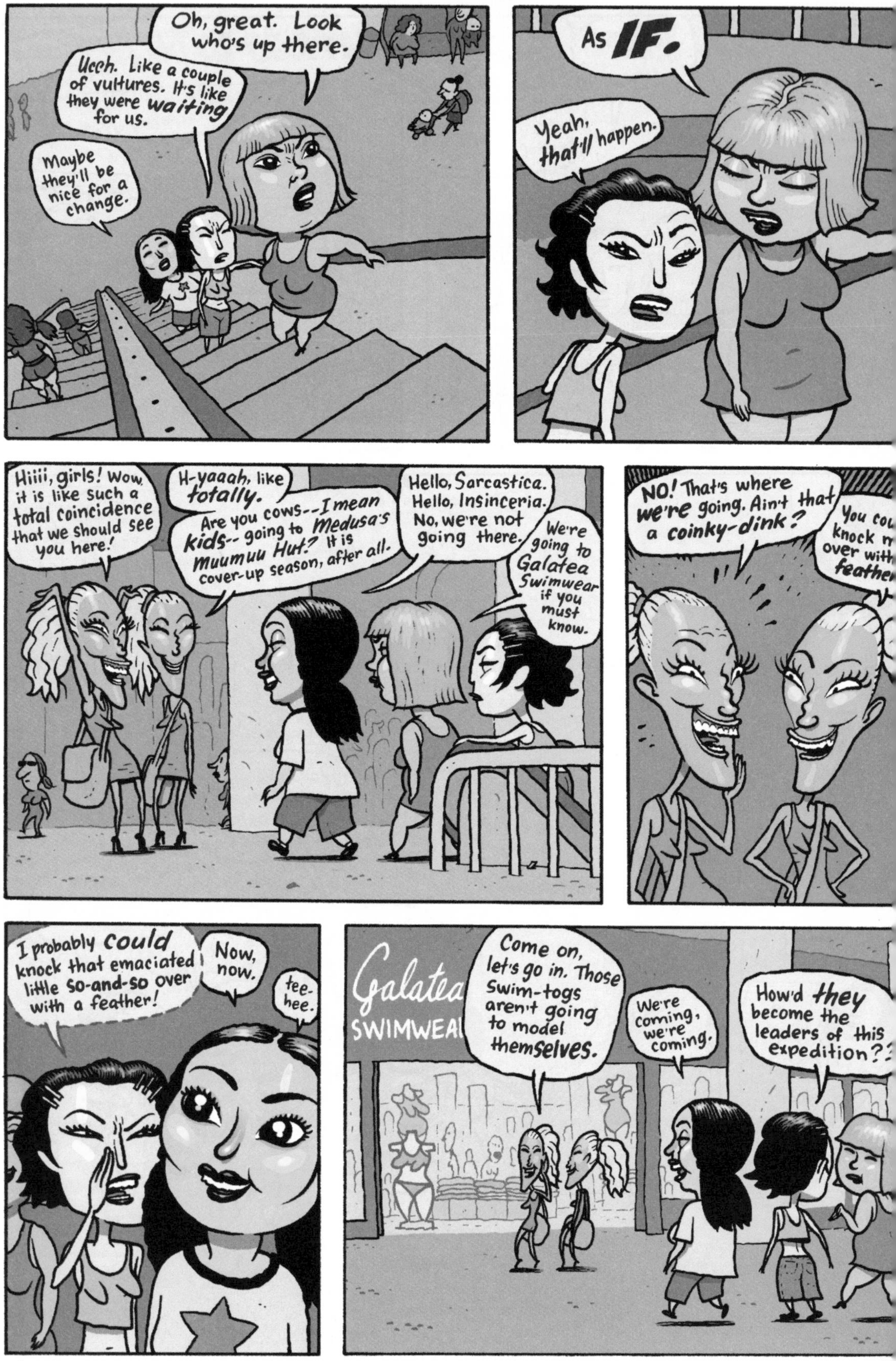

Oh, great. Look who's up there.
Ucch. Like a couple of vultures. It's like they were *waiting* for us.
Maybe they'll be nice for a change.
As **IF.**
Yeah, *that'll* happen.
Hiiii, girls! Wow, it is like such a total coincidence that we should see you here!
H-yaaah, like *totally*.
Are you cows--*I mean kids*-- going to *Medusa's Muumuu Hut?* It is cover-up season, after all.
Hello, Sarcastica. Hello, Insinceria. No, we're not going there.
We're going to Galatea Swimwear if you must know.
NO! That's where **we're** going. Ain't that a **coinky-dink?**
You cou
knock m
over with
feathe
I probably **could** knock that emaciated little so-and-so over with a feather!
Now, now.
tee-hee.
Galatea
SWIMWEA
Come on, let's go in. Those swim-togs aren't going to model themselves.
We're coming, we're coming.
How'd *they* become the leaders of this expedition?

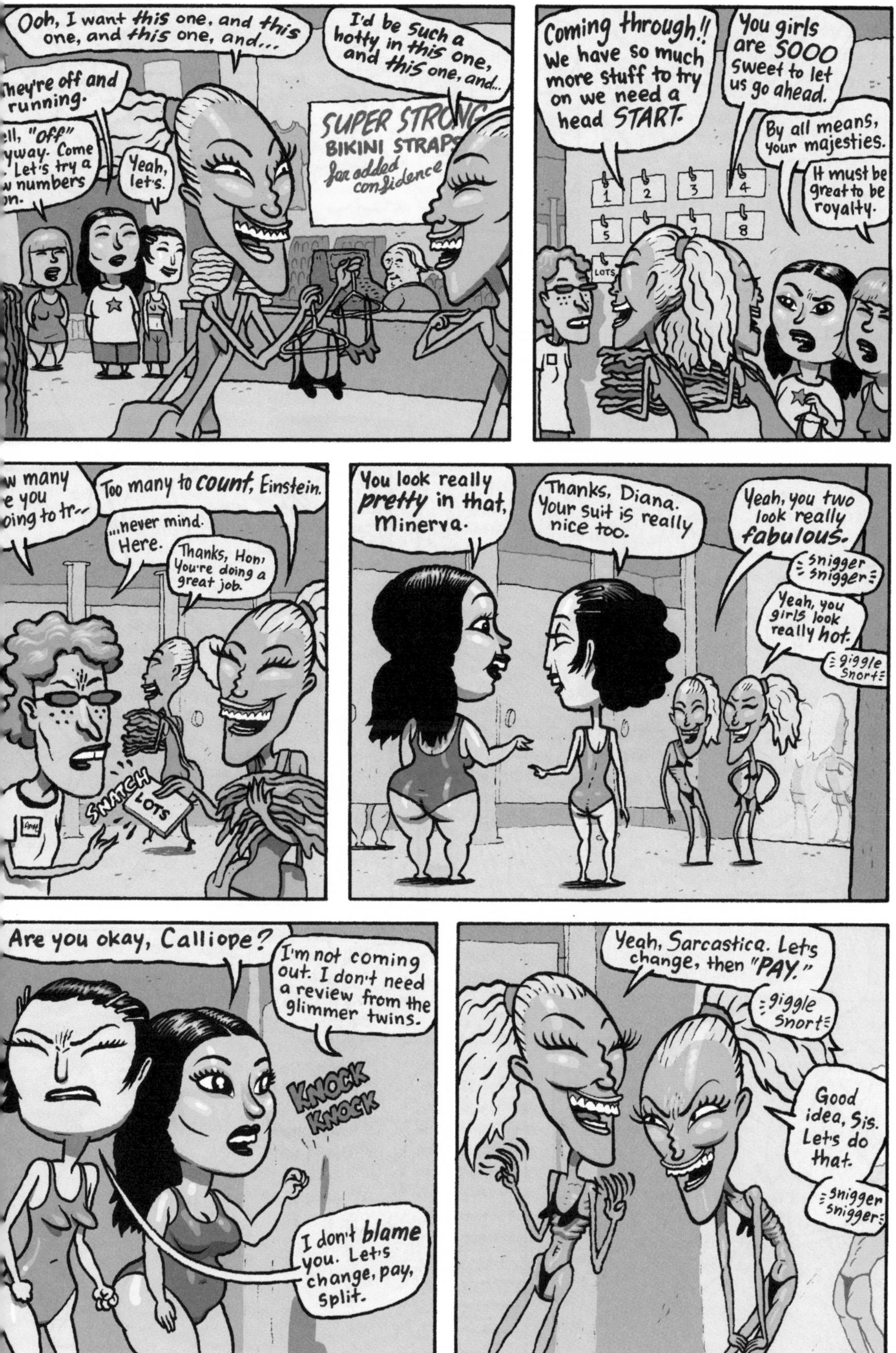
Ooh, I want this one, and this one, and this one, and...
I'd be such a hotty in this one, and this one, and...
hey're off and running.
ll, "off" yway. Come Let's try a w numbers n.
Yeah, let's.
SUPER STRON
BIKINI STRAPS
for added confidence
Coming through!! We have so much more stuff to try on we need a head START.
You girls are SOOO sweet to let us go ahead.
By all means, your majesties.
It must be great to be royalty.
1
2
3
4
5
7
8
LOTS
w many e you oing to tr--
Too many to count, Einstein.
...never mind. Here.
Thanks, Hon. You're doing a great job.
SNATCH
LOTS
You look really pretty in that, Minerva.
Thanks, Diana. Your suit is really nice too.
Yeah, you two look really fabulous.
snigger snigger
Yeah, you girls look really hot.
giggle Snort
Are you okay, Calliope?
I'm not coming out. I don't need a review from the glimmer twins.
KNOCK KNOCK
I don't blame you. Let's change, pay, split.
Yeah, Sarcastica. Let's change, then "PAY."
giggle Snort
Good idea, Sis. Let's do that.
snigger snigger

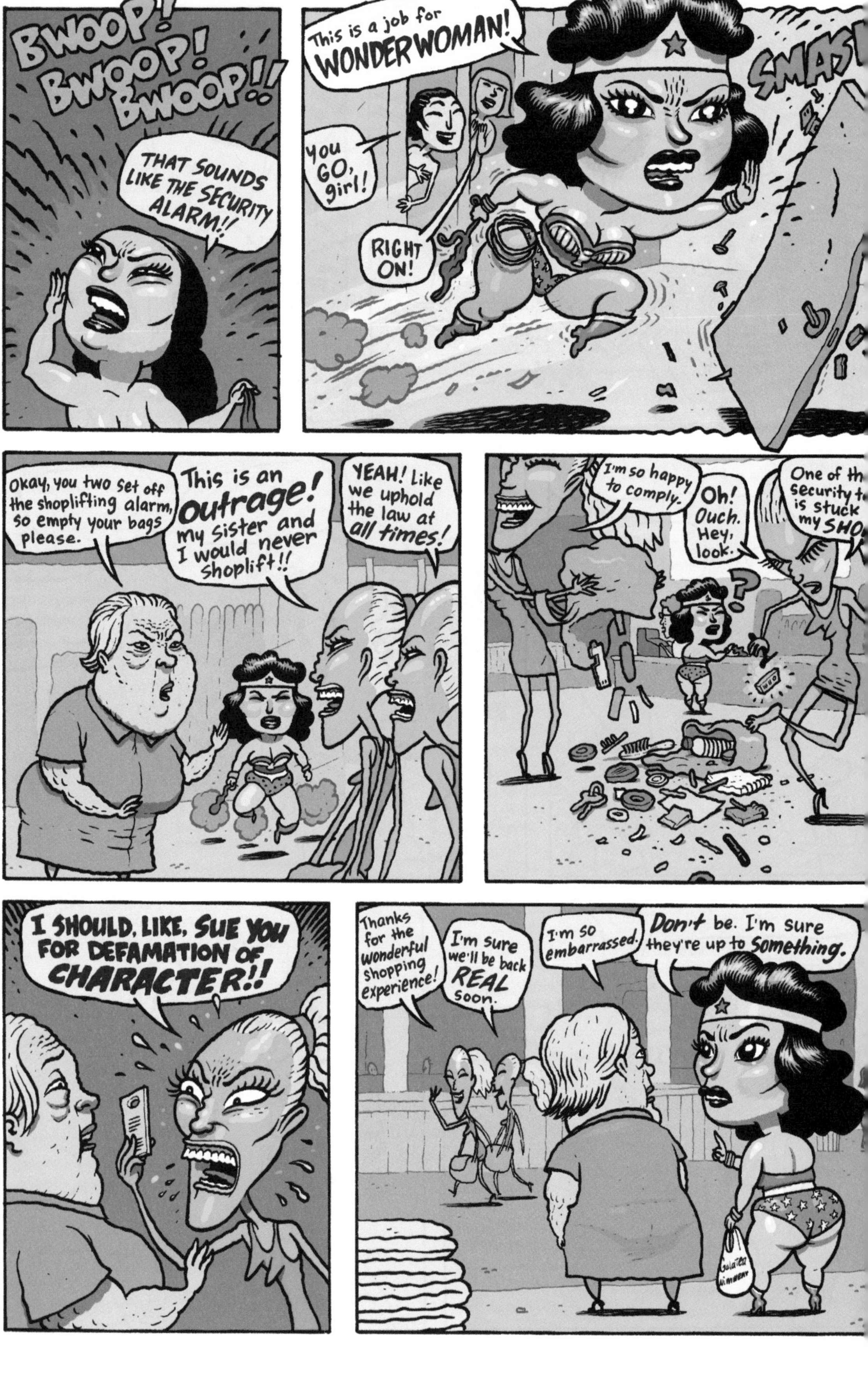

BWOOP! BWOOP! BWOOP!!
THAT SOUNDS LIKE THE SECURITY ALARM!!
This is a job for WONDERWOMAN!
YOU GO, girl!
RIGHT ON!
SMAS
Okay, you two set off the shoplifting alarm, so empty your bags please.
This is an outrage! my sister and I would never shoplift!!
YEAH! Like we uphold the law at all times!
I'm so happy to comply.
Oh! Ouch. Hey, look.
One of th security t is stuck my SHO
?
I SHOULD, LIKE, SUE YOU FOR DEFAMATION OF CHARACTER!!
Thanks for the wonderful shopping experience!
I'm sure we'll be back REAL soon.
I'm so embarrassed.
Don't be. I'm sure they're up to Something.

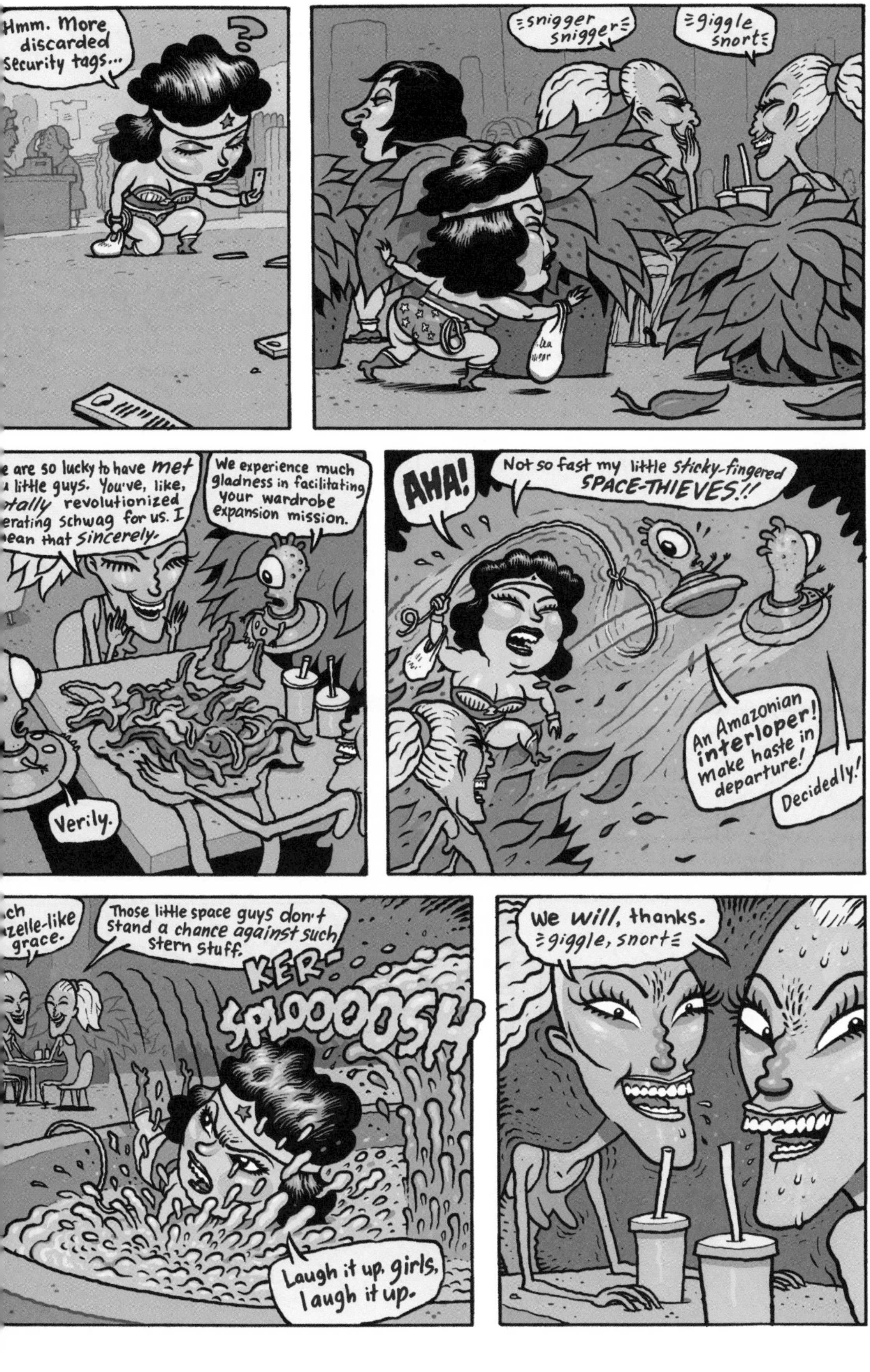
Hmm. More discarded security tags...
snigger snigger
giggle snort
e are so lucky to have met
a little guys. You've, like,
otally revolutionized
erating schwag for us. I
ean that sincerely.
We experience much gladness in facilitating your wardrobe expansion mission.
Verily.
AHA!
Not so fast my little sticky-fingered SPACE-THIEVES!!
An Amazonian interloper! Make haste in departure!
Decidedly!
ch
zelle-like
grace.
Those little space guys don't stand a chance against such stern stuff.
KER-SPLOOOOSH
Laugh it up, girls, laugh it up.
We will, thanks.
giggle, snort

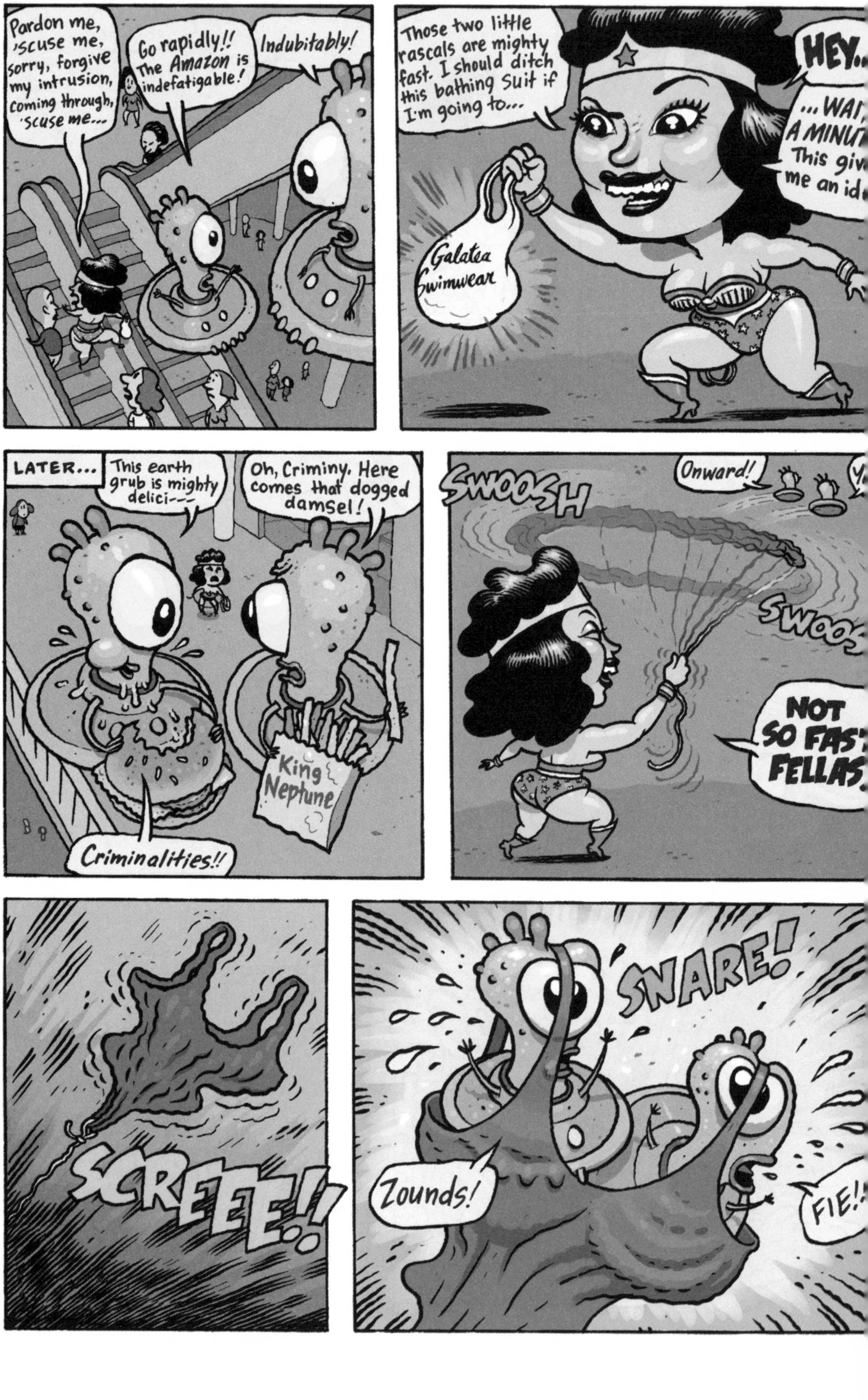

Pardon me, 'scuse me, sorry, forgive my intrusion, coming through, 'scuse me...
Go rapidly!! The Amazon is indefatigable!
Indubitably!
Those two little rascals are mighty fast. I should ditch this bathing suit if I'm going to...
HEY...
...WAI A MINU This giv me an id
Galatea Swimwear
LATER...
This earth grub is mighty delici---
Oh, Criminy. Here comes that dogged damsel!
King Neptune
Criminalities!!
SWOOSH
Onward!!
SWOOS
NOT SO FAS FELLAS
SCREEE!!
SNARE!
Zounds!
FIE!

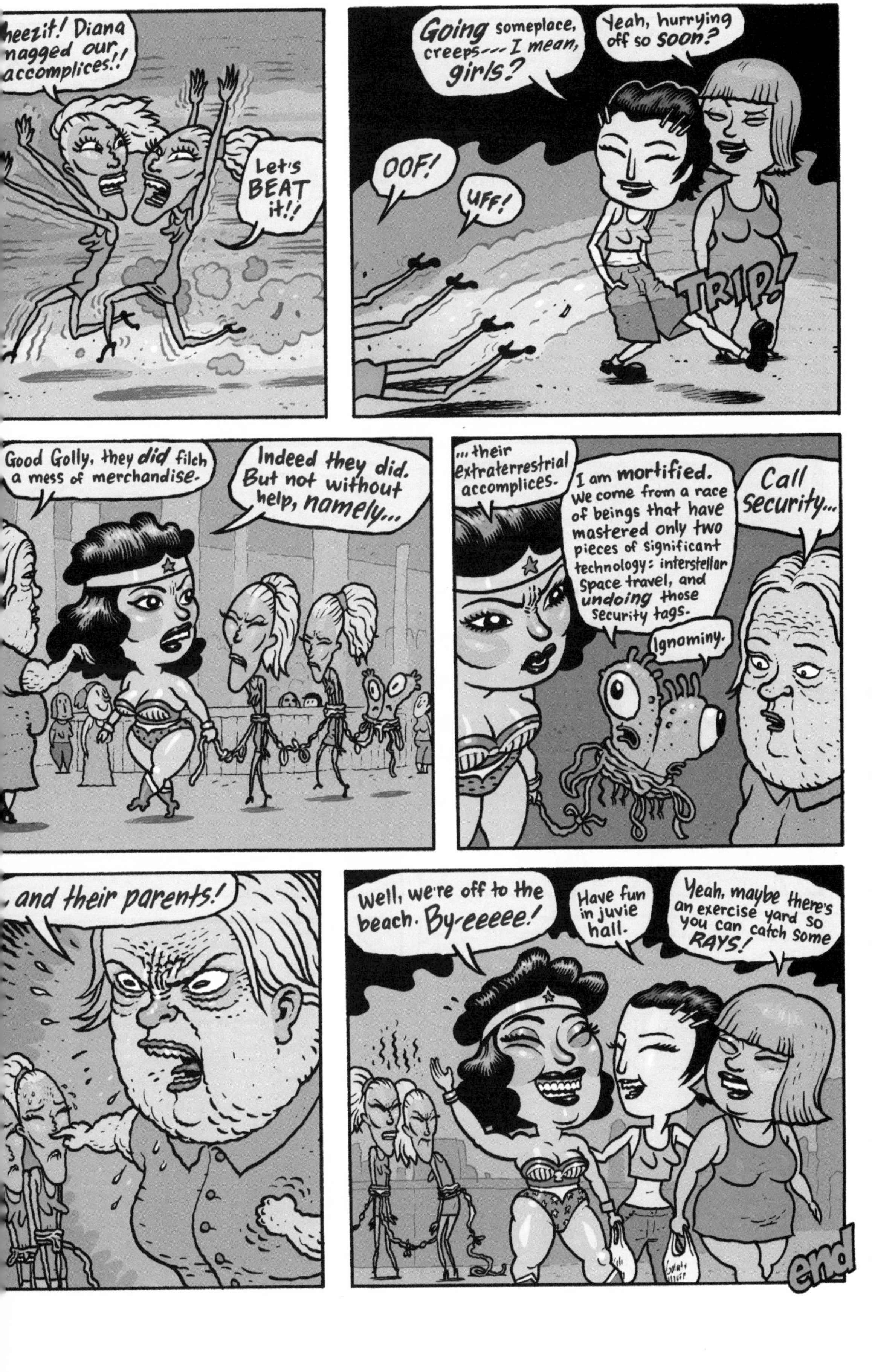
heezit! Diana nagged our accomplices!!
Let's BEAT it!!
Going someplace, creeps--- I mean, girls?
Yeah, hurrying off so soon?
OOF!
UFF!
TRIP!
Good Golly, they did filch a mess of merchandise.
Indeed they did. But not without help, namely...
...their extraterrestrial accomplices.
I am mortified. We come from a race of beings that have mastered only two pieces of significant technology: interstellar space travel, and undoing those security tags.
Ignominy.
Call security...
and their parents!
Well, we're off to the beach. By-eeeee!
Have fun in juvie hall.
Yeah, maybe there's an exercise yard so you can catch some RAYS!
end

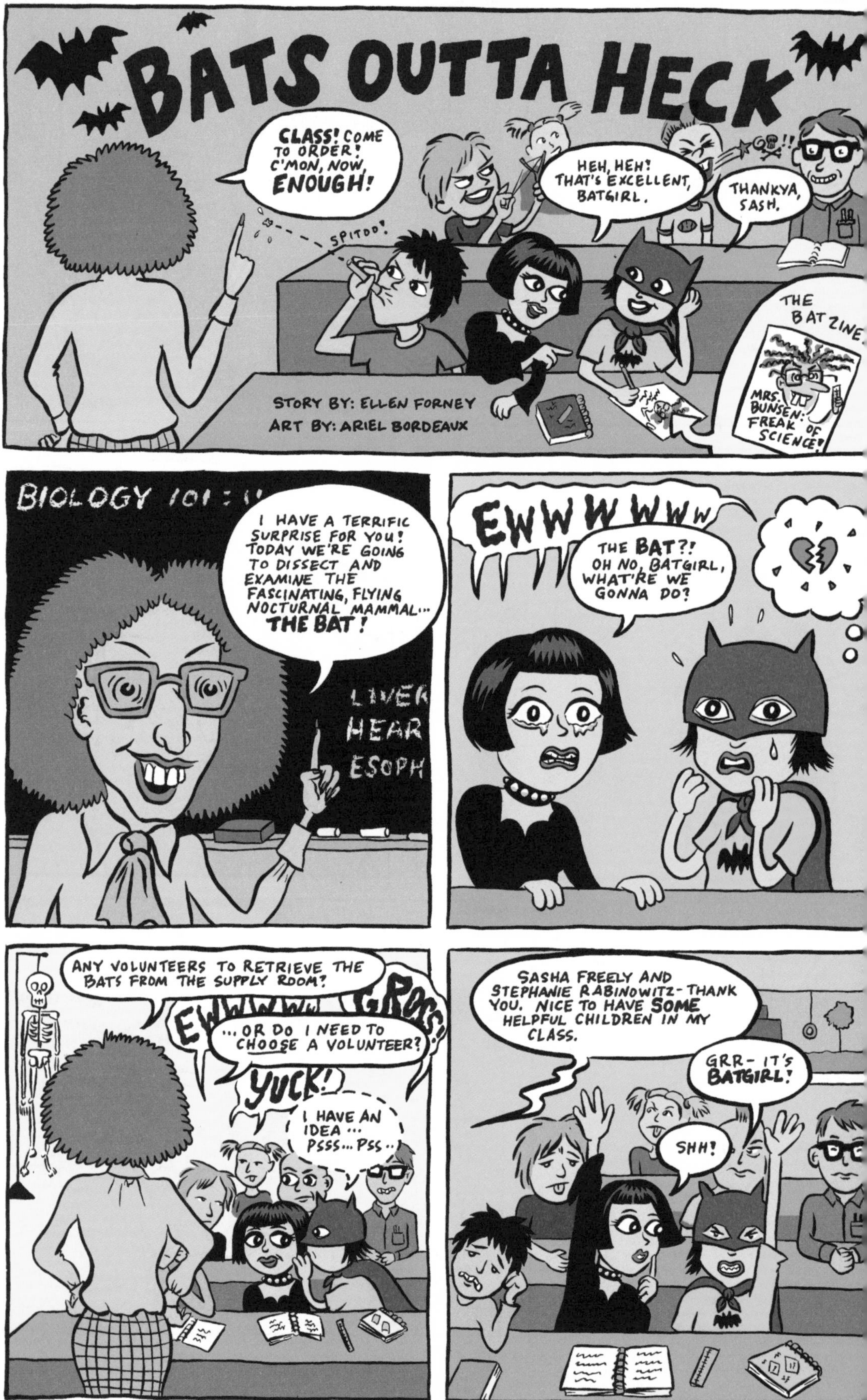
BATS OUTTA HECK
CLASS! COME TO ORDER! C'MON, NOW, ENOUGH!
SPITOO!
HEH, HEH! THAT'S EXCELLENT, BATGIRL.
THANKYA, SASH.
STORY BY: ELLEN FORNEY
ART BY: ARIEL BORDEAUX
THE BATZINE
MRS. BUNSEN: FREAK OF SCIENCE!
BIOLOGY 101
I HAVE A TERRIFIC SURPRISE FOR YOU! TODAY WE'RE GOING TO DISSECT AND EXAMINE THE FASCINATING, FLYING NOCTURNAL MAMMAL... THE BAT!
LIVER
HEAR
ESOPH
EWWWWWW
THE BAT?! OH NO, BATGIRL, WHAT'RE WE GONNA DO?
ANY VOLUNTEERS TO RETRIEVE THE BATS FROM THE SUPPLY ROOM?
...OR DO I NEED TO CHOOSE A VOLUNTEER?
YUCK!
I HAVE AN IDEA... PSSS...PSS..
SASHA FREELY AND STEPHANIE RABINOWITZ- THANK YOU. NICE TO HAVE SOME HELPFUL CHILDREN IN MY CLASS.
GRR- IT'S BATGIRL!
SHH!

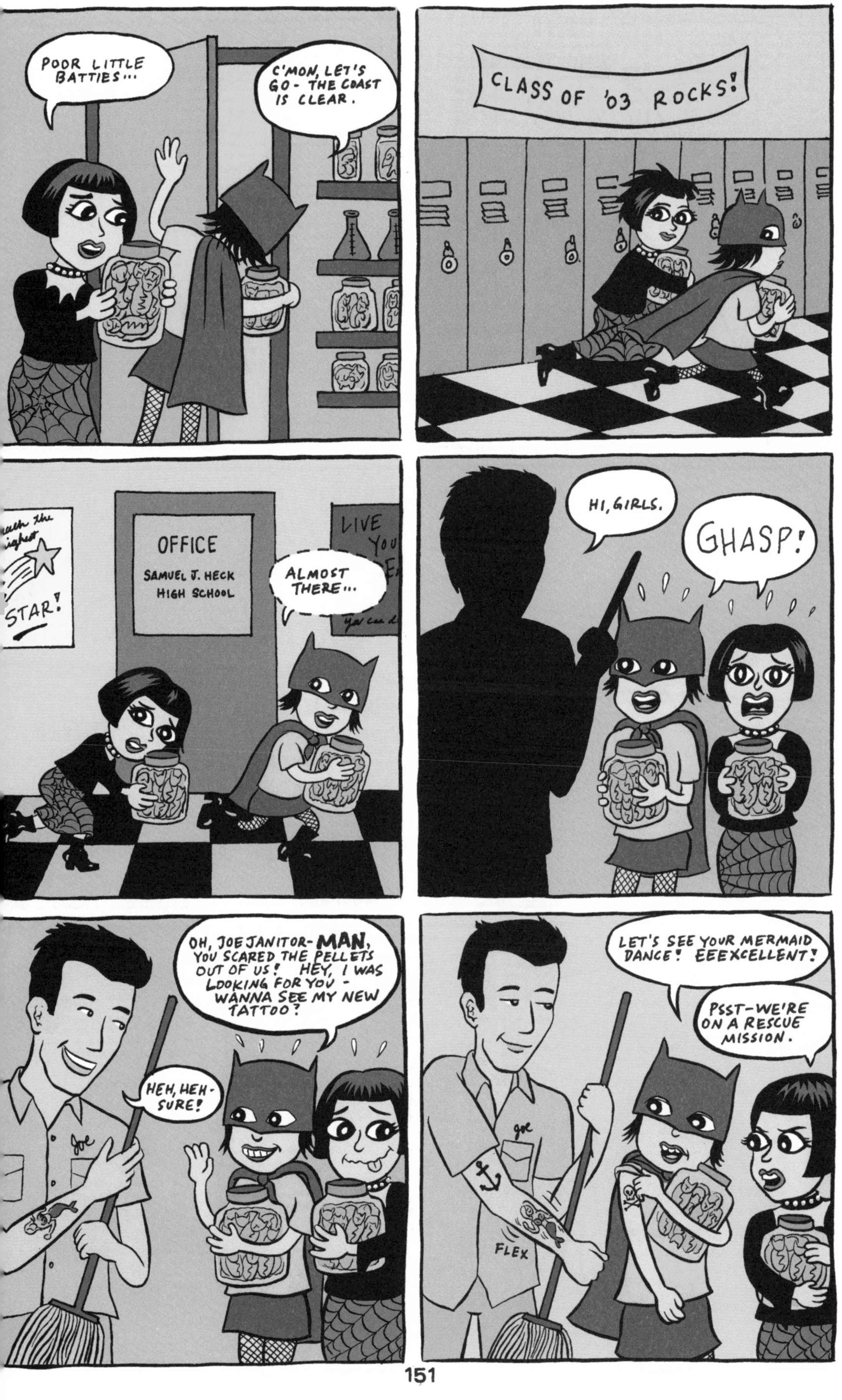
POOR LITTLE BATTIES...
C'MON, LET'S GO- THE COAST IS CLEAR.
CLASS OF '03 ROCKS!
OFFICE
SAMUEL J. HECK HIGH SCHOOL
ALMOST THERE...
HI, GIRLS.
GHASP!
OH, JOE JANITOR-MAN, YOU SCARED THE PELLETS OUT OF US! HEY, I WAS LOOKING FOR YOU - WANNA SEE MY NEW TATTOO?
HEH, HEH- SURE!
LET'S SEE YOUR MERMAID DANCE! EEEXCELLENT!
PSST-WE'RE ON A RESCUE MISSION.
FLEX

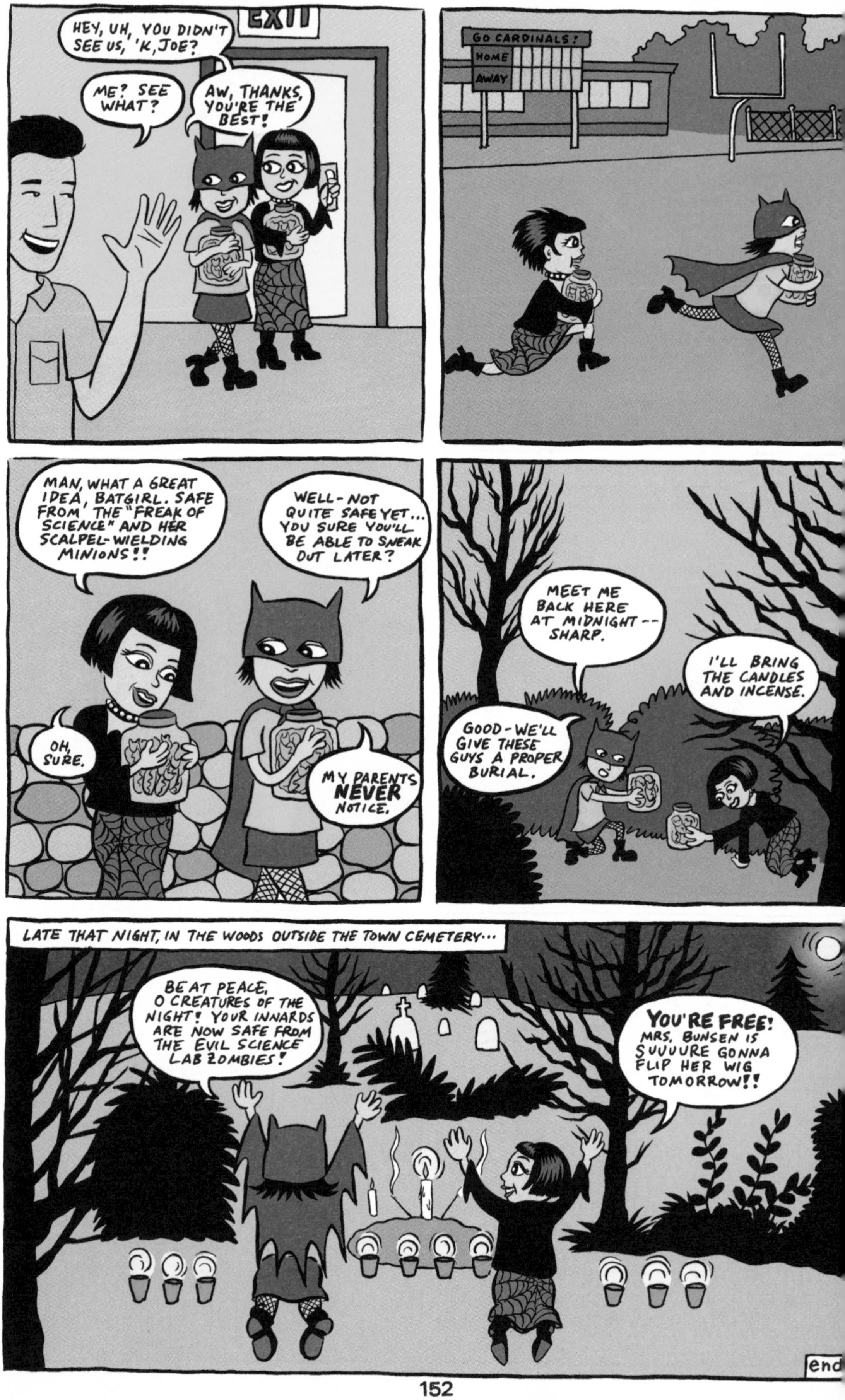
EXIT
HEY, UH, YOU DIDN'T SEE US, 'K, JOE?
ME? SEE WHAT?
AW, THANKS, YOU'RE THE BEST!
GO CARDINALS!
HOME
AWAY
MAN, WHAT A GREAT IDEA, BATGIRL. SAFE FROM THE "FREAK OF SCIENCE" AND HER SCALPEL-WIELDING MINIONS!!
WELL- NOT QUITE SAFE YET... YOU SURE YOU'LL BE ABLE TO SNEAK OUT LATER?
OH, SURE.
MY PARENTS NEVER NOTICE.
MEET ME BACK HERE AT MIDNIGHT -- SHARP.
I'LL BRING THE CANDLES AND INCENSE.
GOOD - WE'LL GIVE THESE GUYS A PROPER BURIAL.
LATE THAT NIGHT, IN THE WOODS OUTSIDE THE TOWN CEMETERY...
BE AT PEACE, O CREATURES OF THE NIGHT! YOUR INNARDS ARE NOW SAFE FROM THE EVIL SCIENCE LAB ZOMBIES!
YOU'RE FREE! MRS. BUNSEN IS SUUUURE GONNA FLIP HER WIG TOMORROW!!
end

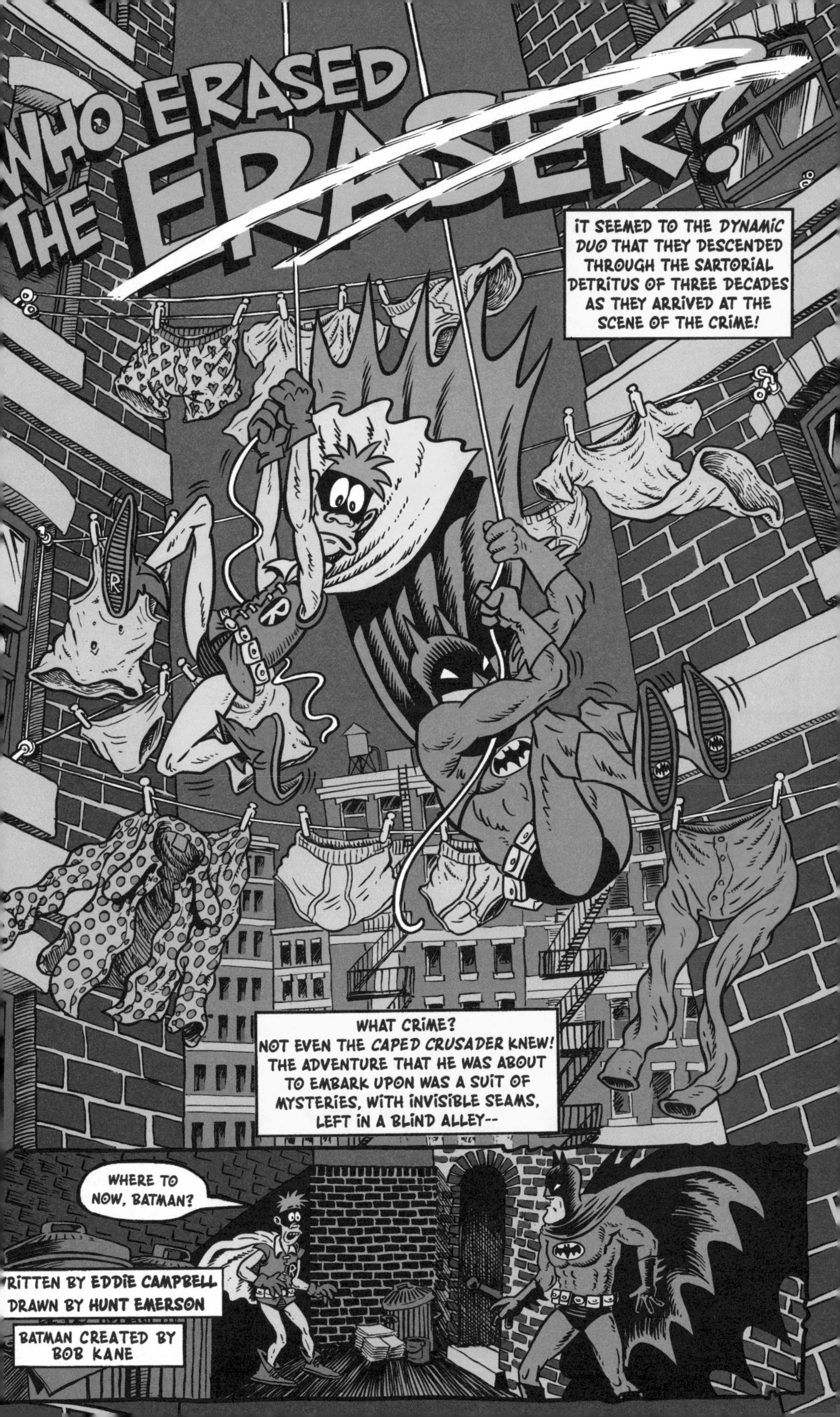
WHO ERASED THE ERASER?
IT SEEMED TO THE DYNAMIC DUO THAT THEY DESCENDED THROUGH THE SARTORIAL DETRITUS OF THREE DECADES AS THEY ARRIVED AT THE SCENE OF THE CRIME!
WHAT CRIME? NOT EVEN THE CAPED CRUSADER KNEW! THE ADVENTURE THAT HE WAS ABOUT TO EMBARK UPON WAS A SUIT OF MYSTERIES, WITH INVISIBLE SEAMS, LEFT IN A BLIND ALLEY--
WHERE TO NOW, BATMAN?
RITTEN BY EDDIE CAMPBELL
DRAWN BY HUNT EMERSON
BATMAN CREATED BY BOB KANE

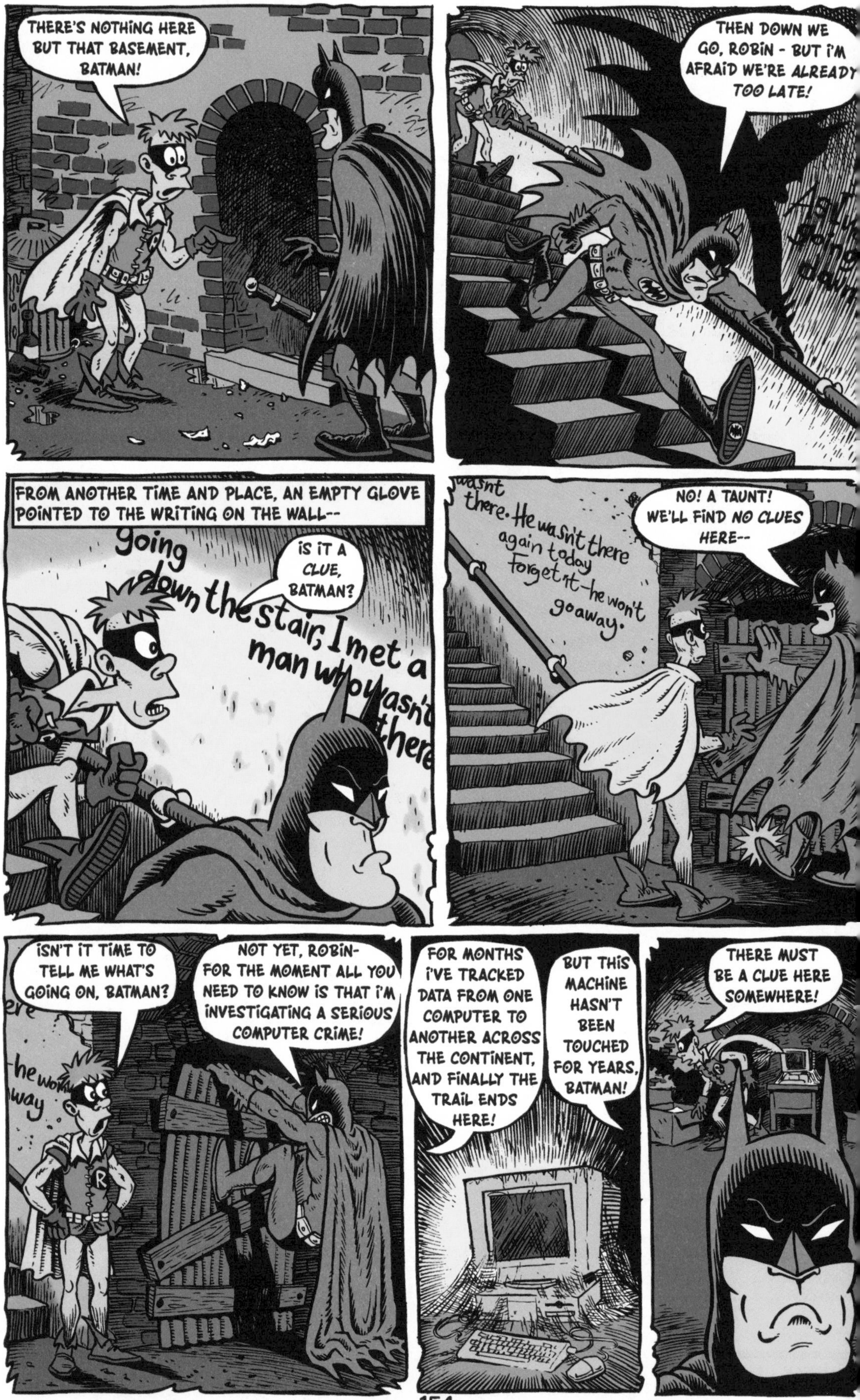

THERE'S NOTHING HERE BUT THAT BASEMENT, BATMAN!
THEN DOWN WE GO, ROBIN - BUT I'M AFRAID WE'RE ALREADY TOO LATE!
FROM ANOTHER TIME AND PLACE, AN EMPTY GLOVE POINTED TO THE WRITING ON THE WALL--
going down the stair, I met a man
wasn't there
IS IT A CLUE, BATMAN?
there. He wasn't there again today Forget it - he won't go away.
NO! A TAUNT! WE'LL FIND NO CLUES HERE--
ISN'T IT TIME TO TELL ME WHAT'S GOING ON, BATMAN?
NOT YET, ROBIN- FOR THE MOMENT ALL YOU NEED TO KNOW IS THAT I'M INVESTIGATING A SERIOUS COMPUTER CRIME!
FOR MONTHS I'VE TRACKED DATA FROM ONE COMPUTER TO ANOTHER ACROSS THE CONTINENT, AND FINALLY THE TRAIL ENDS HERE!
BUT THIS MACHINE HASN'T BEEN TOUCHED FOR YEARS, BATMAN!
THERE MUST BE A CLUE HERE SOMEWHERE!

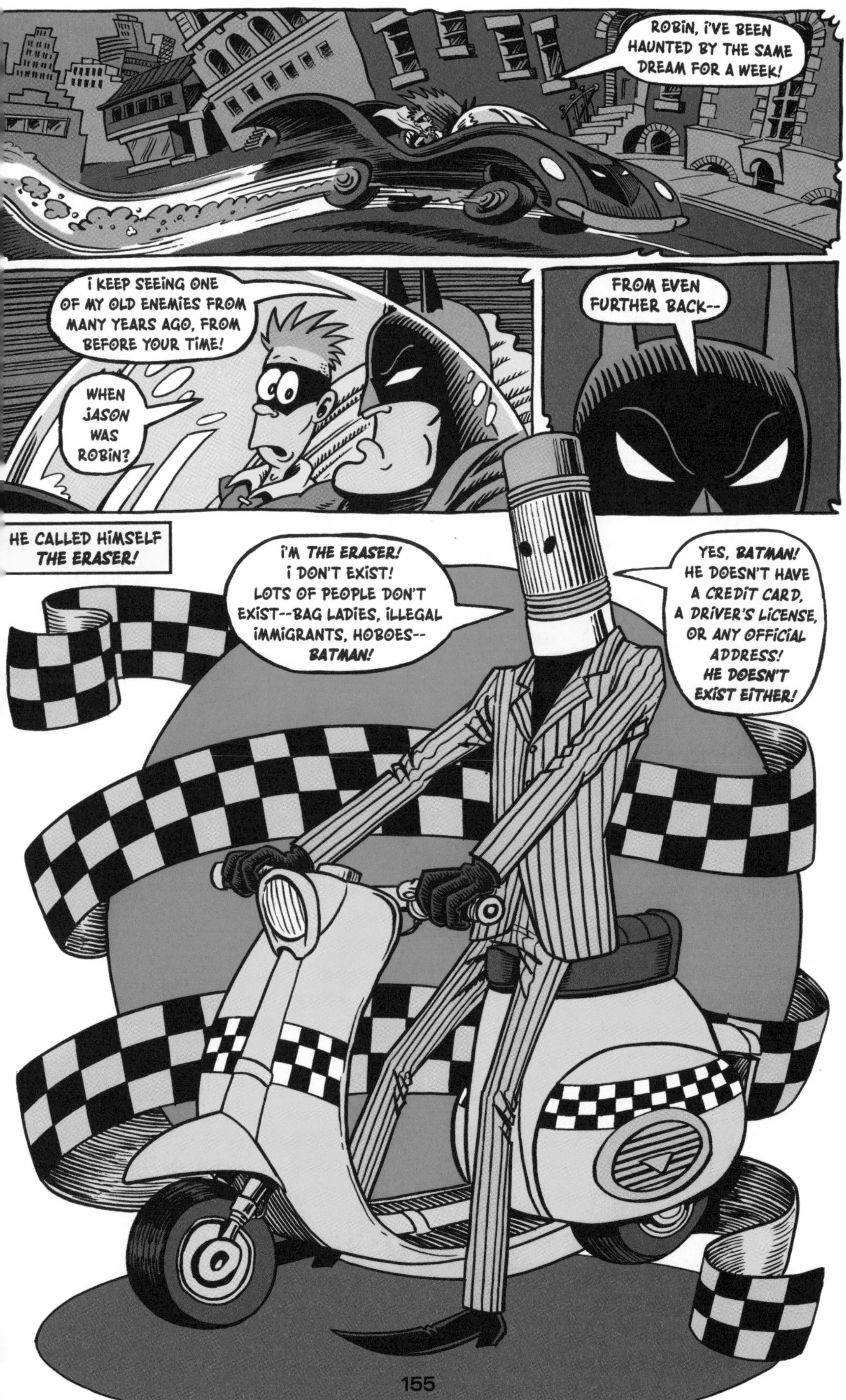

ROBIN, I'VE BEEN HAUNTED BY THE SAME DREAM FOR A WEEK!
I KEEP SEEING ONE OF MY OLD ENEMIES FROM MANY YEARS AGO, FROM BEFORE YOUR TIME!
WHEN JASON WAS ROBIN?
FROM EVEN FURTHER BACK--
HE CALLED HIMSELF THE ERASER!
I'M THE ERASER! I DON'T EXIST! LOTS OF PEOPLE DON'T EXIST--BAG LADIES, ILLEGAL IMMIGRANTS, HOBOES-- BATMAN!
YES, BATMAN! HE DOESN'T HAVE A CREDIT CARD, A DRIVER'S LICENSE, OR ANY OFFICIAL ADDRESS! HE DOESN'T EXIST EITHER!

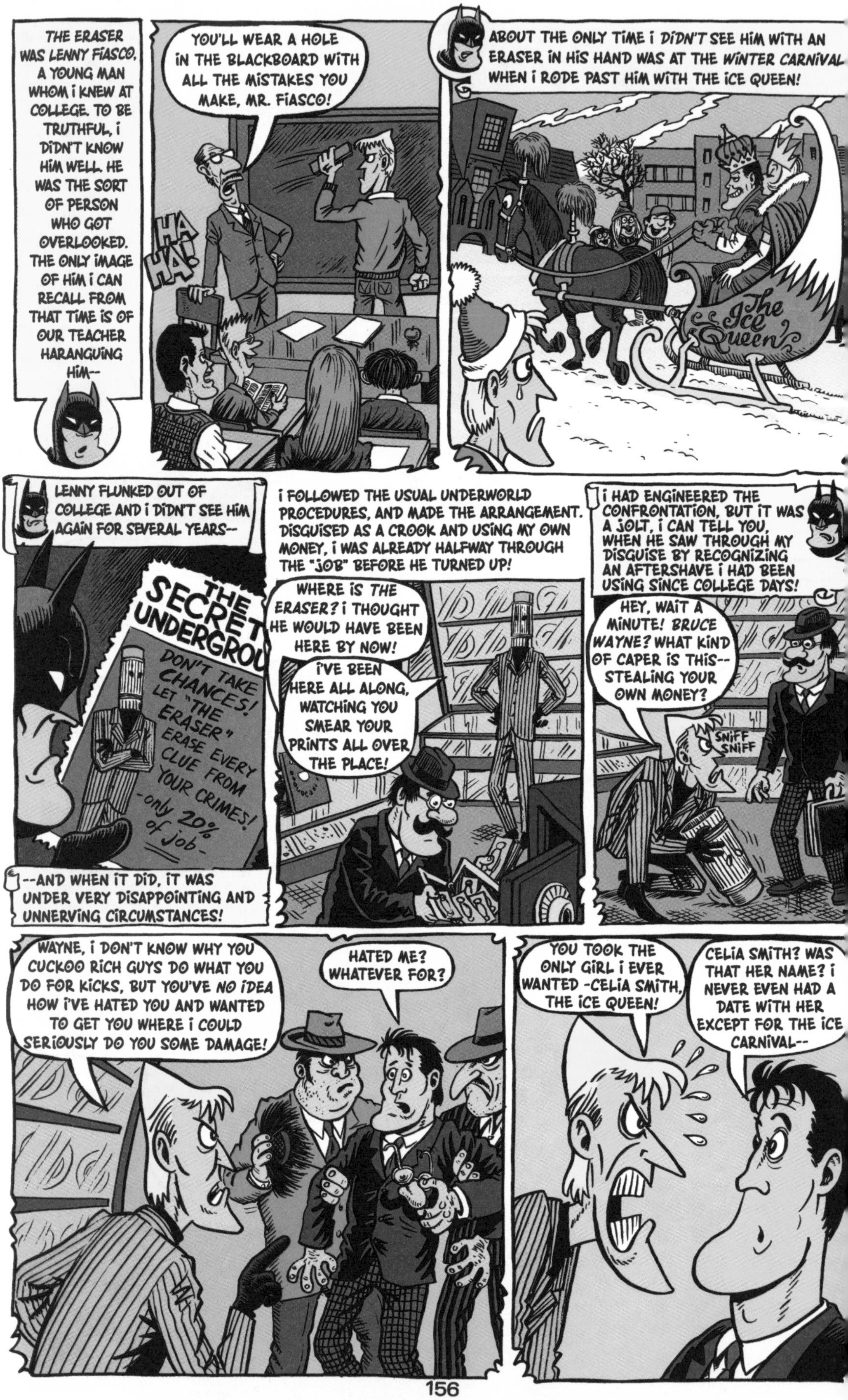
THE ERASER WAS LENNY FIASCO, A YOUNG MAN WHOM I KNEW AT COLLEGE. TO BE TRUTHFUL, I DIDN'T KNOW HIM WELL. HE WAS THE SORT OF PERSON WHO GOT OVERLOOKED. THE ONLY IMAGE OF HIM I CAN RECALL FROM THAT TIME IS OF OUR TEACHER HARANGUING HIM--
YOU'LL WEAR A HOLE IN THE BLACKBOARD WITH ALL THE MISTAKES YOU MAKE, MR. FIASCO!
HA HA!
ABOUT THE ONLY TIME I DIDN'T SEE HIM WITH AN ERASER IN HIS HAND WAS AT THE WINTER CARNIVAL WHEN I RODE PAST HIM WITH THE ICE QUEEN!
The Ice Queen
LENNY FLUNKED OUT OF COLLEGE AND I DIDN'T SEE HIM AGAIN FOR SEVERAL YEARS--
THE SECRET UNDERGROU
DON'T TAKE CHANCES! LET "THE ERASER" ERASE EVERY CLUE FROM YOUR CRIMES! -only 20% of job-
--AND WHEN IT DID, IT WAS UNDER VERY DISAPPOINTING AND UNNERVING CIRCUMSTANCES!
I FOLLOWED THE USUAL UNDERWORLD PROCEDURES, AND MADE THE ARRANGEMENT. DISGUISED AS A CROOK AND USING MY OWN MONEY, I WAS ALREADY HALFWAY THROUGH THE "JOB" BEFORE HE TURNED UP!
WHERE IS THE ERASER? I THOUGHT HE WOULD HAVE BEEN HERE BY NOW!
I'VE BEEN HERE ALL ALONG, WATCHING YOU SMEAR YOUR PRINTS ALL OVER THE PLACE!
I HAD ENGINEERED THE CONFRONTATION, BUT IT WAS A JOLT, I CAN TELL YOU, WHEN HE SAW THROUGH MY DISGUISE BY RECOGNIZING AN AFTERSHAVE I HAD BEEN USING SINCE COLLEGE DAYS!
HEY, WAIT A MINUTE! BRUCE WAYNE? WHAT KIND OF CAPER IS THIS-- STEALING YOUR OWN MONEY?
SNIFF SNIFF
WAYNE, I DON'T KNOW WHY YOU CUCKOO RICH GUYS DO WHAT YOU DO FOR KICKS, BUT YOU'VE NO IDEA HOW I'VE HATED YOU AND WANTED TO GET YOU WHERE I COULD SERIOUSLY DO YOU SOME DAMAGE!
HATED ME? WHATEVER FOR?
YOU TOOK THE ONLY GIRL I EVER WANTED -CELIA SMITH, THE ICE QUEEN!
CELIA SMITH? WAS THAT HER NAME? I NEVER EVEN HAD A DATE WITH HER EXCEPT FOR THE ICE CARNIVAL--

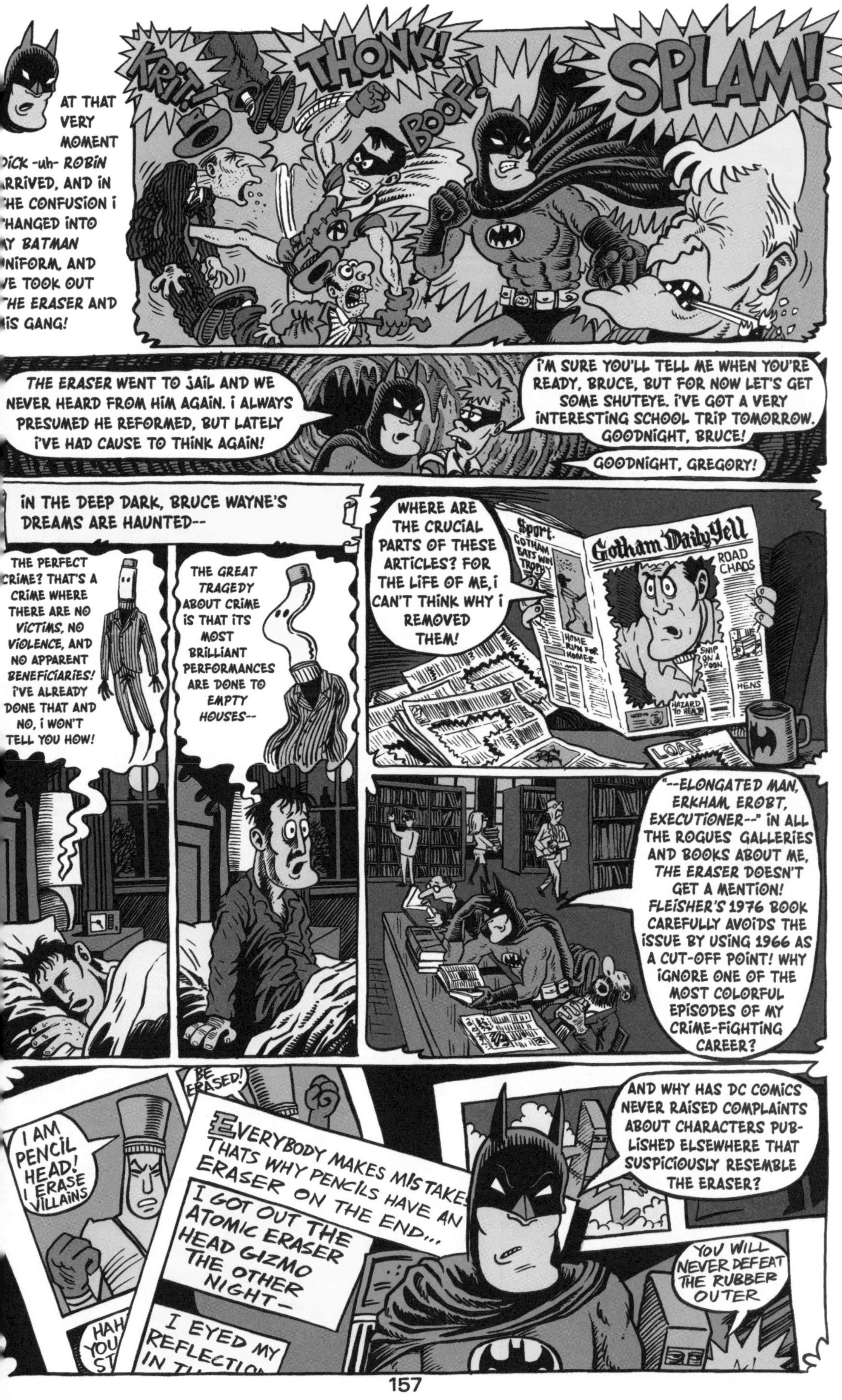
AT THAT VERY MOMENT DICK -uh- ROBIN ARRIVED, AND IN THE CONFUSION I CHANGED INTO MY BATMAN UNIFORM, AND WE TOOK OUT THE ERASER AND HIS GANG!
KRIT!
THONK!
BOOF!
SPLAM!
THE ERASER WENT TO JAIL AND WE NEVER HEARD FROM HIM AGAIN. I ALWAYS PRESUMED HE REFORMED, BUT LATELY I'VE HAD CAUSE TO THINK AGAIN!
I'M SURE YOU'LL TELL ME WHEN YOU'RE READY, BRUCE, BUT FOR NOW LET'S GET SOME SHUTEYE. I'VE GOT A VERY INTERESTING SCHOOL TRIP TOMORROW. GOODNIGHT, BRUCE!
GOODNIGHT, GREGORY!
IN THE DEEP DARK, BRUCE WAYNE'S DREAMS ARE HAUNTED--
THE PERFECT CRIME? THAT'S A CRIME WHERE THERE ARE NO VICTIMS, NO VIOLENCE, AND NO APPARENT BENEFICIARIES! I'VE ALREADY DONE THAT AND NO, I WON'T TELL YOU HOW!
THE GREAT TRAGEDY ABOUT CRIME IS THAT ITS MOST BRILLIANT PERFORMANCES ARE DONE TO EMPTY HOUSES--
WHERE ARE THE CRUCIAL PARTS OF THESE ARTICLES? FOR THE LIFE OF ME, I CAN'T THINK WHY I REMOVED THEM!
Sport
GOTHAM BATS WIN TROPHY
Gotham Daily Yell
ROAD CHADS
HOME RUN FOR HOMER
SNIP ON A POON
HENS
HAZARD TO HEALTH
LOAF
"--ELONGATED MAN, ERKHAM, EROBT, EXECUTIONER--" IN ALL THE ROGUES GALLERIES AND BOOKS ABOUT ME, THE ERASER DOESN'T GET A MENTION! FLEISHER'S 1976 BOOK CAREFULLY AVOIDS THE ISSUE BY USING 1966 AS A CUT-OFF POINT! WHY IGNORE ONE OF THE MOST COLORFUL EPISODES OF MY CRIME-FIGHTING CAREER?
BE ERASED!
I AM PENCIL HEAD! I ERASE VILLAINS
EVERYBODY MAKES MISTAKES THATS WHY PENCILS HAVE AN ERASER ON THE END...
I GOT OUT THE ATOMIC ERASER HEAD GIZMO THE OTHER NIGHT-
I EYED MY REFLECTION IN TH
HAH YOU ST
AND WHY HAS DC COMICS NEVER RAISED COMPLAINTS ABOUT CHARACTERS PUBLISHED ELSEWHERE THAT SUSPICIOUSLY RESEMBLE THE ERASER?
YOU WILL NEVER DEFEAT THE RUBBER OUTER

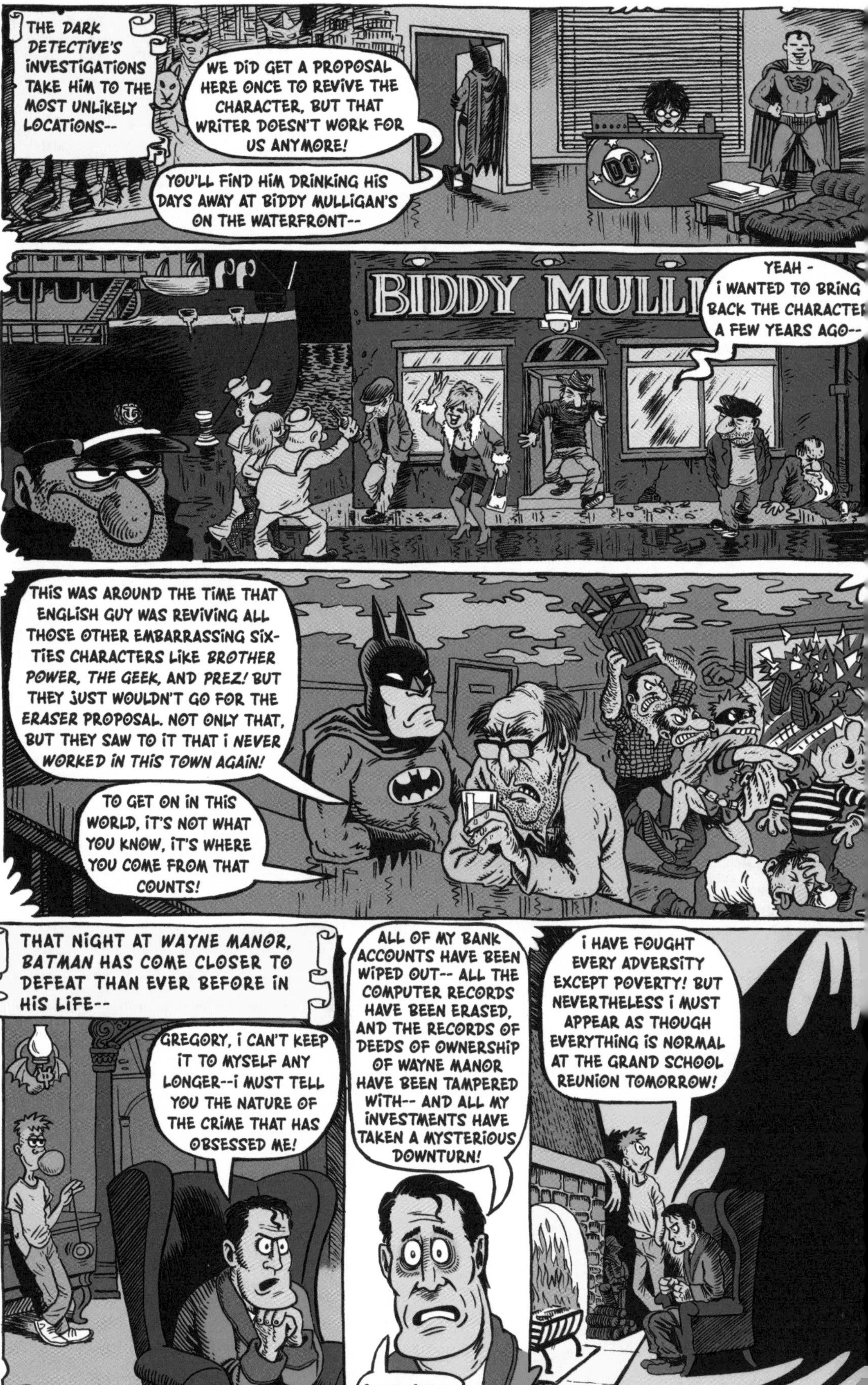
THE DARK DETECTIVE'S INVESTIGATIONS TAKE HIM TO THE MOST UNLIKELY LOCATIONS--
WE DID GET A PROPOSAL HERE ONCE TO REVIVE THE CHARACTER, BUT THAT WRITER DOESN'T WORK FOR US ANYMORE!
YOU'LL FIND HIM DRINKING HIS DAYS AWAY AT BIDDY MULLIGAN'S ON THE WATERFRONT--
DC
BIDDY MULLI
YEAH - I WANTED TO BRING BACK THE CHARACTE A FEW YEARS AGO--
THIS WAS AROUND THE TIME THAT ENGLISH GUY WAS REVIVING ALL THOSE OTHER EMBARRASSING SIXTIES CHARACTERS LIKE BROTHER POWER, THE GEEK, AND PREZ! BUT THEY JUST WOULDN'T GO FOR THE ERASER PROPOSAL. NOT ONLY THAT, BUT THEY SAW TO IT THAT I NEVER WORKED IN THIS TOWN AGAIN!
TO GET ON IN THIS WORLD, IT'S NOT WHAT YOU KNOW, IT'S WHERE YOU COME FROM THAT COUNTS!
THAT NIGHT AT WAYNE MANOR, BATMAN HAS COME CLOSER TO DEFEAT THAN EVER BEFORE IN HIS LIFE--
GREGORY, I CAN'T KEEP IT TO MYSELF ANY LONGER--I MUST TELL YOU THE NATURE OF THE CRIME THAT HAS OBSESSED ME!
ALL OF MY BANK ACCOUNTS HAVE BEEN WIPED OUT-- ALL THE COMPUTER RECORDS HAVE BEEN ERASED, AND THE RECORDS OF DEEDS OF OWNERSHIP OF WAYNE MANOR HAVE BEEN TAMPERED WITH-- AND ALL MY INVESTMENTS HAVE TAKEN A MYSTERIOUS DOWNTURN!
I'M RUINED!
I HAVE FOUGHT EVERY ADVERSITY EXCEPT POVERTY! BUT NEVERTHELESS I MUST APPEAR AS THOUGH EVERYTHING IS NORMAL AT THE GRAND SCHOOL REUNION TOMORROW!

CLASS OF
LOOK AT WAYNE! WHAT MADE ME THINK I COULD DESTROY THAT MAN? I'M SO INSIGNIFICANT TO HIM THAT HE DOESN'T EVEN RECOGNIZE ME AFTER ALL THESE YEARS!
CELIA? OH YES-- OF COURSE-- I REMEMBER NOW--
IF ONLY I'D BEEN BORN WEALTHY-- IT'S NOT WHO YOU KNOW BUT HOW MUCH YOU'VE GOT THAT COUNTS IN THIS WORLD!
OTHAM UNIVERSITY
I ONCE HATCHED A CRAZY SCHEME TO BANKRUPT BRUCE WAYNE, BUT IT RELIED UPON TOO MANY FACTORS BEYOND MY CONTROL - SIMPLE THINGS LIKE CONTINUOUS ELECTRICITY CONNECTIONS AND THE PROJECTED ADVANCES OF TECHNOLOGY! TWENTY YEARS AGO, I SET IT IN MOTION. IT COULD HAVE BEEN THE PERFECT CRIME IF IT HADN'T BEEN SO NAIVE AND FAR-FETCHED!
TONIGHT CLASS REUNION
WHO ERASED THE ERASER?
ERASER
I'M SUCH A SAP!
THE END

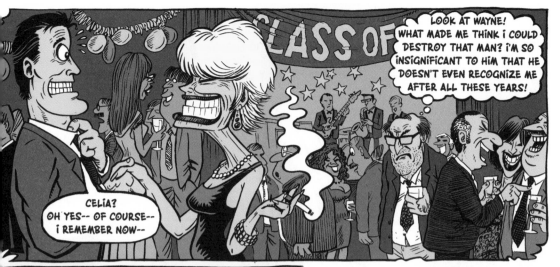

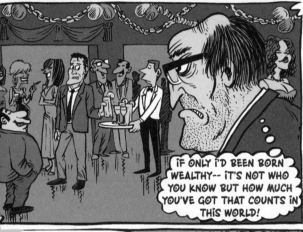

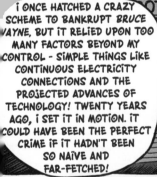

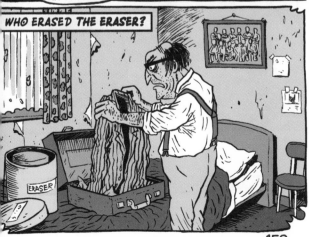

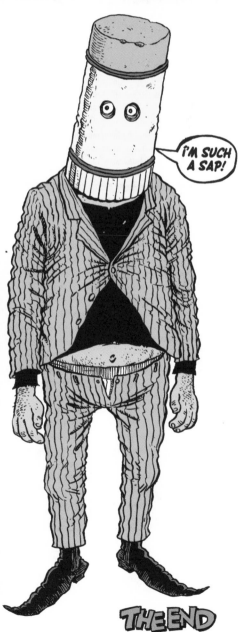

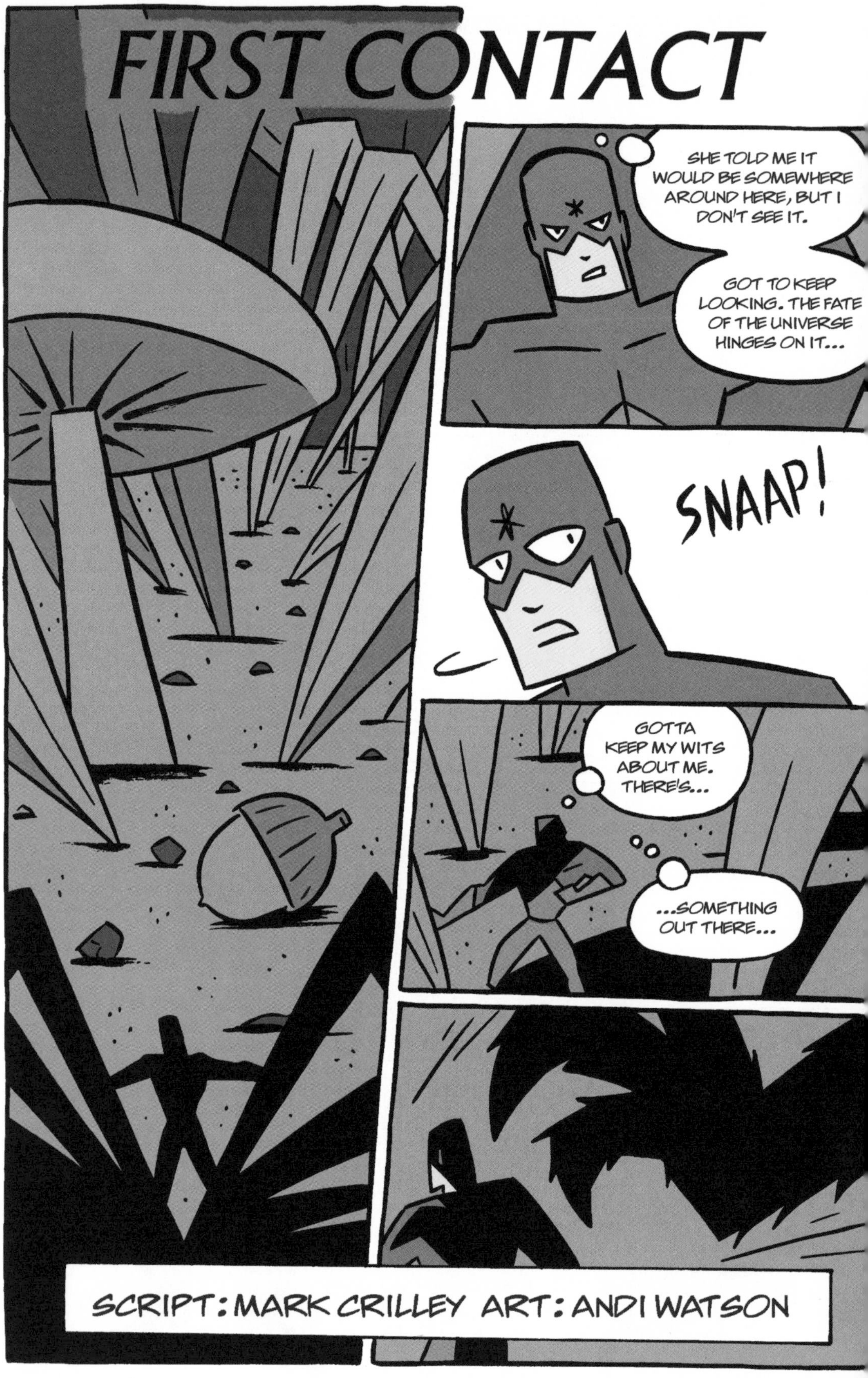
FIRST CONTACT
SHE TOLD ME IT WOULD BE SOMEWHERE AROUND HERE, BUT I DON'T SEE IT.
GOT TO KEEP LOOKING. THE FATE OF THE UNIVERSE HINGES ON IT...
SNAAP!
GOTTA KEEP MY WITS ABOUT ME. THERE'S...
...SOMETHING OUT THERE...
SCRIPT: MARK CRILLEY ART: ANDI WATSON

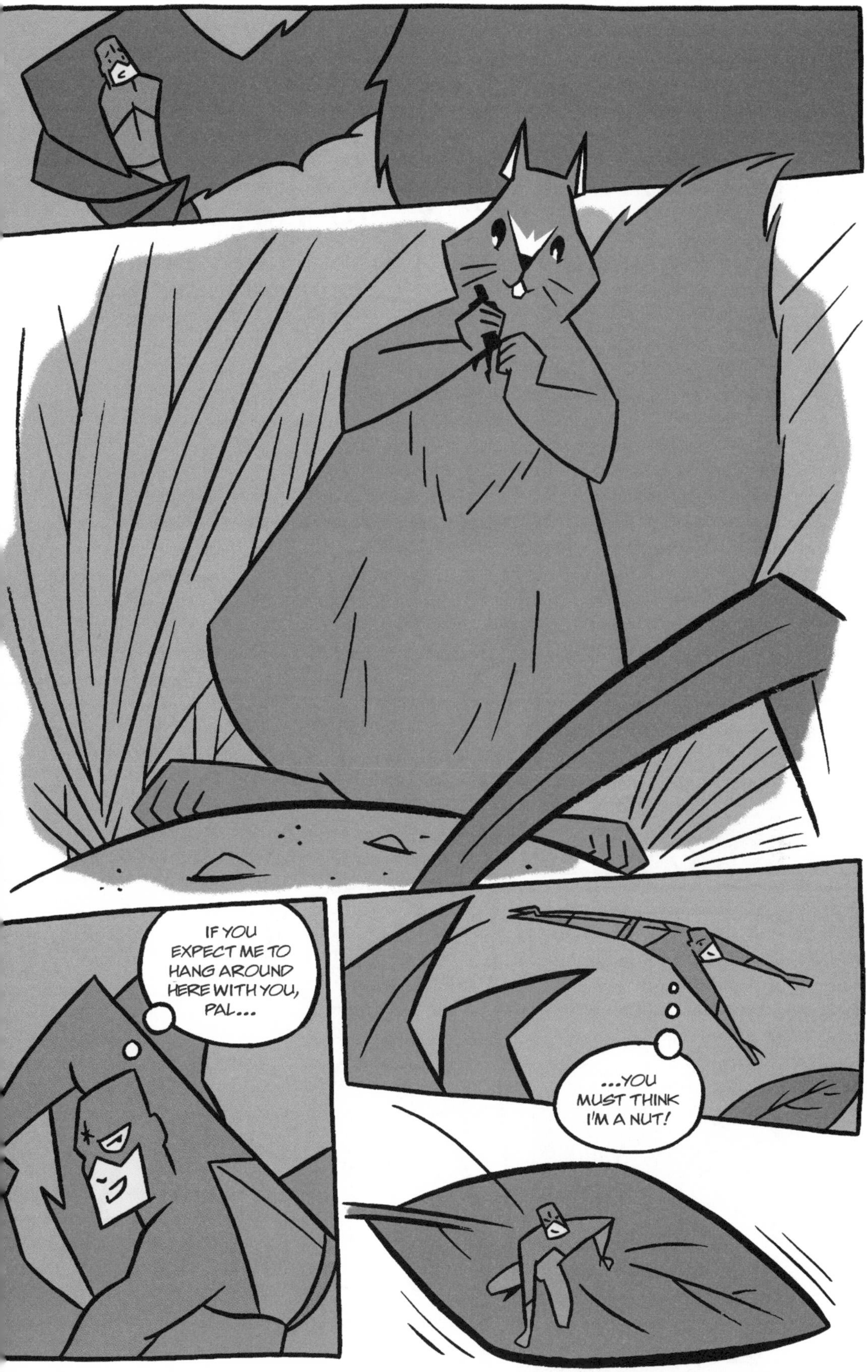
IF YOU EXPECT ME TO HANG AROUND HERE WITH YOU, PAL...
...YOU MUST THINK I'M A NUT!

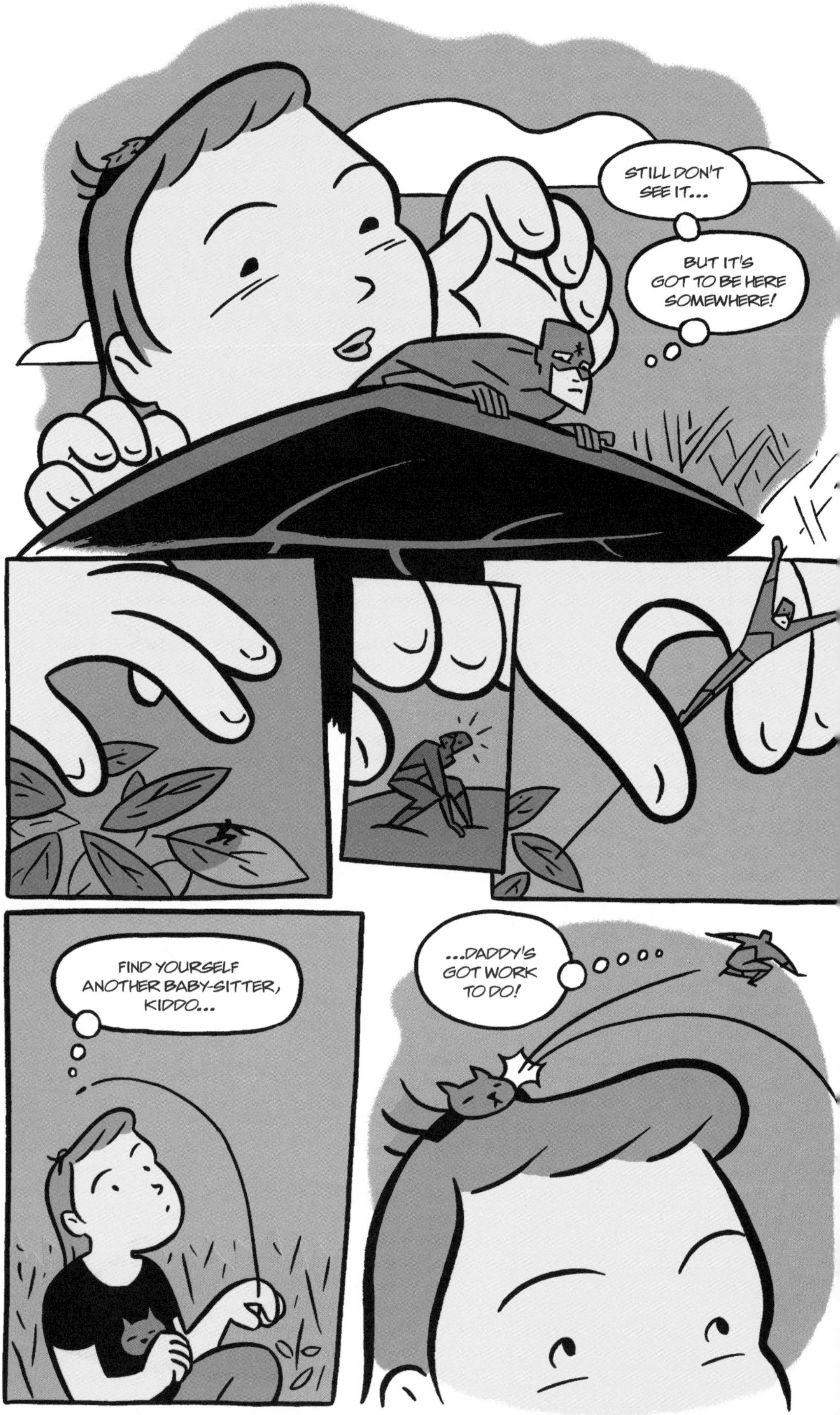
STILL DON'T SEE IT...
BUT IT'S GOT TO BE HERE SOMEWHERE!
FIND YOURSELF ANOTHER BABY-SITTER, KIDDO...
...DADDY'S GOT WORK TO DO!

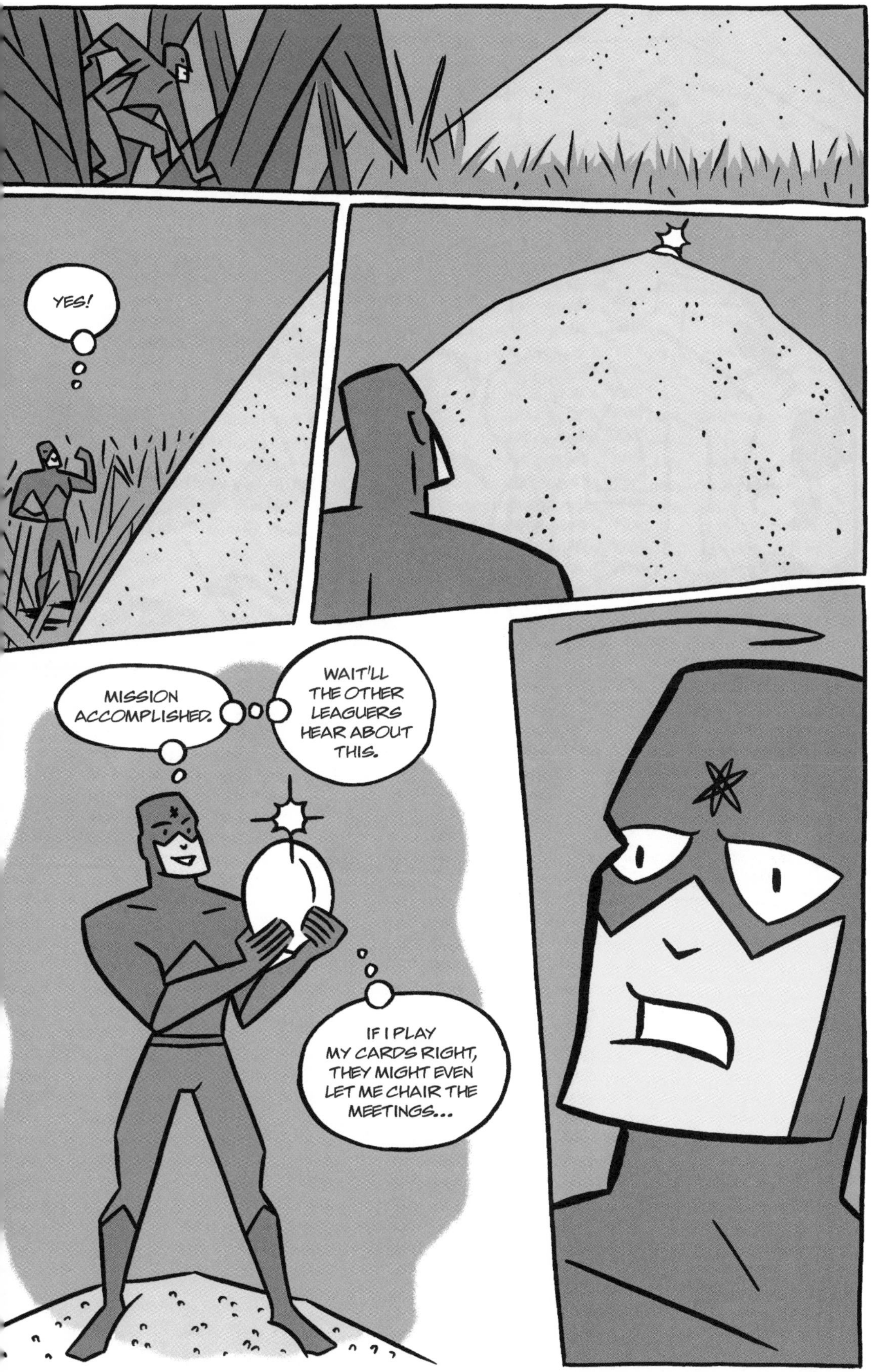
YES!
MISSION ACCOMPLISHED.
WAIT'LL THE OTHER LEAGUERS HEAR ABOUT THIS.
IF I PLAY MY CARDS RIGHT, THEY MIGHT EVEN LET ME CHAIR THE MEETINGS...

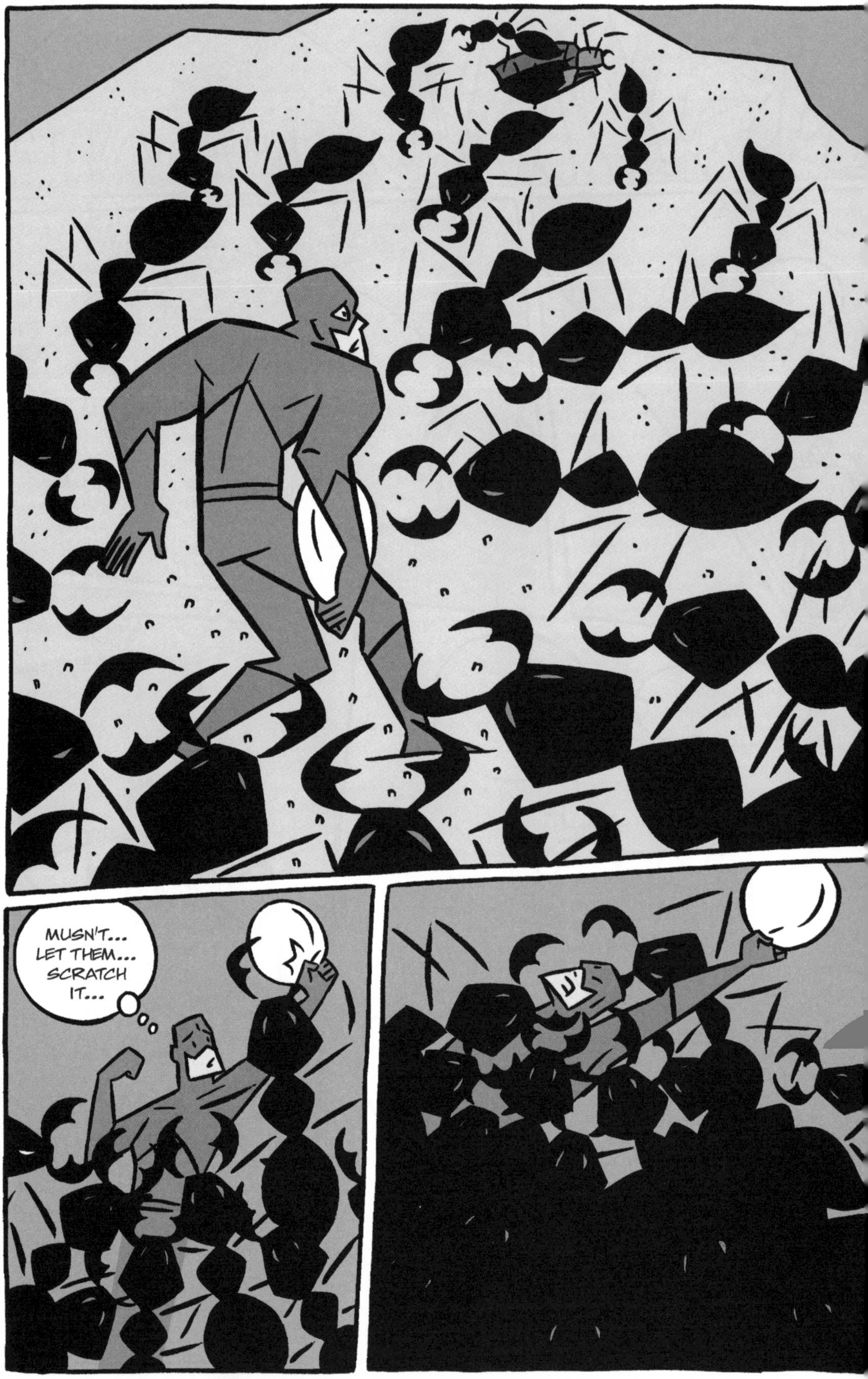
MUSN'T... LET THEM... SCRATCH IT...

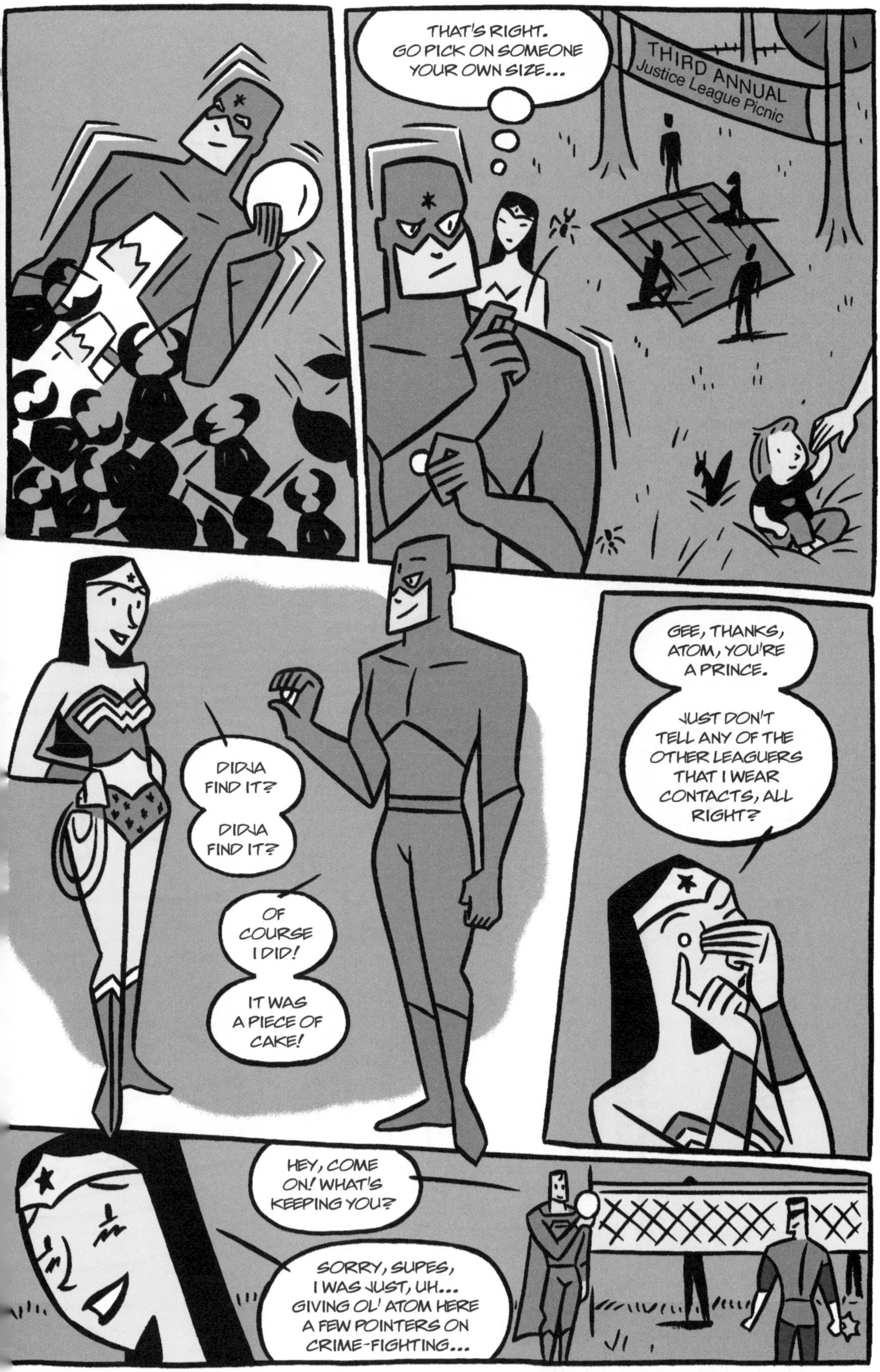
THAT'S RIGHT. GO PICK ON SOMEONE YOUR OWN SIZE...
THIRD ANNUAL
Justice League Picnic
DIDJA FIND IT?
DIDJA FIND IT?
OF COURSE I DID!
IT WAS A PIECE OF CAKE!
GEE, THANKS, ATOM, YOU'RE A PRINCE.
JUST DON'T TELL ANY OF THE OTHER LEAGUERS THAT I WEAR CONTACTS, ALL RIGHT?
HEY, COME ON! WHAT'S KEEPING YOU?
SORRY, SUPES, I WAS JUST, UH... GIVING OL' ATOM HERE A FEW POINTERS ON CRIME-FIGHTING...

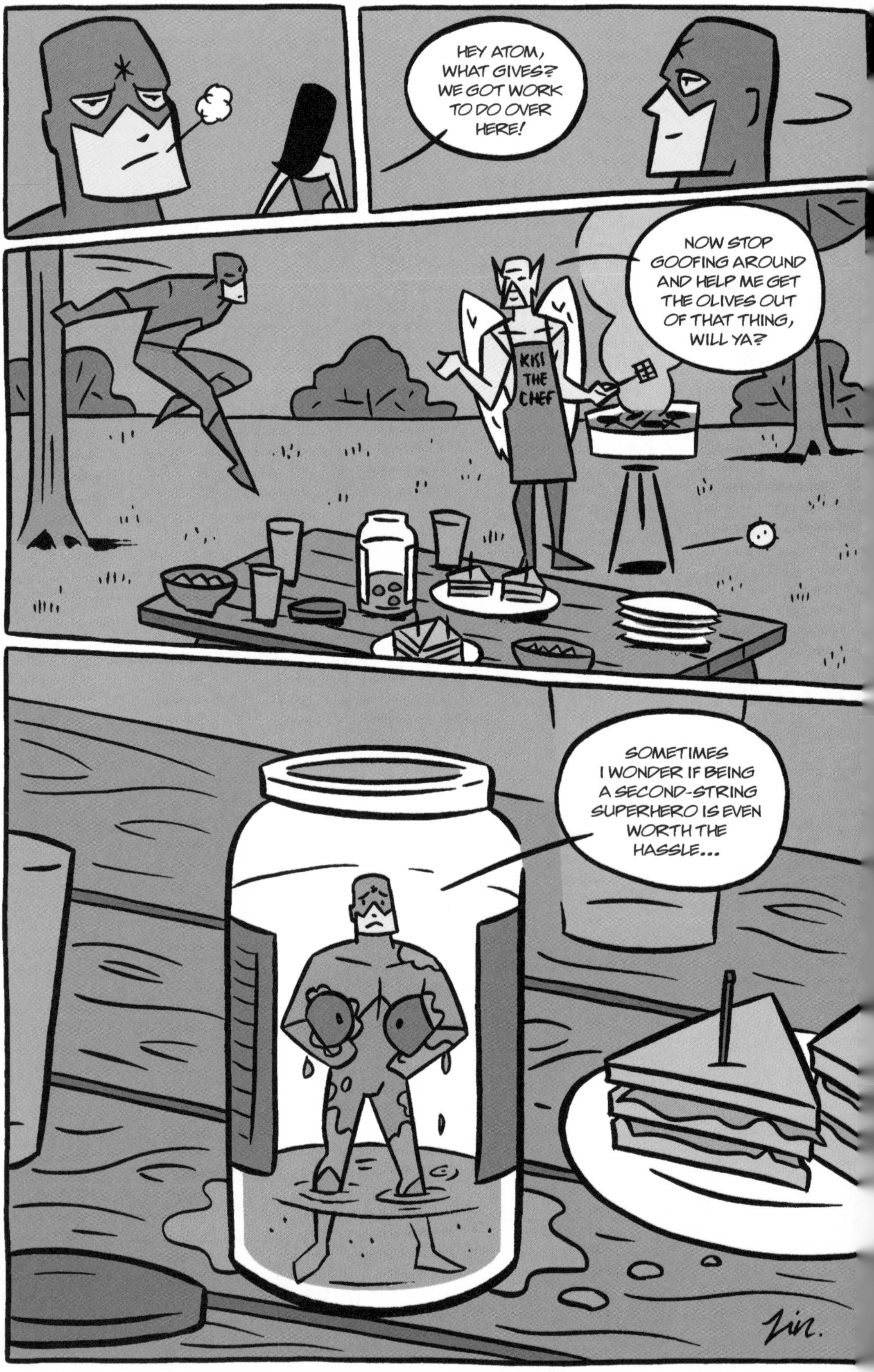
HEY ATOM, WHAT GIVES? WE GOT WORK TO DO OVER HERE!
NOW STOP GOOFING AROUND AND HELP ME GET THE OLIVES OUT OF THAT THING, WILL YA?
KISS THE CHEF
SOMETIMES I WONDER IF BEING A SECOND-STRING SUPERHERO IS EVEN WORTH THE HASSLE...
Zin.

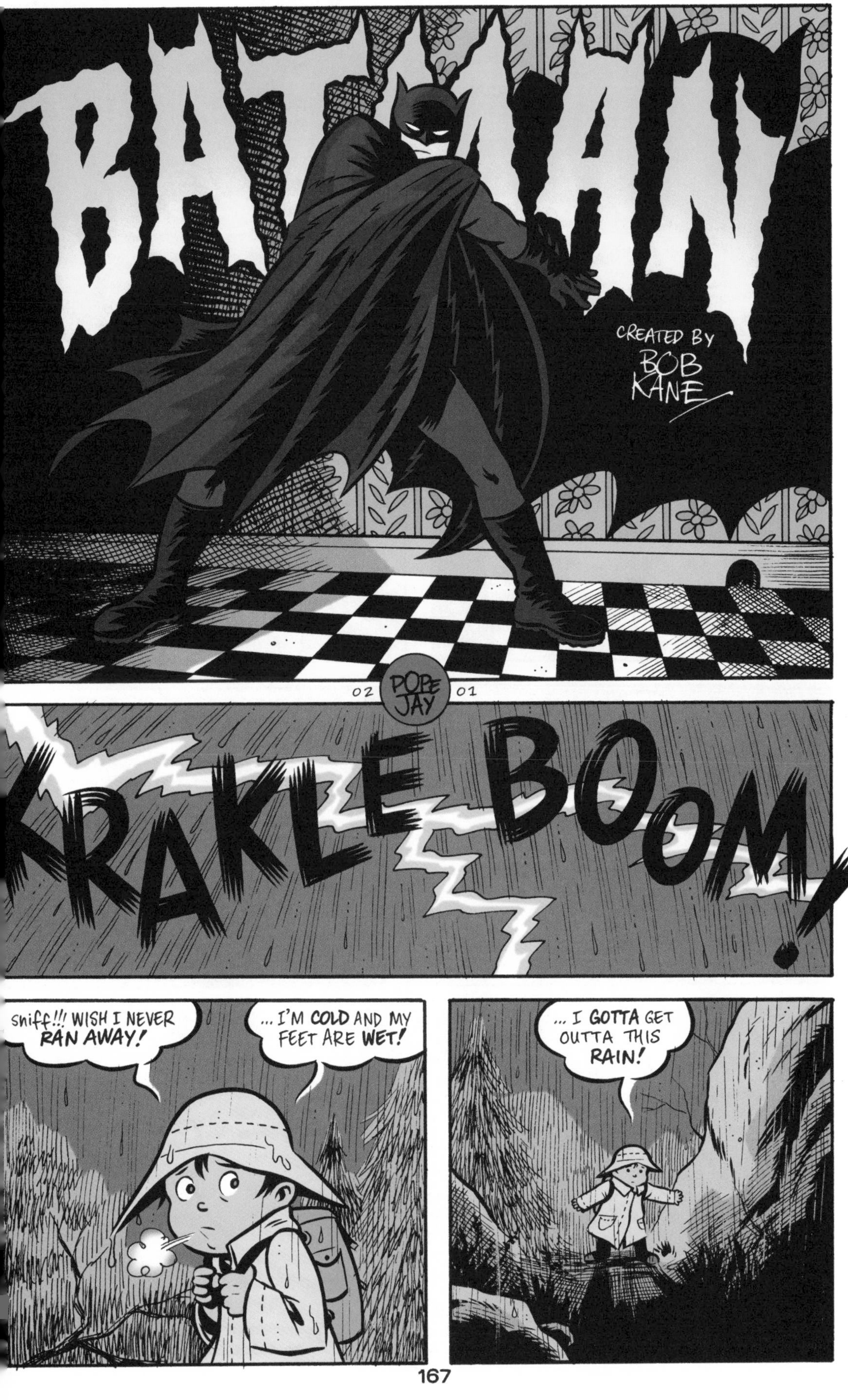
BATMAN
CREATED BY BOB KANE
02 POPE JAY 01
KRAKLE BOOM!
sniff!!! WISH I NEVER RAN AWAY!
... I'M COLD AND MY FEET ARE WET!
... I GOTTA GET OUTTA THIS RAIN!

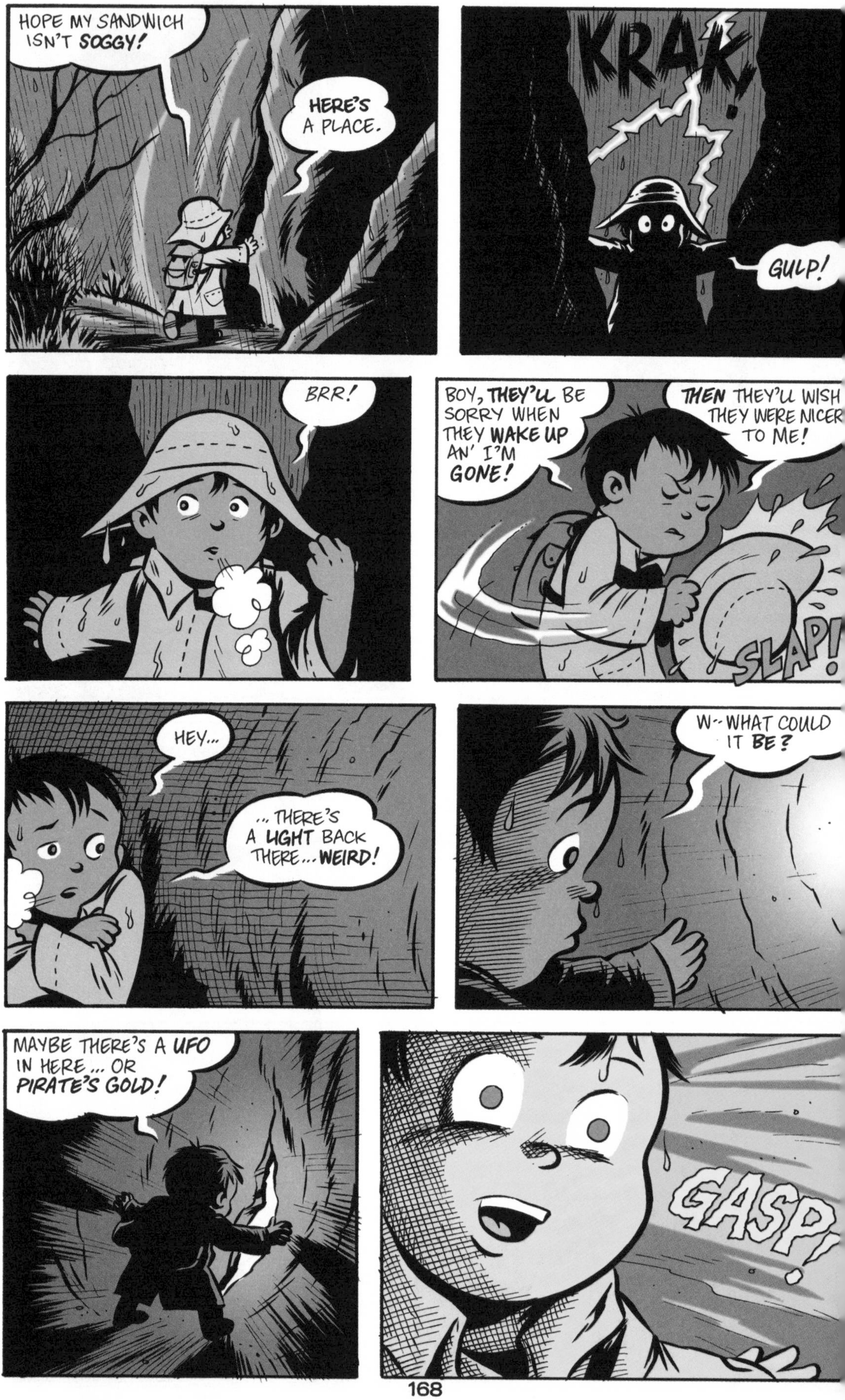
HOPE MY SANDWICH ISN'T SOGGY!
HERE'S A PLACE.
KRAK!
GULP!
BRR!
BOY, THEY'LL BE SORRY WHEN THEY WAKE UP AN' I'M GONE!
THEN THEY'LL WISH THEY WERE NICER TO ME!
SLAP!
HEY...
...THERE'S A LIGHT BACK THERE... WEIRD!
W--WHAT COULD IT BE?
MAYBE THERE'S A UFO IN HERE... OR PIRATE'S GOLD!
GASP!

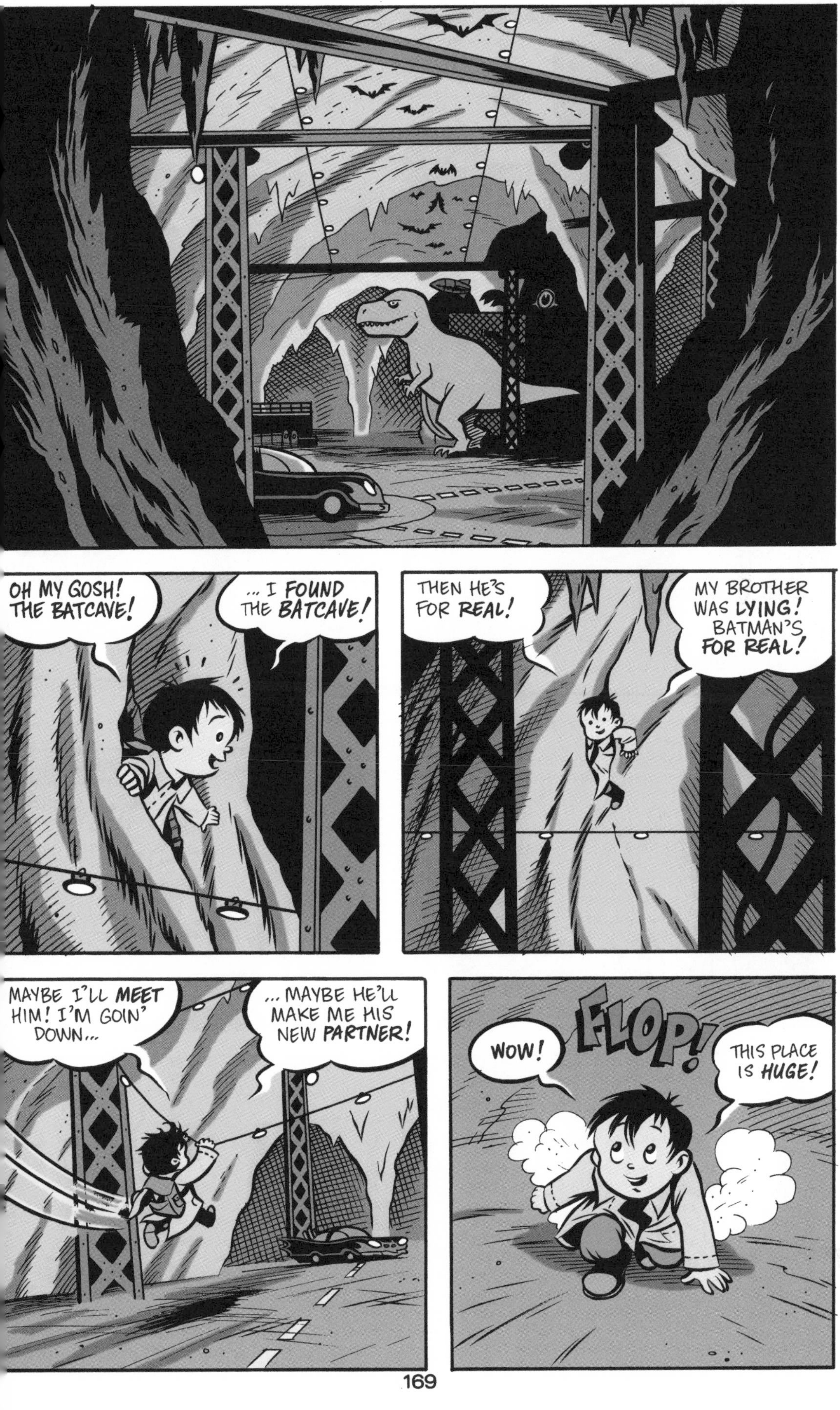
OH MY GOSH! THE BATCAVE!
... I FOUND THE BATCAVE!
THEN HE'S FOR REAL!
MY BROTHER WAS LYING! BATMAN'S FOR REAL!
MAYBE I'LL MEET HIM! I'M GOIN' DOWN...
... MAYBE HE'LL MAKE ME HIS NEW PARTNER!
WOW!
FLOP!
THIS PLACE IS HUGE!

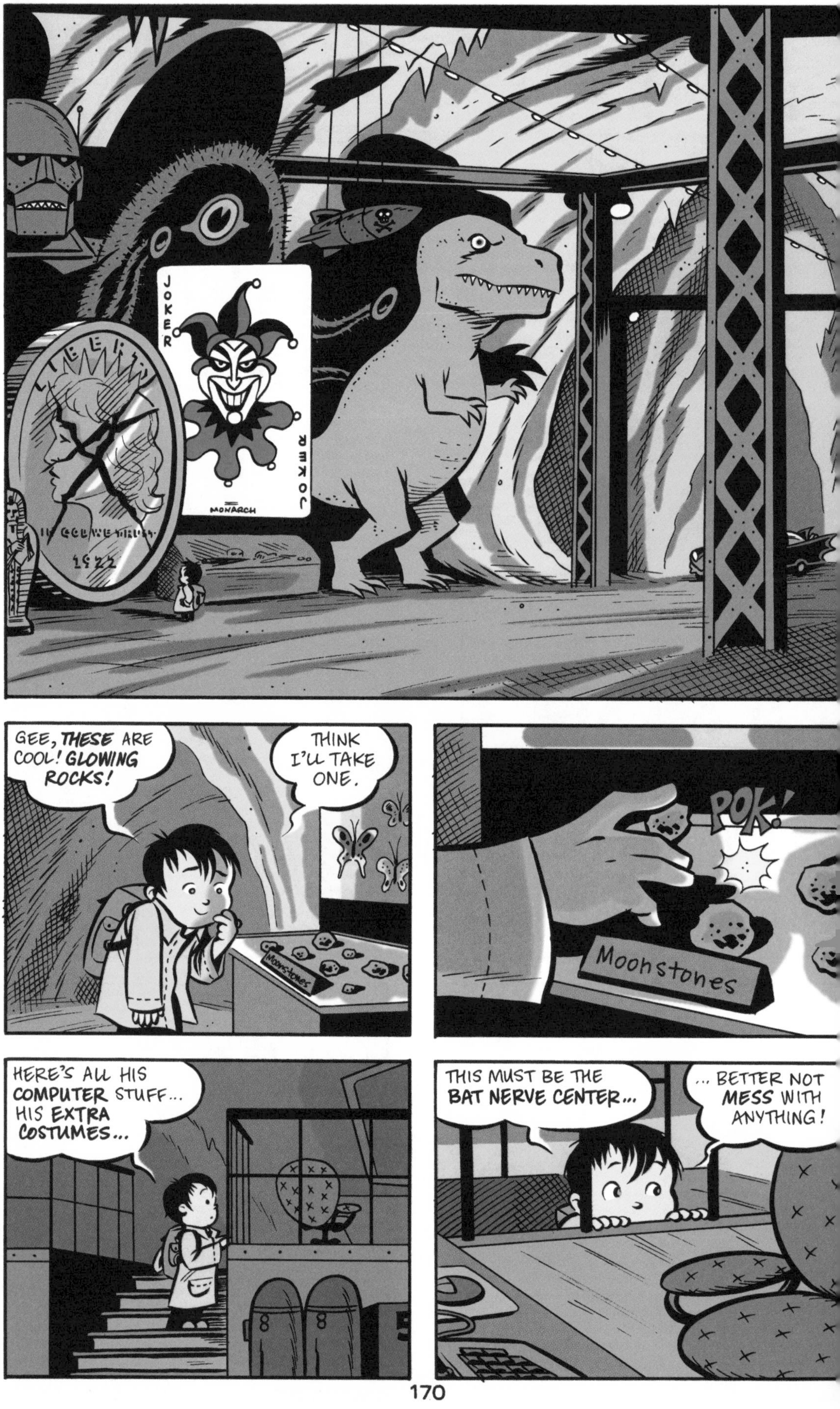

JOKER
MONARCH
GEE, THESE ARE COOL! GLOWING ROCKS!
THINK I'LL TAKE ONE.
Moonstones
POK!
Moonstones
HERE'S ALL HIS COMPUTER STUFF... HIS EXTRA COSTUMES...
THIS MUST BE THE BAT NERVE CENTER...
... BETTER NOT MESS WITH ANYTHING!

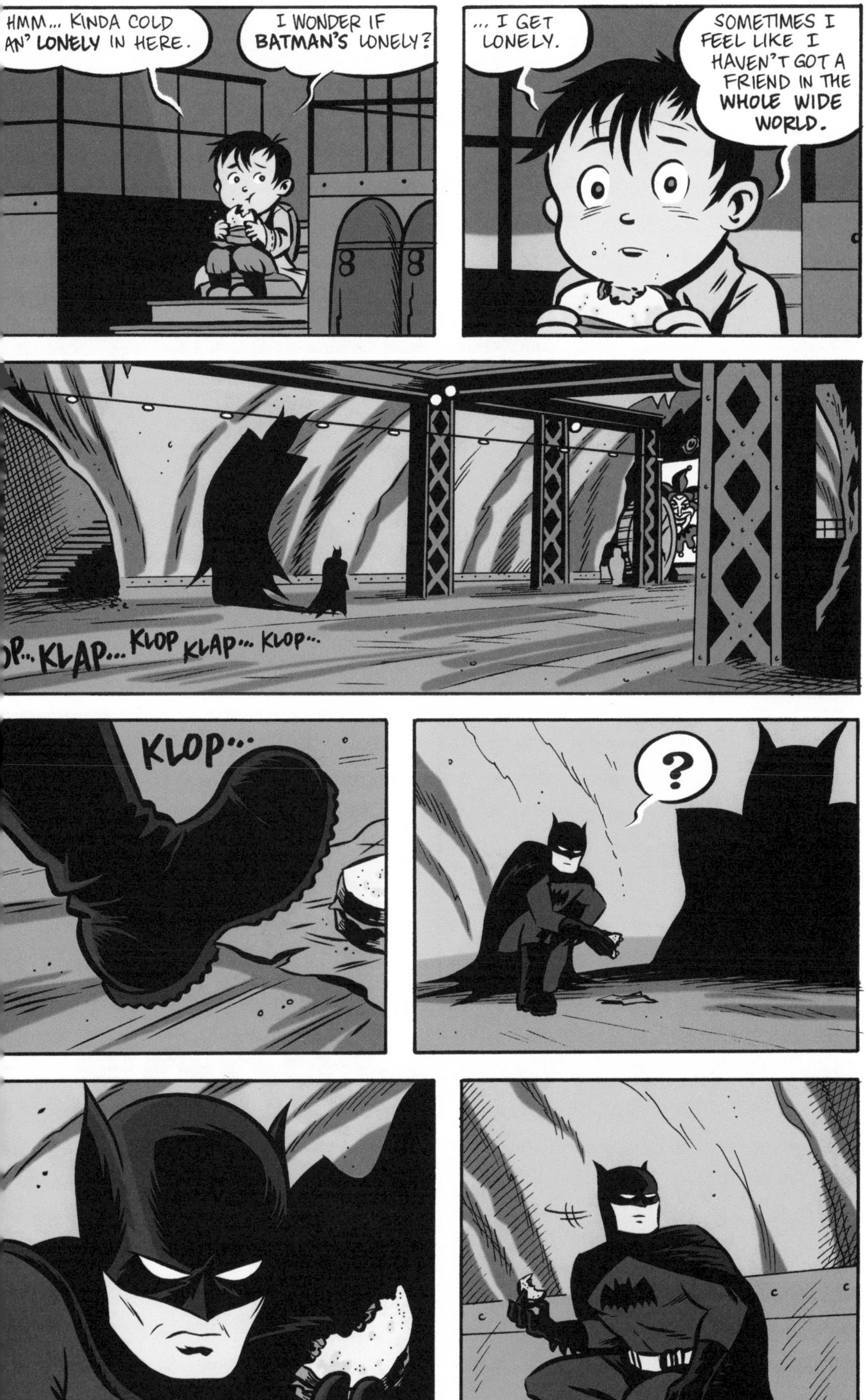

HMM... KINDA COLD AN' LONELY IN HERE.
I WONDER IF BATMAN'S LONELY?
... I GET LONELY.
SOMETIMES I FEEL LIKE I HAVEN'T GOT A FRIEND IN THE WHOLE WIDE WORLD.
OP... KLAP... KLOP KLAP... KLOP...
KLOP...
?

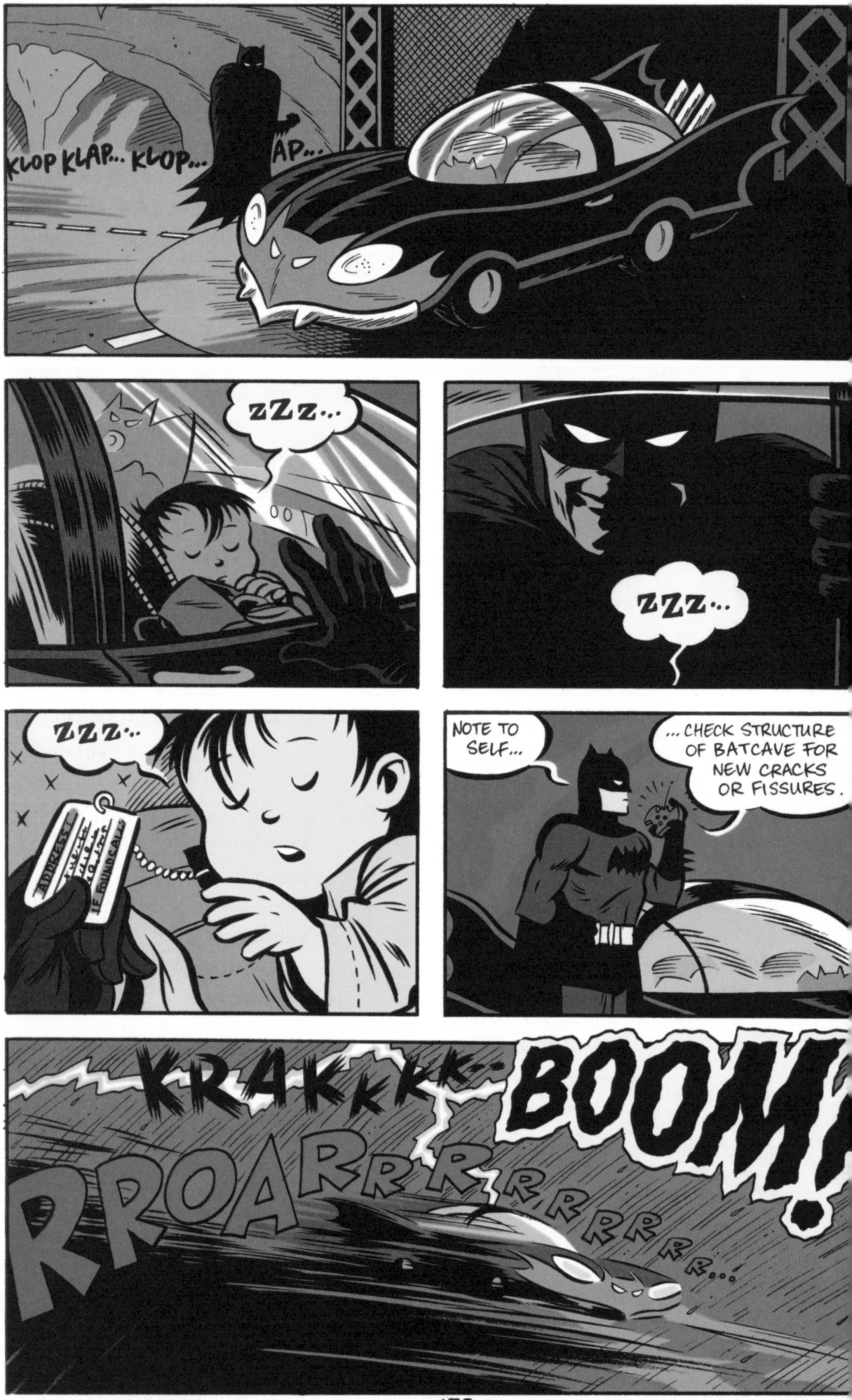
KLOP KLAP... KLOP...
AP...
ZZZ...
ZZZ...
ZZZ...
NOTE TO SELF...
...CHECK STRUCTURE OF BATCAVE FOR NEW CRACKS OR FISSURES.
KRAKKKK-BOOM!
RROARRRRRRRRRRR...

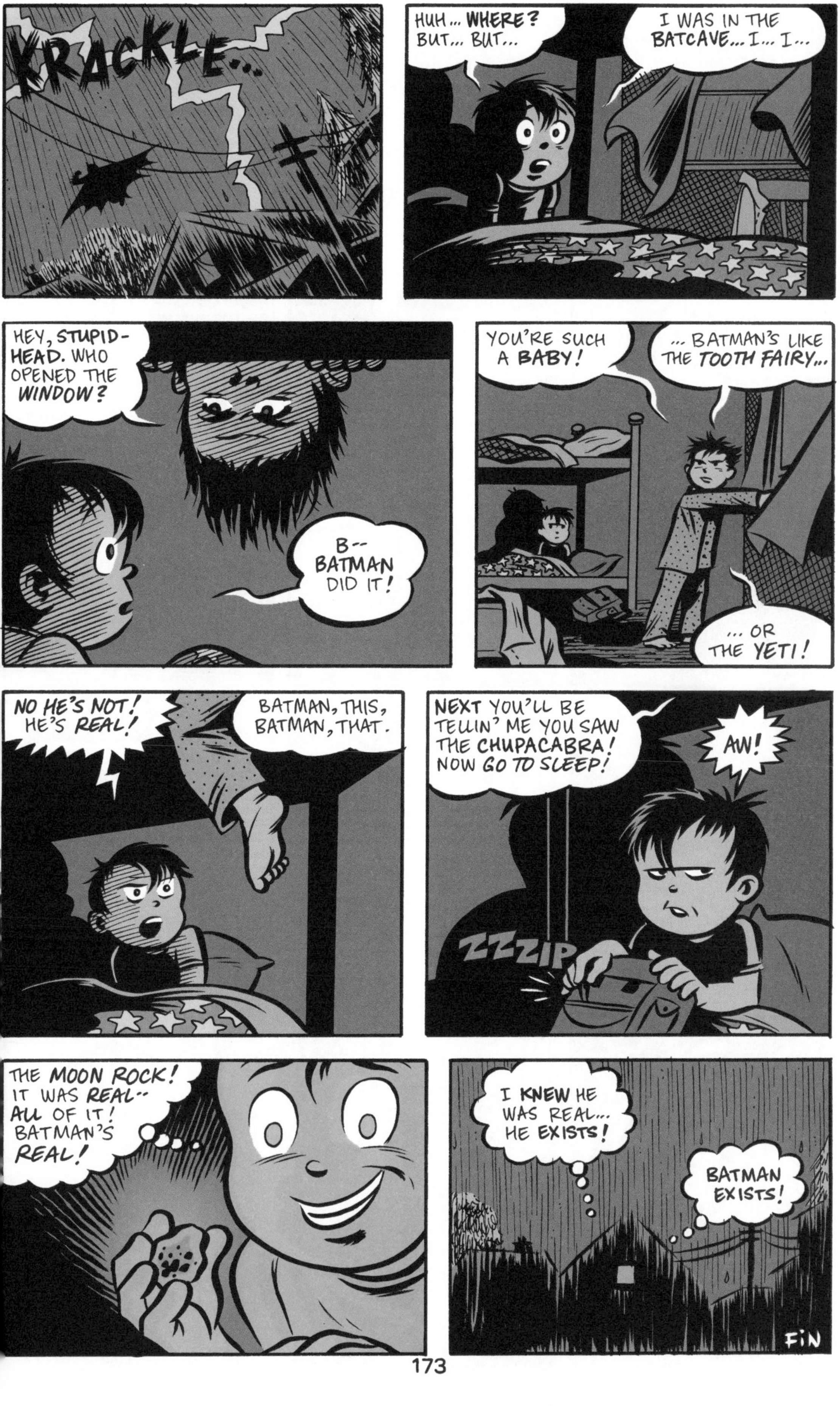
KRACKLE...
HUH... WHERE? BUT... BUT...
I WAS IN THE BATCAVE... I... I...
HEY, STUPID-HEAD. WHO OPENED THE WINDOW?
B-- BATMAN DID IT!
YOU'RE SUCH A BABY!
... BATMAN'S LIKE THE TOOTH FAIRY...
... OR THE YETI!
NO HE'S NOT! HE'S REAL!
BATMAN, THIS, BATMAN, THAT.
NEXT YOU'LL BE TELLIN' ME YOU SAW THE CHUPACABRA! NOW GO TO SLEEP!
AW!
ZZZIP
THE MOON ROCK! IT WAS REAL-- ALL OF IT! BATMAN'S REAL!
I KNEW HE WAS REAL... HE EXISTS!
BATMAN EXISTS!
FIN

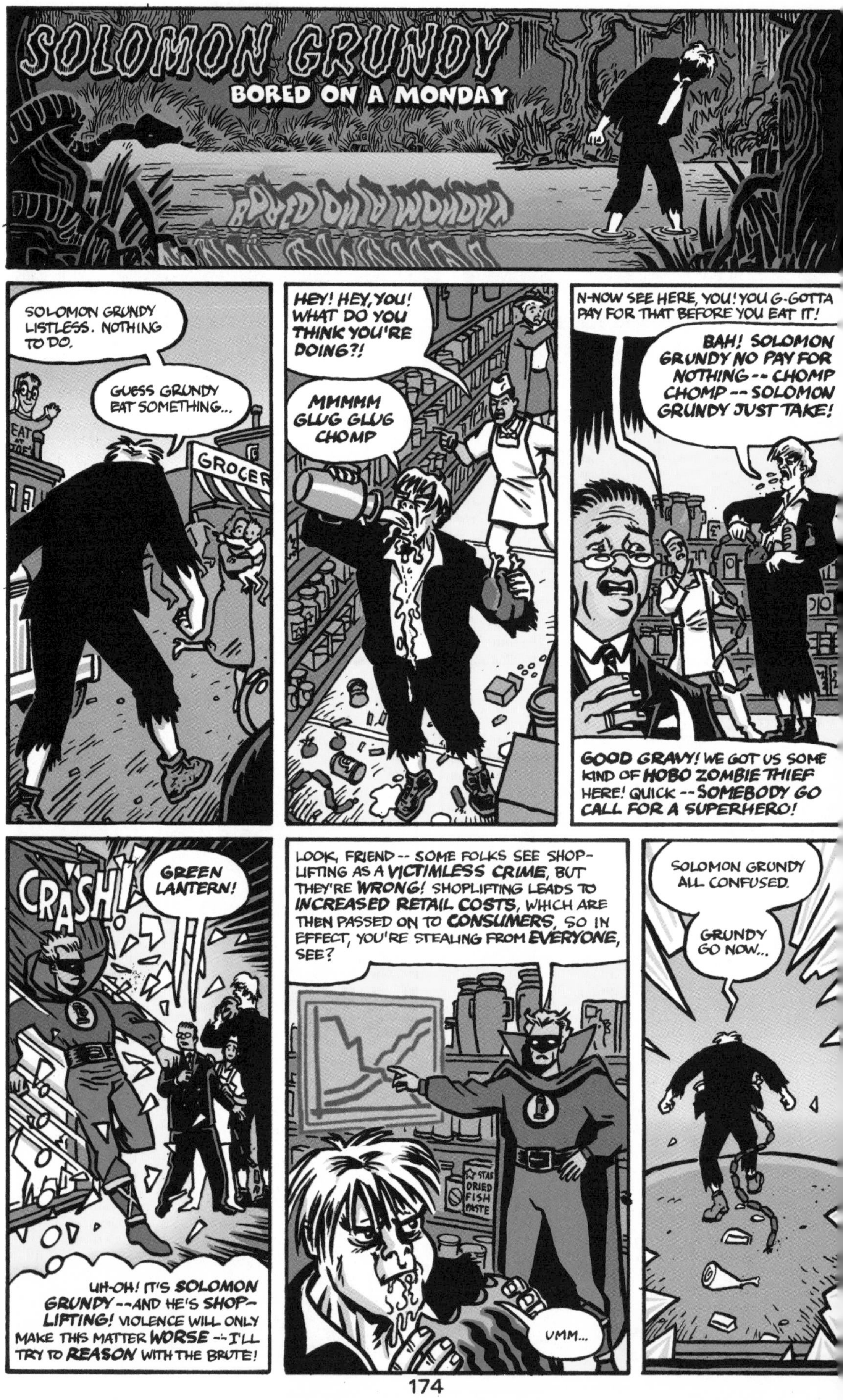
SOLOMON GRUNDY
BORED ON A MONDAY
SOLOMON GRUNDY LISTLESS. NOTHING TO DO.
GUESS GRUNDY EAT SOMETHING...
EAT AT JOE'S
GROCER
HEY! HEY, YOU! WHAT DO YOU THINK YOU'RE DOING?!
MMMMM GLUG GLUG CHOMP
N-NOW SEE HERE, YOU! YOU G-GOTTA PAY FOR THAT BEFORE YOU EAT IT!
BAH! SOLOMON GRUNDY NO PAY FOR NOTHING -- CHOMP CHOMP -- SOLOMON GRUNDY JUST TAKE!
GOOD GRAVY! WE GOT US SOME KIND OF HOBO ZOMBIE THIEF HERE! QUICK -- SOMEBODY GO CALL FOR A SUPERHERO!
CRASH!
GREEN LANTERN!
UH-OH! IT'S SOLOMON GRUNDY -- AND HE'S SHOP-LIFTING! VIOLENCE WILL ONLY MAKE THIS MATTER WORSE -- I'LL TRY TO REASON WITH THE BRUTE!
LOOK, FRIEND -- SOME FOLKS SEE SHOP-LIFTING AS A VICTIMLESS CRIME, BUT THEY'RE WRONG! SHOPLIFTING LEADS TO INCREASED RETAIL COSTS, WHICH ARE THEN PASSED ON TO CONSUMERS, SO IN EFFECT, YOU'RE STEALING FROM EVERYONE, SEE?
STAR DRIED FISH PASTE
UMM...
SOLOMON GRUNDY ALL CONFUSED.
GRUNDY GO NOW...

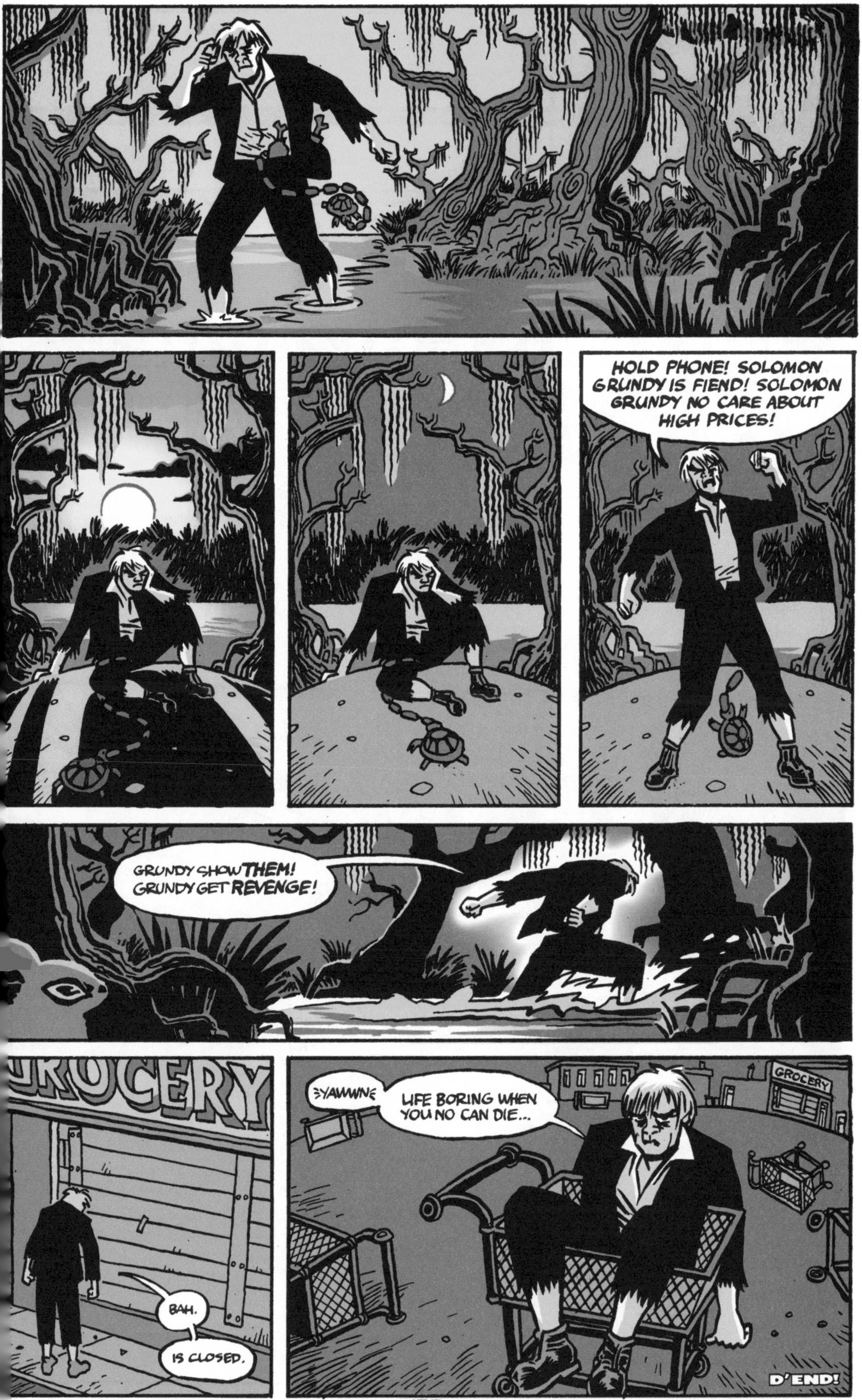

HOLD PHONE! SOLOMON GRUNDY IS FIEND! SOLOMON GRUNDY NO CARE ABOUT HIGH PRICES!
GRUNDY SHOW THEM! GRUNDY GET REVENGE!
GROCERY
BAH.
IS CLOSED.
YAWWN
LIFE BORING WHEN YOU NO CAN DIE...
GROCERY
D'END!

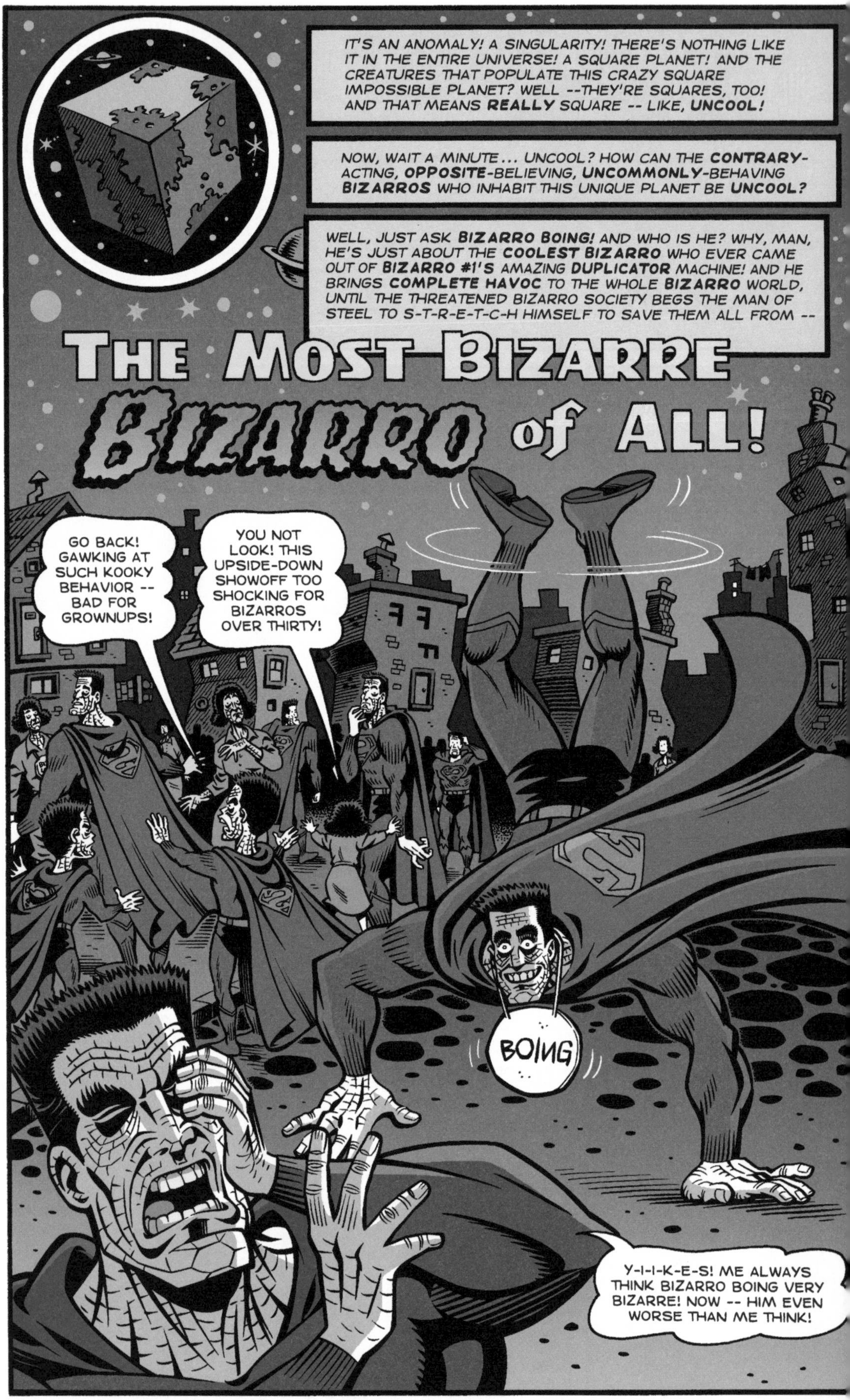
IT'S AN ANOMALY! A SINGULARITY! THERE'S NOTHING LIKE IT IN THE ENTIRE UNIVERSE! A SQUARE PLANET! AND THE CREATURES THAT POPULATE THIS CRAZY SQUARE IMPOSSIBLE PLANET? WELL --THEY'RE SQUARES, TOO! AND THAT MEANS REALLY SQUARE -- LIKE, UNCOOL!
NOW, WAIT A MINUTE... UNCOOL? HOW CAN THE CONTRARY-ACTING, OPPOSITE-BELIEVING, UNCOMMONLY-BEHAVING BIZARROS WHO INHABIT THIS UNIQUE PLANET BE UNCOOL?
WELL, JUST ASK BIZARRO BOING! AND WHO IS HE? WHY, MAN, HE'S JUST ABOUT THE COOLEST BIZARRO WHO EVER CAME OUT OF BIZARRO #1'S AMAZING DUPLICATOR MACHINE! AND HE BRINGS COMPLETE HAVOC TO THE WHOLE BIZARRO WORLD, UNTIL THE THREATENED BIZARRO SOCIETY BEGS THE MAN OF STEEL TO S-T-R-E-T-C-H HIMSELF TO SAVE THEM ALL FROM --
THE MOST BIZARRE BIZARRO of ALL!
GO BACK! GAWKING AT SUCH KOOKY BEHAVIOR -- BAD FOR GROWNUPS!
YOU NOT LOOK! THIS UPSIDE-DOWN SHOWOFF TOO SHOCKING FOR BIZARROS OVER THIRTY!
BOING
Y-I-I-K-E-S! ME ALWAYS THINK BIZARRO BOING VERY BIZARRE! NOW -- HIM EVEN WORSE THAN ME THINK!

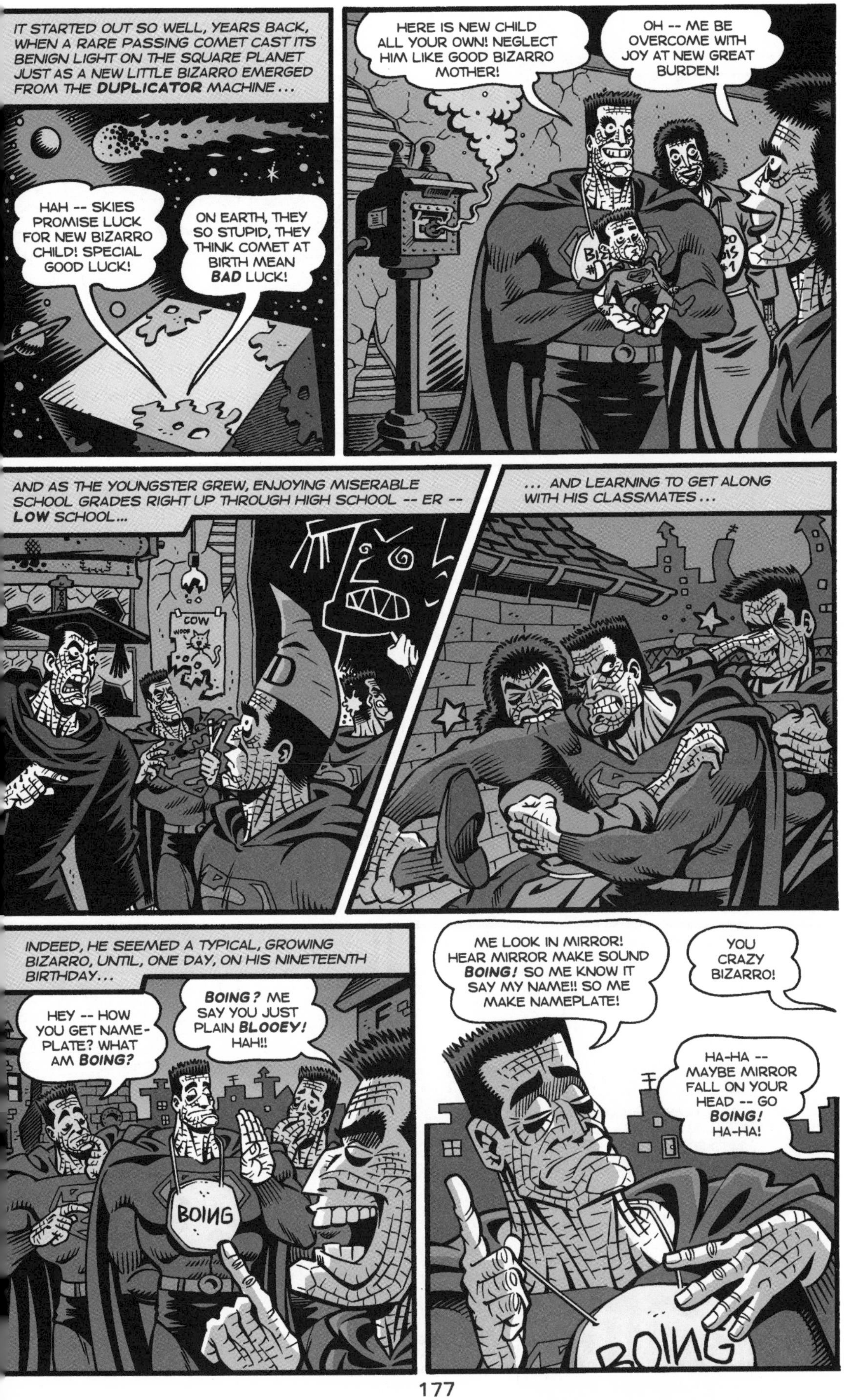
IT STARTED OUT SO WELL, YEARS BACK, WHEN A RARE PASSING COMET CAST ITS BENIGN LIGHT ON THE SQUARE PLANET JUST AS A NEW LITTLE BIZARRO EMERGED FROM THE DUPLICATOR MACHINE...
HAH -- SKIES PROMISE LUCK FOR NEW BIZARRO CHILD! SPECIAL GOOD LUCK!
ON EARTH, THEY SO STUPID, THEY THINK COMET AT BIRTH MEAN BAD LUCK!
HERE IS NEW CHILD ALL YOUR OWN! NEGLECT HIM LIKE GOOD BIZARRO MOTHER!
OH -- ME BE OVERCOME WITH JOY AT NEW GREAT BURDEN!
AND AS THE YOUNGSTER GREW, ENJOYING MISERABLE SCHOOL GRADES RIGHT UP THROUGH HIGH SCHOOL -- ER -- LOW SCHOOL...
COW
... AND LEARNING TO GET ALONG WITH HIS CLASSMATES...
INDEED, HE SEEMED A TYPICAL, GROWING BIZARRO, UNTIL, ONE DAY, ON HIS NINETEENTH BIRTHDAY...
HEY -- HOW YOU GET NAME-PLATE? WHAT AM BOING?
BOING? ME SAY YOU JUST PLAIN BLOOEY! HAH!!
BOING
ME LOOK IN MIRROR! HEAR MIRROR MAKE SOUND BOING! SO ME KNOW IT SAY MY NAME!! SO ME MAKE NAMEPLATE!
YOU CRAZY BIZARRO!
HA-HA -- MAYBE MIRROR FALL ON YOUR HEAD -- GO BOING! HA-HA!
BOING

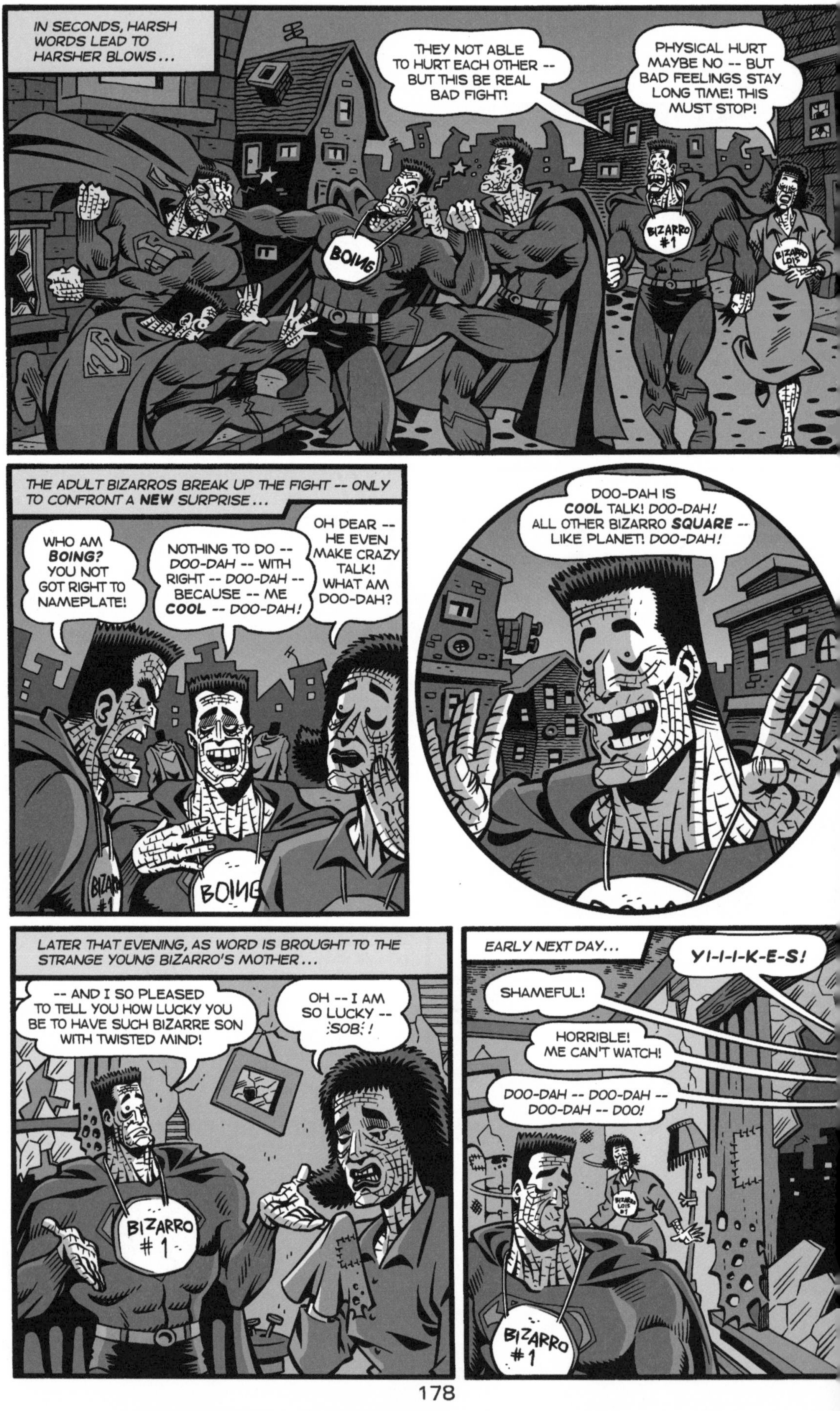
IN SECONDS, HARSH WORDS LEAD TO HARSHER BLOWS...
THEY NOT ABLE TO HURT EACH OTHER -- BUT THIS BE REAL BAD FIGHT!
PHYSICAL HURT MAYBE NO -- BUT BAD FEELINGS STAY LONG TIME! THIS MUST STOP!
BOING
BIZARRO #1
THE ADULT BIZARROS BREAK UP THE FIGHT -- ONLY TO CONFRONT A NEW SURPRISE...
WHO AM BOING? YOU NOT GOT RIGHT TO NAMEPLATE!
NOTHING TO DO -- DOO-DAH -- WITH RIGHT -- DOO-DAH -- BECAUSE -- ME COOL -- DOO-DAH!
OH DEAR -- HE EVEN MAKE CRAZY TALK! WHAT AM DOO-DAH?
BIZARRO #1
BOING
DOO-DAH IS COOL TALK! DOO-DAH! ALL OTHER BIZARRO SQUARE -- LIKE PLANET! DOO-DAH!
LATER THAT EVENING, AS WORD IS BROUGHT TO THE STRANGE YOUNG BIZARRO'S MOTHER...
-- AND I SO PLEASED TO TELL YOU HOW LUCKY YOU BE TO HAVE SUCH BIZARRE SON WITH TWISTED MIND!
OH -- I AM SO LUCKY -- :SOB: !
BIZARRO #1
EARLY NEXT DAY...
YI-I-I-K-E-S!
SHAMEFUL!
HORRIBLE! ME CAN'T WATCH!
DOO-DAH -- DOO-DAH -- DOO-DAH -- DOO!
BIZARRO #1

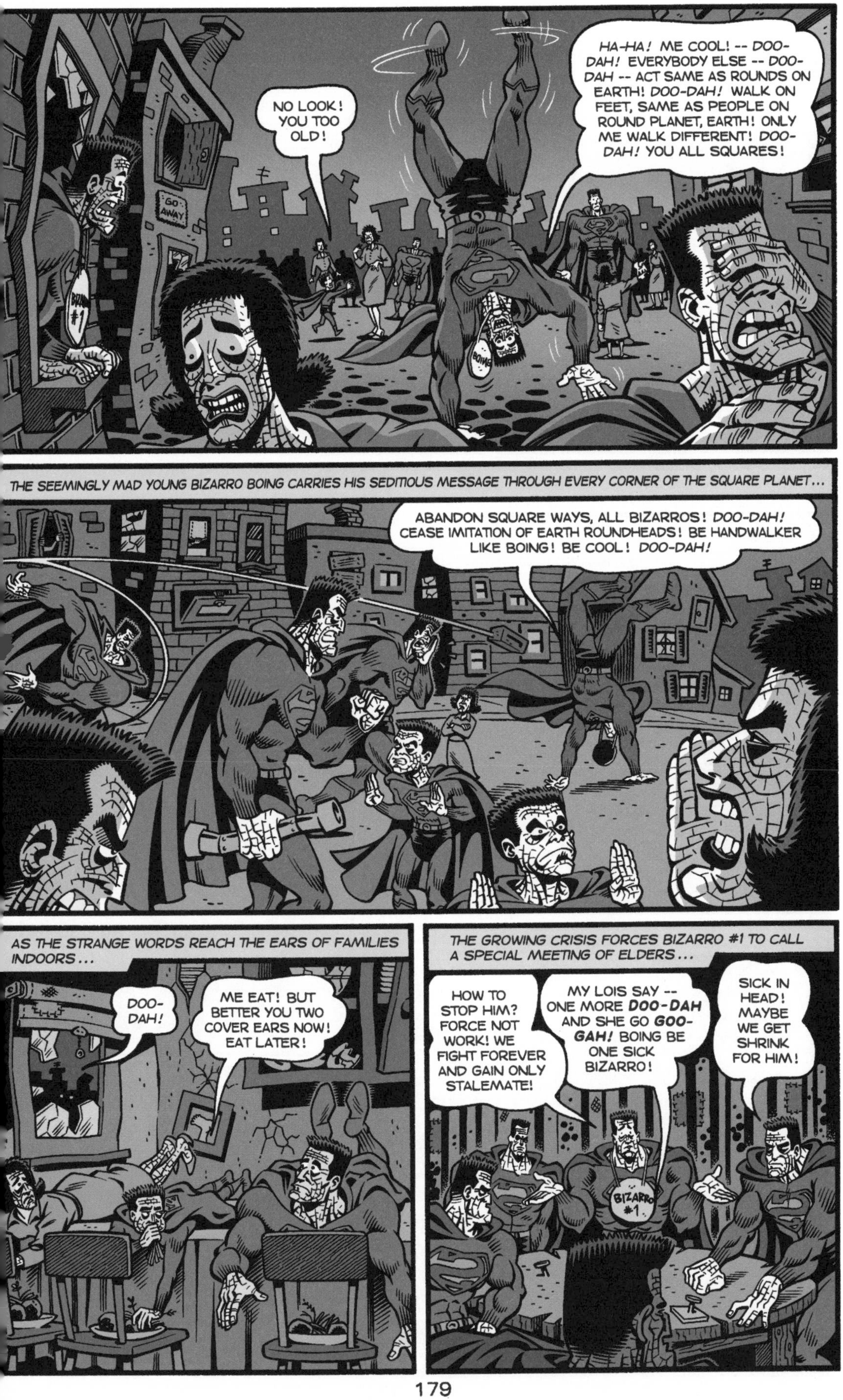
NO LOOK! YOU TOO OLD!
HA-HA! ME COOL! -- DOO-DAH! EVERYBODY ELSE -- DOO-DAH -- ACT SAME AS ROUNDS ON EARTH! DOO-DAH! WALK ON FEET, SAME AS PEOPLE ON ROUND PLANET, EARTH! ONLY ME WALK DIFFERENT! DOO-DAH! YOU ALL SQUARES!
GO AWAY
BIZARRO #1
BOING
THE SEEMINGLY MAD YOUNG BIZARRO BOING CARRIES HIS SEDITIOUS MESSAGE THROUGH EVERY CORNER OF THE SQUARE PLANET...
ABANDON SQUARE WAYS, ALL BIZARROS! DOO-DAH! CEASE IMITATION OF EARTH ROUNDHEADS! BE HANDWALKER LIKE BOING! BE COOL! DOO-DAH!
AS THE STRANGE WORDS REACH THE EARS OF FAMILIES INDOORS...
DOO-DAH!
ME EAT! BUT BETTER YOU TWO COVER EARS NOW! EAT LATER!
THE GROWING CRISIS FORCES BIZARRO #1 TO CALL A SPECIAL MEETING OF ELDERS...
HOW TO STOP HIM? FORCE NOT WORK! WE FIGHT FOREVER AND GAIN ONLY STALEMATE!
MY LOIS SAY -- ONE MORE DOO-DAH AND SHE GO GOO-GAH! BOING BE ONE SICK BIZARRO!
SICK IN HEAD! MAYBE WE GET SHRINK FOR HIM!
BIZARRO #1

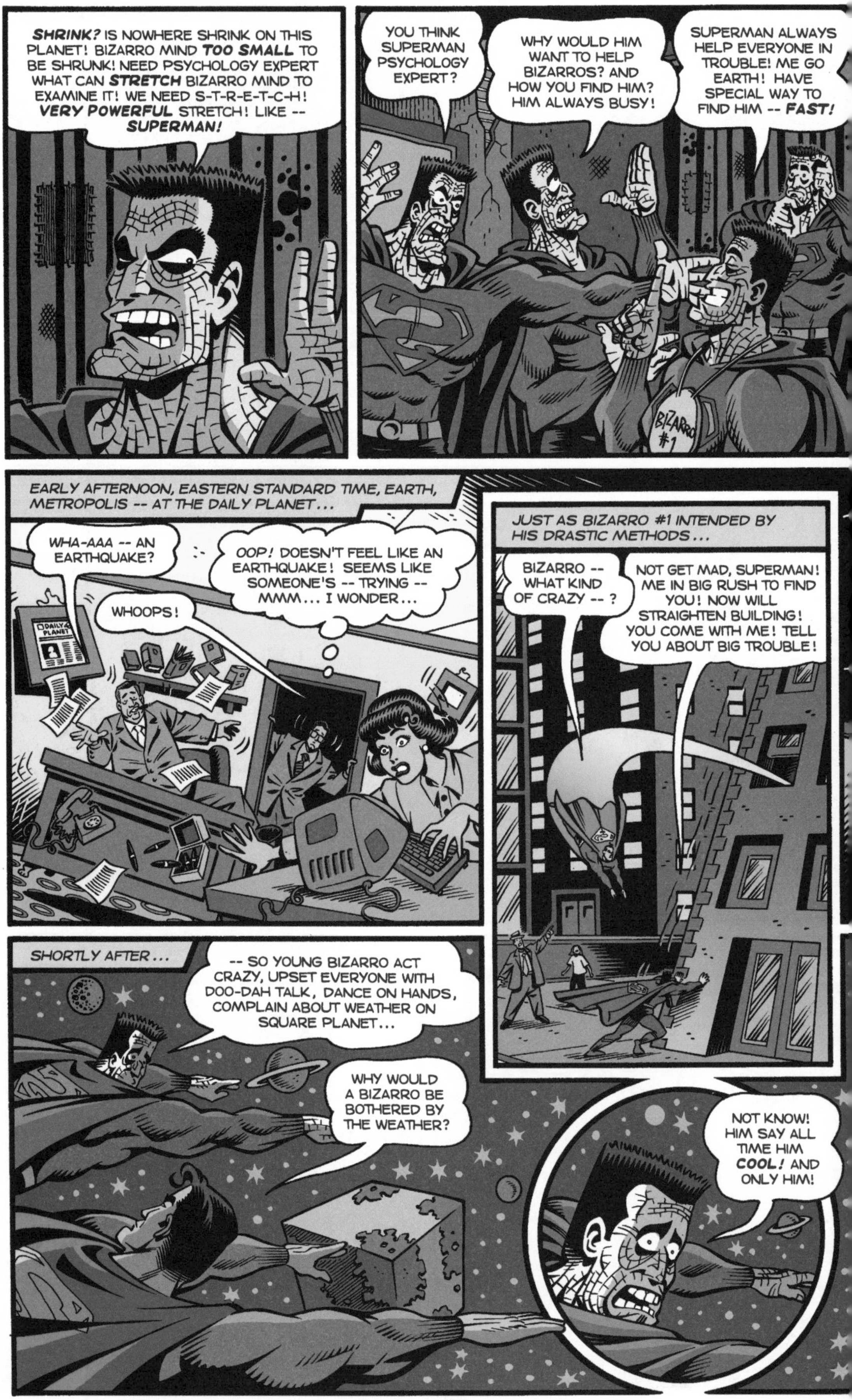

SHRINK? IS NOWHERE SHRINK ON THIS PLANET! BIZARRO MIND TOO SMALL TO BE SHRUNK! NEED PSYCHOLOGY EXPERT WHAT CAN STRETCH BIZARRO MIND TO EXAMINE IT! WE NEED S-T-R-E-T-C-H! VERY POWERFUL STRETCH! LIKE -- SUPERMAN!
YOU THINK SUPERMAN PSYCHOLOGY EXPERT?
WHY WOULD HIM WANT TO HELP BIZARROS? AND HOW YOU FIND HIM? HIM ALWAYS BUSY!
SUPERMAN ALWAYS HELP EVERYONE IN TROUBLE! ME GO EARTH! HAVE SPECIAL WAY TO FIND HIM -- FAST!
BIZARRO #1
EARLY AFTERNOON, EASTERN STANDARD TIME, EARTH, METROPOLIS -- AT THE DAILY PLANET...
WHA-AAA -- AN EARTHQUAKE?
WHOOPS!
OOP! DOESN'T FEEL LIKE AN EARTHQUAKE! SEEMS LIKE SOMEONE'S -- TRYING -- MMM... I WONDER...
DAILY PLANET
JUST AS BIZARRO #1 INTENDED BY HIS DRASTIC METHODS...
BIZARRO -- WHAT KIND OF CRAZY -- ?
NOT GET MAD, SUPERMAN! ME IN BIG RUSH TO FIND YOU! NOW WILL STRAIGHTEN BUILDING! YOU COME WITH ME! TELL YOU ABOUT BIG TROUBLE!
SHORTLY AFTER...
-- SO YOUNG BIZARRO ACT CRAZY, UPSET EVERYONE WITH DOO-DAH TALK, DANCE ON HANDS, COMPLAIN ABOUT WEATHER ON SQUARE PLANET...
WHY WOULD A BIZARRO BE BOTHERED BY THE WEATHER?
NOT KNOW! HIM SAY ALL TIME HIM COOL! AND ONLY HIM!

BUT INSTEAD OF GOING DIRECTLY TO SEE BIZARRO BOING, SUPERMAN HAS ANOTHER IDEA...

WHY YOU NEED FIRST TO LOOK AT DUPLICATOR MACHINE INSTEAD OF BOING?

BECAUSE THE REASON HAS TO BE HERE! SOMETHING HAPPENED TO THIS MACHINE WHEN BOING WAS CREATED TO MAKE HIM SO DIFFERENT!

IT'S KIND OF LIKE A GENETIC PROBLEM, YOU SEE? SO I'LL GIVE IT A SUPER-VISION CHECKOUT!

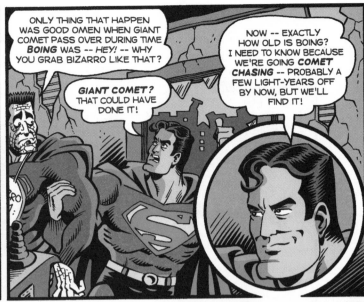

ONLY THING THAT HAPPEN WAS GOOD OMEN WHEN GIANT COMET PASS OVER DURING TIME BOING WAS -- HEY! -- WHY YOU GRAB BIZARRO LIKE THAT?

GIANT COMET? THAT COULD HAVE DONE IT!

NOW -- EXACTLY HOW OLD IS BOING? I NEED TO KNOW BECAUSE WE'RE GOING COMET CHASING -- PROBABLY A FEW LIGHT-YEARS OFF BY NOW, BUT WE'LL FIND IT!

THEN -- MOVING AT SUPER-SPEED, THE TWO SUPER-BEINGS STREAK WILDLY ACROSS THE GALAXY, TRACING THE ESTIMATED MATHEMATICAL ARC THE COMET'S PASSAGE WOULD HAVE GENERATED...

THERE -- THAT HAS TO BE THE RIGHT ONE! I NOT ONLY SEE IT! I HEAR IT! DON'T YOU?

ME SEE, BUT NOT HEAR NOTHING!

YOU CAN'T HEAR IT? WHY, YOU PEOPLE ARE ALL TONE DEAF! DIDN'T YOU KNOW THAT ALL CELESTIAL BODIES EMIT MUSICAL SOUNDS? THE GREEKS CALLED IT "HARMONY OF THE SPHERES!"

AND -- COMET SOUNDS ARE ESPECIALLY STRONG! HM -- MAYBE AT LEAST ONE OF YOU ISN'T TONE DEAF! COME ON!

WHO BE GREEKS?

DA-DEE

THAT'S THE LIKELIEST ANSWER -- THE COMET'S HARMONIC EFFECT MUST'VE PRODUCED A TEMPORARY DISTORTION OF THE MOLECULES IN THE DUPLICATOR MACHINE DURING BOING'S CREATION!

THAT NAME HE PICKED -- BOING! OBVIOUSLY A MUSICAL NOTE HE HEARS ALL THE TIME!

NOW -- LET'S GO FIND BOING!

SOON AFTER, BACK IN BIZARRO CITY...

DEE-DAH -- DEE-DAH -- ME COOL! BUT -- FOOTWALKERS AND BIZARRO SQUAWKERS BE ALL SQUARE -- AND STRICTLY NOWHERE!

POOR FELLOW! HE'S DANCING AND SINGING AT THEM AND THEY DON'T UNDERSTAND! AND NEITHER DOES HE!

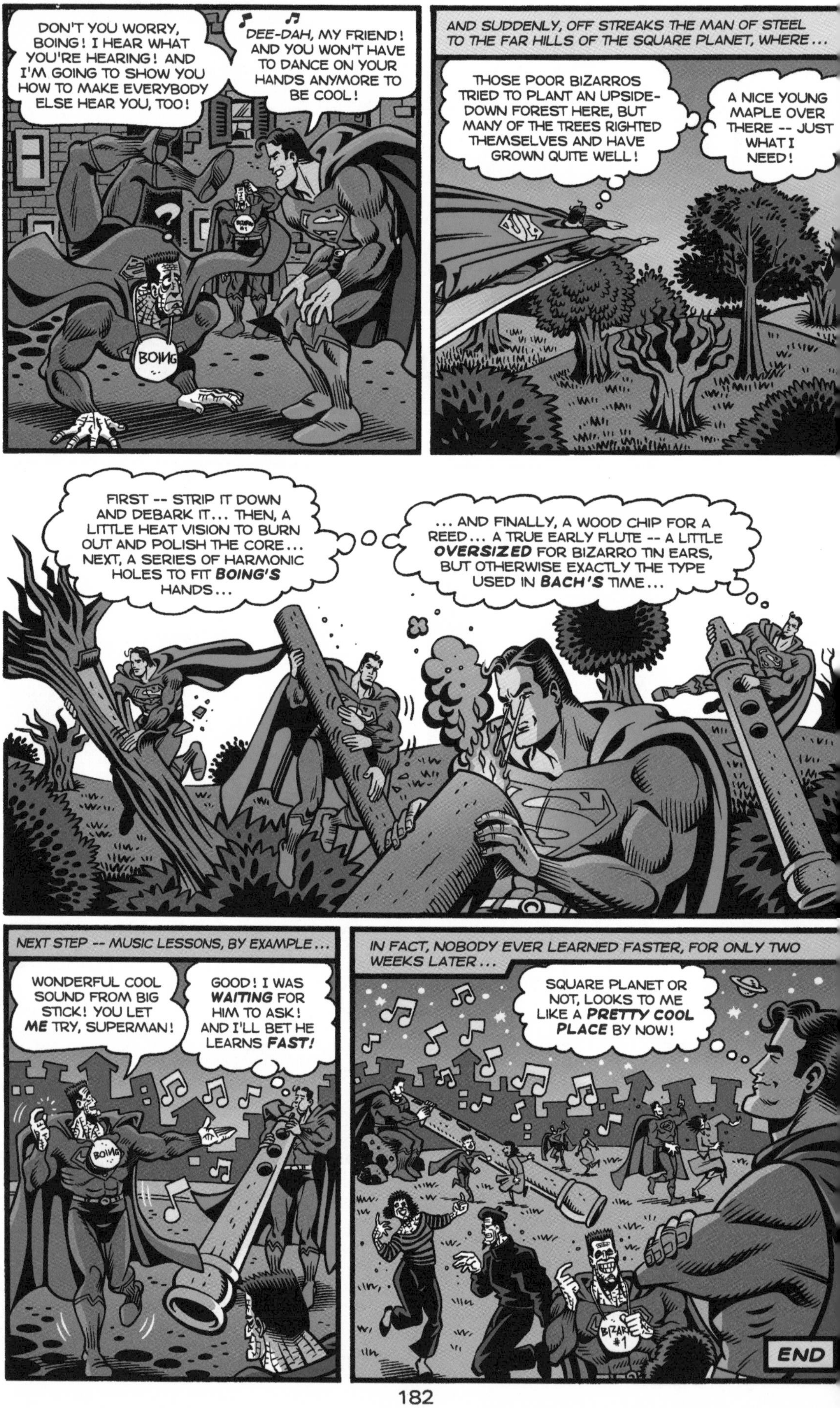
DON'T YOU WORRY, BOING! I HEAR WHAT YOU'RE HEARING! AND I'M GOING TO SHOW YOU HOW TO MAKE EVERYBODY ELSE HEAR YOU, TOO!
DEE-DAH, MY FRIEND! AND YOU WON'T HAVE TO DANCE ON YOUR HANDS ANYMORE TO BE COOL!
BOING
AND SUDDENLY, OFF STREAKS THE MAN OF STEEL TO THE FAR HILLS OF THE SQUARE PLANET, WHERE...
THOSE POOR BIZARROS TRIED TO PLANT AN UPSIDE-DOWN FOREST HERE, BUT MANY OF THE TREES RIGHTED THEMSELVES AND HAVE GROWN QUITE WELL!
A NICE YOUNG MAPLE OVER THERE -- JUST WHAT I NEED!
FIRST -- STRIP IT DOWN AND DEBARK IT... THEN, A LITTLE HEAT VISION TO BURN OUT AND POLISH THE CORE... NEXT, A SERIES OF HARMONIC HOLES TO FIT BOING'S HANDS...
... AND FINALLY, A WOOD CHIP FOR A REED... A TRUE EARLY FLUTE -- A LITTLE OVERSIZED FOR BIZARRO TIN EARS, BUT OTHERWISE EXACTLY THE TYPE USED IN BACH'S TIME...
NEXT STEP -- MUSIC LESSONS, BY EXAMPLE...
WONDERFUL COOL SOUND FROM BIG STICK! YOU LET ME TRY, SUPERMAN!
GOOD! I WAS WAITING FOR HIM TO ASK! AND I'LL BET HE LEARNS FAST!
BOING
IN FACT, NOBODY EVER LEARNED FASTER, FOR ONLY TWO WEEKS LATER...
SQUARE PLANET OR NOT, LOOKS TO ME LIKE A PRETTY COOL PLACE BY NOW!
END

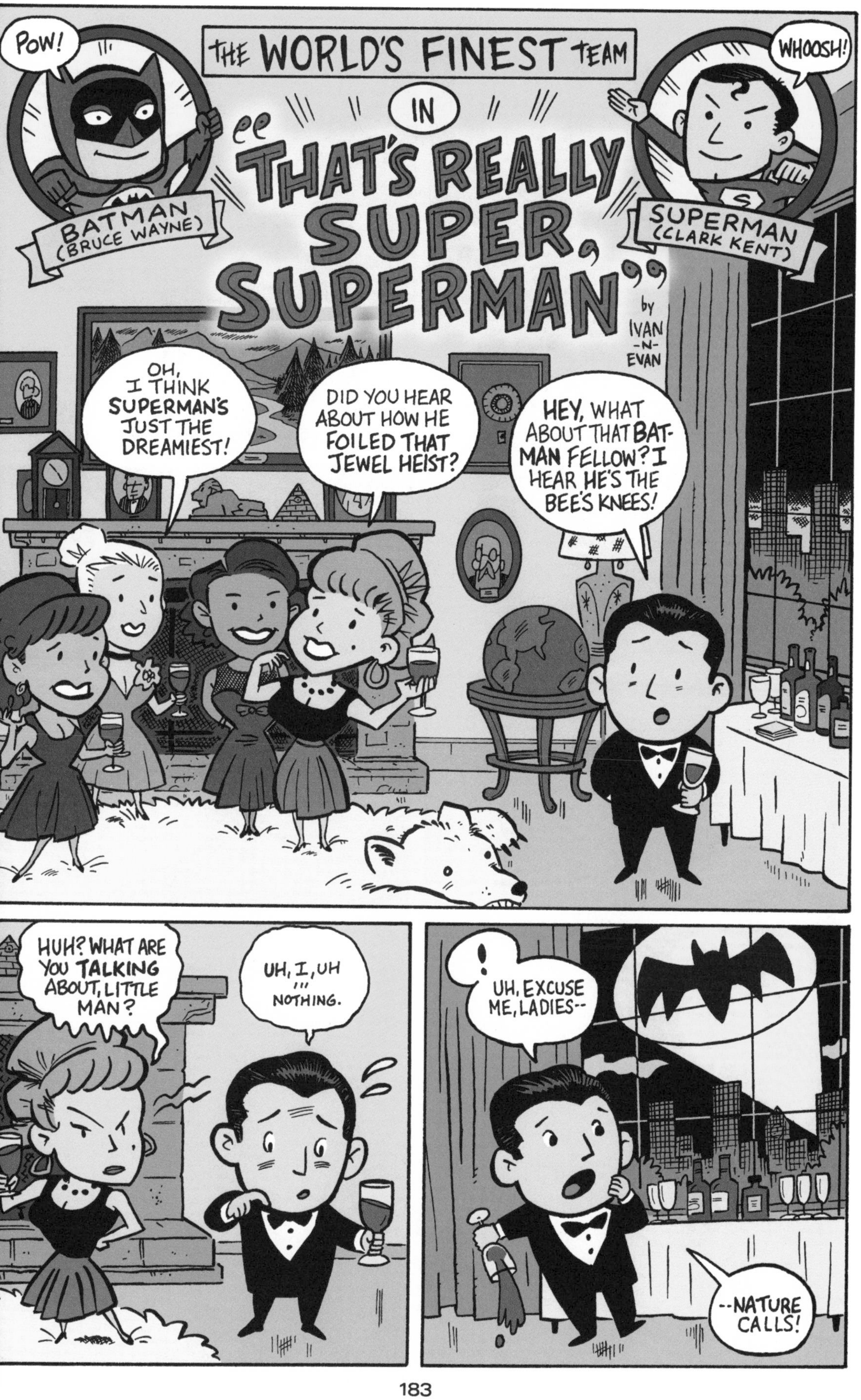
POW!
THE WORLD'S FINEST TEAM
WHOOSH!
BATMAN (BRUCE WAYNE)
IN
"THAT'S REALLY SUPER, SUPERMAN"
SUPERMAN (CLARK KENT)
by IVAN -N- EVAN
OH, I THINK SUPERMAN'S JUST THE DREAMIEST!
DID YOU HEAR ABOUT HOW HE FOILED THAT JEWEL HEIST?
HEY, WHAT ABOUT THAT BATMAN FELLOW? I HEAR HE'S THE BEE'S KNEES!
HUH? WHAT ARE YOU TALKING ABOUT, LITTLE MAN?
UH, I, UH ... NOTHING.
!
UH, EXCUSE ME, LADIES--
--NATURE CALLS!

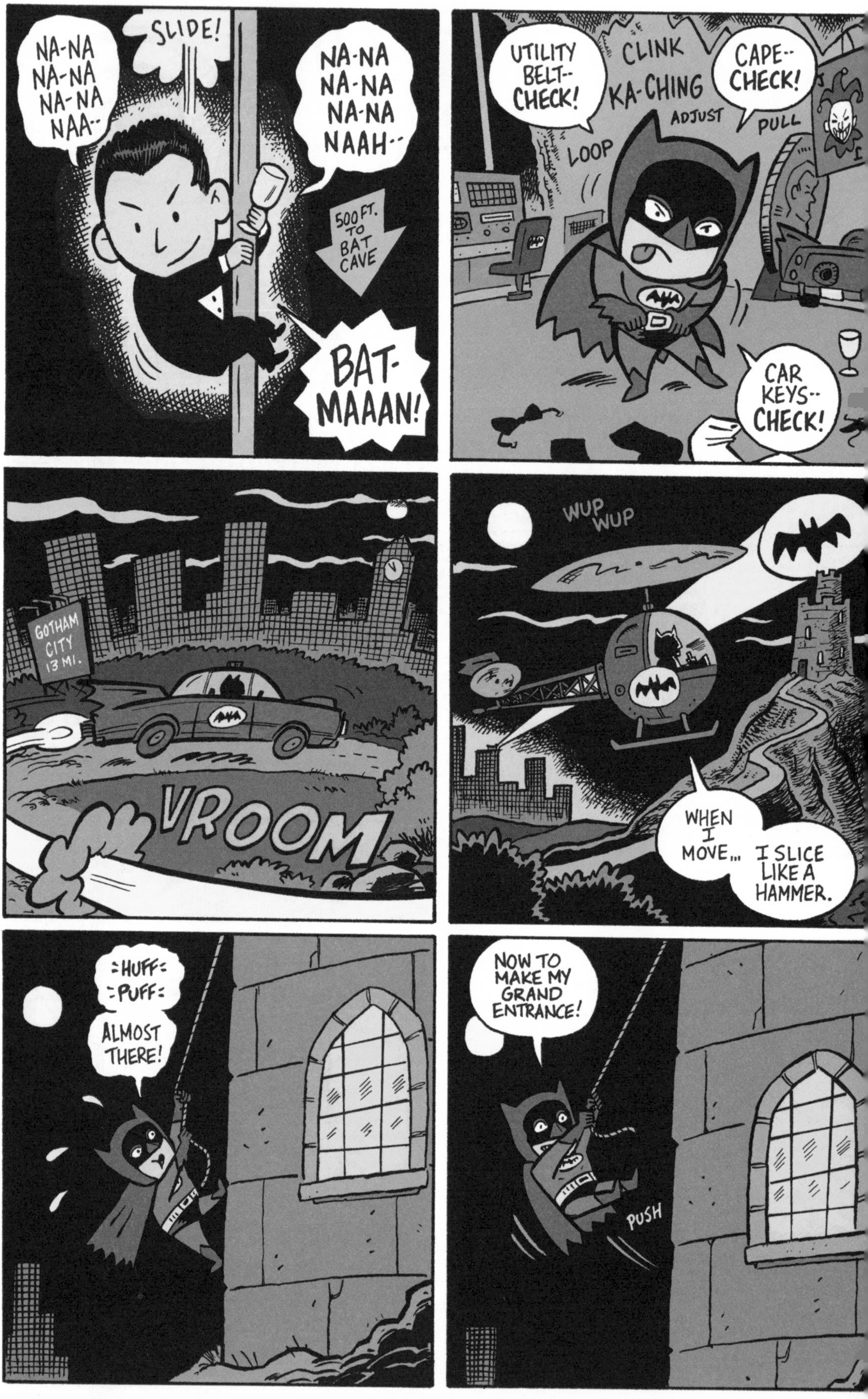
NA-NA NA-NA NA-NA NAA--
SLIDE!
NA-NA NA-NA NA-NA NAAH--
500 FT. TO BAT CAVE
BAT-MAAAN!
UTILITY BELT-- CHECK!
CLINK
KA-CHING
CAPE-- CHECK!
ADJUST
PULL
LOOP
CAR KEYS-- CHECK!
GOTHAM CITY 13 MI.
VROOM
WUP WUP
WHEN I MOVE...
I SLICE LIKE A HAMMER.
HUFF
PUFF
ALMOST THERE!
NOW TO MAKE MY GRAND ENTRANCE!
PUSH

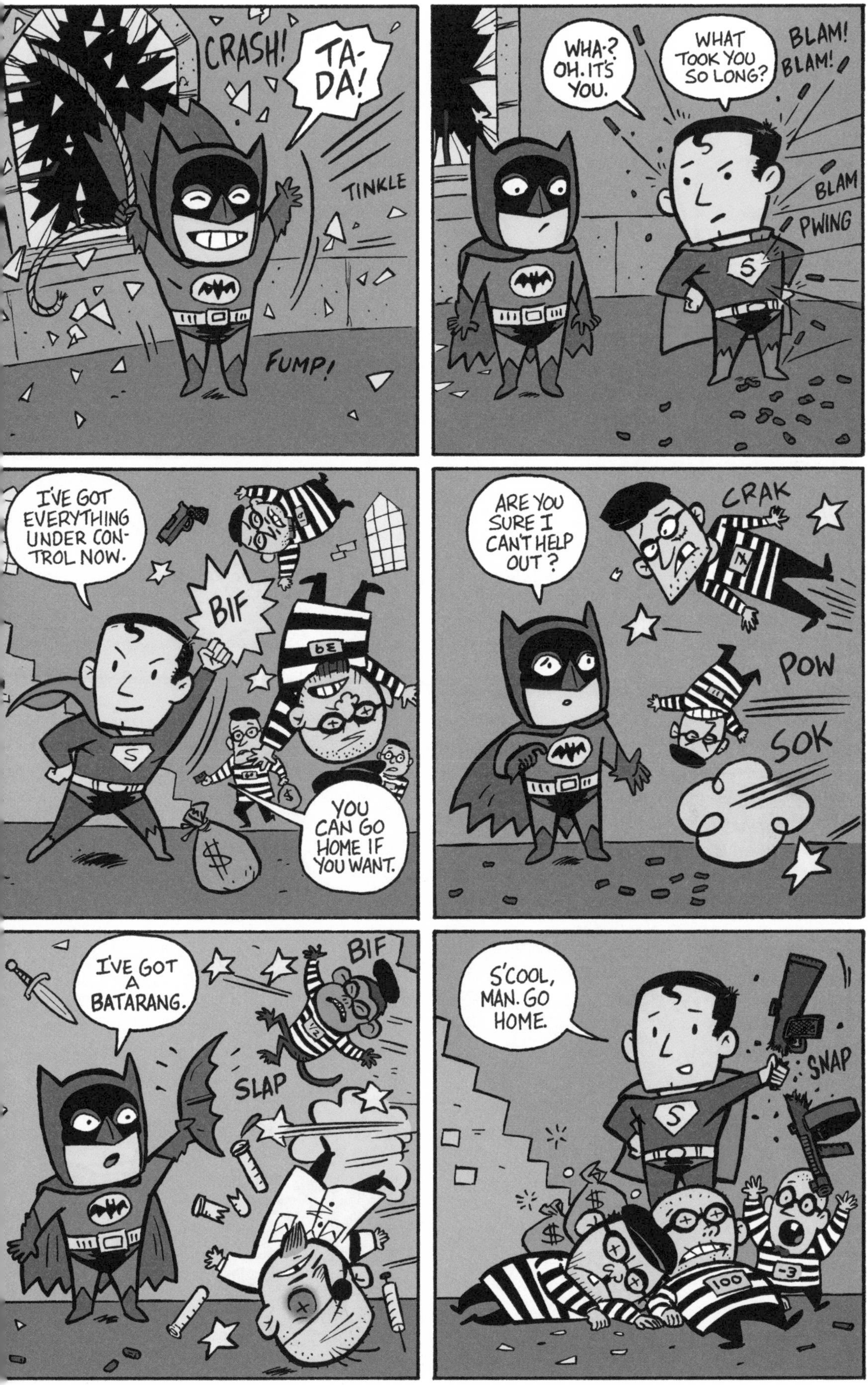
CRASH!
TA-DA!
TINKLE
FUMP!
WHA-? OH. IT'S YOU.
WHAT TOOK YOU SO LONG?
BLAM! BLAM!
BLAM
PWING
I'VE GOT EVERYTHING UNDER CON-TROL NOW.
BIF
YOU CAN GO HOME IF YOU WANT.
ARE YOU SURE I CAN'T HELP OUT?
CRAK
POW
SOK
I'VE GOT A BATARANG.
BIF
SLAP
S'COOL, MAN. GO HOME.
SNAP

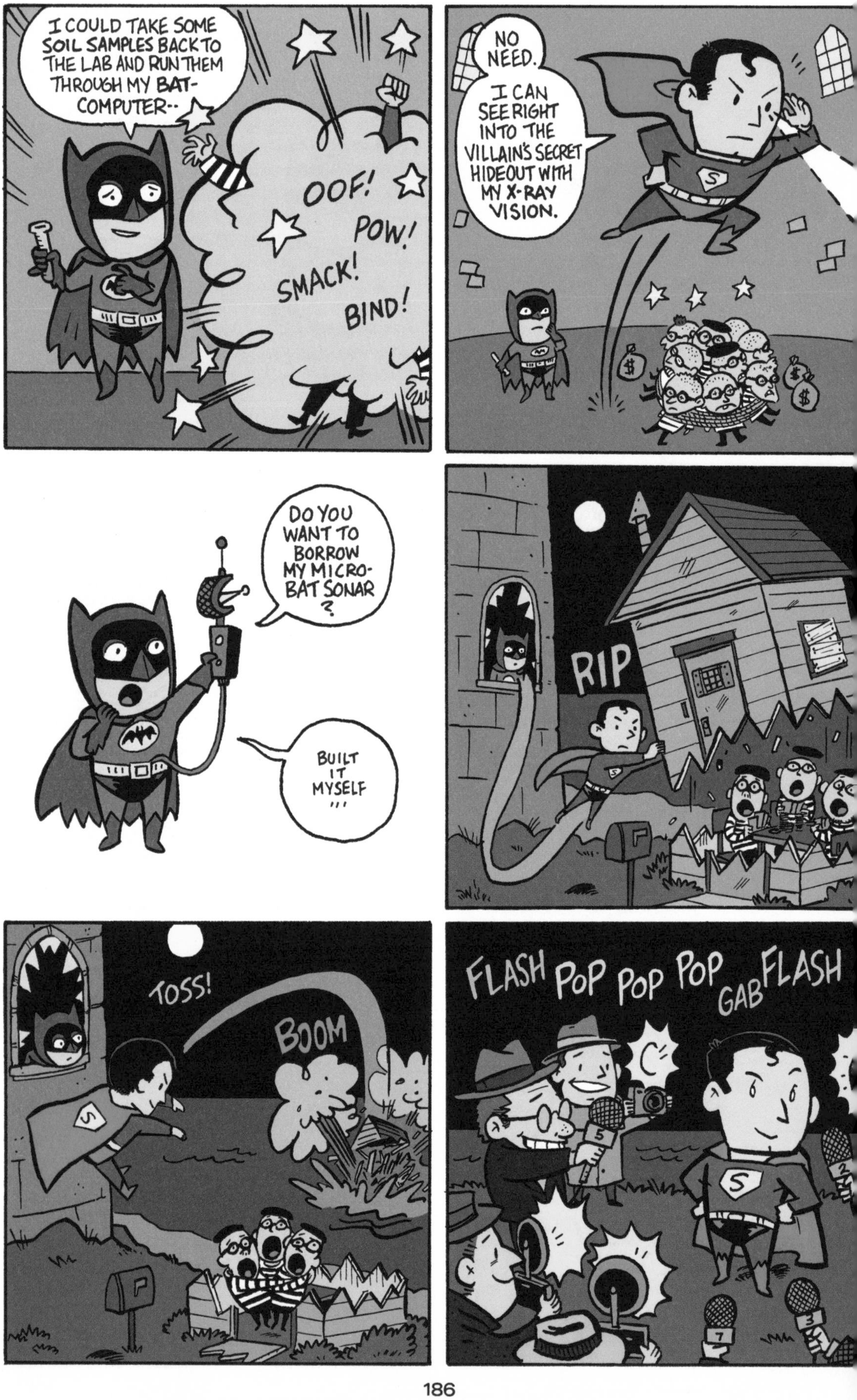
I COULD TAKE SOME SOIL SAMPLES BACK TO THE LAB AND RUN THEM THROUGH MY BAT-COMPUTER--
OOF!
POW!
SMACK!
BIND!
NO NEED.
I CAN SEE RIGHT INTO THE VILLAIN'S SECRET HIDEOUT WITH MY X-RAY VISION.
DO YOU WANT TO BORROW MY MICRO-BAT SONAR ?
BUILT IT MYSELF ...
RIP
TOSS!
BOOM
FLASH POP POP POP GAB FLASH

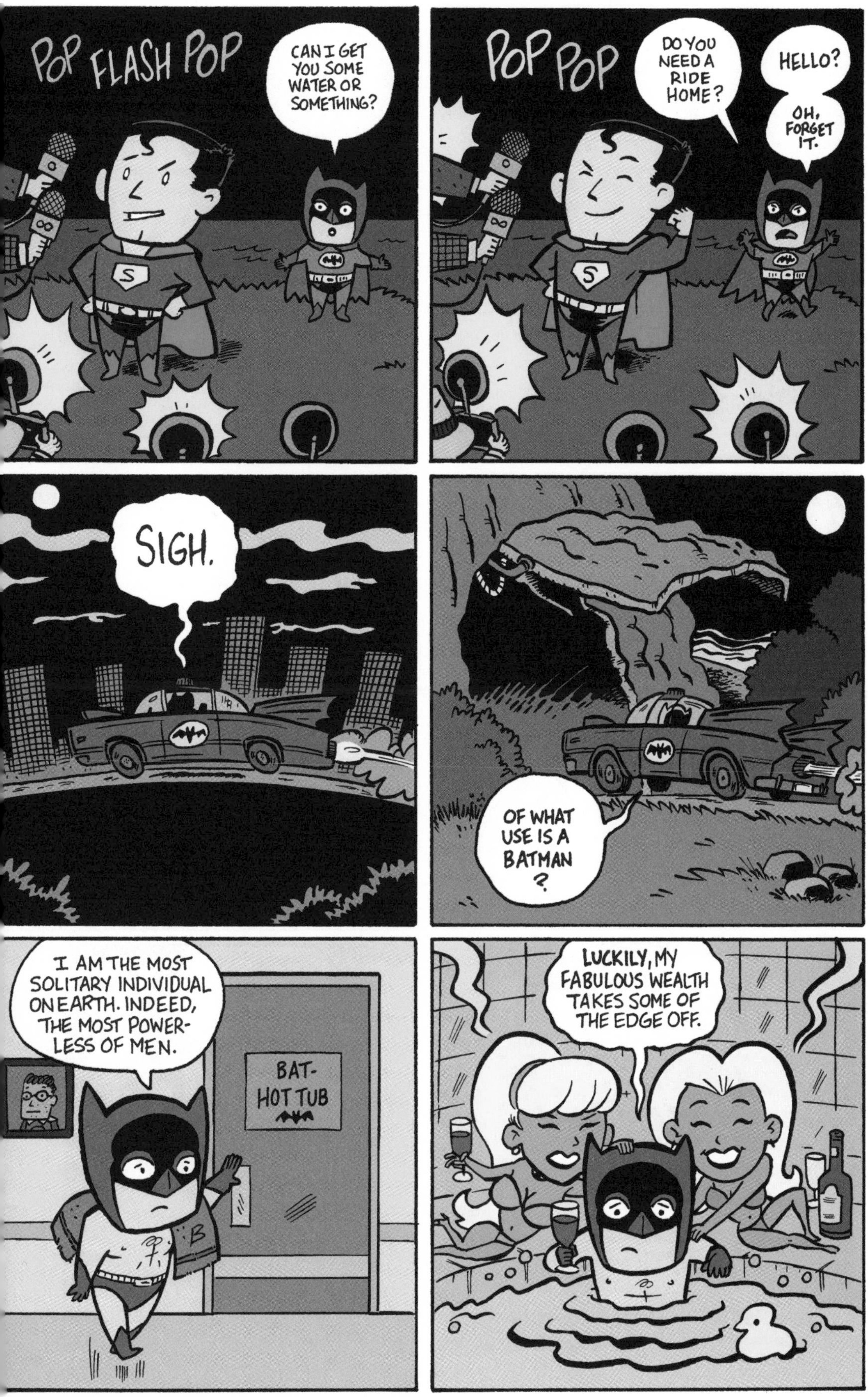
POP FLASH POP
CAN I GET YOU SOME WATER OR SOMETHING?
POP POP
DO YOU NEED A RIDE HOME?
HELLO?
OH, FORGET IT.
SIGH.
OF WHAT USE IS A BATMAN ?
I AM THE MOST SOLITARY INDIVIDUAL ON EARTH. INDEED, THE MOST POWER-LESS OF MEN.
BAT-HOT TUB
LUCKILY, MY FABULOUS WEALTH TAKES SOME OF THE EDGE OFF.

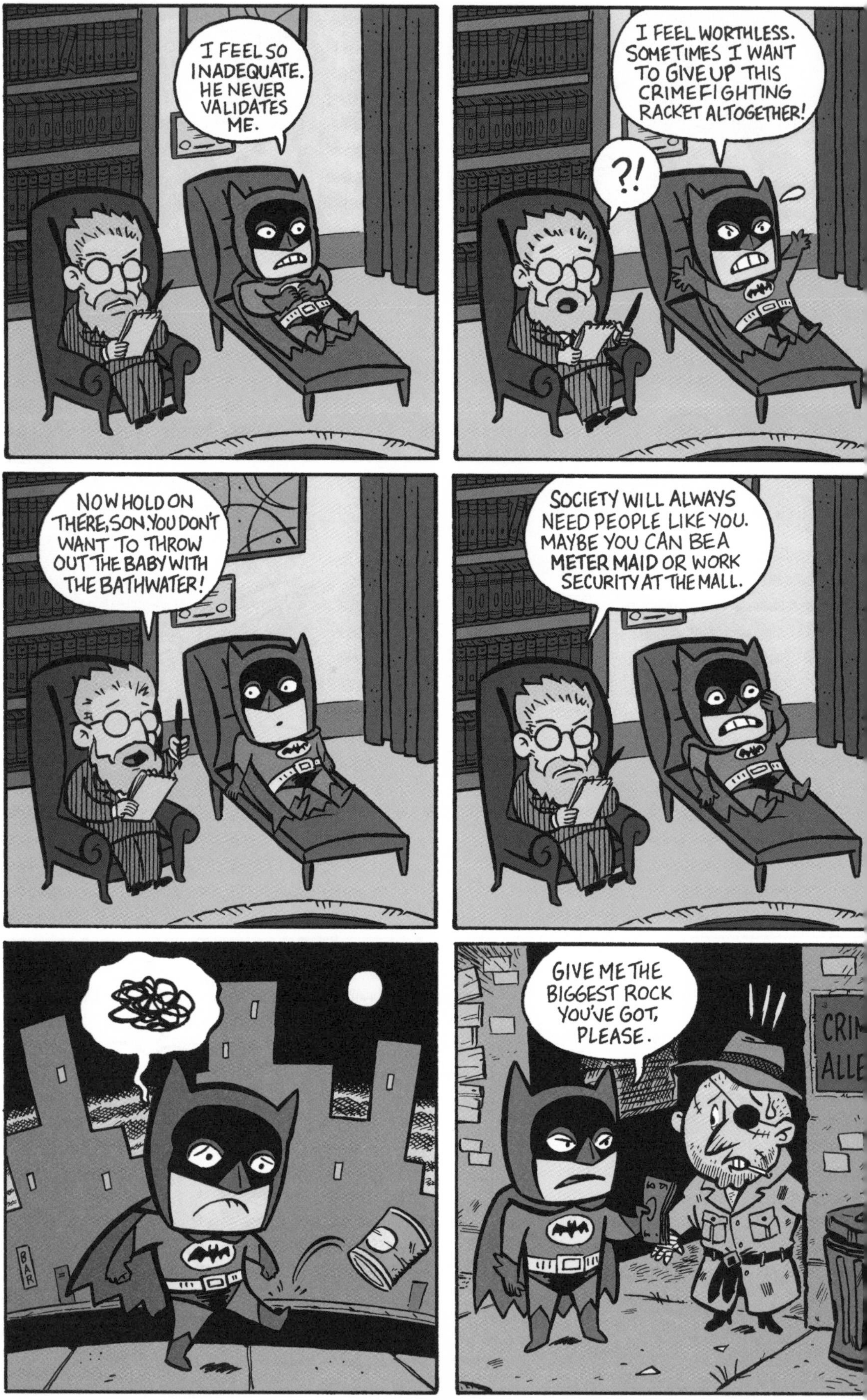
I FEEL SO INADEQUATE. HE NEVER VALIDATES ME.
I FEEL WORTHLESS. SOMETIMES I WANT TO GIVE UP THIS CRIMEFIGHTING RACKET ALTOGETHER!
?!
NOW HOLD ON THERE, SON. YOU DON'T WANT TO THROW OUT THE BABY WITH THE BATHWATER!
SOCIETY WILL ALWAYS NEED PEOPLE LIKE YOU. MAYBE YOU CAN BE A METER MAID OR WORK SECURITY AT THE MALL.
BAR
GIVE ME THE BIGGEST ROCK YOU'VE GOT, PLEASE.
CRIM
ALLE

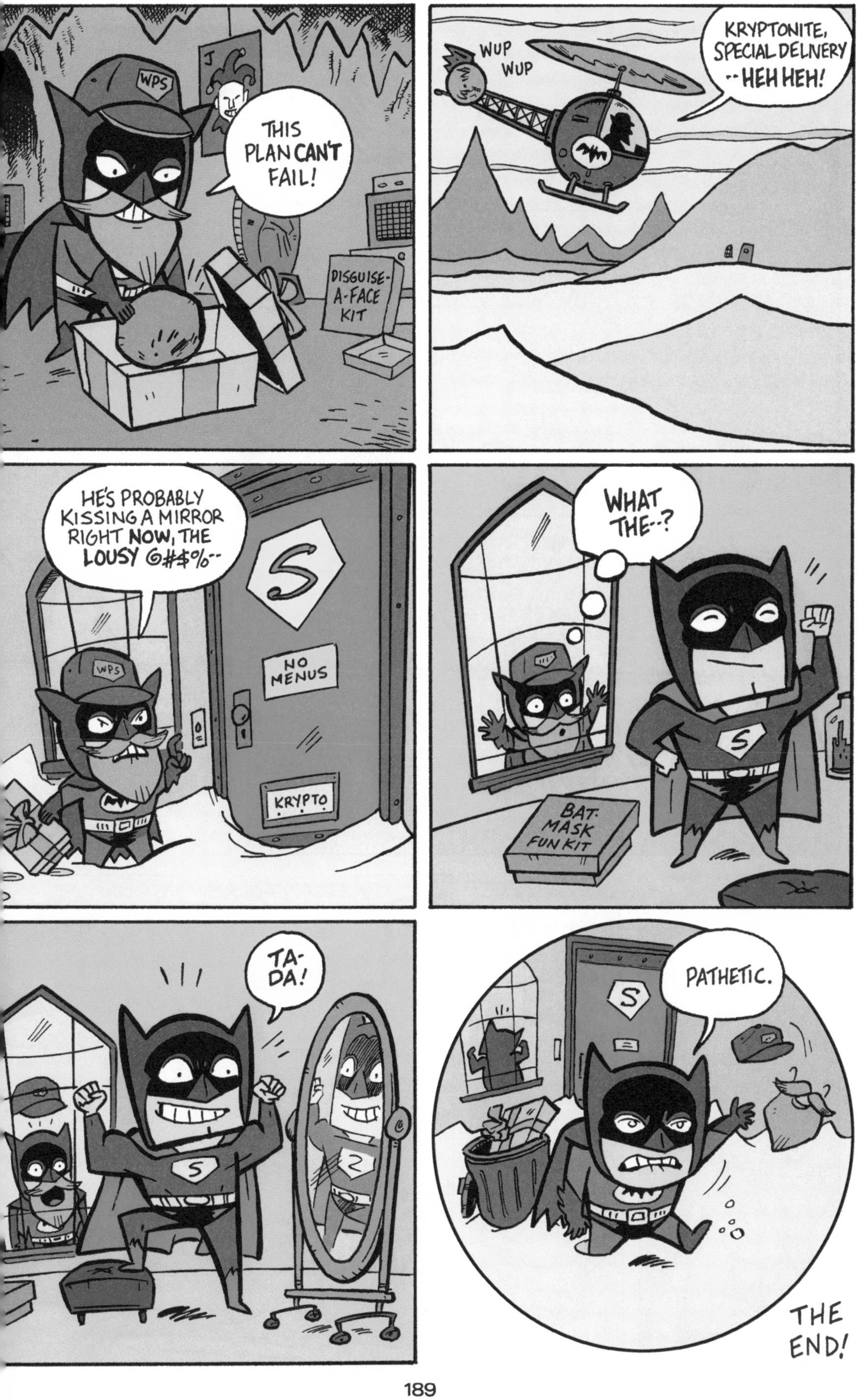
WPS
THIS PLAN CAN'T FAIL!
DISGUISE-A-FACE KIT
WUP WUP
KRYPTONITE, SPECIAL DELIVERY --HEH HEH!
HE'S PROBABLY KISSING A MIRROR RIGHT NOW, THE LOUSY @#$%--
WPS
NO MENUS
KRYPTO
WHAT THE--?
BAT-MASK FUN KIT
TA-DA!
PATHETIC.
THE END!

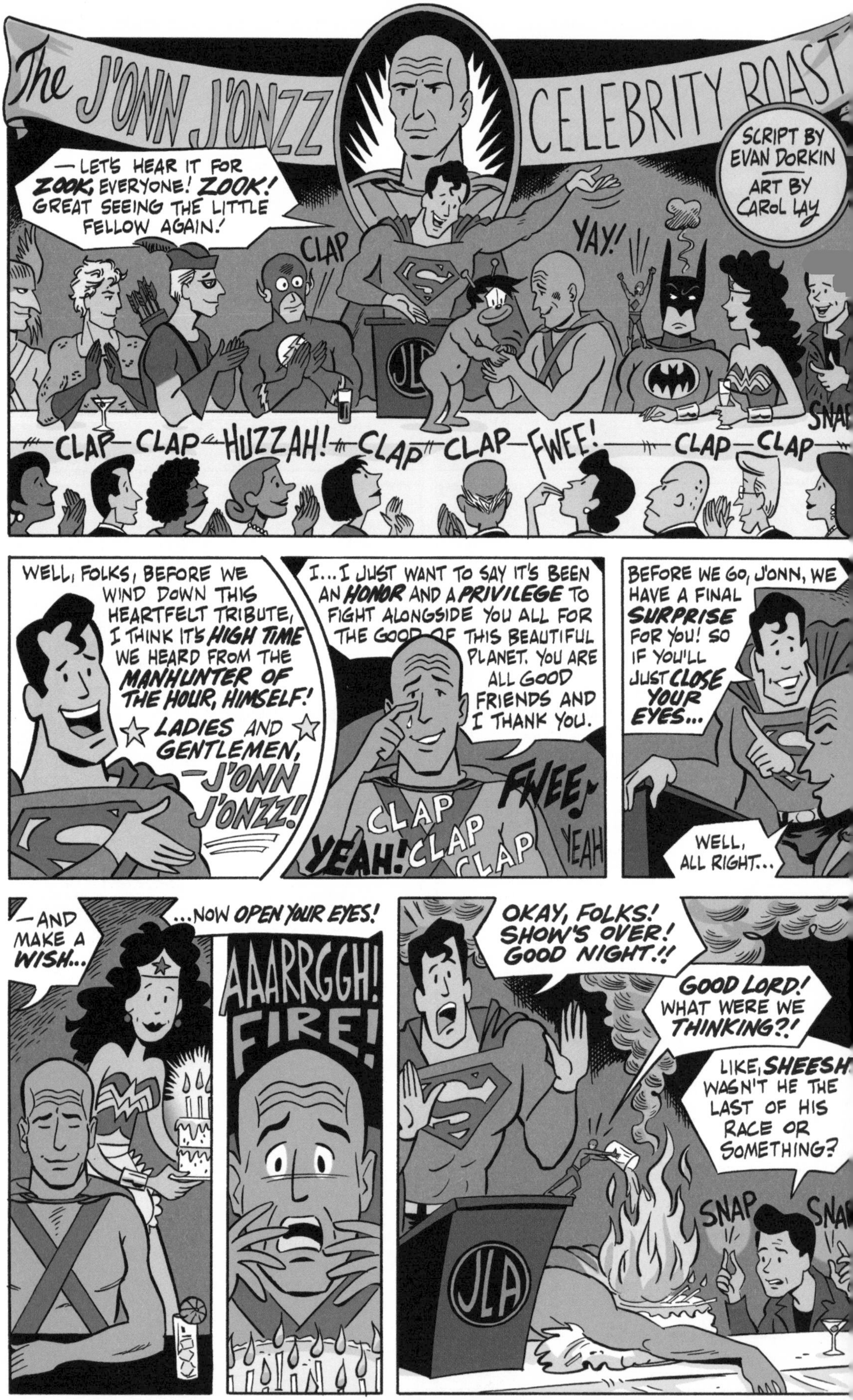

The J'ONN J'ONZZ CELEBRITY ROAST
SCRIPT BY EVAN DORKIN
ART BY CAROL LAY
—LET'S HEAR IT FOR ZOOK, EVERYONE! ZOOK! GREAT SEEING THE LITTLE FELLOW AGAIN!
CLAP
YAY!
CLAP CLAP HUZZAH! CLAP CLAP FWEE! CLAP CLAP
WELL, FOLKS, BEFORE WE WIND DOWN THIS HEARTFELT TRIBUTE, I THINK IT'S HIGH TIME WE HEARD FROM THE MANHUNTER OF THE HOUR, HIMSELF!
LADIES AND GENTLEMEN, —J'ONN J'ONZZ!
I... I JUST WANT TO SAY IT'S BEEN AN HONOR AND A PRIVILEGE TO FIGHT ALONGSIDE YOU ALL FOR THE GOOD OF THIS BEAUTIFUL PLANET. YOU ARE ALL GOOD FRIENDS AND I THANK YOU.
FWEE
CLAP CLAP CLAP
YEAH!
YEAH
BEFORE WE GO, J'ONN, WE HAVE A FINAL SURPRISE FOR YOU! SO IF YOU'LL JUST CLOSE YOUR EYES...
WELL, ALL RIGHT...
—AND MAKE A WISH...
...NOW OPEN YOUR EYES!
AAARRGGH! FIRE!
OKAY, FOLKS! SHOW'S OVER! GOOD NIGHT!!
GOOD LORD! WHAT WERE WE THINKING?!
LIKE, SHEESH WASN'T HE THE LAST OF HIS RACE OR SOMETHING?
SNAP

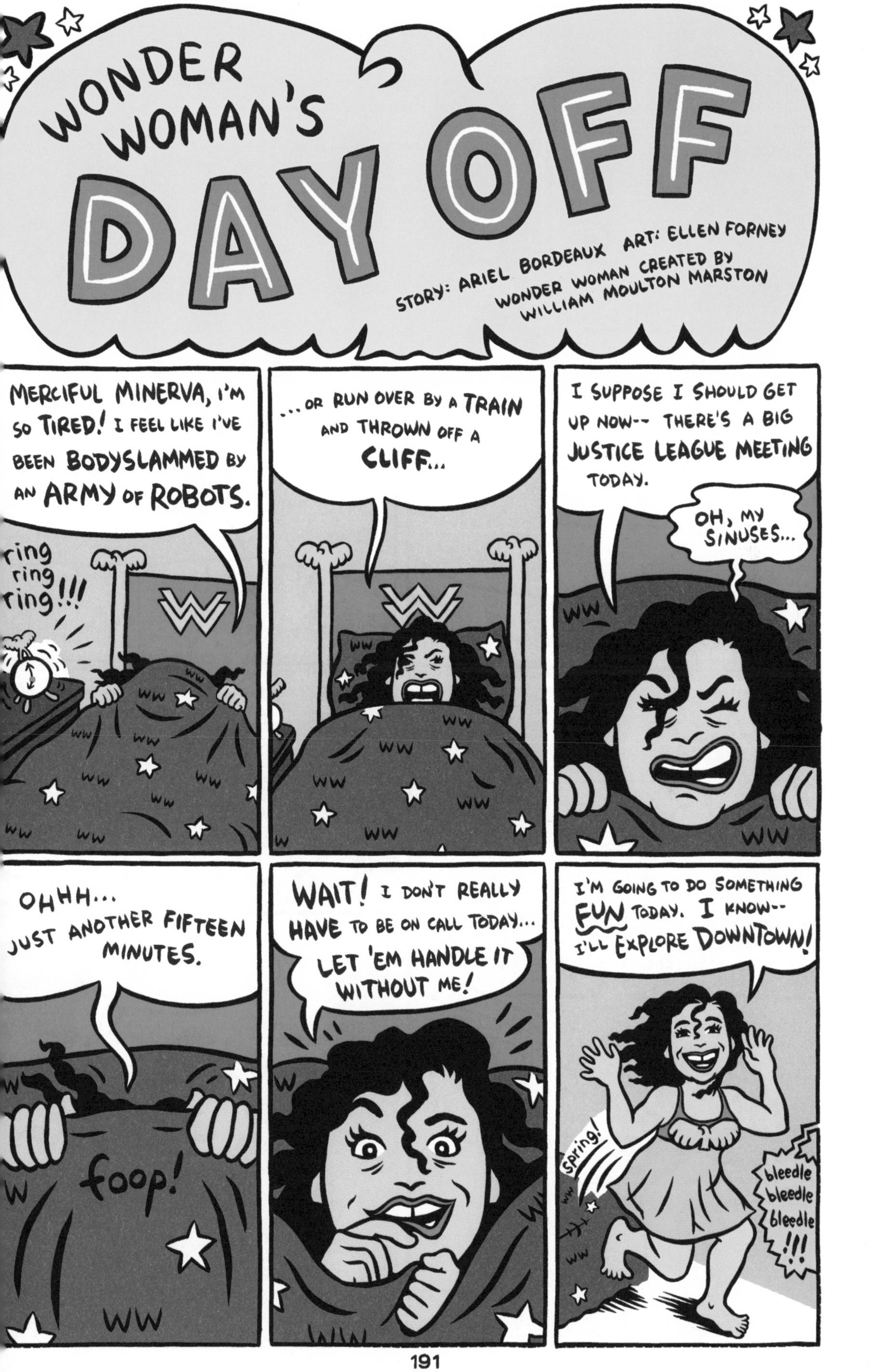
WONDER WOMAN'S DAY OFF
STORY: ARIEL BORDEAUX ART: ELLEN FORNEY
WONDER WOMAN CREATED BY WILLIAM MOULTON MARSTON
MERCIFUL MINERVA, I'M SO TIRED! I FEEL LIKE I'VE BEEN BODYSLAMMED BY AN ARMY OF ROBOTS.
ring ring ring!!!
...OR RUN OVER BY A TRAIN AND THROWN OFF A CLIFF...
I SUPPOSE I SHOULD GET UP NOW-- THERE'S A BIG JUSTICE LEAGUE MEETING TODAY.
OH, MY SINUSES...
OHHH... JUST ANOTHER FIFTEEN MINUTES.
foop!
WAIT! I DON'T REALLY HAVE TO BE ON CALL TODAY... LET 'EM HANDLE IT WITHOUT ME!
I'M GOING TO DO SOMETHING FUN TODAY. I KNOW-- I'LL EXPLORE DOWNTOWN!
spring!
bleedle bleedle bleedle !!!

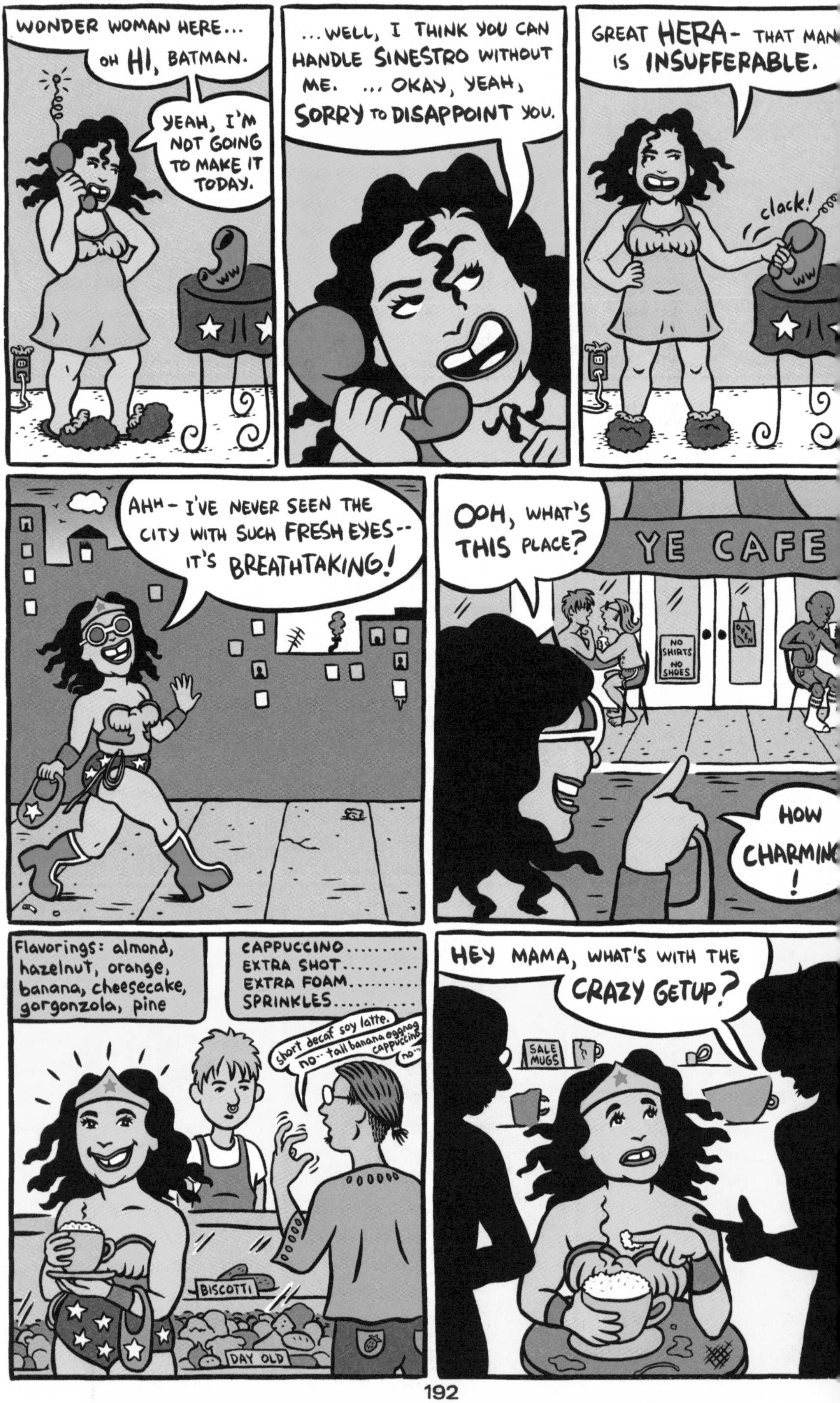
WONDER WOMAN HERE...
OH HI, BATMAN.
YEAH, I'M NOT GOING TO MAKE IT TODAY.
WW
...WELL, I THINK YOU CAN HANDLE SINESTRO WITHOUT ME. ...OKAY, YEAH, SORRY TO DISAPPOINT YOU.
GREAT HERA- THAT MAN IS INSUFFERABLE.
clack!
WW
AHH- I'VE NEVER SEEN THE CITY WITH SUCH FRESH EYES-- IT'S BREATHTAKING!
OOH, WHAT'S THIS PLACE?
YE CAFE
NO SHIRTS NO SHOES
OPEN
HOW CHARMING!
Flavorings: almond, hazelnut, orange, banana, cheesecake, gorgonzola, pine
CAPPUCCINO.........
EXTRA SHOT.........
EXTRA FOAM.........
SPRINKLES.........
short decaf soy latte. no-- tall banana eggnog cappuccino. no--
BISCOTTI
DAY OLD
HEY MAMA, WHAT'S WITH THE CRAZY GETUP?
SALE MUGS

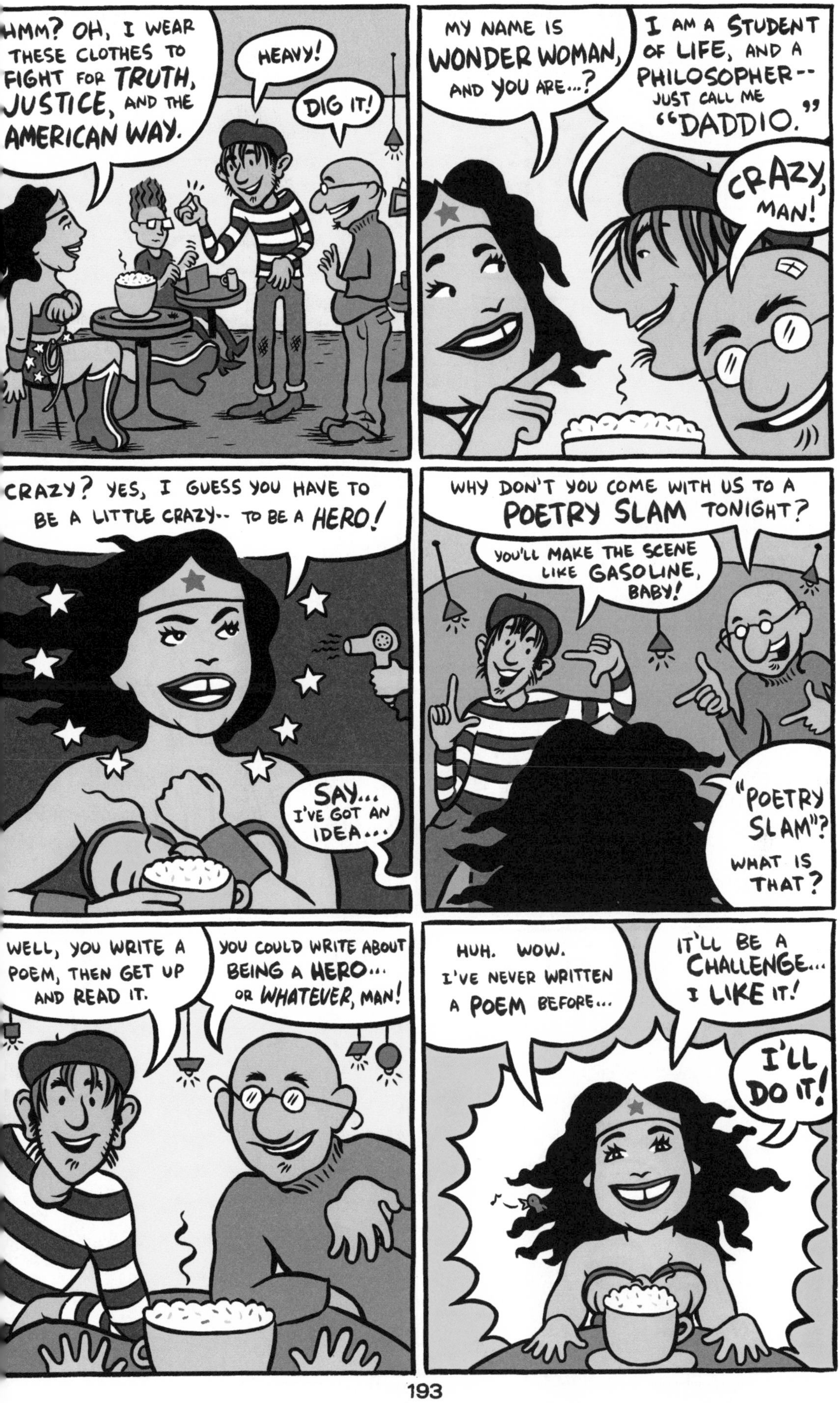
HMM? OH, I WEAR THESE CLOTHES TO FIGHT FOR TRUTH, JUSTICE, AND THE AMERICAN WAY.
HEAVY!
DIG IT!
MY NAME IS WONDER WOMAN, AND YOU ARE...?
I AM A STUDENT OF LIFE, AND A PHILOSOPHER-- JUST CALL ME "DADDIO."
CRAZY, MAN!
CRAZY? YES, I GUESS YOU HAVE TO BE A LITTLE CRAZY-- TO BE A HERO!
SAY... I'VE GOT AN IDEA...
WHY DON'T YOU COME WITH US TO A POETRY SLAM TONIGHT?
YOU'LL MAKE THE SCENE LIKE GASOLINE, BABY!
"POETRY SLAM"? WHAT IS THAT?
WELL, YOU WRITE A POEM, THEN GET UP AND READ IT.
YOU COULD WRITE ABOUT BEING A HERO... OR WHATEVER, MAN!
HUH. WOW. I'VE NEVER WRITTEN A POEM BEFORE...
IT'LL BE A CHALLENGE... I LIKE IT!
I'LL DO IT!

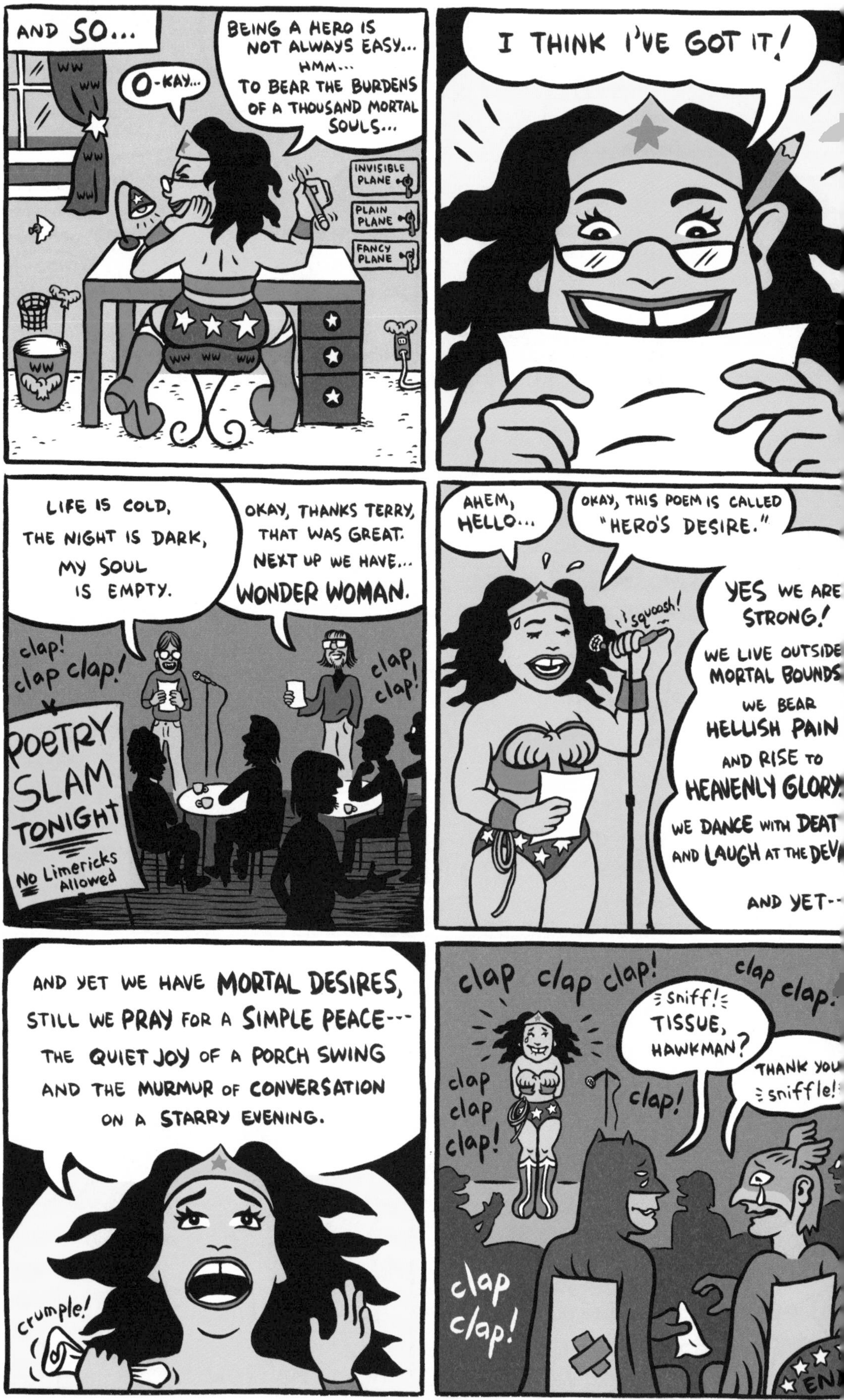
AND SO...
O-KAY...
BEING A HERO IS NOT ALWAYS EASY... HMM... TO BEAR THE BURDENS OF A THOUSAND MORTAL SOULS...
INVISIBLE PLANE
PLAIN PLANE
FANCY PLANE
I THINK I'VE GOT IT!
LIFE IS COLD, THE NIGHT IS DARK, MY SOUL IS EMPTY.
OKAY, THANKS TERRY, THAT WAS GREAT. NEXT UP WE HAVE... WONDER WOMAN.
clap! clap clap!
clap clap!
POETRY SLAM TONIGHT
No Limericks Allowed
AHEM, HELLO...
OKAY, THIS POEM IS CALLED "HERO'S DESIRE."
squoosh!
YES WE ARE STRONG! WE LIVE OUTSIDE MORTAL BOUNDS WE BEAR HELLISH PAIN AND RISE TO HEAVENLY GLORY WE DANCE WITH DEAT AND LAUGH AT THE DEV
AND YET--
AND YET WE HAVE MORTAL DESIRES, STILL WE PRAY FOR A SIMPLE PEACE--- THE QUIET JOY OF A PORCH SWING AND THE MURMUR OF CONVERSATION ON A STARRY EVENING.
crumple!
clap clap clap!
clap clap.
sniff! TISSUE, HAWKMAN?
THANK YOU sniffle!
clap clap clap!
clap!
clap clap!
EN

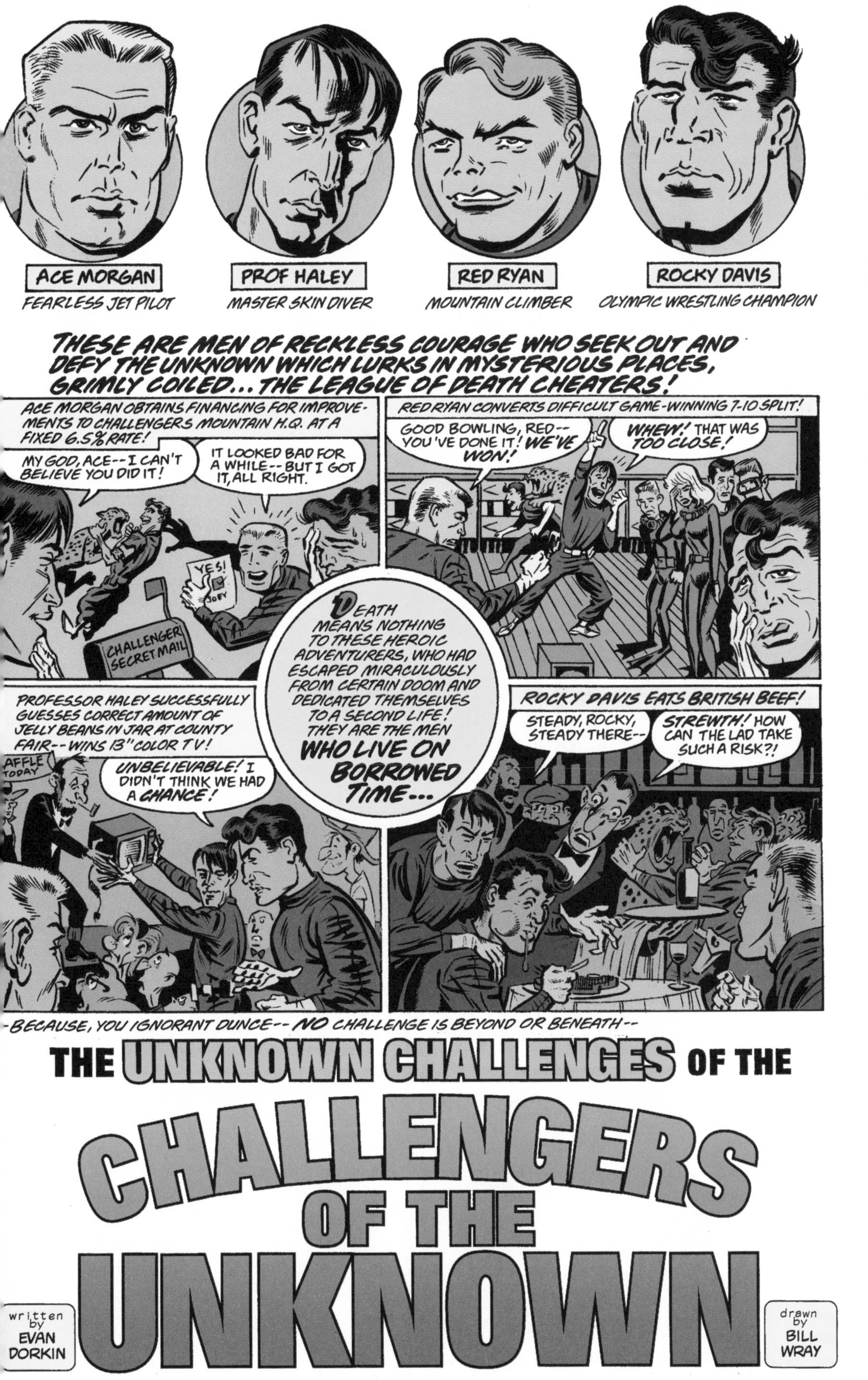

ACE MORGAN
FEARLESS JET PILOT
PROF HALEY
MASTER SKIN DIVER
RED RYAN
MOUNTAIN CLIMBER
ROCKY DAVIS
OLYMPIC WRESTLING CHAMPION
THESE ARE MEN OF RECKLESS COURAGE WHO SEEK OUT AND DEFY THE UNKNOWN WHICH LURKS IN MYSTERIOUS PLACES, GRIMLY COILED... THE LEAGUE OF DEATH CHEATERS!
ACE MORGAN OBTAINS FINANCING FOR IMPROVEMENTS TO CHALLENGERS MOUNTAIN H.Q. AT A FIXED 6.5% RATE!
MY GOD, ACE--I CAN'T BELIEVE YOU DID IT!
IT LOOKED BAD FOR A WHILE--BUT I GOT IT, ALL RIGHT.
YES!
JOEY
CHALLENGER SECRET MAIL
RED RYAN CONVERTS DIFFICULT GAME-WINNING 7-10 SPLIT!
GOOD BOWLING, RED--YOU'VE DONE IT! WE'VE WON!
WHEW! THAT WAS TOO CLOSE!
DEATH MEANS NOTHING TO THESE HEROIC ADVENTURERS, WHO HAD ESCAPED MIRACULOUSLY FROM CERTAIN DOOM AND DEDICATED THEMSELVES TO A SECOND LIFE! THEY ARE THE MEN WHO LIVE ON BORROWED TIME...
PROFESSOR HALEY SUCCESSFULLY GUESSES CORRECT AMOUNT OF JELLY BEANS IN JAR AT COUNTY FAIR--WINS 13" COLOR TV!
UNBELIEVABLE! I DIDN'T THINK WE HAD A CHANCE!
ROCKY DAVIS EATS BRITISH BEEF!
STEADY, ROCKY, STEADY THERE--
STREWTH! HOW CAN THE LAD TAKE SUCH A RISK?!
-BECAUSE, YOU IGNORANT DUNCE--NO CHALLENGE IS BEYOND OR BENEATH--
THE UNKNOWN CHALLENGES OF THE
CHALLENGERS OF THE UNKNOWN
written by EVAN DORKIN
drawn by BILL WRAY

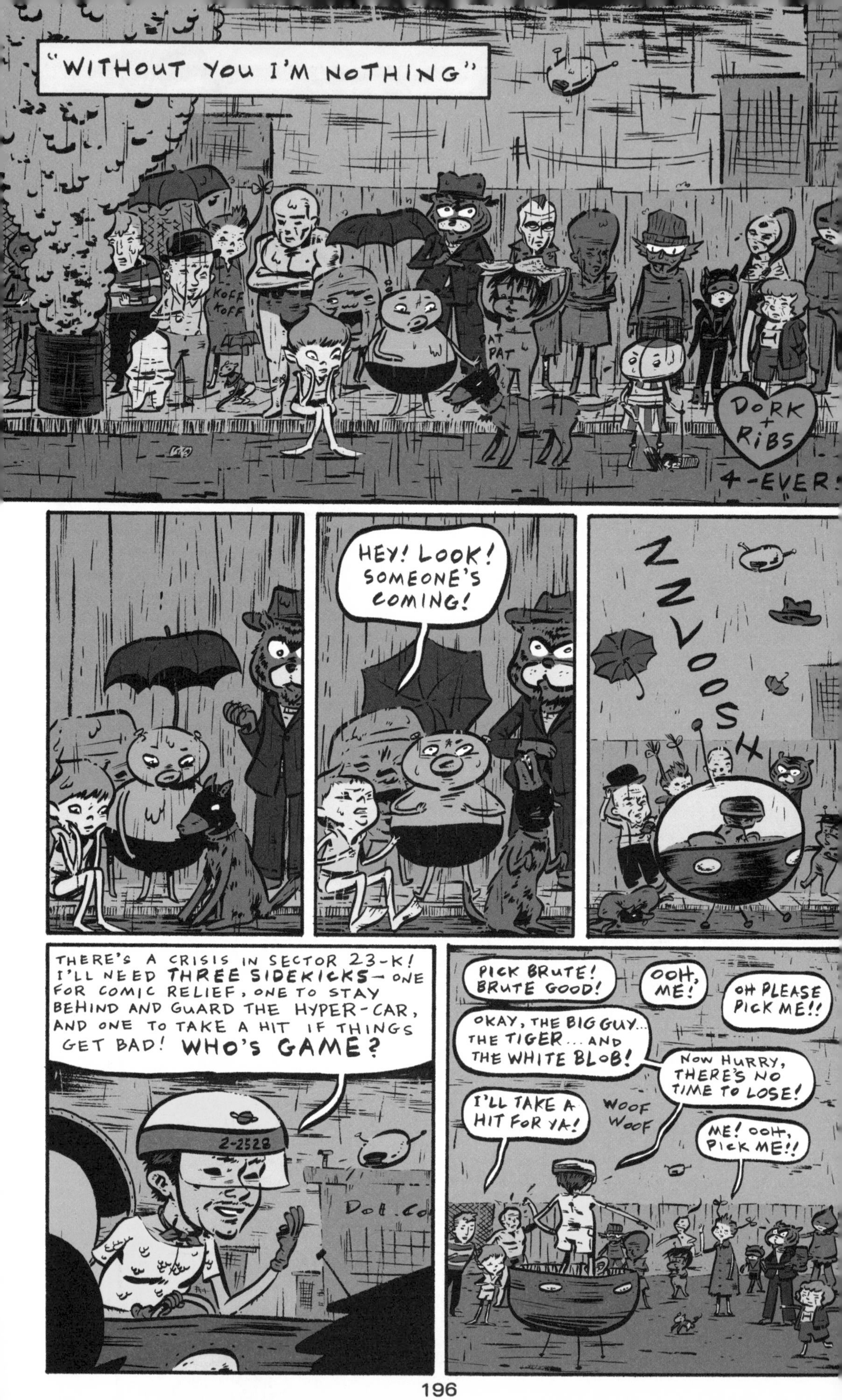
"WITHOUT YOU I'M NOTHING"
KOFF KOFF
PAT PAT
DORK + RIBS 4-EVER
HEY! LOOK! SOMEONE'S COMING!
ZZVOOSH
THERE'S A CRISIS IN SECTOR 23-K! I'LL NEED THREE SIDEKICKS— ONE FOR COMIC RELIEF, ONE TO STAY BEHIND AND GUARD THE HYPER-CAR, AND ONE TO TAKE A HIT IF THINGS GET BAD! WHO'S GAME?
2-2528
Dot.Co
PICK BRUTE! BRUTE GOOD!
OOH, ME!
OH PLEASE PICK ME!!
OKAY, THE BIG GUY... THE TIGER... AND THE WHITE BLOB!
NOW HURRY, THERE'S NO TIME TO LOSE!
I'LL TAKE A HIT FOR YA!
WOOF WOOF
ME! OOH, PICK ME!!

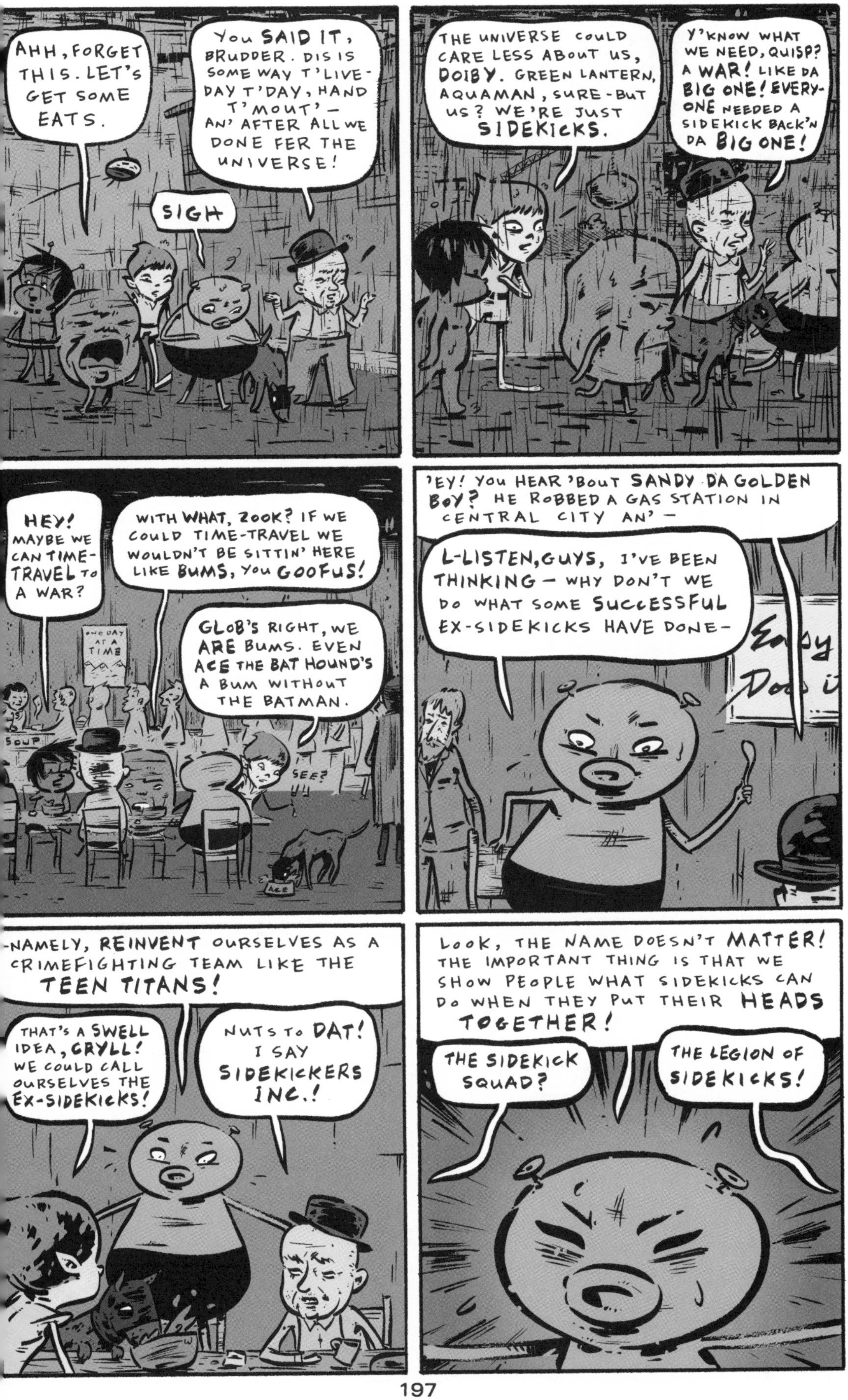

AHH, FORGET THIS. LET'S GET SOME EATS.
YOU SAID IT, BRUDDER. DIS IS SOME WAY T'LIVE-DAY T'DAY, HAND T'MOUT'— AN' AFTER ALL WE DONE FER THE UNIVERSE!
SIGH
THE UNIVERSE COULD CARE LESS ABOUT US, DOIBY. GREEN LANTERN, AQUAMAN, SURE-BUT US? WE'RE JUST SIDEKICKS.
Y'KNOW WHAT WE NEED, QUISP? A WAR! LIKE DA BIG ONE! EVERYONE NEEDED A SIDEKICK BACK'N DA BIG ONE!
HEY! MAYBE WE CAN TIME-TRAVEL TO A WAR?
WITH WHAT, ZOOK? IF WE COULD TIME-TRAVEL WE WOULDN'T BE SITTIN' HERE LIKE BUMS, YOU GOOFUS!
ONE DAY AT A TIME
GLOB'S RIGHT, WE ARE BUMS. EVEN ACE THE BAT HOUND'S A BUM WITHOUT THE BATMAN.
SOUP
SEE?
ACE
'EY! YOU HEAR 'BOUT SANDY DA GOLDEN BOY? HE ROBBED A GAS STATION IN CENTRAL CITY AN'—
L-LISTEN, GUYS, I'VE BEEN THINKING— WHY DON'T WE DO WHAT SOME SUCCESSFUL EX-SIDEKICKS HAVE DONE-
-NAMELY, REINVENT OURSELVES AS A CRIMEFIGHTING TEAM LIKE THE TEEN TITANS!
THAT'S A SWELL IDEA, CRYLL! WE COULD CALL OURSELVES THE EX-SIDEKICKS!
NUTS TO DAT! I SAY SIDEKICKERS INC.!
LOOK, THE NAME DOESN'T MATTER! THE IMPORTANT THING IS THAT WE SHOW PEOPLE WHAT SIDEKICKS CAN DO WHEN THEY PUT THEIR HEADS TOGETHER!
THE SIDEKICK SQUAD?
THE LEGION OF SIDEKICKS!

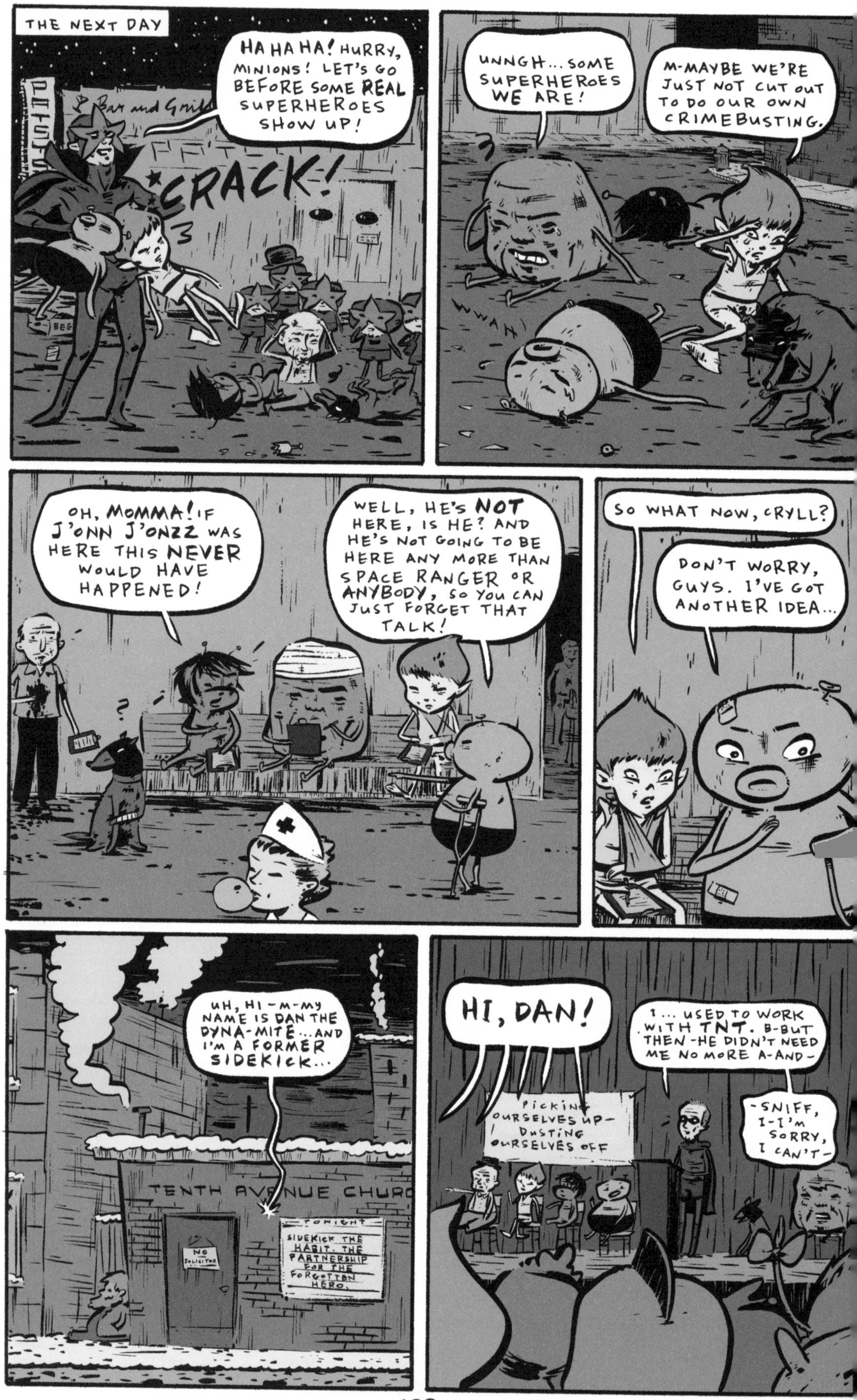
THE NEXT DAY
HA HA HA! HURRY, MINIONS! LET'S GO BEFORE SOME REAL SUPERHEROES SHOW UP!
CRACK!
UNNGH... SOME SUPERHEROES WE ARE!
M-MAYBE WE'RE JUST NOT CUT OUT TO DO OUR OWN CRIMEBUSTING.
WWAH
OH, MOMMA! IF J'ONN J'ONZZ WAS HERE THIS NEVER WOULD HAVE HAPPENED!
WELL, HE'S NOT HERE, IS HE? AND HE'S NOT GOING TO BE HERE ANY MORE THAN SPACE RANGER OR ANYBODY, SO YOU CAN JUST FORGET THAT TALK!
SO WHAT NOW, CRYLL?
DON'T WORRY, GUYS. I'VE GOT ANOTHER IDEA...
UH, HI-M-MY NAME IS DAN THE DYNA-MITE... AND I'M A FORMER SIDEKICK...
TENTH AVENUE CHURC
NO SOLICITOR
TONIGHT
SIDEKICK THE HABIT. THE PARTNERSHIP FOR THE FORGOTTEN HERO.
HI, DAN!
PICKING OURSELVES UP-
DUSTING OURSELVES OFF
I... USED TO WORK WITH TNT. B-BUT THEN-HE DIDN'T NEED ME NO MORE A-AND-
-SNIFF, I-I'M SORRY, I CAN'T-

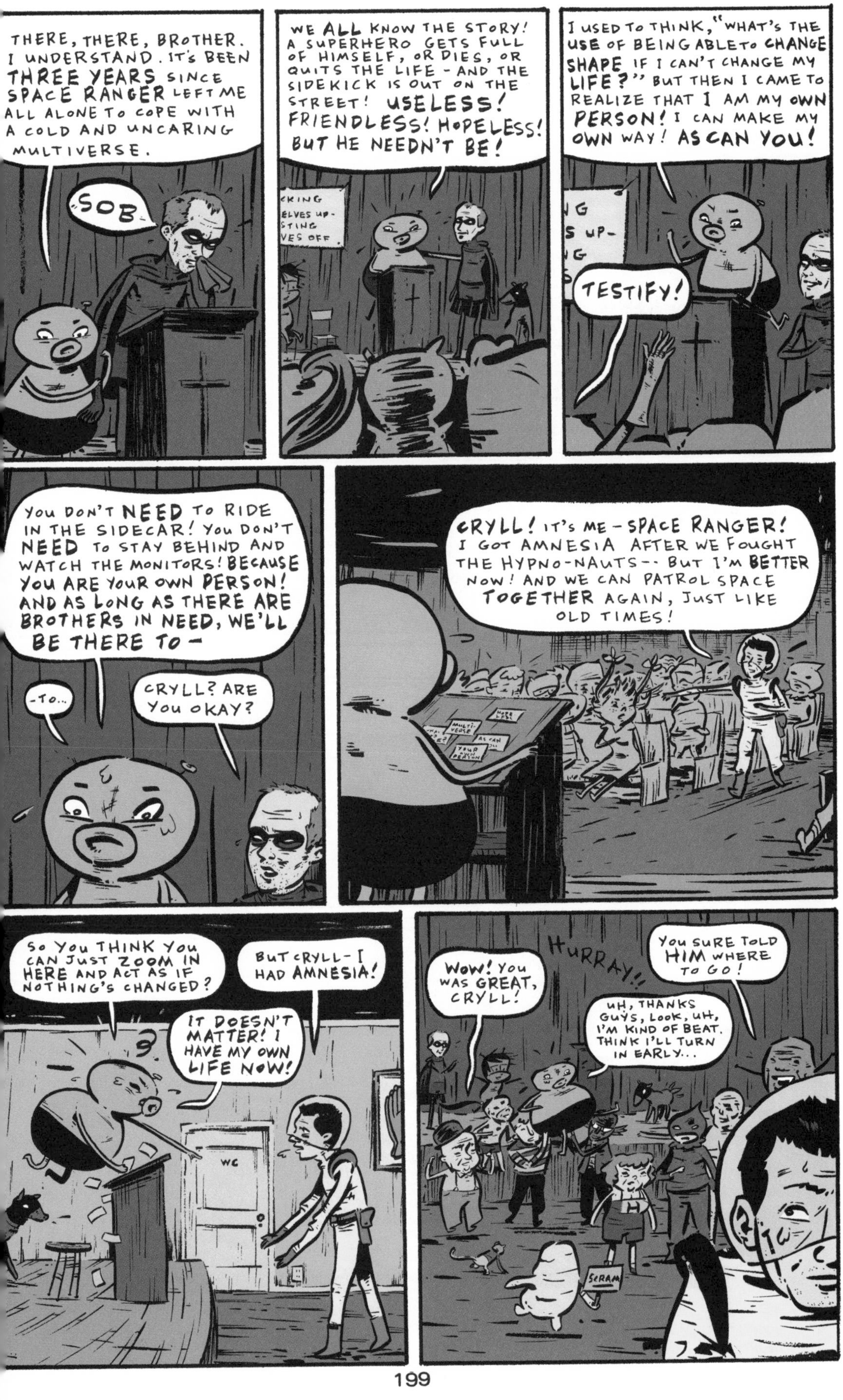
THERE, THERE, BROTHER. I UNDERSTAND. IT'S BEEN THREE YEARS SINCE SPACE RANGER LEFT ME ALL ALONE TO COPE WITH A COLD AND UNCARING MULTIVERSE.
SOB
WE ALL KNOW THE STORY! A SUPERHERO GETS FULL OF HIMSELF, OR DIES, OR QUITS THE LIFE - AND THE SIDEKICK IS OUT ON THE STREET! USELESS! FRIENDLESS! HOPELESS! BUT HE NEEDN'T BE!
I USED TO THINK, "WHAT'S THE USE OF BEING ABLE TO CHANGE SHAPE IF I CAN'T CHANGE MY LIFE?" BUT THEN I CAME TO REALIZE THAT I AM MY OWN PERSON! I CAN MAKE MY OWN WAY! AS CAN YOU!
TESTIFY!
YOU DON'T NEED TO RIDE IN THE SIDECAR! YOU DON'T NEED TO STAY BEHIND AND WATCH THE MONITORS! BECAUSE YOU ARE YOUR OWN PERSON! AND AS LONG AS THERE ARE BROTHERS IN NEED, WE'LL BE THERE TO -
-TO...
CRYLL? ARE YOU OKAY?
CRYLL! IT'S ME - SPACE RANGER! I GOT AMNESIA AFTER WE FOUGHT THE HYPNO-NAUTS -- BUT I'M BETTER NOW! AND WE CAN PATROL SPACE TOGETHER AGAIN, JUST LIKE OLD TIMES!
SO YOU THINK YOU CAN JUST ZOOM IN HERE AND ACT AS IF NOTHING'S CHANGED?
BUT CRYLL - I HAD AMNESIA!
IT DOESN'T MATTER! I HAVE MY OWN LIFE NOW!
WC
HURRAY!!
WOW! YOU WAS GREAT, CRYLL!
YOU SURE TOLD HIM WHERE TO GO!
UH, THANKS GUYS, LOOK, UH, I'M KIND OF BEAT. THINK I'LL TURN IN EARLY...
SCRAM

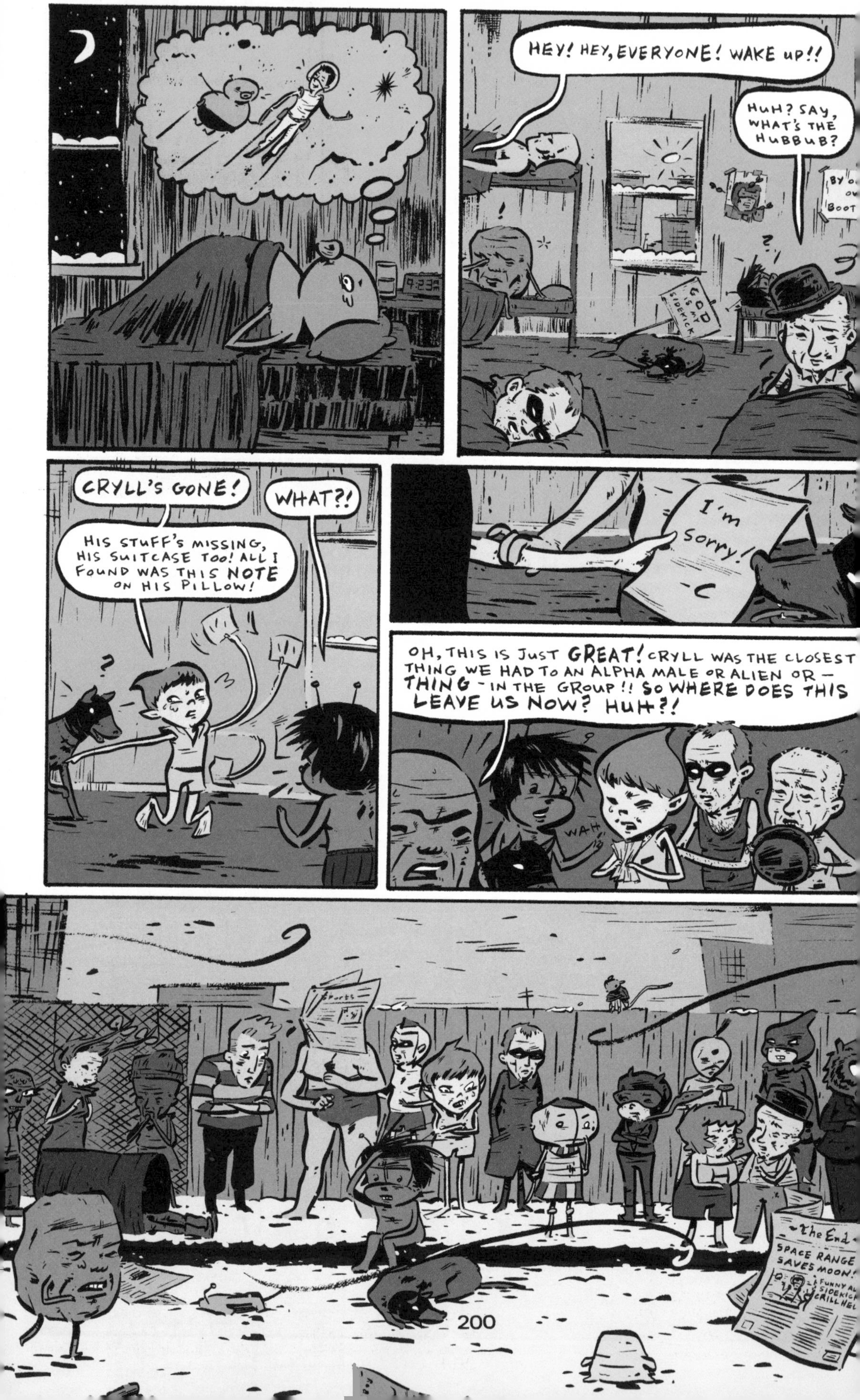
HEY! HEY, EVERYONE! WAKE UP!!
HUH? SAY, WHAT'S THE HUBBUB?
GOD IS MY SIDEKICK
CRYLL'S GONE!
WHAT?!
HIS STUFF'S MISSING, HIS SUITCASE TOO! ALL I FOUND WAS THIS NOTE ON HIS PILLOW!
I'm Sorry! -C
OH, THIS IS JUST GREAT! CRYLL WAS THE CLOSEST THING WE HAD TO AN ALPHA MALE OR ALIEN OR — THING — IN THE GROUP!! SO WHERE DOES THIS LEAVE US NOW? HUH?!
WAH
Sports
The End
SPACE RANGE
SAVES MOON

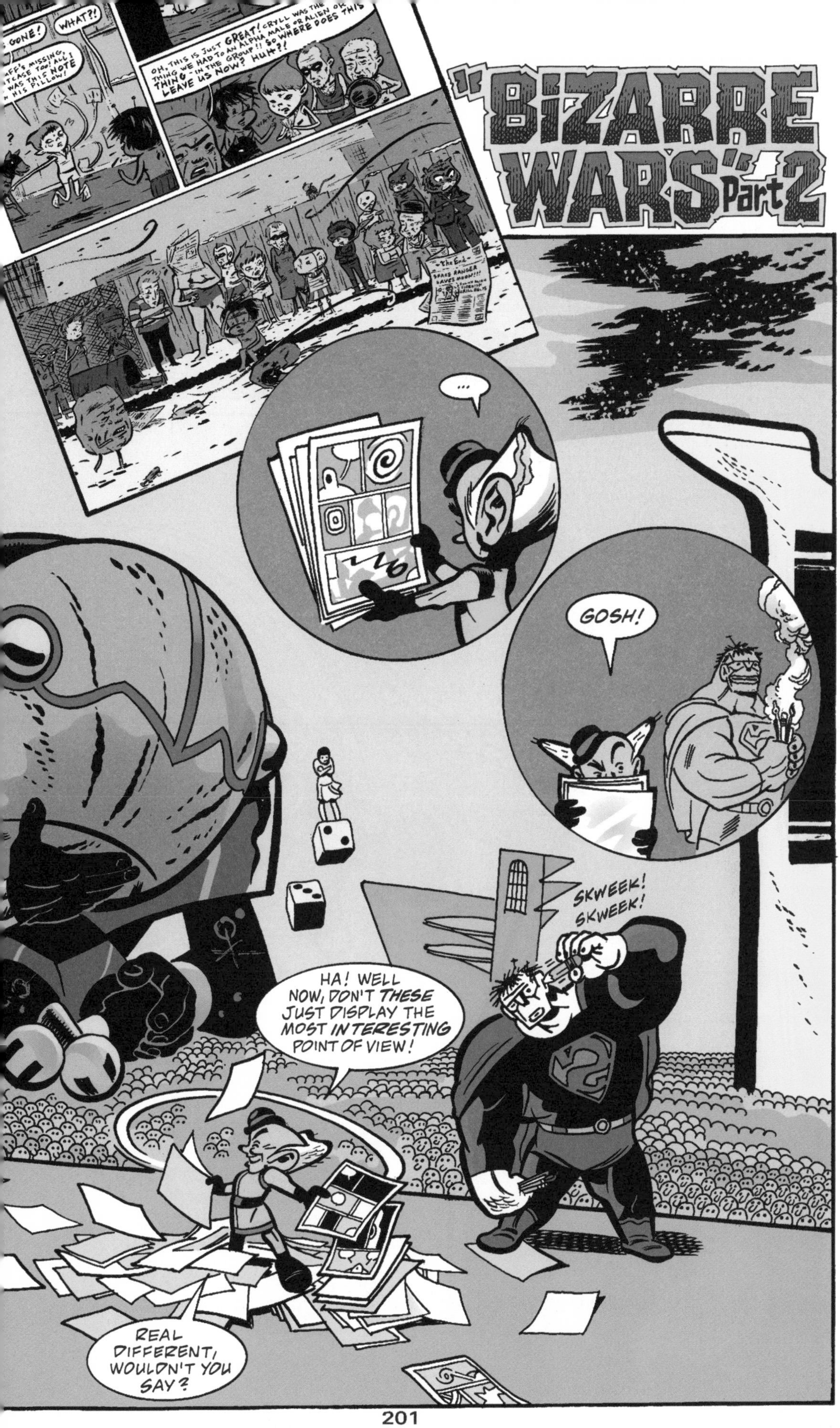
"BIZARRE WARS" Part 2
GONE!
WHAT?!
MISSING, TOO! ALL I WAS THIS NOTE HIS PILLOW!
OH, THIS IS JUST GREAT! CRYLL WAS THE THING WE HAD TO AN ALPHA MALE OR ALIEN OR THING - IN THE GROUP!! SO WHERE DOES THIS LEAVE US NOW? HUH?!
The End
SPACE RANGER SAVES MOON!!!
...
GOSH!
SKWEEK! SKWEEK!
HA! WELL NOW, DON'T THESE JUST DISPLAY THE MOST INTERESTING POINT OF VIEW!
REAL DIFFERENT, WOULDN'T YOU SAY?

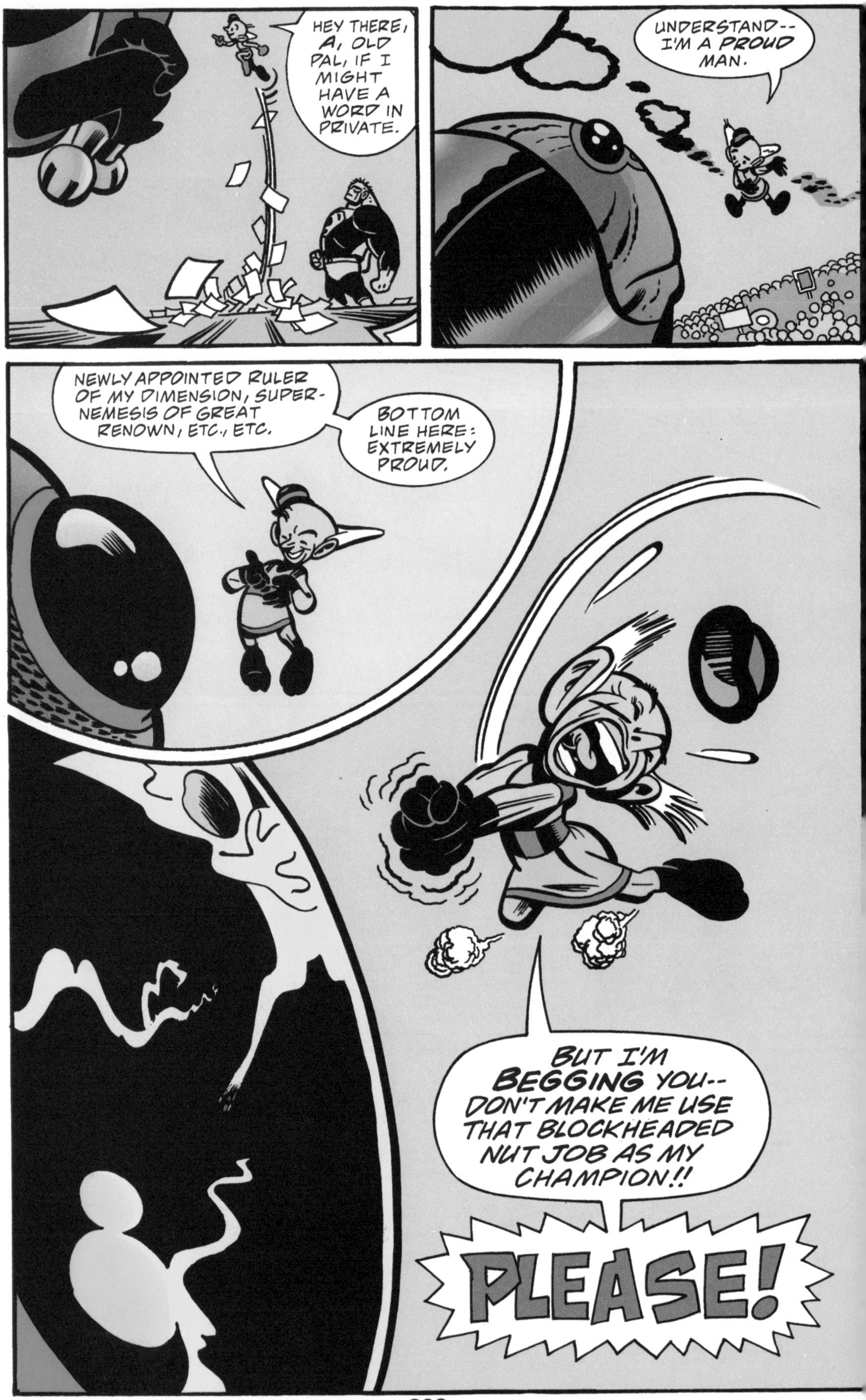
HEY THERE, A, OLD PAL, IF I MIGHT HAVE A WORD IN PRIVATE.
UNDERSTAND-- I'M A PROUD MAN.
NEWLY APPOINTED RULER OF MY DIMENSION, SUPER-NEMESIS OF GREAT RENOWN, ETC., ETC.
BOTTOM LINE HERE: EXTREMELY PROUD.
BUT I'M BEGGING YOU-- DON'T MAKE ME USE THAT BLOCKHEADED NUT JOB AS MY CHAMPION!!
PLEASE!

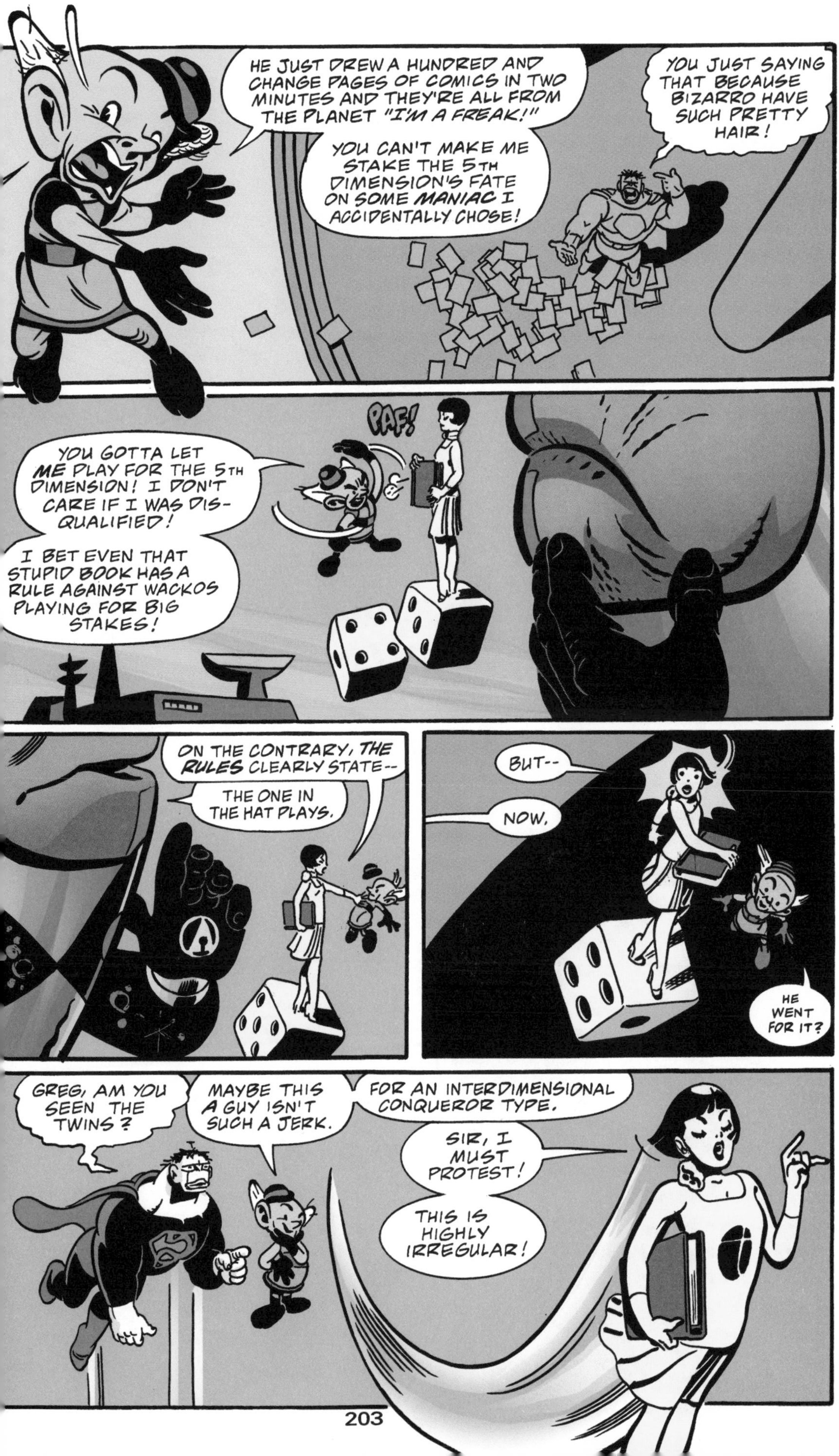
HE JUST DREW A HUNDRED AND CHANGE PAGES OF COMICS IN TWO MINUTES AND THEY'RE ALL FROM THE PLANET "I'M A FREAK!"
YOU CAN'T MAKE ME STAKE THE 5TH DIMENSION'S FATE ON SOME MANIAC I ACCIDENTALLY CHOSE!
YOU JUST SAYING THAT BECAUSE BIZARRO HAVE SUCH PRETTY HAIR!
PAF!
YOU GOTTA LET ME PLAY FOR THE 5TH DIMENSION! I DON'T CARE IF I WAS DIS-QUALIFIED!
I BET EVEN THAT STUPID BOOK HAS A RULE AGAINST WACKOS PLAYING FOR BIG STAKES!
ON THE CONTRARY, THE RULES CLEARLY STATE--
THE ONE IN THE HAT PLAYS.
BUT--
NOW.
HE WENT FOR IT?
GREG, AM YOU SEEN THE TWINS?
MAYBE THIS A GUY ISN'T SUCH A JERK.
FOR AN INTERDIMENSIONAL CONQUEROR TYPE.
SIR, I MUST PROTEST!
THIS IS HIGHLY IRREGULAR!

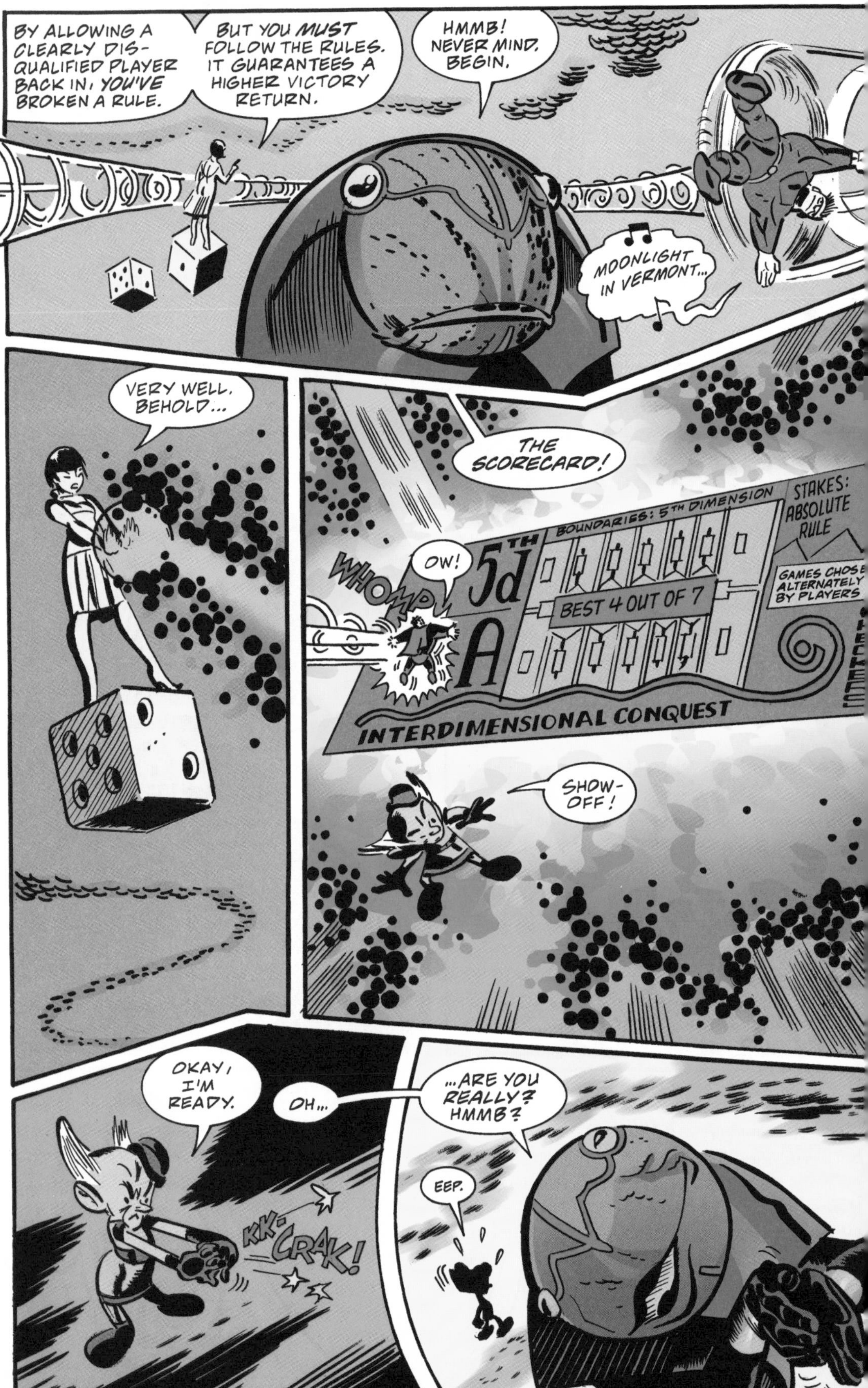
BY ALLOWING A CLEARLY DIS-QUALIFIED PLAYER BACK IN, YOU'VE BROKEN A RULE.
BUT YOU MUST FOLLOW THE RULES. IT GUARANTEES A HIGHER VICTORY RETURN.
HMMB! NEVER MIND. BEGIN.
MOONLIGHT IN VERMONT...
VERY WELL. BEHOLD...
THE SCORECARD!
BOUNDARIES: 5TH DIMENSION
STAKES: ABSOLUTE RULE
5TH
5d
A
BEST 4 OUT OF 7
GAMES CHOSE ALTERNATELY BY PLAYERS
WHOMP
OW!
INTERDIMENSIONAL CONQUEST
SHOW-OFF!
OKAY, I'M READY.
OH...
...ARE YOU REALLY? HMMB?
KK-CRAK!
EEP.

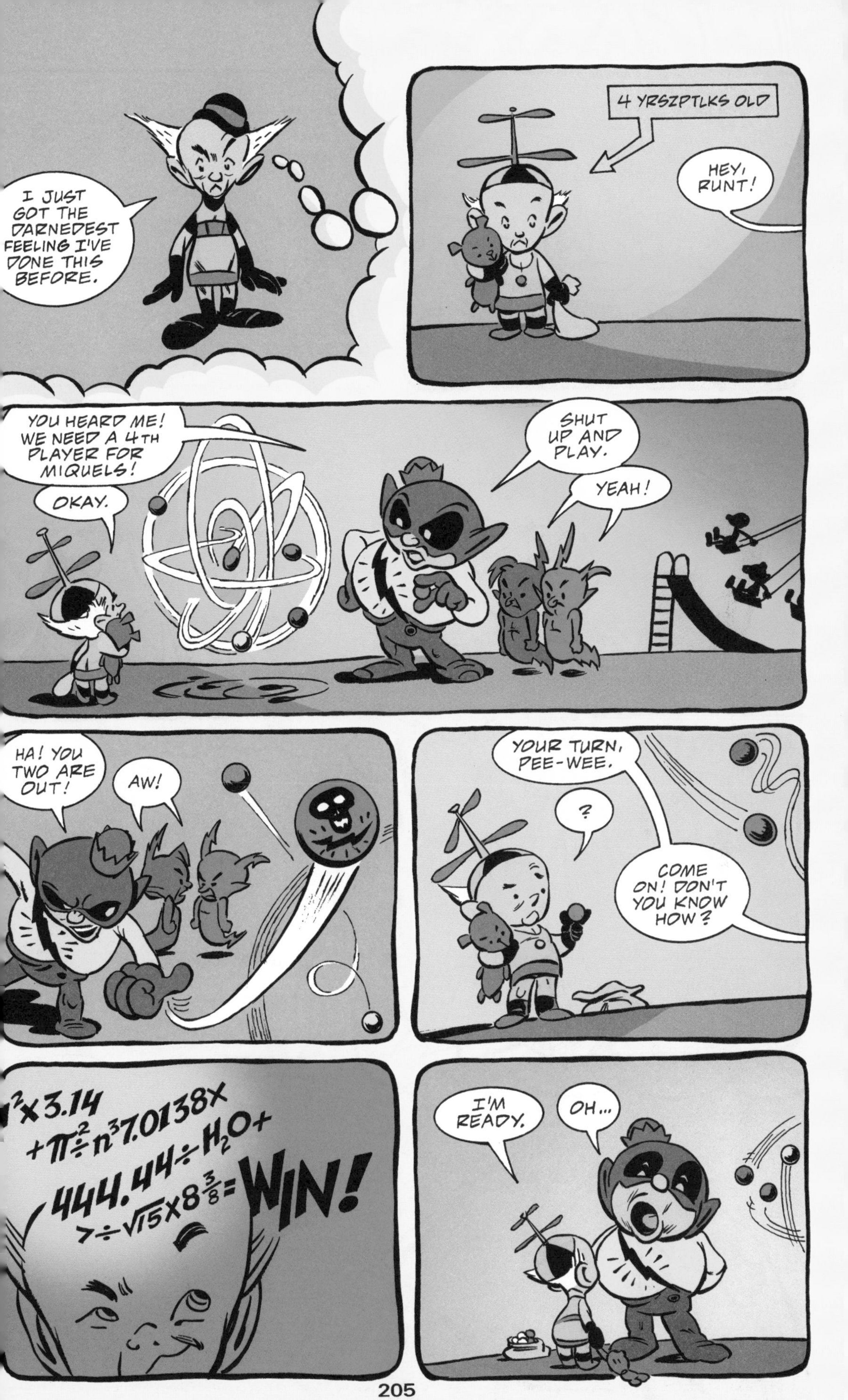
I JUST GOT THE DARNEDEST FEELING I'VE DONE THIS BEFORE.
4 YRSZPTLKS OLD
HEY, RUNT!
YOU HEARD ME! WE NEED A 4TH PLAYER FOR MIQUELS!
OKAY.
SHUT UP AND PLAY.
YEAH!
HA! YOU TWO ARE OUT!
AW!
YOUR TURN, PEE-WEE.
?
COME ON! DON'T YOU KNOW HOW?
$^2\times 3.14$
$+\pi^2\div n^3 7.0138\times$
$444.44\div H_2O+$
$7\div\sqrt{15}\times 8\frac{3}{8}=$WIN!
I'M READY.
OH...

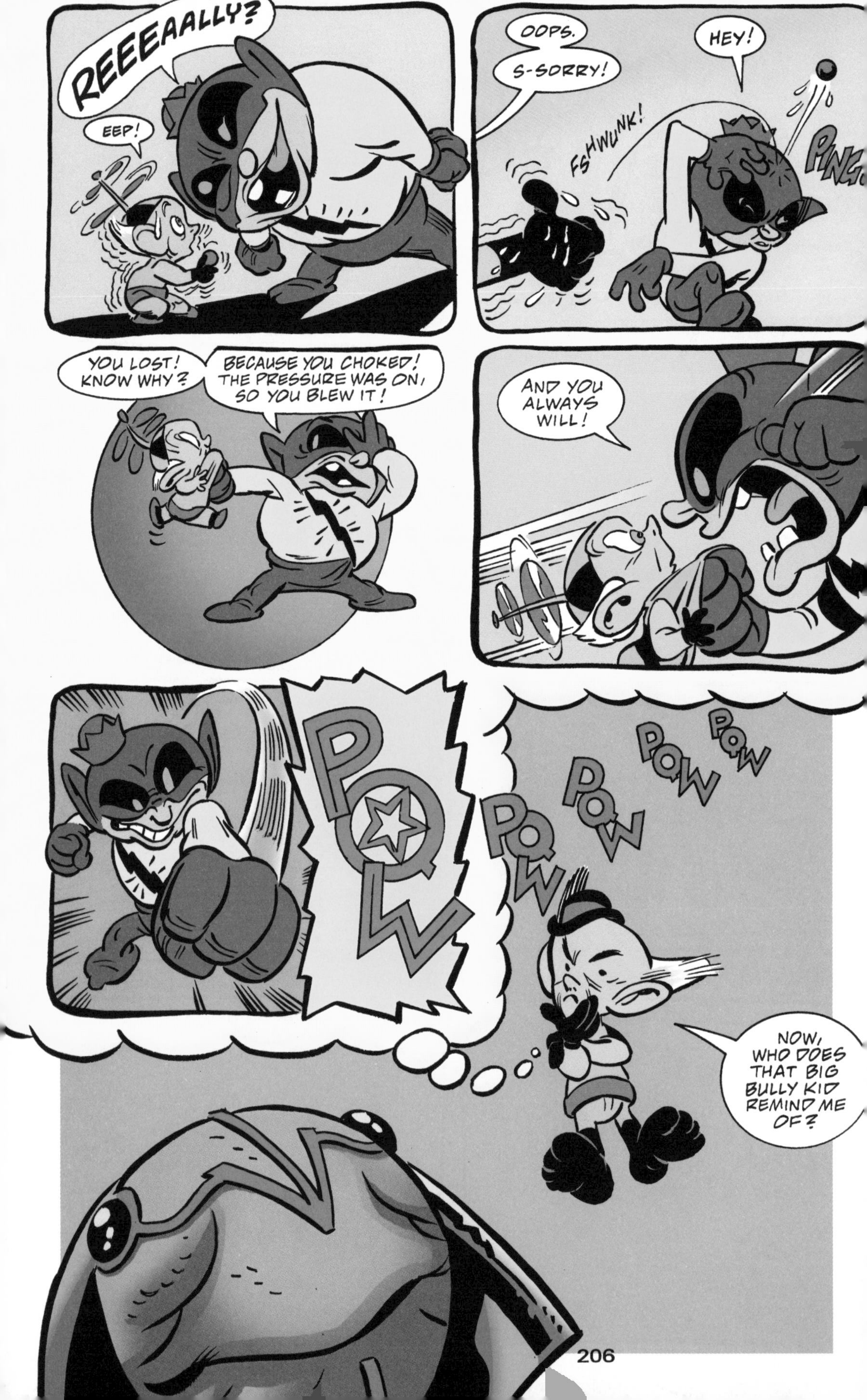
REEEAALLY?
EEP!
OOPS.
S-SORRY!
HEY!
FSHWUNK!
PING
YOU LOST! KNOW WHY?
BECAUSE YOU CHOKED! THE PRESSURE WAS ON, SO YOU BLEW IT!
AND YOU ALWAYS WILL!
POW
POW
POW
POW
POW
NOW, WHO DOES THAT BIG BULLY KID REMIND ME OF?

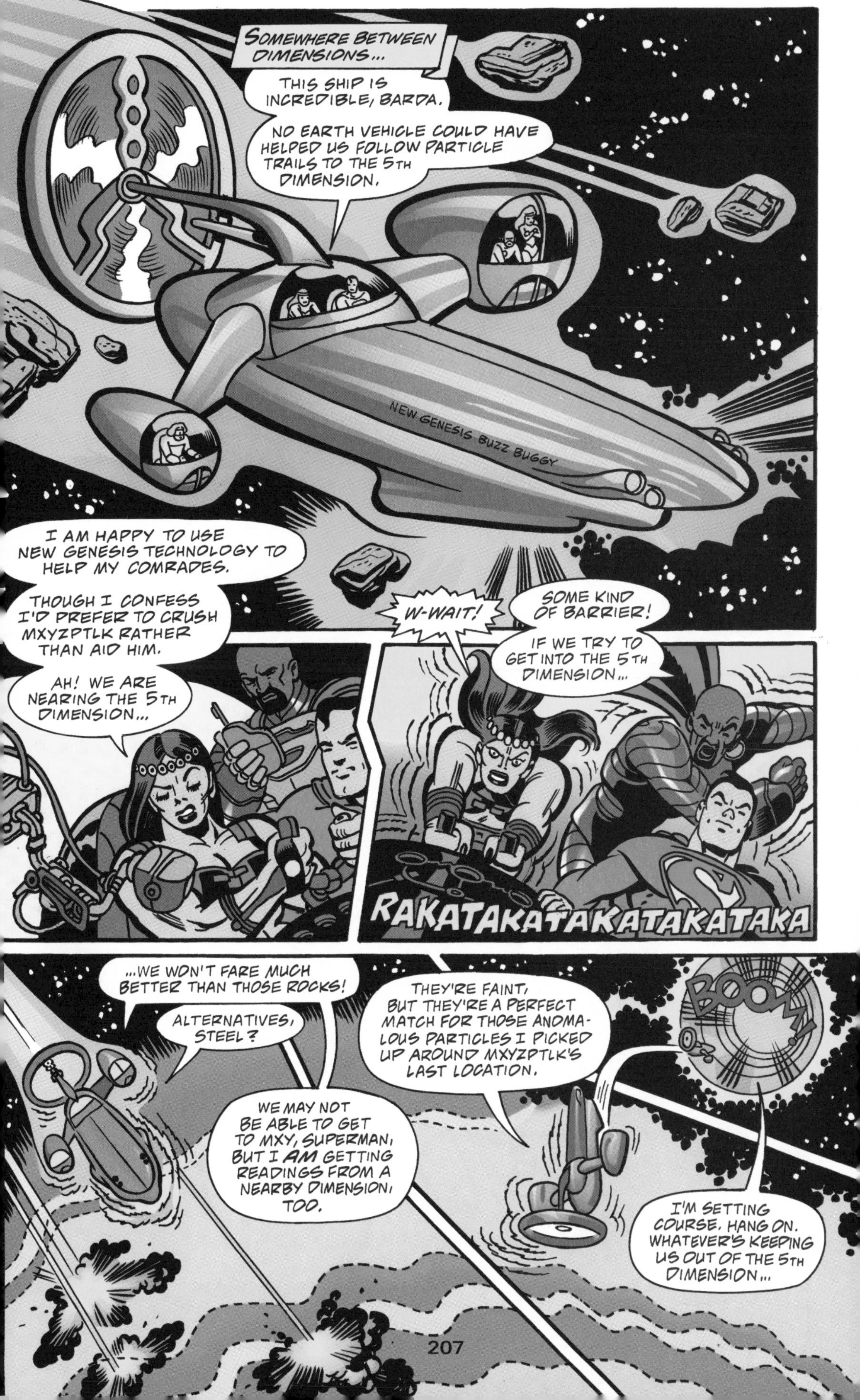
SOMEWHERE BETWEEN DIMENSIONS...
THIS SHIP IS INCREDIBLE, BARDA.
NO EARTH VEHICLE COULD HAVE HELPED US FOLLOW PARTICLE TRAILS TO THE 5TH DIMENSION.
NEW GENESIS BUZZ BUGGY
I AM HAPPY TO USE NEW GENESIS TECHNOLOGY TO HELP MY COMRADES.
THOUGH I CONFESS I'D PREFER TO CRUSH MXYZPTLK RATHER THAN AID HIM.
AH! WE ARE NEARING THE 5TH DIMENSION...
W-WAIT!
SOME KIND OF BARRIER!
IF WE TRY TO GET INTO THE 5TH DIMENSION...
RAKATAKATAKATAKATAKA
...WE WON'T FARE MUCH BETTER THAN THOSE ROCKS!
ALTERNATIVES, STEEL?
WE MAY NOT BE ABLE TO GET TO MXY, SUPERMAN, BUT I AM GETTING READINGS FROM A NEARBY DIMENSION, TOO.
THEY'RE FAINT, BUT THEY'RE A PERFECT MATCH FOR THOSE ANOMALOUS PARTICLES I PICKED UP AROUND MXYZPTLK'S LAST LOCATION.
BOOM!
I'M SETTING COURSE. HANG ON. WHATEVER'S KEEPING US OUT OF THE 5TH DIMENSION...

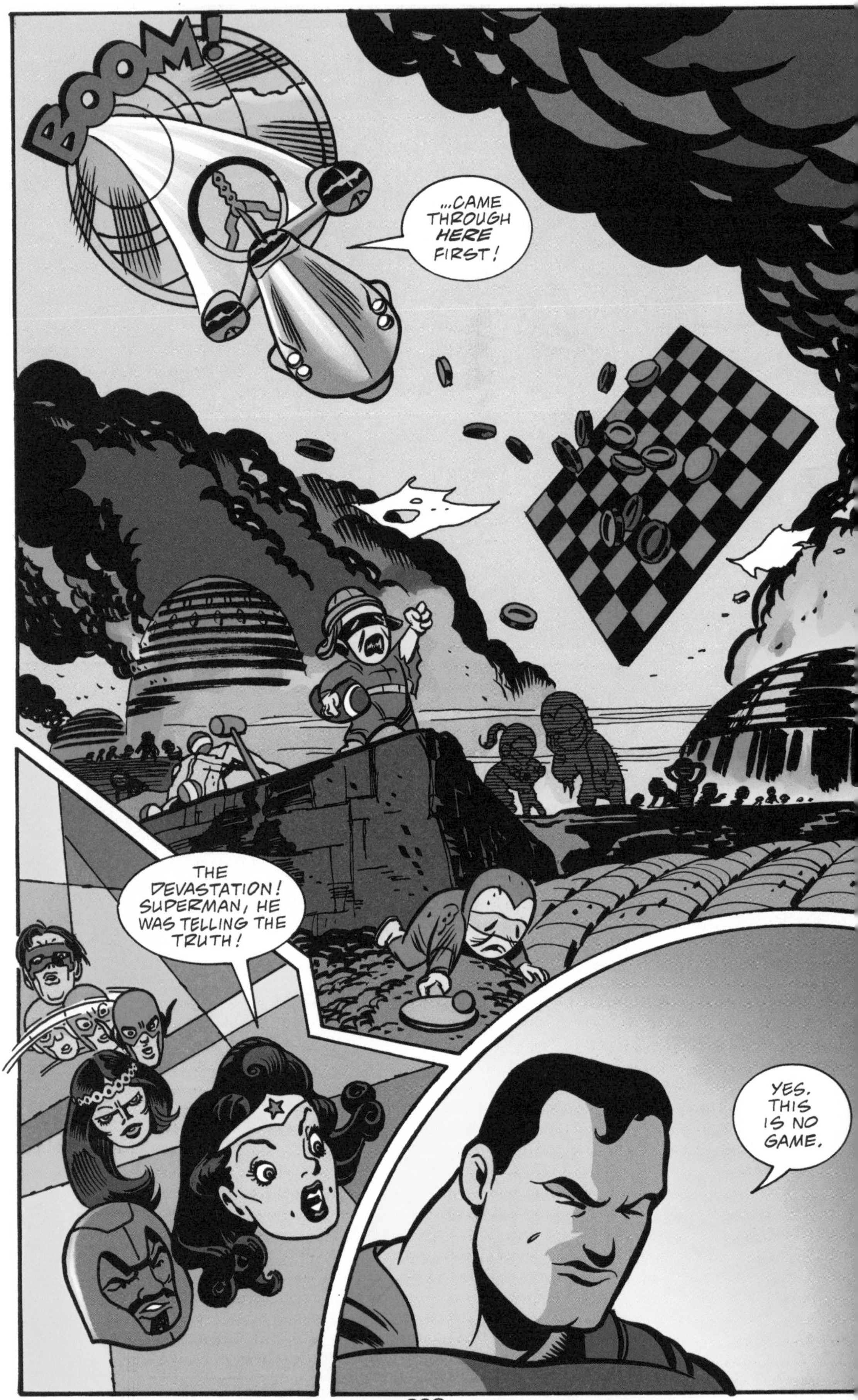
BOOM!
...CAME THROUGH HERE FIRST!
THE DEVASTATION! SUPERMAN, HE WAS TELLING THE TRUTH!
YES. THIS IS NO GAME.

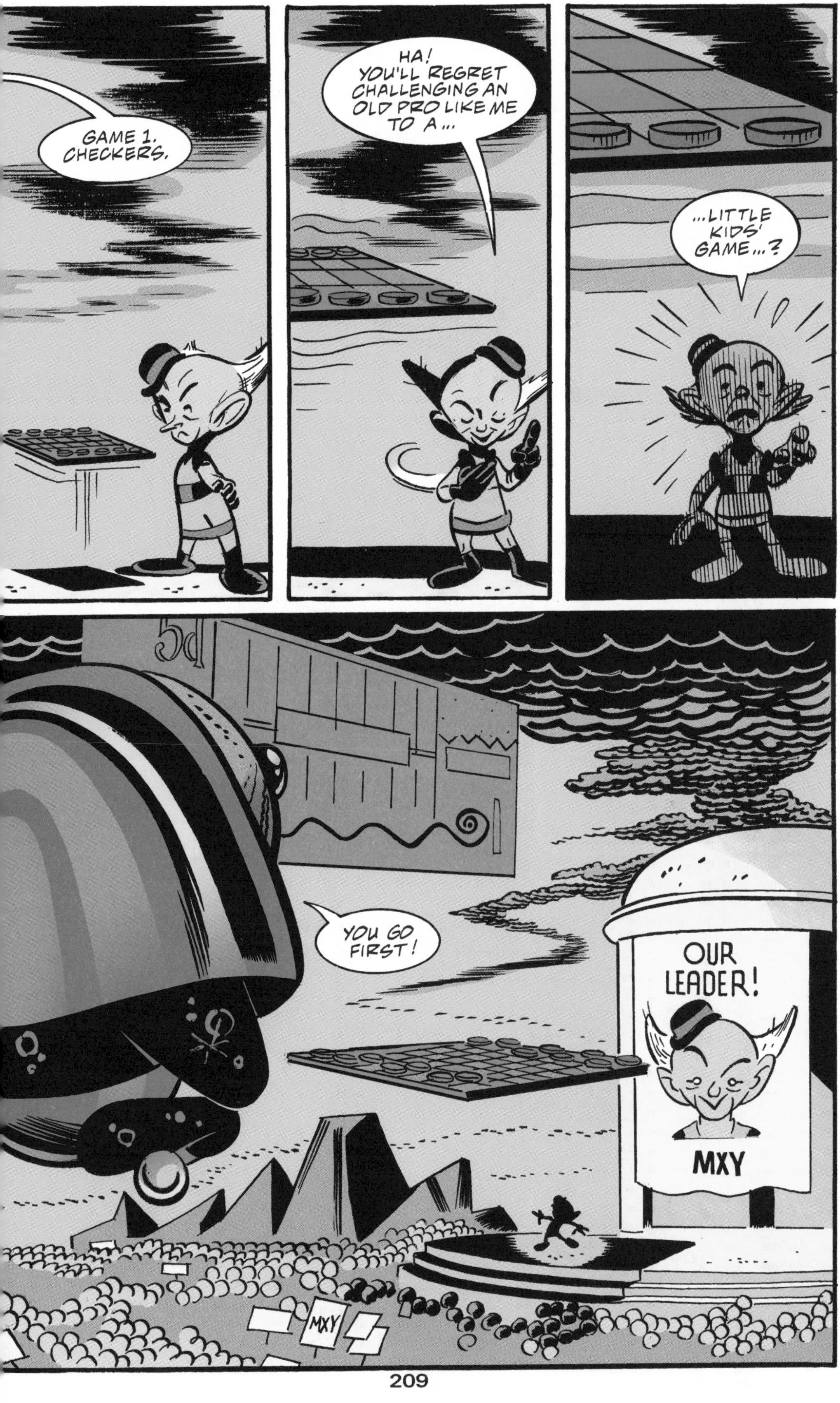
GAME 1. CHECKERS.
HA! YOU'LL REGRET CHALLENGING AN OLD PRO LIKE ME TO A ...
...LITTLE KIDS' GAME...?
YOU GO FIRST!
OUR LEADER!
MXY
MXY

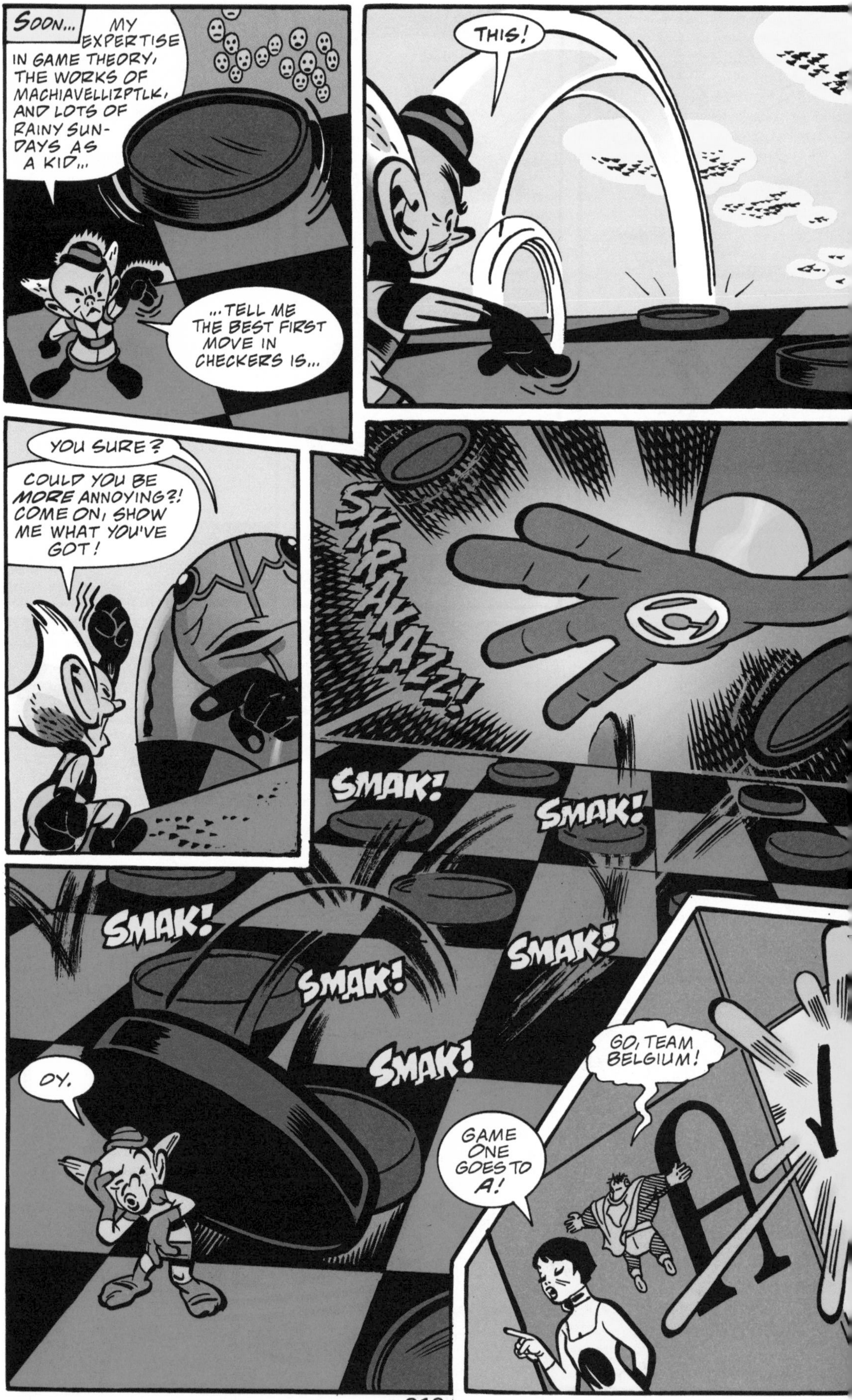
SOON...
MY EXPERTISE IN GAME THEORY, THE WORKS OF MACHIAVELLIZPTLK, AND LOTS OF RAINY SUNDAYS AS A KID...
...TELL ME THE BEST FIRST MOVE IN CHECKERS IS...
THIS!
YOU SURE?
COULD YOU BE MORE ANNOYING?! COME ON, SHOW ME WHAT YOU'VE GOT!
SKRAKAZZ!
SMAK!
SMAK!
SMAK!
SMAK!
SMAK!
SMAK!
OY.
GO, TEAM BELGIUM!
GAME ONE GOES TO A!

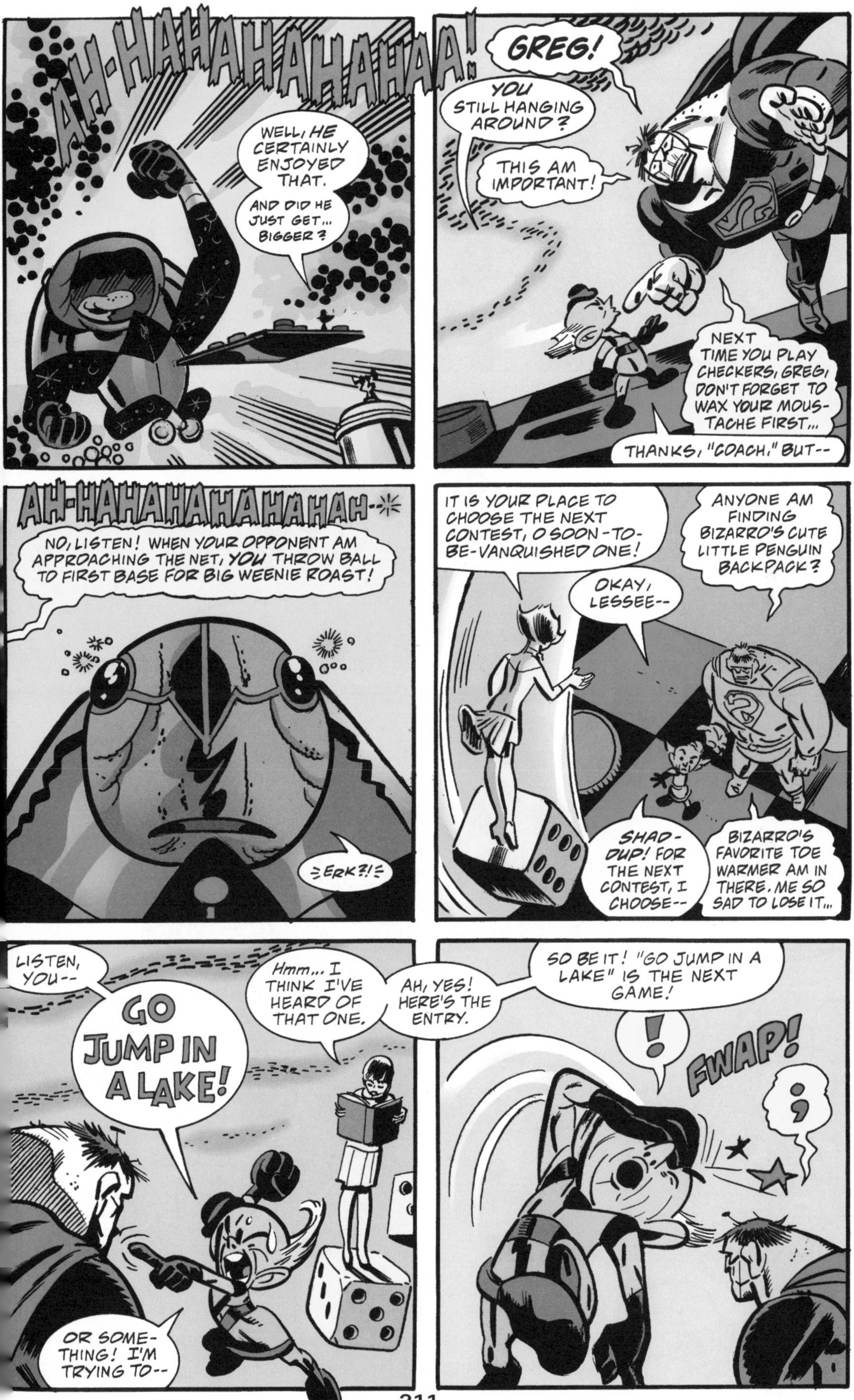
AH-HAHAHAHAHAHAA!
WELL, HE CERTAINLY ENJOYED THAT.
AND DID HE JUST GET... BIGGER?
GREG!
YOU STILL HANGING AROUND?
THIS AM IMPORTANT!
NEXT TIME YOU PLAY CHECKERS, GREG, DON'T FORGET TO WAX YOUR MOUSTACHE FIRST...
THANKS, "COACH," BUT--
AH-HAHAHAHAHAHAH-
NO, LISTEN! WHEN YOUR OPPONENT AM APPROACHING THE NET, YOU THROW BALL TO FIRST BASE FOR BIG WEENIE ROAST!
ERK?!
IT IS YOUR PLACE TO CHOOSE THE NEXT CONTEST, O SOON-TO-BE-VANQUISHED ONE!
ANYONE AM FINDING BIZARRO'S CUTE LITTLE PENGUIN BACKPACK?
OKAY, LESSEE--
SHAD-DUP! FOR THE NEXT CONTEST, I CHOOSE--
BIZARRO'S FAVORITE TOE WARMER AM IN THERE. ME SO SAD TO LOSE IT...
LISTEN, YOU--
GO JUMP IN A LAKE!
Hmm... I THINK I'VE HEARD OF THAT ONE.
AH, YES! HERE'S THE ENTRY.
OR SOME-THING! I'M TRYING TO--
SO BE IT! "GO JUMP IN A LAKE" IS THE NEXT GAME!
!
FWAP!
;

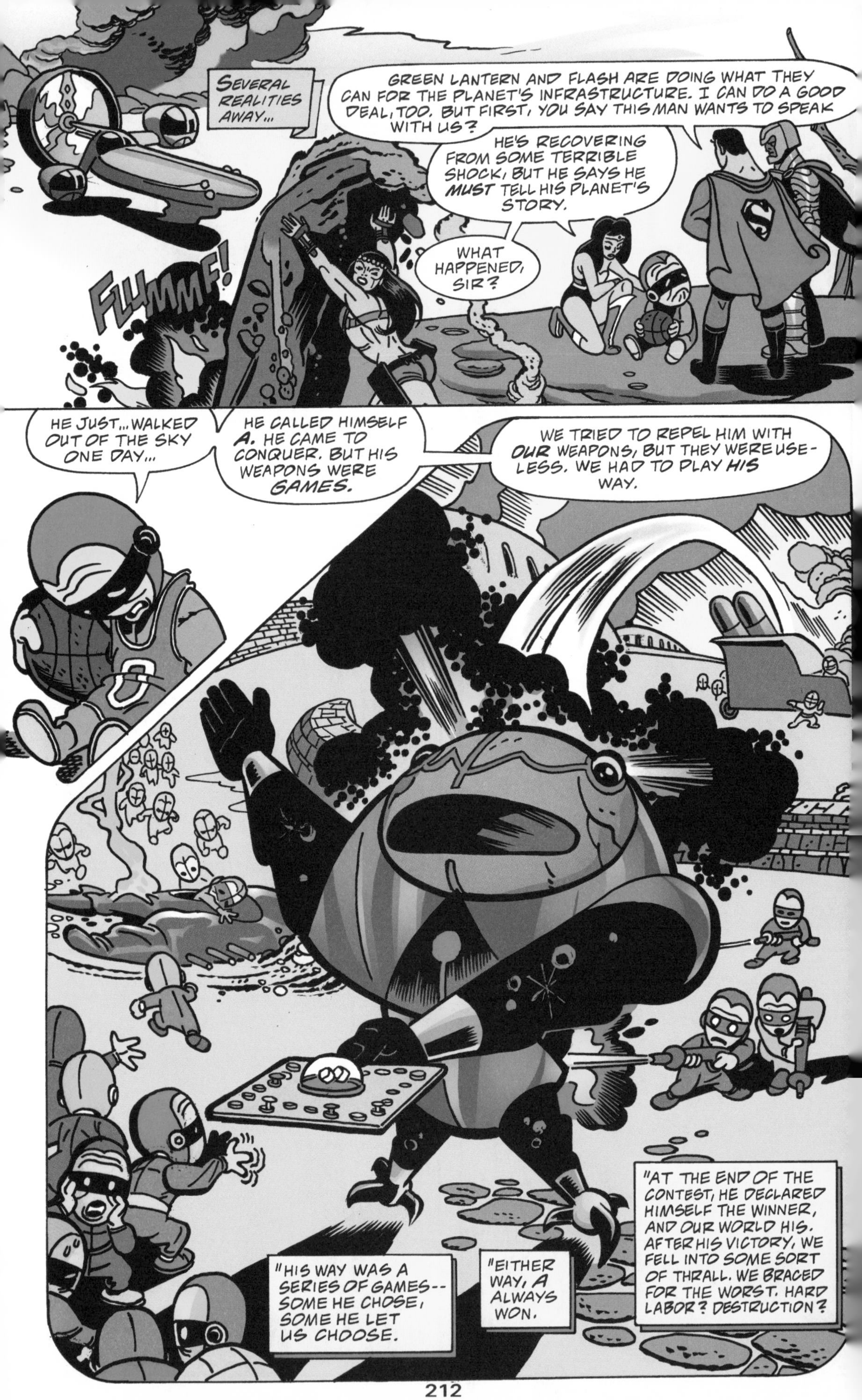

SEVERAL REALITIES AWAY...
GREEN LANTERN AND FLASH ARE DOING WHAT THEY CAN FOR THE PLANET'S INFRASTRUCTURE. I CAN DO A GOOD DEAL, TOO. BUT FIRST, YOU SAY THIS MAN WANTS TO SPEAK WITH US?
HE'S RECOVERING FROM SOME TERRIBLE SHOCK, BUT HE SAYS HE MUST TELL HIS PLANET'S STORY.
WHAT HAPPENED, SIR?
FLUMMF!
HE JUST... WALKED OUT OF THE SKY ONE DAY...
HE CALLED HIMSELF A. HE CAME TO CONQUER. BUT HIS WEAPONS WERE GAMES.
WE TRIED TO REPEL HIM WITH OUR WEAPONS, BUT THEY WERE USE-LESS. WE HAD TO PLAY HIS WAY.
"HIS WAY WAS A SERIES OF GAMES-- SOME HE CHOSE, SOME HE LET US CHOOSE.
"EITHER WAY, A ALWAYS WON.
"AT THE END OF THE CONTEST, HE DECLARED HIMSELF THE WINNER, AND OUR WORLD HIS. AFTER HIS VICTORY, WE FELL INTO SOME SORT OF THRALL. WE BRACED FOR THE WORST. HARD LABOR? DESTRUCTION?

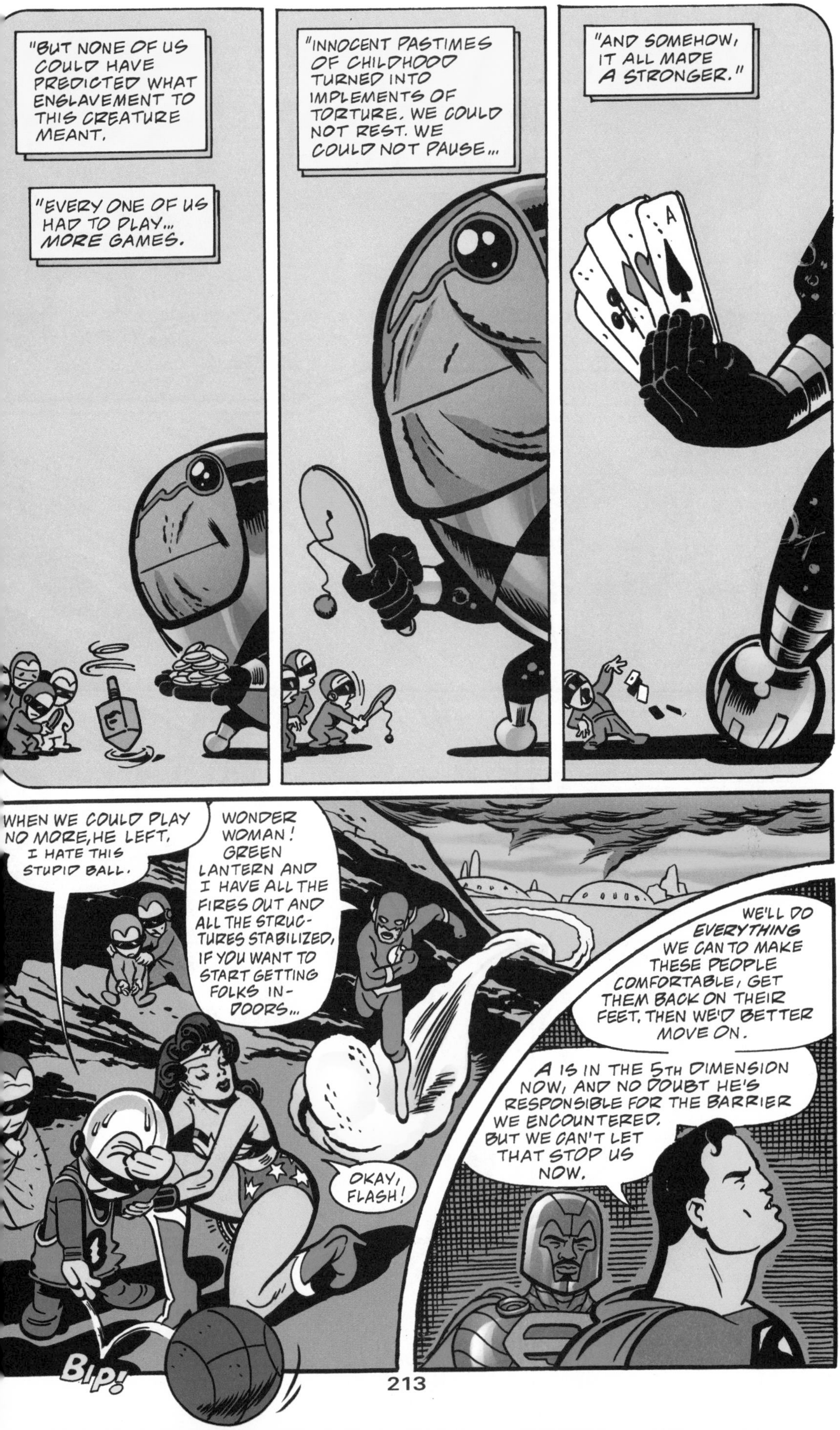
"BUT NONE OF US COULD HAVE PREDICTED WHAT ENSLAVEMENT TO THIS CREATURE MEANT.
"EVERY ONE OF US HAD TO PLAY... MORE GAMES.
"INNOCENT PASTIMES OF CHILDHOOD TURNED INTO IMPLEMENTS OF TORTURE. WE COULD NOT REST. WE COULD NOT PAUSE...
"AND SOMEHOW, IT ALL MADE A STRONGER."
WHEN WE COULD PLAY NO MORE, HE LEFT. I HATE THIS STUPID BALL.
WONDER WOMAN! GREEN LANTERN AND I HAVE ALL THE FIRES OUT AND ALL THE STRUCTURES STABILIZED, IF YOU WANT TO START GETTING FOLKS INDOORS...
OKAY, FLASH!
BIP!
WE'LL DO EVERYTHING WE CAN TO MAKE THESE PEOPLE COMFORTABLE, GET THEM BACK ON THEIR FEET. THEN WE'D BETTER MOVE ON.
A IS IN THE 5TH DIMENSION NOW, AND NO DOUBT HE'S RESPONSIBLE FOR THE BARRIER WE ENCOUNTERED. BUT WE CAN'T LET THAT STOP US NOW.

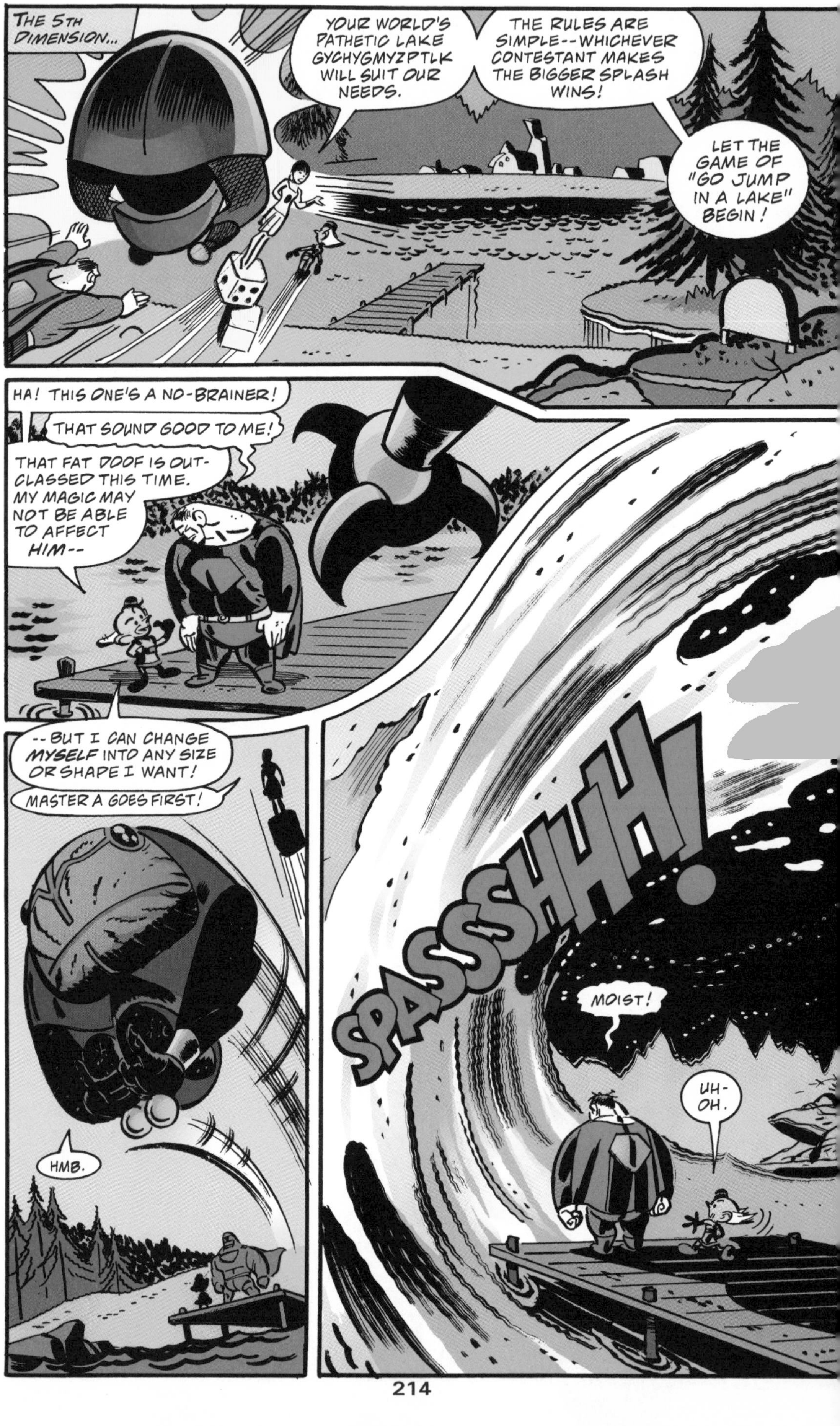
THE 5TH DIMENSION...
YOUR WORLD'S PATHETIC LAKE GYCHYGMYZPTLK WILL SUIT OUR NEEDS.
THE RULES ARE SIMPLE--WHICHEVER CONTESTANT MAKES THE BIGGER SPLASH WINS!
LET THE GAME OF "GO JUMP IN A LAKE" BEGIN!
HA! THIS ONE'S A NO-BRAINER!
THAT SOUND GOOD TO ME!
THAT FAT DOOF IS OUT-CLASSED THIS TIME. MY MAGIC MAY NOT BE ABLE TO AFFECT HIM--
--BUT I CAN CHANGE MYSELF INTO ANY SIZE OR SHAPE I WANT!
MASTER A GOES FIRST!
HMB.
SPASSSHHH!
MOIST!
UH-OH.

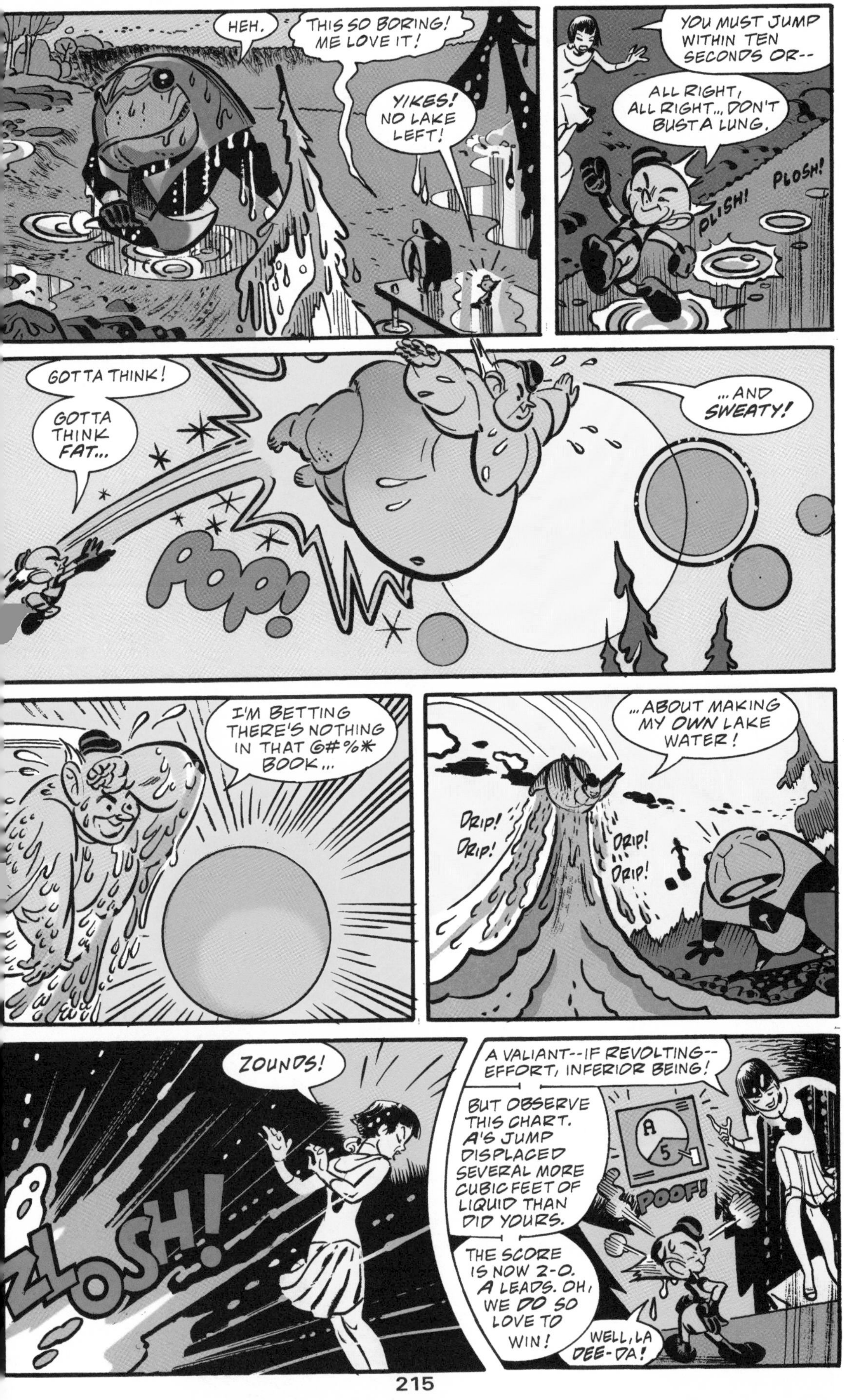

HEH.
THIS SO BORING! ME LOVE IT!
YIKES! NO LAKE LEFT!
YOU MUST JUMP WITHIN TEN SECONDS OR--
ALL RIGHT, ALL RIGHT... DON'T BUST A LUNG.
PLISH!
PLOSH!
GOTTA THINK!
GOTTA THINK FAT...
...AND SWEATY!
POP!
I'M BETTING THERE'S NOTHING IN THAT @#%* BOOK...
...ABOUT MAKING MY OWN LAKE WATER!
DRIP! DRIP!
DRIP! DRIP!
ZOUNDS!
ZLOSH!
A VALIANT--IF REVOLTING--EFFORT, INFERIOR BEING!
BUT OBSERVE THIS CHART. A'S JUMP DISPLACED SEVERAL MORE CUBIC FEET OF LIQUID THAN DID YOURS.
THE SCORE IS NOW 2-0. A LEADS. OH, WE DO SO LOVE TO WIN!
POOF!
WELL, LA DEE-DA!

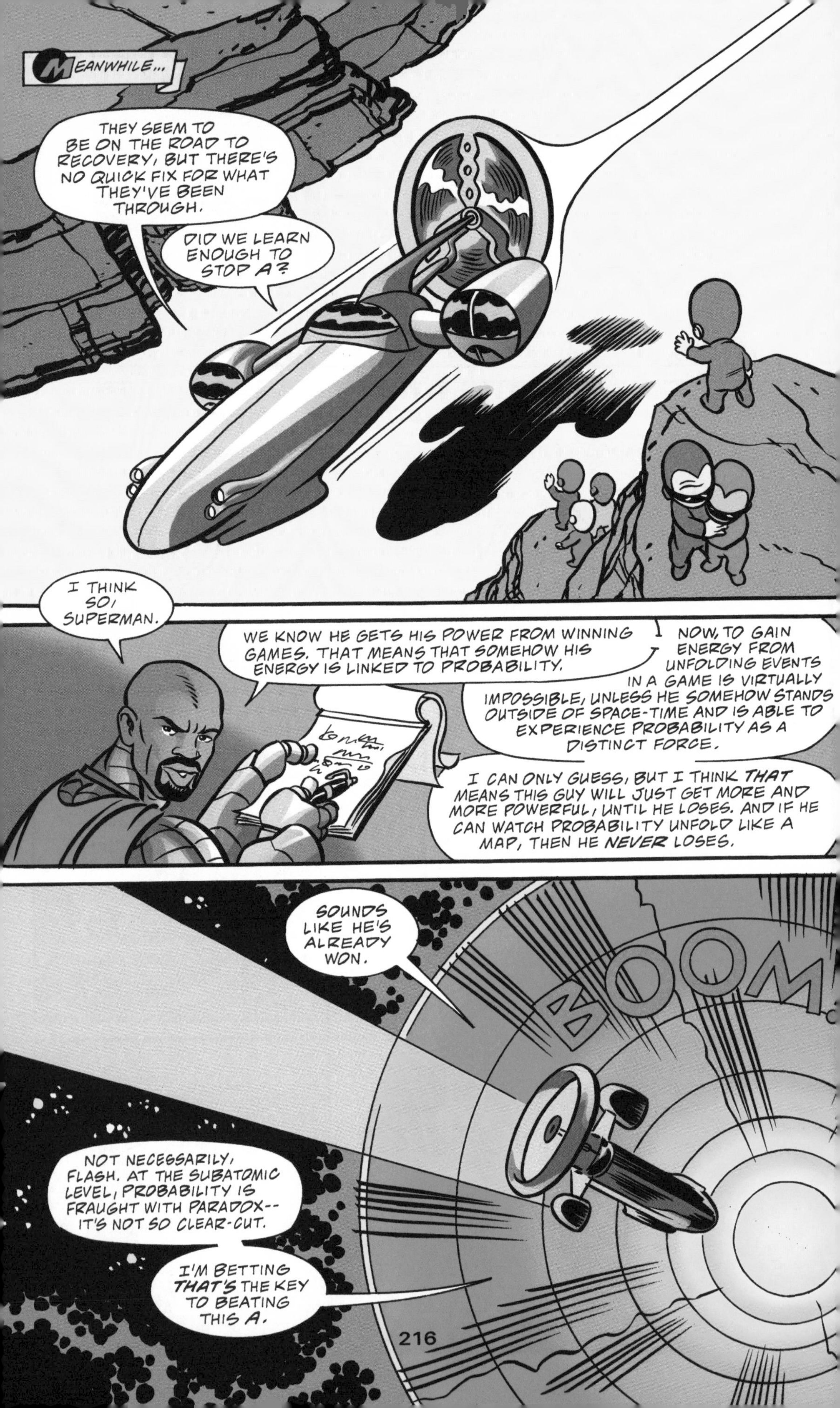
MEANWHILE...
THEY SEEM TO BE ON THE ROAD TO RECOVERY, BUT THERE'S NO QUICK FIX FOR WHAT THEY'VE BEEN THROUGH.
DID WE LEARN ENOUGH TO STOP A?
I THINK SO, SUPERMAN.
WE KNOW HE GETS HIS POWER FROM WINNING GAMES. THAT MEANS THAT SOMEHOW HIS ENERGY IS LINKED TO PROBABILITY.
NOW, TO GAIN ENERGY FROM UNFOLDING EVENTS IN A GAME IS VIRTUALLY IMPOSSIBLE, UNLESS HE SOMEHOW STANDS OUTSIDE OF SPACE-TIME AND IS ABLE TO EXPERIENCE PROBABILITY AS A DISTINCT FORCE.
I CAN ONLY GUESS, BUT I THINK THAT MEANS THIS GUY WILL JUST GET MORE AND MORE POWERFUL, UNTIL HE LOSES. AND IF HE CAN WATCH PROBABILITY UNFOLD LIKE A MAP, THEN HE NEVER LOSES.
SOUNDS LIKE HE'S ALREADY WON.
BOOOM!
NOT NECESSARILY, FLASH. AT THE SUBATOMIC LEVEL, PROBABILITY IS FRAUGHT WITH PARADOX-- IT'S NOT SO CLEAR-CUT.
I'M BETTING THAT'S THE KEY TO BEATING THIS A.

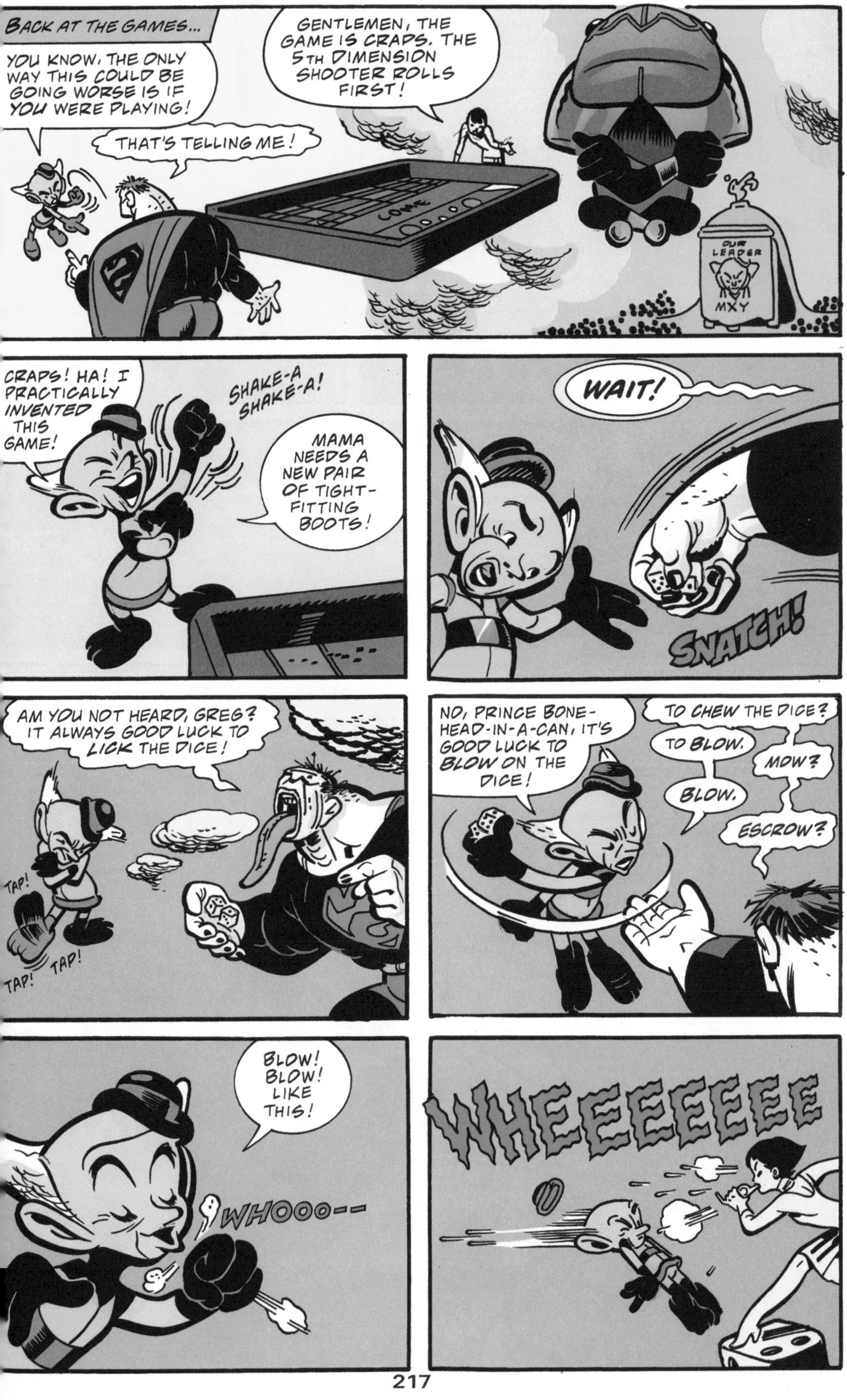
BACK AT THE GAMES...
YOU KNOW, THE ONLY WAY THIS COULD BE GOING WORSE IS IF YOU WERE PLAYING!
THAT'S TELLING ME!
GENTLEMEN, THE GAME IS CRAPS. THE 5TH DIMENSION SHOOTER ROLLS FIRST!
COME
OUR LEADER MXY
CRAPS! HA! I PRACTICALLY INVENTED THIS GAME!
SHAKE-A SHAKE-A!
MAMA NEEDS A NEW PAIR OF TIGHT-FITTING BOOTS!
WAIT!
SNATCH!
AM YOU NOT HEARD, GREG? IT ALWAYS GOOD LUCK TO LICK THE DICE!
TAP!
TAP!
TAP!
NO, PRINCE BONE-HEAD-IN-A-CAN, IT'S GOOD LUCK TO BLOW ON THE DICE!
TO CHEW THE DICE?
TO BLOW.
MOW?
BLOW.
ESCROW?
BLOW! BLOW! LIKE THIS!
WHOOO--
WHEEEEEEE

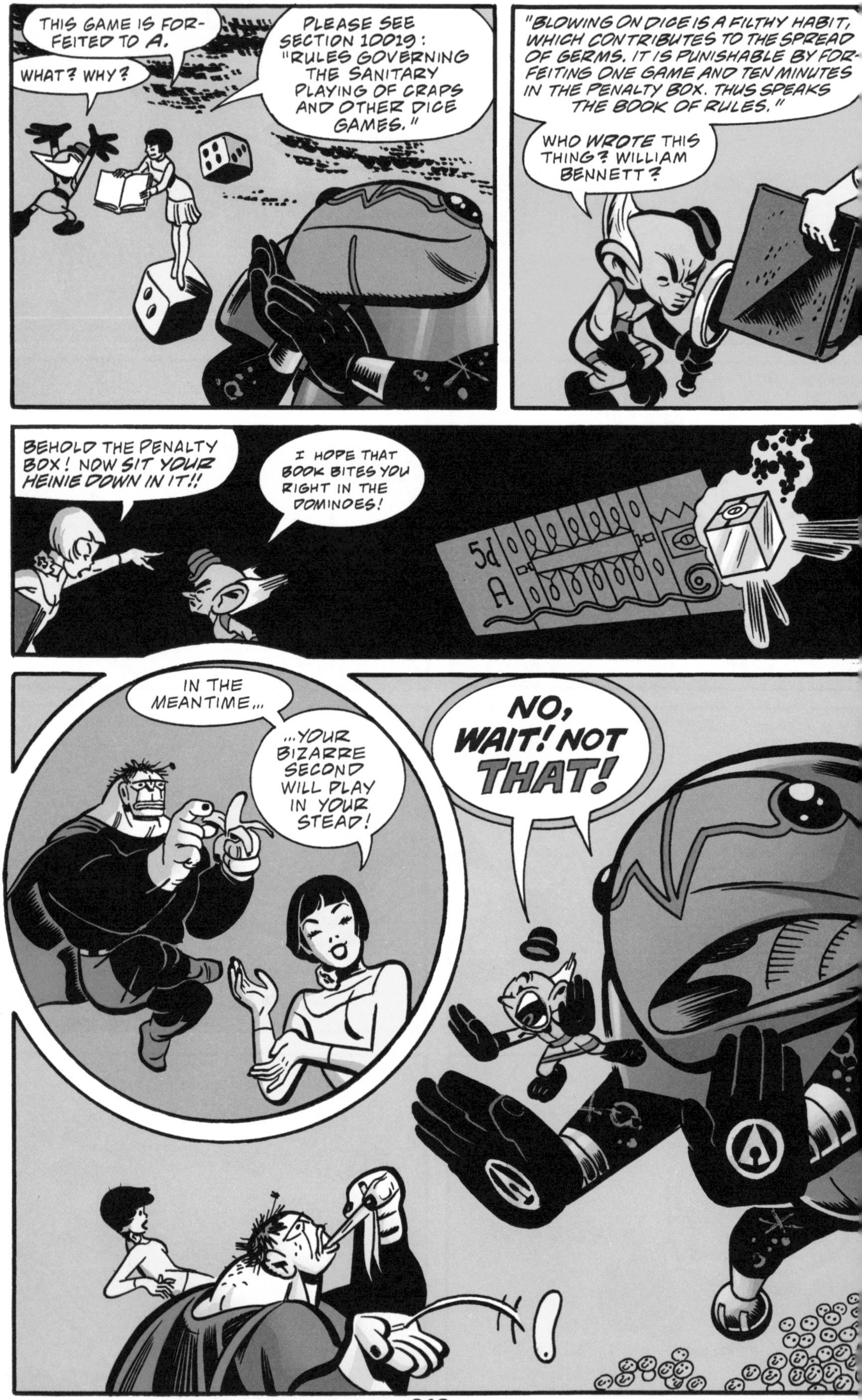
THIS GAME IS FORFEITED TO A.
WHAT? WHY?
PLEASE SEE SECTION 10019 : "RULES GOVERNING THE SANITARY PLAYING OF CRAPS AND OTHER DICE GAMES."
"BLOWING ON DICE IS A FILTHY HABIT, WHICH CONTRIBUTES TO THE SPREAD OF GERMS. IT IS PUNISHABLE BY FORFEITING ONE GAME AND TEN MINUTES IN THE PENALTY BOX. THUS SPEAKS THE BOOK OF RULES."
WHO WROTE THIS THING? WILLIAM BENNETT?
BEHOLD THE PENALTY BOX! NOW SIT YOUR HEINIE DOWN IN IT!!
I HOPE THAT BOOK BITES YOU RIGHT IN THE DOMINOES!
5d
A
IN THE MEANTIME...
...YOUR BIZARRE SECOND WILL PLAY IN YOUR STEAD!
NO, WAIT! NOT THAT!
!

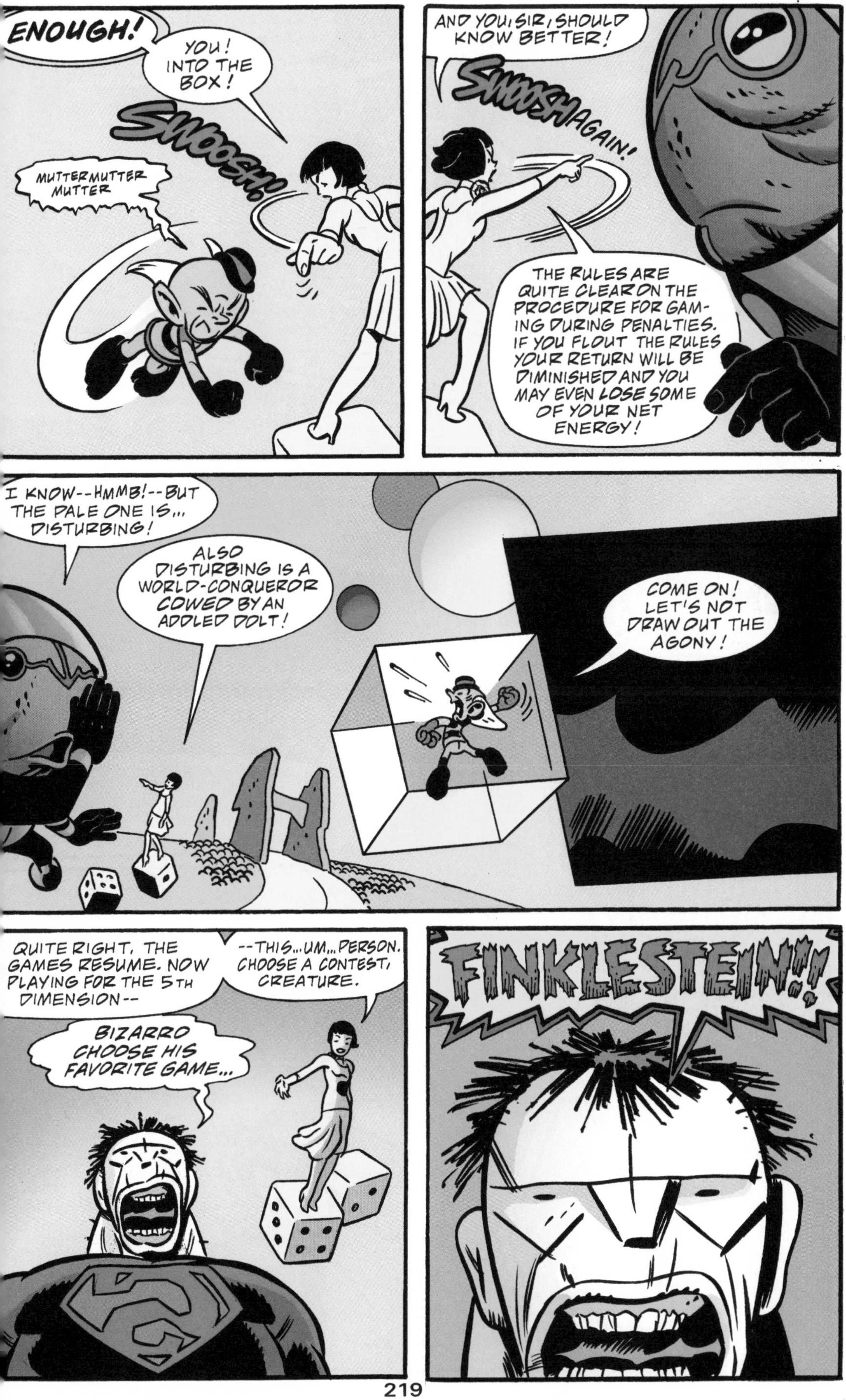
ENOUGH!
YOU! INTO THE BOX!
SWOOSH!
MUTTERMUTTER MUTTER
AND YOU, SIR, SHOULD KNOW BETTER!
SWOOSH AGAIN!
THE RULES ARE QUITE CLEAR ON THE PROCEDURE FOR GAMING DURING PENALTIES. IF YOU FLOUT THE RULES YOUR RETURN WILL BE DIMINISHED AND YOU MAY EVEN LOSE SOME OF YOUR NET ENERGY!
I KNOW--HMMB!--BUT THE PALE ONE IS... DISTURBING!
ALSO DISTURBING IS A WORLD-CONQUEROR COWED BY AN ADDLED DOLT!
COME ON! LET'S NOT DRAW OUT THE AGONY!
QUITE RIGHT. THE GAMES RESUME. NOW PLAYING FOR THE 5TH DIMENSION--
--THIS...UM...PERSON. CHOOSE A CONTEST, CREATURE.
BIZARRO CHOOSE HIS FAVORITE GAME...
FINKLESTEIN!!

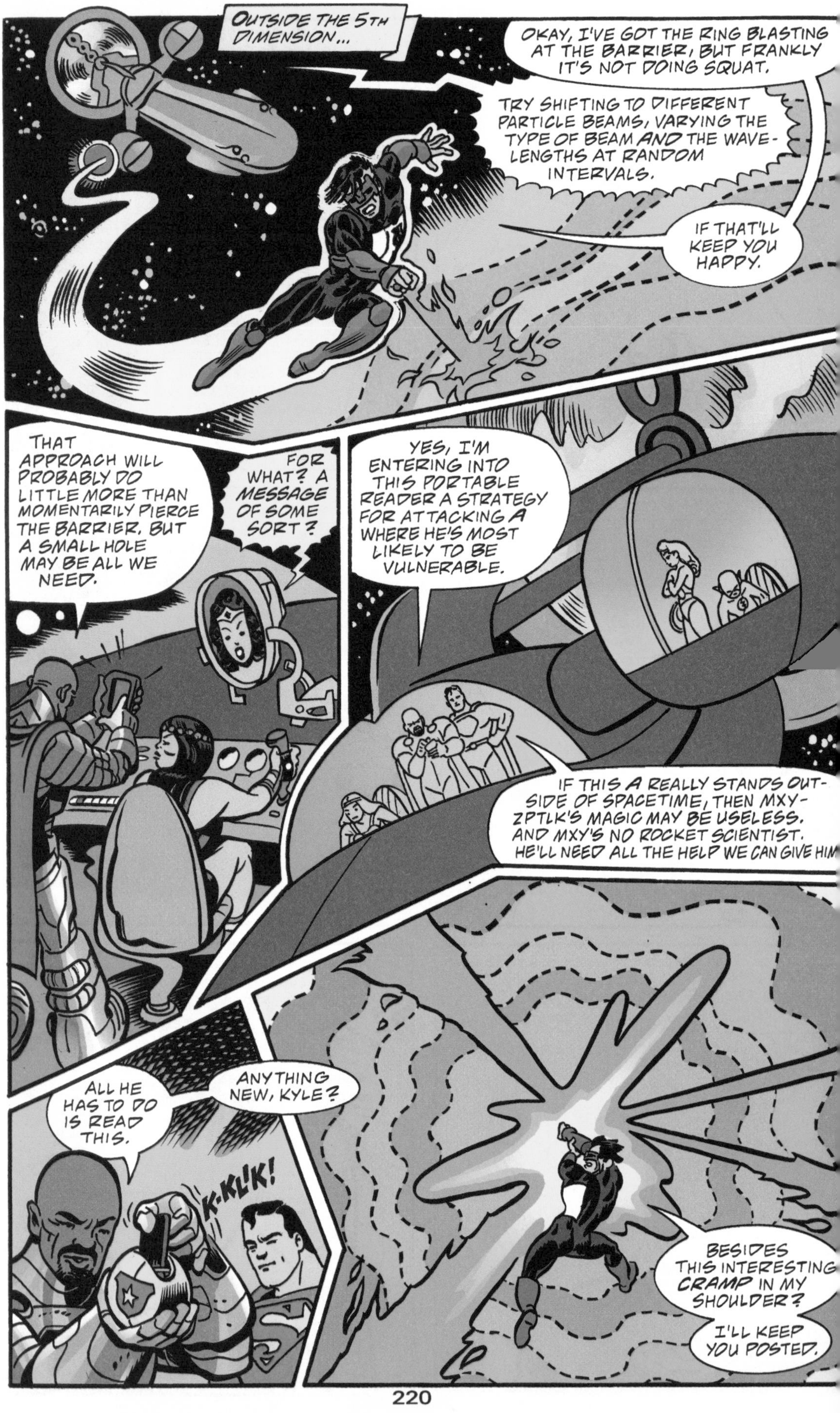

OUTSIDE THE 5TH DIMENSION...
OKAY, I'VE GOT THE RING BLASTING AT THE BARRIER, BUT FRANKLY IT'S NOT DOING SQUAT.
TRY SHIFTING TO DIFFERENT PARTICLE BEAMS, VARYING THE TYPE OF BEAM AND THE WAVE-LENGTHS AT RANDOM INTERVALS.
IF THAT'LL KEEP YOU HAPPY.
THAT APPROACH WILL PROBABLY DO LITTLE MORE THAN MOMENTARILY PIERCE THE BARRIER, BUT A SMALL HOLE MAY BE ALL WE NEED.
FOR WHAT? A MESSAGE OF SOME SORT?
YES, I'M ENTERING INTO THIS PORTABLE READER A STRATEGY FOR ATTACKING A WHERE HE'S MOST LIKELY TO BE VULNERABLE.
IF THIS A REALLY STANDS OUT-SIDE OF SPACETIME, THEN MXY-ZPTLK'S MAGIC MAY BE USELESS. AND MXY'S NO ROCKET SCIENTIST. HE'LL NEED ALL THE HELP WE CAN GIVE HIM
ALL HE HAS TO DO IS READ THIS.
ANYTHING NEW, KYLE?
K-KLIK!
BESIDES THIS INTERESTING CRAMP IN MY SHOULDER?
I'LL KEEP YOU POSTED.

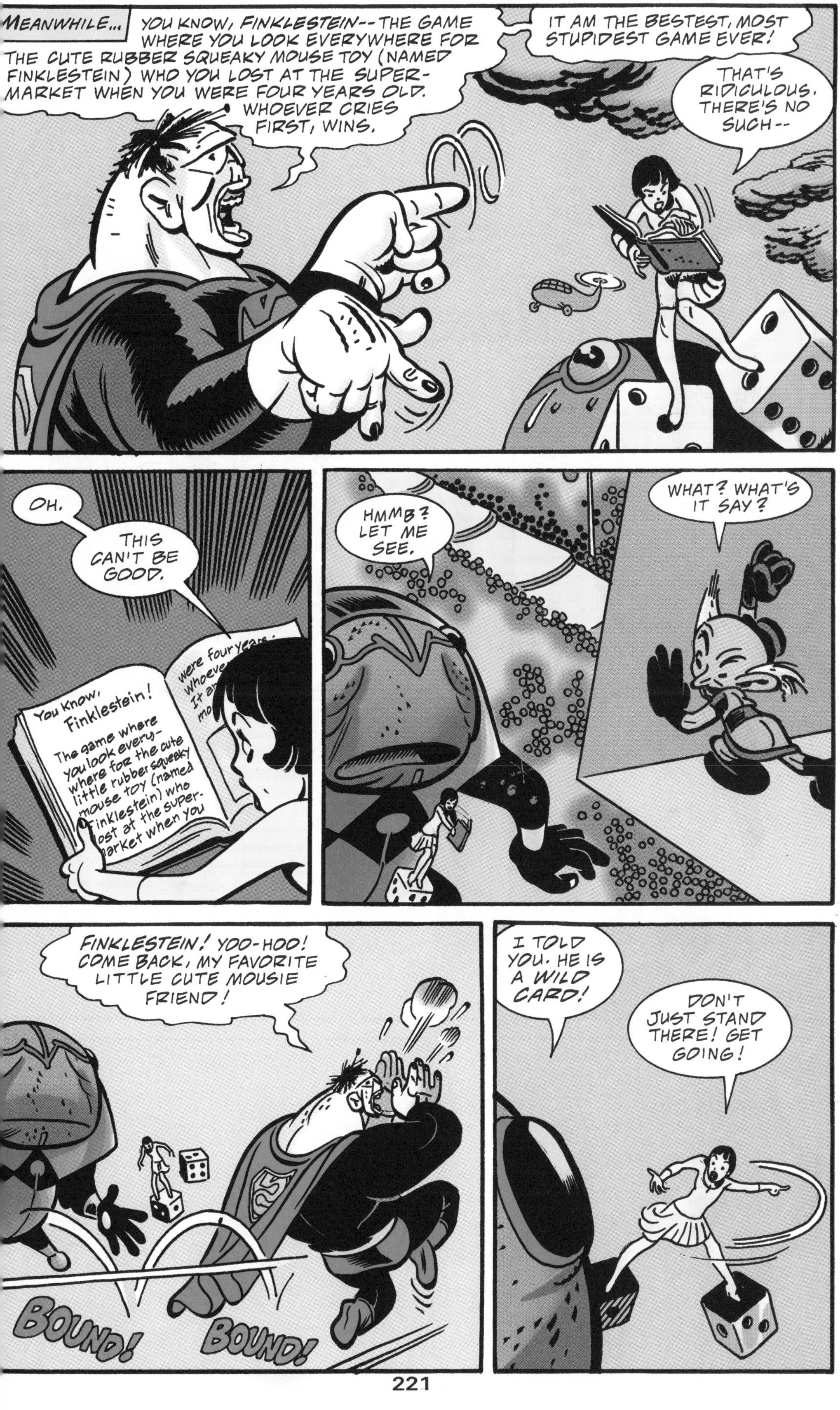
MEANWHILE...
YOU KNOW, FINKLESTEIN-- THE GAME WHERE YOU LOOK EVERYWHERE FOR THE CUTE RUBBER SQUEAKY MOUSE TOY (NAMED FINKLESTEIN) WHO YOU LOST AT THE SUPER-MARKET WHEN YOU WERE FOUR YEARS OLD. WHOEVER CRIES FIRST, WINS.
IT AM THE BESTEST, MOST STUPIDEST GAME EVER!
THAT'S RIDICULOUS. THERE'S NO SUCH --
OH.
THIS CAN'T BE GOOD.
You Know, Finklestein! The game where you look every-where for the cute little rubber squeaky mouse toy (named Finklestein) who lost at the super-market when you
were four years
HMMB? LET ME SEE.
WHAT? WHAT'S IT SAY?
FINKLESTEIN! YOO-HOO! COME BACK, MY FAVORITE LITTLE CUTE MOUSIE FRIEND!
BOUND! BOUND!
I TOLD YOU. HE IS A WILD CARD!
DON'T JUST STAND THERE! GET GOING!

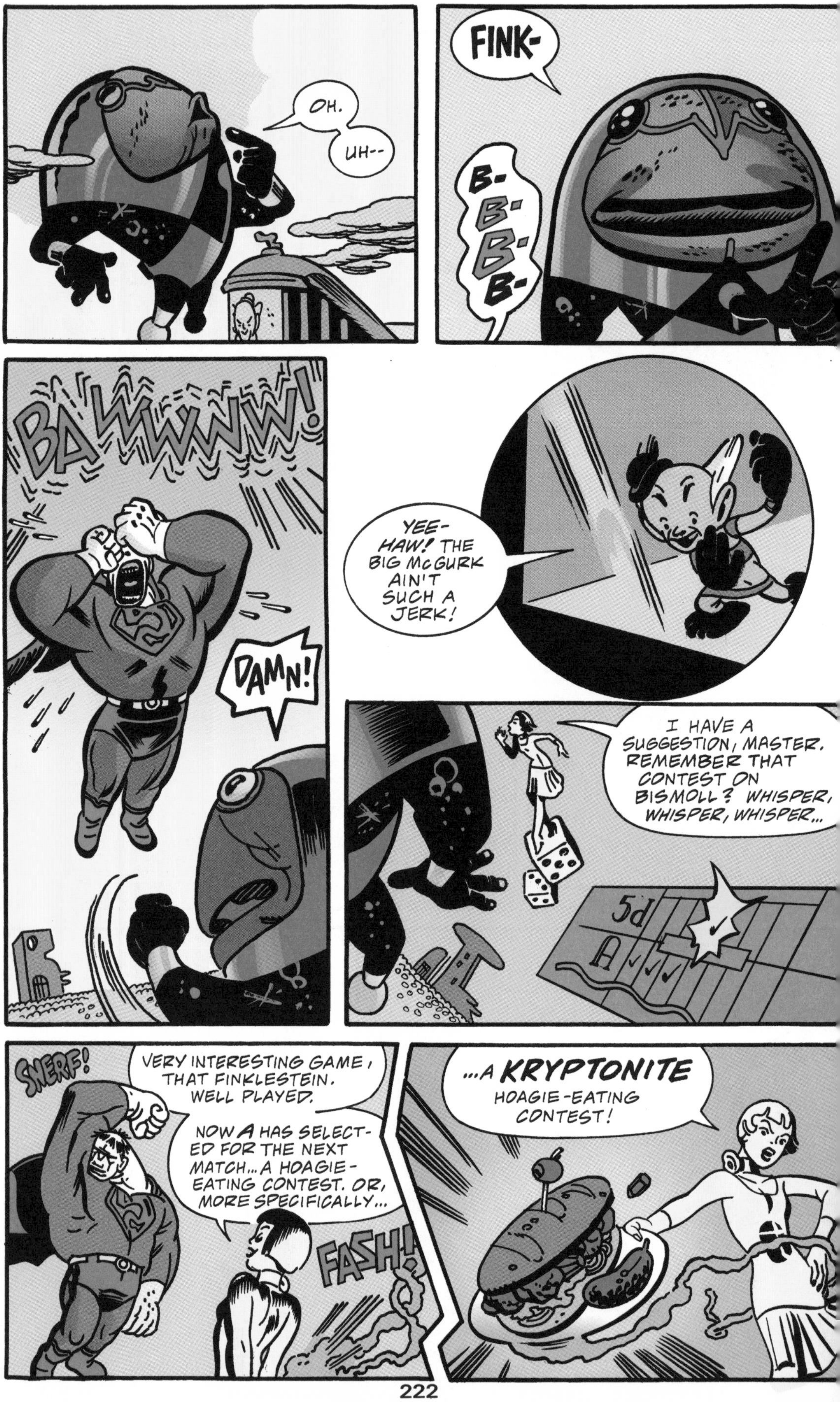
OH.
UH--
FINK-
B-B-B-B-
BAWWWW!
YEE-HAW! THE BIG McGURK AIN'T SUCH A JERK!
DAMN!
I HAVE A SUGGESTION, MASTER. REMEMBER THAT CONTEST ON BISMOLL? WHISPER, WHISPER, WHISPER...
5d
A
SNERF!
VERY INTERESTING GAME, THAT FINKLESTEIN. WELL PLAYED.
NOW A HAS SELECTED FOR THE NEXT MATCH... A HOAGIE-EATING CONTEST. OR, MORE SPECIFICALLY...
FASH!
...A KRYPTONITE HOAGIE-EATING CONTEST!

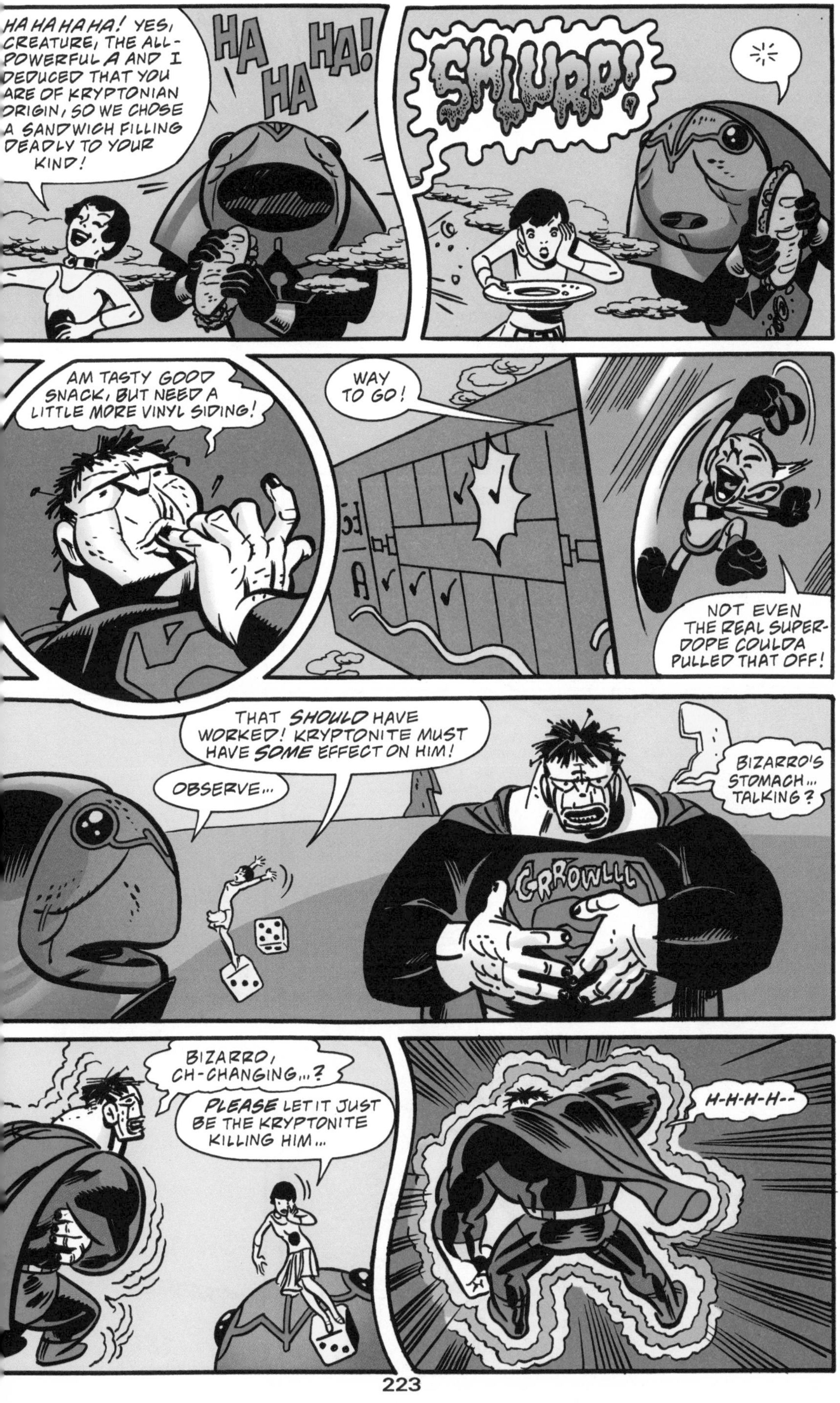
HA HA HA HA! YES, CREATURE, THE ALL-POWERFUL A AND I DEDUCED THAT YOU ARE OF KRYPTONIAN ORIGIN, SO WE CHOSE A SANDWICH FILLING DEADLY TO YOUR KIND!
HA HA HA!
SHLURP!
AM TASTY GOOD SNACK, BUT NEED A LITTLE MORE VINYL SIDING!
WAY TO GO!
NOT EVEN THE REAL SUPER-DOPE COULDA PULLED THAT OFF!
THAT SHOULD HAVE WORKED! KRYPTONITE MUST HAVE SOME EFFECT ON HIM!
OBSERVE...
BIZARRO'S STOMACH... TALKING?
GRROWLLL
BIZARRO, CH-CHANGING...?
PLEASE LET IT JUST BE THE KRYPTONITE KILLING HIM...
H-H-H-H--

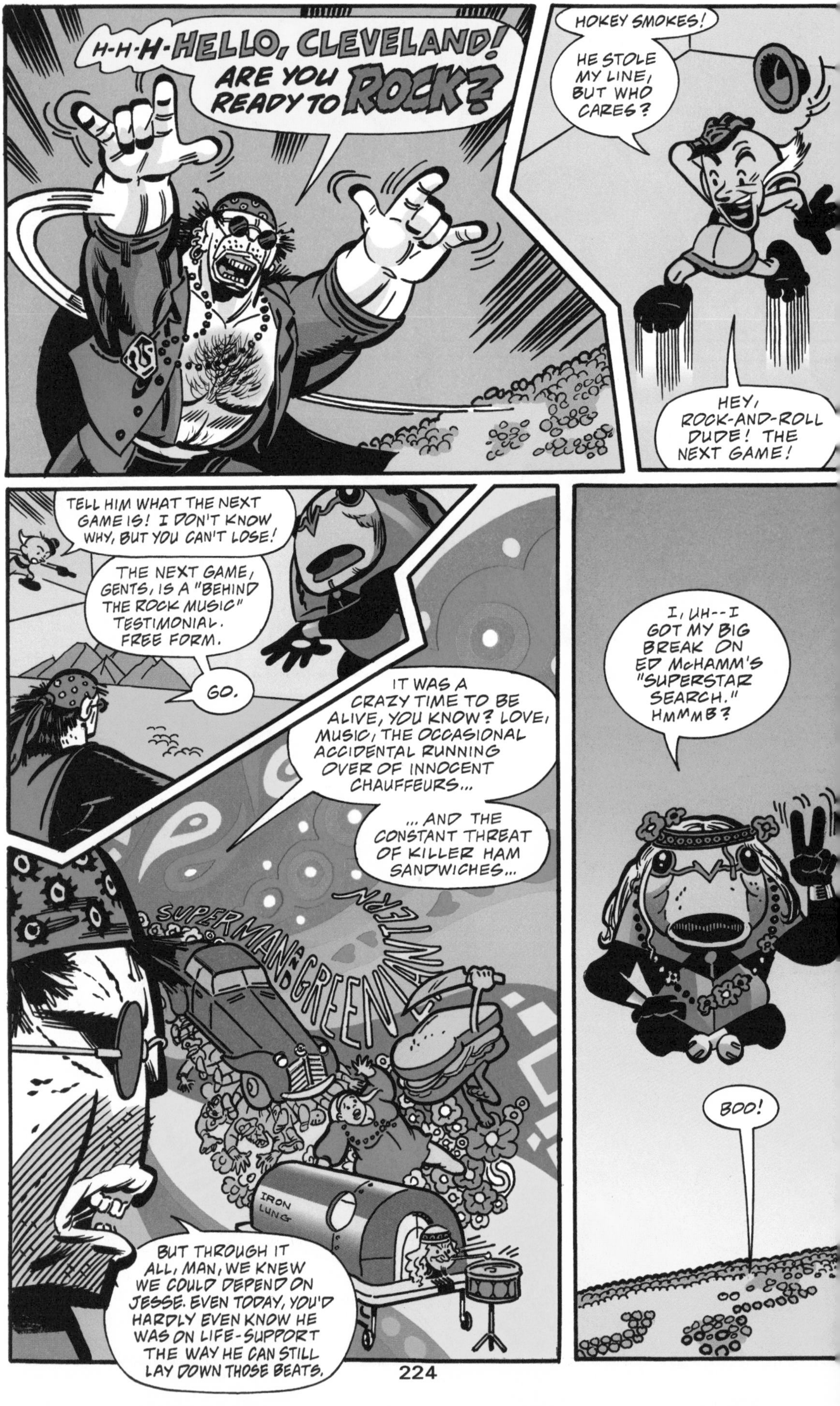
H-H-H-HELLO, CLEVELAND! ARE YOU READY TO ROCK?
HOKEY SMOKES!
HE STOLE MY LINE, BUT WHO CARES?
HEY, ROCK-AND-ROLL DUDE! THE NEXT GAME!
TELL HIM WHAT THE NEXT GAME IS! I DON'T KNOW WHY, BUT YOU CAN'T LOSE!
THE NEXT GAME, GENTS, IS A "BEHIND THE ROCK MUSIC" TESTIMONIAL. FREE FORM.
GO.
IT WAS A CRAZY TIME TO BE ALIVE, YOU KNOW? LOVE, MUSIC, THE OCCASIONAL ACCIDENTAL RUNNING OVER OF INNOCENT CHAUFFEURS...
...AND THE CONSTANT THREAT OF KILLER HAM SANDWICHES...
SUPERMAN AND GREEN LANTERN
IRON LUNG
BUT THROUGH IT ALL, MAN, WE KNEW WE COULD DEPEND ON JESSE. EVEN TODAY, YOU'D HARDLY EVEN KNOW HE WAS ON LIFE-SUPPORT THE WAY HE CAN STILL LAY DOWN THOSE BEATS.
I, UH--I GOT MY BIG BREAK ON ED McHAMM'S "SUPERSTAR SEARCH." HMMMB?
BOO!

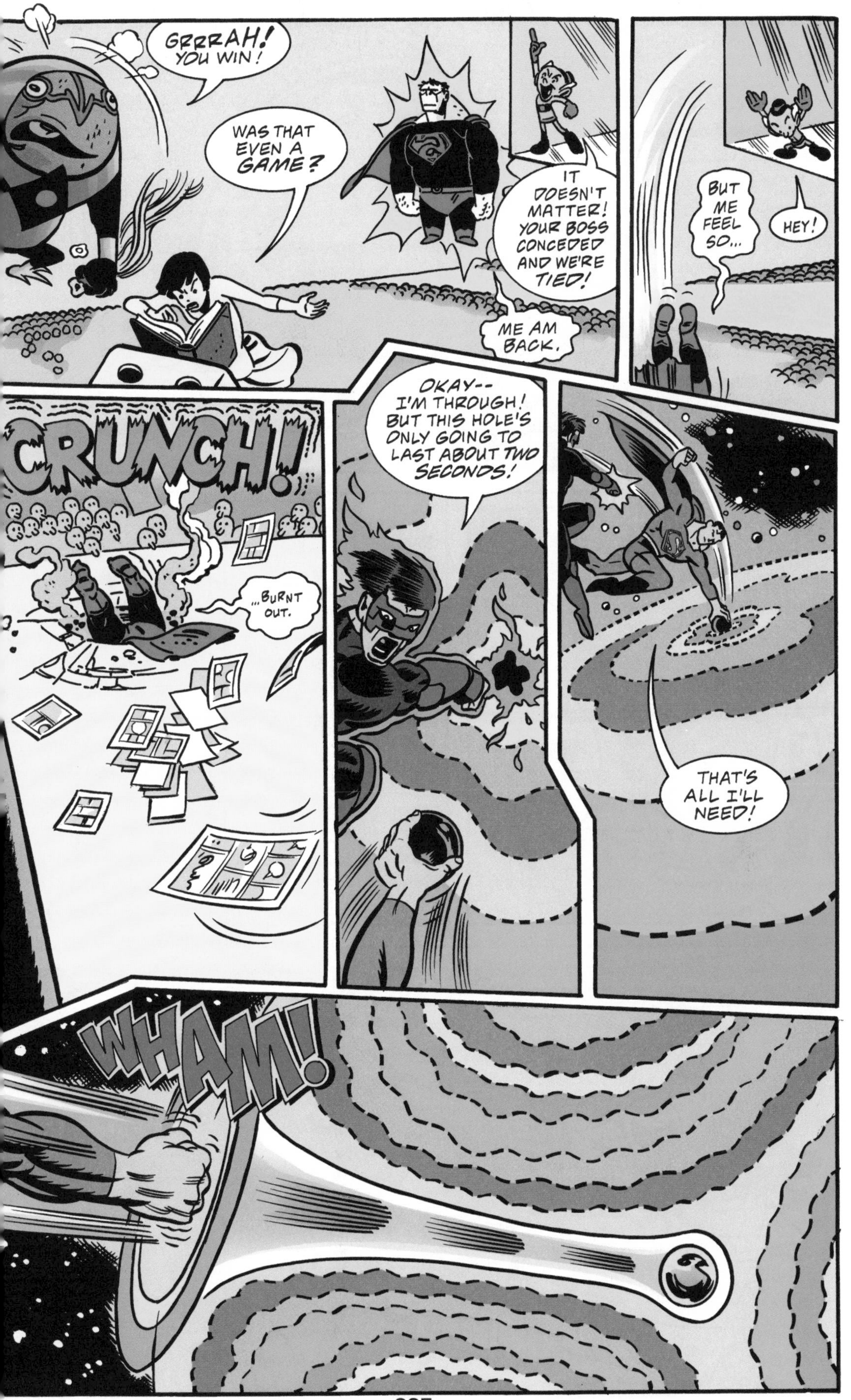
GRRRAH! YOU WIN!
WAS THAT EVEN A GAME?
IT DOESN'T MATTER! YOUR BOSS CONCEDED AND WE'RE TIED!
ME AM BACK.
BUT ME FEEL SO...
HEY!
CRUNCH!
...BURNT OUT.
OKAY-- I'M THROUGH! BUT THIS HOLE'S ONLY GOING TO LAST ABOUT TWO SECONDS!
THAT'S ALL I'LL NEED!
WHAM!

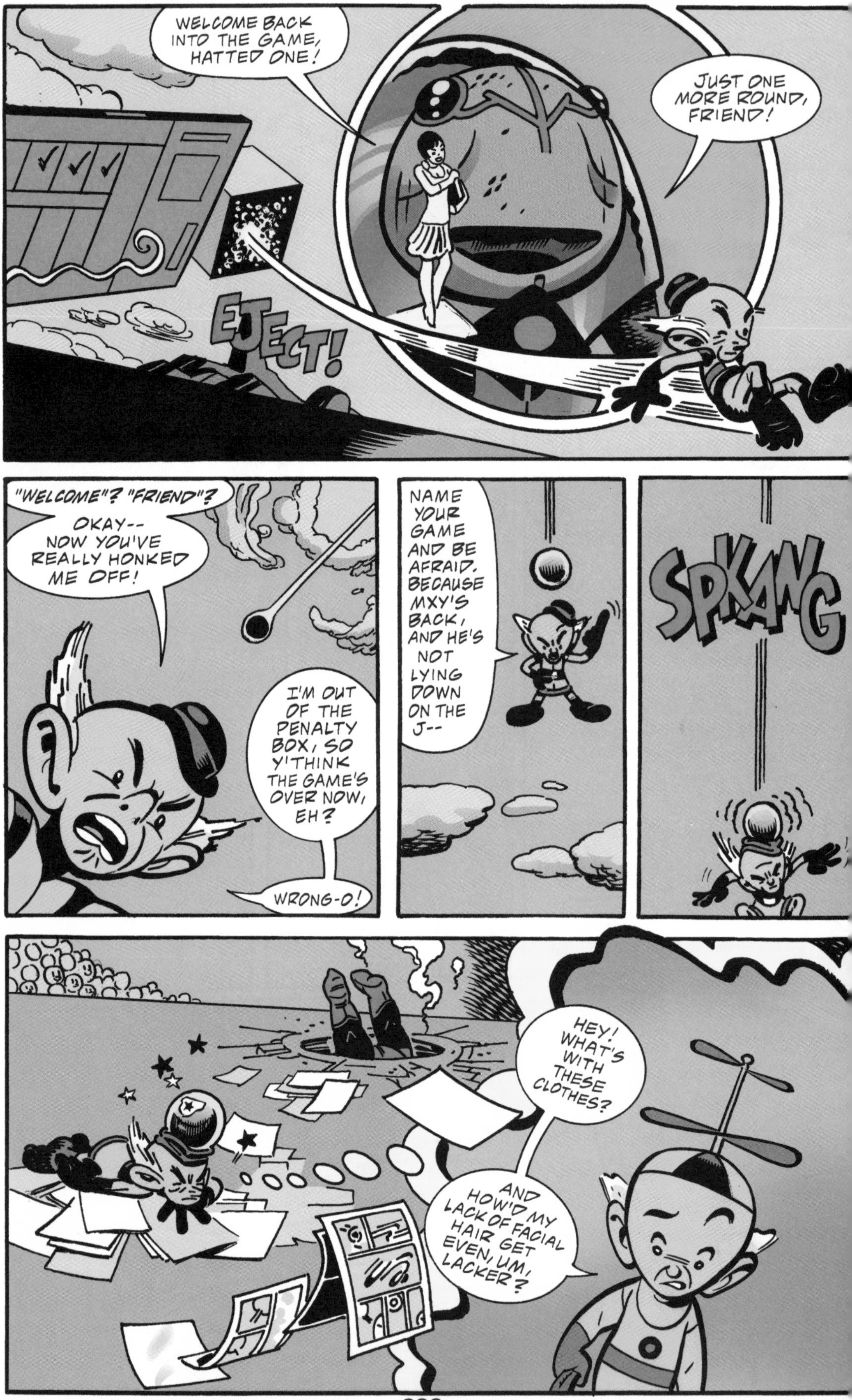
WELCOME BACK INTO THE GAME, HATTED ONE!
JUST ONE MORE ROUND, FRIEND!
EJECT!
"WELCOME"? "FRIEND"? OKAY-- NOW YOU'VE REALLY HONKED ME OFF!
I'M OUT OF THE PENALTY BOX, SO Y'THINK THE GAME'S OVER NOW, EH?
WRONG-O!
NAME YOUR GAME AND BE AFRAID. BECAUSE MXY'S BACK, AND HE'S NOT LYING DOWN ON THE J--
SPKANG
HEY! WHAT'S WITH THESE CLOTHES?
AND HOW'D MY LACK OF FACIAL HAIR GET EVEN, UM, LACKER?

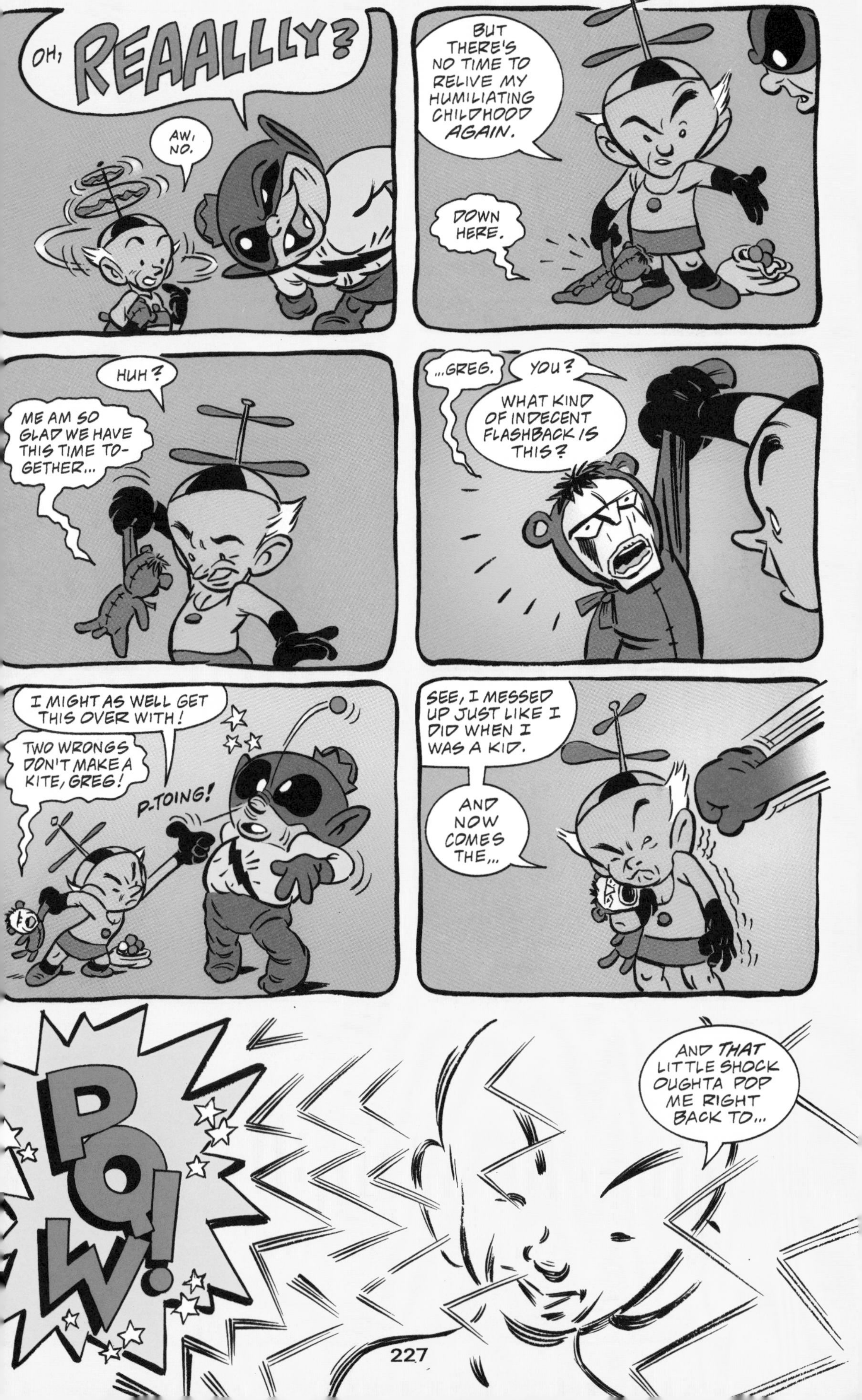
OH, REAALLLY?
AW, NO.
BUT THERE'S NO TIME TO RELIVE MY HUMILIATING CHILDHOOD AGAIN.
DOWN HERE.
HUH?
ME AM SO GLAD WE HAVE THIS TIME TO-GETHER...
...GREG.
YOU?
WHAT KIND OF INDECENT FLASHBACK IS THIS?
I MIGHT AS WELL GET THIS OVER WITH!
TWO WRONGS DON'T MAKE A KITE, GREG!
P-TOING!
SEE, I MESSED UP JUST LIKE I DID WHEN I WAS A KID.
AND NOW COMES THE...
POW!
AND THAT LITTLE SHOCK OUGHTA POP ME RIGHT BACK TO...

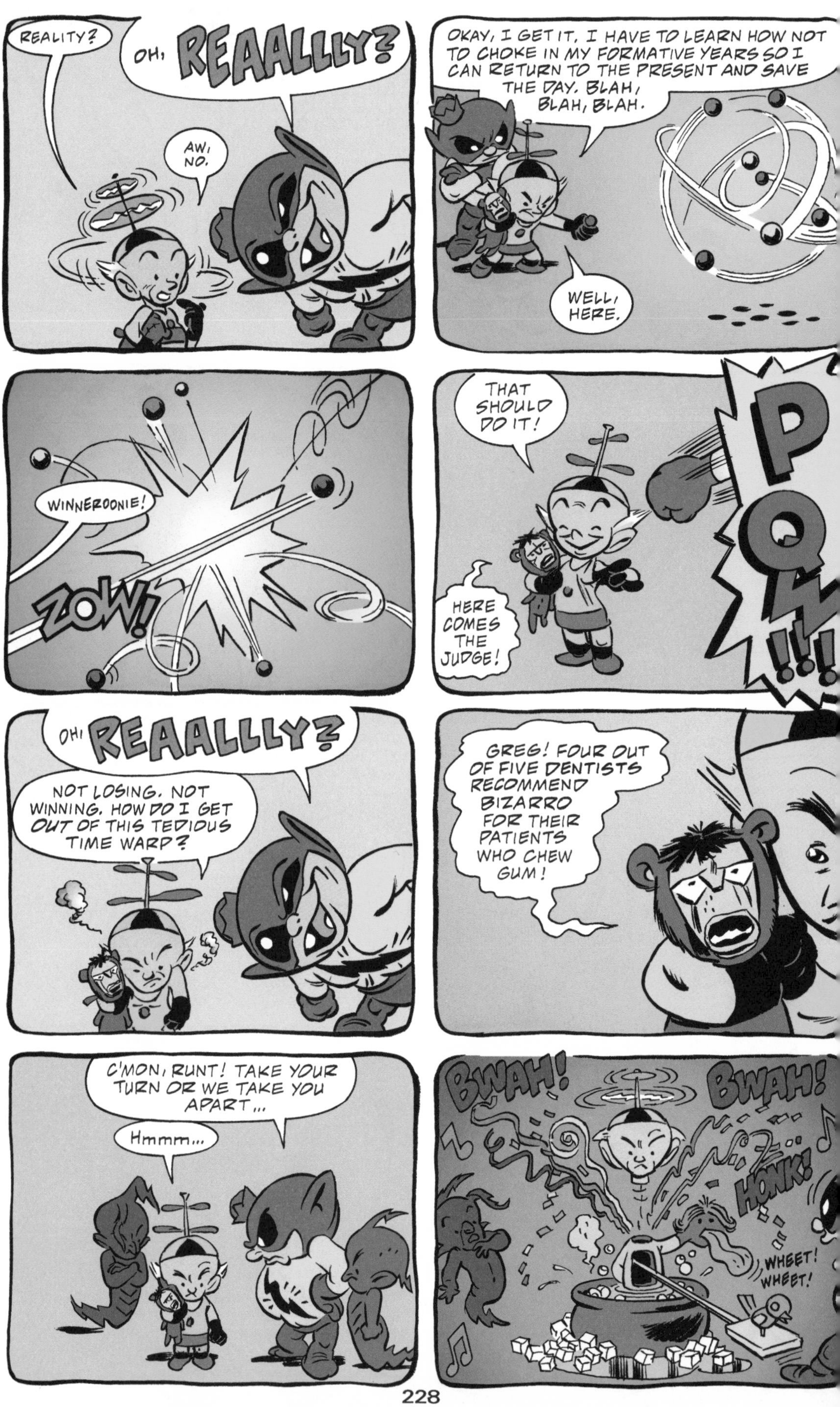
REALITY?
OH, REAALLLY?
AW, NO.
OKAY, I GET IT. I HAVE TO LEARN HOW NOT TO CHOKE IN MY FORMATIVE YEARS SO I CAN RETURN TO THE PRESENT AND SAVE THE DAY. BLAH, BLAH, BLAH.
WELL, HERE.
WINNEROONIE!
ZOW!
THAT SHOULD DO IT!
HERE COMES THE JUDGE!
POW!!!
OH, REAALLLY?
NOT LOSING. NOT WINNING. HOW DO I GET OUT OF THIS TEDIOUS TIME WARP?
GREG! FOUR OUT OF FIVE DENTISTS RECOMMEND BIZARRO FOR THEIR PATIENTS WHO CHEW GUM!
C'MON, RUNT! TAKE YOUR TURN OR WE TAKE YOU APART...
Hmmm...
BWAH!
BWAH!
HONK!
WHEET! WHEET!

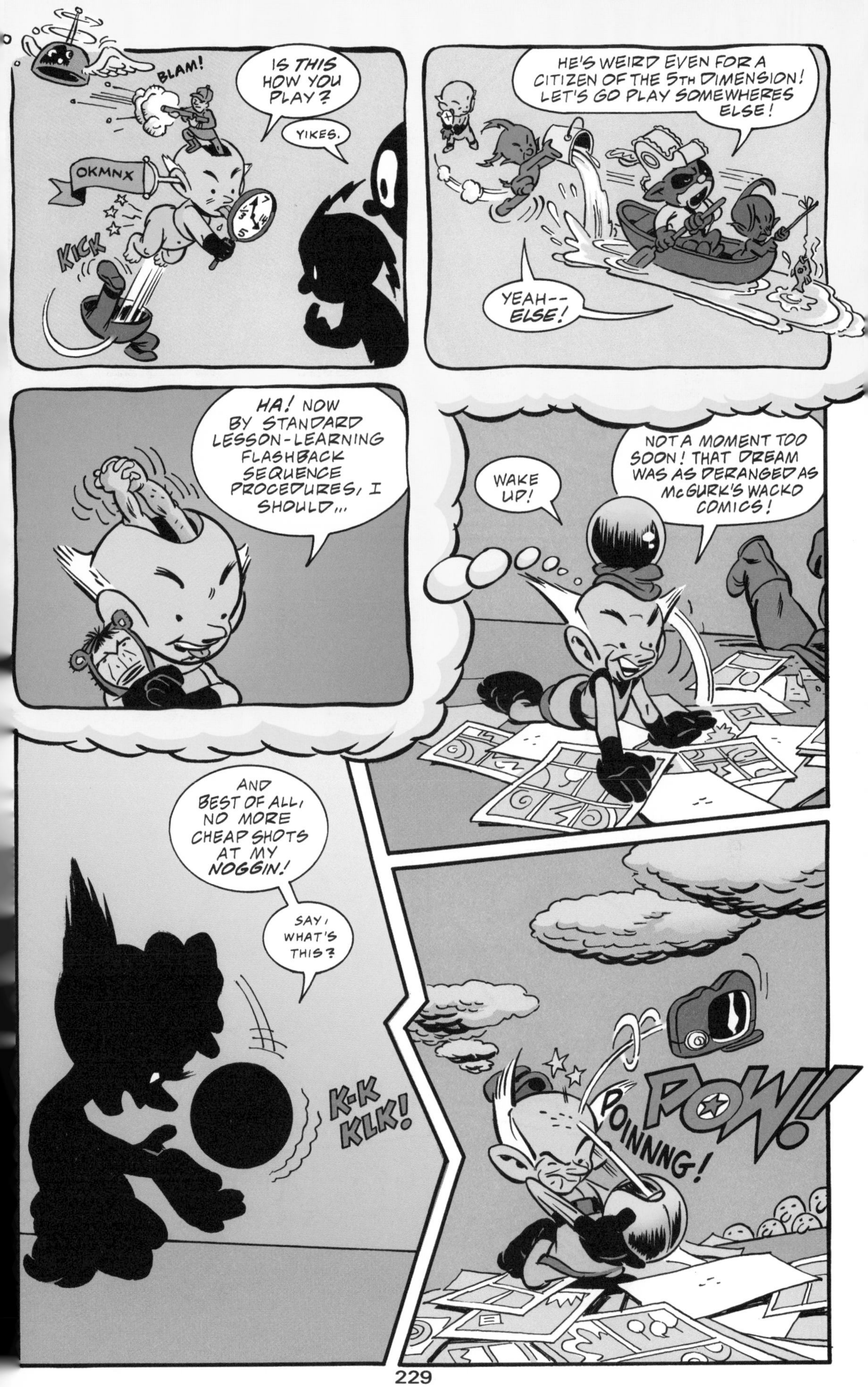
BLAM!
IS THIS HOW YOU PLAY?
YIKES.
OKMNX
KICK
HE'S WEIRD EVEN FOR A CITIZEN OF THE 5TH DIMENSION! LET'S GO PLAY SOMEWHERES ELSE!
YEAH-- ELSE!
HA! NOW BY STANDARD LESSON-LEARNING FLASHBACK SEQUENCE PROCEDURES, I SHOULD...
WAKE UP!
NOT A MOMENT TOO SOON! THAT DREAM WAS AS DERANGED AS McGURK'S WACKO COMICS!
AND BEST OF ALL, NO MORE CHEAP SHOTS AT MY NOGGIN!
SAY, WHAT'S THIS?
K-K KLK!
POW!!
POINNNG!

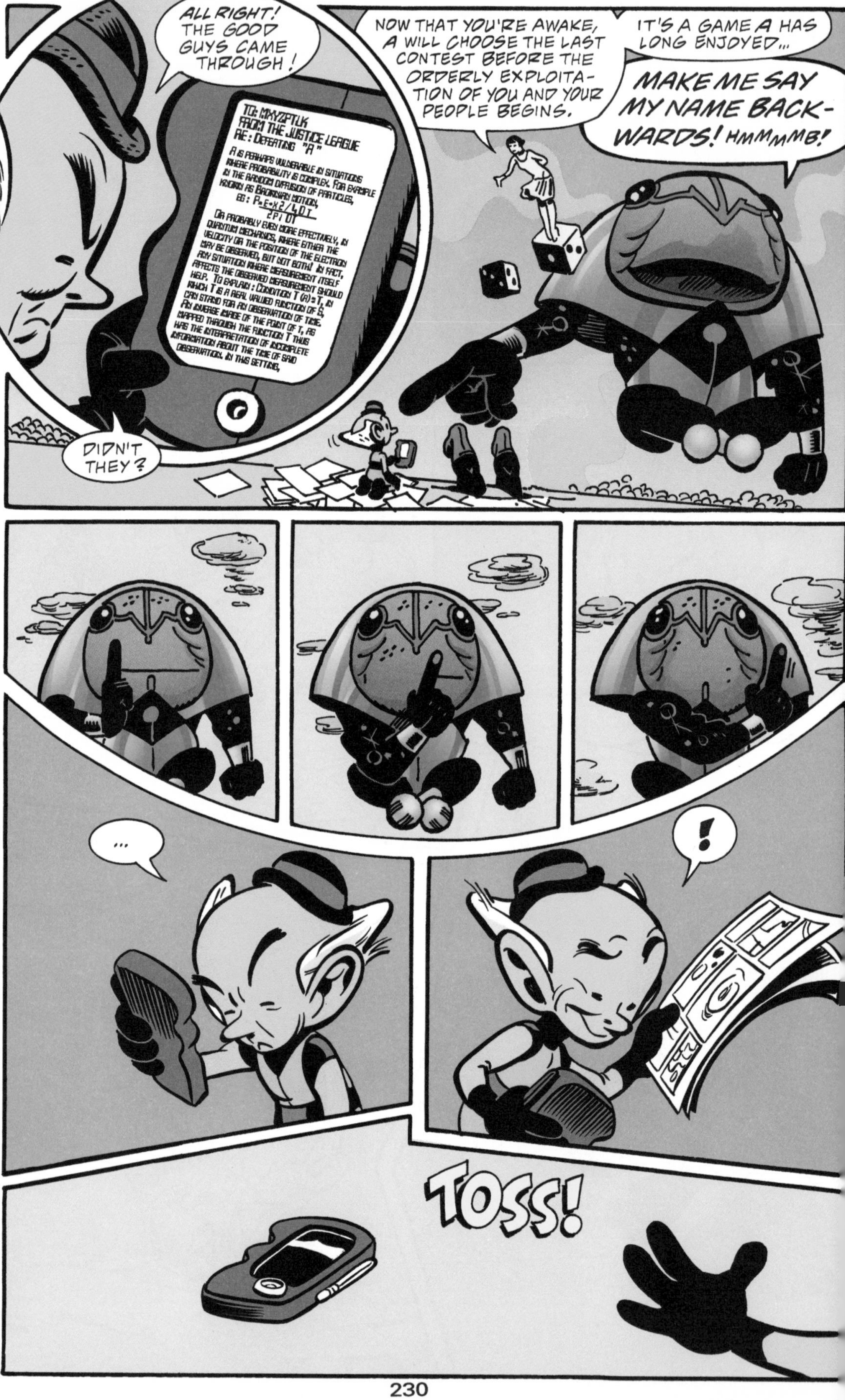
ALL RIGHT! THE GOOD GUYS CAME THROUGH!
TO: MXYZPTLK
FROM THE JUSTICE LEAGUE
RE: DEFEATING "A"
A IS PERHAPS VULNERABLE IN SITUATIONS WHERE PROBABILITY IS COMPLEX. FOR EXAMPLE IN THE RANDOM DIFFUSION OF PARTICLES, KNOWN AS BROWNIAN MOTION,
EG: P=E-X2/4DT / 2PI DT
OR PROBABLY EVEN MORE EFFECTIVELY, IN QUANTUM MECHANICS, WHERE EITHER THE VELOCITY OR THE POSITION OF THE ELECTRON MAY BE OBSERVED, BUT NOT BOTH! IN FACT, ANY SITUATION WHERE MEASUREMENT ITSELF AFFECTS THE OBSERVED MEASUREMENT SHOULD HELP. TO EXPLAIN: CONDITION T (A)=T, IN WHICH T IS A REAL VALUED FUNCTION OF S, CAN STAND FOR AN OBSERVATION OF TIME. AN INVERSE IMAGE OF THE POINT OF T, AS MAPPED THROUGH THE FUNCTION T THUS HAS THE INTERPRETATION OF INCOMPLETE INFORMATION ABOUT THE TIME OF SAID OBSERVATION. IN THIS SETTING,
DIDN'T THEY?
NOW THAT YOU'RE AWAKE, A WILL CHOOSE THE LAST CONTEST BEFORE THE ORDERLY EXPLOITATION OF YOU AND YOUR PEOPLE BEGINS.
IT'S A GAME A HAS LONG ENJOYED...
MAKE ME SAY MY NAME BACKWARDS! HMMMMB!
...
!
TOSS!

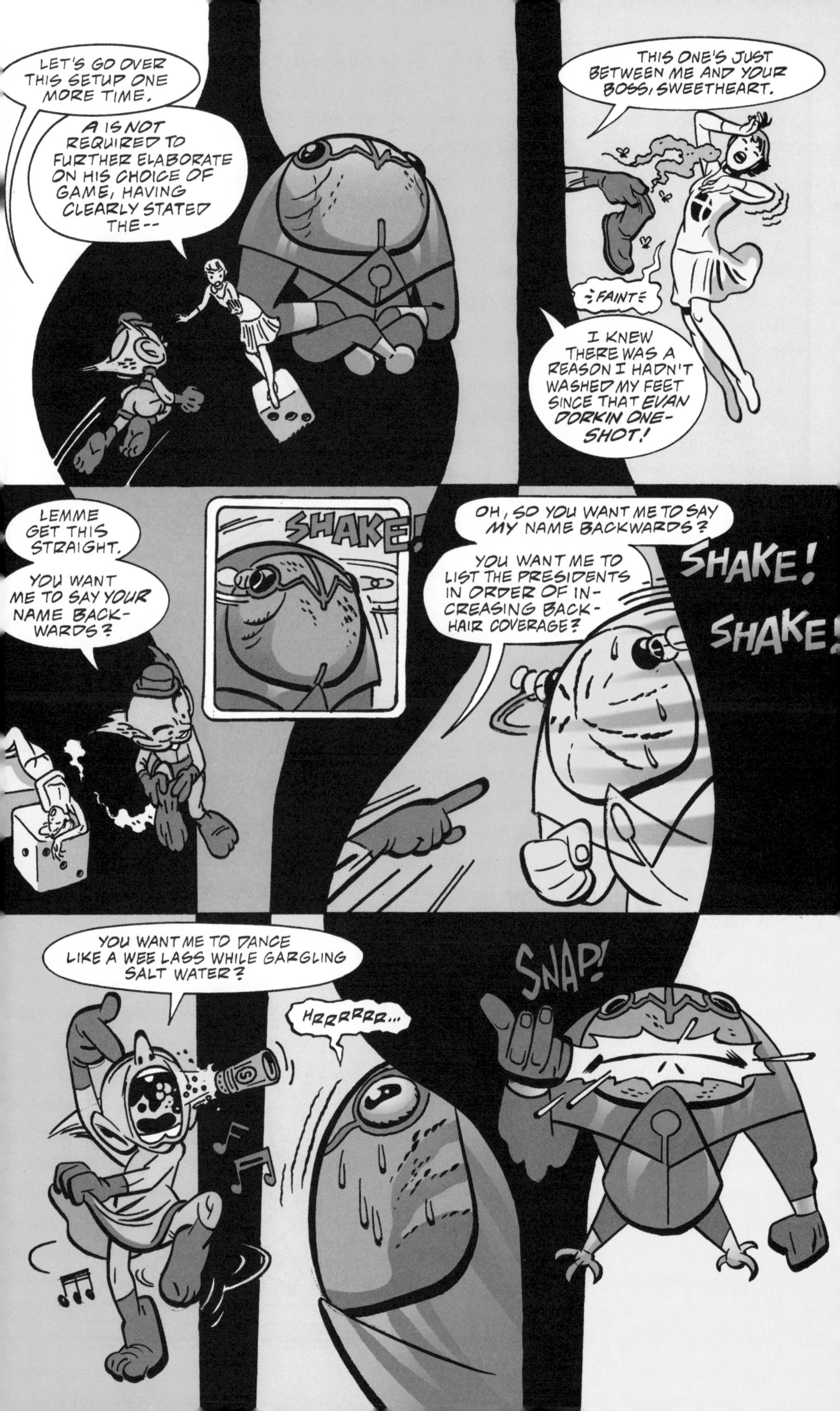
LET'S GO OVER THIS SETUP ONE MORE TIME.
A IS NOT REQUIRED TO FURTHER ELABORATE ON HIS CHOICE OF GAME, HAVING CLEARLY STATED THE--
THIS ONE'S JUST BETWEEN ME AND YOUR BOSS, SWEETHEART.
FAINT
I KNEW THERE WAS A REASON I HADN'T WASHED MY FEET SINCE THAT EVAN DORKIN ONE-SHOT!
LEMME GET THIS STRAIGHT.
YOU WANT ME TO SAY YOUR NAME BACK-WARDS?
SHAKE!
OH, SO YOU WANT ME TO SAY MY NAME BACKWARDS?
YOU WANT ME TO LIST THE PRESIDENTS IN ORDER OF IN-CREASING BACK-HAIR COVERAGE?
SHAKE!
SHAKE!
YOU WANT ME TO DANCE LIKE A WEE LASS WHILE GARGLING SALT WATER?
HRRRRRR...
SNAP!

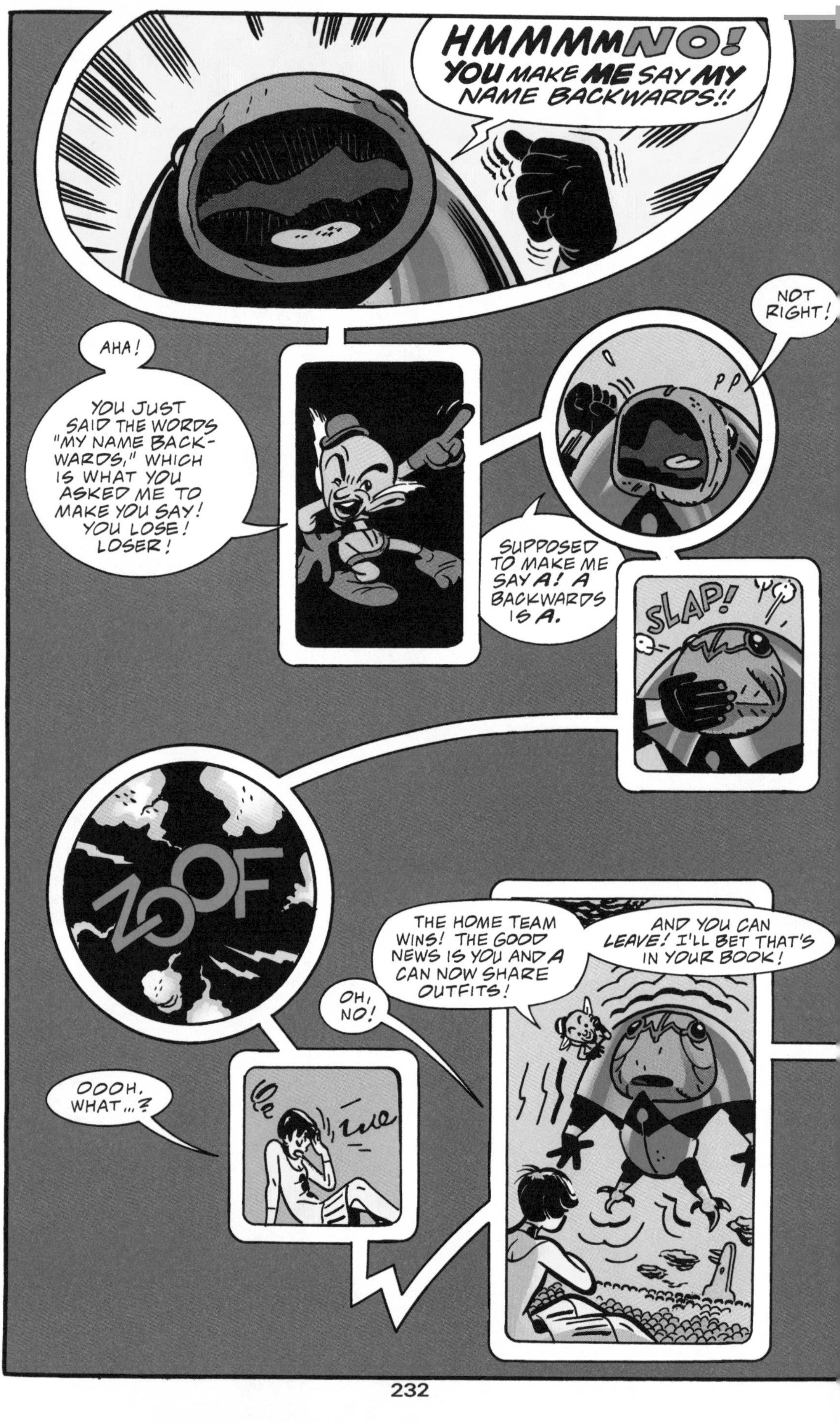
HMMMMNO! YOU MAKE ME SAY MY NAME BACKWARDS!!
AHA!
YOU JUST SAID THE WORDS "MY NAME BACKWARDS," WHICH IS WHAT YOU ASKED ME TO MAKE YOU SAY! YOU LOSE! LOSER!
NOT RIGHT!
SUPPOSED TO MAKE ME SAY A! A BACKWARDS IS A.
SLAP!
ZOOOF
OOOH, WHAT...?
OH, NO!
THE HOME TEAM WINS! THE GOOD NEWS IS YOU AND A CAN NOW SHARE OUTFITS!
AND YOU CAN LEAVE! I'LL BET THAT'S IN YOUR BOOK!

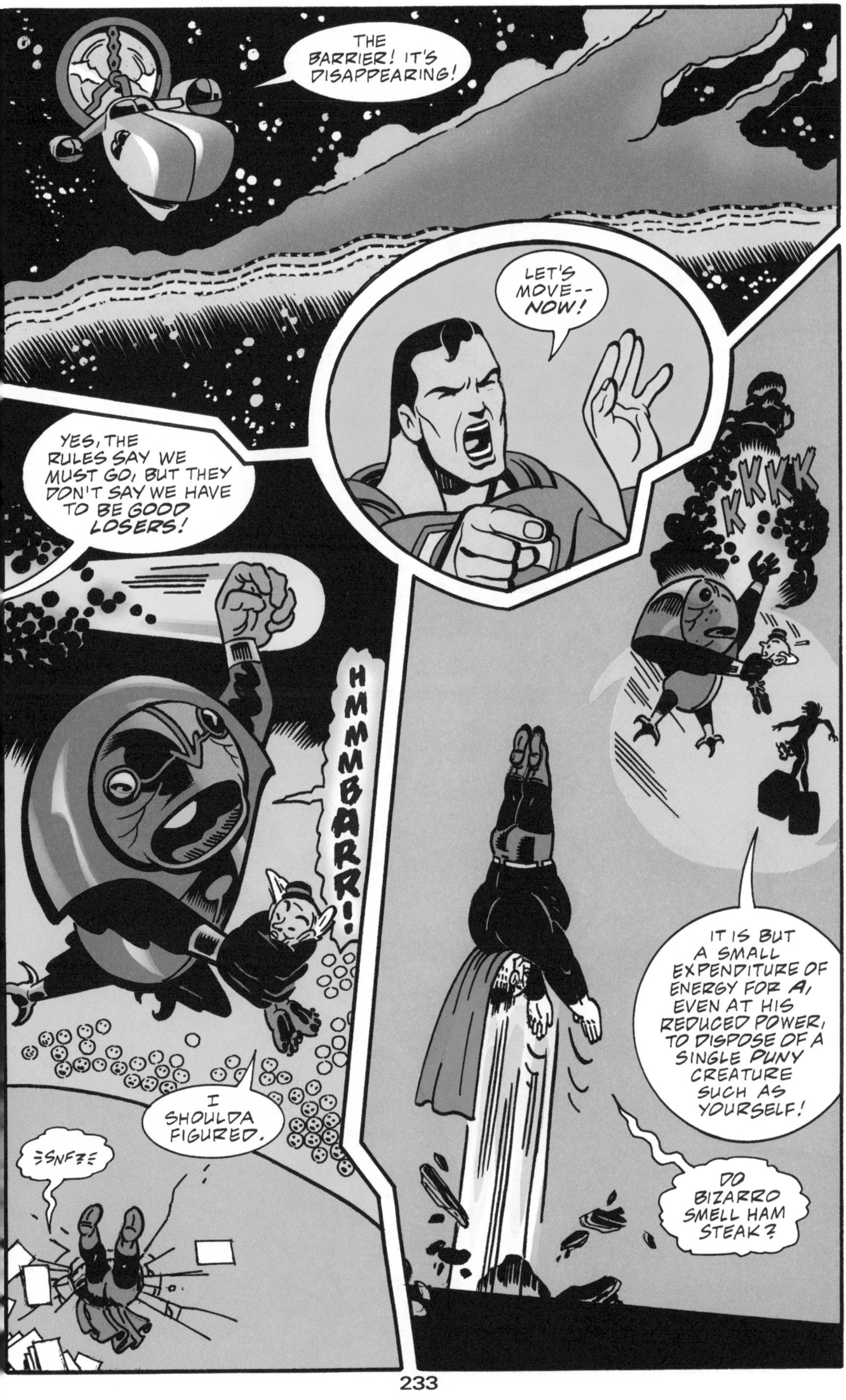
THE BARRIER! IT'S DISAPPEARING!
LET'S MOVE-- NOW!
YES, THE RULES SAY WE MUST GO, BUT THEY DON'T SAY WE HAVE TO BE GOOD LOSERS!
KKKKK
HMMMBARRR!
IT IS BUT A SMALL EXPENDITURE OF ENERGY FOR A, EVEN AT HIS REDUCED POWER, TO DISPOSE OF A SINGLE PUNY CREATURE SUCH AS YOURSELF!
I SHOULDA FIGURED.
=SNF=
DO BIZARRO SMELL HAM STEAK?

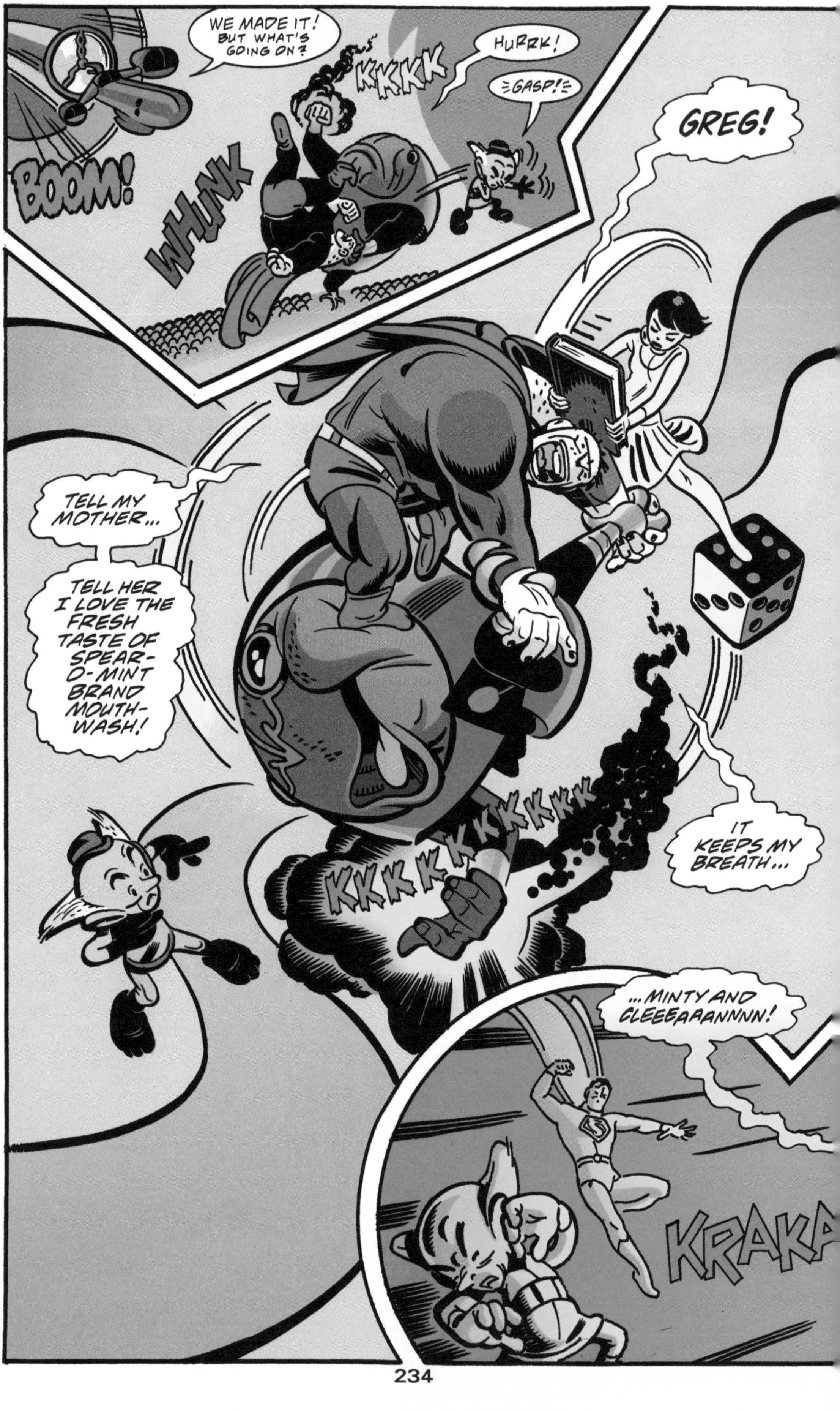
WE MADE IT! BUT WHAT'S GOING ON?
KKKK
HURRK!
GASP!
BOOM!
WHUNK
GREG!
TELL MY MOTHER...
TELL HER I LOVE THE FRESH TASTE OF SPEAR-O-MINT BRAND MOUTH-WASH!
KKKKKKKKKKK
IT KEEPS MY BREATH...
...MINTY AND CLEEEAAANNNN!
KRAKA

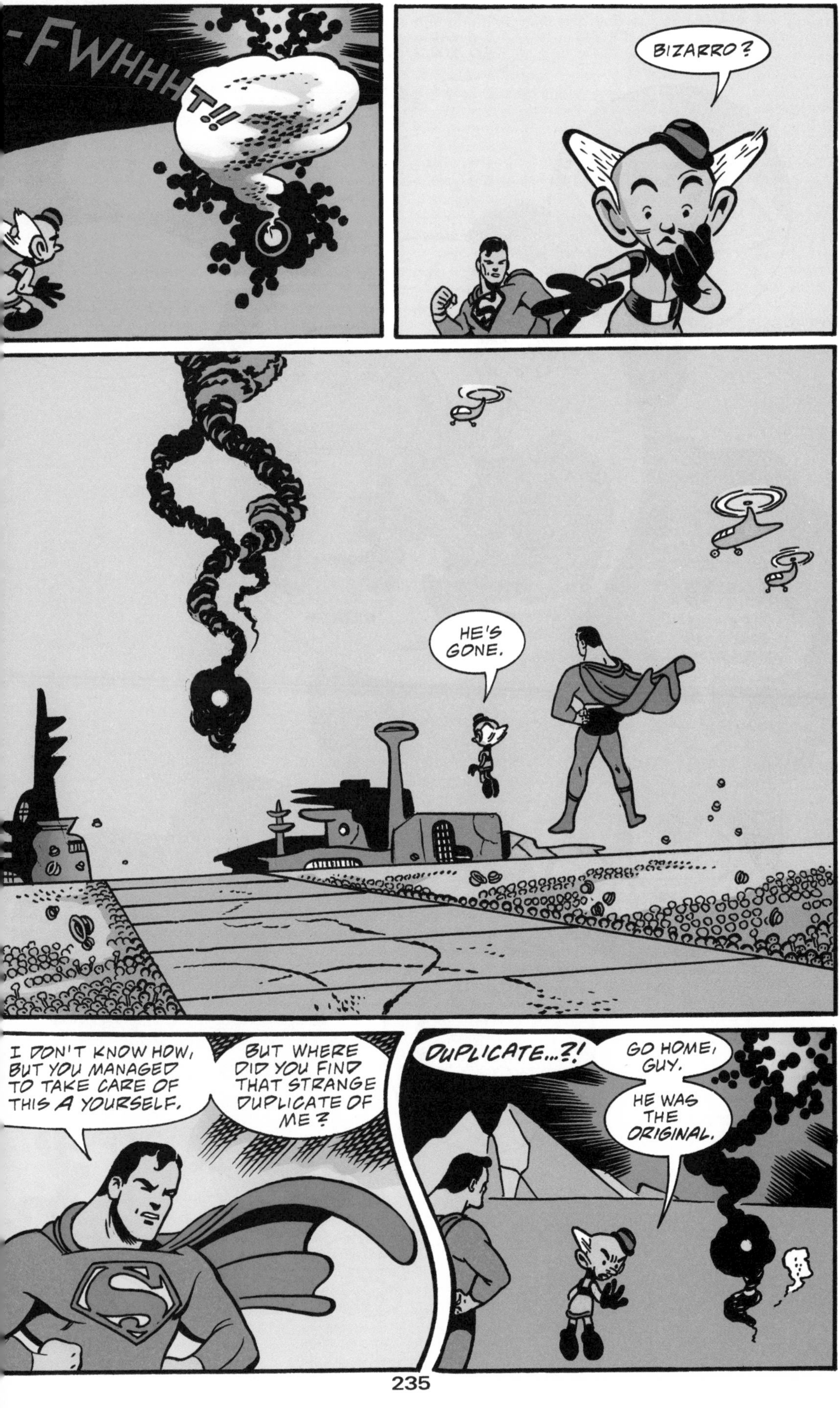

-FWHHHT!!
BIZARRO?
HE'S GONE.
I DON'T KNOW HOW, BUT YOU MANAGED TO TAKE CARE OF THIS A YOURSELF.
BUT WHERE DID YOU FIND THAT STRANGE DUPLICATE OF ME?
DUPLICATE...?!
GO HOME, GUY.
HE WAS THE ORIGINAL.

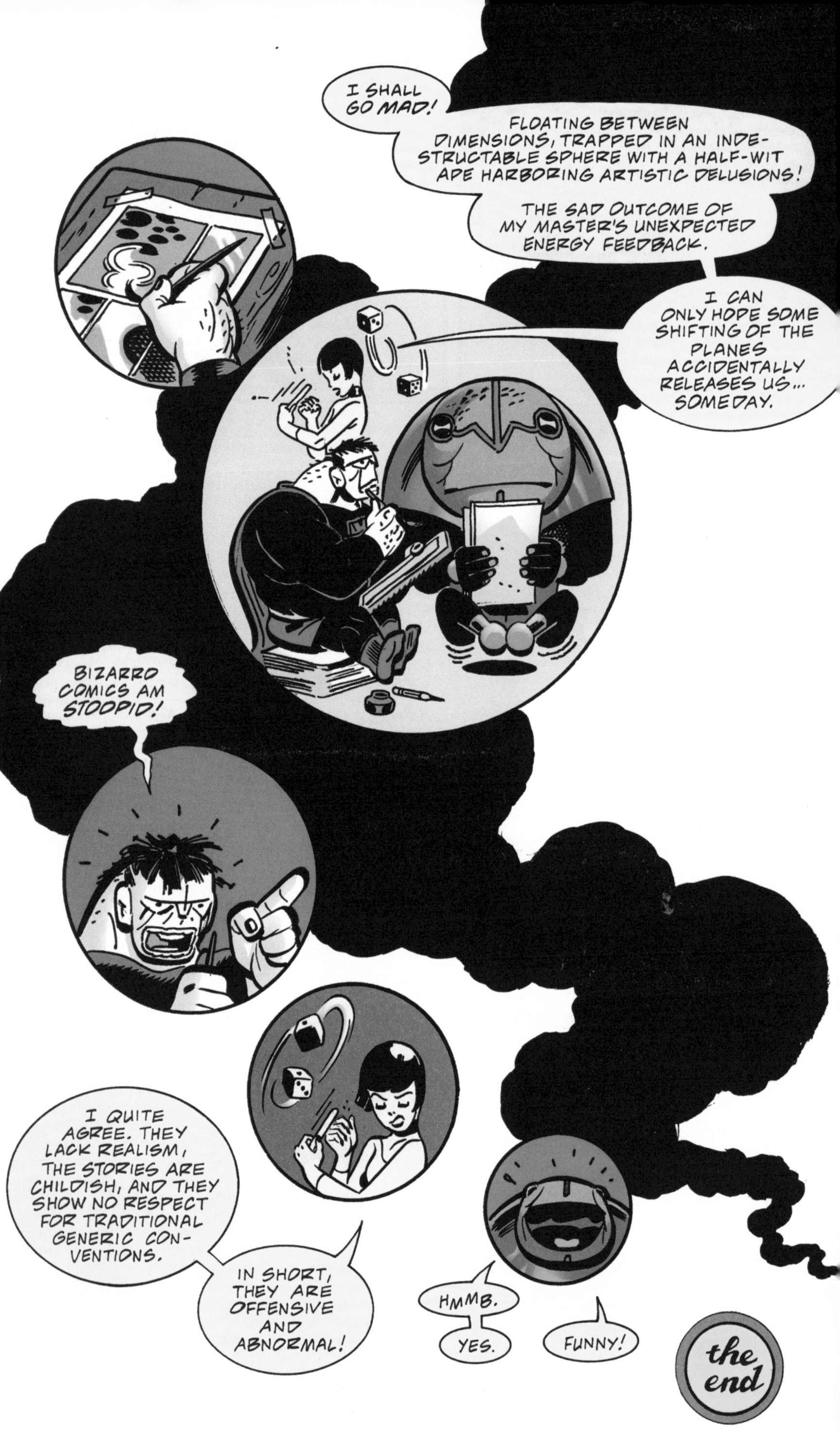
I SHALL GO MAD!
FLOATING BETWEEN DIMENSIONS, TRAPPED IN AN INDE-STRUCTABLE SPHERE WITH A HALF-WIT APE HARBORING ARTISTIC DELUSIONS!
THE SAD OUTCOME OF MY MASTER'S UNEXPECTED ENERGY FEEDBACK.
I CAN ONLY HOPE SOME SHIFTING OF THE PLANES ACCIDENTALLY RELEASES US... SOMEDAY.
BIZARRO COMICS AM STOOPID!
I QUITE AGREE. THEY LACK REALISM, THE STORIES ARE CHILDISH, AND THEY SHOW NO RESPECT FOR TRADITIONAL GENERIC CON-VENTIONS.
IN SHORT, THEY ARE OFFENSIVE AND ABNORMAL!
HMMB.
YES.
FUNNY!
the end

Jessica Abel is best known for her comic-book series of short fiction, *Artbabe*, and her journalistic comics, such as *Radio: An Illustrated Guide*. Her most recent book, a collection of early work, entitled *Soundtrack*, is published by Fantagraphics. She lives in Brooklyn, New York with her husband, Matt Madden.

Kyle Baker is the author of the graphic novels YOU ARE HERE, *The Cowboy Wally Show*, and WHY I HATE SATURN. He is currently working on a graphic novel on the life of King David for Vertigo.

Gregory Benton has had work published in Nickelodeon Magazine. His upcoming full-color book will premiere in the next year.

Nick Bertozzi has a 128-page graphic novel called *The Masochists* published by Alternative Comics. He won an Ignatz Award in 2000 for his map-comic *Boswash*.

Ariel Bordeaux is the creator of the self-published mini-comic *Deep Girl* and the comic *No Love Lost*, published by Drawn & Quarterly. She has also contributed to *Hate*, *Measles*, *Real Stuff* and *Action Girl*.

Ivan Brunetti writes and draws *Schizo*, the fourth issue of which will be out in the fall of 2001. He'll also have a collection of one-panel cartoons out the same summer entitled *HAW!* from Fantagraphics.

Eddie Campbell collaborated on the graphic novel *From Hell* with Alan Moore. It is soon to be a major motion picture. He is also the author of *Alec: The King Canute Crowd* and the *Bacchus* series.

Dave Cooper is the creator of the Fantagraphics series *Weasel*, the first three issues of which buried Dave in a warm avalanche of pointy awards and plaques. He is now preparing for an even heartier crushing with the imminent release of the (by his own account) brilliant *Weasel #4*, and the much-anticipated 100-page "Dan and Larry" collection.

John Costanza, a cartoonist in his own right, is an award-winning comic book letterer.

Mark Crilley is the creator/writer/artist behind the series *Akiko*, which has been collected in four softcover editions and has spawned a series of children's books, the third of which, *Akiko and the Great Wall of Trudd*, has just been published.

Jef Czekaj grew up on the mean streets of Wantagh, a very suburban town on Long Island, New York. His comic "Grampa and Julie: Shark Hunters" appears in Nickelodeon Magazine, and he is the writer/artist of his own *Hypertruck*.

Brian David-Marshall apologizes profusely for anything he may have done in comics in the past.

Stephen DeStefano is best remembered as the artist of DC's 'MAZING MAN and HERO HOTLINE. He has drawn many famous cartoon characters for animation and print, including Bugs Bunny, Ren & Stimpy, Popeye and Felix the Cat.

Digital Chameleon is a group of artists under the stewardship of Lovern Kindzierski, himself a master colorist and award-winning writer.

D'Israeli is a longtime cartoonist on the British alternative scene, drawing *Kingdom of the Wicked*, written by Ian Edginton. His work can currently be seen in the book *Lazarus Churchyard, the Final Cut*, written by Warren Ellis.

Evan Dorkin is the creator of the comics *Milk and Cheese*, *Dork* and *Hectic Planet*. He's written scripts for TV's *Space Ghost Coast to Coast*, *Superman* and *Batman Beyond*. He's at work on an *Eltingville Club* pilot for the Cartoon Network. His last project for DC was the Harvey Award-winning SUPERMAN AND BATMAN: WORLD'S FUNNEST.

Chris Duffy is the Senior Editor of Nickelodeon Magazine. He lives in Brooklyn, New York with his wife, Peggy, and his son, Pete. They have a dog named Lucy.

Sarah Dyer is creator, editor and contributor of the anthology series *Action Girl*, executive producer on the *Eltingville Club* pilot for the Cartoon Network and was nominated for an for an Eisner Award for her coloring work on *Amy Racecar*.

Hunt Emerson has applied his uninhibited drawing style to adaptations of such works as *Lady Chatterley's Lover* and *The Rime of the Ancient Mariner*. He maintains a regular comic strip in the Fortean Times. His most recent collection is *Citymouth*.

Phil Felix lettered many episodes of Harvey Kurtzman and Will Elder's *Little Annie Fanny* in **Playboy** before striking out on his own to become one of comics' most prolific letterers. He teaches at the Joe Kubert School of Cartoon and Graphic Art.

Bob Fingerman is the creator of the critically acclaimed yet temporarily stalled comic book series *Minimum Wage*, as well as myriad other self-created titles such as *Otis Goes Hollywood* and *White Like She*. He makes his home in New York City with his wife, Michele.

Abe Foreu grew up in Louisville, Kentucky, and has been reading and drawing comics since before he can remember.

Ellen Forney has had illustrations in The New York Times, The Village Voice, The Stranger, Mademoiselle, Ms. and The Seattle Weekly. *Monkey Food: The Complete "I Was Seven in '75" Collection* is an anthology of her semi-autobiographical comic strips.

Liz Glass writes and edits a newsletter for a nonprofit organization, the National Alliance for the Mentally Ill. She is married to Kyle Baker and they have two children, Lillian and Isaac.

Matt Groening is the creator of *The Simpsons* (TM, Twentieth Century Fox Film Corp.).

Tom Hart wrote and drew such experimental graphic novels as *The Sands* and *Banks/Eubanks*. His most recent book, *The Collected Hutch Owen*, was nominated in 2001 for a Harvey Award for Best Collection.

Dean Haspiel is the author of semi-autobiographical comix and super-psychedelic romances. His comix appear in *The Billy Dogma Experience* and various anthologies, including his new solo effort, *Opposable Thumbs*.

Sam Henderson is an extremely witty cartoonist who has had his work compiled in T Magic Whistle Blows and Humor Can Be Funny. He is also a contributor to the anthologies Low Jinx, Zero Zero and Measle.

Gilbert Hernandez is part the team behind the acclaimed and influential *Love and Rocke* series. *Love and Rockets Volume Two* began in 2001 and is availa at a comic book store near you.

Matt Hollingsworth, a graduate of the Joe Kubert School of Cartoon and Graphic Art, has been coloring comics f ten years and is best known for his work on Vertigo's PREACHE and WildStorm's TOM STRONG

Dylan Horrocks is the writ and artist of the Ignatz award-nominated comic book *Pickle*, a his graphic novel *Hicksville* wa named a book of the year by Th Comics Journal. He is currently working on *Atlas* for Drawn & Quarterly and scripts THE NAM OF MAGIC for Vertigo.

John Kerschbaum is resposible for a very funny comic bo of his own, *The Wiggly Reader*, published by Fontanelle Press.

Chip Kidd is a groundbreaki book designer. He is also the author of the book *Batman Collected* and the co-author of *Batman Animated*. He is current co-authoring *Jack Cole and Plas Man* with Art Spiegelman, to be published by Chronicle Books.

James Kochalka has his highly distinctive works release from a number of small press publishers, including Top Shelf, Alternative Comics and Highwa Books. His graphic novel *Monke vs. Robot* was nominated for a 2001 Harvey Award for Best Graphic Album of Original Wor

Roger Langridge has done work for DC, Marvel, 2000 A.D. Dark Horse, Deadline, Heavy Metal, Fantagraphics, Les Cartoonists Dangereux, L'Association and "anyone else who talks nicely or offers sweet

rol Lay has done comics for e New Yorker and The Wall eet Journal. Her ongoing comic p, Story Minute, has been lected into three books: *Now sville*, *Strip Joint* and *Joy Ride*.

son Little has had stories lished in the anthologies wn and Quarterly, Zero Zero and Shelf. He is the author of the ic-winning *Jack's Luck Runs t*. Doubleday will release tterbug Follies, the first volume his "Bee" series, in a full-color dcover in September 2002.

e Loughridge is the prietor of Zylonol, the separa- n house that has colored such series as LEGEND OF THE WKMAN, ROBIN YEAR ONE, l the Vertigo graphic novel USE ON THE BORDERLANDS. resides in Savannah, Georgia.

att Madden is a cartoonist l illustrator living in Brooklyn, w York with his wife, Jessica el. He also occasionally writes ut comics for The Comics rnal. His new book, *Odds Off*, ublished by Highwater Books.

m McCraw has been a ter and a colorist on the GION OF SUPER-HEROES ies, and is currently coloring PULSE every month.

t McEown has contributed ries to anthologies such as k Horse Presents, HEART ROBS, FLINCH, and STRANGE VENTURES, and has done imation storyboards for *Static ck* and *Batman Beyond*.

ndy Merrill writes and duces *Space Ghost Coast to ast* and is the beloved voice of k, who'll soon be getting his n show on the Cartoon Network.

ny Millionaire has had ustration work in The New rker and the New York Press, ere his strip, *Maakies*, runs kly. It's been collected into ook, and so has another of his ations, *The Adventures of k Monkey*.

Bill Oakley is one of our field's best and most sought-after letter- ing talents. He's currently applying his calligraphic skills to DC's upcoming BATMAN: NINE LIVES and a new series entitled HAVEN.

Will Pfeifer is an editor and columnist at the Rockford Register Star. He wrote the Vertigo series FINALS and self- published the long-running mini- comic *Violent Man*. His work will appear in *X-Men Unlimited* in 2001.

Paul Pope first came to comics enthusiasts' attention with the self-published comics series *THB*. His new five-issue Vertigo series, *100%*, premieres September 2001.

Brian Ralph created the comic *Cave-In*, selected by The Comics Journal as one of the five best comics of 1999.

Clem Robins has a hip and happening lettering style that adorns the pages of far too many DC Comics to enumerate. He is an adjunct professor of anatomy at the Art Academy of Cincinnati, and his book, *The Art of Figure Drawing*, will be released by North Light Publications in May 2002.

Alvin Schwartz wrote the Superman comic strip during the Golden Age, introduced the Bizarros and is the author of the autobio- graphical book *An Unlikely Prophet*.

Marie Severin is a brilliant cartoonist and colorist whose worked has graced the EC Comics of the 1950s and the Marvel Comics of the 1960s. Currently, she colors SUPERMAN ADVENTURES monthly.

Jeff Smith is the Harvey and Eisner Award-winning creator of the long-running series *Bone*.

Jay Stephens makes TV cartoons like *Jetcat* for Nickelodeon and finds time to do comics for loads of kids' magazines. His previous comics include *Land of Nod*, *Sin* and *Atomic City Clubhouse*. He plans to add a bimonthly book, *Jetcat Clubhouse*, to his workload this spring.

Rick Taylor is the former Director of Graphic Services and Senior Editor of Collected Editions at DC Comics. His coloring credits include IMPULSE, TERMINAL CITY, FINALS, BAT- MAN ADVENTURES and UNDER- WORLD UNLEASHED.

Craig Thompson is the creator of the acclaimed graphic novel *Goodbye, Chunky Rice*. He won the 1999 Harvey Award for Best New Talent. His 500-page nonserialized graphic novel, *Blankets*, will be published by Top Shelf in spring 2002.

Jill Thompson has drawn lots of titles for the Vertigo imprint. She is Will Pfeifer's collaborator on the series FINALS and is the author of the *Scary Godmother* series of graphic novels.

Andi Watson is the Eisner- nominated creator of *Skeleton Key*, *Geisha*, and *Breakfast After Noon*. His new series, *Slow News Day*, will be released by Slave Labor Graphics in July. "First Contact" is his first work for DC.

Steven Weissman is the author of *Champs* and *Don't Call Me Stupid*, published by Fantagraphics. Creator of the crit- ically acclaimed *Yikes* and *Kid Firechief* series, he received the 1998 Harvey Award for Best New Talent.

Bill Wray has worked on such animated series as *Ren & Stimpy* and draws the monthly feature "Monroe" for MAD magazine. He illustrates the covers for DC's DEXTER'S LABORATORY and continues to do freelance work for Cartoon Network.

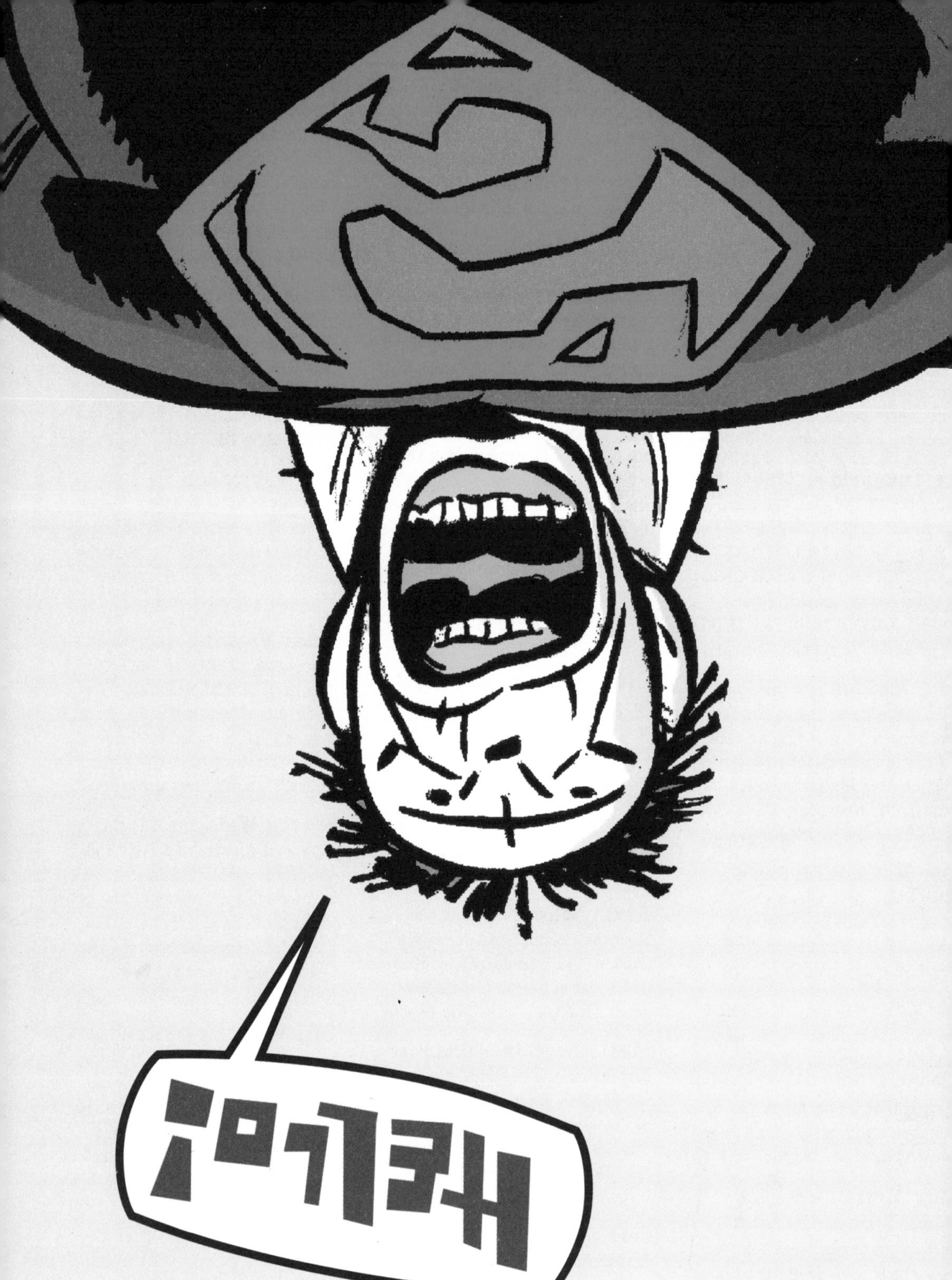
HELP!